THE BIRTH AND GROWTH OF
THE ROYAL NEW ZEALAND NAVY

Official photograph of the Millenium Statue at RNZN Base, Devonport, Auckland.

Permission for use was given by Lt Cmdr Bill Morley RNZN, Public Relations Officer, RNZN Base Devonport

The Birth and Growth of the Royal New Zealand Navy

Jack S. Harker

The Pentland Press
Edinburgh – Cambridge – Durham – USA

First published in 2001 by
The Pentland Press Ltd
1 Hutton Close
South Church
Bishop Auckland
Durham

Email: sales@pentlandpress.co.uk
manuscripts@pentlandpress.co.uk
Web: www.pentlandpress.co.uk

ISBN 1-85821-804-7

Typeset in Monotype Dante 11 on 13 by
Carnegie Publishing
Carnegie House
Chatsworth Road
Lancaster
www.carnegiepub.co.uk

Printed and bound by
Antony Rowe
Chippenham
Wiltshire

In memory of those RN, RAN, RCN, RIN, RSAN, USN, Free French, Dutch East Indies and other allied navy men who gave their all in the defence of our individual and collective homelands

'We Will Remember Them, Amen.'

Contents

Illustrations

Foreword

By Rear Admiral Peter McHaffie OBE
Chief of Naval Staff, Royal New Zealand Navy

WHEN THE AUTHOR APPROACHED ME to write this foreword, I was aware of the great service Jack Harker had done for the RNZN, by recording and publishing the experiences of so many Kiwis who fought in the Second World War at sea.

This book, *The Birth and Growth of the Royal New Zealand Navy* is not a history of the policies and planning that went into the phenomenal growth of New Zealand's naval forces during the Second World War, nor is it simply another account of the campaigns our nation took part in. Rather, Jack has written a sailor's eye view of the war, and of the difficult years that went before, when a small number of dedicated personnel kept the naval profession alive in New Zealand.

Today it is important that future generations of New Zealanders have some understanding of what their forefathers endured, and of New Zealand's contribution to the Second World War at sea. In this book, Jack gives us the sailors' perspective, warts and all, including seasickness, runs ashore and the sudden terror of mines and torpedoes.

During its formative years, the RNZN absorbed the traditions and ceremonies of the Royal Navy, and in the Second World War our small Service proved that it could stand and fight alongside the RN and USN. This is a priceless heritage, but it comes to us at the cost of an earlier generation's lives and health. In this book Jack shows us how those personnel felt, and describes what they did.

I commend this book to you, as a record of service of some of the ships of the RNZN, and of many of their crew. Read it to understand the sailors of past years, who kept the seas open in the face of the enemy to help shape our free world of today.

Peter McHaffie

Peter McHaffie (Rear Admiral)

Foreword

By Russell J. Johnson VRD Cdr RNZNVR (retd)
now Senior Judge

THE BIRTH OF THE ROYAL NEW ZEALAND NAVY in 1941, as the seaward arm of the sovereign forces of a small far-flung member of the British Empire, came during the time when it was needed most during its whole history to date. Formed from the Royal Navy (NZ Division) it was a proven entitiy, blooded most recently in the Battle of the River Plate when the cruiser *Achilles* shared the honours with *Ajax* and *Exeter* in the heroic set-piece battle against the German pocket battleship *Graf Spee* only a little over a year before.

From the earliest days of the Second World War German raiders put our extensive coastline under threat by mining and sinking shipping, and before the year 1941 was out the outlook in the Pacific was very gloomy with the bombing of Pearl Harbour, the Philippines, and the launch of the Japanese assault against South-East Asia. The New Zealand homeland lay under a threat only finally stopped at the battle of the Coral Sea and dispersed by the long slog northwards, eventually culminating in the signing of the surrender aboard USS *Missouri* lying in Tokyo Bay in 1945.

New Zealand then, as now was a small country with a small population, but a strong heart. She supported a large navy, relative to national size, consisting of cruisers, ocean-going minesweepers, armed merchantmen, and scores of coastal craft built or converted for coastal protection. Her ships served in the Mediterranean, the Atlantic, the Pacific, the Indian Oceans and at home. Her sailors served her own fleet and in the fleets of Britain and her allies. Eventually in concert with her allies the ships of the RNZN shared the victory.

The new navy inherited the traditions, the ways and language of its illustrious parent. Jack Harker has told the story of its birth in a way which could only be done by one who was there. From his vantage point in the ships' radio shacks he acquired a contemporary insight into what was going on around him well beyond his own ship and sometimes his own theatre. He kept extensive diaries, and has been a prodigious researcher of the activities of the RN (NZD), and the RNZN during the Second World War for forty-five years. He has interviewed scores of sailors for their memories and built an impressive personal archive.

He tells the story in an engaging, captivating way, with a spin from the bridge and the lower messdecks delivered with equal facility. His story is alive, and peopled by the men who were there. He has recorded stories which would otherwise be lost to memory, against the background of the ships which in Harker's work are part of no mere catlogue but a living part of the navy into which he has personally invested so much.

Russell J. Johnson VRD
Cdr RNZNVR (retd)
Judges' Chambers
Auckland
June 2000

Introduction

HOW FAR DOES A MAN NEED TO GO when delving into the origin of his land? Does he accept the 'Big Bang' and 'Expanding Universe' theories? Does he accept that his Earth's solar system is a minor star comprising the Sun and its satellites, a celestial speck in the vast cloud of countless stars and nebulae, sited inconspicuously near the rim of our multi-million light years diameter Milky Way galaxy which rotates once every quarter of a billion earth years. Man knows little about the Universe, can merely speculate on its entirety, has no conception of what lies beyond it, if there is a 'beyond'. So let us come down to Earth, third planet out from our Sun at a mean distance of 93 million statutory miles. We exist in a life-sustaining atmosphere moistened by cyclical evaporation, condensation, and precipitation of the water which covers two-thirds of our globe. The other third is land divided haphazardly by rivers, lakes, straits, seas and oceans – the largest of these being our Pacific Ocean. It has been theorised that its mass is equal to that of our Moon, and that, some millions of years past, a rogue planet – possibly Venus – near-missed Earth so narrowly that its magnetic attraction sucked out the great mass which has since then been our Moon satellite. In the ensuing turmoil water deluged in to fill the gaping wound, surrounding land changed dramatically, and perhaps during an earthplate breakaway from Australia, New Zealand was formed.

Misting back through time, man evolved to walk the path of tribal civilisation, disputing land tenure, inviting alliance for mutual benefit, then taking neighbours' land and assets by conquest. The pattern still simmers and erupts throughout Europe and Asia whose national borders depend on tenuous treaties, and in lesser tension the rights of self-styled indigenous peoples are arbitrated by governments throughout or bounding the Pacific Ocean.

South Pacific Polynesians quote ancestral origins chanted down through tribal mysticism, so legendary that historical timing is difficult even for the well-meaning researcher, their gods and actual ancestors sometimes inseparable. One might ponder the story of a principal chief, Ngatoro, who fled the ancient wars of Hawaiki and voyaged to New Zealand aboard one of the seven canoes, *Te Arawa, Tainui, Matatua, Takitimu, Kurahaupo, Tokomaru,* and *Matawhaorua*. In a chapter of an early Whitcombe and Tombes

1

Complete Manual of Maori Grammar and Conversation, edited by Sir Apirama Ngata MA LLB, it is written that during a confrontation with Manaia's war party:

> 'Ngatoro was praying and calling on Tawhirimatea to destroy Manaia's thousands. The night and day were divided; then the wind, the rain, the lightning, the thunder, and all the waves of the sea came over Manaia's troops which lay buried in sleep. Ngatoro heard the rumbling noise, the uproar, the disturbance; and after the cries of distress and noise were no more to be heard, the tide alone was dashing against the rocks. Manaia's party had all perished.'
> Ihumanea paused, looked directly at Tauhau. 'Perhaps Ngatoro had his familiar spirits with him?'
>   'Who were his familiar spirits, are they a bad sort of people?' Tauhau asked.
>   'Eh! These fairies [patupairehe] have no fault. They are a lovely race of creatures, their skin is as white as the white peoples,' Ihumanea replied.

Were these white creatures the forest people mentioned in Maori lore; the fish netters who emerged only at night for fear of capture? Ngatoro was a rangitira in the Moa Hunter era. Were there already white people in the land, possibly remnants of the red-haired long-eared whites who fled westward via the Marquesas, to be lost to Polynesian history after that great Easter Island (Rapanui) massacre, ages later in New Zealand frightened to be abroad in daylight to be killed and eaten, perhaps enslaved or taken as wives. It is a question without an answer, so, let us conjecture the arrival of seafaring men from Europe.

A Christian monk, Macrobius AD 395–423 had cartographed a map of the world depicting an undefined land mass in the Southern Hemisphere. Geographers of the time gave it scant credence but the seed was sown. The journeys of Marco Polo (1256–1323) through India and China may have prompted southern exploration, but seafarers found ample trade within Indonesian islands and previously established South Asian coastal centres. Some who ventured to North Australian bays were faced by hostile aborigines and their experiences deterred those already growing rich on known trade routes, so maps created by Ptolemy about AD 200 showed Terra Incognita as the northern boundary of a continent connecting South-East Africa to Southern Asia then on somehow to South America. And that's how things stood until near the end of the fifteenth century when Vasco da Gama's voyage round the Cape of Good Hope shoved Terra Incognita further south.

Only the Mediterranean Sea, North Atlantic and North Indian Oceans had been regularly traversed by maritime trade, the Pacific Ocean not being shown on maps until AD 1513 when Vasco Nunez de Balboa followed a native trail through jungle on the Panama Isthmus, and from a hilltop gazed at the vast ocean. But having no means of sailing upon it, Balboa could only retrace his path and sail back across the Atlantic to report his discovery to the King of Spain. Successive expeditions tried to find a passage through from the Atlantic, then in 1519 the Portuguese mariner Fernao de Magalhais (Magellan) as Captain General of a five-ship fleet, waited off San Lucar near Seville for a favourable wind to fill the sails, then he conned his flagship *Trinidada* downriver and across the Atlantic to the South American coast, followed by the caravels *San Antonio, Victoria, Concepcion* and *Santiago*.

Month by month he drove further south beset by storms and increasingly mutinous crews, until one day when damaged by cold mountainous seas he sought shelter in the lee of sheer granite cliffs rising out of a broad inlet. Later to his surprise, the further he ventured westward into the great waterway, the more it opened out before him until sea stretched away west to an empty horizon. Here at last he'd found the passage for which he'd been commissioned, and in every direction west of southern Patagonia lay that glistening body of water seen six years earlier by Balboa. Now with only *Trinidada, Concepcion* and *Victoria* still under his command, on 28 November 1520 he sailed north-westward in such pleasant conditions that he charted the ocean as the 'Pacific'. Eventually reaching Guam in the Ladrone (Mariana) Islands, he victualled ship and carried on to Cebu in the Philippines, but there on 27 April 1521 at Mactan he was murdered by natives, and in due course *Victoria* arrived back at San Lucar to complete the first known world circumnavigation, under the acting captain general-ship of Juan Sebastian de Elcano whose achievement was not given recognition by the Emperor.

The Pacific's northern latitudes were no longer a mystery but Terra Incognita still showed on maps as imaginary contours of a southern continent counterbalancing all land north of the Equator. Jean Rotz's 1542 map included a land south of Java with an island's west coastline away to the east, this later being identified by Portuguese and Dutch explorers as parts of Australia and New Zealand. The unidentified remains of a six-teenth-century vessel near Raglan, the Tamil bell found in the fork of a North Island tree, and a Spanish-style metal helmet dredged up in Wellington Harbour mud, rekindle speculation that an archival French narrative describes Binot Paulmier de Gonneville's enigmatic voyage, possibly to our South Island west coast in 1503, when unrelenting storms forced him eastward from near the Cape of Good Hope to a heavily wooded country many weeks distant, where he repaired his ship for the return to France.

Sixteenth-century cosmographers still debated their 'round world' theory that there must be an underbelly continent proportionate in mass to that of Europe and Asia, but now called it Terra Australis Incognita. Maritime charts thenceforth showed the southernmost South American link between the Atlantic and Pacific Oceans as Magellan Straits and, later in the sixteenth century Spain's explorer, Alvaro de Neyra Mendana, sailed through it when commissioned to take possession of every island he came across in the Pacific during a further search for the fabled continent.

Circa 1569 the Spanish Basque national, Andreas de Urdaneta, noted that certain Pacific winds blew seasonally from east to west, then changed to blow continuously from west to east, a regular occurrence which when it became widely known, was used by maritime trade until the advent of steam, but this innovation had many years of history to be written before its influence would affect the world. Meantime came England's Spanish galleon plunderer and renowned navigator, Sir Francis Drake, knighted by Queen Elizabeth I for destroying the Spanish Armada, then covertly commissioned in the 1570s to sail *Golden Hind* onto Chile's Pacific coast and relieve King Philip of much of his stolen South American gold and jewellery. Laden to the gunnels with treasure, confronted by adverse winds and knowing that enemy vessels were watching for his return along the usual course, Drake turned north-west and wallowed before benign seas to become England's first circumnavigator.

But a century of Pacific seafaring had not yet discovered that mysterious southern continent, and in 1642 Abel Janszoon Tasman departed Batavia on such a quest aboard his flagship *Heemskerck*, accompanied by the caravel *Zeehan*. Sailing south-west across the Indian Ocean for supplies at Mauritius, he then steered south to the 40th parallel before turning east and surfing on huge following seas until land was sighted. Naming it Van Dieman's Land he continued on his easterly search, and in rough conditions sighted storm-lashed high country in the latitude of Hokitika, but without any indication of a safe entrance, he stood northward and rounded what is now called Farewell Spit, into Golden Bay. Here he anchored intending to land and establish camp, but his ship's boats were confronted by wildly gesticulating natives in great canoes, one of which rammed the leading boat and bludgeoned to death its unfortunate crew attempting to swim back to *Heemskerck*; so Tasman logged the anchorage as 'Mordenaers Baij', then sailed up the west coast to the Three Kings group, called his coastal sightings 'Staten Landt' then returned northward to Batavia, but future charts were soon to indicate his sketchy survey as Nova Zeelandia.

Years of disinterest in Tasman's storm-bound coastal discovery with its cannibalistic inhabitants became decades, then a century, until in 1768 the British Admiralty bought and converted to a survey vessel the little collier *Earl of Pembroke*, renamed it *Endeavour Bark* in deference to an existing warship HMS *Endeavour*, then packed Lieutenant James Cook off in it to Tahiti to observe the transit of Venus. In his confidential safe was a sealed envelope instructing Cook to 'make discovery of the Terra Australis Incognita continent ... bearing due south as far as the fortieth latitude, then if unsuccessful, beating westward to the thirtieth degree longitude, or until you meet the land discovered by Tasman called New Zealand'. This Cook did, going south as instructed then west until the forenoon of 7 October 1769 when an excited shout from the crow's nest announced the first European sighting of New Zealand's East Cape. Cook named it Young Nick's Head in recognition of the youthful lookout, then he traversed and plotted the entire coast of both islands, so accurately that his chartings were still in use late into the twentieth century, The 'Fabled Continent Theory' had now been exploded, Cook possessed New Zealand in the name of King George III, made two more voyages of discovery and survey in the Pacific (1772–1775) and (1776–1777), during the latter of which he was slain and dismembered by Hawaiian natives at Kealakekua Bay, Owhyhee. About this time whalers and sealers were establishing shore bases around New Zealand, and bartering by fair means or foul with its brown-skinned inhabitants, many of whom settled real or imagined grievances by cooking and eating the perpetrators, in addition to some of the innocent immigrants who tried to befriend them.

Exploration, exploitation, colonisation, defence and law. No matter where or by whom, the pattern was and still is universal. Initially New Zealand's security rested with the Royal Navy's Commander-in-Chief India, who on occasions dispatched a sloop or frigate from New South Wales to determine the welfare of villages and townships sprouting in sheltered bays around both main islands. And had the nineteenth-century Royal Navy not then ruled the waves it is probable we would now be seeing the flag of another power atop our flagstaffs. Mr Busby, the British Resident at Kororareka, recorded for 1836 that 150 vessels had anchored in the Bay of Islands, many of them foreign, and an amazing amount of coastal and blue-water shipping is evident in that era from the endless record of shipwrecks about our coasts. Other listings detail the rapid influx of immigrants settling around ports serving districts purchased from recognised Maori chiefs, although inevitably there were quarrels over tenure, British law interpretation, tapu infringements and other Maori/European problems. There were no roads or railways, only river or sea transport, so demands on the Royal Navy increased annually, until England's Home Office decided it was time for residents of New Zealand to shoulder more responsibility for their own government and defence.

In December 1835 Captain Robert Fitzroy arrived at Kororareka aboard HMS *Beagle* toward the end of a five-year world survey, and took to England a distressing observation of Mr Busby's inability as British Resident; this together with impassioned pleas to the Crown by both Maori and Pakeha, determining a House of Lords Select Committee to recommend a stronger political and military representation in the country. Appointed Lieutenant-Governor and authorised to implement a treaty with the Maoris, Captain William Hobson RN arrived in the Bay of Islands with a formal document in English, but Maoris had no written language so a facsimile translated into a script understood by them at that time was signed or moko-marked by representatives of both cultures at Waitangi in February 1840. Copies of these documents were similarly inscribed at venues throughout both islands over ensuing months, and in August 1840 several South Island chiefs acknowledged the Treaty when marking it in Akaroa; British Sovereignty was recognised, and Captain Owen Stanley RN of HMS *Britomart* hoisted the Union Flag ashore during his warship's 21-gun salute.

Now began a continuous flow of Colonial Secretary correspondence requesting naval support in quelling internal strife and allaying fears of foreign threat. In March 1846 Rangihaeata led skirmishes within Wellington's Hutt Valley environs, butchering isolated settlers until Governor Grey, when informed, ordered a siege of the Pahautanui Pah, by men of regiments disembarked from HMS *Driver*, *Calliope*, and the transport barque *Slains Castle*. A longboat from the barque *Tyne* wrecked on Sinclair Head near Wellington entrance, was rebuilt and strengthened on board *Calliope* to mount one of her 12-pounder carronades and a small brass cannon, then, manned by several bluejackets commanded by Midshipman McKillop, it set off in search of a Maori raiding party reported on Porirua Basin shores, each day securing the men's hammocks around their longboat's hull as a protective breastwork which saved many lives. Nearing a suspected hideout McKillop fired a round of canister-shot into dense titri scrub which instantly disgorged a hundred tattooed warriors, yelling and leaping through the mangrove shallows while firing volley after volley of erratic rifle fire. Bullets thwacked against the hammocks and the boat's strengthened planking as, unable to sufficiently swivel his carronade, McKillop shouted for the brass cannon to be discharged at those attempting to scramble inboard over the longboat's quarter. It's barrel disintegrated thunderously in a cloud of smoke without injuring the crew, but it's startling effect together with the bluejackets' telling musketry and good use of the 12-pounder, ended that confrontation, the first in which Rangihaeata personally led his warriors against British navymen.

Being promoted Lieutenant, McKillop was ordered by Governor Grey to capture Te Rauparaha and other chiefs about to join Rangihaeata. Two hundred sailors, police, and militia assembled for the assault on Te Rauparaha's pah, where Plimmerton now stands, and in the dawn raid all of the chiefs were arrested without a shot being fired. *Calliope's* ex-*Tyne* longboat was later employed on the Wanganui River, until its 12-pounder recoil weakened the structure irreparably, the gun then being mounted on the schooner *Governor Grey*.

To assist in the 1860s Maori Wars, government ordered shallow-draft paddle-steamers to be built in Sydney, and existing similar craft on the Murray and Darling Rivers to be purchased by Captain Francis Cadell, a notable marine-engineering adventurer who arrived at Onehunga in 1864 to be ranked Commodore over eight armed steamers, *Avon*, *Gundagi*, *Koheroa*, *Pioneer*, *Prince Albert*, *Rangiriri*, *Sandfly*, and *Sturt*. He was also placed in command of numerous river barges, harbour craft, and defence depots at Port Waikato (Putataka), Newcastle (Ngaruawahia), and Bluff (Maungatawhiri). Under his leadership these and other vessels transported supplies and troops to otherwise inaccessible trouble spots, whilst Royal Navy warships and locally armed craft under separate command provided deep-water transport and gunnery support on the Wanganui River, Thames Estuary, West Coast areas from Port Nicholson northward, and along the East Coast between Napier, Wairoa, and Gisborne (Taranga). But by 1886 the Maori Wars had declined into locally controllable disturbances, so government disposed of its defence flotillas, Royal Navy personnel appropriated to them were returned to their ships and inducted seamen and settlers were released back to their former occupations.

Meanwhile the 'Russian Scare' of 1885 had initiated an earlier demand for national security with a different resurgence of naval activity. Government finance was allocated for two small steamers, *Janie Seddon* and *Ellen Ballance*, to lay and maintain mines, nets, and booms in strategic harbour entrances. Manned by New Zealand Naval Voluntary Artillery recruits, twelve coastal batteries were built on headlands between North Auckland and Invercargill, then four Thorneycroft torpedo-boats arrived from England in 1887 to defend our main ports. And on a broader scale in response to our Premier Sir Robert Stout's revelation that, in the past five years only fourteen Royal Navy vessels had visited New Zealand, against eighteen from Russia, Germany, France, and the United States whose trading vessels had supplied most of the weapons and ammunition to the Maoris during their 1860s insurgence, Admiralty dispatched an Auxiliary Squadron of five *Philomel*-type cruisers and two 750-ton fast torpedo-gunboats to Sydney – Admiralty to maintain and finance its regular Australasian Station Fleet, Australia and New Zealand to proportionately contribute 126,000 pounds sterling annually to upkeep the Auxiliary Squadron.

But apart from a periodic New Zealand visit by one or more of them, these ships remained in reserve pending enactment of the foreign threat which in the end didn't develop so, as F.T. Jane wrote in *The British Fleet* regarding this Auxiliary Squadron, 'In the course of time all of them wore out and were eventually recalled.' Successive events of naval significance

Devonport Naval Base Auckland, Calliope Dock Opening Ceremony, 17 February 1888. Captain Henry Coey Kane RN's HMS *Calliope* enters ahead of HMS *Diamond*. *Calliope* would next year survive the Samoan hurricane which wrecked 3 German and 3 US warships in Apia on 15/16 March 1889.

saw the opening of Devonport Auckland's Calliope Dock in 1888; Admiralty's acquirement of adjacent land in 1892 for a naval base; provision in the 1903 Australia/New Zealand Defence Act for New Zealand naval recruits to serve on the Royal Navy's Australian Squadron cruisers; and in the 1909 Naval Defence Act an accepted NZ Government offer of the total cost of a battle-cruiser for the Royal Navy, with the additional offer of a second one should it be deemed necessary. This second generous offer was declined, and in July 1911 HMS *New Zealand* slid off the stocks at 1,700,000 pounds sterling, with the final payment being made in 1945. During her 1913 New Zealand visit she was presented with a Maori cloak and told that if it was worn by the Captain in action his ship would emerge unscathed, and during each of the First World War Heligoland, Dogger Bank and Jutland engagements in which she fought with distinction, word went round the ship: 'Everyfing's orright, matey, Skip's got 'is fevver coat on.'

But let us return to 1905 when for 800 pounds sterling our government acquired the 805-ton sail and steam gunboat HMS *Sparrow*, then at Sydney in reserve. Built by Scott Shipbuilders, Greenock, with teak planking on a steel frame, she was launched in 1889 and armed heavily for her size with six 4″ B.L. guns, two 3-pounders and three machine guns; her triple expansion engine drove her at 13 knots maximum, and she was rigged as a three-masted barquentine for cruising during her eleven years service on the Cape of Good Hope Station. There at times she saw action interspersed with entertainment, both being provided by sultans and rival chiefs about the Mozambique Channel and its nearby islands. In August 1896 with her sistership HMS *Thrush* in company, she joined the 3rd Class cruiser *Philomel* in a punitive action against the rebel-held fortified Zanzibar Palace and the rebel-manned cruiser *Glasgow*, which had been gifted to the British-friendly Sultan of Zanzibar shortly before his overthrow and assassination. *Glasgow* was sunk at her moorings by gunfire which also silenced shore batteries and wrecked the palace fortifications, then landing parties from *Philomel*, *Sparrow* and *Thrush* killed several hundred insurgents before the remainder surrendered.

At Wellington in 1906 *Sparrow* was renamed *Amokura* when she decommissioned as a warship of New Zealand's War Department to become a Merchant Marine training ship, thereafter embarking boys aged 13 to 15 for two-year periods wherein they were given naval training, navigational skills, and when secured alongside her Wellington berth, the boys were marched ashore for a general education by the Marine Department schoolmaster. After shaking down new entries in Cook Strait, *Amokura* visited South Island ports, the West Coast sounds, the islands south of New Zealand, the Chathams away to the east, and the Kermadecs 600 miles north-east, to check outposts and replenish supply depots for shipwrecked mariners; one example being the rebuilding and storing of Curtis Island's corrugated-iron shack which had been vandalised by Count von Luckner's German crew aboard the scow *Moa*, during his First World War attempted escape from internment at Auckland's Motuihi Island. From 1907 to 1921 *Amokura* trained 527 New Zealand boys, but with *Philomel* becoming the New Zealand Division of the Royal Navy's stationary training cruiser, *Amokura* was sold to the Westport Coal Company for use as a coal hulk in Wellington where the enamel and gilt scroll work on her decorative stern gradually deteriorated. In 1940 the Union Steamship Company bought her for continued use as a Wellington-based coal hulk, then in 1953 she was sold to a Mr Orchard to become a jetty-cum-storeship at St Omer in Kenepuru Sound, Marlborough, where it is possible she was broken up in 1955.

CHAPTER I

The Saga of Admiral Count Reichsgraf von Spee

FROM THE SIXTEENTH to the nineteenth century Britain extended her sphere of influence to all corners of the Earth, becoming rich and powerful to the extent that her Royal Navy was recognised internationally as the World's maritime policeman; but several pugnacious nations of the early 1900s were throwing down a gauntlet – to cite one, Germany, who from 1900 to 1906 launched fourteen battleships and wrote a programme including thirteen more, plus an avalanche of new and modernised cruisers, destroyers, submarines and auxiliaries. But over the centuries Britain had established a network of safe anchorages for bunkering, victualling, ammunitioning and refitting her warships on foreign stations; many of these harbours being operated under the British flag through annexation and colonisation, treaties, or merely due to bi-national high-rank personal friendships.

Let us turn back the calendar to a mild November 1913 evening in Hong Kong's capital, Victoria, where Vice Admiral Count Maximilian Reichsgraf von Spee had arrived on a goodwill visit from his China Coast naval base at the German colony in Tsingtao. Born in 1861 in his father's Dusseldorf castle, Maximilian entered the German Navy in 1878, was commissioned in 1882, saw action in China's Boxer War, became CNS North Sea 1908–1910, then C-in-C Far East Station in 1913. Right now his modern 24-knot 8.2″ heavy cruiser SMS *Scharnhorst* rode at anchor off the Fleet Club, close to Captain Brand's aged 18-knot 6″ cruiser HMS *Monmouth*; and the German C-in-C had invited both countries' diplomats, naval officers, and their partners, to a farewell banquet for the British warship. In animated conviviality beneath glittering chandeliers, gold-epauletted naval dress surrounded an expansive mahogany table attended by white-coated servants; tall, silver candelabra glistened on a wealth of delicate porcelain and embossed silverware fronting every chair. A bell at the head of the assembly subdued the high-spirited camaraderie, then von Spee rose to address his British and German guests.

'Gentlemen and partners, "The King of England!" Gentlemen and partners, "The Kaiser!"' He raised his glass and 200 glasses reciprocated. The stern-faced, trim-bearded, tall, Catholic Admiral continued: 'Gentlemen and

Sie Majistat Schiff SMS *Scharnhorst* Flagship German Far East Squadron
1913/14, a similar 8.2″ gunned heavy cruiser to SMS *Gneisenau.*

ladies, this is a happy and a sad occasion; happy for you of His Majesty's
Ship *Monmouth* who will tomorrow sail for your homeland, England; but
sad for us of Sie Majestat Schiff *Scharnhorst* who will see you depart Hong
Kong at the conclusion of your foreign commission. Charge your glasses
as we wish our Englander friends, Aufweidersehn!'

The banquet resumed, men sweated and ladies perspired throughout the
'lancers', 'quadrilles' and 'military two-steps', and ended near dawn when
officers selected their partners for 'The Last Waltz'. A leisurely year would
pass. In an arena 9,000 miles south-east across the vast Pacific Ocean that
'Till we meet again' awaited.

On Sunday, 28 June 1914 whilst touring Sarajevo, Austria's Archduke
Francis Ferdinand was assassinated and in consequence, a month later,
Austria-Hungary declared war against Serbia, this initiating a domino effect
of treaty-obligated fists-up between allies and enemies throughout Europe,
Russia and Asia. Britain entered the ring against Germany on Tuesday, 4
August, threw a punch at Austria-Hungary on the 12th, then it was 'all
on', even Japan declaring war on Germany on the 23rd. This latter com-
petitor, whose fleet had grown since it thrashed Admiral Rozhdestvenski's
Russian Fleet at Lushun (Port Arthur) in 1905, now made the German base
at Tsingtao untenable, so von Spee, still wearing his flag on *Scharnhorst* at
present in the Caroline Islands' Ponape Harbour, led his heavy cruiser
Gneisenau south-eastward for a look into Apia, as Samoa had recently been
wrested from Germany by New Zealand forces. Finding no ships within,

Spee went east and threw a few shells onto the hill-slopes beyond Tahiti's Papeete, then he continued south-east toward Chile whose ports were known to be German friendly. There his squadron would coal and victual, obtain information about enemy warship and mercantile movements, and when joined by his light cruisers *Dresden, Leipzig* and *Nurnberg,* hazard the thousands of miles of coastal routes.

First Sea Lord Winston Churchill, thinking Spee's squadron would operate off Asian coasts, learned it had left footprints across the Pacific and was currently coaling in Valparaiso. He ordered Rear Admiral Sir Christopher Cradock to take his South American Squadron to the Chilean coast, vetoed Cradock's cabled request for adequate support, and sacked Admiral Sir Doveton Sturdee from the post of Director of Naval Operations when he disagreed with Churchill's veto. Consisting of the outdated cruisers *Good Hope* (Flag), *Monmouth, Glasgow,* and impeded by the armed merchant cruiser *Otranto,* it was evident this SA Squadron would be no match for Spee's five fast, heavy and light cruisers, but Cradock, although aware of the impossibility of victory, or the small chance of inflicting crucial damage on his adversaries, rounded the Horn and on the stormy Saturday night of 31 October 1914 engaged von Spee off Coronel. Excerpts translated from a letter written by Admiral von Spee just days after Coronel, describe that fateful night:

My ships were scattered whilst searching for the enemy seaward of the small coaling station of Coronel near Concepcion, *Gneisenau* alone being with me at 1625 when two ships identified as *Monmouth* and *Glasgow* were sighted. Soon *Good Hope* and the armed merchant cruiser *Otranto* were seen astern of them as we closed at speed. The enemy was trying to manoeuvre to windward of me but I steamed at 20 knots into a heavy sea, on a parallel course while wirelessing *Leipzig* and *Dresden* to join. After sunset an easterly moon shining between broken low cloud assisted my squadron's gunnery when I closed to five miles and made the signal to open fire: *Scharnhorst* against *Good Hope*; *Gneisenau* at *Monmouth*; *Leipzig* at *Glasgow*; *Dresden* at *Otranto*. *Good Hope* although bigger

Rear Admiral Christopher Cradock and his flagship HMS *Good Hope.*

than my flagship, was not so well armed, and we having been in the Pacific for two years had practised gunnery throughout. We had learned that Cradock's ships were crewed by naval reservists who had not yet seen their guns fired and, *Monmouth* with only some of her 6″ guns able to bear, was soon overwhelmed by *Gneisenau*'s 8.2″ broadsides, and *Glasgow*, hit numerous times appears to have withdrawn into rain squalls and escaped. Many fires were observed about *Good Hope*, then a terrific explosion, but it seemed she kept on retaliating from 4500 metres range, until the action ceased after 50 minutes when my gunlayers lost their targets in the smoke and dark. After 2040 we steered north-west toward distant gun flashes, where *Nurnberg* whilst speeding to join me had found the crippled *Monmouth* who soon capsized and sank. Unfortunately the heavy seas and lack of visibility forbade most attempts at rescue. We have been victorious, and intending to ensure that Chile interned *Good Hope* if she succeeded in making a port, I visited Valparaiso and heard that Cradock was not one of *Good Hope*'s survivors when she foundered. *Dresden* has informed me that the armed merchant ship *Otranto* quitted the line early in the action and I think escaped; while it is reported the English have a Queen Class 12″ battleship hereabouts. Should it have been in company we may have got the worst of it.

This in fact was the old training ship *Canopus*, scheduled for scrapping in 1915 but at the outbreak of war hastily manned by reservists and sent south with some of her boilers defective. On her arrival in the Falklands, Cradock cabled Churchill this information with a rider that as he was about to round the Horn in search of Spee's squadron, *Canopus* being too much of an encumbrance would follow as escort for the colliers. There has been debate about Cradock's decision but as one of the old ironside's senior officers later remarked: 'Our value would have been extremely minimal in that weather, 13 knots maximum, secondary armament probably awash, and our four antiquated main guns in charge of an RNR lieutenant who had yet to see the inside of a 12″ turret.'

Meanwhile to avoid Chilean internment, *Glasgow*'s Captain Luce had nursed his damaged cruiser back round the Horn to Port Stanley where he was ordered north to Rio de Janeiro. There the British Minister, Malcolm Robertson, had 'arranged' per a Brazilian government associate, for another friend, Senor Enrique Lage, to make his personal dry dock available for a week. And immediately *Glasgow* entered, her shell-pierced hull was re-paired, scraped and painted, while local technicians swarmed inboard making good her many defects. So good was this Brazilian refit that within several days she steamed north to become a unit of Rear Admiral A.P. Stoddart's squadron of 23 to 26-knot 6″ cruisers, *Carnarvon*, *Cornwall*, *Kent*, *Glasgow*, *Defence*, and the AMC *Orama*, similar to *Otranto* which had been sent to Sierra Leone with boiler problems.

Here we might ponder some history of the Falkland Islands, a name bestowed in 1690 in favour of the Admiralty Secretary, Lord Falkland. French adventurers later named them *Les Isles Malouines* which Spain translated to *Las Malvinas*. In 1764 Louie-Antoine de Bougainville settled sealers at one of its eastern upthrusts and named the harbour Port Louis; then next year Commodore John Byron RN possessed West Falkland, founding and naming Port Egmont after the Earl of Egmont, First Lord of the Admiralty. French claims were ceded to Spain in 1767; a Spanish force from Buenos Aires expelled the British garrison in 1770, but Spain agreed to British re-establishment in 1771, an occupation lasting only three years until it withdrew and left a Spanish community at Port Louis which they renamed Soledad; but in 1811 they too departed. Circa 1820 the Buenos Aires Governor had a flag erected in the Falklands which he declared to be *Territorie da la Plata*, resettling Soledad, and in 1831 confiscating the boats of three United States sealers. An American sloop immediately landed troops at the settlement, razed the Argentinian fort and evicted the colony. Finally Britain who didn't recognise any of these disturbances, sent two frigates in 1832 to repossess Port Egmont, then in 1833 Soledad's Argentinian garrison surrendered to a Royal Marine and Bluejacket force and watched surlily as the British Union flag broke out atop their flagpole. Civil administration was established in 1841 and after many years Argentine is still attempting political or military possession.

But back to November 1914 when the enigma of Admiral Von Spee's whereabouts since departing Valparaiso was giving Admiralty Intelligence a headache over doubtful to possible sightings, including a week's old one from Easter Island where an English farmer had sold beef and mutton carcases to the German squadron, he being unaware of the war due to his only outside world communication being by an infrequent Chilean supply vessel. Churchill and his First Sea Lord, Sir 'Jacky' Fisher, were now giving serious thought to Port Stanley, their only base for colliers and storeships tendering to the needs of British warships in that windswept, storm-infested South Atlantic region, and the nearest habitation to wireless telegraphists manning Britain's powerful and strategically sited W/T station.

'How soon can you get something down there to counter Spee's squadron, John?'

'Well ... two battlecruisers refitting Devonport ... they complete Friday 13 November ... '

'No, not good enough ... don't like the date either, so pass me that pad.'

Within minutes Churchill had drafted the signal reproduced below, agreed to his naval chief's minor amendments, then handed it to his signal officer for cyphering and delivery to Admiral Sturdee, the recently dismissed

Churchill's Message (No. 435).

Director of Naval Operations, now appointed Vice Admiral C-in-C South American Station.

On Wednesday, 11 November 1914 in the bleak Devonport forenoon, Admiral Sturdee mounted the 18,000 ton, 26-knot, eight 12″ gunned battlecruiser *Inflexible*'s gangway, to be piped aboard as his flag broke out atop her foremast peak, commissioning rites ensued on the massive quarterdeck, then men were marched off for'ard while all senior and departmental officers welcomed the C-in-C in their wardroom. Later that day Sturdee led his sistership *Invincible* out through Plymouth Sound, and south at economical speed to Sao Vicente for a Cape Verde Islands coaling stop, before the prearranged rendezvous off Brazil's Abrolhos Rocks where Rear Admiral Stoddart's cruisers and colliers awaited his arrival. Next day, Friday, 27 November, this imposing fleet stood well out to sea for secrecy en route to Port Stanley which they entered on Monday, 7 December.

Already a cyphered message from Rio de Janeiro's British Minister, Malcolm Robertson, had been cabled and radioed to the Falklands' Governor, Mr Allardyce, warning him of a possible Argentinian invasion supported by Spee's squadron. To counter this the local garrison had dragged *Canopus*'s smaller weapons uphill about the entrance; then the obsolete battleship was moored where her four 12″ guns covered the entrance, and where their maximum 11-degree elevation could be aimed over Sapper Hill to be directed by an observation post established there for that purpose. Sturdee having invited the Governor aboard and learned of these preparations, assumed that Spee's ships were thousands of miles away in the Pacific, so he signalled wartime harbour routine, ships queuing to bunker alongside colliers, duty watchkeepers below, those off watch eyeing the township in anticipation of possible liberty. But what of the German squadron?

After Coronel, Spee resolved to place the German Ensign on Port Stanley's flagstaff. Several thousand miles south of Valparaiso, at Puerto Montt, Germans were being recruited into a reservist force to augment another enlisting in Punta Arenas, the world's most southern city, sited northside near the centre of Magellan Strait. These when equipped would follow as a garrison after Spee's squadron had taken over Port Stanley and the adjacent wireless station; colliers and storeships were to be captured intact; then a resident of Tierra del Fuego, Baron von Maltzahn, would assume Governship to which he'd already been appointed.

Although perturbed by rumours that two RN battlecruisers had left Devonport for the area, confirmation didn't reach the German Admiral and he proceeded as planned. But luck was deserting him, placing before him decisions which would seal his fate. He captured the Canadian sail-collier *Drummuir* off Staten Island and escorted her back to Beagle Bay, this delaying his invasion attempt by four days whilst refuelling his cruisers from the sailing ship's 3,000 tons of coal; thus it was 6 December before they signalled readiness to proceed, unaware that Sturdee's fleet was within hours of entry to the target harbour.

Having disposed of his political visitors, Sturdee RPC'd *Carnarvon*'s Rear Admiral Stoddart and his Flag Lieutenant, Humphrey Pakington, aboard *Invincible* to dinner followed by madeira in the late twilight wherein Sturdee began to reveal his plans: 'Tomorrow after coaling, my fleet will round the Horn ...', an unfinished disclosure interrupted by the Chief Yeoman who said that Sapper Hill was reporting indistinct smoke on the horizon. But before this was substantiated night descended and the matter went into idle discussion. 'German warship? Most unlikely, they're well out in the Pacific where soon I intend to run them down. Bloody imagination or a cloud probably!'

At daybreak aboard *Carnarvon*, Lieutenant Pakington was shaving when passed a signal through his cabin door: 'EMERGENCY. ALL SHIPS. Prepare to weigh. Raise steam immediately for full power. Acknowledge.'

Now the sound of running feet – strident bugle calls – steam vents blowing – imperious voices about approaching enemy. Then a God-awful BAAANNNGGG and a jolting concussion as *Canopus* fired her four 12″ low over Sapper Hill.

Ships lying haphazardly about the inner and outer berths were belching raw soot, anchor cables rattled inboard, securing lines to colliers smoked back in through fairleads, while flaghoists, signal lamps and semaphore tried to establish sanity out of the confusion. Fleet trapped at anchor? Unprepared? Anticipating a deluge of German naval shells, which didn't arrive? So one by one with captains cursing and ignoring seniority, ships' bows swung seaward to the thrust and drag of opposing propellers; first out *Kent*, then *Cornwall*, *Carnarvon* followed by the battlecruiser *Inflexible* and finally Sturdee's flagship *Invincible* with 'GENERAL CHASE' whipping at her top halyard. Fate's pendulum was favouring Sturdee; it was 'TALLY HO!', individual captains demanding more and more revolutions, closing the gap between their cruiser and a selected column of smoke on the sun-drenched horizon. Gradually mastheads and fighting tops materialised, then shortly before 1300 their upperworks when Admiral Spee ordered his light cruisers to detach and escape south. Too late; *Invincible* had detected the attempt and, requiring *Carnarvon* to remain, Sturdee ordered *Glasgow*, *Kent* and *Cornwall* to 'PURSUE AND DESTROY!'

Spee's heavy cruisers had opened fire and the battlecruisers retaliated with initial wides and shorts. The German shells being more accurate straddled *Invincible* who helmed away out of *Scharnhorst*'s and *Gneisenau*'s 8.2″ range, continually correcting her falls of shot until the longer range

12″ were obtaining percentage hits. At 1458 Sturdee asked Stoddart to position *Carnarvon* to relay visual signals when and if smoke or distance hampered communication, then he brought both battlecruisers onto a parallel course with Spee's heavy cruisers and recommenced firing. The British salvoes were gaining accuracy, and although *Inflexible* sustained superficial damage their concentrated gunnery was inflicting crucial punishment; flames and smoke-blackened steam geysering high between *Scharnhorst*'s forward funnels; shells piercing armoured steel upperworks before exploding and hurling secondary armament out of their ports, then her masts shattered and collapsed as she developed an evident list.

Still the battle raged. *Gneisenau*'s Captain Maerker, on being told the Admiral's flag was half mast, signalled *Scharnhorst*'s Captain Schultze: 'Is the Admiral dead?' and was answered by Spee's own reply: 'No. I am uninjured. You were right after all, Captain Maerker', a generous acknowledgement of Maerker's Beagle Bay insistence that the battlecruiser rumour should be checked before approaching Port Stanley. Already flames were gushing from long gashes in *Scharnhorst*'s hull, but her wake still foamed as she drove on with her main turrets firing regularly, until her list increased spasmodically when interior bulkheads collapsed, and her foc'sle became awash from every wave encountered. More cordite clouds billowing far to the north as both British ships fired. Minutes ticked by then waterspouts reared hundreds of feet either side. Tremendous detonations shook the ship end to end as armour-piercing projectiles drilled deep inside before obliterating men and metal. Smoke now enshrouded the stricken heavy cruiser, her funnels hung awry as she slewed while losing way, rolled slowly bottom-up while *Gneisenau* surged past unable to assist, seeing their sister-ship mates clambering up her barnacled underbelly, soon to be sucked under with her as she foundered.

That fate now hovered over *Gneisenau*. *Invincible*'s and *Inflexible*'s turrets were tracking onto their new target; devastating everything above her armour belt, shells penetrating deck after deck to explode in her boiler rooms, to incinerate or scald screaming stokers on coal-strewn foot-plates fronting exploding boilers and shattered furnaces, to mercifully punch great chasms down through double-bottoms for an inrush of unrestrained ocean.

At 1725 she lay helpless, relentlessly pounded as she wallowed in early evening South Atlantic swells, a dying gladiator reluctantly laying over at 1802, then vanishing to leave hundreds struggling amongst the flotsam of those sub-zero waters.

Miles south of this main action *Nurnberg* and *Leipzig* were undergoing similar punishment, their 4.1″ armament being no match for *Kent*'s and *Cornwall*'s fourteen 6″ each plus *Glasgow*'s two 6″ and ten 4″. *Nurnberg* came under fire from *Kent* at 1800 and went down at 1927; *Leipzig* was engaged by *Cornwall* and *Glasgow* at 1900 to be sent under at 2123; only *Dresden* managed to break clear and escape during the early chase.

One of *Glasgow*'s young officers (later Vice Admiral H. Hickling RN of Turangi NZ), recalled *Leipzig*'s final moments:

> When it was obvious she had fired her last round we and *Cornwall* lowered our seaboats and rowed to within 40 yards to be among survivors in those freezing waters. Men were still heaving lashed hammocks overboard and leaping in after them. But already she was laying over until flat on her side where I saw a group of German sailors singing as they held aloft the Imperial German Navy Ensign. Then she went down and men drowned before our eyes when we could not drag them aboard, even though searchlights probed here and there to assist. Too intent on grasping feebly upraised hands I didn't see her go under, and when I looked there was only a ghostly column of smoke and steam to mark her grave. Back in Port Stanley as those rescued went over gangways onto lighters, our nearest cruisers cleared lower decks and, in recognition of the German squadron's overall gallantry, rendered them three rousing cheers.

SMS *Dresden* had gone into hiding among the treacherous maze of uncharted channels separating high granite upthrusts forming the south-western tip of Cape Horn, and although Admiral Sturdee's cruisers searched week after week, it remained for a *Cornwall* telegraphist to be the instrument of *Dresden*'s fate by intercepting her signal to a collier, ordering a rendezvous in Juan Fernandez Islands' Robinson Crusoe Bay, the one-time home of Alexander Selkirk. There on Sunday, 14 March 1915 she was cornered by *Kent*, *Glasgow*, and the armed merchant cruiser *Orama*, but immediately they opened fire *Dresden* raised a flag of truce. Lieutenant Wilhelm Canaris (Admiral Canaris who was executed in the Second World War for conspiracy against Hitler) was sent by boat to *Glasgow* with a letter of protest against this attack in neutral territory; however, having read it through, Captain Luce dismissed him back to *Dresden* with a written ultimatum: 'Haul down your flag, sir, inside ten minutes of receiving this final message or your ship will be destroyed.'

Those ten long minutes ticked by; the German Imperial Navy Ensign stayed up, surrounding hillsides echoed to the rumble of Royal Naval gunfire then, opening her seacocks while men placed delay-fused demolition charges in all magazines, *Dresden* abandoned ship in time to be well clear when she erupted and sank; her dead and wounded being taken to Valparaiso for burial or hospitalisation.

Germany's Far East Squadron no longer existed, nor did the male side of Spee's aristocratic lineage. His elder son Leutnant zur see und Adjutant Otto Ferdinand Maria Hubertus Reichsgraf von Spee, was lost with *Nurnberg*. His younger son, Leutnant zur see Heinrich Franz Irenaus Maximilian Hubertus von Spee, went down in *Gneisenau*. He, Vizeadmiral und Chef des Kreuzergeschvaders, Count Maximilian Johannes Maria Hubertus Reichsgraf von Spee, 1st and 2nd Class Iron Cross, died with his flagship *Scharnhorst*.

So the austere German Vice Admiral led his spectral troupe off-stage at the curtain-drop of Act I. Then after the briefest of intermissions it rose again to introduce some of Act II's star performers – Sir Eugen Millington-Drake KCMG – his years-long friend, Uruguayan Minister of Defence, General Alfredo Campos – Kapitan zur see, Chef des Panzerschiff Hans Langsdorf – Commodore South American Station, 'Crack-o-dawn' Henry Harwood – then an imposing cast in the preludes of a play to be billed as '*La Batalla del Rio de la Plata*'.

During a July 1919 Buenos Aires to Southampton passage, the meat ship *El Paraguaya* called in at Montevideo where young Eugen Millington-Drake went ashore and met Lieutenant Henry Harwood, Torpedo Officer of HMS *Southampton* secured at the same wharf; C-in-C South American Station's cruiser flagship had been invited to visit Uruguay, the only South American country to have severed relations with Germany in the First World War. The SA Station was vast and its RN cruisers patrolled Pacific coastal waters extending south from Peru's Callao, down the length of Chile to the Argentinian and Patagonian regions, round the Horn and north along their Atlantic shores to Uruguayan marine territory, then up Brazil's long coast to the wide Amazon outflow. In the two years Harwood served during that commission he made a point of contacting service and political dignitaries, learning their languages and studying each country's attitude to Britain and Germany, becoming a courteous and successful ambassador.

Harwood's career was punctuated with promotion periods in Naval Staff Colleges succeeded by positions of higher responsibility aboard foreign station ships, until August 1936 when he returned to the South American Station as Commodore-in-Charge with his burgee atop *Exeter*'s foremast. Again he played golf with Millington-Drake who now directed Britain's diplomatic posts in Uruguayan Montevideo and west across the River Plate in nearby Argentinian Buenos Aires. He dined and exchanged friendly views with his long-acquaintance Uruguayan ministers and service chiefs, but was more circumspect with Argentinians. He discussed with his other cruiser captains and senior staff the problems to be faced in the event of another war; and in 1937 during squadron visits to South American Pacific ports, won Chilean Government gratitude to Britain when Admiralty hurried *Exeter* to Talcahuano where there'd been a devastating earthquake. Harwood's seamen, electricians, varied technicians, medical staff and cooks, gave unstinted assistance week upon week until local authorities signified their ability to cope.

German and British factions had for decades vied for favour from South America's populace and aristocracy, while German propaganda insinuated British exploitation of those engaged or employed, so, in October 1938 it was decided that during a tour of South American capitals the Marquess of Willingdon, Lord Milne, would present long-service medals to those employed by British companies – gold for thirty years – silver for twenty-five – bronze for twenty. Inscribed '*Con los felicitaciones del Marques Willingdon*' and bearing his family crest, they were presented together with a parchment in Spanish, recording his Montevideo presentation speech commending every branch of service to Britain throughout Uruguay. Later in response to requests that company pensioners might also be rewarded, a local mint was contracted to produce similar medals for presentation at the Central Uruguay Railway Headquarters. Then there ensued such pro-British sentiment that when the Marquess was found to be a British Field Marshal, an invitation from the Minister of Defence, General Campos, to stay a month at the Legation over February/March 1939 was readily accepted by Lord and Lady Milne. Uruguayan defence and political elite gloried at ceremonials such as the '*Parade des Presidente Lancers*' in century old uniform worn during independence; and at the pomp arranged for the Lord and Lady at '*Escuela Militar and Escuela Navale*' where they awarded Willingdon medals to both services, this time gold, silver, bronze, according to seniority. On all these occasions they were accompanied by General Campos who too would in a short nine months be called onstage to perform in the *Graf Spee* drama.

We go back now to a sundrenched Saturday, 30 June 1934 at Wilhelm-shaven. Teutonic throngs amid pomp and splendour surround Supreme Commander German Forces Adolf Hitler, and Grand-Admiral Erich Raeder. Highly polished brass instruments of a naval band glisten, rendering muted airs as Huberta von Spee is guided to an electronic console on the Reich-Fuehrer's red-white-and-black festooned podium. A public-address system names Germany's third pocket battleship *Admiral von Graf Spee* in honour of Huberta's father; then she presses the button to launch Raeder's future commerce raider.

Only some of those spectators were aware that just the previous day, units of Britain's Home Fleet had visited nearby Swinemunde, and that the recently commissioned *Achilles*' liberty men would fraternise with *kriegsmariners* in Kiel on 7 July before returning to Sheerness, but none predicted the South Atlantic clash in just five years' time between these friendly warships. Right now *Graf Spee* was being towed to her fitting-out yard from where, after eighteen months, on Wednesday, 1 January 1936 in sleet-driven conditions she headed for the Kattegat fully crewed, ready to test her two huge triple 11″ turrets, her secondary dual 5.9″ mounts, an array of A/A weapons, her torpedo tubes, and her eight 7,000 hp diesel engines specially designed to assure 28 knots if needed, plus all the German electronic gadgetry evolved to that period; and when clear of the moles she stopped to crane her Arado float-plane inboard.

Meanwhile on Tuesday, 31 March 1936 alongside one of Sheerness's drab wet granite wharves, 'Down-unders' off their decommissioned *Diomede* were recommissioning *Achilles* on loan to the NZD under Captain Irvine G. Glennie RN, a First World War destroyer skipper ranked captain in 1933. They would work up their new cruiser with ships of the Home and Med Fleets based at Gibraltar, keeping in mind the probable resumption of a global war with Germany, the increasingly evident opponent. They would then bring their ship home to New Zealand via the Panama Canal, en route catapulting off the Walrus to survey and land on island lagoons inside atolls, sufficiently spaced down through the Pacific Ocean for a proposed Vancouver-Auckland flying-boat route.

CHAPTER II

HMS/HMNZS Philomel, 5th of the Name, Mother of our RNZN

H IS OR HER MAJESTY'S SHIPS *Philomel* date back to 1806 when a Brid-port-built 384-ton 18-gun sloop was so named at her launching. During one of her relentless attacks on French vessels attempting to breach the Royal Naval blockade of Toulon in 1809, she destroyed some of the heavily laden storeships before three Tricolour frigates bore down on her, but being a fast sailer she lured them toward the 74-gunned line-of-battle ship *Repulse*, whose accurate broadsides soon saw the frustrated frigates wearing away to sanctuary within Toulon's inshore defensive battle fleet. In October that year she escorted British troops to the French-occupied island, Ithaca, where her softening-up bombardment led to a successful amphibious assault, followed by the French garrison commandant's surrender aboard *Philomel*. But only eleven years after her launching, and shortly after the Napoleonic Wars, she and many other Royal Navy ships were sold to defray wartime expenses.

The second *Philomel*, a 230-ton, 10-gun sloop launched in 1823 at Ports-mouth, participated in the 1827 Battle of Navarino against the Turks, an engagement wherein she suffered one man killed and seven wounded. Her short navy career ended in 1833 when she too was sold out of the service, but 1843 saw the Plymouth commissioning of *Philomel* number three, the 360-ton, 8-gun brig whose honours board recorded her action at the 1845 Battle of Obligado, also her 1851 confrontation against Nigeria's unruly King of Lagos; then nineteen years later she was sold out of reserve. *Philomel* number four emerged from Deptford in 1867 as a 663-ton screw gunboat which took part in the 1874 destruction of Masmaah Fortress in the Gulf of Oman, then in 1875 she steamed east in a flotilla to assist the Perak Expedition in Malaya, before she too went under the War Asset Realisation Board auctioneer's hammer in 1885.

Four years now elapsed before the keel of *Philomel* the fifth was laid down at Devonport, England. Over the months her steel-framed skeleton materialised, then her bronzed-steel plating, internal partitions, fire-brick furnaces, boilers and triple expansion power plant, reciprocating engines, bridge, masts, guns and everything necessary for a 3rd Class 2,575-ton, 7,000 hp, 19 knot, coal-fuelled cruiser, armed with eight 4.7" B.L. guns, eight 3-pdrs, four water-cooled machine guns, two torpedo tubes, and 217 complement. Finally fitted out from Captain's cabin to boys' messdeck, she lay alongside under the Red Duster, still crewed by dockyard artisans and a nucleus of RN departmental officers already appointed to the ship with Captain Charles Campbell.

Engaged at that time on her design was a Mr J.H. Narbeth, father of the 1945–6 Chief Constructor to our New Zealand Naval Board, Mr J.H. Narbeth; and so entwined with the Royal Navy of the late 1800s were we, that in 1946 an Invercargill resident, Mr J.W. Puckey, remembered visiting the cruiser with his father who was Foreman of England's Devonport Yard in 1890. He recalled noting a hammer mark on all rivets to testify that each had been tested; and he recalled *Philomel's* 28 August 1890 launching with Naval Traditions by a Royal Marine band, interspersed among speeches and ceremony before she took the water. Seven months thence she underwent English Channel trials, but another eight months passed until 10 November 1891 when she commissioned for service on the then designated Cape of Good Hope Station, a point of interest being that although steam driven, she was rigged to use her Admiralty issue of: 2 Fore Gaffsails, 1 Gaff Topsail, 1 Trysail, 1 Main Gaffsail, 1 Main Trysail, 1 Fore Skysail, 1 Foretop Skysail and 1 Main Skysail. But while stepping the foremast, a rigger noticed that it was stamped 'Devonport Dockyard 1757', which the dockyard officials recorded, and although a 1950s NZNB request was made to Admiralty for details, especially of its previous use in action, the reply regrettably could furnish no further information.

On 10 November 1891 Captain Campbell attended at Admiralty House to be briefed on *Philomel's* Cape of Good Hope Station commission, but working up exercises and a return to Devonport yards to have a chart room built into the forebridge, delayed her Simonstown arrival until June 1892. At this time Britain and South Africa were still embroiled in some fifty years of skirmishes and warfare over territories, gold mining, and Charles James Fox's 1834 Slave Abolishment Act which the Dutch population resented. Therefore during her first six years on station *Philomel* did endless sea-time, intercepting persistent slave-trade dhows and larger vessels whose masters had no compunction in heaving the chained slaves overboard as soon as they saw her mastheads. As a diversion she assisted in the Bohemie Creek expedition, and in 1896 joined Rear Admiral Rawson's flagship *St George*, together with the gunboats *Sparrow*, *Thrush* and *Racoon* in defeating Sayyid Khalid's rebel hordes who had assassinated the Protectorate Sultan of Zanzibar, occupied his palace, and seized the cruiser *Glasgow* recently gifted to him by Britain. In an hours' long naval bombardment *Glasgow* was sunk, the palace fortress was destroyed and the few rebels not killed or captured by landing parties, fled. In 1897 *Philomel* assisted in the Benin

Expedition before being recalled in 1898 to Devonport for an extensive refit after which she returned in 1899 to the 'Cape' Station, for more operations in the 2nd Boer War which ended on 31 May 1902 under the Vereeniging Treaty, five days after the death of Sir Cecil Rhodes (Founder of Rhodesia, now Zimbabwe).

Philomel paid off at Devonport in March 1902, thereafter lying at anchor in the Firth of Forth for five years, but the Kaiser's naval building upsurge was worrying Britain, so anything with propellers and guns had to be recommissioned. She was towed en route to Ireland's Haulbowline Yards by the cruiser *Hampshire* (lost with all hands including Lord Kitchener en route to Russia, 5 June 1916). Then having been given a major facelift and a new commanding officer, Captain John R. Seagrave, she joined the Mediterranean Fleet in 1908, gaining RN recognition and Sicilian Government acclaim for her ship's company's assistance tirelessly rendered at that year's catastrophic Messina earthquake, subsequently doing strenuous service quelling unrest in Somaliland. Eventually the unrelenting Red Sea heat took its toll but after a spell back in England she sailed for the Persian Gulf on 19 August 1909, restricting the operations of known gun-runners over the next two years, at the conclusion of which she was made available to the New Zealand Government, thus giving birth to the Dominion Division of the Royal Navy. Arriving in New Zealand waters accompanied by her sister ships *Psyche* and *Pyramus* in mid-1914, she sailed alone to Wellington where on 15 July at the authorisation of Governor-General Lord Liverpool, Captain P.H. Hall-Thompson CMG RN hoisted his Commodore burgee, an appointment which also carried the role of Naval Adviser to the government.

Two days earlier RN officers and men who'd volunteered for a three-year commission on New Zealand's cruiser had arrived as passengers on the *Arawa*, those returning to England left the ship, and the first draft of New Zealand seamen and stokers humped their bags and hammocks up *Philomel*'s for'ard gangway and into their various messdecks. Then days later, with an auspicious farewell, the cruiser departed for a shake-down cruise in Marlborough Sounds, a brief excursion curtailed by her recall from Picton to be brought onto a war footing with 'called-up' reservists. On Saturday, 8 August, four days after New Zealand declared war against Germany, she again steamed out from Wellington, this time to join *Psyche* and *Pyramus* at Auckland. It was well known that Vice Admiral Count Maximilian Reichsgraf von Spee's Far East Squadron based at Tsingtao, China, comprised the 8″ heavy cruisers *Scharnhorst*, *Gneisenau*, and the light cruisers *Emden*, *Dresden*, *Nurnberg*, and *Leipzig*, which operating together would be a threat to Pacific maritime trade. At present Western Samoa flew the German ensign, and should it be garrisoned with enemy troops, Spee could use Apia as a coaling base. It was essential that this should be forestalled, preparations for such an operation had been pigeon-holed in the Defence Department's 'TOP SECRET' safe for months, and on a blustery Saturday, 15 August *Philomel*, *Psyche* and *Pyramus* escorted the 'Samoa Expeditionary Force' aboard the USSCoy transports *Moeraki*, *Monowai*, trailed by their collier *Waipori*, out of Waitemata Harbour en route to New Caledonia. There at Noumea they were joined by France's heavy cruiser *Montcalm*, together with Australia's battlecruiser *Australia*, and *Melbourne* which coaled from *Waipori* while *Philomel*'s lower-deck men toiled for hours, bunkering ship from barge loads of convict-made ingots of compressed coal-dust, pitch, and tar, each weighing 14 pounds.

At last everything was ready for departure, Admiral Patey's flagship *Australia* had busied her halyards with flags, while other signalmen were semaphoring and flashing leaving-harbour instructions to each ship, but soon after passing Amedee Lighthouse the trooper *Monowai* grounded on coral sand; her stores and military equipment had to be lightered off before she could be towed astern, then twenty-six hours later, at high tide on Sunday, 23 August when her troops re-embarked she signalled readiness to proceed.

Now adequately protected against a chance interception by Admiral von Spee's German squadron, *Monowai*, *Moeraki* and *Waipori*, steamed eastward under a clear tropical sky indistinguishable on the horizon from an unruffled blue sea. A coaling stop at Suva, then on again toward Samoa with *Psyche* dispatched ahead to give ample warning if Spee's squadron had already arrived at Apia. It hadn't, *Psyche* had entered under a flag of truce, the remainder came to anchor throughout Sunday forenoon, 30 August, blue-jackets and troops surrounded the town's small German garrison, and after an official German surrender Samoa was proclaimed to be a British possession.

Simultaneously with New Zealand's occupation of Samoa, an Australian expedition escorted by the cruisers *Sydney* and *Encounter* was on its way to haul down the German Ensign at Rabaul so, immediately Admiral Patey was assured there would be no uprising in Apia, he left *Philomel* in charge and departed with *Australia*, *Melbourne* and *Montcalm* to cover the Australian convoy now nearing Port Moresby. And probably fortunately for the little New Zealand cruiser she and her now empty troopships were ordered to return home, being days later near the Tongan Islands when loud German naval transmissions indicated the proximity of Spee's Pacific Squadron. On Sunday, 23 August when Japan declared war against Germany, Admiral von Spee's cruisers were at Ponape Harbour in the Caroline Islands two thousand miles from their China Station base at Tsingtao. It would have been unwise to return there so Spee bunkered all ships to capacity, then steamed south-east at the speed of his slow attendant colliers. Having stopped at Christmas Island to water and coal the squadron, he arrived off German West Samoa in mid-September, but finding Apia now strongly garrisoned under the New Zealand Ensign, and being convinced by deliberate Royal Navy W/T ruses that the battlecruiser *Australia* and numerous cruisers were in the vicinity, he steamed away eastward, detached the light cruiser *Nurnberg* to cut the Trans-Pacific cable at Fanning Island, then continued on to replenish at Valparaiso. But in attempting to invade the Falkland Islands months later, he was defeated by Admiral Stoddart's battlecruisers and cruisers which within twenty-four hours eliminated the German Far East naval threat.

Meantime back in Auckland on 12 September 1914, Captain Hall-Thompson and his senior officers were briefed on the ships' next operation as one of the escorts for New Zealand's 1st Expeditionary Force about to depart for Egypt. She would sail on the 23rd with HMNZ Troopships Nos 8 and 12, *Waimana* and *Star of India*, to join those from Wellington in mid-Tasman. But typical of decisions and counter-decisions between service chiefs and politicians, *Philomel* and her transports were barely out of sight of our coast when they were ordered back to port. Parliament had insisted on a stronger naval escort before the main body could sail, and the Auckland contingent must be brought down to Wellington.

'Another bloody snafu,' from messdeck grouchers, 'flamin' war'll be over before we get there.' So farewellers did it all over again from Auckland's wharves and waterfronts when *Philomel* and her two charges helmed round North Head en route to the capital where week by week more ships arrived, the NZ-stationed RN cruisers *Psyche*, *Pyramus*, and our own *Philomel* all swelling city pub patronage until the agreed day of departure.

Immediately government had announced its intention of sending an Expeditionary Force to assist Britain at war, New Zealand's General Officer Commanding, Major General Sir A.J. Godley, required each Military District – Auckland, Wellington, Canterbury, Otago – to recruit an infantry battalion comprising four double companies. Lieutenant Colonels, majors, captains and lieutenants were appointed to each 2,000-strong regiment, then within short weeks the whole New Zealand force embarked fully equipped for dispatch overseas, Wellington District Battalion on the appropriated liners *Maunganui* (Commodore), *Limerick* and *Arawa*. Horse stalls had been installed along all promenade decks, and multi-thousand citizens crammed into Newton Park on Wednesday, 23 September for the farewell parade, inspected by Lord Liverpool and followed by speeches from the Prime Minister, Minister of Defence, and Wellington's Mayor. Then as soon as the contingent marched back aboard through flag-waving throngs excited by reverberating drumbeats and blaring bugles, *Limerick* and *Arawa* moved out to anchor mid-stream; but rumours of a delayed departure were confirmed within the week when both troopships secured back alongside near *Maunganui*.

Four more liners carrying the South Island troops berthed on 28 September, and it was rumoured that uncertainty over Germany's Pacific Squadron's whereabouts was keeping the convoy in harbour until Admiralty could supply an adequate escort. All horses with their cavalrymen were disembarked and railed to Trentham or other temporary camps, companies of foot soldiers were marched out to Wellington's rugged hills to fight mock battles, while those recruited from the Fielding district returned there to be entertained on the racecourse by ladies' groups who provided entertainment and lavish delicacies. Then with the arrival on Thursday, 15 October of Britain's 16,000-ton, $4 \times 9''$, $10 \times 7.5''$ gunned 23-knot heavy cruiser *Minotaur* and Japan's battleship HIJMS *Ibuki*, all units re-embarked and moved out to anchorages in readiness for next daybreak's final departure.

Early-morning Eastbourne and Hutt Valley chimney smoke was overclouded by dense funnel emissions as the ten transports and their six escorts raised steam, weighed anchor and swung out into Cook Strait at last on the way to Egypt. A brief pit stop at Hobart for coal, water, provisions, and a full marching kit parade through the city centre and miles out into suburban countryside, delighted Tasmanians, young and old bringing refreshments to the troops each time the column rested. Cakes, fruit, massive enamel jugs of home-made fruit drinks were handed round the perspiring men immaterial of rank, all the way out and all the way back aboard, where cases of apples had been shipped throughout the day. But across the Australian Bight from 23 to 28 October things were anything but friendly as huge seas lifted bows high above oncoming cold rollers, wrestled the transports viciously port to starboard, then surged away midships to leave them tottering, propellors thrashing air, bows crashing down into seething chasms, hopelessly seasick men bruising and breaking limbs against each ship's steel obstructions. Out on the convoy's flank *Philomel* shipped mountainous seas down her starboard waist, seas which rivered through her foc'sle messdecks when she plunged, then surged aft to flood her covered quarterdeck, officers' cabins and wardroom passages when her stern shuddered deep into foaming troughs.

Stokers struggled for footholds on the heaving boiler-room plates, opened furnace doors to rake slag from roaring white-hot coals, shovelled more in and slammed the doors to contain those angry spitting flames.

Four nights out from Hobart the Antarctic-born storm roared away eastward, stewards and quarterdeck men rehabilitated *Philomel*'s Captain's cabin and officers' quarters, messdecks were dried out and made livable, and daybreak saw the convoy and escorts once more steaming in correct formation, soldiers and navymen again topsides, anxious for their first sight of Albany's offshore islands. Bright sunshine greeted the New Zealand convoy as it steamed into King George Sound to anchor near an armada of liners carrying Australia's Expeditionary Force; colliers, storeships and water barges servicing them day and floodlit night throughout the next fortnight, until dawn on Wednesday, 11 November when the combined convoy, thirty-six transports and their escorts, steamed down the sound in single line ahead formation, a magnificent spectacle of Dominion allegiance to the King. And when clear of land the Australian liners, still in their peacetime colours, were disposed in four long columns, with New Zealand's transports already overpainted drab grey bringing up the rear in two columns. But *Sydney* and *Melbourne* had taken the place of *Philomel* and *Pyramus* who were now days up the Western Australian coast, dispatched there to search for Germany's light cruiser *Emden*, recently reported by Indonesian Intelligence to be making for the Indian Ocean. It was not however to be the New Zealand cruiser's hour of glory; on 22 November, when eleven days away from Albany, *Sydney* raced north-eastward trailing black smoke and high-pressure steam; wireless signals from Cocos Island only sixty miles distant were reporting a suspicious warship entering harbour and refusing to answer flashlamp enquiries. *Ibuki*, who'd taken *Sydney's* place on the outer screen, hoisted an immense Japanese battle-flag, belched clouds of coal smuts and raced off after her, only to be recalled with a reminder that her role was protection of the convoy; and some three hours later *Sydney* broke W/T silence with a self-evident coded message saying she had sighted the enemy and was about to engage. *Philomel*, then near Christmas Island, raised full steam and headed towards the coded position, but about noon the Australian cruiser again morsed the ether with the tremendous news that she'd shelled the German cruiser *Emden* which ran herself onto a reef to avoid sinking. A terse signal and not descriptive of the gunnery-wrought wreckage, crumpled funnels, shattered upperworks and fallen masts, later described by boats sent to administer to *Emden's* many wounded and take prisoner those not killed. Cheers resounded throughout ship after ship of the convoy as each received news of *Sydney's* victory, *Ibuki* lowered her battle-flag, and *Philomel* received a cyphered message directing her to Singapore from where she escorted three French transports to Aden.

When crossing the Equator all ships paid traditional respect to Father Neptune, but *Arawa's* hilarities ended with probably New Zealand's first war-service fatality when Captain E.J.H. Webb of the NZ Medical Corps dived into Neptune's pool from atop an adjacent deck house; unfortunately there was insufficient depth and he remained unconscious with multiple head and neck injuries until he died days later in a Colombo hospital. Shortly after the convoy's arrival, *Sydney* steamed slowly up harbour past the New Zealand ships whose troops had been cautioned to 'Stand quiet as she passes!'; a mark of respect for rows upon rows of stretcher cases covering her decks from the battered *Emden*.

Meanwhile *Philomel* had deposited her three French transports in Aden where she was ordered to patrol the Red Sea, unenviable weeks of onerous sea-time in suffocating lower-deck heat, sweat rashes, insipid warm drinking water and only salt water for personal hygiene, occasionally an unidentified vessel to stop and board in case it might be aiding Turkey after her declaration of war against the British Empire. There was the day that New Zealand transports signalled 'Haere mai, Haere mai to taua hoa' from afar, as the Expeditionary Force, now joined by the three French troopers, passed endlessly from mid-forenoon to dusk. There was the day that she fired her first angry shots of the War, bombarding and destroying the Mocha seaport shipyard which had been building dhows for the Turks. Then there was *that* day when she received radioed orders to proceed to Suez dockyard for an overdue refit, but Suez had inadequate facilities and *Philomel* immediately left for Tor, a British quarantine station on the Sinai Peninsula said to be under seige by Turkish forces. Thirty men were landed with two Maxims, Captain Hall-Thompson moored his ship where the guns could cover the station's perimeter, but on the third day, 23 December, nothing had occurred and she was ordered to Port Said then out again on Christmas Day 1914, sole escort for nine newly camouflaged liners to Malta. Not a White Ensign among a harbour crammed with warships, all flying the Tricolour; Britain had made her central Mediterranean base available as Headquarters for the French Fleet operating in the Adriatic; one French dreadnought lay at anchor minus most of her bows due to torpedoing; many cruisers and destroyers were awaiting repair, and others were alongside giving leave to the throngs of matelots enjoying Malta's bawdy entertainment. Yet there was a month in dock for *Philomel*, weeks in the care of Maltese nurses for her worst heat-affected cases, and nights in the care of Malta's navy-minded femininity for both officers and men, after which the little cruiser and her 250 ship's complement departed fully rejuvenated and ready for their next assignment.

When Turkey's alliance with Germany put Allied Suez Canal shipping under threat, Britain declared Egypt to be one of her protectorates and took military measures to safeguard the vital waterway, especially from attack across the desert lands south of Turkey. Plans were being implemented preparatory to full-scale landings north of Syria, and on 29 January 1915 *Philomel* departed Malta for Port Said, there being ordered to destroy Alexandretta Gulf sea and coast traffic wherever encountered or made aware of, and to oversee the landing of troops at Alexandretta town, to cut a rail line following the ancient camel route from Baghdad. Rather than undergo a bombardment of his unfortified town by *Philomel*, the local sheik agreed to destroy all trains and rolling stock, but not having any explosives or demolition experts: 'Could it be done under a truce by the British navy and army?' 'Certainly!' A time at the marshalling yards was negotiated, safe-viewing areas were arranged for both Turkish officials and British brass, then ground-shaking detonations cart-wheeled locomotives, goods wagons and all manner of railway apparatus high over mud buildings in dust-clouds black with disintegrating debris, eminently enjoyed by Arab and British spectators and everyone topside on *Philomel* at her nearby anchorage. Other coastal landings accomplished varying results, one being the spectacular derailment of a train-load of enemy troop reinforcements which turned out to be unfortunate camels in the first train to arrive; the second locomotive with its carriages full of troops screeched to a stop short of the carnage and reversed rapidly out of sight. Then followed a tragic day on Monday, 8 February, after a softening-up bombardment of an intended beachhead, where the landing party was to intercept a caravan of pack camels making for Alexandretta. This time it was a ruse and 200-plus riflemen greeted the 2 officers and 15 ratings with an intense but erratic fusillade. Dragging their wounded into a shallow gully, those able to shot each Turk daring to approach until dark when the men retired to waiting boats, leaving three dead, one of them a New Zealander, Able Seaman Knowles RNR.

About now Captain Hall-Thompson received a written ultimatum from the local Turkish Governor and his Syrian Ottoman Army C-in-C, General Djemal Pasha. If the Captain of HMS *Doris* wasn't executed for killing several Arabian civilians during a recent bombardment, five British ser-vicemen would be drawn by ballot from many imprisoned at Damascus, and summarily shot. Reply letters from British agents and intelligence officers previously embarked at Famagusta, convinced the Governor that not only his life, but those of his army C-in-C, and his Commandant Rifat Bey, would without fail be forfeited if the retribution threat took place. More correspondence gave a Turkish assurance that it hadn't been intended to take war prisoners' lives, but HMS *Philomel* should depart to look after Britain's own interests which would now assuredly be in danger.

Within days the cruiser *Bacchante* relieved *Philomel* which now spent weeks traversing north and south through the Suez Canal, on one occasion scaring the hair up on everyone's neck when she hit a mine laid in the waterway at night by the Turks, but fortunately when retrieved it was found to be faulty. Her next task was to tow two shallow-draft gunboats from Suez to Mesopotamia, but when they both filled and sank during stormy weather in the Red Sea *Philomel* coaled at Aden, then sped to Berbera where she mustered crew volunteers for a 'Camel Corps' to capture or eliminate British Somaliland's Mad Mullah. However, this operation died in its hilarious infancy and all the volunteers nursed their sore backsides back to unsympathetic mates' messdecks. GHQ Aden telegraphed Captain Hall-Thompson to embark a platoon of miscreant natives hijacked from Berbera bazaars. Each evil-smelling 'volunteer' carried his own ancient firearm with or without ammunition; they were transported along the coast to the worst trouble spot, Shallub, offloaded into the surf through which they struggled ashore, rifles and gear held high; and as *Philomel*'s Captain later wrote: 'I doubt if they ever did much damage to the Mullah and his dervishes.'

Mid-June found the ship's company waving to men of the NZ Expeditionary Force manning gun and searchlight posts along both canal embankments as the ship coursed north back into the Med. Previously friendly Senussi tribesmen at points along Libya's coast were reported to be preparing to aid enemy landings near Sollum, but several rounds of 4.7 lobbed close to insurgent leader camps seemed to do the trick and Intelligence said the threat no longer existed: 'Would you be so kind as to buzz off down to Aden?' So *Philomel* once more parted Biblical waters then sped down the Red Sea 'with all despatch', British troops at Sheik Othman fortress only twenty miles from the strategic port were being hard pressed by Turkish armed forces and some of the garrison were retreating towards Aden while other British troops had been driven away from the port's freshwater wells. *Philomel*'s landing parties had already been armed, and a mobile wireless telegraphy unit mustered with them for immediate transfer to the front lines on arrival, as were those of more RN ships coming in to anchor, then no sooner were these bluejackets in place than a general charge was made on the enemy, taking some of his trenches but being driven back out by Turkish counter-charges. It was not going to be easy. The fortress at Sheik Othman was vacated, then retaken as reinforcements arrived, and three more of *Philomel*'s ship's company died among the many army and navy lives lost in that four months' savage fighting up to late October 1915. Aden was no longer under threat, but a crisis was now arising in Persia.

Captain Hall-Thompson entered Navy Office Aden to be informed that German 'Drang Nach Osten' agents were influencing Islamic Kurd and Arab leaders against Britain so, because of his previous affable dealings with the heads of coastal villages, he would take *Philomel* into the Persian Gulf and:

(i)   Protect British shipping.

   (ii) Revisit your Sheik associates and regain their allegiance if need be.

   (iii) Act immediately as you deem fit should you encounter any threat to British interests ashore. Any threat to allied interests should be reported by W/T to Navy Office Aden or Navy Office Bombay for further decision.

So, apart from an occasional maintenance and repair docking at Bombay, *Philomel* cruised the Persian Gulf for almost fifteen months as Senior Officer afloat, investigating problems at Muhammerah, Abadan, Bushire, Kuwait and lesser ports, sounding her way through the Shatt-el-Arab shallows to board and check unlisted vessels near the Tigris/Euphrates delta; anchoring off Kuwait and landing armed units, when the Sheik was threatened by Persian troops violating the border west of Shahpur; and progressively suffering from the torments of dhobi-rash and other extreme-heat afflictions. There was little relief from monotony, but once when coaling at Bahrain *Philomel* left post-haste, rounded Qatar Peninsula and raced to the vicinity of two villages just north of Abu Zabi. There, two Arab headmen had been reported to be in conflict, each had some ancient muzzle-loading ship's guns but they were critically short of cannonballs. To exterminate their neighbours' habitats and harems, tribesmen charged the smooth-bore weapons, man-handled heavy round-shot into the muzzles and shouted vile imprecations as they fired with an ear-shattering BAANNNGGG and a dense cloud of rolling smoke. The missiles bounded to a stop well wide of their target, the 'enemy' rushed out, retrieved whatever they could and rolled them into the snouts of *their* already charged cannons. Another almighty BAANNNGGG, clouds of acrid smoke, and thus the 'battle' raged, shot after retrieved shot to the shouted insults of whirling-dervish fanatics.

    This was observed for an hour by Captain Hall-Thompson before he was rowed ashore under a flag of truce, told each sheik in turn that their confrontation must cease within a week, 'Or else!' But on returning to Sharjah in company with HMS *Clio*, *Philomel* found smoke palls still alternating over the villages' intervening desert; so both offended chiefs were brought off to the Captain's cabin, where the wrath of Allah echoed off its walls to be heard along the wardroom passage and out onto the quarter-deck. Then finally after Hall-Thompson's declaration that all the guns would be destroyed or confiscated if their problem wasn't resolved forthwith, a written agreement was put on the table between them; they were left alone for more long minutes, after which the now seemingly mollified Islamic neighbours appended their signatures. Sweetened black coffee was brought in to cement their new friendship, whilst each loudly eulogised the others' 'inestimable merits', and reiterated his unending faith in Allah's friend, Great Britain.

Philomel's complement of English, Scots, Irish, Australian, Newfoundland, Maltese, Somali, Abyssinian, Arabian, and some sixty New Zealand navy men were long overdue for a rest away from the Gulf's heat-induced torments. But enemy agents were still encouraging coastal tribes to carry out acts of sabotage against Gulf communications, so Persia's principal port, Bushire, was taken by British land and sea forces, and Gurkha platoons were transported to all telegraph stations along the eastern and northern Persian Gulf coastal telegraph line, by *Philomel* and *Pyramus*, who signalled Maori greetings on joining company once more.

Philomel, apart from her March 1902 to February 1908 lay-up in reserve, had now completed some twenty years service, much of it in tropical heat. On 3 January 1917 she departed Muscat for another Bombay docking, but this time it became evident she needed a complete overhaul and updating, boilers, engine, armament, the lot.

'Costly?' from an Admiralty estimator.

'Yes, too damned costly. Send her back to New Zealand as is. They can use her as a training ship.'

'What a good idea,' to conclude the conversation.

So she helmed south around Australia and arrived Wellington on Friday, 16 March, thence continuing her war career downgraded to a coastal and primary harbour guardship, most of her eight 4.7″ guns being removed to arm merchantmen, as were her seven 3-pounders and Maxim machine guns. On Thursday, 19 July 1917, Captain Hall-Thompson, having commanded *Philomel* right throughout her overseas war service, looked wistfully about his cabin, glanced at the empty cabinet from which his wife and family photographs had been packed, shook hands and talked warmly with his personal servant, then went out to greet his successor, Lieutenant Commander C.J. Kelly RNR, who'd been brought out of his retirement to take *Philomel* into hers.

However, shortly after she paid off into maintenance care Navy Office Wellington recommissioned her as a depot ship for the minesweepers *Nora Niven*, *Simplon*, and the chartered whaler *Hananui*, whose crews, supplemented by officers and ratings from *Philomel*, spent the next fifteen months sweeping up and destroying forty-seven of the sixty mines laid by Germany's raider *Wolf* off Farewell Spit and other areas. Then with the Armistice signed in Paris by German plenipotentiaries on Monday, 11 November 1918, her remaining ship's company laid aft onto the poop for the Minister of Defence's congratulatory speech, mentioning that *Philomel* as a New Zealand-owned light cruiser had carried our flag with honour, as had the many New Zealand officers and ratings of the Australasian Naval Force serving throughout the War aboard the cruisers *Pyramus* and *Doris*. He then gave a glowing report on hundreds of New Zealanders who'd gone to England and served on RN ships, especially those who'd crewed fast, armed-motorboats at the Zeebrugge and Ostend actions. Before he left the ship he witnessed the decommissioning ceremony, watched her ensign and commissioning pennant being lowered to the Navy's bugled traditional, then reported to the Navy Board that *Philomel* would henceforth be reduced to care and maintenance pending a future decision on her use, and in the interim as from February 1918, there would be no specifically appointed Commanding Officer.

Worldwide, disarmament was the catch-cry, but there were those in Parliament still determined that our Dominion should be fully responsible for an on-station modern cruiser, 'on loan from Admiralty to train new entries sufficiently to man two cruisers within foreseeable years'. And three years later in 1921, when the Big Powers of the First World War were still denuding their navies to decrease expenditure, New Zealand was about to upgrade hers. But oil was now the in-thing as fuel for warships, and her ports didn't have storage facilities, coal yes, so Admiralty loaned the coal burner *Chatham* instead of the more modern oil-fuelled cruiser *Canterbury* then being considered.

Two months after her January arrival in Wellington, a 14 March 1921 Order in Council constituted the New Zealand Naval Board, comprising the Minister of Defence as Chairman, the Commodore as Naval Adviser and Commander-in-Chief New Zealand Station, a Second Naval Member, and a Naval Secretariat to be seconded from the Internal Affairs Department staff. Admiralty agreed that their Flower Class sloop *Veronica*, already based in New Zealand, would continue to be manned entirely by RN personnel and maintained financially by the British Government, but henceforth to be under the control of CCNZ as would a second sloop, *Laburnum*, on her arrival; and to upgrade the Dominion's naval status, a 20 June 1921 Order in Council designated the force as the New Zealand Division of the Royal Navy. Recently it had been decided to recommission *Philomel* as a stationary training ship to be based in Auckland's naval dockyard; Wellington Harbour Board technicians and naval ERAs toiled ceaselessly on her boilers and propulsion units to make her seaworthy, then with *Chatham* in company, Commander J.G. Walsh RN blanketed Eastbourne's environs with the thirty-year-old cruiser's coal smuts while departing, en route Auckland on her final self-powered port-to-port passage.

At first she anchored off Devonport Reserve, and in May 1921 recruiting commenced throughout New Zealand so effectively that thirty Seaman Boy and twenty-four Stoker applicants were selected, and when two months later *Chatham* departed Auckland on a Pacific Islands cruise half of the trainees were drafted to her. Meantime, reorganisation of the dockyard was proceeding apace. *Philomel* assisted by the tugs *Te Awhina* and *William*

C Daldy used her engines for the last time to go in astern shore-side of the Training Jetty; corrugated-iron-roofed wooden lecture rooms and a chapel were erected along the sea wall; and far side of the grassed parade ground-cum-sports field, a recreation room, a canteen, and a sick bay; but new entries were hustled along the jetty and up the old cruiser's midship gangway, then directed aft onto the quarterdeck to be sworn in and enlisted. This done they quickly absorbed the discipline of living aboard an actual warship and, on completion of their three-month Stoker course or twelve-month Seaman Boy course they were drafted to a cruiser; now well acquainted with parts of a ship, messdecks, bathrooms, drying rooms; quarterdeck to be saluted on crossing the brass strip; defaulters' table to be ordered 'OFF CAP!' for award of the Training Officer's degree of punishment; and that uneasy lift and roll as the bow wave of a passing vessel surged under *Philomel*.

This then was to be the role of our little cruiser, immobilised later when her engine and boilers were craned out and taken away to obscurity, strict discipline with the threat of cane lashing, dismissal from the Service as the most severe punishment; legendary Chief and Petty Officer Instructor names, some brutal, some not – 'Tojo' Vincent, 'Con' Canty, 'Gate' Atkinson, 'Tiddler' Smith who looked and grimaced like the film star Edward G. Robinson, Jim 'Doin's', 'Arty' Smitheram – and a 1930s Training Officer, Lieutenant 'Pug' Thew, athletic, manly and upright, blond and blue-eyed, strict but fair and popular. Some of us were trained as Wireless Telegraphists by PO Tel 'Pots' Sissley, others by appropriate instructors in gunnery, still more as torpedomen, but all with Germany's *Kriegsmarine* instilled as our future opponent. And here perhaps it might be appropriate to list the commanding officers who had occupied the old cruiser's Commanding Officer's Cabin:

Capt C. Campbell RN	10 Nov 1891	17 Oct 1894
Capt M.P. O'Callaghan RN	18 Oct 1894	9 Mar 1898
In reserve	10 Mar 1898	31 Nov 1898
Capt J.E. Bearcroft RN	1 Dec 1898	18 Mar 1902
In reserve for sale, no buyer	19 Mar 1902	31 Jan 1908
Capt J.R. Seagrave RN	1 Feb 1908	26 Jul 1909
Cdr V.G. Gurner RN	27 Jul 1909	16 Jan 1911
Cdr N.I. Stanley RN	17 Jan 1911	18 Sep 1911
Cdr G.N. Ballard RN	19 Sep 1911	14 Jul 1914
Capt P.H. Hall-Thompson RN	15 Jul 1914	19 Apr 1917
Lt Cdr C.J. Kelly RNR (Rtd)	20 Apr 1917	Feb 1918
Care and Maintenance only	Feb 1918	4 Aug 1920
Cdr J.G. Walsh RN	5 Aug 1920	31 Dec 1922

A/Cdr A.W.S. Agar VC DSO RN	1 Jan 1923	10 May 1923
Cdr I M. Miles OBE RN	11 May 1923	3 Dec 1925
Cdr F.C. Bradley RN	4 Dec 1925	24 May 1928
Cdr N. Clover RN	25 May 1928	1 Jan 1931
Cdr E.L. Berthon DSC RN	2 Jan 1931	9 Nov 1933
Cdr B.C.B. Brooke RN	10 Nov 1933	4 May 1936
Cdr C.B. Tinley RN	5 May 1936	31 Aug 1938
Capt H.M. Barnes RN	1 Sep 1938	13 Oct 1940
A/Cdr D.A. Bingley OBE RN	14 Oct 1940	21 Mar 1941
Capt E. Rotheram RN	22 Mar 1941	31 May 1942
A/Cdr J.C. Elworthy RN	1 Jun 1942	14 Apr 1946
Lt Cdr P. Phipps DSC RNZNVR*	15 Apr 1946	16 Jan 1947

* Vice Admiral Sir Peter Phipps KBE, DSC & bar, VRD, m.i.d., US Navy Cross. Born Milton, Otago, 7 June 1909; bank clerk; RNZNVR 1928–46; CO HMS *Bay* (Channel Convoys) 1940–1; HMNZS *Scarba* 1941–2; *Moa* 1943; *Matai* and *Arabis* (S/O 25th M/S Flotilla) 1944–5; transferred RNZN Feb 1946; CO *Philomel* 1946–7; Exec Officer *Bellona* 1948; CO *Tamaki* 1949–50; Naval Assistant, Second Naval Member 1950–3; Captain, 30 June 1952; Commodore 2nd Class, 7 June 1957; Rear Admiral, Chief of Naval Staff, 30 June 1963; Vice Admiral, Chief of Defence Staff, 1 July 1963; Retired 30 June 1965.

HMS/HMNZS *Philomel* ended her 56-year service as a warship, training ship, and depot ship, on Thursday, 16 January 1947, when her colours were lowered and her name was bestowed on our Devonport Naval Shore Establishment. She was bought for £750(NZ) by Strongman Shipping Company Ltd who had her towed to the shallows of Coromandel Harbour. There they stripped everything useful in building their twin-screw coaster *Coromel*, after which the little old relic's hulk was towed to the 100-fathom line off Cuvier Island and sunk ignominiously by explosive charges; not a bugle note to honour her demise; not one Navy Board member with sufficient foresight to have her preserved in Auckland Harbour, moored perhaps inside the Western Viaduct where sea cadets and naval reserves could establish their headquarters on board, gangways ship to shore as access for the public to be shown over the Mother of our Royal New Zealand Navy.

CHAPTER III

NZ Warships between the Wars

HMS *Chatham*, 'City' Class light cruiser, 5,400 tons, 548' long, 25,000 hp, 25.5 knots, coal fuelled, turbine driven, armament 8 × 6" single-mounted guns, 1 × 3" A/A, 4 × 3-pdrs, 4 Maxims, 2 × 21" torpedo tubes, 440 complement, built 1911 at Chatham Naval Dockyard.

During the First World War she escorted troopships to the Dardanelles and bombarded Turkish gun emplacements; she outgunned and sank the German cruiser *Konigsberg* in a one-to-one engagement off North-West Africa; then on Monday, 29 May 1916, while seaward of Yarmouth, Norfolk, on her way to join Jellicoe's battlefleet off Jutland, a mine blasted away most of her bows, necessitating a stern-first tow 130 miles back to Chatham. There she was repaired and put back into service for the remaining months of the Great War, after which in 1918 she went into reserve at the Nore until 1920 when Admiralty made her available 'on loan' to New Zealand.

Wednesday, 26 January 1921 dawned sultry over Waitemata Harbour, its sub-tropical strands of morning mist distorting up Auckland's many volcanic upthrusts to dissipate in the heat of our mid-summer forenoon sun. Mount Victoria's signalmen were already busying their halyards with international flags, rattling the shutters of a 15" carbon arc lamp and relaying by telephone initial messages received from HMS *Chatham*. Seen off Whangaparaoa as an indistinct blur under a curtain of smoke, the four-funnelled cruiser slowly materialised from Hauraki Gulf, rounded North Head, and secured City-side to a tremendous public welcome.

There, immediately her quarterdeck gangway had clanged down on Princes Wharf, she was boarded by a stream of official dignitaries politely manoeuvring for places of prominence, while their ladies chatted coyly with the ship's gold braid until our Governor General, Lord Jellicoe, mounted the awning-shaded dais to address Captain Alan G. Hotham RN and his officers. Others including the Prime Minister Sir William Massey, the Minister of Defence Sir Heaton Rhodes, and finally His Worship the Mayor of Auckland J.H. Gunson, spoke of this momentous naval occasion in New Zealand's maritime history. Those invited retired to the wardroom, a few elite entered the Captain's cabin, and HMS *Chatham*, 13th British warship of that name, became the country's first unit of our NZDRN.

She had recommissioned on Friday, 1 October 1920 under Captain Hotham; left Chatham on the 21st for Trinidad, then frog-hopped down a line of Atlantic and Pacific coal stops: Balboa 23 November, San Diego 8 December, Honolulu 21–26 December, Fanning Island 1 January 1921, Pago Pago 8–10 January, Apia 11 January, Suva 16–17 January, Port Fitzroy (Great Barrier Island) 22–26 January for a scrub-down, repaint and polish in preparation for her Auckland arrival.

But she was not the first HMS *Chatham* to visit our shores. The 7th, a 131-ton, 4-gun brig launched circa 1780, accompanied Commander George Vancouver's *Discovery* from April 1791 to 1795 on a Pacific exploration, and excerpts from *Chatham's* log state that on 2 November 1791 both ships entered New Zealand's Dusky Sound, to shelter and repair damage sustained in their storm-driven Tasman Sea crossing from Australia. *Chatham's* Commanding Officer Lieutenant Broughton then wrote that having departed Dusky Sound on 22 November bound for Otaheite, they parted company during a gale, and on 23 November he approached a barren land inhabited by hostile natives. Unable to establish friendly relations, he nailed to a tree a square of lead inscribed with particulars of his possession for the King – 'of this land which I have named Chatham Island'. And as a coincidence of Lieutenant Broughton's sighting and naming of Chatham Island, Commander Vancouver had several hours earlier sighted and claimed other islands of the group which he charted as 'The Snares'. Both ships being unaware of their proximity proceeded independently to a rendezvous in Tahiti, then sailed north together in execution of sealed orders to retrieve Nootka Sound Canada from the Spaniards; which they did.

So, on to 1921 at Auckland from where Captain Hotham, now Commodore Commanding New Zealand Station (CCNZ) and wearing his burgee on *Chatham's* foremast, was joined at sea by Australia's cruiser HMAS *Melbourne* for inter-Dominion naval exercises, the first of an annual sequence throughout ensuing decades. But even though *Chatham* was only nine years old, some politicians queried her worth as protection of our sea routes, one saying she should be used for bringing fruit from the islands. Admiral Jellicoe at that time Governor General of New Zealand, pointed out that light cruisers were essential for trade protection, and added that Admiralty was willing to exchange oil-fuelled cruisers for *Philomel* and *Chatham*. They would be much faster at no expense to the Dominion.

In 1923 the light cruiser *Dunedin* (Capt A.R.M. Ramsay DSO) sailed from Portsmouth as a unit of the 'Special Service Squadron', and on arrival in New Zealand she was transferred to the NZ Div of the RN, becoming flagship of the New Zealand Squadron in place of *Chatham* which on 24 May 1924 left to become flagship of the East Indies Station. Then in January 1926 *Dunedin's* sister-ship *Diomede* (Capt J.S.M. Ritchie RN, a New Zealander from Dunedin) arrived in Auckland to a Mayoral Reception at which

CCNZ, Commodore Alister Beal, read from his recent report to NZNB that 'The Dominion now has on loan two modern cruisers of a very efficient type.'

Two years passed, then a tragedy arose when the aviators Hood and Moncrief departed Sydney in early January 1928 on a single-engined flight to New Zealand. Crowds awaited the intrepid aviators' arrival, but as night approached, excited anticipation turned to ominous despair, especially for the fliers' relatives and Hood's brother Les Hood NZD–572, a stoker on *Dunedin* lying alongside Calliope Wharf, with half the ship's company still in towns about New Zealand on Christmas leave.

Commodore Swabey immediately asked Commander H.L. Morgan to ready the ship for sea. One lad, Ralph Hemingway, born in Rotherham, England, had come to New Zealand on a farmhand scheme near Taihape, joined the NZDRN's Class 19 on 2/11/26 as NZD–847, Boy 2nd Class, and fourteen months later on 7 January 1928, shuffled up *Dunedin's* gangway shouldering his bag and hammock. As he recalled the event:

We were not supposed to join her until later that month when all seasonal leave would be completed. However this emergency arose about the fliers and our draft was expedited. *Dunedin* went to sea almost immediately with half her ship's company still on leave, these being brought down by *Diomede* which sailed days later. Our search focused mainly in the Taranaki Bight on the assumption that farmers in the vicinity of New Plymouth had heard an aircraft passing low overhead at night. For our part we got a hammering, a tough baptism for boys who weren't supposed to keep night watches; but I remember doing my stint as bridge messenger, sick all the time, coming off the Middle Watch and laying on the Rec Space deck, then staggering to the Boys Messdeck right forward alongside that stinking capstan engine. Neither *Dunedin* nor *Diomede* had a show of seeing anything night or day as it was so bloody rough over the five days we searched. By the way, *Philomel's* crest those days depicted only the bird of that name, now someone has changed it to a topless bird of the human species.

Ralph Hemingway was rated Petty Officer in May 1946 and PO Stoker Les Hood (DSM on *Achilles* at the Plate) took his discharge as a Chief Mechanician on 25/9/45.

His & Her Majesty's Royal Fleet Auxiliary *Nucula*

(*Nucis nuculidae* – The Clam Nut.)

Completed in September 1906 for C.T. Bowring & Coy at Newcastle's Armstrong Whitworth Yard, No 776 came off Wallsend Slipway to become the 6,120dwt, 370' × 68.5' tanker *Hermione*. When fully laden she had a summer draught of 24′ 4″ which gave her a main deck freeboard of 6′ 3″. Three coal-fired furnaces heated three boilers for her triple expansion engine, which turned her single shaft to produce 10 knots at full load. Being at the worldwide change from coal to oil fuel, she was converted to burn oil in October 1907 and could thereafter raise steam on either.

Her seven tanks port and eleven starboard, separated by a fore-and-aft bulkhead, enabled her to onload 6,200 tons. *Hermione*'s seamen's accommodation portside and firemens' to starboard, reached 35′ aft from the stem, with small separate concrete-floored ablution-rooms containing wash basins under the foc'sle overhang. Engineer and seaman officers had small cabins in the 25′ long bridge structure midships, with some in the 95′ poop above her power plant right aft.

In 1908 *Hermione* was sold to the Orient Steamship Coy, Kisen Kaisha, Tokyo, who renamed her *Soyo Maru*, and until the First World War sent her regularly to California for oil. A First World War Service List indicates that on Wednesday, 7 April 1915 Admiralty purchased and recorded her as 'RN Oiler No 73' which they chartered to the Anglo Saxon Oil Coy who renamed her *Nucula*. From 24/9/17 to May 1919 she appeared on the 'List' as Admiralty Oiler No 220; but *Janes Warships 1919* does not list *Nucula* among its summary of RFAs, so there is the possibility that she had been purchased by Anglo Saxon, then chartered to Admiralty who repurchased her in June 1922 as an RFA on the China Station. On Saturday, 1 September 1923, during an intense Japanese earthquake, she was dispatched to Nagasaki as one of the RN's relief vessels, evidently remaining there until November when she returned to her Tokyo anchorage.

In May 1924 the coal-burning cruiser *Chatham* was replaced on the New Zealand Station by the oil-fuelled cruiser *Dunedin*; her sistership *Diomede* had been pencilled-in for loan to the NZD in 1925, and the oil-fuelled sloops *Leith* and *Wellington* would eventually replace the coal burners *Veronica* and *Laburnum* which although not manned by New Zealanders, were based in Auckland.

A lot of Admiralty head-scratching resulted in *Nucula* being offered as a tanker on loan, conditional that NZNB maintain her on a basis similar to the one in operation regarding previous loan vessels. Agreements were signed and *Nucula* made her way south from Hong Kong, refuelling *Dunedin* in Suva en route.

On 20 March 1925 *Philomel*'s CO, Commander I.M. Miles OBE RN, asked CCNZ who would do *Nucula*'s impending Marine Survey: 'The Navy or a Marine Surveyor?'

'Uhmm, yes, a good question. Why not give the job to Marchant?'

So Lieutenant Commander (E) J. Marchant got the nod four days later. Then, 'No, John, we'd better check with Admiralty.'

More delays while Admiralty reiterated that their loan condition from the date of *Nucula*'s transfer made NZNB responsible for repairs, manning, and an annual classification of the ship in Lloyd's Register, 'therefore, arrangements should be made for all *Nucula*'s surveys to be carried out by Lloyds' nominations'.

Finally the matter was resolved and the Survey proceeded. Then endless correspondence ensued between *Nucula*'s Master, *Philomel*'s Commanding Officer, Navy Board Wellington, CCNZ, NOCA, the Merchant Marine Guild and its various Maritime Unions. There were problems over crewing but at last *Nucula* ploughed east in water-ballast, on her first errand to Richmond San Francisco to pump 6,200 tons of Californian crude into her tanks, and create another string of signals to Navy Office regarding crew member desertions and sickness, transfers to US hospitals, engagement of US merchant seamen or firemen replacements, arrangements for hospitalised crew to be paid in equivalent US currency, and for their repatriation to New Zealand as Matson Line passengers. Even the exact amount of apples, flour and other victuals purchased in San Francisco had to be approved by NZNB, so it is understandable that the list showed an ample supply of Bayers Aspirin for Captain Attwood and his First Officer.

A round trip to Richmond or San Pedro took almost two months, which made it necessary for a tank to be installed in the Devonport Dockyard to maintain a supply of fuel while *Nucula* was away from Auckland. Records show that after discharging 3,000 tons into the Base tanks she paid off until the remaining 3,200 had been pumped into the cruisers, when on 13 July 1931 she recommissioned under the Merchant Shipping Act and departed via Bora Bora to Richmond, arriving 7 August and sailing nine days later direct to Auckland, a return trip which Captain Attwood logged as uneventful in generally good weather.

Next year on Monday, 30 May 1932 when Navy Office endeavoured to engage a merchant crew at reduced rates, there were weeks of confrontations over wages and conditions; NZNB considered manning *Nucula* with naval men but eventually the Merchant Shipping Guild conceded and a crew of seamen vied for engagement; the unavailability of a 3rd Cook being overcome by the 1st and 2nd agreeing to share the absent 3rd's duties, *and pay*. *Nucula* left for Richmond weeks behind schedule, arriving back in Auckland on 1 December to discharge 5,400 tons of crude into the Base tanks, after which Captain Attwood paid off the crew and *Nucula* once more anchored in Rotten Row off Orakei. There she would lie under the care of a few registered watchkeepers who rotated 24-hour shifts until the next commission; some of her crew would obtain dockyard employment, but they were depression days and many wouldn't.

Owen Olsen as an early 1930s boy had longed for a marine engineering career, not a possibility with experienced men long out of work, but an uncle knew Captain Attwood and said; 'Take this note and go and talk to him.' Which he did.

'What makes you want to go to sea, lad?'

'Always wanted to go to sea, sir.'

'Alright, I'll give you a job but it's a dog's life.'

'That won't matter, sir, I still want to go to sea'.

Owen was signed on next trip as a Crew Attendant (Mess Boy), first port of call Colombo for provisions and Persian Gulf charts. On leaving Hauraki Gulf, Owen, who hadn't been out of sight of land before, experienced his first bout of green-seasickness when *Nucula* contorted slowly on the groundswell; his head temperature rose, his eyes rolled and he agonised on his knees while being sick in the heads.

'Here, boy,' a crewman advised, 'tie this lifebelt round yourself, take this mug of salt water, get over to the lee side and get it down in one go.'

Owen did so, mug of salt water straight down – and straight up – 'Never been seasick since.' A day or so north as *Nucula*'s bluff bows white frothed the intense blue Pacific calm, he gazed enthralled while passing Norfolk Island, then he grew amazed at the vast expanse of ocean traversed day in and day out before northing up Queensland's coast inside the Great Barrier Reef, anchoring nightly due to dangerous coral upthrusts, then safe sailing through Torres Strait, the Arafura Sea, Timor Sea and into the Indian Ocean.

'Heat,' Owen recalled. 'Everyone kangaroo leapt across the steel decks to avoid blistering their feet.' A short stop in Colombo and on up through the Arabian Sea and around Qatar Peninsula into the Persian Gulf where one night the cruiser *Leander* signalled *Nucula* to stop. At that time, three years prior to being loaned to the NZD, she as a unit of the East Indies Station was on anti-contraband patrol off Muscat; *Nucula*'s steaming lights weren't bright enough and she'd been followed under suspicion: 'Show a few more lights. Bon Voyage.'

In Abadan two or three firemen were transferred ashore to hospital with respiratory problems; 'Heat!' Owen repeated. 'Seamen were still kangarooing across the steel decking. God help those poor sods in our boiler room!' And having been there in *Leander* circa 1940, I agreed.

On her way back fully laden, *Nucula* secured to a Colombo buoy and Owen spent several hours ashore before waiting on a quay for the bumboat taking provisions out to his ship. When it arrived a well-dressed man boarded for transport out to a Shaw Savill liner and, in conversation, he said he lived in Kitchener Road, Takapuna.

'Oh, anywhere near old Doctor Leonard's rooms?'

'Yes, he's my father and I'm also a doctor.' Their boat was easing in to the liner's sea-gangway. 'Why not come aboard and we'll continue this talk over a few drinks?'

Some hours later Owen was taken back to *Nucula*, rather disgruntled at his quarters in comparison to those of his Takapuna acquaintance, the liner's Medical Officer; but his confidence in the old tanker was about to be fully restored.

Fully laden, *Nucula* had left Abadan on Tuesday, 15 May 1934, experiencing temperatures around 110 fahrenheit down though the Gulf but gradually easing on the way to Colombo. Thereafter conditions changed until several hundred miles south of the Line she encountered rising south-easterlies, which worsened as she changed course off South-West Australia's Cape Leeuwin for the long easting in the Roaring Forties. After passing Wilson's Promontory she wallowed, decks awash, before a howling south-easterly which made steering almost impossible. Then the climax came at 0100 Sunday, 17 June when a rogue hillside of water crashed inboard, cataracting down hatches and ventilators to her engine-room and boiler-room where men struggled ankle-deep to maintain power. Hours later another massive sea smashed the lower bridge and carried away steam-pipe casings along the lower deck.

Daylight showed endless cliffs of storm-driven Southern Ocean rearing astern, shrieking gusts shredding spume from their crests as they towered over the poop then thundered inboard, wrenching deck fittings from their rivets, leaving railings a distorted tangle. In the trough of two wide-spaced swells and at great peril to the ship, Captain George Attwood asked for emergency speed and ordered the wheel hard over. *Nucula* came round slowly, deep laden and sluggish, momentarily awash end to end with only the poop, upper bridge and foc'sle above water; but she made it before cresting head-on and surging down the hundreds of feet slope into the following trough. Throughout that day men aft had to remain there, as the catwalk had been rendered unsafe, twisted out of shape. One man who attempted to stagger forward was inundated and nearly torn from a loosened rail. Cabins, messdecks, even the wheelhouse, were flooded. Darkness came without relief and it is doubtful *Nucula* would have survived had she been kept stern-to as the hurricane heightened.

Another day broke with bad visibility, gale-tormented black cloud sweeping over just above the masts, seas being shipped continuously and a rogue one caving in a side of the navigating bridge, heaving the starboard lifeboat out of its chocks and contorting heavy steampipes on the poop.

Throughout those perilous nights and days the tanker had slewed and yawed drunkenly, her bows being brought back against the seas time after time by Chief Engineer Bullimore's engine-speed manipulations and Captain Attwood's orders to his helmsman, preventing *Nucula* from broaching and becoming a Lloyd's 'Luten Bell' statistic.

Wednesday morning, 20 June, saw the four-day storm abating, so the water-logged tanker was brought back onto her course for Auckland, a disgruntled sea shouldering her starboard quarter; bleary-eyed men seeking a brief sleep before relieving their mates; and Captain Attwood, Chief Officer George Fraser, Chief Engineer Bullimore, and Chief Steward John Yates relegating their duties to 2nd Officer Pine and other certificated officers, with the understanding they were to be awakened instantly if conditions reverted.

When interviewed by the press in Auckland, crew with a lifetime at sea said they'd not seen anything worse: 'Before Attwood brought her head into the storm, three successive rollers drove over the fiddley and we thought *Nucula* was done for. We owe that man our lives.' A First World War destroyer man who'd been through North Sea blizzards said he'd never seen anything like this: 'She's not pretty to look at, but the old girl proved she has floating powers and won't be put down. And our cooks; right through the worst of it they provided hot drinks; we didn't want food so maybe that made it easier for them.'

Chief Engineer Bullimore said his engineers and firemen had kept the shaft turning throughout: 'and that undoubtedly saved the ship. Without a break the engine-room and furnace crews were at their posts, meals snatched as best they could. At one stage the masthead electric light fused and a seaman went up to replace it with a kerosene storm lamp; that man was brave.'

Nucula nursed her wounds quietly in warm winter sunshine, secured at Calliope Wharf where someone pointed to her starboard paravane stanchion, 2.5″ diameter solid steel twisted like a piece of fencing wire, boat davits similarly distorted, catwalk unrecognisable and the bridge a shambles: 'Rather you than me on that trip, mate.'

However, her schedule for the remainder of 1934 seems to have been more placid according to archives:

Place	Arrived	Departed	Remarks
Auckland	23/6/34	30/6	Ship repaired. Replenished Base tanks. Ship commissioned.
Bora Bora	9/7	12/7	Refuelled *Dunedin*.
Apia	17/7	18/7	Refuelled *Diomede*.
Colombo	18/8	18/8	Picked up charts.
Abadan	28/8	3/9	Load tested oil.
Colombo	13/9	13/9	Returned charts.
Auckland	10/10	24/10	Docking etc.
Colombo	20/11	20/11	Picked up charts.

Abadan	30/11	6/12	Load tested oil.
Colombo	16/12	16/12	Returned charts.
Auckland	12/1/35		

Being aware by the mid-1930s that international shipyards were turning out tankers averaging 12,000-ton fuel capacity, New Zealand's Defence Department gazetted an area of reclaimed land near Stanley Bay for the site of a 12,200-ton oil fuel tank, this storage becoming necessary with NZNB's decision to replace *Diomede* and *Dunedin* with two Leander Class cruisers, and Admiralty's decision to replace their two NZ-based coal-fired sloops with two modern ones fuelled by oil.

Well off-coast in early June 1935 *Nucula* cleaned out her tanks, entered Calliope Dock for minor repairs and departed for California on her normal run, stopping at Suva to refuel *Dunedin*; then on her way back from San Francisco, waiting in Bora Bora to replenish *Diomede* and *Dunedin* between 24 and 30 July during their Hawaii and Pacific Islands cruise.

Next year the old tanker departed Auckland 1/8/36, bound Bora Bora with 700 tons of oil for *Dunedin*, and 150 tons for *Wellington* onto whom she also off-loaded 2.5 tons of potatoes, 2 tons of flour, 560lb of onions and a manifold of small necessities. She then continued eastward to Nuku-hiva in the Marquesas where on 19 August, 1,000 tons of fuel were pumped into *Achilles* while the new cruiser's crane and working parties transferred 5 tons of potatoes, 8 cwt of onions, 10 cwt of ironbark pumpkin and 2,000 apples from *Nucula* who then continued on her way, this time to Los Angeles for 6,500 tons of oil from San Pedro's Texas Oil Coy installations. Departing there on 3 September she arrived Auckland on 30 September 1936 and once more paid off.

Each time *Nucula* commissioned for a trip to California, a wireless operator was engaged to carry out the ship's 0350 and 1050 GMT morse schedules on 6600kc/s and, as an ex-telegraphist in *Philomel*'s small 'New Daventry' W/T Station off Clover Avenue, I recall those weak signals barely readable through atmospheric conditions:

FA7 de GNXP = QTC2 = AR [*Philomel* from *Nucula* = I have 2 messages for you.] GNXP de FA7 R QSA4 QRM QRU GM K AR [*Nucula* from *Philomel* = Receiving you strength 4 under atmospherics. I have nothing for you, Good Morning, go ahead].

His messages would be read with great difficulty – generally daily weather reports and the ship's position until nearer either destination when Captain Attwood's expected time of arrival would be included. Various documents have applied different call signs to *Nucula*, in Lloyd's 1925 Register, GRWP;

in their 1939/40 Register, GVTQ; but when prefixed with GV the 4-letter call signs were usually applied only to front-line warships and when I worked her in the mid to late 1930s she used GNXP.

Having only a 6,500-ton capacity *Nucula* was kept busy between 1934 and 1937, when the NZD's two cruisers and Admiralty's two NZ-based sloops needed frequent refuelling during their extensive Pacific Ocean duties; additionally when in Auckland on 12 February 1937 she pumped 5,300 tons into the visiting RAN Squadron cruisers and destroyers, then departed for Nukuhiva to give *Dunedin* 600 tons before continuing eastward to arrive San Pedro about 15 March and ingest a full load.

Back in Auckland she pumped this into the Base tanks and on 19 April was off again for another San Pedro fill-up; this time needing to send Oil Burner E. Church and Able Seaman T. Finnemore to San Pedro's 'Seaside Hospital', thereby involving Los Angeles' British Consul who on 17 May accepted responsibility for their welfare, also arranging all the International and Maritime Union correspondence necessary to sign on two Americans, Able Seaman R. West and Crew Attendant F.C. Brown for *Nucula*'s return trip to Auckland.

Numerous messages between the British Consul, CCNZ, NOW, NOCA, Captain Attwood, and *Achilles*, alleviated the international and maritime hiccups and at 2030 on 10 June 1937 I receipted *Nucula*'s ETA signal. She requested a tug on arrival, said her crew would pay off on Saturday, 12 June at Auckland's Government Shipping Office, quoted the amount of residual US currency she would be transferring to *Achilles*, and concluded that NOCA should make arrangements for the two US crewmen's passage back to the States on the first available liner.

Morsed 'Good evenings' ended that routine, and it basically ended *Nucula*'s service as an RFA on the New Zealand Station. She remained on hire from Admiralty at a greatly reduced rate as a stationary fuel hulk; her topmasts, derricks, lifeboats and commission flags being removed except for the mandatory red danger flag midships, and over the next three years she was moved to Shoal Bay and other harbour anchorages dependent on the need for her oil, or for its replenishment.

In July 1940 she was given a Western Viaduct berth for two weeks, so that respondents to her advertised sale could inspect and tender a purchase price for the ship and pages upon pages of items, columnised down from several tons of lubricating oil to the smallest engine-room nut and bolt, and the last Officers' Mess teaspoon. Those two weeks extended over another eighteen months until the Auckland Harbour Board demanded her removal to provide berths for essential wartime shipping. She was mentioned in Lloyd's 1939/40 Register but not thereafter, and Admiralty's final claim for her hire was recorded in July 1941.

Came that sun-drenched January day in 1947 when tugs moved the old tanker to Calliope Wharf where her oil was pumped into the Base tanks and once more she was advertised for sale. A.C. Ratcliffe Ltd., an engineering company of Penrose, purchased her for scrapping at Western Viaduct; on Thursday, 24 July a floating crane started extracting her engine and other useful equipment, then on Monday, 10 September she was returned to her Shoal Bay moorings pending a decision on her final disposal. Negotiations by the RNZAF for her use as a bombing target broke down and, on Tuesday, 23 October in pleasant spring conditions, she passed around North Head under tow by *William C Daldy*, steadied astern by the smaller tug *Coralie*. Next day the tow was transferred to Auckland's Marine Department tug *Manawanui* YTL622 (Master William Stanaway), who slipped the line as instructed in position 036 deg 27 min S, 176 deg 02 min E, approximately 11 miles ENE of Cuvier Island. Scuttling charges placed in her engine-room were detonated by timed fuses; she foundered ignominiously in deep water beyond the 100-fathom shelf, and a sequence of her final hours was photographed from the attendant tug *Seebee*.

HMS *Veronica*

Flower Class, *Acacia*-type, coal-burning fleet minesweeper built in Britain's 1915 Emergency War programme; later converted to a sloop; 1,200 tons, 1,800 shp, 17 knots, 77 complement, 2 × 4″ guns, depth-charge racks, 2 saluting guns and 3 machine guns. Approx 1,300 miles at 8 knots on 150 tons of coal.

Replying to a question in New Zealand's House of Representatives in 1920, Prime Minister William Massey outlined Admiralty's intention to base three sloops in Suva to protect Britain's South Pacific interests, but later in that year's session he said that in further UK/NZ consultations it had been agreed:

(i)   Only two sloops would be dispatched.

(ii) For bunkering and dockyard convenience they would base in Auckland.

(iii) They would be manned and financed entirely by the RN.

(iv) They would be under the command of Commodore Commanding New Zealand Station (CCNZ).

William Henry Clifton was born at Enfield, London, on 22 February 1897, and when several years later his mother died he was placed in a naval institution for serving members' boys. On 18 July 1912 William was given the Service Number J 18648 on being enlisted at HMS *Ganges* training establishment, thence over subsequent years he served on the destroyer *Russell*, tug *Jason*, battleships *Vanguard* at Jutland in 1915 and *Prince George* at Dogger Bank in 1916, then the armoured cruiser *Hercules* on which he continued to serve when she was converted to the aircraft carrier *Courageous* in 1919. When Leading Seaman Clifton read aloud an Admiralty circular that men were required for a three-year commission on sloops being fitted out for the South Seas, some of his messmates applied with him, then in the day-to-day routine aboard *Courageous* forgot about their application until weeks later on arrival in Portsmouth.

'Do yuh hear there. Leading Seaman Clifton, Able Seamen Ross, Faulkner, Jones and Hansen report to the Regulating Office. Leave to Second Part of Port Watch. Duty seaboat crew man the starboard seaboat. At the double.'

Right now the five ratings were ignoring the Bosun's repeat call as they mustered at the Regulating Office to be put through the aircraft carrier's drafting routine and be handed train tickets to Pembroke.

'You're in charge of the draft Clifton. Here's your instructions. *Veronica* [Commander F.H.L. Lewin], Pembroke Dry Dock. And you watch those girls in Tahiti!'

'Don't you worry about me, Freddie boy, I'm thinking about them right now.'

On 22 February 1920 Bill Clifton shepherded his small draft westward by bus and train, merging with groups from other ships and depots also making their way to the Welsh naval dockyard sited on the south side of Milford Haven. Ordnance buffs were still checking gunnery controls and communications to the bridge. Clifton, who had been gun-captain on similar 4″ guns aboard *Courageous*, instructed *Veronica*'s new gun crews in this latest technology and, after week-by-week sea trials in St George's Channel, liberty men were warned that the ship was under sailing orders. Bunkered to capacity and victualled for many long days at sea, *Veronica* slid down the Haven on a cold Tuesday, 23 March 1920 with Commander Lewin and his bridge staff remarking wistfully about the ruins of Monkton Priory. How long it would be until they caught up with their wives who would right now be booking passage to New Zealand, how long would it take for this east-about voyage halfway round the world?

The sloop coaled and stored at Gibraltar, added fresh water to requirements at Port Said, sweltered down through the Suez Canal and Red Sea to Aden where dockside Arabs humped coal inboard in monstrous bags, skinny coal-black coolies ant-trailing up and down gangplanks as they bunkered again in Colombo for that tropical leg via Singapore to Darwin. Sweat. Nothing but sea, endless sea and sweat. Then came the unwelcome news that *Veronica* had been ordered to survey specified parts of North-Western Australia before continuing her delivery voyage to New Zealand.

In Darwin at high tide men walked ashore across a horizontal gangway, sought the nearest corrugated-iron pub to drink lukewarm beer, brushed thirsty flies off the rim of their handles as long, slow-moving fan blades circulated fetid air, then at night clambered down iron rungs in the pilings, 40 feet and more to where the ebbing tide had lowered the deck of their ship.

On completing their surveys *Veronica* continued on to Sydney where messdeck rumours indicated that the sloop had been ordered back to England. Bill Clifton and some of his mates decided they'd had enough of the Royal Navy and, going in civilian clothes to the Mercantile Marine Union Office signed on to an American freighter about to sail for San Francisco, but the skipper, on being told they were British naval deserters, roared: 'You Pommies get back to your ship before I send for a patrol to escort you back in irons!'

This they did so surreptiously that the matter of desertion didn't arise; they bought back the navy uniforms they'd sold to messmates, disposed of their recently purchased civvies, then underwent Commander Lewin's punishment for being two days AWOL. According to Clifton's widowed wife, now Mrs E. Vigers in her 90s in Hastings, *Veronica* did more surveys around Niue Island and the Kermadecs, then arrived Auckland on Monday, 14 February 1921. The ship's company was given a belated two weeks Christmas Leave in watches; the 'Sydney deserters' went north to the gum fields from which they didn't return. William Henry Clifton aliased his surname to Clark, and circa 1936 when they were granted a King's Pardon, Bill Clark (Clifton) wasn't aware of it until 1938 when he chance-met one of them in a Kaitaia hotel.

Meantime *Veronica* had cruised the South Pacific, entertained remote island chiefs and their retinue on her awning-shaded quarterdeck, corrected incorrect latitude and longitude positions of partially submerged reefs for Admiralty charts, and appeared in newspaper shipping notices as she arrived in or departed from New Zealand ports, to disembark or embark RNVR(NZ) ratings and officers doing their annual sea-time training. On occasions when working out of Auckland in company with her sistership *Laburnum* for the cruisers *Diomede* or *Dunedin* 6" shoots, she would tow the huge black-hessian-covered battle-practice target from its anchorage midway between the Naval Base and the nearby Cable Wharf, off which HM Cable Ships *Iris* or *Recorder* were periodically moored.

Over the ten years since arrival in Auckland *Veronica* would do her annual docking maintenance, return ammunition to her magazines, victual ship then ease alongside Auckland's Western Wharf to bunker sufficiently for the first of her 1,500-mile island stretches about New Zealand's vast area of Pacific responsibility, coaling interim at Fiji, American Samoa, sometimes Tahiti, then returning to Auckland for brief spells with wives and families originated in New Zealand or brought out from the United Kingdom. So she and her 1922-arrived sister-ship *Laburnum* wiled away those peaceful years until – Tuesday, 3 February 1931.

Commodore Geoffrey Blake had attended '8-o'clock' colours then retired to his quarters on *Dunedin* which lay ahead of *Diomede* alongside the Sheerlegs Jetty. Both cruisers sparkled, just repainted blue-grey, quarterdeck bulkheads enamelled, decks holystoned, all steelwork and gun muzzles burnished until they glinted like chrome plate. At 1430 they would be on their way to the Bay of Islands for that year's Waitangi Treaty celebrations.

Betsy Chapman, *Philomel*'s Paymaster Commander's wife, was preparing their Calliope Road clifftop house for their son Tony's 10th birthday, which was to be held coincidental with Pat's, that day's ten-year-old daughter of Padre Trevor Robson and his wife Kathleen. K had been helping, it was hot, windows open as the forenoon ran on. They bundled the ten-year-olds out to go down and remind their fathers to be up there by midday.

But something was wrong in the base, men running, trucks piled with paraphernalia heading for the cruisers, cars disgorging nurses and civilian doctors at *Dunedin*'s gangway, and *Diomede*'s siren whooping as she eased stern-first out into midstream. Pat tugged a lieutenant's sleeve: 'Have you seen Dad, he's to come to my birthday at midday!'

HMS *Dunedin*.

'Sorry Pat, he won't be there, he's out there on the *Diomede*.' Nothing further as he hurried toward the flagship.

Just then Tony appeared and they scampered uphill as he gabbled about a *big* earthquake, bursting into the room to be quietened as Betsy and K listened to an unscheduled 'YA' link-up: 'catastrophic earthquake in Hawkes Bay, Napier and Hastings in ruins, road, rail, telephone and all other communications totally destroyed ... only link is by wireless transmission from HMS *Veronica* which is believed to be aground in Ahuriri Harbour. Further information will be released as it comes to hand.'

Commander H.L. Morgan DSC RN had long since relieved *Veronica*'s previous commanding officer, and now on the bridge at 0600 he made courtesy signals to the big refrigeration ships *Northumberland* and *Taranaki* at anchor in Napier Roads, before also lying off the entrance awaiting the Harbour Master's arrival. Shortly after seven the pilot boat approached and as Captain Whyte-Parsons clambered aboard, *Veronica* weighed and proceeded inside where she secured alongside West Quay; official calls being arranged for 1500, other considerations being discussed over a pink gin, after which the Harbour Master departed and normal harbour routine continued.

At about 1045 off-duty watchkeepers were preparing for an after-lunch run ashore in the sun-drenched town, some leaning on guardrails looking at the Norfolk Pines fronting Napier's popular esplanade, when the ship shook violently, a momentary still, then an unearthly rumble and indescribable crashing and grating with the ship being violently whipped and shaken. Through clouds of dust men saw the road and wharf distorting, wharfside sheds swaying and adjacent warehouse walls cracking then disintegrating in rubble covered by collapsed roofing. People were running to safety in the heaving streets, stumbling and regaining their feet only to stagger about as though drunk. One by one the ship's mooring lines parted as she thumped against the pier and surged outward, until her stern swung seaward and she remained held only by the for'ard spring. Throughout this frightening experience Ahuriri Harbour bed had risen and water was torrenting out of the inner harbour so, realising that it would soon leave *Veronica* grounded, Commander Morgan had the ship's furnaces drawn then drafted a signal to inform CCNZ of the drastic situation: a sequence which covers those fateful hours:

1054 To CCNZ = Serious earthquake Napier. No damage to *Veronica*.

1114 From CCNZ = Do you require assistance of cruisers?

1122 To CCNZ = Yes. *Veronica* hard and fast ashore.

1141 To CCNZ = Impossible to estimate damage, feared extensive, water rising, ship afloat, had to draw fires, am now raising steam.

1151 From CCNZ = What assistance is required?

1153 To CCNZ = Medical assistance required. Feared considerable loss of life. Am landing all assistance possible.

1157 From CCNZ = Proceeding Napier with *Diomede* and medical assistance.

1218 To CCNZ = Buildings down, fires raging everywhere, all medical assistance possible required. Shocks still recurring.

1254 To CCNZ = Broadcast message for assistance sent to all ships.

1301 To CCNZ = Have informed Wellington. Houses destroyed, fires. Many dead and injured. Medical assistance required.

1309 To CCNZ = SS *Northumberland* offered assistance, ordered her to land doctor and men. Have opened HQs at Police Station.

1313 To CCNZ = All local communication destroyed, acting as W/T link to Wellington. Impossible state damage to Napier. Have landed all available men.

1319 From CCNZ = Sailing 1430. ETA Napier 0700 with 3 doctors, 15 nurses and med stores. Anything further to report?

1331 To CCNZ = Situation appalling, whole town appears to be afire.

1337 To CCNZ = Advised by Nav Sec to keep watch with ZLW. *Northumberland* has ample food aboard. Told to land all available food.

1347 From CCNZ = Am keeping watch on 111kc/s.

1413 To ZLW = Nothing further to communicate. Fires still raging. Thousands are homeless. Much food required.

1421 From ZLW = Prime minister anxious you supply information of medical needs.

1445 To ZLW = To Prime Minister. As much as possible. Whole town wrecked. Fires still raging. Continuing shakes.

1445 To CCNZ = Maintaining watch on 111kc/s. Calling ZLW every 15 mins.

1450 From CCNZ = Report present Napier situation & changes to ZLW, also to me.

1456 To CCNZ and ZLW = Impossible estimate present damage, very critical, have taken over as SNO. Endeavouring to organise situation ashore. Have help from SS *Northumberland* and *Taranaki* Every available man landed and refugees coming aboard. *Veronica* will remain in Inner Harbour in touch with situation ashore.

1520 To CCNZ = SS *Cumberland* passing Portland Island offered to assist. Told her to call off Napier when she will be further informed.

1600 From ZLW = SS *Northumberland* told render all possible assistance and advise CCNZ re navigational matters off Napier.

1605 From ZLW = SS *Cumberland* told to anchor in Napier Roads & await instructions.

1627 To CCNZ and ZLW = Information received that Waipawa and Waipukurau suffered equally with Napier and Hastings. Med assistance urgently required there, & organisation for food etc. in all towns. Am endeavouring to do this at Napier but assistance is urgently required elsewhere.

1726 From CCNZ = Have not ordered *Laburnum* down to Napier as she would not arrive until Thursday. Assume food supplied by merchant ships arrive by that time. If *Laburnum* can be of value she will be sent forthwith.

1731 To CCNZ = Do not think *Laburnum* will be required here by Thursday, but she may be required at other places.

1731 From ZLW = Following med assistance despatched.
Auckland – 5 doctors, 15 nurses, by naval vessels.
Wellington – 7 doctors, 23 nurses.
Gisborne – 5 doctors, 5 nurses.
Palmerston – 8 doctors, 10 nurses.
Adjacent towns – 13 doctors, 24 nurses.

1734 To CCNZ = Situation ashore still obscure. Damage & loss of life worse than I thought, water supply completely failed, food shortage probable. Have organised food depots. I understand all surrounding towns are equally or worse affected.

1756 To SS *Cumberland* = Request you remain Napier till *Dunedin* and *Diomede* arrive.

1832 From SS *Taranaki* & *Northumberland* = Request permission to return men to ship for the night.

1833 Reply = Propose to keep men ashore for the night. Please send all available electric torches. Urgently required.

1919 CCNZ to *Laburnum* = Proceed to Auckland and stand by to bring further medical assistance if required.

2000 To ZLW for Watson & Co = Films, developer, thermometers urgently required by Dr Biggs.

2019 From CCNZ = *Important*. When situation is clearer to you I shall be glad if you will forecast what action you would propose on arrival of cruisers including working parties etc. required ashore. We have onboard 5 doctors, 11 nurses, 54 stretchers, portable X-Ray, 5 marquees, 34 tents, 400 blankets, 125 seamens beds, 200 ground sheets, 80 shovels, 31 picks, 5 boilers, numerous kettles, mugs, Deal spars, scantlings etc. also additional medical and surgical chests & miscellaneous medical stores.

2020 To *Diomede* = Request you answer all calls on 500kc/s.

2028 From CCNZ = The Public is anxious to know extent of damage and casualties so far as they can be ascertained. Would you prepare a list of your observations up to the present time and send to me for retransmission, sorry to trouble you.

2037 To CCNZ = *Cumberland* arrived and waiting instructions on arrival of *Dunedin* and *Diomede*.

2051 To CCNZ = Have just returned from going round area. Practically all stone brick buildings destroyed, many still blazing. Hundreds of wooden buildings shaken to ground, some totally some partially. Casualty list very heavy, impossible estimate number yet. Water supply failed, fire brigade incapable of handling all fires. Populace quiet, appear stunned by magnitude of disaster. I have organised a food depot and am policing the streets. Several temp'y hospitals have been organised and *Veronica* is forming an X-Ray station. All destitute women and children who care to are onboard *Veronica*. Shocks still recurring.

2105 To *Taranaki* & *Northumberland* = Request you hasten supply of food.

2136 From *Cumberland* = Am prepared to send Chief Officer and 20 men if required, and medical stores.

2137 To All Ships= All lights, navigational and otherwise out at Napier.

2140 From *Northumberland* = Ahuriri Bluff light is now working.

2203 To CCNZ = Ref your 2019. Following organisation submitted. Doctors and medical stores to be distributed as follows: Race Course. 9 doctors, 6 nurses, Portable X-Ray, 2 marquees, 15 stretchers, 200 blankets. *Nelson Park* 2 doctors, 3 nurses, 2 marquees, 15 stretchers. Botanical Gardens.

2 doctors, 3 nurses, 1 marquee, 15 stretchers. *Veronica* 9 stretchers. Bell tents, beds, ground sheets, boilers and remaining blankets, cooking utensils etc. to Nelson Park as it is considered the best HQs for destitute and homeless. I consider a strong Marine Detachment should be landed for police duties, and that demolition and fire parties should also be landed. Whyte-Parsons and I will come out by launch on your arrival and put you wise to the situation as we know it. I have asked local authorities who are available to meet you onboard *Veronica* about 0800. Fresh water and sterilizers are required.

2210 To *Taranaki* & *Northumberland* = Thank you for the wonderful way you have responded to my requests and wishes.

2230 To ZLW = Marquees urgently required.

2249 From CCNZ = Thank you for your 2203. Most helpful and will be arranged. It may be after 0800 before I reach *Veronica*. Will approach the anchorage with caution. ETA 10 miles off Napier 0700.

2250 From ZLW = Food, tents, blankets being sent by train. Min of Defence and Mr Masters leaving by road.

2257 From CCNZ = Are water tank lighter, tugs or additional water transport available?

2311 To CCNZ = No water tank available. 2 small tugs may be available but not before 0800. Will make endeavour to provide transport to land men and stores. SS *Taranaki* has offered to take off refugees.

2337 To CCNZ = Medical assistance has arrived by aeroplane and car, I think situation is slightly easier but that only refers to rescued people able to get to medical centre.

As a result of *Veronica*'s morsed information to CCNZ, *Diomede* and *Dunedin* had embarked doctors, nurses and stores, then proceeded 'with all dispatch' to Hawkes Bay; while en route informing NZNB and government of the disaster so that immediate action could be implemented; broadcasting navigation warnings to all ships in the area; and informing the press of authentic news so that unfounded rumours might be kept in check.

Colin Malcolm NZD860 a Leading Torpedoman on *Dunedin*, was among the 270 seamen and stokers and sixty anti-looting armed marines landed by boat from the cruisers' anchorage well offshore. What the earthquakes hadn't wrecked that initial day and night had since been destroyed by fires which subsequently raged throughout the town and permeated the air with a nauseating stench of burnt flesh. Working parties were assigned different areas, and Colin's group was detailed to search the ruined Public Hospital and Nurses' Home for the injured and dead. Many night-duty nurses asleep that Tuesday forenoon when the catastrophe struck were killed by falling masonry, others were badly injured as they attempted to escape from their collapsing quarters. Hospital patients had died or suffered similarly, bringing tears to the eyes and lumps in the throats of navymen, inured to disaster in the First World War but now confronted with the grisly task of extricating young and aged from the rubble, then trying to make their corpses presentable for relatives' identification.

Four of Colin's mates were lifting a concrete slab from a nurse's body when the cadaver emitted a terrifying moan, giving them such a fright that they dropped the slab and stood petrified, but Padre Robson, who'd experienced the carnage of Flanders, had just arrived on a motorbike he'd found still rideable.

'Come on lads,' he encouraged them. 'It's not her ghost; that was air filling her lungs when you took the weight off her chest.'

Reassured but shaken, they ignored the repeat moan when the slab was removed, took splintered masonry from the girl's face and body, then laid it out with others awaiting transport to a temporary morgue.

It was lunch break, Robbie had powered off on his 'borrowed' bike and the group sat in tree shade for a meal. One young seaman was using the blade of his pussers dirk, hungrily spooning corned beef to his mouth from his ration tin when an old salt casually remarked, 'Say, Spinnaker, you didn't wash that blade I saw you getting concrete out of the nurse's legs with.'

Able Seaman Speight's knife poised mid-air to his mouth; his face turned pale green and his eyes rolled as he staggered behind a tree to be sicker than he'd ever been in the worst of seas.

After lunch break Robbie was back helping to shift concrete blocking a heavy cupboard door behind which there were sounds of life. This they crowbarred open and out rushed a wild-eyed apparition – SWISSHH – as it ran sunblinded into a startled seaman's arms.

'HEY LAD! BELAY PANIC STATIONS!' Then more quietly; 'The Devil's not after you, son, you'll be alright.'

'I *am* alright,' the terrified boy sobbed, 'But Christ, I'm bloody starving.'

Later that day when demolishing a partly ruined building, a severe quake rushed everyone across the road where they looked back and saw the three-storey wall still standing, just as another shake had them racing centre-road with rubble crashing behind them. A sequence of nervous laughs as they stood deciding who'd climb an extension ladder against the standing wall, as someone had to affix their hauling-down wire but so far they were short of a volunteer. Just then an old ex-maritime captain appeared and started up the swaying rungs: 'Don't worry about me, lads, better me than you if it crashes, I've had a good innings.' Fortunately the tremors had stopped; the ancient mariner arranged the purchase, and some more before that day's clangour and billowing dust subsided after the last wall came down.

Meantime CCNZ had been attending meetings where civic authorities discussed future moves. As many of the dead were not yet formally identified it was necessary to defer their interment until known relatives were contacted, but without electricity the morgues couldn't cope; there were insufficient graveyard allotments so it was essential to create a common grave adjacent to the Park Island Cemetery, where local preachers and Padre Robson would officiate at a mass funeral, the government being so informed.

Prime Minister George William Forbes declared Friday, 5 February as a day of national mourning, flags throughout New Zealand to be flown at half-mast and all churches to observe intercession services for the Hawkes Bay earthquake victims and, from South Africa, Lord Baden Powell decreed that scouts worldwide would wear black armbands for one year to mourn New Zealand scouts killed in the disaster.

In Napier's exceptional summer heat that Friday, 6 February 1931, trucks laden with rough planked coffins chalk-marked with the victim's name or simply NOT IDENTIFIED, began to arrive at the Marine Parade Court House for registration, and at 3 p.m. the long cortege moved slowly off to Park Island's new cemetery. There in a long, wide, deep trench excavated by naval explosives in the hard sun-baked clay, 101 coffins were laid side by side. Local ministers spoke for the dead, after which Chaplain George Trevor Robson MC NZDRN commended Napier's ex-Service victims to God; *Dunedin's* bugler sounded the *Last Post*, mourners bowed their heads throughout a minute of silent reverence, then *Reveille* terminated the non-denominational funeral.

An excerpt from Commodore Geoffrey Blake CB DSO's Enclosure (a), NZ Submission No 51 H/31 of 8 March 1931, dispatched from HMS *Diomede* at Whangaroa, stated:

> Item 15. A survey of damage to *Veronica* was made shortly after arrival. Although the ship was considered seaworthy, it was considered essential to get her clear of the Inner Harbour as soon as possible and send her to Auckland for docking and repair. As the work of assisting local organisations was almost complete and the Marines were being relieved by a Territorial Force, I ordered *Veronica* to sail at high Water on Tuesday 9 February, and *Diomede* to escort her to Auckland. A fine weather forecast also influenced my decision. Some difficulty was experienced in getting *Veronica* out of the Inner Harbour and eventually she had to be towed out stern first, owing to there being insufficient water to turn her around. Her steering gear also jammed. She sailed p.m. the

same day, *Diomede* sailing later and keeping in close touch. A fine weather passage was experienced and *Veronica* arrived at Auckland a.m. Thursday 12th February.

Item 16. *Dunedin's* Marines were withdrawn a.m. Wednesday 11th February. After I inspected the town and interviewed the Chairman of the Relief Committee to make certain that no further assistance was required, *Dunedin* sailed for Auckland p.m. the same day.

Item 17. On Thursday 5th February the Commodore put forward the following appeal for subscriptions towards the Prime Minister's Relief Fund.
To the Officers and Men of the New Zealand Squadron. Earthquake Relief Fund.
'The earthquake has wrecked Napier, Hastings and surrounding districts. Those who have seen the conditions realize that apart from their personal losses, the majority of the population are ruined and a large number of their homes destroyed. Under these circumstances, I appeal to the officers and men of the New Zealand Squadron to help those hard stricken people who have shewn fortitude and courage. Napier has always shewn to the Navy many kindnesses and much hospitality, which we can do well to remember at the present time and endeavour in some small way to show our sympathy with our friends in this desperate affliction through which they are passing. It is proposed to send a subscription from the New Zealand Squadron to the Prime Minister's Relief Fund.

[The sum raised was £500]

Item 18. In conclusion I consider that the work done by the Navy during this very trying period was of great value, apart from the purely practical aspect. There is no doubt that the whole population was stunned and I think they would have remained in a more or less stupefied condition unless they observed some action being taken. It was in this capacity that the Navy contributed an essential service. Confidence was restored and a lead given which was soon responded to. The officers and men worked very hard and cheerfully, some of the work of digging out bodies being very unpleasant. They cleared the main thoroughfares, thus facilitating communications and demolishing many dangerous buildings. They established temporary telephone communications, were instrumental in getting the water supply under weigh, started a food depot and were a body who could be called on for any useful duty. On all sides I received a grateful appreciation of their services.

(Sgd.) Geoffrey Blake.
COMMODORE COMMANDING
NEW ZEALAND STATION.

Hawkes Bay and East Coast provincial towns would lie in ruins for weeks, months; modern technology would be incorporated in their resurrection from the dust and rubble. Not granted CCNZ permission to remain and assist the grieving population, Robbie returned to Auckland aboard *Diomede*, then motored back with K in their 1928 Austin 7, to marry an RN officer to a Hawkes Bay grazier's daughter, en route crossing distorted rail bridges with K guiding the wheels while walking cautiously backwards, and driving on grassed roadsides due to wide and deep road fissures in which unfortunate cars still lay on their sides, inextricable.

HMS *Wakakura*
'The Canoe of Learning'
'Te Manuwao a Kingi Hori te Rima o Niu Tireni'

The Royal Naval Volunteer Reserve (NZ) was inaugurated at Auckland in 1925, then at Wellington, Canterbury, and Otago, in 1928, at the end of which year there were sixty-three 'Wavy Navy' officers and 420 ratings on the books.

In January 1925 Navy Board's Chief of Staff recommended the purchase of a steel trawler, capable of mounting a 4″ gun and suitable equipment to train 'Rockies' in seamanship, minesweeping, deep-water diving and gunnery. Cabinet approved his proposal in that September and made approaches to Admiralty who said: 'Ahhh, we've got just the thing: TR–1: a Castle Class minesweeper built at Port Arthur, Ontario in 1917: 429 tons gross. It's got a gun already; and, shhh, you can have it for £5,000 sterling – as is, where is.' The 'where is' was Sheerness Navy Yard's 'Rotten Row', among dozens of similar First World War sweepers; her 'TR–1' identification was scraped off with lots of rust, and, renamed *Wakakura* she then commissioned under the command of Lieutenant R.A. McDonald RN on a sunny Thursday, 8 April 1926.

Weeks passed quickly, stores and victuals came onboard daily, and on Monday, 14 June, with a brand new White Ensign declaring her importance, she laid a screen of funnel smoke over herself and the Thames/Medway confluence when heading for the English Channel en route to New Zealand. And that's when the 'As is' bit manifested.

Engine-room gremlins brought her to a standstill day after day between coaling stops on the way to St Vincent in the Windward Islands. There, dockyard mechanicians got her mobile for the short run to Port o' Spain, Trinidad where more extensive repairs to the propulsion unit, plus a bunkerfull and a deck-load of coal kept her shaft revolving throughout the Panama Canal and north to California's San Diego Navy Docks. Here, head-scratching USN experts solved enough problems to set her on a course for Honolulu, but heavy Pacific weather hampered progress and once more she broke down, wallowing bows-on at the end of a sheet-anchor rope while morsing the ether for assistance, fortunately provided by the nearby US cruiser *Pittsburgh* who towed her into Pearl Harbour. This time her machinery and boiler were given a thorough going-over in Hawaii's naval dockyard; then the Maori-designated 'Canoe of Learning' retraced the course of ancient Polynesian seafarers without further incident, apart from the apoplexy she caused Navy Office and Parliament wallahs on her January 1927 arrival in Auckland, just ahead of a wad of bills mailed to the Defence Department for her en route repairs totalling some $80,000 US, almost £20,000 sterling. That wily 'As is' clause had upped her from 5,000 pounds sterling to 25,000 give or take a quid or two; but thenceforth until the Second World War she trained hundreds of RNVR (NZ) mariners who later served the country admirably.

She also taught many lessons to the permanents who crewed her around our stormy coasts as a *Philomel* tender. Pre-war the New Zealand Division of the Royal Navy was paid monthly and consequently remained permanently in debt; more so on *Waka* whose pay inevitably went to the wrong port, thus stretching each month to five or six weeks. But fortunately while I served aboard pre-war as Sparkie, cum Signalman, cum Captain's Cook alternate days in harbour to allow PO Steward George Tunnicliffe a run ashore, our Skipper, Lieutenant Peter North-Lewis RN, had rich Welsh parents. So, he and our illicitly bottled 'neaters' staved off abject poverty. We borrowed from him until the NZ Post Office caught up with the ship, and we traded gin bottles of neat rum for meat, bread, greens and groceries from eager shopkeepers and Union Steamship Company coasters in ports we regularly visited; especially Oamaru which had no pubs. It did have a moulting penguin which Ned Broad plucked off a horizontal pier stringer to become the messmate of our Kawau Island wallaby, rescued from its dead mother's pouch and reared on board with condensed milk. The penguin recuperated on a diet of fish and fresh water, but Joey relished cigarettes or tobacco left unguarded, vegies from the greens screen, and manila or coir mooring lines which needed constant splicing.

Both pets went missing in Akaroa, maybe a lucky kidnapping before Joey turned all our mooring lines into wallaby pellets to be dropped ad lib on our bunks and mess table. The Sunday we were leaving, many strollers gathered on the wharf to watch with interest as Skip issued his usual orders for getting the bows in and stern out. He then asked for 'Full Astern', and that's when the evolution went awry. A local wharfie was supposed to slip our for'ard line off the top of a bollard he was standing by; but he hadn't done so; there was blind panic as sightseers ran shrieking from the quaking planking from which we'd yanked its main support. The Lord heard his name mentioned a lot as the air turned blue, then: 'Oh well, back to Lyttelton. Left hand down a bit.'

Twenty-four hours later after our Gunnery Officer Joe Woodward had introduced our Cantabrian volunteers to the perplexities of the 4″ gun, we were off Port Levy on a placid surface shafted yellow by a brilliant moon. A Christchurch rockie had the wheel, Skip's unmelodious flat voice was singing dolefully to his distant Wellington heart-throb, and I sat off watch in my tiny W/T office sited in one corner of the huge wheelhouse. My voice-pipe to the bridge was branched to a mouthpiece above the wheel, either for economy or convenience. At times Ned Broad, Brigham Young, Bill Yates or some other of *Wakakura*'s pirates would open my soundproof door to ask about the weather forecast or maybe whatever semi-official directives we'd received from Navy Office, and none of them were above hatching up some hairbrained mischief, particularly during a full moon.

This time the door opened and Ned asked politely: 'How's it going, Sparkie?' I should have spotted his half grin, but he'd already leaned over my swivel chair and put his face close to the intercom mouthpiece to drawl in a soft Welsh accent: 'Twenty degrees port wheel, helmsman,' and he was gone. 'Twenty degrees port wheel on, sir,' echoed clearly through the copper piping as I locked up and disappeared also. Already *Wakakura* was scribing a phosphorescent arc in Pegasus Bay, while Skip, who'd checked my shack and found a locked door, was engaged in hot dispute with the unfortunate reservist, and I was looking for Ned to tell him he had no known parents.

Apart from the usual daft errands reservists were dispatched about the ship on, such as the lengthy period one lad stood in the boiler room when sent down by Snowy Bowden to ask the on-watch stoker for a long weight, *Wakakura*'s complement behaved reasonably sanely.

'Telegraphist on the bridge' was Skip's normal voicepipe command to get me topside, and this time it came shortly after I'd biffed off a quick: ZLB de GXPD = QTP Bluff = 0850 AR. which told Awarua Radio that His Majesty's Ship *Wakakura* was about to enter Bluff Harbour at ten minutes to nine that morning. ZLB morsed receipt of my transmission, keyed an abbreviated 'Good Morning' and signed off. But minutes later when he was calling me urgently, I'd switched off my receiver and climbed to the bridge where Skip was pointing to the Bluff lighthouse. Its keeper Wally Kay, an ex-navy signalman, was flashing us a message so fast I couldn't read it, never could and hadn't previously needed to; so we disappeared around the headland with Lieutenant North-Lewis purple with rage at my ineptitude, me ashen in mortification, and Wally Kay telephoning Bluff's harbourmaster that *Wakakura* had ignored his warning to stand off.

Wakakura eased alongside a wharf audience of serious-faced marine officials who, when invited on board, demanded an explanation. Unusual Foveaux Strait currents together with an abnormally low tide had left barely 16 feet of water over the bar, and we drew 16 feet aft; we'd endangered King George's boat, and possibly worse we may have dislodged a lot of oysters, so, I was 'Stood Down' at the table for a court martial. However, my captain liked the massive steaks and onions I smothered his plate with when it was my turn at the frying pan. The morning after a Picton Royal Yacht Club dance I'd warned him that the Club Commodore intended reporting his whisky-induced indiscretions to Navy Office Wellington; he'd sought out the Commodore and fixed that one; so now back at sea with time to ponder, he sent for me to suggest I might prefer his punishment rather than the verdict of a Naval Court. I accepted readily, he somehow mislaid Commissioned-Gunner Joe Woodward's submissions, had the charge modified and entered his decision in the ship's correspondence. From that 'Dog Watch' until all hands including himself were competent in all aspects of visual signalling, I would instruct everyone off watch on a complete V/S course.

Eventually we had a ship's company so competent in recognising international flags and reading flashing and semaphore, that I was rarely disturbed at sea, and even Skip would voice down the pipe anything he wanted logged after an Aldis lamp conversation at night or day with a passing vessel. En route north from Dunedin with a hold full of Otago Rockies proud of their spotless uniforms, our tall funnel's eternal smuts became their despair, faces begrimed, clambering up the vertical lower messdeck ladder with snow-white towels in search of a bathroom. 'Ahhh yes,' in subdued anticipation by Bill Yates, 'down aft, port waist, just bang hard on the door and go in.'

Soon there were yells of outrage from whichever of our two officers had been caught naked, crouched knees to chin in the half-size OFFICERS ONLY bath. For the ship's company and reservists there were four galvanised basins close-set in a row under the gun-deck overhang; if possible you sluiced yourself down without pouring too much over the man either side; you cleaned your teeth, shaved, washed your socks and whites in the gallon of water each tip-basin held. But *Waka* being top-heavy due to our foc'sle gun and oversized wheelhouse, ensured that every ablution attempt at sea became a nightmare experience. Even most emergences from our messdeck right up in the bows were doomed as she plunged deep under oncoming seas, staggered skyward and cataracted tons of wintry ocean over the gun platform and down onto the unfortunate she'd been waiting for.

We slogged north from Lyttelton to roll at anchor offshore at Kaikoura, where local fishermen boiled up a forty-gallon drum of crayfish over old tractor tyres, while we rolled a firkin of Ballins Heavy Ale from the pub and helped it along with our bottles of Nelson's Blood. Next day we somehow weighed anchor and took on a Cook Strait free-for-all against a dirty-fighter southerly which did its best to roll us bottom up. I sat with a foot on each wall of my tiny office, copying Tinakori Hill Wellington's international marine radio's morsed transmission: XXX XXX XXX, the urgency signal which triggered auto-alarms in single-operator merchant-men, a pause long enough to get them out of bed, then: QRT QRT QRT de ZLW ZLW ZLW = MOST IMMEDIATE AR.

This made slowly to clear the air for something really urgent. GBXZ GBXZ GBXZ de ZLW = MOST IMMEDIATE = ALL BRITISH MER-CHANT VESSELS AND MEN OF WAR FROM ADMIRALTY = A STATE OF WAR HAS BEEN DECLARED AGAINST GERMANY = AR.

There were more messages and instructions, but no answers. All ships had been warned to observe W/T silence except in dire urgency or to report the enemy.

Coaling in Wellington, we bustled up the east coast to Auckland and entered Calliope Dock for a bottom clean, then later at the Orakei dolphin around which ships revolve to correct their compass settings, we circled slowly at the end of a long mooring line while everyone including the duty stoker gazed shoreward. The rope broke and we did it again. The furnace hadn't gulped a banjo full of coal, so, eventually when asked for 'FULL AHEAD' to do an ordered power trial, there wasn't sufficient steam. 'YOU,' the Captain yelled at someone strolling along the waist, 'DOWN BELOW! AND YOU AND YOU. YES DAMN IT. YOU TWO AS WELL. GET ON THE END OF A SHOVEL!' *Waka* had never gone so fast; we passed Rangitoto Beacon at well over her rated 8 knots and, while pulsating at 12-plus off Tiri Tiri the inevitable happened, BAAANNNGGG and a cloud of steam up the stokehold hatch followed by a scurry of panic-stricken stokers and involuntary assistants when a main steam gland blew.

Three hours later, with insufficient power to steer down the outboard side of *Philomel* jetty to our berth, between the dock head and *Leander*'s stern protruding from the Cruiser Wharf, there was 'that feeling in the air'. *Waka* crabbed onward, nudged sideways by a Waitemata Harbour rip. I stood at the binnacle voicepipe, centre bridge, repeating Skip's orders as he stood forward for a better view of the bows.

'Half astern' calmly. 'Half astern' down the pipe to our ERA. 'Half astern on, sir!' loud. Nothing happened! There wasn't enough pressure to reverse our prop.

'FULL ASTERN!' With luck we'd miss the dock caisson forty feet above the empty dock bottom. By now I'd been swept aside and Skip was yelling down the pipe for 'EMERGENCY ASTERN!' but all available pressure had long since burst out through that ruptured gland. Then luck decided our future, instead of shoving our 430-ton trawler through the caisson to drop on inrushing sea into the empty dock, we struck a patch of reverse current which heaved us headlong into stone walling twenty feet south of the dock gate. *Wakakura* sculptured an eight feet inverted V in the concrete decking, split our bows and anchor hawse as the stem buckled, and upended the training whaler crane which promptly dropped the whaler with timber-smashing noises. Officers viewing the incident from *Leander*'s quarterdeck recovered in time to rush over a portable pump which probably saved us from being the NZD's first wartime loss; the dock was still intact, and handy, but several weeks passed before we rose on its flooding waters to now enter the War, this time against the enemy, but first to cross to Western Viaduct's coaling wharf.

On completion and after hosing down our decks, we sloshed ourselves with soap suds, then watched with trepidation as Nobel Explosive's topsail schooner *Huia* berthed astern. What faith! 'Her Skipper can't have heard of *Wakakura*,' Brigham Young mused aloud as we made for Fred Gleeson's pub at the bottom of Hobson Street to wash down any remaining coal dust. Next forenoon all was ready for our departure; there was a brisk easterly blowing which wouldn't make things easy, as *Wakakura* tended to veer to port when going astern, no matter where our helmsman put the rudder.

'LET GO AFT; SHORTEN IN FORE'ARD,' by voice trumpet. A moment to ensure both orders had been obeyed, then, 'Wheel, fifteen degrees starboard.' 'Fifteen degrees starboard wheel on, saah.' 'Half ahead,' to the engine-room. Everything was going smoothly as the stern eased out and our freshly painted bows squeezed wharf fenders, 'Stop engine.' 'LET GO FORE'ARD' by loud hailer. 'Full astern' down the pipe and repeated back up. And! Now was the time for that gust to make things awkward. *Wakakura*'s obstinate left drift, an onsetting current, and a second puff of wind swung us back in. Instead of gliding handsomely off into manoeuvring water we rasped along the length of *Huia*'s gleaming white hull, baring her timbered planking and bringing down her shrouds with our foremast yard. Brigham Young's foreboding had materialised. Captain Samuel J. Atkins who'd previously brought her safely through fires, storms and groundings, invented a new dictionary full of sailing-ship terms about the Navy, never before heard as far away as Queen Street; and we shot off around North Head out into the sanctuary of Hauraki Gulf. There, after several days target towing for *Leander*'s gunners, our Commanding Officer, Lieutenant Peter North-Lewis RN, got an official commendation for his ship's efficient compliance with every order received either by W/T or V/S, both night and day; a pat on the back he may not have earned but for that wise decision to administer his punishment, in lieu of my pending court martial.

I transferred to *Leander* for her Middle East and Mediterranean role, leaving the old *Waka* to continue her private war against the New Zealand Navy, Merchant Navy, and various Harbour Board installations around our coast. Her wartime exploits are briefed in the *Official History of New Zealand in the Second World War – Royal New Zealand Navy*. And her post-war career is mentioned in *The Shoestring Fleet* written by her ex-RNZN skipper and owner who ran cargoes across the Tasman until 1952 when she was scrapped in Auckland.

CHAPTER IV

1915–1930 – NZ Involvement in Samoa

SAMOAN ISLANDS. Tropical. Reaching westward along the 14 degree south latitude, this lengthy archipelago constitutes Nu'unomanu (Rose Island) sited at 168 degrees west longitude; Ta'u and Manui'a Islands 140 miles to the west; another 72 miles west to Tutuila with its sheltered deep water Pago Pago American Naval Base; a further 36 miles west to the main island Upolo (cap. Apia); then a final 12 miles to neighbouring Savai'i Island with its 6,100-foot Mount Silisili being the highest of this 280-mile chain of volcanic upthrusts. Verdant and precipitous they had been inhabited for 3,000 years by a Polynesian race of mild-mannered people whose culture evolved similarly to that of other developed civilisations. Elected village headmen, or women, were given power tempered by lesser advisers. Above these were prominent governors of central and outlying districts; Upolo's districts including parts of Savai'i Island becoming what we might term 'Central Government', the remainder of Savai'i Island being self-governed, while Manui'a Island away to the east also managed its own affairs, but adjacent Tutuila Island was regarded as a sub-district of eastern Upolo.

Perhaps the first European to sight one of Samoa's islands was the Dutch Admiral Jacob Roggeveen who on 14 June 1722 watered at remote Ta'u Island, but being one in the race to discover the fabled Southern Continent he gave it scant record. Next, in 1768, came Francois Louis de Bougainville who whilst plotting a distant island in the area, recorded skilled Polynesians in outrigger canoes; then he too cruised on in search of the Southern Continent. Nineteen years later another French expedition, led by Jean Francois Perouse on *Le Astrolabe* accompanied by *de Boussole*, anchored in Tutuila Bay; but when filling water containers a skirmish with islanders erupted. *Le Astrolabe*'s Captain de Langle and the entire watering party were bludgeoned to death and in consequence the Samoan Islands were avoided for decades by informed seafarers.

And so it remained until 1830, when the London Missionary Society sent the Rev. John Williams to Savai'i to introduce Christianity. Within twenty years European settlers had established their form of government and, circa 1861–5, during the American Civil War, US enterprises bought land for cotton growing, so much so that by 1873 Samoans had sold more of their land to Americans than actually existed. To arrive at a solution Albert Steinberger represented himself, and was accepted, as a US Government agent given powers to arrange an American takeover, but soon he was suspected of acting in collusion with German interests. Early in 1876 Washington denounced him, British, German and US consuls had him arrested and he was deported aboard HMS *Barracuda* to Fiji. In the unrest which followed, Samoans were encouraged by a Hamburg Shipping Co agent to hoist Tamasese Titimaea's personal flag, this igniting a mini-civil war involving US, British, and German warships which bombarded rival Samoan villages. Then on 15 March 1889 the problem was resolved by a violent hurricane which wrecked three German and three US warships at anchor in Apia Harbour, only Captain Henry Coey Kane's HMS *Calliope* managing to steam out to sea. He came back three days later to participate in the clean-up and burial services for the 186 German and American navymen lost.

Three months later in Berlin a tripartite treaty recognised Samoan neutrality and independence, with her citizens guaranteed the protection of Britain, Germany, and the United States of America. But this temperamental mandate lasted barely ten years until in 1899 a more realistic settlement was reached: America was given Tutuila; Germany received the rest of Samoa by forfeiting all rights to Anglo/German disputed territories in Africa and certain other disputed Pacific islands; and Britain concentrated on the problems involved in her African, European, Indian, Chinese, South American, and other colonial interests.

One of the late nineteenth-century settlers in Upolo was a Swede who married a Samoan chief's daughter, thereby inheriting land on which to build his house and produce children, one, Olaf Frederick Nelson, growing to be a man of immense build and strength of character. He adopted his family motto (Man submits to reason, not force) under which and being well conversed in Samoan, German and English languages he became prominent from 1910 onwards among white traders and Samoan chiefs protesting at unfair German taxes.

At the outbreak of the First World War, Britain's Secretary of State, Sir Lewis Harcourt, cabled New Zealand's Governor General, Earl Liverpool, a request to seize Samoa and its W/T station atop the hill behind Apia. Infantry Companies of the 5th Wellington Regiment commanded by Lt Col Harcourt-Turnbull, and a similar contingent from the 3rd Auckland Regiment commanded by Lt Col Harry Fulton were encamped near Wellington for departure on 11 August 1914. But due to delays in providing adequate escorts to reinforce New Zealand's three old 2,200-ton 4″ P-Class cruisers, *Psyche* (SNO Captain Herbert Marshall RN), *Philomel* (Captain Percival Hall-Thomson RN), *Pyramus* (Captain Viscount Kelburn RN), that date was amended.

It was understood that Admiral von Spee's Far East Squadron based at Tsingtao would defend German territories and islands about the north-west Pacific, and the only unit capable of outgunning his 8″ heavy cruisers *Scharnhorst*, *Gneisenau*, and lesser warships *Dresden*, *Leipzig*, *Nurnberg*, *Eitel Friedrich*, and *Kormoran* was Australia's fast 19,000-ton 12″ battlecruiser *Australia* (Adm. Patey), who with his 6″ cruisers *Melbourne* and *Sydney* had been dispatched to the Bismarck Sea region to await Graf von Spee's ships. But after a fruitless five-day search Patey arrived at Bougainville then coaled at Port Moresby whilst awaiting further orders.

On Saturday, 15 August the New Zealand transports *Monowai* and *Moeraki* departed Wellington under escort, expecting to rendezvous east of Gisborne with the Australian squadron which however was still in Port Moresby, so they returned to the capital. Ministerial and Defence ears reddened whilst reading Admiral Patey's diatribe about their lack of intelligence; but eventually pieces of the communication jigsaw came together, the convoy again sailed, bunkered and provisioned in Suva before going on to Noumea where they found *Australia*, *Melbourne* and France's old cruiser *Montcalm*, then, escorted by the Australian, French and New Zealand warships, sailed once more for Suva. There this time they embarked fifteen prominent Samoan chiefs resident in Fiji, their role being to assure Samoans that similar to their experience in Fiji, Samoans could rest assured of virtual freedom of custom and speech under British administration. Then on 27 August 1914 when clear of land the troops were each issued 150 rounds of .303 ammunition, 'not to be fired unless necessary to take the German W/T Station'.

At daybreak on Saturday, 29 August men streamed topside on *Monowai* and *Moeraki*. There, miles across an undisturbed leaden ocean, sunrays were revealing the tops of Upolo's 3,300-feet high Mount Fito and lesser Mount Vaea. Everywhere the New Zealand troops and returning Samoan chiefs looked there were those familiar escorts, *Philomel*'s siren warning nearby cruisers as, bow waves creaming and her wake boiling, she sped a cable astern of *Moeraki* to assume *Pysche*'s vacated station. Away in her van position, laying a browning cloud of funnel smuts, huge turret guns training to port across her massive quarterdeck as she altered course, *Australia*'s foaming wake ploughed a widening arc. Down both escort columns above *Pyramus*, *Melbourne*, and two colliers, the overhead airspace mushroomed then hung black and heavy above vertical shafts of unburned fuel. Colourful flags ran up halyards, were acknowledged, then ran down. The convoy was to stand offshore while *Psyche* flying a flag of truce went alone into Apia, there to present Admiral Patey's terms for German Governor Dr Schultz's 'unconditional surrender of Apia and all Imperial possessions under his control. The W/T Station must cease transmission or be destroyed by gunfire. Etcetera etc.'

The half-hour deadline came and went. So did more half hours. Then *Psyche* emerged in a hurry back to Admiral Patey with the German reply. In Dr Schultz's absence from Apia, Acting-Governor Rimberg had dictated a letter saying he had ordered the W/T Station to be 'packed up', no resistance to be attempted by citizens or local police, as Apia had only an antiquated saluting gun and some ceremonial rifles of antique vintage, and he expected Admiral Patey to observe the 'Principles of Nations' Rights' signed by Britain at the 2nd Hague Convention.

The landings now proceeded at previously selected beaches. During the day's preliminaries in Apia, everyone massed before Government House to see the German Flag lowered by Private Bayley and replaced by the British Union Flag; shortly after which, on Governor Schultz's arrival back from an outlying village, New Zealand's first Governor of Samoa, Colonel Robert Logan, regretfully placed him under arrest for transport to New Zealand.

There on Monday afternoon, 31 August 1914, town and city billboards blazoned huge headlines, while paperboys waved folded copies of late editions and loudly announced New Zealand's first First World War military success.

The way was now clear for the 1st NZ Expeditionary Force to go overseas so, on Friday, 16 October 1914, 7,761 officers and ranks of the main body, and 738 of the 1st Reinforcements, departed Wellington in the transports *Arawa*, *Athenic*, *Hawkes Bay*, *Limerick*, *Maunganui*, *Orari*, *Ruapehu*, *Star of India*, *Tahiti*, and *Waimana*, escorted by Australia's heavy cruiser *Minotaur*, Japan's heavy cruiser *Ibuki*, and New Zealand's 3rd Class light cruisers *Philomel*, *Psyche* and *Pyramus*, on their 48-day voyage to Alexandria. Throughout the war forty-three Reinforcements totalling 102,438 men would be convoyed overseas to the Middle Eastern and European battle-fronts; but back now to Samoa.

Within Colonel Logan's 1914–18 term as governor, Samoan life proceeded much as it had under the German flag, Sino-Samoan marriages being forbidden and fraternisation severely restricted, but such laws were often breached even during Colonel Robert Tate's 1918–23 administration; an unhappy start when on 7 November 1918 the Union Steamship Coy's vessel *Talune* brought the 'Spanish Flu' to Apia from Lyttelton and one in every four Samoans died. Olaf Nelson's name once more featured when he translated Samoan complaints for a local newspaper concerning the lack of medicines made available throughout the epidemic; then in 1920 as a rich trader he part-financed the formation of a Citizens Committee which petitioned against continued high taxation.

These petitions were ignored by Colonel Tate, and by the 3rd Administrator, General George Richardson 1923–8, who tended to govern over-militarily. But to try and pacify Nelson he gave him a minority seat on the Legislative Council, and in 1926 at Wellington he attended a meeting with New Zealand's Prime Minister Gordon Coates, Minister of Foreign Affairs William Nosworthy, and Minister for Cook Islands Maui Pomare, at which he detailed Samoan problems similar to the 1909 Mau opposition to unsatisfactory German dictates. Their objectives were reasonable, law-abiding, and based on a desire for welfare betterment embracing all ethnic races resident in Samoa. Nosworthy made plans to visit Samoa in November but on Richardson's request they were postponed until May 1927. Meantime civil unrest was festering under restrictive legislation until Nelson cabled Nosworthy that Samoa seemed like a military camp under martial law. On 21 December 1927 Governor General Ferguson signed an order authorising Richardson to deport Nelson for five years and this was carried out. Even this did not suit Richardson and on 13 February 1928 he cabled Nosworthy, requiring an immediate show of naval force in Samoa. NZNB readied the cruisers *Dunedin* and *Diomede*; Commodore T.G.B. Swabey made accommodation available on his flagship for an External Affairs officer, Carl Berendsen, then with *Diomede* maintaining position in *Dunedin*'s rumbling wake, both cruisers sped north to enter Apia on Tuesday, 21 February 1928 and anchor off the reef on which SMS *Adler*'s rusting hull still spoke of that fateful hurricane thirty-nine years past in March 1889.

Having been barged ashore Commodore Swabey, on his way to meet General Richardson at Government House, passed shops picketed by barefooted Samoans in Mau uniform – short-sleeved white singlet and knee-height blue lavalava with two white stripes above the hem. Everywhere there were Mau members armed with crude batons and heavy sticks, but as they showed no animosity he saw no reason to mount an armed confrontation. Instead he signalled the cruisers to give leave until the last boat from Customs Wharf at 2100 and within an hour the dust of Beach Road's unsealed surface was being lifted by 300 friendly NZDrs whose casual attitude created instant goodwill.

Meantime Swabey attended a Legislative Council meeting at which invited Mau representatives laid bare their *matais'* grievances about poll taxes and restrictive legislature. In turn administration officers declared the laws to be just and more than equitable; then towards evening the meeting ended in sour confusion when Richardson tabled a bill authorising arrests for 'wearing Mau uniform', 'refusal to disband from unauthorised meetings', 'failure to assist police when required' and other anti-Mau legislation. Within hours police were reporting arrangements being discussed by Samoans for a show of civil disobedience on Friday, 24 February. Swabey with no alternative, dispatched armed Royal Marine and seamen contingents ashore, some to Tivoli Wharf and others to Customs Wharf in order to surround and contain on Beach Road some 400 Mau for civil arrest.

Offering no resistance they fell in as ordered and were marched off to Alcazar Garage from where they were trucked to Vaimea Gaol; then to highlight the General's lack of wisdom the Mau marched in another 150 demanding to be arrested for creating an area of disturbance, and, to exacerbate Richardson's dilemma down came the rain, torrential, continuous. Commodore Swabey insisted the near 600 arrested be moved immediately from Vaimea's bogged and polluted conditions, but when they were moved to a slack-wired compound erected on Richardson's orders across harbour at Cape Mulinu'u, the Mau leaders insisted that the remainder of their movement be impounded there also.

Now arose one, Tupua Tamasese, who in previous discussions at Wellington's Parliament Buildings to improve Samoan relations, had been treated discourteously. The latest show of naval force had induced him to assume Mau leadership in matters advised by collective Samoan chiefs; at an open court presided over by Chief Judge William Woodward at Mulinu'u he declined the Judge's suggestion that he plead for the several hundred impounded, this leaving Woodward no option but to find them all guilty, each sentenced to six months imprisonment. Obviously impossible, Richardson then attempted mollification but this was politely refused by Tupua Tamasese. He declined a position of intermediary involving mass pardons and the election of prominent Samoans to the Legislative Council, and when Richardson's verbal threats fell on deaf ears the General was left wielding the hasp of a bladeless sword.

Up till now, as impounded Mau politely defied Royal Marine sentries when breaking camp at Mulinu'u, the 'Royals' under instructions to show friendliness, merely grinned and looked elsewhere; so, intent on imprisoning the head Mau, Richardson sent local police to arrest Tupua Tamasese, but this too failed when the village Mau mustered in strength and threatened the constables with home-made batons. Commander Robin Jeffrey RN considered the police having neglected to use adequate force were in no danger and, not having the authority to cause bloodshed by using firearms or bayonets, he waited long enough to be assured the police had gained control of the situation, then marched his men back to their boats lying off Customs Wharf.

Finally, the General asked Commodore Swabey to take a dozen or so captured ringleaders aboard *Dunedin* for deportation to Niue. The New Zealand Government refused permission as it was considered internationally illegal. Richardson had to release all Mau from the Mulinu'u compound, and on Friday, 9 March 1928 *Dunedin* led *Diomede* out of Apia en route for New Zealand.

Richardson's five-year term as Administrator had done little for New Zealand; he still smarted over Tupua Tamasese's pacifist victory, and he badgered Wellington for reinforcements to overthrow the Mau. But the External Affairs Department had had enough, so Nosworthy recalled the General on the premise that a change of administration was vital. The new man, Colonel Stephen Sheppard Allen, with Cambridge University degrees in law and maths, First World War decorations, a farmer and Mayor of Morrinsville, started off on the wrong foot by also wanting Samoa to march in military step. He arrived in Apia in May 1928 with a strong force of Military Police recruited from ex-Western Front servicemen armed with batons, bayoneted .303 rifles, Colt sidearms, and two Lewis guns. With a display of Empire glory he stood at the salute, watching his flag run up the staff just denuded by that of the Royal Marine and seamen platoons which left in March when their cruisers departed.

Samoans and Mau adherents had mellowed under the Navy's friendly attitude, but Colonel Allen's SMP brigade was soon to make things worse than ever. Almost immediately armed squads were dispatched to remote villages, laying waste to *fale* furnishings and rough-treating frightened women and children while searching for *matai* and Mau documents. Tupua Tamasese was chased and arrested at his village, then on 6 December he was charged before Chief Justice Woodward with tax avoidance and resisting arrest, being sentenced to six weeks gaol on the first count and six months on the second; the terms to be served in New Zealand at Allen's request. Tamasese disembarked from *Tofua* at Auckland on Boxing Day 1929 and went directly to Mt Eden Prison.

Gaoling him in New Zealand backfired as had previous high-level attempts to subdue Samoan Mau. Ex-Reform Party Minister of Cook Island Affairs, Sir Maui Pomare, the Church Leader Reverend Walter Averil, and eminent Auckland lawyers, took up the gauntlet on his behalf, culminating in the Supreme Court in late January 1929 when perhaps the most eminent lawyer, Alfred Hall Skelton, tabled a writ of Habeas Corpus, insisting that the 'Samoa Act 1921' had been ignored in transferring Tupua Tamasese from Samoa to New Zealand. The presiding judge did not agree, Tupua remained in Mt Eden Prison, editorials and public opinion down-rated New Zealand's administration of Samoa, and thousands packed town hall meetings demanding reform. But all this was refuted by government assertion that under New Zealand rule Samoans were the most healthy Polynesians, proven by their marked rate of child production.

By mid-1929 many lips were shaping the name of another Mau leader, Tagalo Fumuina, who led several uniformed followers to Apia's Administration Building in front of which he loudly read a speech. He was not arrested. But on Saturday, 15 June, when Colonel Allen's now unarmed

SMP saw Tagalo in the centre of a number of approaching Mau, it was anticipated he would arouse trouble from streets full of Mau ostensibly shopping.

Tagalo Fumuina was on the list of wanted tax evaders, but when an SMP constable attempted to arrest him other Mau interfered. Swinging batons the SMP forced their way through obstructing participants who retaliated with previously lavalava-hidden cudgels and, after the inevitable melee bleeding Mau and battered SMP were assisted from the dust-clouded road. Tagalo Fumuina was bundled into a police van and taken to Vaimea Prison on remand for a week until tried and sentenced to nine months in gaol; then an Order in Council rearmed all European police with loaded Colts plus ten extra rounds. In future they would carry batons and handcuffs at all times.

In November 1929 the Mau petitioned King George V to transfer the Mandate over Samoa from New Zealand to Great Britain but, unfortunately for New Zealand, King George's parliament had escalating problems concerning one, Adolf Schicklegruber Hitler; they ignored the petition, thus spraying high-octane kavakava on a Samoan conflagration soon to be known as 'Black Friday'.

Apia's Christmas celebrations 1929 were over, the small island trader *Lady Roberts* was due from Pago Pago, and on 28 December crowds were gathering at daybreak to welcome relatives and Hall Skelton who'd come up from Auckland to Pago Pago on *Niagara*. A typical Samoan feast had been prepared for him in the knowledge that he was here as a lawyer, to gather information supporting Olaf Nelson in a case to be heard in Auckland's Supreme Court. A big Mau march was expected any moment, and Colonel Allen had instructed Police Chief Arthur Braisby to arrest all wanted Mau offenders participating. Braisby had laid his plans: five constables armed with Webley pistols would make any such arrests, eighteen others armed with batons would wait in the Police Station as support if required, others with a Lewis gun were posted on the British Club balcony overlooking a Beach Road bridge across which the march would pass.

Shortly after daybreak an approaching band heralded the Mau parade, its base drum being pounded by the massive Mau Secretary Mata'utia Karuna who was wanted on several charges. On seeing him by binoculars from Custom House, Braisby telephoned Police Sergeant Waterson to have him apprehended, but when a constable tried to drag him to the roadside all hell broke loose. Waterson yelled for his men to get their rifles from the Police Station and was clubbed to the ground, but he managed to extricate himself and break clear down Ifi'ifi Road. A following constable, Will Abraham, wasn't so fortunate and he was clubbed to death in an adjacent lane. Waterson, a First World War machine-gunner, mounted the station Lewis gun and fired a burst over the heads of those milling at the intersection of Beach and Ifi'ifi Roads, its rounds being seen spitting into the sea by passengers on the now Custom Wharf berthed *Lady Roberts*. Yells of rage, screams of pain, and the uproar of an all-in melee were punctuated by rifle fire and the occasional staccato of Lewis gun bursts; among and above all being Tupua Tamasese's stentorian exhortations for the Mau to stop fighting: 'STOP! FILEMU SAMOA! PEACE SAMOA!' A shot rang out and he slumped badly wounded, in pain but still calling loudly for the fighting to stop.

At about 6.30 a.m. it did and there was quiet, an eerie quiet, as dust settled along Beach Road while dead and wounded were spirited away.

Colonel Allen's initial report to Finance Minister Sir Joseph Ward stated: 'near 2,000 Mau armed with clubs, machetes and knives in the affray – Constable Abraham and two Mau killed – two police and some 30 Mau injured – Tupua Tamasese shot and in hospital'. But the actual number of Mau and innocent Samoan dead soon rose to eight with about fifty injured. Tupua Tamasese died on Sunday morning the day after he was shot; 3,000 Samoans and Europeans attended his funeral on Monday, then the recriminations from both sides surfaced. Parliament on 11 January voted in a bill authorising Colonel Allen to declare the Mau insurrectional, so he again asked for military assistance to 'for once and all, quell the Mau entirely'. With *Diomede* away in Chatham Dockyard for her triennial refit, the newly appointed CCNZ, Commodore Geoffrey Blake CB DSO RN, arrived in Apia on *Dunedin* at 1600, Sunday, 12 January 1930, immediately going ashore for discussions with Colonel Allen at his Administration HQ.

January 1930 was wet, tropically wet, excessively humid and enervating; and with Commander Jeffrey again in charge of shore patrols, landing parties suffered agonies while crossing cold streams high up in the ravined jungle, constantly bitten in the mosquito-infested sodden bush, coming out to coastal villages whose forewarned inhabitants had already fled. On one occasion Able Seamen Bill Yates, 'Spud' Murphy, 'Bobo' Page, Stokers Paddy Duigan, Bob Sawyers, Les Hood and numerous others were 'quietly' approaching a village at night to surprise and capture Mau activists at sleep in their *fale*. One section would creep around 'quietly' to form a line of no escape on the far side. When given the order, section two would advance at the lope with bayoneted rifles at the low port. Those Mau would be trapped and taken. The first strategy went off without alarm 'RIGHT! GO! GO!' and off went strategy two in total dark as intended.

'YOWWPS! CHRIST, I'VE HAD MY BLOODY THROAT CUT!' from Bill Yates as an unseen wire clothes line threw him backward onto the ground. Blood coursing down his chest he stumbled after his mates, this time with his rifle forward at the present. 'SHHITT! BLOODY SHHITT!'

he screamed involuntarily as skin tore off both legs on an unseen concrete trough. By now silence was unnecessary and he staggered into the darkened *nu'u*, where both detachments were now using torches inside *fale* after *fale* from which male Mau had hours previously fled.

Wide-eyed women and children answered their queries in unintelligible Samoan; the search was called off; bedraggled and dispirited with bandages round his throat and legs seeping blood, Bill kept pace with the returning party – *but* his worries weren't yet over. Given permission to obey nature he downed trows in hip-high grass, right over a hornets' burrow. His yells of pain brought men running to his aid sure that he was being ambushed and killed, but they too were set upon by the enraged swarm and the whole detachment went pounding down the hillside trail beating off the airborne assault. Laughing Samoans watched the 'enemy' in retreat, an enemy glad to be launched back out to their anchored cruiser, where Bill Yates queued with less serious casualties in the sick bay flat.

For this naval assignment *Dunedin* had shipped a Hobsonville Gypsy Moth float-plane and its pilot Flight Lieutenant Syd Wallingford. Day after day he grazed treetops, powering over ridges and gliding down through gullies to find bands of Mau in clearings. These he morsed back to *Dunedin's* W/T operators, but having been entertained by their first sight and sound of an aeroplane the quarry were well away before search parties arrived. On 25 January 1930 the Commodore realised the futility of further naval endeavours, the flagship's Sick Bay was crammed with cot and stretcher cases totally exhausted and putrescent with ulcers caused by scratched mosquito bites. Most Samoans were supplying their hunted groups with food. Tupua Tamasese's successor Tamasese Me'ole unsuccessfully asked Allen for talks; but both he and Commodore Blake had already conceded their inability to contact, much less arrest, Mau bands in the rain-drenched rugged terrain; and they were now cabled from New Zealand that the militant Seamens Union was refusing to work ships loading replenishments for administration purposes in Samoa.

Then to put a stain on the Navy's good-humoured participation to date, during a 21 February patrol, Able Seaman 'Shorty' Colson tripped and fell while chasing some running Mau, his pistol triggered and the bullet dropped a youth who died while Colson was trying to resuscitate him. Although at the inquiry Chief Judge John Luxford exempted him from blame, as did the Mau, Colson grieved over his tragic misadventure, especially at the burial to which his particular platoon had been invited.

Days later on Monday, 3 March in Tamasese Me'ole's *vale* at Vaimoso, New Zealand's Minister of Defence John Cobbe, Colonel Allen, Commodore Blake, Commander Jeffrey, and Native Affairs Secretary Frank Lewis, met fifty paramount chiefs. That meeting produced scant goodwill, nor did one on 4 March or another next day. Back in Wellington Cobbe told Cabinet that civilian diplomats should replace military men as Samoa administrators if there was to be any possibility of appeasement; *Dunedin* departed Apia on 12 March with sixty men on her sick List, and on 17 March Allen cabled Sir Joseph Ward that since the cruiser left, the Mau had been quiet.

Brigadier-General Herburt 'Bunty' Hart's appointment as Administrator lasted from 1931 to 1936; his term did nothing to appease, or to inflame, the Mau, after which civilians were given the post. And all subsequent visits by New Zealand warships right through to Samoan Independence in 1962 were made and welcomed in friendship.

CHAPTER V

Proposed BOAC Flying Boat Pacific Route

Tropic islands, romantic, tragic. Since forever, the lowest forms of marine life have secreted a lime substance skeletal structure on or in which to live and die. Thriving in warm seas these polyp colonies have thrust up from the crests of submarine mountains to be dangerous reefs or inhabitable atolls, some enclosing lagoons, others freshwater lakes.

One great underwater range, the North-West Christmas Island Ridge, reaches south-south-east from the western Hawaiis almost to the Society Group, climbing from a 12,000-feet seabed to a 600-feet submerged backbone whose peaks and coral growths have emerged to trace its course. North of the Equator these upthrusts are called the North Line Islands; south, the South Line Islands, but we will be interested in only those punctuating a proposed mid-1930s British flying-boat route from Vancouver to Auckland, so a brief description of each will acquaint us with their history.

Kingman Reef: 6 deg 24 min N 162 deg 23 min W. A low triangular atoll 9 miles long by 5 miles wide, with a deep lagoon. Discovered 1798 by Captain Edward Fanning of the US trading schooner *Betsy*. Named after a Captain Kingman in 1853; annexed to the US on 10 May 1922; used later by Pan American Clippers as a fuel depot between Honolulu and Pago Pago.

Fanning Island: 3 deg 51 min N 159 deg 22 min W. An atoll 30 miles in circumference, its ring of land only several hundred yards wide and 10 feet high, enclosing a lagoon. Discovered 1798 by Captain Fanning of *Betsy*; annexed to Britain in 1888 by Captain William Wiseman RN of HMS *Caroline* when surveying the Pacific cable route. Cable station 1902–1963. Commercially owned by Fanning Island Plantations Ltd, subsidiary of Burns Philp, Sydney.

Christmas Island: 1 deg 59 min N 157 deg 30 min W. 150 miles SE of Fanning Island. Discovered 1777 by Captain James Cook of HMS *Resolution*. 100 miles in circumference, an irregular shape lying NW to SE with a lagoon in the NW area. It is the world's largest coral island and has over

100 lakes up to 2 miles in diameter; possibly visited by early Spanish explorers but imprecise maps cause doubt. Bay of Wrecks named due to easterly exposure casualties. Good anchorage off Cook Island to the south of 'London' settlement, and north of 'Paris'. Pre-European artefacts and stone statues found. Worked by US Guano Coy in 1858. Formally possessed for the US by USS *Narrangansett* in 1872, but despite US Govt protest, annexed to Britain by Captain Sir William Wiseman of HMS *Caroline* in 1888. Leased in 1902 for 99 years to Lever Pacific Plantations who planted 73,000 coconut palms. Lease sold in 1913 to Father Emanuel Rougier under the name of Central Pacific Plantations Ltd; managed by his nephew from 1932 when Rougier died, until the mid-1930s depression. Garrisoned in the Second World War by NZ and US troops, then used until 1948 by America as a Honolulu to Bora Bora flying-boat stop. Copra enterprise continued by Gilbert and Ellice Islands Colony. Used for British nuclear tests from 1956 to 1964.

We have retrogressed a time-scanner to the eighteenth century; years have sizzled back on the read-out, it decelerates through 1900 and 1800 then the counter stops at 1777. A sparkling early morning tropical ocean fills the screen, and a video voice monotones that we are about to locate Captain Cook's sloop HMS *Resolution* and the expedition's 2nd I/C, Commander John Clerke's smaller HMS *Discovery*. Under full sail with *Resolution* a nautical league to starboard, they were ploughing northward, urged on by rhythmic blue swells shouldering their wooden rudders and lathering their waterlines, heaving both ships' broad sterns high to reveal marine growths accumulated over the two months since leaving Otaheite's Matavai Bay.

In his unpretentious cabin Cook sat dusting dry his log entry recording 1,217 mean distance miles from the Society Islands' main anchorage, 112 since crossing the Line at 158 degrees of West Longitude during the last dogwatch yesterday, 23 December. He rose to see that the morning watch handed over satisfactorily.

'LAND HO OFF THE STARBOARD BOW!' disrupted his intentions. The crow's nest lookout was pointing away to the north-east where he'd discerned a blur of surf on the horizon. Cook's chair clattered to his cabin planking as he reached down for a telescope and joined his astronomer Bayly near Lieutenant King on the poop.

Already top-gallants were being furled as lower-yard seamen worked successive halyards, masts and mains. Through their megaphones straddle-legged bosuns roared orders up into the rigging, and quartermasters loudmouthed directives to their helmsmen to spin the wheel in sympathy with the swinging yards. Now canted to port with all sails taut, *Resolution* led *Discovery* northward until well seaward of a reef which stretched beyond sight as a surf-pounded barrier to the calm waters inside. Finding no entrance, Cook stood his ships clear throughout the night and closed again at dawn, this time locating an opening and making a cautious landing inside the barren atoll, which he named Christmas Island in deference to it being 24 December. The festive season was celebrated, then forage parties landed daily to provision ship with turtles and fish, while Cook, Bayly and King were rowed to an islet in the entrance, there setting up their instruments to observe the 30 December moon eclipse which Cook entered in his journal.

> There was too much cloud for the beginning of the eclipse to be seen, and I was forced to discontinue observing for a time, under the strain of the awkward angle of my telescope combined with the fierce heat of the sun reflected by the coral sand. As Bayly and I had similar telescopes my timing for the end of the eclipse should not have differed as it did – 24 minutes; perhaps it was in part, if not wholly owing to a protuberance in the Moon which escaped my notice but was seen by both other gentlemen. [Later in the journal he continued] there is little growth of any foliage and no inhabitants, but there are many lagoons and abundant birds, turtles and fish. We have planted some coconut palms, sprouting yams, and sowed melon seeds. On Eclipse Island I have left a seaman's bottle enclosing my inscription to the honour of Georgius tertius Rex. From a plentiful spot on Eclipse Islet alone we have taken three hundred excellent green turtles.

Closing his journal Cook went out into the poop's still morning air to ready his ships for an anticipated offshore breeze. Soon there was the usual noise and activity associated with departure, as men on *Resolution*'s and *Discovery*'s capstan spars winched in their anchors to the rhythm of each ship's fiddler. Longboat crews strained at their oars to drag the sloops' blunt bows seaward and tow them ponderously through the reef entrance. Outside they wallowed under slack sails while boat after boat swung inboard. A slight shimmer riffled the mirrored surface, and announced the day's awakening breeze. A gentle gust barely moved the heavy canvas but it sufficed to cause eddies around the sloops' rudders. More persistent pressures made their sails bang and fill; spars on each mast took the strain, were swung aslant to gain every ounce of momentum until low whitecaps raced after both vessels now heeling with surging waterlines, once more on their voyage via the 1,500 miles distant Sandwich Islands to the cold North Pacific.

Cook's expedition took him from Kauai in the Hawaiis to America's north-west coast, up to Vancouver Island and Nootka Sound at the US-Canada border, north to Alaska, then back to Hawaii and his untimely 13 February 1779 death at Kealakekua Bay. Cook, Clerke who assumed command until he died of ill health at Siberia's Kamchatka Sound on 22 August 1779, and

NZDRNs on *Neptune* at Kiel for Germany's Naval Week and the 1936 Berlin Olympics. Note Nazi Youth guide in khaki shorts.

Gore who carried the assignment through to its conclusion, are now immortalised in history.

HMS Resolution: built in Fishburn Yards, Whitby, in 1770 as the 462-ton collier *Marquis of Granby*. Bought by Admty Nov 1771 and renamed *Drake*. Bottom copper sheathed, fitted out as a 12-gun sloop with 120 personnel.

HMS Discovery: built Whitby 1774 as the 298-ton brig *Diligence*. Purchased by Admty Jan. 1776 and renamed *Raleigh*, bottom copper sheathed, three masts mounted instead of original two, classed as a 'ship' but later referred to as a sloop mounting 8 four-pounders 8 swivel guns and 8 musquetoons; 70 personnel.

Not wishing to offend Spain who still rankled over the Falkland Islands the previous year, and who had no love for Drake or Raleigh *Drake* was renamed *Resolution*, and *Raleigh* became *Discovery*, these name changes being considered prudent due to Spain's substantial Pacific presence at that time.

The recorder on our time machine flashes forward to the year 1936; we have witnessed the discovery of one island; in the intervening century and a half all of those protruding above the surface have been discovered, named and charted, physically fought over or wrangled about in international courts.

In 1935 as a 19-year-old Wireless Telegraphist on HMS *Dunedin* at

Dunedin (CCNZ) and *Diomede* in Wellington Harbour, New Zealand, 1935.

Invercargill's Bluff Harbour, I was among those rudely awakened pre-dawn and rushed by bus, train and ferry via Dunedin, Lyttelton, Wellington and Auckland to bring *Diomede* up to war strength. Admiralty had required NZNB to send one of her cruisers to be a unit of the Red Sea Force based at Aden, for protection of British interests in the area during Mussolini's rape of Haile Selassie's Ethiopian Empire. Months later with Abyssinia

Achilles towing target. Note rake party (bottom left) plotting *Rodney's* 16″ fall of shot from 12 miles. Off Gibraltar 1936.

conquered by Italian forces, *Diomede* carried on through the Mediterranean to Sheerness where we packed our bags and hammocks before humping them along the cold granite wharf to *Achilles*. Secured directly ahead of us she had been loaned to the New Zealand Division of the Royal Navy in exchange.

For a wet month from March 1936 we frequented Sheerness, Chatham, and London pubs in which we drank dark brown ale and vied for competence on shove-hapenny boards, night clubs where long-legged burlesque girls kicked high on smoke-clouded stages, and sparsely lit street corners where the asking price was half a crown. In April we sailed for an extensive work-up with our sister-ships *Neptune*, *Orion*, *Leander* and others of the 2nd Cruiser Squadron based at Gibraltar, at night when on liberty singing lustily in the Rock's cabarets, and by day hiring taxis to cross the Spanish border into La Linea ostensibly to see a bull fight but in reality to frequent the town's *casa de tratos*. By mid-July we'd convinced *Orion's* CS2 that we had made no more mistakes than any other ship of the Home Fleet, but his 2nd C/S had to quit Gibraltar with the Battle Fleet *Rodney*, *Hood*, *Warspite* and the carrier *Furious*, because Britain was in no mood to aggravate Italy in the current international situation, so we 'cleared lower deck' for a talk by Captain Glennie who spoke of the imminent Spanish revolution, said Intelligence at Ceuta was reporting massed Italian war planes in Morocco, then read out the purport of a CCNZ order that *Achilles* should make her way through the Panama Canal to the Pacific.

Achilles, 5 August 1936, in the Panama Canal en route to New Zealand.

Twelve days later we were swimming in Kingston, Jamaica's Bourne-mouth Baths; several more and we were lining our foc'sle and waist while passing Japan's antiquated cruisers *Iwati* and *Ukuma* near the Canal's massive Culebra Cut; then at Balboa we sat amazed through a French blue movie watched by white and brown residents with their girlfriends and wives. Finding the actors more hilarious than erotic we left with notions about renowned Coconut Grove, only to be disenchanted by Mother Judger's ageing and tawdry hostesses, thus with an air of virginal smugness we made our way to a US Navy canteen chow-line, then back aboard.

At the Pacific Equator en route to commence a Navy Board directive to survey atolls suitable for flying-boat pit stops, King Neptune found most of our crew guilty of trespass within his Domain, and those without prior documented initiation were brought before his throne for sentence; instant lathering and shaving by his barbers and bears, then back-flipped into the royal pool already rigged in preparation. This canvas contraption remained throughout ensuing days and nights, a boon to below-deck watchkeepers who raced along the midnight foc'sle and porpoised over the four feet sides into cool clear water – that was, until the night I arrived first and leapt exultantly into the air over the top and into more air: some stupid bastard had drained the pool and I landed like a spreadeagled frog, sandpapering skin off arms, legs, chin and more vital unmentionables. To add to that

Achilles, 1936, Captain Glennie standing centre.

discomfort a tattoo inflicted in Balboa had pussed up to an ulcer on my arm, a painful lump rose in my armpit, and there was raw flesh from head to toe. On Wednesday 19 August we refuelled from the NZ Navy tanker *Nucula* at Nukuhiva in the Marquesas, levitated about the ship while reading scented love-letters, our first mail for many months, then Captain Glennie ordered a course for Christmas Island just north of the Equator.

During the leisurely approach in idyllic conditions our Navi gave a briefing of the 300,000-acre island, saying that *Achilles* would be anchoring in one of Cook's soundings off an entrance through which he had passed in 1777. And now in 1936 our ship's boats were taking parties through that same gap, into a vast lagoon lined by white coral sand backed by spindly scrub. Monstrous sharks cruised around our whalers and cutters until we left the open sea, dozens of screaming gulls fought over the bait or spinners on lines trailed astern, and immediately the boats grounded, most were over the side splashing in those tepid crystal-clear shallows. Others searched among tangled vegetation for nesting bosun-birds to yank out their long red tail feathers, while yet more taunted giant coconut crabs with sticks. The red feathers would be sold readily to Auckland's milliners.

Back on board, Captain Glennie stood boyishly excited among men watching a fighting 12-foot shark being hauled tail first up a davit for dissection; its ominous stomach bulge disgorging a large turtle and the remains of an adult goat. Meanwhile our Walrus had been scanning the lagoon for submerged obstructions and coral growth hazards to future flying-boat landings; photographs were taken and survey parties motored

Walrus Supermarine.

about the most favoured area, taking precise soundings before going ashore
to reconnoitre and map possible sites for buildings and storage tanks. Then
on completion of a week's findings *Achilles* called at Fanning Island cable
station which had been wrecked in 1914 by Admiral von Spee's light cruiser
Nurnberg. It had years since been fully restored, and currently some 300
islanders were working a copra trader's plantation, so we leaned outboard
to watch a 20-foot shark take a leg of mutton bait, snap the 3/4″ line
without flinching, then glide back under the ship's keel to wait in anticipation.

Further north-west off Kingman Reef our Walrus was revving its motor
at the end of the extended catapult, readied for blast-off in a lightening
dawn, but someone noticed smoke on our eastern horizon and the launching was cancelled. The roaring motor droned to a sputtering kick-back and
stopped. The box girder telescoped into itself then swung fore-and-aft to
appear innocent as an American destroyer sliced into the bay. Her crested
bow fell; she eased slowly to within a few cables and anchored as her bridge
lamp flashed:

'What ship and captain?'

'Warship *Achilles*. Captain I. G. Glennie RN.'

'Bon voyage,' in curt dismissal.

We were more heavily armed, three times her weight and probably
more modern; but Kingman Reef was American full-stop. Britain was a
fairly consistent upholder of international marine protocol; Ian Glennie

knew he'd been caught with his fingers in the cookie jar so we departed pink eared for Canton Island down in the Phoenix Group. Although plastered with concreted-in American claims, it had just as many British headstones dating back into the eighteenth century. We stayed long enough to concrete-slab another one for George, impressing into it the declaration: 'HMS *ACHILLES*, Captain I.G. Glennie RN. 28 August 1936.' But they omitted the fact that it was one day after my 20th birthday.

This claim *Achilles* was prepared to dispute but the Yankee destroyer didn't appear. Our Walrus Supermarine 'Pussers Duck' concluded several hours over the lagoon, finished photographing, did a few surface landings and power-offs, then sat preening itself on the catapult cradle. We cruised sedately down to Hull Island for the wardroom to entertain the Bishop and his entourage, while those off watch sought remote beaches to annoy more plate-sized crabs and seabirds with saleable tail feathers. Meantime our Duck amazed natives who'd never heard of an aeroplane let alone seen one; it belched radial flames when roaring low over coconut-palmed villages en route to do more photographing for posterity, and confounded Hull Islanders as they saw it splash down and putter alongside to be craned inboard. Then there were similar exhibitions at Nukunono before bypassing Minerva Reef on our way to Auckland, where perchance the writers of those scented letters might yet be waiting.

CHAPTER VI

Achilles *Arrives Auckland –*
September 1936

W IVES, SWEETHEARTS, RELATIVES, and *Philomel* ratings massed along
Calliope Wharf to greet *Achilles* when we berthed on Sunday, 6
September 1936; then at Princes Wharf two weeks later with the cruiser
open to visitors we were deluged by a friendly Auckland public. We came
off watch for meals in messdecks filled with civilians, went through packed
passageways to bathrooms where doors were opened by young women
embarrassed at finding us under steaming showers; and we almost had to
bar our 'Heads' doors to inquisitive, happy people.

Recrossing Waitemata Harbour *Achilles* lay dormant at the naval base
while Tubby Wrightson, Ginger McCrudden, Dave Ingram and I operated
New Daventry W/T Station, the rehashed ingredients of *Philomel's* antiquated shortwave transmitter. When tuned it lit a 40-watt light bulb dangling
from a looped wire around the interior aerial-lead; its rugby ball shaped
valve glowed a brilliant mauve; and when keyed the transmitter emitted
harsh, rude noises. Using our callsign FA7 on naval schedules, and the NZ
Naval Station commercial callsign LL6 when working Portishead Radio in
England, we handled the Navy's service and personal correspondence until
Achilles refired her boilers and our cruiser's modern radio equipment did
the routines more efficiently.

Throughout late 1936 and early 1937 *Achilles* endeared herself to appreciative North and South Island visitors shown around the ship above and
below deck; town hall dances to our popular Royal Marine band; wardroom
entertainment for the elite, upperdeck amusement for hordes of excited
school-kids; and impromptu reunions with schoolmates who returned next
day to talk about the dance and moan about their hangovers. In Taranaki
Bight we engaged in mock battles with Australia's cruisers and destroyers,
before entering Wellington to beat them at most field sports, although in
aquatics, beer drinking and leg pulling we came second, but unfortunately
for *Sydney* she crunched Pipitea Wharf and departed immediately for
Cockatoo Dockyard's panel beaters.

June through August were the winter months selected by Navy Board
for one of our cruisers to show the flag around Pacific islands under New
Zealand mandate. *Achilles* over the past nine months had exhibited herself

in most New Zealand ports so, now crammed with canned and dried provisions to replenish shipwreck depots on uninhabited atolls, we steamed north from Auckland on 12 June 1937. Five meteorologists on the Kermadec's Sunday Island were given fresh and canned food, newspapers, books, and building materials to enlarge their Weather Reporting Station. At Nukualofa the 6-foot tall 18-stone Queen Salote received full naval recognition as her barge approached, then a multi-bosun-piped salute when she stepped onto the awning-covered quarterdeck to be greeted by Commodore E.R. Drummond. Enthroned in 1918, the Tongan Queen later married Prince Tugi, and now aged thirty-seven she ruled benevolently over her 38,000 subjects plus 2,000 whites and a huge gnarled royal turtle, said to have been in its infancy when seen by Captain James Cook on visiting and naming the group the Friendly Isles.

Falcon Island, three hours steaming from Nukualofa, had a habit of changing its appearance or disappearing altogether. In 1865 HMS *Falcon* named and charted it as a reef; another ship logged it as a mile and a quarter long, 153 feet high island in 1885; others reported it awash in 1894; three miles long and 50 feet high after an eruption thereabouts that same year, but completely submerged in 1895. As a low reef it surfaced in 1918, and in 1927 it was again an island. HMS *Veronica* logged it as steaming and smoking in 1928; the 1930 *Mariners' Almanac* recorded it as 1.2 miles in length by 475 feet in height; in 1935 when we saw it from HMS *Dunedin* it hadn't altered, but on 20 June 1937 as we looked at it from *Achilles*, our navigator was charting it as an island one mile long and 50 feet high.

We cruised 500 miles north to Apia, the port and main town of a more stable upthrust inhabited by Samoans under some form of New Zealand jurisdiction. Here the population wasn't as firmly founded as its island, having been governed by Germany until 1914 when the British War Cabinet told New Zealand to occupy the enemy-held territory, then aroused to rebellion against a 1928 New Zealand imposition of taxes, unknown even under German administration. Landing parties from NZDRN cruisers quelled that uprising but it erupted again in January 1930, this time backed by a paramount Samoan chief, and it wasn't until 1936 that friendly relations were established.

Just a year later *Achilles* secured to one of Apia's large buoys seaward of a wave-lapped reef supporting the deteriorating remains of Germany's nineteenth-century gunboat *Adler*. In 1889 she'd been driven broadside onto the reef by a hurricane which wrecked or sank other warships anchored nearby. America's cruiser *Trenton*, corvette *Vandalia*, and sloop *Nipsic* foundered; Germany's corvette *Olga*, 900-ton gunboats *Adler* and *Eber* went aground; but the Royal Navy sail-and-steam cruiser *Calliope* visiting from New Zealand, slipped her moorings and powered by Westport coal fought her way out to sea at less than one knot. As she struggled past the doomed *Trenton*, Rear Admiral Kimberly USN led his men in an unheard round of rousing cheers. And now as we looked across those sunbathed tranquil waters at the broken *Adler*, we thought of the 200 German and American sailors who didn't make it ashore, the intervening forty-eight years were as yesterday. Tannoy-relayed bugle blasts interrupted our reverie, then: 'CLEAR LOWER DECK FOR LEAVING HARBOUR! CABLE PARTY MAN THE PORT WHALER! HOIST ALL BOATS! EVERYONE OUT OF THE RIG OF THE DAY, OFF THE UPPERDECKS!' There was more but we were already disappearing below.

In turn *Achilles* offloaded stores for New Zealand's Resident and his two dozen Cook Islands' subjects at Nassau; then Pukapuka, Manahiki, Raka-hanga, and Tongareua in the Tokelaus – Tongareua (Penryhn) at that time being the world's richest pearling lagoon. Its mountains of rotting oysters stank, and the two white traders who employed 350 Polynesians, wore Colt 45s to deter anyone with illegal thoughts about the lustrous beauty of those perfect pearls displayed on black velvet for genuine buyers. We returned aboard to an atmosphere of excitement in the Main W/T Office: Navy Office Wellington had ordered us to set a continuous watch on Amelia Earhart's international frequency.

It was the era of pioneer aviators: Moncrief and Hood overflying New Zealand in bad visibility to be lost when flying from Australia; 'Smithy' and his 'Southern Cross' crew applauded by thousands on arrival at Wigram Aerodrome in Christchurch, then lost somewhere west of Java; our success-ful aviatrix Jean Batten breaking long-hop records around the world; and now America's Amelia Earhart, the wife of millionaire publisher Putnam, missing. Months previously she'd attempted a west-about Equatorial world flight. Her red Lockheed Electra co-piloted by Captain Harry Manning and navigated by Lieutenant Commander Fred Noonan USN had arrived at Honolulu from Oklahoma, but the undercarriage was damaged when at-tempting an overload take-off for Howland Island on their second leg. The Lockheed was transported back to America for repairs, Captain Manning rejoined his ship SS *Roosevelt* and seasonal headwinds dictated an east-about route for the second attempt. Leaving this time from Miami, Florida, Amelia accompanied by Fred Noonan touched down in successive countries for two-thirds of the circumnavigation.

Their next leg, from Lae, New Guinea to Howland Island would take eighteen hours but they'd done longer hops. A 30 June press release from Lae said fuel-line repairs had necessitated a departure postponement, then a 2 July bulletin reported the fliers' 10 a.m. lift-off on the 2,250-mile journey, and the world anticipated that Amelia was about to become the first flier to make an equatorial circuit. The amount of scientific apparatus carried had earned them the nickname 'Flying Laboratory', but the Lockheed Electra lacked adequate radio equipment – no D/F, no International Distress Frequency, only a low-power transmitter tuned to 3105kc/s using the callsign KHAQQ. Five hours out from Lae they radioed their speed at 140 knots, altitude 7,000 feet. When halfway to Howland they spoke to a San Francisco coastguard station, but several hours later the drama started. A fragmentary message read by the coastguard cutter *Itasca* based at Howland said: '281 north Howland xxxxx call KHAQQ xxxx beyond north xxxxx don't hold xxx with us xxx much longer above water.'

KHK Honolulu was heard broadcasting that the New Zealand cruiser *Achilles* had picked up the aviators; this was repeated by station KGU which was in contact with *Itasca*; then the radiograms poured in from all parts of the States offering unlimited finance for the sole rights to the story of our rescue. Over the next few days we told Navy Radio NPM Pearl Harbour there'd been a public misrepresentation by American newscasts; our 2nd W/T Office telegraphist had logged scraps of Amelia's distress message received through intense meteorological interference. Her weak signals were not heard again and the enigma of the Lockheed Electra's disappearance has lived on in myth and conjecture into the twenty-first century; there have been many theories but only one can be true.

The US battleship *Colorado* with her three float-planes, carrier *Lexington's* sixty aircraft and three destroyer escorts, the coastguard cutter *Itasca*, US destroyers *Ontario* and *Swan*, the Matson Liner *Mariposa*, a flying boat from Hawaii, the British freighter *Moorby*, HMS *Achilles* and the sloop *Wellington* from New Zealand, the Japanese aircraft carrier *Kamoio*, survey vessel *Koshu* and a fleet of Nipponese fishing boats from the Marshal Islands, all participated in that search covering thousands of storm-handicapped square miles; reefs and islands to all points of the compass from Howland Island were air-searched but drew a blank. Nothing. Snow blizzards previously unknown in the area hampered ships and aircraft, prolonged gales reduced visibility to mini-miles, lessened the chances of ditched aircraft survivors and made endless vigils a lookout's nightmare; then the need to refuel demanded that *Achilles* depart for Honolulu. There on 16 July 1937 a newspaper column read in part:

> The San Francisco Chronicle says it has learned unofficially that Mrs Putnam was – 'engaged on a high patriotic service, which is better left undisclosed as to detail' – This recalls former rumours that she intended to become unofficially lost for the purpose of claiming islands in the Pacific.

The question of ownership of Canton Island arose in Britain's House of Commons on 19 July 1937. Quoting an alleged statement by USS *Avocet's* commanding officer, that America did not recognise Canton Island as a

British possession, Foreign Minister Anthony Eden replied that the British Ambassador to America had communicated to the United States Government a copy of the Order in Council of 18 March, whereby Canton Island and named others were incorporated in the Gilbert and Ellice Islands colony. Asked if any reply had been received from the United States Government, Mr Eden said: 'I do not think the communication requested a reply.'

From our central Honolulu berth we drove out to Pearl Harbour, passing Hickam Field, Wheeler Field, Bellows Field, Naval Air Stations at Barber's Point, Ford Island and Kaneohe, and Marine Corps Airfields wherever the Navy and Army had left a space. Not all the US 3rd Fleet had joined in the Earhart search; seven 30,000-ton Tennessee class battleships lay close together at Ford Island; the cruisers *Astoria*, *Augusta*, *Honolulu*, *Phoenix*, *Raleigh* and others, hid a cluster of submarines and lesser vessels from view; thirty or so destroyers lay side by side across the bay from Pearl City and two aircraft carriers accompanied by their crash destroyers were making way towards the Pacific Ocean. Days later having explored the possibilities in Honolulu's 'Enlisted Men Only' fleshpots our money-belts were empty, so *Achilles* curtsied to Diamond Head as her bows caressed Waikiki Beach's offshore rollers, on our way to Hawaii Island's Kealakekua Bay where in December 1778 Cook had written in his journal:

> At 11 o'clock in the forenoon we anchored in thirteen fathoms of water in the bay which is called by the natives Karakakooa. The ships became crowded with natives, and we were surrounded by a multitude of canoes. I had nowhere in the course of my voyages seen so numerous a body of people assembled. Besides those who came off to us in canoes, all the shore was covered with spectators, and hundreds were swimming round the ships like shoals of fish. We could not but be struck with the singularity of the scene.

No more was entered in his journal and later he died at that very place, the incident being recorded by Lieutenant James King as follows:

> an accident happened which gave a fatal turn. The boats had fired at some canoes and killed a chief. The islanders armed themselves and a general attack followed. Our unfortunate Commander was stabbed in the back and fell with his face in the water. His body was immediately dragged ashore and surrounded by the enemy who showed a savage eagerness to share in his destruction. Thus fell our great and excellent Commander. They dismembered his body but later contritely returned it for sea burial.

Achilles also anchored in thirteen fathoms of water, but 'Karakakooa' was now deserted. We cleaned and repainted the memorial obelisk, photographed Commodore E.R. Drummond and Captain I.G. Glennie to either side of it, then departed south with mail and stores for Fanning Island.

After Fanning we steamed south-east to Christmas Island where a colonisation party, comprising a portable W/T transceiver, a lieutenant, a
telegraphist, a signalman and several ratings, was landed together with a
civilian. He, Mr Cowie, would remain in residence as Administrator, but
at the required term of occupancy *Achilles* retrieved our naval personnel
and cruised 856 miles south to Canton Island. There our motor boat towed
a lengthy flag-pole ashore, work parties concreted in a huge galvanised-iron
footing surrounded by anchored eyebolts, the already rigged mast was
worked erect by blocks and tackle, all stays were tautened, then to a
traditional fanfare the British Union Flag went aloft to put the island's
ownership beyond doubt. Here also we landed an officer, a telegraphist
and his transceiver, and two seamen; our dated communications were
meticulously recorded throughout the necessary colonisation period, then
all were embarked and we departed for Hull Island. Its original mast erected
in 1889 was replaced with appropriate ceremony, witnessed by the island's
one white trader and his four dozen copra-working Polynesians, four of
whom came aboard as passengers on our way further south.

At Nukunono in the Tokelaus, 300 miles from Hull Island, the 250
populace was governed by a native magistrate who embarked for the short
journey to his main island, Fakaofa. So, while he discussed his peoples'
economy with a more senior Tokelauan magistrate our working party found
the British flagpole to be in good condition, and a couple of new flags sufficed
to renew colour between the island's two enormous whitewashed churches
whose RC and Protestant ministrations vied for prominence. Thus *Achilles*
concluded our historic voyage through the past; cleaning, repainting or
replacing nineteenth-century poles and neglected monuments recalling Captains Cook, Edwards, Wilkes and others who in their day mapped faraway
Pacific islands, unknown to that era's Western civilisation as is the outer
space being probed by today's astronauts and scientific gadgetry.

Achilles' Hull Island passengers padded down our gangway at Suva to
be lost in the dust and aroma of copra traders and bustling Indians. I packed
down the scrum of our 1st XV which defeated Fiji, drank afterwards in the
nearby Club Hotel and suffered from its renowned pink gins at that night's
dance. Then next day when out sailing on the keeler of my dance partner's
father, I lost my dream girl to my shore-going oppo Athol Johnston who
I'd invited for the day's excursion, on top of which the Jaunty sent for me
on return aboard. I'd altered Romeo's leave card so that he could come
ashore; so days later on arrival in Auckland on my 21st birthday, my
stoppage of leave had not ended and I polished brass fittings on the bridge
while watching streams of innocents stepping ashore. Also from the bridge
I could see *Leander* berthed astern, recently arrived from England in place
of *Dunedin*.

CHAPTER VII

US & UK Flying Boats in Auckland. Achilles Recommissions in Portsmouth

*A*chilles ARRIVED IN AUCKLAND on Thursday, 26 August 1937 at the completion of her Pacific islands' flagpole maintenance, to find *Leander* secured at Calliope Wharf, having just arrived from England in exchange for *Dunedin* and already involved in various trophy challenges. She took the Blackwood Rugby Shield, but lost the Cole Soccer Cup challenge to *Philomel* from whom *Achilles* took it; then repeated her performances for the more prestigious Horne Soccer Cup.

Early Saturday leave enabled all off-watch personnel from the cruisers, sloops and base, to jam-pack every available liberty boat, offload at Auckland's Admiralty Steps and overflow already public-compacted trams and buses bound for Eden Park. It was a cold blustery day and 58,000 rueful spectators saw the 1937 Springboks down our All Blacks by 17–6. Then followed real tragedy during the next week's Diomede Cup sailing race around Waiheke Island. *Achilles'* 2nd cutter out in the lead across Tamaki Estuary capsized in a fierce squall. Auckland RNVR's whaler pulled out of the race to rescue the crew, and *Leander's* galley having been signalled that it wasn't required, took the lead and drove away out of sight, only to be overturned by another storm-driven gust with no other boat nearby. Before any of the following contestants arrived, Leading Seaman Forbes, Able Seaman Paterson, and Ordinary Seaman Tasker were swept beyond reaching hands and were lost in the white-capped frenzied seas; intensive searches were of no avail and their bodies were not found for two weeks. Servicemen die. At Waikumete Cemetery Padre Robson committed their bodies to the earth from which they came, a volley from high-port rifles and the bugled Last Post honoured their naval service, then our funeral contingent re-entered waiting transport. Life goes on.

On Sunday, 26 December 1937 the result of *Achilles'* Pacific atoll surveys materialised when Pan America's *Samoan Clipper*, piloted by Captain Edwin Musick, thundered low over Devonport on his final leg from Pago Pago, alighted on Waitemata Harbour's cleared path and motored triumphantly to an anchorage at Mechanics Bay. Then next day, Monday the 27th, New

Samoan Clipper at Auckland prior to leaving for Pago Pago. She was lost en route during January 1938.

Zealand-born Captain John Weir Burgess circled his Empire flying-boat *Centaurus* over Auckland City in bright summer sunshine. Taking off from England's Hythe Airport he had made stops in Europe, Arabia, India, Burma, the Netherlands East Indies, and Australia before crossing the Tasman. Naval and Harbour Board boats had cleared enthusiastic yachts and powered pleasure craft from a wide stretch across the Waitemata; and now with all four engines revving or easing off according to wind shifts he swung low around holiday crowds covering Mount Victoria, roared over house-tops above the Naval Base, then throttled back onto centre harbour and ploughed the huge amphibian to its anchorage fifty yards abreast of Captain Musick's *Samoan Clipper*.

Meantime there were matters of personal import for men of both cruisers. Christmas leave had taken hundreds to distant home towns; weddings were binding many to the girls of their dreams; Cardinal Huff was confounding uninitiated matelots in Queen Street pubs; and draft chits were being uplifted from Regulating Offices by men sent ship to ship or ship to shore. At Admiralty Steps awaiting the 7 a.m. pinnace we read the *Auckland Herald* progress of Captain Musick's return flight to Honolulu; days later his 3 January 1938 arrival; then his Sunday, 9 January departure south, overnight stop at Kingman Reef, and Pago Pago arrival on the 10th. It would have been a 12-hour flight to Auckland as he carried excess fuel, and by now Auckland Radio stations were broadcasting half-hourly reports. Shortly after lift-off Captain Musick said one engine was leaking oil, he would be returning to Pago Pago immediately and they were jettisoning fuel to lighten the aircraft for landing. That was the last message heard from the *Samoan Clipper*. Next day a Tutuila-based US minesweeper found burnt debris and a life jacket several miles offshore, then the theories started: had he feathered the sick motor too abruptly, tearing it from the wing and igniting fractured fuel lines? There were endless perhaps's; but today in Auckland there is only Musick Point Marine Radio Memorial to commemorate the American flier and his crew who were lost with the VIP passengers they carried.

Two months passed, the tragedy was all but forgotten and *Leander* lay ahead of *Achilles* at the Cruiser Berths on Tuesday, 7 May 1938. Men streamed down both ships' gangways to join with the ships' companies of *Philomel*, *Leith*, *Wellington* and *Wakakura*, mustering along Calliope Wharf on the eve of Rear Admiral E.R. Drummond's departure, to hear his farewell speech followed by an introduction to his successor, Commodore H.E. Horan. Formalities over we dispersed, and within weeks *Achilles* was cruising north to avoid the chills of an approaching winter.

Whilst visiting the Tongan Islands we won all rugby fixtures against native teams at Nukualofa, climbed Vavau's Mount Yalau to admire the tropical panorama, dived through a submerged passage into an immense aerated cavern, and pulled the 2nd whaler inside Swallow Grotto to strike Bell Rock and marvel at its resonant chimes. Then at American Samoa an outbreak of rubella kept us quarantined aboard, likewise at Funafuti where the Captain's barge brought off Ellice Islands' Commissioner and five islanders awaiting passage to Nukufitau; but owing to our German measles epidemic *Achilles* bypassed their destination and disembarked them at Niutao in the colony's northern extremity, after which Navy Office Wellington cancelled the remainder of our cruise and ordered us direct to Auckland where our affected went into Auckland Hospital's isolation wards. It was nearing the end of *Achilles'* three-year commission, and as soon as health authorities declared the ship clean we departed on a farewell cruise to Lyttelton, Dunedin and Wellington. As per custom RN officers from aristocratic families freighted out their personal cars, speedboats and yachts for their entertainment in New Zealand ports, and on this commission a Jaguar and a Ferrari had been craned inboard for stropping down to waist-deck ringbolts, thereafter arousing intense interest as they snaked at speed among the antiquated traffic of Christchurch and Dunedin. But en route up-coast to Wellington we battled a howler from the frozen Antarctic, and mountainous roaring forties crashed onboard to inundate all messdecks while completely ruining the unlucky owners' treasured cars.

Fortunately this had no effect on the ship's company mode of transport. Those days, men in naval uniform rode free by rail between

Onehunga-Auckland, Petone-Wellington, Port Chalmers-Dunedin, Bluff-Invercargill, and Lyttelton-Christchurch; and as a bonus, station attendants turned a blind eye to sailors sleeping in carriages standing overnight for the early morning run to each port. Even so, our meagre monthly pay rarely survived a week after which we were at the mercy of the ship's usurers, mostly old RN salts growing opulent on their 2-pound repayment for every one pound borrowed. So we put ourselves in favour with our girlfriends' fathers by smuggling them duty-free cigarettes, tobacco, and our bottled tots; the source of these gifts rarely being questioned by recipients who in many cases had experienced the First World War's trenches, and the early 1930s breadlines. Back in Auckland we threaded our way through Queen Street's boulevard of friendly people, caught bustling trams to our girlfriends' suburban homes and brought them back to the city's many theatres, escorted them in their ball gowns to town hall civic dances for the ship, and endured mayoral speeches before tall broad-shouldered Royal Marine Bandsman Percy Hines twanged and strummed his huge base fiddle, setting the tempo for our popular Marine Band. We danced the night out, walked our partners to their near or distant homes, then walked miles back to the Blue Boat Jetty. Street kids and thugs had not yet been invented and strangers of the night caused no concern.

But it hadn't been decided which fuel stops were most suited for Britain's Pacific air route and *Leander* drew the short straw. She too carried a Supermarine Walrus powered by a Pegasus nine radial-cylindered engine, mounted midway nose to tail between the wings and high above the fuselage, its four-bladed propeller facing aft and pushing instead of pulling. Pilot Lt (A) Nicholl and Navigator Lt (A) Logan occupied the cockpit, and Telegraphist Air-Gunner 'Hooky' Mortimer hid inside a huge pair of padded earphones in his tiny W/T space below. If necessary he would mount a machine gun on the fore or aft ring and be Z4's gunner, but until New Zealand went to war he would mount and aim the amphibian's camera at indicated targets, some official. Able Seaman Stan Summers as parachute maintainer became general handyman during crane launching and retrieval, and if he was absent bits got knocked off wingtips, floats, and tail by over-zealous handling parties; these being the occasions when Rigger RAF Cpl Jack Ison would vividly acquaint them with their lack of wedded parents.

Singling up for departure on Monday, 7 November 1938 under a warm blue sky, *Leander*'s parts-of-ship stood in neat white lines about her decks and upperworks, while foc'sle, waist, and quarterdeck men ran in wires for later stowing. Captain J.W. Rivett-Carnac DSC RN spoke quietly by phone to his wheelhouse, engine-room, and upperdeck officers. Coir fenders flattened under bow pressure, foc'sle wires smoked in steel fairleads as more turns were taken around restraining bollards, then gradually her stern eased outward from the cruiser wharf. Now a more urgent sequence of intercom directives.

'Let go fore'ard.'

'Wheel midship.'

'Full astern both.'

Leander's propellors whirlpooled mud to the surface, a spreading whirlpool through which she glided astern into navigable water to come to a standstill then pick up way ahead. On passing *Philomel* her strident 'Still' was answered by another bugle glinting on the training cruiser's signal deck. Imperial Airways VIPs, New Zealand Chiefs of Staff, and SOI Wellington relaxed and moved about the bridge in less self-conscious attitudes, pleasantly assured by the ease with which the Captain took his ship to sea. It was a novelty for them to cast their eyes about the swiftly passing harbour, to see the gleaming War Memorial Museum atop Auckland Domain, floating cranes and workers still preparing Mechanics Bay as a flying-boat terminal, and in the distance beyond Orakei Basin a long trail of smoke heralding the Limited from Wellington. Several rusting tramps at anchor in Rotten Row awaited tugs from Japan, where they would be melted down to become our future enemy's ammunition; this being publicly surmised those days. As *Leander* breasted Devonport's Esplanade Hotel a vehicular ferry waited, engine idling, her Auckland-bound passengers waving beside their cars. At the Passenger Ferry Wharf *Makora*'s tall stack belched coal smuts and steam as she moved off to cross the harbour. More passengers on her upper and lower decks waved. Torpedo Bay's grey sheds slid by to port, then stilted Bean Rock Lighthouse away off the starboard bow with Kohimarama and St Heliers in the distance, as *Leander* rounded North Head to see Rangitoto overlording Hauraki Gulf. Special sea dutymen were being piped and it was nearing tot-time so afternoon watchkeepers drifted below for a clean-up and dinner before their midday takeover.

Leander's ship's company had already christened her the Grey Funnel Line Tramp because of the crated stores, fuel drums, galvanised-iron water tanks and the conglomerate of gear to be offloaded at various stencilled destinations; and at Suva from 11 to 17 November more deck space was forfeited to the requirements of colonial authorities, when laden barges bumped alongside to keep the crane and handling parties busy. Three days later *Leander* rolled lazily on a deep anchor off the airway site at Hull Island, preparing to ferry stores and building material ashore. All that day her boats pulled towards the reef, surfing low swells into calmer water where men waited waist deep to manhandle the heavy cutters and whalers to the coral beach. Bulky containers were humped to tents erected in spaces cleared of small coconut palms, then at dusk radio contact was made with the shore party's telegraphist to ready everyone for embarkation and, with the last boat hoisted, the ship cruised leisurely four days to Christmas Island.

Again in deep water several hundred yards offshore, preparations proceeded for surveys to be finalised to Imperial Airways wallahs' satisfaction in Britain. Z4 shuddered downwind on the athwartship telescoped catapult, gunning the motor to a thundering full throttle then easing back to an uneven sputter while awaiting radio contact with the 2nd W/T operator. Lieutenant Nicholls made thumb gestures to the grinning ACO whose gently circling hand-flag gradually increased its revolutions, another crescendo of power, the flag whipped down and acrid fumes belched as the catapult's chamber-charge detonated. The ungainly Duck hurtled across ship with its nine radials exhausting flames, propeller screaming as it scythed thin air, amphibian dipping dramatically then spiralling around the ship in the first of many ship-launchings, until a Fijian contractor formed a runway for Z4 to lower her wheels and operate ashore over the next two days. Previously plotted and newly located coral obstructions were photographed throughout the main lagoon, then all were demolished by spectacular underwater charges, until *Leander*'s Imperial Airways dignitary declared the flying-boat water-strip suitable for use.

Z4's RAF crew, by now inured to their CPOs' and POs' messdeck neat rum, were accepted as seasoned seafarers and played darts, ukkers, mahjong, and 500 in the neighbouring tinfishmens' mess. They lost their money at the illicit crown and anchor board on paydays, and they competed skilfully at tug-o-war, quoits, and deck hockey; but swimming and water polo were a 'no-no' due to the prevalence of large sharks seen gliding out from under the bilges each time a bucket of gash went down the chute. Some were hauled thrashing frantically up davit falls at the end of 3/4″ lines to be dispatched with a knife and dropped back in, but an 8-foot 200-lb groper brought up from maxi fathoms was craned inboard and photographed to convince future disbelievers.

At times an English-speaking French trader with his wife and daughter were invited to Wardroom dinners and entertainment, most popular for them being evening films and Marine Band musicals on the quarterdeck. They exported copra when trading vessels arrived, and expressed regret at the proposed airway base, having chosen their idyllic life among the Christmas Islanders in preference to the hurly-burly of civilisation. But those who braved the power-cutter's warm drenching through the surf to go ashore, found the lure of Hollywood's South Sea Isles to be largely a myth; instead of hula-skirted Dorothy Lamour and other seductive beauties reclining on palm-shaded lawns, there was rough coral sand infested by dinner-plate coconut crabs with enormous claws threatening from wide-mouthed burrows. Instead of cool clear streams when thirsty, there was the ship's warm insipid distilled water in those galvanised iron tanks floated ashore. *Leander* departed Christmas Island on 27 November for a few hours at Fanning Island, then cruised south-west 1,052 miles to Gardner Island where working parties repaired and painted years-old signs declaring the island to be a British possession.

Here there was a diversion for some who clambered aboard the substantial remains of the several-thousand-ton trader *City of Norfolk* which had been beached in 1925 due to an uncontrollable cargo fire. She'd grounded halfway onto the reef at full tide, and successive low tides left her after section hanging dry until she broke her back, so now when boarded there were only burnt-out ghostly decks thoroughly stripped over the years by locals. This concluded the NZDRN's participation in establishing trans-Pacific flying-boat bases; *Leander* returned to Auckland for Christmas 1938 and joined in the New Year midnight hilarities fronting Queen Street's GPO. Then in response to an Admiralty Top Secret directive to NZNB, she intensified her Hauraki Gulf exercises with Hobsonville's RNZAF aircraft during 1939's summer and autumn months; while 12,000 miles around the world, Adolf Schiklegruber's frenzied outpourings were rallying the Nazi movement to grandiose heights. Now known as Adolf Hitler, *der Fuehrer*, his panzers rumbled along concrete autobahns recently built to echo the tramp of his goose-stepping armies; and our Empire's Service Chiefs were more and more embarrassed as Britain's Prime Minister, Neville Chamberlain, soft-shoed back and forth across the Channel with entreaties for European appeasement.

Meanwhile Imperial Airways flew via Africa, India and Australia to New Zealand, but Pan American Airways flew the Pacific in easy stages from San Francisco to Auckland, and New Zealand's TEAL Airways purchased its own flying boats, *Aotearoa*, *Awarua*, *Mataatua*, and *Takitimu*, which winged the air-routes to Sydney and Fiji; huge, ponderous, beautiful; now only one remaining as a living memory in Auckland's Museum of Transport and Technology.

Back in Auckland on Sunday, 2 December 1938, the Dockyard Gates had been opened to relatives and friends of men on *Achilles* as she prepared to depart for England. At the foot of the gangway, kiddies clung to the legs of NZD fathers about to go aboard, and young women sobbed in the arms of RN men not expected to return. Bugles blared, bosun pipes shrilled; the dockside gangway had been craned ashore and the ship's tannoys were ordering: 'CLEAR LOWER DECK FOR LEAVING HARBOUR'. Men lined up in No 6s at their department stations stood motionless as *Achilles* saluted NOCA while passing *Philomel*. Waving farewellers along Queen's Parade stopped running, faded behind the Ferry Building. Waitemata Harbour became a memory as did features of Hauraki Gulf in seemingly short hours, when clouds over our New Zealand coast dropped below *Achilles'* western horizon. In Suva we eased gently against the fenders of a surprised *Leander*, removed the guardrail gates and shoved a short gangway over to seek shipmates at rum-up while Postie transferred bags of mail taken aboard at Auckland.

On Tuesday, 13 December we gazed contemplatively at Moorea's granite spires, the beauty of its vegetated slopes, the inviting entrance to Baie du Cook; but ahead across the channel Papeete's carnal anticipations awaited those already forgetting the wonders of nature. Our main W/T had morsed 'FJP' Tahiti our 1000 ETA, it had also told their Port Health Officer about the ship's clean bill of health, and as *Achilles* negotiated Baie Faaa's coral reef entrance, those entitled to liberty were already in their No 6 white drills, slightly bored during our duty Crusher's reading of the dire penalties proscribed within King George's Rules and Admiralty's Instructions relating to misdeeds in foreign ports. We knew them off by heart and I silently recalled Papeete as an Ord Tel of *Diomede*, when they roped me bum-up over my hammock atop a table on No 4 gun deck to receive six lashes. I'd blithely walked into a brawl outside Quinn's Bar, but my broken nose and blood-spattered whites had done little to convince *Diomede's* Commander 'Curly' Farquhar of my innocence.

Now four years hence as a Ldg Tel, my off-duty watch joined matelots of the French sloop *Zelee*, drank Manuia and Hinano beer interspersed with Pomard Burgundy in bars along dusty Bir Hakeim, then shuffled about smoke-hazed dance floors to lively tamures and lazy hulas. The tempo, the beer, the wine, dispersed caution as some went arm in arm with pretty vahines into dimly lit parks off Rue Jeanne d'Arc, anticipating a romance which was shattered by the ship's sirened general recall. A sudden squall had deflected off Passe Avarapa and shouldered *Achilles'* stern against a submerged reef on which she stuck. Impatient boats rushed everyone aboard, all hands were mustered starboard side on the foc'sle to 'Jump and Frolic' in time-tested tradition for such emergencies, and probably due more to a rising tide than to our semi–intoxicated evolution, it proved successful.

Next night in Quinn's someone loudmouthed: 'Hey lads! Cop the intruders!' All eyes turned to see a group of *Achilles'* officers barging through the swing doors riotously accompanied by a gaggle of French officers, including Colonel LaFayette intent on being introduced to 'Ze matelots orv sur maritime de'guerre *ACHILLE*!' The din increased. Corks popped. Brandy spilled and an esprit de corps developed; a polite but enduring cordiality evident between wardroom and messdecks throughout the remainder of *Achilles'* journey 'Home'. Tombola, boxing, wrestling, and cinema shows were organised in each waist, and a deck-ukkers tournament played on a massive painted-canvas board with 12″ coloured discs and a 9″ cubed dice rolled from a bucket and won by the wardroom team; in all a ten-day carnival atmosphere attended constantly by Captain Glennie until we rejoined the Navy to enter Balboa.

En route from Papeete, he had asked for a power trial to determine whether or not the grounding had affected his cruiser, so all boiler rooms were manned. Already steaming on two in 'A' boiler room the ship could create a substantial wake at 19 knots, and with two more in 'B' boiler room our bow wave crested the foc'sle at 26. Then 'C' room's Chief Stoker nodded Okay through the crescendo of roaring furnaces and their howling forced-draught fans, when sign-queried by his Watch Lieutenant (E), who acknowledged by finger before speaking into his padded telephone to the bridge. Topside there was exultation as bridge staff heard Captain Glennie reply: 'Right! Let's see what she can do!' Skip's usually impassive countenance now exhibited a boyish enthusiasm. *Achilles* smashed through low swells without dipping, burned paint off the single stack hip as she passed 29, 30, 30.5–31–32, leaving an angry white-water turbulence extending back towards the horizon. 'She's touching 34, sir!' from No 1 whose eyes sparkled as he turned from the engine-room phone, apprehensive lest the Owner accept things as they stood. Captain Glennie knew his ship had already exceeded her designed power and speed, but memories of his First World War destroyer exploits were awakened. He paced the bridge port to starboard, then quietly put the question again. '36, sir!' as No 1 replaced the phone on its hook. The word spread fast, 'Straight up man. We've hit 36. We're doing 42 miles a bloody hour!' No smoke, only blue-tinged intense heat waves streaming aft to scorch the maintop mast. Gradually the power was reduced, fell below the intended 72,000 horse power. *Achilles* still cut water at 28 knots, decreasing as boiler after boiler went through its shut-down routine, until night fell and 'A' room's superheated furnaces maintained economical steaming. Men yet topside looked up at a star-studded black velvet ceiling lazily etched by both masthead navigation lights.

Christmas Day was celebrated at sea; on Boxing Day the uninitiated were sentenced at King Neptune's Court and formally punished, and *Achilles* arrived into a riotously festooned Latin Panamanian festivity on Sunday, 31 December 1938. Multi-coloured men and women burlesqued and sang into the night's bawdy extravaganza. '*Manana nostros estar ocupado! Esta noche hacer el amor!*' '*Olvidar manana. Manana estamos en el asilo!*' (Tomorrow we work. Tonight we make love; forget tomorrow, tomorrow we will be in the poorhouse.) Latin girls walked straight out from glossy magazines; crimson hibiscus in their blue-black hair, crimson lips parted in laughter, white teeth sparkling, black eyes reflecting night lights. A hush descended near midnight, paying reverence to the dying year. Seconds were long minutes. Then a cacophony of clanging church bells, deep-throated ships' horns, howling sirens, car hooters, train whistles, claxons and cheering humanity revelling in a night now slashed by waving searchlights and high-bursting rockets spattering rosettes of momentary splendour. Panama was half an hour of handshakes and fantasy, friendly senoritas inviting kisses and not being denied. Sanity returned slowly, searchlights extinguished, the din abated and mass pyrotechnics deserted the black overhead arena. Most of *Achilles*' liberty men awakened in their half-empty messdecks; but many stragglers misfooted on early daylit gangways and air-walked for'ard into 1939, a year about to see warfare unprecedented in human history.

Shortly after leaving Panama *Achilles* rose on the waters of Mira Flores and Gatun locks, traversed the canal and received UK mail from RMS *Rangitata* at Colon. She refuelled at Kingston Jamaica's oiling jetty then shifted to Townside Wharf to be given 14 shillings Jamaican for our NZ pound, not as profitable as the deal accorded HMS *York*'s paymaster at the same wharf, but better than the one negotiated by SMS *Duisburg* berthed astern, these exchange rates being discussed with the *kriegsmarines* and Royal Navy men watching our soccer team beat the German side by 2 goals to 1, before shaking hands at the stadium gate and being wished '*Auf wiedersehen*'. Two days out the barometer bottomed, creating danger sufficient for all hands to be denied the upper decks. Towering following swells topped by hurricane-torn crests crashed onto the quarterdeck, broke portholes and flooded officers' cabins before torrenting forward over torpedo mounts and bursting into the extended-shelter waists to geyser up port and starboard hatchways onto both boom-decks. The Walrus and various boats were damaged, the entrapped baker had to be rescued through a hole torch-cut from the keyboard flat, and Navi measured the swells at 70-feet peaks spaced four ship lengths apart. The 500kc/s operator was logging SOSs but their given positions were distant and *Achilles* had her own problems in keeping stern-on to the huge seas. Lookouts reported the topmasts of a tramp which suddenly loomed atop a nearby crest, propeller thrashing air before she slid a mile to port into our own trough, riding steady in the translucent walled valley until again swept skyward on the next giant upsurge.

On the second night a large ship's masthead lamp answered Captain Glennie's query:

'What ship? How is it with you?'

'USS *Augusta*. Managing 14 knots. How about you?'

'HMS *Achilles*. No problems.'

And as his clipped reply was being keyed to the American cruiser battling into those rollers on which *Achilles* surfed northward, Skip muttered: 'Lying sod, be lucky if he's doing five.' The storm raged several days, rolled and sank trawlers, broke a tanker midships and destroyed vessels other than those whose distress calls had been received. It lessened eventually and a bleak sun broke through devoid of warmth, debris was cleared from the chaos below, flats and messdecks were squee-geed and mopped reasonably dry, and our battered cruiser arrived in the Channel with her Imperials anxious to step ashore among loved ones not seen for three years. But the ship anchored off Spithead in bitter sleet, to be made presentable after the Atlantic ordeal, weighing next morning at daybreak and proceeding into Portsmouth to secure alongside *Hood* whose decks were crowded by close relatives and friends. Here and there as *Achilles* warped in against the world's largest warship, cries of recognition erupted among the masses, spreading along the battlecruiser's length until everyone laughed and talked deck to deck unmindful of the cold wind-swirled drizzle. Still fallen in we joked with RN messmates, heckled them about their alien affections down under, but felt for them in this moment of reassociation, stopped chaffing and wished them happy reunions at dispersal as they ran en masse to intership gangways.

In time *Achilles* shifted to Pitch House Jetty near Nelson's flagship *Victory*; all Imperials had gone on Foreign Service Leave, and we *foreigners* sought our own entertainment locally or 'up the line in The Big Smoke'. We went aboard *Victory* and stood reverently at the spot where he fell at Trafalgar; we glanced inside his spacious quarters; we walked stoop-shoulders through her low-beamed gun-decks one below another; then we negotiated ladders down to her powder and shot magazines just above the bilges. Those lower decks, painted red to camouflage the sight of blood during battle, still exuded an imaginary stench of death, echoed faint yells of agony as surgeons' saws and knives amputated shattered limbs; and those massive oaken timbers still trembled from the roar of *Victory*'s broadsides. Almost hypnotised we emerged topsides expecting to be surrounded by fallen masts and cannon fire, to join in the bygone cheering as, wreathed in flame and enveloped in gunpowder fumes, ship after British ship broke through Villeneuve's French and Spanish lines of battle.

We read those late 1930s newspapers still talking about 'Peace in our time' but it was apparent the Axis powers were intent on European domination. It was also apparent that the Royal Navy wasn't wilting under Hitler's and Mussolini's aggrandisement, and on Thursday, 28 September 1938, a day before the Munich Four Power Agreement between Britain's Chamberlain, France's Daladier, Germany's Hitler, and Italy's Mussolini, the Royal Navy was ordered to mobilise. And now five months after 'Munich', cranes were working on *Hood*'s side armour, while blue sparks all around Portsmouth Dockyard indicated an upgrading of warships of every class. The British Navy was preparing. January 1939 became February, New Zealanders returning from an unexpected two weeks' leave, found *Achilles* re-ammunitioned and stored, a new draft of loan Imperials embarked, and everyone eager to depart for Auckland.

CHAPTER VIII

Preparations for War

IN JANUARY 1939 Navy Office Wellington received TOP SECRET correspondence from Admiralty, detailing RN policy in the event of war against
Germany; it reinstituted First World War sea route strategy, and detailed
British and French naval dispositions to be readied by 1 August 1939 in
named oceans: 'By such means we have in the past succeeded in protecting
shipping on essential routes,' the memorandum advised, 'and it is intended
to rely on these again, adapting them to problems under review.'

In Portsmouth's drear early-February conditions, NZD stragglers from
Achilles' long leave entered their messdecks to find many strange faces,
replacing Imperials who'd been drafted elsewhere on conclusion of their
recent three-year loan to New Zealand. And two weeks later *Achilles*
punched through a truculent Bay of Biscay's weather which confronted her
right down the coast of Portugal and around Cape Trafalgar into Cadiz
Gulf. She slewed dramatically into Gibraltar Straits, and entered Gibraltar
Bay with everyone now topside for the view before falling in for entering
harbour. *Achilles* saluted flagships and returned the salutes of lesser commanding officers while negotiating columns of men-o-war, slipped inside
the inner harbour to ease alongside '42-Berth', then disembarked the many
draftees brought down to strengthen undermanned ships dispatched urgently to the Atlantic Fleet's strategic base.

Gib hadn't altered since my month ashore there in 1936, so I headed for
a small dress shop familiar to me, but my little seamstress was no longer
on the staff so within hours I was across the border to La Linea, walking
the dusty road to the flower-surrounded white stucco cottage in my
memory. House after house stood gutted, pitiful reminders of Spain's Civil
War. The one I had visited so often no longer gleamed white. Familiar
shrubbery and flowerpots were invaded by thorns and weeds, infiltrating
broken walls and entwining throughout wrecked masonry and collapsed
roofing. The iron bed protruded, twisted, brass embellishments dulling.
The brass-framed mirror hung askew, glass shattered by bomb blast; never
again would it reflect those laughing eyes and long black tresses. I asked
at the nearest occupied dwelling and received a torrent of impassioned
Spanish explanation: '*Mama mia mi marinero! Su modista muerto. Por el amor
de dios! Insurgente aeroplano bomba en las horas dela noche!*' As I walked away
the old woman still gesticulated in describing that night of terror and death.

As I made my way back to the bus for Gibraltar the sun ceased to warm me; there was now no colour in that afternoon's cloudless blue sky.

We took station without error in fleet manoeuvres, taught our new Imperials more than we'd learned from their predecessors, exercised night and day with other cruisers, and we became increasingly confident in *Achilles'* new owner, Captain Edward Parry, who'd entered the Royal Navy in 1905. Apart from minor disturbances promptly quelled by insurgent troops, the Spanish Civil War had ended. So, on Monday, 27 February 1939 Britain officially acknowledged Franco's Republic Leader status, but British, French and Dutch warships still ensured international shipping safety within Spain's territorial waters; and already the threat of Round Two in Germany's bid for expansion was being recognised by Western leaders.

Achilles cleared Gibraltar on Monday, 20 March, stayed two days in Malta where some were measured for 'tiddley' uniforms while others posed for studio portrait photographs, these being assured of delivery in Alexandria; but the ship steamed directly to Ismailia 30 miles into the Suez Canal and a lot of unhappy men bemoaned their losses, only to be overjoyed shortly after anchoring when Maltese agents brought all the purchases on board.

Now the first of two widely separated events was about to occur, events which were to occasion *Achilles* much inconvenience in her initial war

Achilles' Walrus, 1 April 1939. Capsized on take-off from the surface off Jiddah in the Red Sea.

operations. On April Fool's day in the Red Sea 70 miles west of Jiddah, Captain Parry asked for the Walrus to be catapulted off, but leprechauns in its mechanism turned the exercise into a surface launching. The pilot, his observer, and Telegraphist Peter Trent had already manned the aircraft which was then craned overboard, slipped, and left to taxi clear as the ship picked up speed. All seemed to be normal until the RAF corporal yelled that the plane was digging a wing under and capsizing. *Achilles* came about quickly and dropped the manned seaboat in time to rescue L2241's crew before it disappeared. At the enquiry it seemed the water-rudder used for taxiing had unknowingly become jammed to port, this swinging the Walrus onto her side during take-off. 'Bloody hard luck, eh Pilot?' over pink gins at the Wardroom bar that night, 'Never mind old chap, there's a spare for us at Hobsonville.'

Week by week the world also was gyrating out of control, steered by a psychopathic Nazi whose Wehrmacht was goose-stepping over borders one by one, while his counterpart, Benito Mussolini, not content with Libya as a colony, had overrun Abyssinia in 1935 then in April 1939 seized Albania. Britain and Russia conferred on 14 April; Britain introduced conscription a week later; on the 22nd Hitler renounced the Anglo-German Naval Treaty and his Non-Aggression Pact with Poland. Teutonic military marches blared from Radio Berlin. Britain signed a Defence Agreement with Turkey on 12 May, responded to by an immediate Military Cooperation Compact between Italy and Germany. France and Turkey did likewise on 23 May, then Britain and Poland on the 26th. Nation by nation the world was creating teams, headlined in newspapers, shown on Metro-Goldwyn-Mayer newsreels in theatres, and dramatised in radio newsflashes as *Leander* and *Achilles* shadow-boxed each other around Hauraki Gulf, interspersed with Trentham Camp frolics. *Achilles* then embarked New Zealand's 5th Governor General, his retinue, and his family for a Pacific Islands cruise.

Lord Galway, Sir George Vere Arundell Moncton-Arundell, Eighth Viscount, PC GCMG DSO OBE KG StJ MA (Oxon), born 1882, had served with distinction in the First World War and in 1935 had relinquished his post of Colonel Commandant, Honourable Artillery Company in England, to represent the King in New Zealand. As such, and for this cruise, he occupied CCNZ's suite on *Achilles'* quarterdeck, and at our forepeak flew his huge rectangular royal-blue emblem with its gold lion above a gold crown prominent over the gold letters DOMINION OF NEW ZEALAND. His daughter walked the quarterdeck in tropical silks which engendered messdeck wagers as to the colour of her panties, a wager settled unobtrusively by boat crews when she climbed up and down the Jacob's ladder to visit remote islands.

And now came the second event related to our Red Sea Walrus loss three months previously. *Achilles* approached Aitutaki in the Cook Group on Saturday, 15 July in ideal tropical weather, having just repaired the plane's wingtips after they bumped the ship's side when last hoisted inboard. This day K5783 catapulted off perfectly to zoom low over Aitutaki's wildly excited population, completely stealing the show. The islanders hadn't seen an aeroplane and the Governor General happily accepted second place in the forenoon's activities, the highlight about to be a foreshore thronged with spectators when *Achilles* approached adjacent deep water to retrieve the Walrus. As always, she swung her stern to broom an expanse of still surface, onto which K5783 alighted in two lengthy leaps before puttering alongside the slowly moving cruiser now only mini-hundreds of yards offshore. Already in safety-harness atop the upper wing, Peter Trent reached up for the weighted grab expertly lowered by Jackie Alder, the crane driver. Grab coupled to lifting-eye, wing-tip tracing wires affixed, Peter thumb-upped for hoist. Then the effluent hit the punkalouvre. The grab unclamped and *Achilles* was dragging her amphibian onto its side by the tracing wires. Before going under with the upturned plane sinking on top of him, Peter gulped a lungful of air, fought his harness catch which refused to disengage, had to expel air, gasped and swallowed water; but just when he thought this was the end, a massive air bubble rolled along the submerged lower wing and took him with it to the surface, minus the harness which had parted although tested to several hundred pounds breaking strain.

Not hearing the string of profanity from the pilot Lt (A) Bill Sykes, an enthusiastic boat crew drove the whaler straight into the bottom-up Walrus and stove a hole aft in its fabric hull, much to the disgust of Peter who was now scrambling about in search of fixing-eyes for an attempt at salvage. Hereabouts the whaler backed off, carved a long gash in the submerged wing which instantly exhaled all its air, and without sufficient buoyancy K5783 sighed profoundly while foundering irretrievably in the crystal-clear depths. *Achilles* arrived back in Auckland with her catapult unoccupied for the second time, Hobsonville had spare Walrus parts but no Walrus, war was imminent and she would have to enter the ring without her aeronautic eyes.

On Monday, 21 August 1939, Kapitan zur See Hans Langsdorff eased his *panzer-schiffe Graf Spee* out of Wilhelshaven at night, avoided shipping in the North Sea and along the Norwegian Coast, negotiated in darkness the waters between Iceland and the Faroes, then turned south to be in a position near Cape Verde Islands off the bulge of Africa by 3 September when Hitler intended to invade Poland. Other German warships and U-boats had made for their war stations, as had units of Britain's and France's navies. New Zealand's Prime Minister informed NZNB on 24 August that his government had adopted the Empire War Book's 'ALERT STAGE'. *Achilles* and

Leander were recalled from their Hauraki Gulf exercises, with *Leander* docking on arrival for bottom cleaning and painting, after which she stored and ammunitioned to full wartime capacity while *Achilles* took her place on the chocks. All hands including chiefs and petty officers laboured, with rostered breaks for meals, until both ships were readied on Monday, 28 August, then a 'MAKE AND MEND' saw a sea of white caps surging towards Devonport's buses and ferries, liberty boats shuttling hundreds to Admiralty Steps, and trams dispersing those who lived in Auckland suburbs. There were family arrangements to be made quickly by men from *Achilles*, which would be the first to sail according to leaked confidential correspondence that one New Zealand cruiser be dispatched to the West Indies.

At 0900 Tuesday, 29 August Captain Parry received his sailing orders, and as *Achilles* lay waiting at Calliope Wharf in latitude 37 degrees South, about to sail for South America; right about then *Graf Spee* in the Atlantic was going south through latitude 37 degrees North, en route to her appointed war station. Few on either vessel may have known it, but the two ships were not entire strangers. On 30 June 1934 as the pocket battleship was launched at Wilmshaven, *Achilles*' liberty men were fraternising with *kriegsmariners* in Kiel; and at a later date in the English Channel both captains engaged in a friendly race which left *Graf Spee* far astern. Now, with Captain Parry's 'sealed orders' directing his ship to South America's Pacific coast and then the Atlantic, both ships would deviate and converge repeatedly, and Fate was already guiding the thoughts of Captain Langsdorff aboard *Graf Spee*, Captain Parry on *Achilles*, and Commodore Harwood C-in-C South America Station who would shortly shift his flag from *Cumberland* to *Ajax*.

OPTHALMIC SURGEON
Cecil A. Pittar, Doctor

This brass plate advertised the rooms in which a telephone jangled, summoning the young medico from a consultation with his partners. 'Yes, certainly sir. Admiralty Steps one o'clock. Right, sir, leave it to me.' Then turning to his audience he wished his share of the practice into their bemused care, grabbed his kit of implements and with hurried goodbyes, fled. Within the hour he'd taxied home for his Surgeon Lieutenant RNVR (NZ) uniform, tried to explain to his bewildered loved ones, and arrived at the Steps to be whisked by *Achilles*' speedboat across Waitemata Harbour to the cruiser. Now including the Reserve Doctor and two of *Leander's* junior officers her war complement consisted of well-trained long-service men and officers, 246 Imperials and 321 New Zealanders. Seaman Gunner Archibald G.H. Shaw NZD1030 had joined in the early 1930s from Ngongotaha Rotorua, and as *Achilles* passed Takapuna Beach he stood near LTO Colin Malcolm who was very unofficially sending an Aldis lamp farewell to his Mon Desir pub-mates. Grinning at the tall dark-haired gunner Colin asided: 'Wonder when we'll see Auckland again, Archie. That's our last link with New Zealand,' as he replaced the signal lamp. Archie Shaw wouldn't; but right then they speculated idly before heading for separate messdecks as the cold wind intensified.

Both were topside again later when *Achilles* cleared lower deck to lay aft where Captain Parry outlined the tension between Britain and Germany, saying that at present there were only 'strained relations', the ship's destination was Balboa, and there he would receive instructions for joining the West Indies Squadron. 'Carry on, Commander,' as he made for his quarters. Coromandel's granite cliffs loomed close to starboard but Great Barrier Island hid behind sea-level cloud to port as *Achilles* passed Channel Rock, while the dispersed off-watch audience marched off the slowly heaving quarterdeck. Dusk descended cheerless, New Zealand disappeared in sullen lightning-slashed thundercloud miles astern, and the ship quivered stem to grumbling propellors as Frank Stennett sought the warmth of his swaying hammock. In three hours he would relieve Neville Milburn at the Main W/T H/F bay, to copy Tinakori Hill Wellington's ZLP2/4/5/6 navy morsed broadcast. Frank and Neville lived 25 miles apart in England, mere miles from the Birkenhead shipyard which built *Achilles*.

Two days from Auckland an anticyclone developed, the ship dried out and part-of-ship exercises started with turret crews exhorted to increase their rate of fire, damage control parties becoming faster to their posts at dummy alarms, W/T operators getting quicker to their 2nd, 3rd, D/F, and remote control positions, and boarding parties mustering with their weapons at whichever sea-boat was piped. Endless other evolutions from boiler rooms to director tower were repeated at haphazard hours day and night to sharpen everyone before joining the West Indies Squadron. At meal breaks and between drills, men listened to the BBC news, castigated Chamberlain for his cap-in-hand policy, yet hoped for a peaceful outcome. But on Sunday, 3 September Britain's patience ended, an ultimatum to Hitler that he withdraw his troops from Poland within twenty-four hours expired, and a State of War between Britain and Germany now existed. Among the codes and cyphers addressed to *Achilles* was one diverting her from Balboa to Valparaiso; fuel needed to be conserved for whatever might occur on this 6,600-mile trip, perhaps the world's longest port-to-port sea route, so economic speed had to be maintained.

Next day's BBC news reported the U-boat sinking of the liner *Athenia* with the loss of 122 passengers; British troops had landed in France; the Russian Army was massing along Poland's eastern border; two U-boats were sunk in the North Sea by RN destroyer depth-charges; and RAF bombers had attempted to disrupt the entrance to the Kiel Canal.

From a hot mirror surface at 1030 Tuesday, 12 September *Achilles* saw the snow-capped Andes Range rising on her eastern horizon, only hours now to her first port of call, and at all vantage areas about the ship barefooted off-watch men in shorts only were being sent below by Freddie Loader the Jaunty, and the Crusher Eric Tollerton: 'Right Benson! Last warning! Thought you sparkers had more bloody sense. Get below for Christ's sake!' Loader rarely put a man in the rattle but he gave explicit advice. Near 1330, Spanish *casas* and *cabanas* blended into distant foothills backdropped afar by 23,000-foot Aconcagua and 22,000-foot Tupungato, everyone out of the rig of the day had vanished and *Achilles* entered harbour under her biggest and cleanest flags, her saluting guns crews banging off a 21-gun Foreign Nation recognition, followed shortly by another thirteen for Rear Admiral Garcia aboard his 30,000-ton battleship *Almirante Latorre*. Then later that afternoon Captain Parry's shore visit to Chile's Director of Naval Services occasioned a return courtesy by Chile's C-in-C, Vice Admiral J. Allard who also received a thirteen-gun salute when leaving *Achilles*, and even though neutrality allowed a belligerent warship to refuel with only sufficient to reach a neighbouring nation, Allard instructed his port authority to refuel *Achilles* to capacity: 'In the event,' he said over the telephone, 'she may be required to proceed at full speed in an emergency.' During their talks Captain Parry remarked that at Jutland in the First World War, *Almirante Latorre* had been the Royal Navy's battleship *Canada*; and Admiral Allard who had trained as a cadet at a Royal Naval College, added that one of his classmates named Bell had served on *Canada* at that and other engagements, concluding: 'I believe that he is now Captain of *Exeter* in the South Atlantic Squadron.'

Apart from Chilean warships and merchantmen at anchor and alongside, there were neutral cargo vessels about the harbour, also a square-rigged three-masted German training ship apparently unarmed, and the German tramps *Dusseldorf* and *Dresden* claiming sanctuary under international law that, until belligerent warships were 24 hours at sea they were not obliged to sail. Valparaiso wore an air of old Spanish architecture, its 200,000 population thought little about the War and the city remained fully illuminated at night, but only the Captain, the Canteen Manager, and Postie went ashore, so nonwatchkeepers enjoyed their first all-night-in for weeks, tiring of looking shoreward and soon seeking their hammocks. Messdeck after messdeck darkened as its occupants slept; all but the tinfishmen who awakened with hacking coughs. Acrid smoke stung their eyes and throats from McKenzie's smouldering jersey draped to dry above the electric heater, and later as it floated away on the tide, fresh air replaced the pungent wool-smoke, angry remonstrations subdued and mollified torpedomen resumed their interrupted dreams. Next forenoon at a refuelling berth *Achilles* ingested 1,385 tons of Chilean crude, a chilling-room full of Argentine beef, crate upon crate of local greens, sacks of spuds, and the British Consul's written relief at seeing New Zealand's cruiser on the coast. 'CLOSE ALL WATERTIGHT DOORS AND SCUTTLES' blared through lower-deck speakers, men dispersed to their 2nd Degree of Readiness stations, and *Achilles* bugle-saluted Chilean warships passed on her way out of harbour.

Captain Parry blew into a bridge mike to ensure he wasn't talking to himself, then said, 'Our presence has been reported by the Chilean media, so I intend to make that evident in as many ports as possible. Our stay in each will be limited by international law and you will have little shore leave. While at sea our last ports of call will have been passed on to enemy agents, so the ship will remain in a state of readiness for action.' A click in each speaker terminated the broadcast, and as Ian Grant, an O/D from Tainui near Dunedin, was passing P2 A/A gun he heard: 'Sea-time mate, yures of rotten bluddy sea-time on this stinkin' Grey Funnel bastard.' You'd need to know the RN three-badge killick whose naval eulogy bore no malice to the service he loved. Ian Grant knew but couldn't resist quipping: 'Stow it, Stripey, you're making my heart bleed!' after which he dodged round P2 and fled from the old salt's pretended wrath.

Claude Mason-Riseborough's action station was in B-turret as its left gun's No 5 handler of the loading tray's 6″ projies and cordite charges. His normal day-duty was Navigator's Yeoman in the Chart Room, a 'quiet number' assisting Navi with chart corrections which arrived continually by W/T or by confidential mail, to be pencilled in worldwide or locally, wherever navigation lights and beacons were extinguished or otherwise damaged or removed, wherever there were newly notified minefields, hazards, or prohibited areas offshore of neutral countries. Daily Claude rewound the ship's mechanical chronometers at a specified time and logged the + or − seconds gained or lost during the elapsed 24 hours; he updated the Weather Synopsis Chart for forecasting purposes, and he pigeon-holed used charts before unrolling adjoining ones onto the Chart Table for Navi to pore over with his pencil, dividers and parallelogram, laying off courses and speeds necessary to estimate times of arrival at specified positions or ports. That done Claude would clean and polish *Achilles'* 'Monkey's Island', the Bridge Compass Platform, then return to give the Chart Room similar attention; but during Navi's and Claude's absence Torpedoman 'Chang' Williams, who frequented the adjacent Starboard Torpedo Control Bridge, had ample time to peer though a chart room porthole and memorise the cruiser's proposed destinations and, within the hour a new 'buzz' would ripple throughout the ship; highly amusing to Navi but of concern to Commander Neame whose nickname had long since been appended by the ship's day-workers.

When Commander Neame first joined *Achilles* his 'Daily Orders' were promulgated with minutes sliced off meal breaks; where it had been customary after breakfast for 'both watches' to fall in at 0805 it became 0755; after lunch 1305 became 1255 etcetera, so it was natural for some self-appointed baptist to christen him 'Nickabit', which stuck. And now with Chang Williams' forecasts being surreptitiously passed about the ship, Nickabit initiated a clause in his Daily Orders which was read and dramatised by messdeck mimics: 'The ship's company is entreated to refrain from disseminating false reports of indeterminate authenticity.'

That night on the Chilean coast lookouts with night-glasses picked up five vessels, none German; extra lookouts were posted during daylight hours to detect the merest indication of smoke beyond all horizons, and to relieve encroaching monotony interdepartmental teams were organised for deck hockey in the waists, wrestling and tug-of-war contests on the spacious wooden quarterdeck, where a ring was set up occasionally for a supervised grudge-fight to be settled when two normally friendly messmates turned sour over some trifling incident. Nickabit who in earlier years had been a PTI, still exhibited his prowess by doing a standing jump over the quarterdeck capstan, always appeared on deck smartly turned out, was recognised by all for his efficiency, and ensured after these rare 'three 3-minute round decisions' that the two shook hands and left their messdeck rancour in the ring.

Meanwhile in the Atlantic well west of Cape Verde Islands on 3 September, *Graf Spee* in company with her 22-knot newly built tanker *Altmark*, was ordered further south and, while refuelling on the 7th was fortunate to escape discovery by the County Class cruiser *Cumberland* on her way to join Commodore Harwood's squadron near Rio de Janeiro. Langsdorff had ordered his Arado float-plane aloft while *Graf Spee* and *Altmark* lay side by side. In circling the horizon, by the wildest chance the aircraft detected a warship's mastheads at maximum visibility, closed sufficiently to identify it as British, estimated that its course would take it within sight of the stationary German ships, then flew back to warn Langsdorff by morse-lamp in ample time for him to move east-south-east until nightfall. Had *Cumberland* been on her zig instead of the zag, the Arado wouldn't have seen her until too late to warn *Graf Spee*, and the 31-knot 8″ cruiser could have shadowed the slower enemy until reinforcements arrived.

But fate had other plans for *Graf Spee*, and now *Achilles* was 280 miles south of Valparaiso, entering Talcahuano with her upperdecks ceremoniously manned, her saluting guns having paid their respects, and her Royal Marine Band playing British naval glories as she drew alongside a wharf drenched with Chilean naval and civil VIPs on that hot 14 September forenoon. Three German freighters, *Orsono*, *Tacoma* and *Frankfurt* rode at anchor under sanctuary, and to confirm their status *Achilles'* cutter pulled around each in turn, photographing anything resembling a camouflaged gun or otherwise suspicious, especially the German seaman waving a swastika flag and baring his backside. These gestures and successive two-finger insults evoked hefty Kiwi-blurted raspberries in response, then five hours later the cruiser departed on an uneventful night search en route to Puerto Corral. Again shortly after arrival and a check for disguised enemy raiders she headed south, this time lingering beyond the horizon before doubling back for a quick look at nearby Isla Mocha's Caleta-dela-Fragata anchorage, where in 1578 Sir Francis Drake had anchored his *Golden Hind*.

No *Golden Hind*, no enemy shipping, just an empty bay. No radar or satellite reflectors to detect vessels over the ship's horizons at sea, not even her two lost amphibians with their several hundred square mile search capability, only a suspect M/F D/F contraption to heighten Captain Parry's chances of interception above those of Nelson. Most of the enemy freighters had already sought refuge as ordered by W/T at the outbreak of war, but their cargoes were sorely needed by the Fatherland and Captain Parry was trying to outwit them. He cruised past Constitucion, then San Antonio, boarded two tramps bound for La Serena and found their papers legitimate, unfortunately closed Coquimbo where his presence was made known to a German ship with steam up, then missed another German by mere hours when 70 miles off Talcahuano for a second look.

Telegraphist Milburn had excitedly copied the enemy freighter *Lahn*'s 500 kc/s traffic report to Talcahuano Marine Radio, saying she was entering harbour after leaving Sydney on 25 August. In Huasco there were Norwegians, Americans, Britishers, evident by long-range telescope, but no Germans so *Achilles* cruised on. Where was this goddam war? Nothing but monotony, abruptly dispelled by a BBC announcement that the Royal Navy carrier *Courageous* had been torpedoed and sunk in the English Channel, probably by a U-boat; there was a large loss of life.

Dawn actions came and went, men secured from quarters and dressed for entering Callao, the port of Peru's capital Lima. Parts-of-ship were manned, gun salutes were exchanged, and international protocol was observed when Peruvian dignitaries experienced the hospitality of Captain Parry's quarters. But within the hour there was pandemonium, officers saluted parting guests at the gangway then raced for ladders to the bridge, bugles hustled mooring parties and special-sea-dutymen topside, yet all was too late. Parry still scanned the main W/T signal announcing the merchantman *Leipzig*'s arrival in territorial waters leading into Callao, and his secretary had just opened a confidential bag delivered by a British Intelligence courier, containing a Consul report that *Leipzig* had left Guayaquil, 650 miles north, on 19 September, her departure and expected time of arrival at Callao being made known to the British Consul there within an hour of her sailing.

Captain Parry's official memorandum of the incident made uncomplimentary references to local British Intelligence, then concluded: 'since the Consul's message was not received until after *Leipzig* had anchored on 21 September, this episode is inexcusable.'

That afternoon after resecuring, *Achilles'* cutter photographed all suspect aspects of five German freighters at anchor, being harangued by their crews who shook their fists, made Nazi salutes and shouted German insults; but not so some groups of women and children gathered aft making furtive friendly waves. Then as the cutter passed a Yankee passenger-freighter exhibiting many of the fair sex, American men made good-humoured throat-cutting actions while the women blew kisses until out of range. And later when Postie returned onboard, he told of British and German seamen brawling ashore, due to swastikas and explicit sex cartoons about Germany's intentions with Britain having been painted on the British vessels. One German was killed, and badly beaten-up men of both sides were now fraternising in a local Peruvian cooler awaiting trial.

Being the only RN cruiser on South America's entire Pacific Coast, *Achilles* was informed by Britain's Minister to Peru that the English liner *Orduna* would leave Balboa on 24 September with VIPs and valuable consignments for Puerto Paita, Callao, and Valparaiso; and German vessels in harbour or at sea might try to seize the liner. Parry suggested by signal to C-in-C A & WI that *Achilles* remain in Peruvian waters meantime; and to retain secrecy the British Naval Attaché to Chile flew from Santiago with intelligence about enemy maritime movements. With this information, *Achilles* darkened ship that night and slid out of Callao in search of a German freighter reported off Puerto Paita. Four merchantmen answered challenges correctly but when the cruiser entered the Peruvian harbour at daybreak, she found the fast German motor-vessel *Friesland* just anchored and down to her Plimsoll line with cargo. It was now time to refuel, the ship's company was becoming testy, so Parry took his ship 40 miles north to Talara, an oil port on Cape Parinas, where at an American-Canadian oil company jetty, he gave off-duty men their first wartime run ashore. Only 4 degrees south of the Equator it was hot, but high in the barren hills after a hectic truck ride punctuated by minor breakdowns, liberty men were shown through the company distillery before being entertained at lavish tables under overhanging foliage. Here attended by men and women of the refinery staff they ate and drank until satiated, later being whisked downhill in their antiquated conveyances to Talara's English Club for another bender and an all-night dance. Meanwhile 900 tons of Peruvian crude had been pumped inboard; formal and informal *adios* were exchanged at dawn when inebriated men were helped out of the dance hall. Then after 0900 Divisions *Achilles* departed in search of an elusive *Orduna*; Captain Parry having to break W/T silence twice to be updated on her position before effecting a rendezvous and escorting her to safety, a safe passage not available to all shipping in the Atlantic.

Seventy miles off Pernambuco on 30 September, Langsdorff sent the Britisher *Clement* down with twenty-five rounds of 5.9″ then five rounds of 11″ after missing her at close range with two torpedoes. On 2 October the Brazilian ship *Itatinga* landed thirteen of *Clement*'s survivors at Bahia with varied descriptions of the raider, and on 9 October *Clement*'s Captain Harris, who'd been taken onboard *Graf Spee* for questioning, prior to being transferred to the Greek tramp *Papalemos*, was put ashore at St Vincent in the Cape Verde group. Harris certified the raider as a pocket battleship and claimed her to be *Admiral Scheer* which he'd seen painted on her stern, so now notified of the type of raider they were hunting, Admiralty cast a broader net, but it would be weeks before it enmeshed the intended monster.

Having delivered *Orduna* to Callao, Parry authorised leave for Red Watch day-men, a regrettable choice of colour in retrospect when local authorities complained that nearby Lima was being hazarded by men from *Achilles*. A patrol sent ashore to investigate arrested two sparkers in the final round of a boozy fight, then spent hours rounding up stragglers for the 2300 liberty boat; but well after midnight when the ship sailed, Telegraphist Tim Foley and Able Seaman Sammy Wilson were still engrossed in Lima's street of *casa de tratos*. Day after day escorting *Orduna* port to port, multi hours outside waiting for her to reappear, then on 10 October back to Valparaiso where the Captain's friend Almirante Allard agreed to three days in harbour because, he said: '*Achilles* is a belligerent warship, yes, but I consider her to be unseaworthy for three days, no?' to those about to protest. The news spread as an epidemic throughout the ship: 'LEAVE! There'll be tons of it!' And so there was with Red Watch onboard while Blue and White did the town; Blue Watch onboard the second day; White the third. It soon transpired that local senoritas were *extremo simpatico*, no mock modesty, your partner for the night meant just that; and laughing groups of *Achilles*' sailors were newspaper-photographed walking arm-in-arm with German cadets off the interned three-masted training ship *Priwall*. Beyond Chile's three-mile territorial zone they would be at war, fight to kill, but here both countrys' seamen shouted each other drinks, and ate together at 'Neptune's Bar' whose enormous German owner cooked succulent steaks. Parry was praised by the Port Captain for his ship's company behaviour and, as a goodwill gesture a Chilean destroyer escorted *Orduna* inside territorial waters all the way from Iqueque where *Achilles* had last deposited her. Men who slept in Monte Carlo Hotel's luxurious beds last night, had been warned by the owner's Belgian wife that there were rumours of a U-boat awaiting the cruiser's departure on Friday, 13 October; it is possible Captain Parry was alerted more officially; and even the ship seemed loath to sail on a Friday 13, fouling her anchor and delaying departure for long hours. So all boilers were flashed, everyone went to his action station, and *Achilles* finally left at speed on a zig-zag course until well clear of Valparaiso, when Skip announced: '*Admiral Scheer* is operating in the South Atlantic and we have been ordered there to participate in the search for her!'

After sinking *Clement* on 30 September, Langsdorff cruised west until 5 October when he captured the British freighter *Newton Beech* near Ascension Islands, next day deciding her to be too slow as a store ship and sinking her within hours of sending *Ashlea* down. Three days later he sank the 8,000-ton *Huntsman*, and on 22 October only 100 miles from St Helena, the *Trevanion*. By now he had many extra mouths to feed, intercepted Royal Navy signals indicated that he'd stirred the hornet's nest in Freetown, so he rendezvoused with *Altmark* for fuel and stores, transferred his prisoners onto her then set a course for the Indian Ocean. Unlike Royal Naval ships who had the advantage of wartime harbours, German warships had to remain at sea and keep their whereabouts undisclosed, thus making it difficult to maintain crew morale as *Graf Spee*'s Commander portrayed in this interpretation of the German entry in his diary on 30 September:

> The weather at present is exceptionally beautiful for these latitudes. The sea is calm, and bright sunshine gives an agreeable temperature. Life in a sanatorium could not be more pleasant. With our daily exercises there are no more sick and we are much fitter. Another practice for action. We go aft where Captain Langsdorff tells us there are 100 Iron Crosses for the crew because of our successes, but they should be for every man onboard, so a few only wear the Cross for those who did not receive it. We are also told the ship will try to return home in January. It is of great value that the Captain makes these talks from time to time. Questions are thus answered beforehand and speculation avoided. In the evening our cinema showed *Ninon*, a Louis XIV period theme with little moral and much love.

After *Achilles*' high-speed departure from Valparaiso she rendezvoused with RFA *Orangeleaf* who'd been dispatched via Panama Canal for the purpose, but refuelling in the rough conditions proved impossible so that night, with all lights doused, both ships sidled into Tongoy Bay to operate in secrecy, meantime transferring bags of flour, rice, sugar, boxes of butter and tea; 1,300 tons of oil were pumped into *Achilles*' fuel tanks while her Blue-boat idled about the entrance with its depth charges primed for instant use, as gunners and lookouts with high-power night glasses scanned the bay for telltale phoroscent periscope trails or a U-boat silhouette. BAAANNNGGGG! Nerves shattered momentarily as men froze in their tracks. A bridge lookout yelled: 'WHAAATIN BLOODY HELL WAS THAT?' Then all eyes lifted to the burst of boiler-pressure-vent steam spearing into the dark high above the funnel. Apparently the blow-off was heard for miles as within minutes Yeoman Jack Robertshaw reported the lights of a speeding boat approaching round a headland, and minutes later its occupants were discernable as a Chilean policeman and his patrol-boat coxswain, Jack's night glasses showed their look of apprehension as they saw the darkened cruiser, then they swung the tiller and disappeared on full throttle. No need now for secrecy as the anchor cable rattled noisily below, and *Achilles* was over the horizon before dawn with *Orangeleaf* smashing through her wake at maximum revs. Chile's coast was endless, at times rough, at times calm. Into Ancud Gulf's translucent depths, walled either side by sparsely vegetated sheer granite reminiscent of our South Island sounds; a few hours waiting off German-populated Puerto Montt while being told by the British Resident that a U-boat had stored and refuelled there three days ago; then on again into San Quinton Sound, where in 1914 Vice-Admiral Count Maximilian Reichsgraf von Spee coaled his flagship *Scharnhorst*, her sistership *Gneisenau* and the squadron's lesser cruisers, before losing his and his two sons' lives, and all but one of his Far Eastern Fleet to RN Admiral Sturdee's battlecruisers and cruisers which engaged him from their Falkland Islands' base.

Out through San Esteban Gulf into a broadside snow blizzard from which a Norwegian tanker loomed ominously close, with seas breaking over her foc'sle to lash her bridge with driven spray. *Achilles* entered Magellan Straits on 20 October with sunshafts revealing glistening snow-capped peaks backdropping a rust-streaked Chilean tramp. By mid-forenoon she was negotiating cold Froward Reach at latitude 54 degrees south, before turning for the run up Brunswick Peninsula with Terra del Fuego away to starboard. Then shortly those topside with binoculars were seeing the world's southernmost city, Punta Arenas, straight-roaded blocks of red-roofed buildings beneath snow-covered hills, all readable signs in English; 150 miles further west the Andes eased down to rolling *campina* protected from bitter Atlantic storms by Gabo des Virgens, but without the virgins' protection *Achilles,* according to one linguist, 'battled fru the worst bollickin we've ever ad'. Ladders were wrenched adrift, booms and boats were damaged, off-duty hands were piped down, and those who could were soon cocooned in their hammocks for warmth and security. Lookouts continually wiped their lenses, endeavouring to penetrate sub-zero sleet for first sightings of the Falklands as *Achilles* smashed through mountainous combers, seas burying her foc'sle and pounding A-turret before creaming onto B-gundeck and torrenting down both boom-decks. Assisted by D/F bearings Navi located Port William at 2000, but she dragged her anchor in the 70-knot blow and Parry stood out to sea again for safety. Then near 0800 on the 22nd with the storm abated, he re-entered Port William in bright sunshine to anchor off Port Stanley.

It was the Sabbath; leave had been granted until 1800; the few local dwellings opened their doors and invited men in for sumptuous plates of bacon and eggs; but Falkland's Governor had declined Parry's request for the local cinema and hotel to be opened, so Red and White watch had to be content with Port Stanley's small Scottish-type inn's service through opened windows. The guid lawd and the guid taverner found 'nae fault with a wee drammie or twae on such arn occasion, ye mind'. The talk got louder, the patronage denser as bottles of Scotch were passed over the sills, fights erupted on the way back aboard, and a thoroughly abusive Chief ERA who told the OOW: 'I'm a Chief Engineroom Artifishur of thuree ge-ge-generashuns of artifishurs, and YOOUH cahhn't puput me in cells!' woke next morning with sunrays glinting through the vertical bars welded across an opened porthole of one of *Achilles'* for'ard lock-ups.

Meanwhile there'd been a top-level reshuffle: Force G's Commodore Harwood would transfer his burgee from *Exeter* to *Ajax*, which would be joined by *Achilles*; and Force G's two intended destroyers *Havock* and *Hotspur* were diverted to the West Indies Station. *Exeter* and *Cumberland* would remain with Force G under Commodore Harwood, but C-in-C Atlantic at Freetown would co-ordinate their movements if necessary with those of Simonstown's Force H, *Sussex* and *Shropshire* plus Gibraltar's Force K, the carrier *Ark Royal* and battlecruiser *Renown*; thus creating a widely spread force of 8″ cruisers with a carrier and battlecruiser in support to meet any foreseeable situation from the central to South Atlantic Ocean. Additional to these groups the C-in-C had on call various other British and French ships comprising three battleships, two battlecruisers, five aircraft carriers, fourteen cruisers, a destroyer flotilla and a submarine flotilla, all wearing the White Ensign; plus two battleships, two battlecruisers, an aircraft carrier, five cruisers and numerous lesser warships, all flying the Tricolour of France. On paper this looks top-heavy compared to Germany's available raiders and so it was intended to be; but with electronic detection gadgets still on drawing boards or hatching in scientists' dreams, satellites and nuclear power unheard of, the ocean was reasonably easy to hide in and British warships quickly ran out of fuel.

Fully stored and refuelled on 24 October *Achilles* left Port Stanley, steamed north at 17 knots in weather warming day by day, and joined *Exeter* well east of Montevideo at 0730 on the 26th. One of Commodore

Harwood's greeting signals said his ship hadn't been in a port for thirty-seven days, he was about to leave for the Falklands and en route he would meet and transfer his flag onto *Ajax*, *Exeter* then continuing south for a week's R & R. Several hours after that short rendezvous, *Achilles* joined the big County Class 8″ cruiser *Cumberland* and for the remainder of October ambled along in her wash, constantly cleaning paintwork and decks bespattered by her three-funnel oil smuts. Both ships would patrol the area east, north, and south of Rio de Janeiro while *Ajax* when rejoined by *Exeter* would search near and far waters off the River Plate; one at a time each cruiser would be detached for a week in Port Stanley. This news cheered even those who thrived on despondency, until PO Tel Harold Sheirtcliff's loud 'Miserable pack of bastards!' headlined Mickey Savage's response to NZNB's recommendation for a 3-shilling per day rise in seamens' pay; and Parliament authorised ninepence. Eventually *Cumberland* took her unburned soots south, and the foc'sle became clean enough for stripped-down sun-worshippers as *Achilles* patrolled in sight of the Brazilian coast jungle, before fog blanketed everything and ships' horns bellowed soulfully as the cruiser rounded Cabo Frio into clear air when entering Rio on 10 November.

A square mile of *burdels* and *casa de tratos* attracted some, others toured the adventurous city, going up Sugar Loaf by cable-car, mingling with sunbathers on swarming beaches, losing money at night in casinos, dancing into early morning hours, then trying to find their way back to the ship. Able Seamen Tommy Collins and Ray Synnott took the ship's motorskiff and broke ship; Brazilian police found the abandoned Blue-boat but not its pirates who were still ashore in Rio when their ship sailed; so back to patrols, monotonous goddam patrols, emphasised as a P2 gunner moaned: 'If only we could see a flippin Gerry boat scuttle 'is bloody self.'

CHAPTER IX

Battle of the Plate

As *Achilles* DEPARTED Rio de Janiero on Sunday, 12 November 1939 her ship's company envied the throngs enjoying Copacabana Beach and frolicking in its sparkling surf, but hours after saluting Brazil's old battleship *Sao Paulo* inbound ahead of her destroyer escorts, Rio's many experiences were talk-exhausted memories. Then three days out in unsettled seas *Achilles* rendezvoused with France's reserve-troops transport *Massilia* from Buenos Aires, escorted her to Rio's approaches and waited outside intending to take her part-way to Sierra Leone, but missed her when she sailed at night in dense fog. Other ships were intercepted in clear areas, checked and wished 'Bon Voyage', one being *Highland Monarch* who stubbornly presented her stern until Parry identified his cruiser and signalled: 'Sorry if we startled you.' A dour Scots burr could almost be detected in the liner's flashlamp reply: 'We've got our 6″ and 3″ gun trained on your bridge and are frightened by no man.' Ignoring this rebuff *Achilles* escorted her to within sight of the glow above Rio, watched as she melted into the harbour lights, then doubled back to protect more appreciative shipping named in Admiralty's Daily Traffic List for the area. Other confidential information was morsed from Naval W/T stations covering the South Atlantic, including one cyphered message to all warships, reporting sightings of *Admiral Scheer* in the vicinity of Madagascar.

Disguised as *Admiral Scheer*, *Graf Spee* had prowled the Capetown-Perth route in early November without success, until inclement weather decided him to try nearer Madagascar. Langsdorff sighted the small Dutch freighter *Holland* but thought she was too near Lourenco Marques so remained distant, saw nothing else for a week, then boarded the 700-ton British tanker *Africa Shell* but sank her on finding that she'd discharged her cargo of aeroplane fuel at Quilemane. Now a prisoner on *Graf Spee*, *Africa Shell*'s Captain Dove protested that his ship had been sunk in neutral Portuguese East Africa's territorial waters, and demanded that Captain Langsdorff countersign a written claim to be presented post-war at an International Court. Langsdorff invited the irate Britisher into his chart room, indicated a marked position 24 deg 48 min S – 35 deg 01 min E, which placed the incident 7 miles off coast and therefore 4 miles outside territorial waters; then in his ornate cabin he produced a bottle of William Grant & Sons Special Reserve 'Glenfiddich' pure malt Scotch whisky while explaining:

'Salvaged from your country's *Clement*' and adding, 'believe me, Captain Dove. I don't like sending merchant ships to the bottom, no sailor does.' Having appended a disclaimer, he then signed Dove's document.

Later that November, after returning via deep latitudes to the Atlantic with a dummy funnel and a canvas B-turret, *Graf Spee* resembled *Repulse* so much that *Altmark* and other German auxiliaries drifting in their South Atlantic lair tried to escape. Here it was learned that although the pocket battleship had been at sea only since July, numerous defects required dockyard repair, there were cracks in her diesel mountings, and the Arado spotting plane's last engine was useless which nullified aerial reconnaissance, so Langsdorff prepared a lengthy memo for his staff officers, which continued:

> Item 5 ... From today henceforth, contrary to recommended tactics, we will meet enemy warships at the risk of losing our ship. Evasive tactics have for some time displeased me, but come what may, this for me is the best decision. It would be a pity to return home without a baptism of fire – a cruiser or some warship not superior to us would be a fine finale to our cruise. Enemy wireless communication has stopped as a consequence of our sinking *Africa Shell*. The English are taking protective measures in the Indian ocean; a bit slow perhaps, but they do things properly. They can not know that we are back in the South Atlantic, and having refuelled from *Altmark* we will take down our disguise.

> Item 6 ... *Graf Spee* needs a dockyard overhaul. Her period of commerce raiding is concluding and the necessity to avoid naval action no longer applies. I anticipate being able to close an enemy at speed, and sink or damage it so as to eliminate it as a shadower.

> Item 7 ... After a minor machinery overhaul I intend to operate in the general South Atlantic area where I sank *Trevanion*, until December 6; then dependent on my diesels, to:

> (a) ... Return to Germany.

> (b) ... Operate against River Plate traffic, then return to Germany.

> (c) ... *Altmark* shall await in an area convenient to either eventuality.

While *Graf Spee* shivered in southern latitudes, *Achilles* traversed the Brazilian coast with her sundrenched foc'sle covered by tanned off-watch torsos, but days thence toward the patrol's southern extremity, men venturing topside were experiencing a *pampero* common to the Plate Estuary through which *Ajax* and *Achilles* crashed at speed in that violent summer storm, searching for the German freighter *Lahn* who'd just morsed her entering harbour signal to Montevideo Marine Radio. Weeks back on the Chilean coast *Achilles* had missed her by 70 miles when she entered Talcahuano Harbour, and now not only *Lahn* but also *Tacoma* had made it to Montevideo after a furtive trip south round the Horn. Parry refuelled his cruiser and resumed those monotonous Brazilian coast patrols; put the searchlight on an unlisted American liner whose rails were soon lined by bed-clothed passengers, approached Rio Grande do Sul in daylight to deter the German freighters *Rio Grande* and *Montevideo* from making an Intelligence-reported bid for home, verified that the German merchantman *Sao Paolo* was still in Cabedelo, then heard a Brazilian newscast describing *Achilles* as a pocket battleship. Off Cap San Roque at the patrol's northern extent on 2 December Parry turned 180 degrees for the 1,500 miles down to Rio, came under scrutiny from Brazilian aircraft when closing their harbours to visually identify German ships in port, then made directly for Montevideo under radioed orders to refuel there on 8 December. Meanwhile an interrupted distress transmission from *Doric Star* in the eastern South Atlantic had said she was under attack by a battleship.

Uruguayan authorities permitted Captain Parry 48 hours in Montevideo, sufficient to give Blue and White watches a night each ashore, then the ship was ordered to meet *Ajax* 300 miles east of Cabo Santa Maria on 10 December.

Fortune changed for *Graf Spee* after her unsuccessful Indian Ocean interlude. Two days after refuelling from *Altmark* she sank *Doric Star*, next day *Tairoa*. Then German High Command informed Langsdorff that *Highland Monarch* had left Montevideo on 5 December, four British vessels were raising steam there for departure in convoy, HMS *Achilles* might be their escort; and *Andalusia Star* had departed Rio de Janiero on the 8th.

'If steaming north-east', Langsdorff surmised, 'the ships from Montevideo could be in our vicinity soon.' His last kill had been the Britisher *Streonsalh* on 7 December, and to date having sunk more than 50,000 tons of enemy commerce this extra 30,000 tons would put him above *Emden*'s First World War tonnage. *Graf Spee* cruised quietly into the night of 12 December, a still night pregnant with stars.

As instructed, *Achilles* joined Commodore Harwood's flagship at sea on 10 December, transferred mail and confidential bags taken aboard at Montevideo, and exercised constantly until *Exeter* arrived from the Falklands on Tuesday the 12th. All three captains and their staff officers then assembled aboard *Ajax* to be acquainted with the Commodore's intentions regarding a possible engagement:

'My policy with three cruisers versus a pocket battleship, is to attack at once by day or night.' He continued with precise details of the tactics to be adopted, ending with an instruction to his three captains, 'Act without further orders, so as to maintain decisive gun range.'

Waiting boats returned the officers to both nearby cruisers and now the three exercised at speed, maintaining W/T silence and manoeuvring by semaphore, flag hoists and signal lamps as if they'd worked together for months; *Exeter* deploying afar on one of an imaginary enemy's quarter, with *Ajax* leading *Achilles* out to the other, thus engaging the enemy ship from two directions astern and making her split her firepower; *Exeter*'s two forward 8″ turrets counterbalancing the combined forward 6″ turrets of *Ajax* and *Achilles*. They exercised this tactic at dusk to have their target silhouetted against a setting sun, adjourned for an evening meal and again at late supper, scrambled to 'Action Stations' for a night encounter, and were cursing Harwood's hunches' near midnight when 'Secure from Action Stations' sounded.

Middle Watch men relieved their offsiders just returned to complete the First, and almost four hours later junior rates from each department crept into their messdecks with torches, making sure they shook the right hammocks containing Morning Watchkeepers:

'Hey Peter,' with a gentle shake of the shoulder, 'Wake up Peter, it's ten to four.'

'Uh! Okay Nev, yep I'm awake – you shaken Stan?'

'Yes, there's only Stennett, can't find his hammock ...' an unfinished sentence as he shook the wrong man and disappeared amid well-flavoured abuse. Within fifteen minutes all changeovers had been completed and those now looking after each cruiser sipped thick pussers cocoa. The remainder slept.

ALARM RATTLERS BLARED!

Men swinging from hammocks swore. 'JEEZ MAN, I've only hit my f...in' scratcher!' Some halfwit was yelling 'SCHNELL SCHNELL GOMEN-HEIR ENQUICKEN. RAUS! RAUS!' P2's Stripey was struggling into his tattered overalls, mouthing invectives punctuated with 'Roll on me bleedin' twelve!' And aloft in his Director Control Tower, Lieutenant 'Dicky' Washbourn was going through his usual Dawn Action Stations routine, acknowledging telephoned reports from each 6″ turret captain, the TS computer table deep in *Achilles*' bowels, the various W/T remote positions, and lastly the bridge. But again as in every previous daybreak there were empty horizons; dawn stand-to secured and men resought their yet warm hammocks. PO Tels Stan Keeley and Peter Trent were among some who'd taken cups of tea onto the foc'sle instead, were shading their eyes against the day's rising sunrays, and were looking for an almost indiscernible wisp of smoke being pointed at by a nearby group. On *Achilles*' Signal Bridge Eddie Telford was spelling out flashlamp words from *Ajax*, telling *Exeter* to investigate; but being several miles nearer and first to detect the smoke, *Exeter* had anticipated the command and was already altering course while increasing speed. Stan's cup followed Peter's over the side as they raced below to the Main W/T Office, not waiting for the alarm rattlers.

Achilles' signalmen were watching *Exeter* through telescopes, now reading her flag-hoist – FLAG N TACKLINE NUMERALS THREE TWO TWO – yelling its purport: 'ENEMY IN SIGHT BEARING 322 DEGREES' Immediately followed by 'POCKET BATTLESHIP.' This was no exercise! Captain Parry had been informed from the DCT that a pocket battleship's mast and fighting top were evident through the rangefinder. 'Right, Guns, keep me informed.' Then replacing the phone he told Chief Yeoman Martinson to hoist *Achilles'* battleflags, so 'Bully' had the New Zealand Ensign hoisted to the foremast peak while he sent a signalman running aft to the mainmast yelling 'MAKE WAY FOR THE DIGGER FLAG!' which was run up its halyard to whip proudly at that peak: the first time a New Zealand cruiser had gone into action flaunting its country's ensigns as its battle banners.

Meanwhile, seated centre-bridge on his stool, Captain Parry had been issuing orders explicitly but calmly: 'Sound the alarm, Pilot, open out to four cables astern of *Ajax* and keep loose formation. Weave when she fires at us, but don't use too much rudder. Warn the engine-room we will be requiring full speed shortly.'

Commodore Harwood was leading *Achilles* onto a converging course and increasing speed to close the range, while *Exeter* opened out westward as if repeating yesterday's exercises.

On *Graf Spee* Langsdorff thought he'd intercepted the cruiser and convoy in High Command's last situation report on Montevideo. 'Probably a cruiser and two destroyers,' he briefed his bridge staff. 'No great problem, but perhaps a little longer before we can get at the convoy.' *Exeter* had now been identified at 20,600 metres, the two destroyers several hectometres more distant, no sign yet of the British freighters. Hearts leapt throughout the *panzerschiff* as an ear-shattering crash shook her end to end. The crew had experienced gunnery previously, but not this full-charge blast from all six 11″ barrels. Livid flames lanced the unusually smokeless salvo, hurling two tonnes of destruction at the 17-kilometre distant enemy cruiser, aiming where she was expected to be in seventy seconds but, without the Arado to radio falls of shot, corrections would have to be applied by rangefinder observation. Before his third salvo, Langsdorff was told the two smaller ships were *Ajax* and *Achilles*. He could easily out-range their 6″ gunnery, but *Exeter's* known 8″ were falling too close for comfort, so he ordered both his triple 11″ turrets to concentrate on her.

At 0620 *Exeter's* Captain 'Hooky' Bell authorised Y-turret to open fire even though both aircraft were being readied to launch. Now all six 8″ were engaging in a deafening crescendo, reducing elevation continually as the range decreased, then just as the first spotter prepared to catapult off, an 11″ shell landed short, exploding in a thunderclap of screaming fragments which instantly killed the starboard torpedo tubes' crew and two of the tween-deck damage control party. Essential gunnery control circuits were severed, both aircraft were wrecked, and almost simultaneously an 11″ shell pierced B-gundeck to screech down through the Sick Bay and out the port side without detonating. Minutes later as B-guns fired, their turret took a direct hit, killing all inside and putting it out of action. Shrapnel blasted up through steel decks and bulkheads, dropping men at their stations and killing almost all in the wheelhouse and on the bridge. Captain Bell's staff lay dead or dying and, although severely wounded in the face he made off for the After Control to command the few officers able to assist. A- and Y-turrets continued firing, obtaining a direct hit near the enemy's funnel, then some on her waterline which caused her to turn away under a smoke screen. Captain Bell was passing his orders via a chain of seamen, all realising they could be incinerated any moment if the petrol showered everywhere from the two wrecked aircraft ignited, but the chain remained as Bell's only communication link, keeping the ship's remaining guns firing at their enemy now only six miles to starboard.

Achilles' Main W/T sat directly over the port forward screw and it was evident from its vibrating power that this was the real thing. Loose articles jinked off operators' desks as the ship began to tremble, all four propellers rumbling with the increase in revolutions. Men in the Coding Office swayed and grabbed for support when a heavy WHOOOMMPH indicated the ship's opening salvo, shockwaves thrust a cloud of dust from overhead ventilation ducts, lights flickered then steadied. More resounding gun-blasts. The 500kc/s operator removing his headphones as *Ajax's* main transmitter smote his eardrums. Keying dead slow for the benefit of merchantmens' 1st mates, she broadcast the International Safety Signal – TTT TTT TTT – to activate auto-alarms, waited for their receivers to be switched on, then warned all shipping in the vicinity: CQ CQ CQ de GEBT GEBT GEBT = Naval battle in progress. Position 3434S 4917W. All ships keep clear = 0620 AR.

At about 0630 the light cruisers' gunnery worried their enemy so much that her turrets were trained off *Exeter*, straddling *Ajax* with towering columns of blackened water from 11″ upheavals while the 5.9s whirred overhead apparently unable to be corrected for range. All ships were now firing, *Graf Spee's* 11″ and 5.9s, *Exeter's* remaining 8″ A- and Y-Turrets, and the light cruisers' sixteen 6″ as they could be brought to bear. Men at *Achilles'* and *Ajax's* exposed stations shouted between their ships' crashing salvoes, pointed their mates to *Exeter* where smoke and flames showed that she'd been hit; cheered loud when explosions were seen on *Graf Spee*, then cheered louder when told the enemy's fore'ard turret seemed to be out of action. But her after turret and secondary armament still punished *Exeter* mercilessly, flames and smoke obvious in many places, then a midship burst higher than the others.

Harwood had to draw the fire off her, agreed to his captain's suggestion that they close the range to increase the effectiveness of their 6″ salvoes, and led *Achilles* onto a converging heading.

The tactic proved right, *Graf Spee* being more in danger from the light cruisers, again swung her 11″ away from *Exeter*. Now being targeted, *Achilles* weaved to confuse the enemy gunners' aim, but a near miss exploded abreast the bridge, spattering the upperworks and DCT with fragments. Men cried out in agony as hot metal tore their flesh. Neville Milburn slumped, heard the explosion and opened his mouth to exclaim but made no sound, his headphones clattered to the Control Tower deck as his life ebbed. Alongside him Frank Stennett raised his hands to his shattered head and toppled lifeless through a manhole onto the rangetaker below. Milburn now fell through the same hatch and lay across them. The Spotting Officer's assistant, Royal Marine Sergeant Trimble, jerked forward and slumped with a moan. Eddie Shirley with his head and shoulders above the tower roof checking the distance to *Ajax*, collapsed with a cry of surprise onto the DCT deck where 'Guns' Washbourn swayed, shaking his bloodied head over the Rate Officer 'Nippy' Watts. Marine Trimble had recovered and although badly wounded, placed a gauze pad on Milburn's neck to stem the blood, but as they laid him down he coughed and died. Relief telegraphists soon arrived to find their W/T circuits were out, all communication cables had been severed and gunnery corrections were relayed man to man until repaired, but even then falls of shot were seen landing uncorrected. The Director Layer yelled to the man on his left; 'Hey Archie, you're not putting the corrections on, are you alright?' No answer from the Sight Setter who sat rigidly holding his control wheel. There never would be. Archie Shaw's dead body was removed and Ordinary Seaman Rogers squeezed past to take over, perhaps young, but well trained as shown when flashes about *Graf Spee*'s top structure indicated hits.

On the bridge splinters had slashed through Captain Parry's calves, bringing him down holding on to the binnacle. Chief Yeoman Lincoln Martinson also fell with his legs smashed. He was taken by stretcher to the Sick Bay but Parry insisted on being assisted back to his high-chair, his rank being ignored as well as his protests while a Sick Bay tiffy administered first aid. Other attendants and stretcher bearers eased bodies and wounded out of the DCT, laying the dead on the bridge and taking the injured below. Leading Seaman Harry Beesley had just urged his P1 4″ A/A gun crew to take cover behind their unshielded weapon: 'Come on Ian, get behind the bloody gun before the next bastard arrives.' But another from the pocket battleship landed short as he spoke. He was moving behind Ian Grant when the young O/D dropped with his chest shattered. Ordinary Seaman Marra had also dropped to the gun-deck writhing in pain with wounded thighs and a hot splinter embedded in his backside; so to get him down to Sick Bay Harry hoisted him onto his back, arms gripped around his shoulders, face alongside his ear. At the nearest hatch Harry turned to take him down backwards, not realising Marra's butt stuck out so far until he backed it straight onto the hatch combing. 'OWWW YOU BASTARD HARRY!' right in his ear, 'OHHH FOR CHRIST'S SAKE! OWWWW.' The injured lad was now out cold, not hearing Harry's mumbled apologies while being deposited at a first aid post for more professional treatment.

At 0640 two more 11″ shells hit *Exeter*, one wrecking A-turret and the other starting fierce fires amidship. She disappeared in smoke which cleared to show her firing her after turret. A further shell smashed her Navigation Office, Armament Office, and RCO, killing most of their occupants before it passed through the Signal Deck and burst on S1 A/A gun, detonating its ready-use ammunition with catastrophic results. With her for'ard compartments flooded through a waterline implosion she ploughed on, foc'sle almost awash, her masts swaying ominously as she pitched over low waves.

Ajax and *Achilles* were now exceeding 33 knots when *Ajax* took a direct hit on her after superstructure, the 11″ missile penetrating several compartments and cabins, passing through X-turret trunk and wrecking its gunhouse machinery, then exploding in Commodore Harwood's quarters, part of the shell-casing drilling into Y-turret rotation track to lock it from turning. Both her after turrets were now out of action with many of their crews dead or injured and an hydraulic ammunition hoist for one of her B-turret guns ceased to function, leaving only three of her eight 6″ guns operative.

Intent on finishing *Exeter* off, Langsdorff concentrated his fire on her from only four miles, but again worried by 6″ damage from the light cruisers at five miles and closing rapidly, he had to haul round onto a north-west course to use his forward turret as a deterrent. Meanwhile 'Attack with torpedoes' flew at the flagship's upper yard, and just as *Achilles'* Torpedo Officer Lieutenant Woodhouse sensed his moment of glory, *Ajax* turned across his line of fire to launch hers. Langsdorff's lookouts reported the torpedoes approaching, he helmed hard to comb them, but in presenting *Graf Spee's* stern prevented her forward 11″ and starboard 5.9s from bearing onto the light cruisers. With good effect Harwood had used his own theory of attacking from both quarters of an enemy's stern, and had scored telling hits from less than four miles.

Again Langsdorff altered course to fire torpedoes at 0731, these being morsed by *Ajax's* plane as: 'Torpedoes approaching you, they will pass ahead.'

But taking no chances the Commodore ordered both ships onto a direct approach heading, and in so doing decreased their rate of fire when only the forward guns could be aimed. It was now that Harwood was informed about a risk of running short of ammunition, and this led to an immediate change of tactics; action would be deferred until nightfall when he could close sufficiently to make full use of the ships' torpedoes.

Langsdorff also had problems: holed in the bows and unable to maintain high speed because of flooding, his diesel fuel contaminated and escaping from ruptured tanks, his 5.9″ gunnery circuits disrupted among twisted steel in which many lay dead, he radioed German High Command details of his predicament, advising no chance of shaking off his pursuers, and stating his decision to make for Montevideo to which Grand Admiral Raeder replied: 'Your intention understood.'

Throughout the forenoon *Ajax* and *Achilles* tailed the fleeing pocket battleship at some 30,000 yards, closing periodically to 23,000 to worry him with rapid salvoes, then breaking beyond range under heavy smokescreens when 11″ shells fell close, one rumbling over *Achilles* to erupt near *Ajax*, bringing down her main-topmast and causing additional casualties. So the chase continued with *Exeter* falling astern, crippled but still requesting permission to participate, signalling: '18 knots available, one 8″ gun one 4″ gun and port torpedoes serviceable', but being ordered by Harwood to try and make it to Port Stanley, 'Good luck Hooky'.

Up till now the British ships had been under the impression they were fighting *Admiral Scheer*. Admiralty had no reason to believe otherwise since 9 October, when *Clement*'s Captain Harris said that's what she was when he was released by Langsdorff to *Papalemos*, and put ashore at Bahia, but now p.m. 12 December they were about to learn the truth.

Early that evening Langsdorff tried a final ploy to escape, by morsing Harwood he had just sunk an outward-bound vessel: GVBK GVBQ de DTGS = Please pick up lifeboats of British steamer = AR.

GVBK was *Achilles*' international callsign, GVBQ denoted *Ajax*, and DTGS belonged to *Graf Spee*. With no need for further subterfuge Langsdorff had authorised the use of his correct identity, but the ruse didn't work, as when sighted and queried by *Ajax*, the supposed sinking steamer *SS Shakespeare* reported herself unharmed.

Nearing Punta del Este at sunset Harwood attempted to get *Graf Spee* silhouetted for a torpedo attack, but again those 11″ guns foiled the manoeuvre and both cruisers retired behind smoke. About now Harwood took *Ajax* outside English Bank to head off Langsdorff if he tried to make a dash for open water, this leaving *Achilles* as the sole pursuer. At 2048 off Punta Negra, *Spee* opened fire to the delight of Uruguayan spectators whose car headlights delineated the dark coastline; *Achilles*' four turrets immediately responded and at 2056 obtained hits at the base of the big warship's funnel. She altered course out of range then swung back to fire again at 2132, 2140 and 2143, but his time being inside Uruguaya's territorial waters

Captain Parry withheld permission to retaliate. Then at 2350 *Graf Spee* called Montevideo Marine W/T to say she was entering harbour, so *Achilles* rejoined *Ajax* and they withdrew under Harwood's orders to: 'Patrol the area from the Uruguayan coast to a line 120 degrees from English Bank. *Ajax* to cover the southern area, and both ships to move back to cover their respective estuary areas at dawn.'

Ordered by Hitler to scuttle *Graf Spee* in Montevideo Roads, Langsdorff invited his captive British mercantile-marine captains to remain onboard until their release could be arranged with the British Ambassador; they had negligible choice. He then supervised a funeral service ashore for his thirty-six dead, saw to the welfare of the injured and 1,100 about to be interned, and in the privacy of his quarters wrote lengthy accounts of the battle. It was now time to avoid having his pocket battleship interned.

At sea at 1000 on Thursday, 14 December 1939 the patrolling British cruisers held funeral rites for their dead; Captain Parry reading the service aboard *Achilles* and concluding:

Ian Grant	NZD 1734	Ordinary Seaman
Archibald H Shaw	NZD 1030	Able Seaman
Neville J Milburn	D/SSX 23288	Ordinary Telegraphist
Frank Stennett	D/JX 148899	Telegraphist

whose earthly remains we now commit to the deep.

That eerie sound as each weighted hammock slid from under the White Ensign and plunged . . . 'into the sea which has claimed them'. The realisation of life with the bugling of 'Reveille'. A hoarse 'ON CAPS! RIGHHHT TURRN! QUUICK MAARCH!' off the heaving quarterdeck and back to duty.

Although *Cumberland* had rejoined at speed from the Falklands, converging reinforcements were yet several days' steaming distant. Men catnapped in turns at their posts, waiting. It was now 1845 on 17 December, *Graf Spee*'s deadline for internment; everyone knew it and the anxiety showed. *Ajax*'s Sea Fox reported the pocket battleship under way, turning seaward on leaving Montevideo. Harwood signalled his cruisers to their battle stations, his orders: 'The object of tonight's action is destruction of the enemy.'

The force was advancing in single line ahead formation – *Ajax* – *Achilles* – *Cumberland*, battle-flags taut at mastheads, lookouts reporting distant smoke.

The Sea Fox was again transmitting: '*Spee* appears to be preparing to scuttle.' Then: 'SHE IS BLOWING HERSELF UP!'

Harwood ordered all ships to increase speed and follow him into Montevideo Roads where the huge warship's self-destruction could be observed;

thunderous explosions were witnessed that night by foreign correspondents ashore, by the city's population and, at about 2300 by the three cruisers as they approached *Graf Spee*. Captain Parry had ordered all off-duty hands topsides on *Achilles* to witness the end of their big German adversary. Dull explosions still accompanied new eruptions of flame and smoke along the fiercely burning pocket battleship, evoking renewed inter-ship cheering until group after group went below, officers to their wardroom bar, tired men to their hammocks.

Phases of *Graf Spee*'s self-destruction.

Top Left: Initial blast and mushroom cloud.
Top Right: More explosions.
Bottom: Still burning the next day.

High-priority cables had already informed Admiralty and C-in-C South Atlantic that *Graf Spee* had destroyed herself in the Montevideo Roads, so now the ether pulsed with cyphered messages recalling Force K's carrier *Ark Royal*, battlecruiser *Renown* and cruiser *Neptune* to Freetown; Force H's County Class cruisers *Sussex* and *Shropshire* to Cape Town; and other reinforcements to their area bases.

In Borombon Bay while *Ajax* and *Achilles* refuelled from RFA *Olynthus*, Commodore Harwood boarded *Achilles* to say he would be taking *Ajax* into Montevideo and was sending *Achilles* further up the Plate Estuary for a spell in Argentine's Buenos Aires; but shortly after heading upstream Parry was recalled. Evidently *Graf Spee*'s crew had been interned in the German-minded city, they were permitted on trust to be given leave from their camp, and it was an inappropriate time to visit; instead the ship would accompany *Ajax* to the Falklands, en route endeavouring to intercept *Graf Spee*'s supply ship *Altmark* known to have some 300 British merchant seamen in her holds. Both cruisers deployed at horizon distance with the flagship's Sea Fox airborne during daylight hours, but there were eleven million square miles of the South Atlantic in which to hide, leaving minimal odds on finding *Altmark* within the several hundred able to be covered by their air-and-sea search.

On Thursday, 21 December, when nearing the Falklands, an *Olynthus* seaman taken aboard *Achilles* at Borombon Bay for a peritonitis operation died, and at 1500 his body was committed to the deep with full naval honours; then both cruisers streamed paravanes for their Port Stanley entry.

There, heavily listed to port with big holes in her bows, no foremast, funnels and upperworks peppered by shrapnel, and her for'ard turrets askew, *Exeter* presented a sorry sight but she raised a resounding response to the flagship's lusty cheers while gliding past, closely followed in her eddying wake by *Achilles* who also rendered and received hat-raised throaty acclamations of victory. Then later in the small town's pub, where *Exeter*'s hospitalised walking wounded stood evident in their civilian coats and remnants of uniform, it was learned that two *Achilles'* leave-breakers left behind in Rio on 10 November, had somehow got to Montevideo where they gave themselves up to *Exeter*'s gangway corporal during an early December port call for fuel. A Captain Bell report accompanying their transfer back to *Achilles* now saved them from a court martial trial for desertion: 'During the action these two New Zealand ratings were seen in many dangerous situations, entering blazing compartments repeatedly to drag injured men out, assisting fire parties and joining wholeheartedly in damage control.'

Thomas Collins, Able Seaman NZD1352, born Waikouaiti, was lost with HMS *Neptune* off Tripoli, North Africa, in the early hours of Friday 19 December 1941. Ashley Raymond Synnott, Able Seaman, retired from the RNZN post-war, attained a Master's ticket and skippered Union Steam-ship Company coasters for the remainder of his working years.

There had been all manner of intrigue and counter-intrigue by Monte-video's British and German diplomats to foster Uruguayan friendship. Britain's Ambassador to Argentine, Sir Eugen Millington-Drake KCMG, had been involved in Uruguyan affairs prior to the First World War. In 1919 he had met and become a friend of the South American Station flagship HMS *Southampton*'s young Torpedo Officer, Lieutenant Henry Harwood, who over ensuing years sought and befriended South American service and political dignitaries at every opportunity, throughout successive years and promotions until he became the Station C-in-C. Eugen Millington-Drake and Henry Harwood had years since become trusted friends of General

Top Left: Captain Hans Langsdorff.
Top Right: *Ajax* minus her main topmast in Montevideo.
Bottom Centre: Eugen Millington-Drake with Rear Admiral Harwood on board
Ajax in Montevideo days after the battle.

Alfredo Compos, Minister of Defence in Uruguaya's Government which was the only South American one to sever relations with Germany in the First World War, so one might question Langsdorff's decision to enter Uruguayan Montevideo instead of nearby Argentinian Buenos Aires.

Once done however it appears that the decision was unwise, as exemplified by translated excerpts of a letter written by Captain Langsdorff on 17 December 1939 to the German Minister at Montevideo expressing his dismay at the existing predicament:

The German Reich Minister at Montevideo	Kapitan-zur-see Hans Langsdorf
Herr Otto Langmann	Panzerschiff Admiral Graf von Spee Montevideo 17/12/39

Before leaving Montevideo I wish to express through you my deep gratitude for the numerous demonstrations of sympathy and help from the people of Uruguay, I shall never forget them.

Also, I wish to express my great pleasure to the Uruguayan authorities, especially when consideration is given to the grave situation which has arisen between us, for the quick assistance which was given to the *Graf Spee* to my wounded and the honours rendered to my dead.

With great sorrow on my part, they have mixed with these truly humanitarian sentiments a profoundly disagreeable one.

According to your communication referring to your visit to the Foreign Relations Minister of the Uruguayan Republic, you are obliged to consider as definite the time fixed by Cabinet for 8pm on the 17th of December for the sailing of *Graf Spee*. This notwithstanding the fact that urgent repairs required to make the ship navigable cannot possibly be completed by this time.

Against such a ruling I protest in every way. The points of my protest are as follows:

(1) In accordance with Art 17 of the 13th Hague Convention you are allowed to concede to belligerent warships in neutral ports time necessary to make good defects which are essential to safe navigation. There is a precedent in South America which dates from 1914 when the British cruiser *Glasgow* was allowed to make repairs over a period of weeks. In order to make good the repairs to my ship I have asked for 15 days.

(2) The technical commission of the Uruguayan Government have been able to convince themselves that the fighting ability of *Graf Spee*, both machinery and armament have suffered little so that I am not allowed to repair either of them. This same commission also convinced itself that the hull was safe against the dangers of navigation. Besides, states

of the galley and bakery would prohibit a long stay on the high seas considering the number of crew. Such repairs are covered by Art 17 previously quoted and 72 hours did not allow these repairs to be carried out.

(3) In spite of the intense efforts being made it has not been possible to repair the damage in the time fixed even with the help from firms in Montevideo. This fact should have been understood and a new investigation ordered. Work was also hindered by the Customs authorities at 1800 on December 16th. I also state that the determination of the Uruguayan Cabinet forces me to leave Montevideo with a ship that has not been repaired and that is unsafe to navigate. Voyage on the high seas would endanger the crew of more than a thousand men. In this I do not refer to the danger of enemy origin but exclusively to the general dangers of navigation.

(4) The decision of the Cabinet represents a flagrant violation of the hopes of carrying on the war more humanely in accordance with the article of the Hague Convention already quoted. I for my part protest strongly against their decision.

(5) On the morning of the 13th December I attacked the English cruiser *Exeter*. In the fight the *Ajax* and *Achilles* also took part. Once the *Exeter* had been put out of action by me, I resolved to enter Montevideo to effect repairs. I also knew that British Government only recognised territorial waters as extending three miles from the shore. Once my ship had entered this zone which is Internationally owned by several South American States I respected their neutrality by ceasing fire in spite of favourable visibility. I opened fire on a British cruiser stationed off Labos Island after she had opened fire and the shells were falling close to my ship.

(6) In spite of the fact that I do not recognise the action of the Uruguayan Cabinet at the same time I shall respect the time limit they have fixed. I blame the Government for not allowing me to make my ship fit to navigate in accordance with the Hague Convention. I cannot argue against the control of this country with my ship which has suffered badly in battle although she can still be fought. Under these circumstances there remains no other solution than to sink my ship. I shall blow her up close to the shore, disembarking beforehand as many of the crew as possible.

[signed] LANGSDORFF
KAPITAN-ZUR-SEE

Around noon on Wednesday, 13 December an American ornithologist, Mike Fowler, had returned to Montevideo from his latest bird life expedition in the Uruguayan forest, steering his dilapidated truck through milling crowds on his way to Manolo's all-night bar where letters and messages were kept pending his infrequent returns. Near the Palacio Salvo an American United Press newsman waved him down and told him about that morning's naval battle. Wide-mouthed bystanders listened excitedly. Mike got excited too – if the warships entered the Plate Estuary he might see them from his top-storey room – he had one of the latest H/F transceivers – he'd radio the fight direct to his New York agents who would broadcast it worldwide – chance of a lifetime for such a scoop! 'Come on, McTavish!' Manoel Herrera McTavish was an unkempt beachcomber of doubtful birth, a Manolo pub habituate and a self-appointed camera and radio bearer on Fowler's forest expeditions.

Throughout the day Punta del Este's lighthouse keeper had been telephoning ball-by-ball incidents for display on noticeboards surrounded by eager crowds:

ACHILLES HAS BEEN SUNK sent local Nazis on a celebration spree until a 7 p.m. bulletin quashed the rumour:

A GERMAN BATTLESHIP IS PASSING PUNTA DEL ESTE PURSUED BY AJAX AND ACHILLES.

By now the coast road from town to East Point was a grandstand for parked cars, their passengers yelling and pointing at distant gunflashes, those with car radios hearing Fowler's commentary and naming each ship as it came closer, others remarking about the huge rooster's tail brought up by *Achilles* as she raced through the shallows. Every hillock, every rooftop, every vantage point was crowded till well after dark when cars queued agitatedly on the road back to town, where lighted windows shone in the Presidential Palace, in the Port Authority building, the Defence Headquarters, Foreign Ministry, French and British Legations, and the German Embassy.

Inside each of those buildings the final rounds of '*La Batalla del Rio de la Plata*' would be contended; diplomats skilled in intrigue would vie for Uruguayan friendship; Eugen Millington-Drake would transfer there from Buenos Aires to propound Britain's rights; and *Graf Spee*'s Oberleutnant Rasenack would days later rebuke the Uruguayan Government in print as these translated excerpts indicate:

By adroit propaganda Millington-Drake has gained Uruguayan affection toward Britain ... they like him for his attendance at all athletic events ... he congratulates winners if they are Uruguayan ... he donates trophies and flatters local people. He, an Englander with all the advantages on his side, now confronts our captain in this diplomatic contest for our ship's fate ... he will try by all means to obstruct our proposals ... meanwhile the Uruguayan Government sends us to the devil.

Two large Nazi flags topped *Graf Spee*'s masts when Langsdorff sailed at 1815, having minutes previously telephoned Hitler with his scuttling proposal, asking for alternative instructions but being told that as *Graf Spee*'s commanding officer he was in charge of the situation.

At 1845 *Graf Spee* waited mid-channel for two launches from the German freighter *Tacoma* to which all married men were transferred, then she proceeded southward followed by *Tacoma* expecting to be called alongside to refuel the pocket battleship with 1,600 tons of diesel.

Fowler's voice interrupts a samba, tells the world that hundreds of crew are leaving *Graf Spee* and going below on *Tacoma* with their gear ... 'is this big Nartzi battlewagon gonna do a win or die breakout with a reduced crew?'

Montevideo is crammed with recently arrived newsmen of many nationalities. Sunday dawns and crowds cover the waterfront. Churchill smokes endless cigars in his London War Office, ecstatic as Fowler's commentary indicates British ascendency. President Roosevelt in the White House chaws intently on a long Havana. Hitler rants and raves at Admiral Raeder in his Berchtesgaden lair. Men on *Ajax, Achilles*, and the recently arrived *Cumberland*, express flowery derision on hearing that *Renown, Ark Royal*, and France's battleship *Dunkerque*, have arrived outside Montevideo, and Commodore Harwood says: 'Nice thinking, Millington,' to no one in particular on his bridge.

But Captain Langsdorff can't be sure.

Mike Fowler sees large Nazi ensigns unfurl on *Graf Spee*'s topmasts, sees white water swirling above her propellers, his voice is almost hysterical as she gathers way; then it subdues as she heads for Recalda Buoy marking the channel to Buenos Aires: 'Isn't she going to take on the Brits? If you look aways out south you'll just see them, small dots makin' smoke.'

In *Achilles'* A-turret Billy McKenzie is nervously cracking a joke, none laugh, they feel the tremor as their cruiser picks up speed, they anticipate another flurry of intense combat. Parry has asked for revs for 25 knots in compliance with Flag G Numeral 2 Numeral 5 whipping taut atop *Ajax*'s main halyard; turrets are training ominously, their guns elevating and depressing in preparation.

Throughout *Graf Spee*, torpedo heads have been manhandled into magazines, into turrets, everywhere it is intended to destroy top-secret equipment. Timed switches have been connected to accumulators. Captain Langsdorff brings his ship to anchor and the demolition party salute him as they hurry down the sea gangway to a waiting motor boat; he turns aft and salutes wistfully before leaving his ship; he steps into the launch and orders the coxswain to make for Buenos Aires.

They are stopped by the Uruguayan gunboats *Huracan* and *Zapican*, but are allowed to proceed when Langsdorff produces his Uruguayan government order that he quit Montevideo. He advises *Huracan*'s commander to clear all craft from the area and glances at his watch.

Fowler's H/F commentary to New York is being rebroadcast on M/F by Radio Montevideo, his voice rises, almost trips over his tongue with excitement: 'That Brit navy squad with their little popguns ... hold it! ... *Tacoma*'s boat is pulling away from the *Spee!*' Moments later listeners hear him again: 'Two Uruguay gunboats are stoppin the Nartzi launch ... Now they're all quittin thu area, AND FAST! OH MY GAWWD! A mighty spear of flamin debris has shot up somewheres about the fightin top—' Mike's voice is lost in a loud crash, screams, yells, buckling noises then profanity as he resumes: 'Sorry folks if I scared yuh'all,' breathlessly. 'Thu goddarn table I was standin on collapsed!'

Locals in high-rise buildings had seen *Graf Spee* leaving harbour, seen her stop with all sorts of activity around her, then backdropped by a glorious sunset they saw the violent drama unfold. First a small flash, followed within seconds by an enormous explosion and an erect column of smoke-blackened flame mushrooming soundless high over her fighting top. Dead silence, radio, people, motionless until a resounding thunderclap and buffeting shockwave rattles doors and windows. More booming concussions; compounding the raucous clamor of Montevideo's myriad spectators, almost delirious.

Back out at sea aboard *Achilles*, Gunnery Officer Dicky Washbourn has been kept informed of *Graf Spee*'s movements by *Ajax*'s aircraft; his head emerges from the 6″ DCT hatch and he shouts up at the 4″ tower: 'RELAX FELLAHS, THE BASTARD'S BLOWN HERSELF UP!'

'Cyclone' McGlone is whooping, right throughout the ship everyone is hollering, shaking hands and patting backs in unembarrassed relief. It is their moment of glory. But hours later the anti-climax pervades each cruiser; there have been acts of selfless bravery, devotion to duty, inherent efficiency, and there is a cost. *Exeter* has 61 dead, 23 critically wounded, others not so badly; *Ajax* 7 killed several critical in Sick Bay; *Achilles* 4 dead, 3 seriously injured. Men will lay aft to stand head bowed as last rites are intoned, the rattle of high-port rifle salutes, projectile-weighted hammocks containing messmates' or officers' bodies will slide from under White Ensigns over upended burial boards to their eternal rest.

Days later, on Tuesday, 19 December at Buenos Aires' Florenclo Varela naval barracks, Captain Hans Langsdorff addressed many of his interned crew concluding: 'A few days ago it was your sad duty to pay homage to your dead comrades. Perhaps in the near future you may be called on to undertake a similar task.' Only one, perhaps two of his most intimate staff perceived that significance as, wishing the assembly goodnight, he paid them tribute with an Imperial German Naval salute then left.

Next morning grief-stricken *kriegsmariners* listened in mute disbelief as *Graf Spee*'s Executive Officer announced their revered captain's death. His Flag Lieutenant, Kurt Diggins, had left him penning letters late at night, shut the door quietly and heard nothing while retiring well after midnight to his bed. Then before breakfast he knocked twice on the Captain's door, no answer, entered the room and found Hans Langsdorff in full uniform lying on *Graf Spee*'s naval ensign, shot through the temple, service pistol alongside his left hand. In accordance with naval tradition he had ensured the welfare of his ship's company, then followed his ship to its end.

Ajax, *Achilles* and *Exeter* had won the first decisive naval encounter of the Second World War but there would be many more throughout the six years conflict to follow

To expose Joseph Goebbels' lie to the German public that the British force had been damaged beyond repair, Churchill insisted on *Ajax*'s and *Exeter*'s return home – but quick – so Port Stanley's meagre facilities worked wonders to make *Exeter* seaworthy enough to meet Churchill's demand.

Before returning north, 'Hunch' Harwood (nicknamed thus because of his intuitive early December reasoning that Langsdorf's final killings were bringing him towards the Plate Estuary) shifted his flag from *Ajax* to *Achilles* pending the arrival of relief cruisers, then shifted it again to *Hawkins* off Rouen Bank on 28 January 1940. Captain Parry then steamed *Achilles* to within a hundred yards of *Graf Spee* which was already a mass of twisted metal, charred by fire, rusting from exposure with a high tide lapping her big gun muzzles. He dipped his flag to the Uruguayan guardship anchored nearby, then turned for a last rendezvous with *Hawkins*. Now promoted Rear Admiral, Henry Harwood stood bare-headed on the old cruiser's quarterdeck, listening to and visibly moved by the New Zealand crew's genuine rendition of 'For he's a jolly good fellow' followed by 'Now is the hour ...' repeated immediately as 'Po ata rou ...' by the ship's few Maoris and many New Zealanders. Then as *Achilles* moved away he waved to the ship, raised a handkerchief to his eyes and walked toward the door of his quarters.

Engine-room telegraphs jangled for more revolutions and Navi laid a course for Port Stanley en route home. Falkland Island farewells. Fog lifting off Cabo Virgens. Then the early morning watch lights of Punta Arenas, before daylight revealed Magellan Strait's glaciers glinting from cloud-pierced sunrays. Day after day setting the clock back half an hour in rising temperatures. 'Tolly' the Crusher amassing bundles of requests to recommence shaving, his RPOs organising leave chits, train and Cook Strait ferry passes, and at last the SRE radio relaying 2YA through messdeck speakers, then 1YA, and 1ZB with Phil Shone's familiar voice. The Gulf, Rangitoto, flags adorning inner harbour ferries and berthed shipping, as *Achilles'* band arrayed on X-gundeck played the victorious cruiser past *Philomel* and *Leander*. Bugled salutes were exchanged then *Achilles* crossed the sparkling harbour to berth alongside Central Wharf's mass of near hysterical welcomers.

Newsmen photographed official and privately tender greetings, caught Captain Parry laughing and chatting with dignitaries and raced off to ensure inclusion in that evening's *Auckland Star*. Then at 1100 with Central Wharf cleared, the ship's company fell in for the march up Queen Street, an easy drumbeat pace as the long four-abreast column passed under a wharf-shed banner inscribed:

BRAVO ACHILLES THE AUCKLAND HARBOUR BOARD THANKS YOU.

The ship's Royal Marine band is now blaring louder, the parade wheels into Queen Street, base drum booming, side drums rattling above swelling cheers. Over Quay Street an enormous banner sways in light airs, says:

WELL DONE ACHILLES. THE GOVERNMENT AND PEOPLE OF NEW ZEALAND WELCOME YOU BACK.

Thunderous applause; the ship's band resounds off streamered buildings; airforce bands; army bands; Highland pipe bands; civil bands all adding to the pounding beat of marching men from every service. They march proud.

HAERE MAI HAERE MAI HAERE MAI.
WELCOME FROM DUNEDIN
CHRISTCHURCH GREETS YOU.
NAPIER'S GREETINGS.

Stretched across every intersection and from intervening buildings for the length of Queen Street there are banners from thirty-five New Zealand cities and towns, flags and garlands, streamers above a third of Auckland's population crowding both sides of the route. It snows confetti onto radiant pretty faces, onto laughing and cheering men's faces. Victoria Street intersection (Battleship Corner to the Navy) comes and goes; military marches reverberating, rising and falling; bugles glinting; big drums pounding. Wellesley Street, wide, the Civic Theatre; girls jumping up and down, throwing kisses. Now the vast open space fronting Auckland's Town Hall. Band Major's ordering their drummers and musicians into designated positions; commands screaming above the tumult to deploy units before

Achilles' victory march up Queen Street, Army support.

the flag-draped massive dais; *Leander* detachment; *Philomel* detachment; RNZAF; RNZAC; Cadets; Scouts; Guides; schoolchildren in their thousands with teachers in control. All tightly wedged. Speeches long or short according to egotism, replied to by Captain Parry. A hush – a drum roll – complete quiet under blue skies – then 'God Save the King' sung in a swelling uplift by 100,000 patriotic voices.

Achilles files into the Town Hall for an official luncheon while Lady Davis as Mayoress entertains next of kin in the Concert Chamber. More speeches and Captain Parry's reply; Grace by Auckland's Bishop; the luncheon; then singly and in greater numbers men find their way to loved ones; home; to visit friends; friendly pubs; back into Auckland's wartime life.

CHAPTER X

Leander *Goes West*

WITH *Achilles* on the South American coast, and with the RN sloops *Leith* and *Wellington* dispatched by Admiralty to Singapore, *Leander* became the New Zealand Station workhorse. On 30 August 1939 in preparation for war, she embarked an advance party of army personnel and sped 3,000 miles north to Fanning Island cable station, a vital mid-Pacific link in the Empire's communications; en route on 3 September learning that war had been declared against Germany. Some of her complement had been drafted to *Achilles* before she left Auckland and Navy Office Wellington had been busily informing all RNVR headquarters what types of ratings and officers should be called up immediately. Stan Roy, an Otago RNVR telegraphist, yawned acknowledgement when called by his mother to get up; it was 6.45, a dark Dunedin morning as he followed his Dad through the bathroom, talked as usual at breakfast, then biked off to work. At 8.40 a.m. he was called to the office phone, unusual, not encouraged unless essential. A voice was trying to conceal its excitement: 'Is that Mister Stanley Roy?' 'Yes, I'm Stanley Roy.' 'You are to report to RNVR Head-quarters immediately – Yes that's right, you're wanted there straight away.' Shortly after 10 a.m., having rushed home to tell Ma, he was standing in the familiar dockside Reservist building with Jack Baker, Ralph Bowler, Nathaniel Millar and George Gibbs, all being handed travel warrants for that morning's 11.35 train to Lyttelton, ferry to Wellington, and next afternoon's Limited to Auckland, there to report directly to *Philomel's* Regulating Office. 'Yes, yes, yes,' in answer to their anxious questions, 'and there'll be a P & T van waiting at the Auckland Station. Now, GET WEAVING! And lads, good luck.' On 13 September when *Leander* berthed at Calliope Wharf, Stan Roy humped his recently issued kit and hammock up her gangway, on his way with other reservists to their various mess-decks.

Two weeks later the cruiser wallowed off Campbell Island in sub-Ant-arctic gales which rolled her dangerously, wrenching whole banks of lockers off bulkheads and crashing them down among fragmented crockery, wrecked bread bins and mess-gear ankle deep in sugar, tea, the overturned gash-can and infiltrated ocean. Finding nothing but sheep and nesting albatrosses on the tussocked slopes bounding Campbell Island's navigable inlets, *Leander* searched Auckland Island's Port Ross and Carnley Harbour before being recalled to Wellington then Auckland. But Navy Office wasn't satisfied, The German freighter *Erlangen*, having loaded in New Zealand ports, had sailed from Dunedin on 28 August to coal at Port Kembla for her long journey home, and instead of heading for Australia she'd been sighted on the 30th off Stewart Island. Intelligence knew she'd been warned away from British Empire ports and, estimating that she'd have insufficient coal to reach South America, sent *Leander* down for another search of the islands deep below New Zealand. But again she came away empty handed and it was two years before events proved that her quarry had in fact been there.

In April 1941 while establishing a coast-watching station on Auckland Island, an expanse of felled trees was found at the extremity of Carnley Harbour. Then in late July 1941 the cruiser *Newcastle* intercepted *Erlangen* to the north-east of Montevideo. When challenged she set herself on fire, but on being taken in tow she sank. Her log revealed that she had concealed herself in a deep inlet overhung by trees at the head of Carnley Harbour's north arm, there bunkering with 500 tons of sawn Rata tree trunks to augment her remaining coal. Then assisted by improvised canvas hatch-cover sails she departed 7 October and reached Chile's Puerto Montt on 11 October, from there sailing around the South American coast in nightly stages to reach Buenos Aires.

So, back to late 1939 when thousands of volunteers were encamped throughout New Zealand, training for its 1st Echelon 2nd Expeditionary Force, while arrangements were being discussed with London for their transport overseas. A pocket battleship had been reported near Madagascar, and the possibility of her intent to attack the proposed New Zealand/Australian Army convoy somewhere along its route needed top-level consideration. On 29 November NZNB advised Admiralty that *Leander* was being held in Auckland at twelve hours notice in the event the pocket battleship might be reported in New Zealand waters. If so *Leander* would shadow the enemy until favourable night conditions enabled an attack by gunfire and torpedoes. But as it transpired, the raider, *Graf Spee*, returned to the Atlantic where *Ajax*, *Achilles* and *Exeter* forced her to scuttle herself in the Plate Estuary; so preparations for escorting the 1st Echelon were finalised.

Admiral Andrew Cunningham dispatched the battleship *Ramillies* to Wellington to strongarm the RAN's 8″ cruiser *Canberra* and New Zealand's smaller *Leander*. Their convoy of fast liners comprised *Empress of Britain*, *Orion*, *Strathaird*, *Rangitata*, *Dunera*, and Poland's *Sobieski*, the latter two going down to Lyttelton for the South Island troops and being escorted back out through Godley Heads by *Leander* on 5 January 1940. Next forenoon in Cook Strait they were signalled into allocated dispositions within the main body from Wellington then, led by *Ramillies* at 18 knots with *Leander* and *Canberra* on either beam, the six liners in two columns surged westward for an easy Tasman Sea crossing, some waiting outside Sydney Heads while others entered to top-up fuel tanks, and hours later emerging with Australia's transports *Empress of Japan, Orcades, Orford, Otranto,* and *Strathnaver* manoeuvring into convoy formation. The County Class *Australia* was now to starboard of *Ramillies* as the eleven liners turned south for Bass Strait; while *Leander* returned to Auckland.

There were essentials such as lawns awaiting attention in New Zealand, the 6 February 1940 Waitangi Treaty Centenary to be celebrated with our naval parade in black-booted, white-gaitered No 6s white belted, their polished 303s white strapped with gleaming fixed bayonets, and *Leander's* Royal Marine band glinting as it rendered past Royal Naval glories. Then ten days later in Hauraki Gulf, she did a reduced-charge, full-calibre attack against *Wakakura's* towed battle-practice target, leaving the trawler's skipper and his crew to pick up the bits of shattered framework and tow the target back inside.

By late February the 2nd Echelon had assembled in camps close to Wellington, fully trained and equipped, eager to go overseas in those adventurous days, while our government haggled with Whitehall about the inadequacy of Admiralty's escorts, and the need for more anti-raider groups along the proposed convoy routes. So delay followed delay for weeks until 24 April when *Leander* arrived in the capital, having been told by the Minister of Defence before leaving Auckland: 'It is the policy of Government that in future one cruiser will remain on the New Zealand Station while the other is overseas under Admiralty control. *Achilles* has been recalled and you will operate in whatever capacity Admiralty suggests and Government approves.'

And now in Wellington's cold rain men chased their caps along Feather-ston Street to the amusement of pedestrian capitalists inured to such vagaries. The Royal Mail liner *Andes* had gone to Lyttelton for South Island's contingent, and *Empress of Britain, Empress of Japan,* and *Aquitania* had already embarked North Island's troops who were exploiting an unofficial freedom of the city. HMASs *Australia* and *Canberra* arrived four days later, and this time *Canberra* went to Lyttelton as escort while *Leander* frequented New Zealand's Centennial Exhibition functions until Thursday, 2 May 1940 when farewellers gathered in cold blustery conditions to be drenched while waving bravely to the departing transports. It was rough in Cook Strait where *Canberra* signalled *Andes* into position, but rougher still when the convoy pounded into an obstinate Tasman at 18 knots with no soldiers apparent on their promenade decks, and few sailors topside on the cruisers.

A brief fuel stop at Sydney, no leave, then out into the wake of Britain's

RNVRs mustered at Wellington HQ before embarking on *Aquitania* for
overseas with 2nd Echelon 2nd NZEF, May 1940.

73,000-ton *Queen Mary* and lesser *Mauretania*, accompanied overhead by
RAAF Avro Anson long-range reconnaissance bombers.

Telegraphists were reading a constant stream of messages transmitted
and repeated inter-station on Sydney, Melbourne, and Perth Naval W/T
H/F bands; while men off-watch in their messdecks were listening to
newscasts detailing Chamberlain's inadequacy, then next day his resignation
and Winston Churchill's takeover as Prime Minister. Germany was invading
Holland, Belgium, Luxembourg – British troops were pouring into Belgium
as *Leander* entered Fremantle for a Friday and Saturday ashore with thousands of Anzac servicemen. Up the line to Perth's unstinted hospitality,
ribald friendship in each pub: 'The bloody war can wait a pair of flamin'
days, right Kiwi?' 'Suits me Wallaby, here, grab this beer for your drongo
mate,' an almost impossible manoeuvre in the clamour fronting every bar
in town.

By midday Sunday, 12 May the escorts and transports, except *Queen Mary*
and *Mauretania* who were too big for entry, had refuelled, and a forest of
waving femininity waved goodbye as each ship passed inside the crowded
breakwater and out into the Indian Ocean. Only ten days from Wellington's
early winter, men were experiencing increasing heat, 100 degrees fahrenheit
in the Main W/T office and considerably more in the boiler rooms; then
on Tuesday afternoon three soldiers were reported overboard from *Empress
of Japan*, but although *Leander* searched until dark, two of them drowned
or were taken by sharks, the other being rescued by his own troopship.
Then next day after being sentenced to ten days in cells, Seaman Boy Lloyd

leapt over *Leander*'s guardrails and she left the line again, fortunately finding the now much wiser lad, ensuring he made it safely into confinement. On the 15th, BBC shortwave said Holland had capitulated after destroying all fuel reserves and ordering its naval and mercantile ships to Allied ports; the Dutch East Indies were declared neutral; and because of Mussolini's suspected leanings toward Germany all Allied shipping was being diverted from the Mediterranean. So, with the short route via Suez Canal no longer available, our convoy now nearing the Indian Ocean equator changed course south to the Cape route, and *Leander* detached with orders to join Cunningham's Mediterranean Fleet recently established at Alexandria. RN cruisers and destroyers from distant stations and the Royal Australian Navy were being incorporated into squadrons and flotillas there; one Australian cruiser, HMAS *Sydney*, several hours ahead of *Leander*, signalling: 'Hello Kiwi, see you soon,' when leaving Colombo as we entered to refuel. And as soon as dipsticks registered full tanks she manoeuvred out of the closely packed Ceylonese port, sped at 25 knots across the Arabian Sea to gulp oil from Aden's Anglo-Iranian pipeline terminal, then hurried north through Bab el Mandeb Straits into the Red Sea.

Below-deck temperatures were now up to 130 to 145 degrees fahrenheit, turning signal pads to pulp when sweat rivuletted down telegraphists' arms and off their pencils as they copied constant transmissions. Off Perim we passed the Senior Naval Officer Red Sea Force's (SNORS) flagship *Liverpool*, then when entering the Gulf of Suez, the old cruisers *Carlisle* and *Durban* going south with four new destroyers *Khartoum*, *Kandahar*, *Kimberley* and *Kingston*, to replace *Sydney* and *Leander* who'd initially been allocated to SNORS's squadron. Fleet dispositions were under reorganisation almost hourly as Admiralty concurred with Cunningham's requirements in the worsening Mediterranean situation. Her 29-knot Red Sea transit had burned all paint off the lower half of *Leander*'s funnel, red rust was blooming where bow waves had stripped the ship's side since leaving Wellington, so while at anchor among a mass of Suez shipping awaiting Canal entry, the cruiser vanished under a festoon of ropes attached to planks, supporting overalled matelots armed with pots of crab-fat and long-handled brushes. A Canal pilot embarked during the First Dog and Port Tewfik glided to obscurity behind khaki-coloured brick buildings, tall palms and struggling shrubbery; then a monotony of scorched desert reaching eastward beyond rusting relics of the Great War, wavering lake mirages, and away to a range of barren hills floating in the haze of burning atmosphere.

From the bridge and foc'sle men shaded their eyes to peer at the ribbon of water stretching ahead to eternity, saw it fading in the short Egyptian twilight, then remarked on the simplicity of canal marking when the ship's port and starboard searchlights stabbed the darkness, illuminating reflectors widely spaced along either bank. *Leander*'s phosphorescent bow wave rippled lazily along the compacted earth slopes in places stone walled, rose up her bows as she increased revolutions through the waterway's lakes, then fell away completely near midnight when PO Sig's 'Nifty' Chapman flashed his ship's pennants to Port Said's cruiser guardship *Gloucester*, before we anchored off Navy Office. At 0400, having picked up Mediterranean charts, bags of mail and correspondence, we were under way again, arriving ten hours later at Alexandria and easing gently between flotillas of destroyers, lines of battleships, gaggles of Sunderland flying boats, and ominous black-hulled submarines side by side near the cruiser billet. 'Leave till 2300!' Although granted permission to discontinue shaving, men's unkempt early stubble didn't deter those packing liberty boats beyond normal capacity.

On completion of the Afternoon Watch liberty men just managed to make the 1630 pinnace, had their No 6s saturated by a wind-blown chop, and were landed miles from town at a timber-yard jetty when the coxswain lost his way to No 14 Naval Steps. Suburban trams rattled by our long line of gesticulating Kiwis without stopping, and Gyppo natives materialised shouting: '*Bak'sheesh* master!', begging for cigarettes, begging for '*Filoosh piastres* master!' They got a lot of abuse, and disappeared near armed sentries guarding camouflaged oil and petrol tanks. We forced our way aboard an open bus, whose native passengers objected when leaned over or jammed into corners until it arrived at Mohammed Ali Square. Now among throngs of odorous Arabs in long gowns, clean Egyptians in European clothing, and smartly dressed French girls arm-in-arm with French matelots, we were at a loss, explored modern seven-storey business and shopping centres, and wandered through drab streets of native housing alive with urchins and skinny thugs. With 96 piastres for £1 sterling we felt rich, ate in the Fleet Club for 3 pias, drank in Stanley Bay's Acteon Cafe for 10 pias a glass of coloured meths said to be whisky, but refused advances from Sister Street's bacchantes outside their tawdry bedrooms. We ignored massive posters advertising donkeys having sex with exotic Eastern girls, paid for a more natural but equally immoral stage show packed by local inhabitants, then emerged into fresh air to take the reins from an obliging gharry owner who let us drive it along the waterfront. By 9 p.m. it was pitch dark and side streets were avoided, but street vendors still wailed: 'Clean fruit, sahib! Watches mastah, torches! Scarabs genuine from the pyramids! Beer, good for the Kiwi!' Then sidling close they whispered, 'Here, you want girl, Spanish Fly. Verry verry clean girl for you only, Kiwi!' It had taken them little time to know where these new sailors had come from, but they wasted their breath and it was time to find the Naval Landing. No boat at the timber yard. Another hour wasted in total dark trying to find a naval boat, anything that floated, eventually contacting Greentree and Randall to share a feluccah owner who agreed to everything said, rowed for a while until the wind filled his sail, then sped off into the unknown – rounding the stern of a dimly visible battleship whose sentries yelled blue murder, passing moored flying boats and destroyers who all roared invectives from the dark, then fouling a Tribal Class destroyer's mooring cable and being directed to *Leander* by a sleepy young OOW. It was now nearer 2 a.m. than 2300 when leave expired, but being some of the first back aboard we were told to disappear for'ard.

Even though the fleet was not yet at full strength it appeared formidable, categorically comprising in allocated areas:

Battleships	Cruisers	Destroyers	
Warspite	*Calypso*	*Stuart* (Aust)	*Ilex*
Valiant	*Capetown*	*Vampire* (Aust)	*Isis*
Malaya	*Gloucester*	*Vendetta* (Aust)	*Dainty*
Royal Sovereign	*Leander* (NZ)	*Voyager* (Aust)	*Decoy*
Resolution	*Neptune*	*Waterhen* (Aust)	*Janus*
Ramillies	*Orion*	*Hereward*	*Juno*
Lorraine (Fr)	*Sydney* (Aust)	*Hostile*	*Hero*
Atlas (Greek)	*Duquesne* (Fr)	*Havock*	*Hasty*
	Duquay Troin (Fr)	*Hyperion*	*Mohawk*
	Tourville (Fr)	*Imperial*	*Nubian*
	Suffren (Fr)	*Defender*	*Diamond*
		Also a flotilla of French and Greek destroyers and Submarines.	

Aircraft Carrier	Submarines
Eagle	*Osiris – Phoenix – Oswald*

Fleet Repair Ship
Resource

Additionally there were submarine and destroyer mother ships, Royal Fleet Auxiliaries, tugs, water-barges, boom-defence-vessels, steam pinnaces, and a massive floating dock; while ashore the harbour and naval buildings were ringed by searchlight units, A/A batteries, and harbour defence balloons tethered to heavy vehicles in readiness for sending aloft against air intrusion if necessary. Over the next five days all ships exercised a complex network of W/T communications to be used as a massed fleet at sea, and during air attack in harbour. Alexandria's overhead defence was set out as an imaginary three-dimensional cube, made up of hundreds of smaller cubes each given a number and identity letter. The whole area was covered by radar, and each ship and shore battery was allocated one cube to fire at when its letter and number was morsed by W/T from the controlling ship *Valiant*. Thus any intruder detected in those segments would immediately encounter bursting anti-aircraft shells. Using dummy ammunition the fleet's A/A gunners soon excelled at day and night firing, their 4", 5.5", multi-barrelled short-range weapons, and even high-angle main armament being aligned in anticipation; but as yet it was 'For Exercise' only and the 'Enemy' were aircraft from RAF bases.

There were diversions; a bus trip to the Sphinx, Pompei's Pillar, and the Pyramids – 45 piastres including tea and tips; but insufficient time to absorb those monuments of ancient civilisation; and a second one cancelled on its scheduled Saturday, 1 June. All leave was restricted to 1600 with the ship 'under steam for 1900'. No longer a unit of the 7th Cruiser Squadron's 2nd Division *Leander* again transited the Canal, telescopes and lookout glasses focused on a bevy of white-skinned service women frolicking in the shallows of Ismailia's beaches, then later suffering an intense heat change south of Tewfik en route to Aden to become SNORS' flagship. But a W/T message directed the ship to Port Sudan to embark Rear Admiral A.J.L. Murray and his staff there. No admiral on the stone wharf awaiting our arrival, surely not one of the gowned Sudanese peering up as we peered down, so relax. Four hours passed in idle contemplation, then the big cruiser *Liverpool* arrived; Captain Horan and some of *Leander*'s officers were downgraded to lesser cabins as humping parties sweated intership with VIP baggage, half of SNORS' personal liquor was spirited below to become one of *Leander*'s best-kept secrets, and Rear Admiral Murray silently resolved to find the New Zealand cruiser lots of rotten jobs in retaliation.

Meantime Sudan's southern neighbour, Italian Somaliland, hosted a sizable force of destroyers, submarines, and military aircraft at Massawa, a theoretical stone-throw distant; their Marchetti Savoia bombers being among the world's largest and their fighters reputedly fast. Intelligence who'd been probing Il Duce's mind, expected him to take sides with der Fuehrer on account of Britain's and France's retreat in the face of Germany's military might. *Leander*'s messdeck tacticians were taking bets on Musso's hour of decision, and a rendezvous with the RN sloop *Grimsby* was ordered and kept to instruct her secretly to intercept and board the Italian ammunition ship *Umbria*, reported by Admiralty cypher to be leaving the Canal for Massawa. Having given *Grimsby* his orders Admiral Murray returned to Port Sudan, keeping his cruiser's whereabouts unknown to the nearby Italian naval base. Legally Italy was neutral and still was when *Grimsby* ushered *Umbria* to an outside anchorage covered by 6" defence batteries.

An armed guard from *Leander* boarded her to ensure her captivity, but that evening they flashed a message that she was being scuttled. Intense activity. Tugs and fire-fighting gear were dispatched, but with none eager to be aboard if she blew up, she settled on the bottom with only her mast tips showing; her Captain and crew now under armed escort for questioning.

'My instructions,' he said, 'were to destroy my ship and cargo in the event of capture, when my country declared war on your country.'

'But Italy has not declared a state of war to exist,' from Admiral Murray.

'Maybe not,' in perfect English, 'but your sloop would not have intercepted me unless war between us was imminent. So his action must be recorded as piracy.'

Further interrogation of the Captain and his officers revealed that her seacocks had been opened and their shafts hacksawn off to prevent closure. But now her cargo of aircraft fuel, ammunition and casks of fulminate of mercury were no longer a threat. Within hours SNORS was told that Italy had declared war on the Allies; the sixty-eight prisoners in *Leander's* recreation space filed down a gangway into waiting army trucks semi-circled by prone machine-gunners behind cocked weapons and, at 2300 on Monday, 10 June 1940 *Leander* sailed, convinced she would see action inside the hour.

She stalked a blacked-out vessel in an area where no British ships were listed, remained all night at the first degree of readiness while working round to have her nicely positioned for a dawn attack, then cursed the wasted hours when she identified herself as a British tramp. Where were all those Italian merchantmen heard only hours ago on the 500kc/s marine frequency, their submarines and destroyers D/F'd and plotted; now not a whisper on any manned W/T receiver, not a ripple on the Red Sea's sun-burnished surface. Only heat. Continual thirst and sweat. Then over by the first day's setting sun, bombers from the direction of Italian Eritrea. Raucus undulating bugles rushed gunners to their A/A mounts; S1 and S2 twin 4″ swung to meet them, multi-barrelled .5″ swivelled and elevated while the 6″ turrets tracked to be on target with breeches flashing open to receive fused shells. Rangefinders locked on to the distant aircraft, passing continual corrections for range and elevation to gunnery control, and the main W/T transmitter hummed and glowed awaiting notice from the bridge to inform Aden Naval W/T she was being attacked by eight enemy aircraft. 'Why doesn't the bloody skipper open fire?!' The leading bomber was flashing identity as they roared low overhead in two waves, Wellingtons from Aden's Khormaksar Airfield returning from raids on Asmara and Gura; but the original leader of their nine-plane flight had been shot down.

With the Walrus scouting ahead for minefields, submarines and surface vessels, *Leander* continued south, diverting to Kamaran Island for an Italian Somaliland prisoner and his armed guard awaiting passage to Aden, streamed paravanes for Perim Strait's night passage and got a hell of a surprise when the port one snagged something big and tore adrift. After sun-up in the Gulf of Aden, Signalman Sammy Goddard swapped messages with HMAS *Hobart* who said she'd repulsed several air attacks already, and added that Italian bombers had killed civilians and servicemen in raids on Aden's city centre which was heavily damaged. Then hours later the towering rock heights of Aden wavered under a blazing sun, outer harbour shipping miraged clear above the surface and buildings assumed bizarre shapes, all gradually resuming normality as we negotiated the 'safe channel' through Aden's defensive minefields.

After *Leander* moored off Post Office Quay, liberty men found most shop windows shuttered, doors locked, and the owners away in outlying regions for safety, but a pair of enterprising French brothers still operated their second-storey verandahed restaurant overlooking the square and nearby waterfront. Here as opposed to the smoke-filled NAAFI Canteen's typical 'bangers, beans and mash', one could sit at clean white table-clothed tables beneath large overhead electric fans enjoying iced lime and lemon, before being served chicken, chips and eggs suspiciously like the ovum and original seagull, but in that relaxed atmosphere, reminiscent of a distant civilisation. Almost within hailing distance *Leander* lay secured fore and aft to buoys, K-Class destroyers similarly moored ahead and astern of her, with Austra- lia's cruiser *Hobart* passing up-harbour to refuel at the pipeline terminal; and further out but no longer in the war several Italian freighters rode at anchor, displaying White Ensigns lazily furling and unfurling above the ships' red white and green national flags. In fading twilight men retraced the route to their 2030 boat and were soon below in familiar messdecks cluttered with occupied slung hammocks, Middle Watch men almost naked on tables and stools in the dark, asleep before being shaken minutes before midnight. Some off-watch groups went topside into Aden's relatively less heat, to sleep on their opened hammocks, but others still preferred their messdeck niche and braved the stench of sweating bodies.

On Saturday, 15 June the BBC said French forces were retiring from Paris to avoid its destruction, France was still fighting and Britain had offered Reynaud a Franco-British union; dramatic; but we were involved closer at hand in the opening rounds of war with Italy. The Norwegian tanker *James Stove*'s SOS from 10 miles outside Aden said she'd just been torpedoed. Planes and A/S vessels saw a disappearing periscope near nightfall but depth-charge attacks were unsuccessful and it seemed the submarine had escaped; a destroyer rescued the tanker's survivors as she blazed out of control and SNORS ordered her to be sunk by gunfire. Two days later a destroyer made an uncertain asdic contact in the same area, then on Wednesday forenoon the A/S minesweeper *Moonstone* radioed success. Working close inshore she depth-charged a contact and instantly became engaged in a close-range duel as a huge black conning tower emerged. Manoeuvring to comb two torpedo tracks speeding at her, *Moonstone* slammed repeated 4″ shells into the Italian's conning tower and surfaced hull, machine-gunned men overboard as they scrambled down casing-ladders endeavouring to reach their for'ard and rear guns, then crunched alongside to put a boarding party on the now stationary submarine. Her captain, bridge officers and topside crew were lying around dead, exploding shells had wrecked her upperworks, and gaping holes made it impossible for her to dive. Having secured her against scuttling, collected her codes and mine charts, and a decoded message indicating a night rendezvous with another submarine in the Persian Gulf, *Moonstone* towed her victim, *Galileo Galilei*, into Aden amid loud applause from anchored merchantmen and warships. SNORS immediately radioed the escort vessel *Shoreham* to keep *Galileo Galilei*'s tryst, and grinned satisfaction days later when informed this was done, ramming and sinking the surprised enemy sub at night when it surfaced.

Any success right then was heartening. Over two weeks we'd heard about naval and army losses at Dunkirk, heard our west European allies being overthrown in rapid sequence, found ourselves at war with the 1914 ally Italy, saw America standing aloof as a neutral observer, and realised that with Premier Reynaud ousted by Marshal Pétain, the French fleet could soon be under Nazi Grand Admiral Raeder's control. But not being 'top brass' we let Churchill and Cunningham do the worrying, felt that the Royal Navy would assert dominance over all oceans including Il Duce's Mare Nostrum, and two-fingered *Hobart*'s loudmouths as she passed on alternate departures and re-entries. Probably for close liaison with Aden's RAF and Military Commandants, Rear Admiral Murray kept *Leander* in harbour as a mast to put his flag on; so we thumped off lots of 4″ A/A shells at high-level bombers; winced when thumped back by their near misses; then expressed pleasure in the cooler temperatures at sea en route Perim Harbour on 24 June for a look at the destroyer *Khartoum*. Only her funnel and upperworks showed above oil-covered water. Somehow one of her torpedoes had fired from its tube during maintenance, exploding in her after structure and breaking her back. *Kandahar* had already embarked her ship's company and departed for Aden, so *Leander* was left the task of retrieving confidential material and semi-secret equipment from the mess of thick oil and debris, transferring it aboard by her cutter and whalers, then cleaning up at nightfall as Admiral Murray relaxed, remembering his purloined wine and spirits.

Meantime from across the Gulf of Aden in French Somaliland, SNO Djibouti reported seven determined bomber raids on shipping and harbour

installations; and closer at hand the Greek freighter *Kastor* ran aground on
a submerged reef. She needed assistance to get off, so Ralph Greentree and
a portable transceiver were loaned to an Arabian tug, which arrived
simultaneously with two Italian bombers and spattered them with heavy-
machine-gun bullets, driving them off then hauling *Kastor* free to re-enter
harbour. About now the A/A cruiser *Carlisle* who'd been dispatched to
Djibouti because of her new-fangled radar installation and massive anti-aircraft armament, detected approaching enemy bombers and alerted shore
batteries who joined in a concerted barrage which downed plane after
low-flying plane. Later arrivals flew higher and wasted their bombs on the
port's surrounding barren countryside. Again meantime, *Kingston* had
depth-charged a contact off the Eritrean coast, but had to return to Aden
to refuel. Air reconnaissance reported two enemy destroyers and a submarine on their way from Massawa to the damaged submarine's assistance,
so SNORS decided it was time for him to do some seatime, that night in
company with *Kingston* and *Kandahar* he sped north to intercept them. Few
off duty remained below, preferring the cool wind created by the 30-knot
dash, entertained by phosphorescent bow waves illuminating the three
ships' sides when cresting foc'sle high, disappearing, turmoiling above the
rumbling propellers and cataracting away astern into the dark as luminous
rivers.

Dawn stand-to came and went without incident, the forenoon wore on,
aircraft lookouts changing hourly for alertness; *Kingston* cleaving whitecaps,
flinging spray while morsing: $O-A = 1 AC - 325 - 4 - 11 = AR$. She was
already firing at the 4-mile distant, 11,000-feet-high enemy aircraft bearing
325 degrees. *Leander*'s twin 4" mounts swung, elevated and fired, reloaded
elevated again and fired, again and again. Earsplitting blasts that left heads
ringing. Black smoke erupted high around a shining speck. Towering
discoloured waterspouts rose between *Leander* and *Kingston* as shockwaves
thwacked our hull, their muffled detonations lost amid our gunfire. Then
silence followed by a bugled 'All Clear' as the Italian disappeared toward
Massawa to report our presence. But *Kingston* was flashing SNORS she'd
seen a periscope, and was told to attack it, while a lookout on *Leander*'s
after searchlight platform was yelling about a torpedo track seen sizzling
across our immediate wake. Now mere miles south of Massawa it seemed
the British force wasn't welcome, and although the earlier reported Italian
destroyers had not yet appeared, *Kandahar* away to port was signalling the
bearing and distance of another submarine, this one stationary in the
off-beach shallows.

With his glasses focusing on the distant speck, Admiral Murray ordered
the destroyer to destroy it by gunnery, our Walrus recently catapulted off
armed with A/S bombs, to meantime spot and report *Kandahar*'s fall of

shot; but unable to contact the destroyer by W/T, the amphibian was telling our 2nd Office operator *Kandahar*'s shells were landing between the beach and the submarine whose two guns were retaliating. SNORS curtly ordered *Kandahar* to assume seaward screen and *Kingston* to close the enemy to destroy it by torpedoes. Once more the Walrus radioed a sequence of misses, having watched the trails spearing either side to end abruptly on the beach. Murray wasn't happy.

'Captain Horan,' as he turned to our cruiser's popular skipper, 'please see what your Walrus can do about that blasted submarine.'

'Certainly, Sir, although I'd like to blow the cobwebs out of our six–inch.'

'Give the aircraft a bowl first, then we'll see.'

Ship-to-Walrus messages ensued and the ungainly amphibian plummeted through sporadic defensive gunfire to release its bombs. Near splashes but no explosions. A spiral climb for height then down he came again with better effect, one bomb bursting close enough to convince the submariners it was time to go, yet even as they took to their inflatable the target was still intact. SNORS' face and neck had gone a deeper shade of red. Bridge officers refrained from comment.

'Alright Captain Horan, let's see what your New Zealanders are re-nowned for.'

All four turrets had been training inshore as *Leander* cruised up and down the line of activity, ranging on the submarine since the DCT's crew first locked on to it, each turret's Guns Ready lights glowing red on the bridge repeater. The briefest of telephoned exchanges, then warning tinkles as firing mechanisms activated. *Leander* whipped full length and men in exposed positions winced when the eight-gun reverberation smote their ears, when acrid cordite fumes stung their nostrils and lungs. *KK KK* morsed through earphones to indicate an immediate straddle. Stress lines vanished from the Admiral's face:

'Ask your Gunnery Officer to destroy the enemy, Captain.'

'Aye Aye, sir,' a pause, then a thumbs-up to 'Guns' standing by his intercom.

'ALL GUNS, RAPID SALVOES!' and *Leander* was engulfed in a thunderous chaos of mayhem in messdecks and below deck offices. Now no more a menace to shipping, the distorted *Evangalista Torricelli* had been lifted bodily and turned forty degrees; our bridge again talked freely, and SNORS signalled the Walrus: 'Bloody great spotting!' But this atmosphere of *bon volonte* was short-lived. Bugles were chasing men to 'REPEL AIRCRAFT!' stations as the drone of large aircraft intensified above low cloud. At several thousand feet they passed over in waves of three to attack from different directions. With radar control a thing of the future, P1 and P2 4″ gun-crews were firing steadily until restrained by their mounts' upperworks-protection stoppers, when S1 and S2 commenced firing as the passing bombers were now appearing in *their* sights, triple airscrews turning ever so slowly, Italian emblems so distinct. One Marchetti Savoia rocked visibly in a shellburst at 2,000 feet, then columns of angry water erupted between *Leander* and *Kandahar* as again that day they reeled to near misses, cupped their ears against the sharp crack of 4″ guns and heavier concussions when the 6″ fired. More Savoias emerged from distant cloud to roar overhead through everything thrown up at them.

For brief moments some not required in the RCO ran for the unmanned port and starboard Torpedo Remote Control platforms to see the conflict. *Leander* was heeling hard in a lather of boiling wake, slewing dramatically to be an elusive target. Speed was vital. Five big bombers were wheeling in arrowhead formation, straightening in a shallow dive with throttles wide open, their target *Kingston*, a weaving foc'sle hidden aft of her raked funnel by dense rolling smoke. Nearer and nearer, their combined fifteen engines a crescendo obliterated by the thunder of gunfire and exploding bombs. *Kingston* showed through a gap in the towering black waterspouts, her bows angling slowly skyward, her rolling smokescreen now pillared vertical: 'SHE'S BEEN HIT! THE POOR BASTARD'S SINKING!' But as we ran back to our RCO someone was shouting that she was safe.

Right then there was *Leander* to consider, more imperatively ourselves. Things had been too easy for our cruiser and the Italians had that in mind. As this flight retired out of range another approached to attack, and for an eternity it seemed, we were in a nightmare of booming explosions, crashing gunfire, the reverberating beat of multi-engined bombers, wave after wave rumbling overhead through curtains of close-barrage retaliation. Massive shapes swerved low above swaying aerials, climbed into the distance and turned for their next approach. At times *Leander* raced through the deluge of collapsing upheavals; at times men topside glimpsed the two destroyers cleaving peaceful blue seas some miles abeam, still firing but ignored while *Leander* became the quarry. An exceptionally loud detonation impacted against our hull. A string of heavies had exploded 40 feet abreast along our length, screeching fragments inboard to richochet into every imaginable crevice from foremast crow's nest to the Ship's Company Heads, penetrating thin bulkheads but not causing injury. Then eventually with their ammunition expended the enemy flew away, this time not to regroup, not to turn and come thundering in again, but to return to their Massawan base.

SNORS was ordering *Kingston* and *Kandahar* onto our port and starboard quarters for the long run home; men were still shaken, but jubilant when congratulatory flashlamps indicated kills for the Admiral's gunners. They'd seen one go down in an almighty splash and flame-tongued explosion;

watched another trailing ominous black smoke while flying away erratically; and now they were learning that others had been observed in the distance, downed by *Leander*'s fused 6″ shellbursts. *Kingston* reported many leg injuries to her crew at the time her bows impacted skyward, a sizable defect list would require attention when convenient, but meanwhile she was operational in essential capacities: 'Would you please embark a cook with compound leg fractures?' The three ships had fought off determined attacks throughout two long hours; sixty-five 'close'-category heavies were observed exploding near one or other of the force; the destroyers' ammunition expenditure and claimed hits were being assessed; and a walk past the 418 brass cylinders stacked in *Leander*'s waist confirmed the fight her 4″ A/A gunners had just experienced. Countless rounds of small-arms ammunition were being listed for replacement, also thirty-two fusable 6″. Men now expressed complete confidence in the gunnery department, also in 'Crash' Horan for the contortions he'd put *Leander* through to avoid being bombed; and that night in all messdecks men were hearing Radio Roma's news in English saying: 'Our Massawa based heavy bombers today attacked a British cruiser and its destroyer escorts in the Red Sea. Some of the enemy ships were left in a sinking condition. Three of our aircraft falled to return to base.'

Early next morning *Leander* was in line astern at 10 knots negotiating Aden's safe channel. 'Blackie' shouldering a long-handled mallet stood by the anchor cable shackle, ready when so ordered to belt out its locking pin, while he and the foc'sle party were taking in whatever attractions the harbour and its shipping offered. In this Aden heat their uniform usually comprised a pair of worn-out underpants and a pair of Arabian sandals; and one similarly attired lad was peering from the open Rec Space door when a comedian grabbed his vital parts from behind. It hurt, and the startled youngster's 'LET GO!' needed no loud hailer. Blackie's mallet swung involuntarily; away went the pin; the released anchor cable bounded along the foc'sle and down its hawse; and pandemonium erupted. Emergency orders had *Leander*'s propellers thrashing madly astern, taking headway off as *Kandahar* and *Kingston* shot past to port and starboard, fortunately avoiding a collision and the minefield, as *Leander* came to a shuddering standstill, all the port cable out and some of its links stretched. She cautiously winched it in then proceeded redfaced to her moorings off Steamer Point; this perhaps concluding A.J.L. Murray's introduction to the New Zealand Division of the Royal Navy. Having decided he could concentrate more effectively on his overall Red Sea Force if domiciled ashore, he took his flag and retinue off *Leander* with her Communication Department's blessing. No longer the Admiral, we would decode only those messages addressed to *Leander* or any groups she might command at sea.

CHAPTER XI

Leander *in the Red Sea, the Indian Ocean and the Med Fleet*

ADEN ON 29 JUNE 1940 was hot, it was always hot, and the ship's tween-decks were unbearable; deadlights clamped down over closed scuttles, punkalouvres ventilating hot air, and off-watch men sweating asleep on tables, the hammock netting, the stools, the deck. Shortly after mooring our gunners ran to Air Defence Stations, banged off more 4″ shells at Massawa's Savoias then ceased firing when signalled that Khormaksar had scrambled its fighters. The bombs intended for Aden and the fleet had been dropped on nearby Crater City, and when sirens ashore wailed the undulating All Clear we relaxed through four hours until piped below, doors and all intakes shut against an approaching sandstorm. Above, to the south, north and east the sun blazed, but the hot air was already being compressed against Aden's barren rocks by a dark wall of driven sand a thousand feet high, all of the west in breadth. It rasped everything in its path, blanketed shipping as it plunged *Leander* into total darkness while rumbling over. All electrical gear was switched off to prevent damage so we breathed foul air in pale secondary lighting and wondered how men in our boiler-rooms were coping, fortunately in harbour routine only one was needed, its forced draught fans were kept running and apart from burnt sand among its furnace waste there was negligible effect.

Next forenoon *Leander* wallowed ahead of HMS *Shoreham* and HMISs *Changte* and *Hindustan*, to be tormented for three days by the gale of yesterday's sandstorm, white-capped rollers reaching under the propellers to heave our sterns high with no regard for stability. We were to rendezvous at noon on 2 July with *Leander*'s first of many Suez-bound convoys taking weapons to the 8th Army, but hours passed in dispersed search before their escort cruiser *Ceres*' masthead lamp signalled their position. Eventually the stragglers were found and shepherded into two columns at 8 knots, relentless walls of Arabian Sea crashing down on their plunging foc'sles, continuous reprimands being flashed to rusting tramps emitting dense smoke.

Days later with the storm a memory, some of the ships distorted into Aden's heat-crazed air; we sent our mail to *Ceres* who was being relieved by *Carlisle*, and by 1900 were off Perim in encroaching darkness. Mussolini had told the world his Massawa-based air and naval forces had closed the Red Sea to Allied shipping, but here to expose the lie stretched ten merchantmen – *Beacon Street, British Hope, British Architect, Anna Odland, Svenor, Akbar, Tubor, William Strachan, Drava,* and RFA *Plumleaf* – being escorted north by the cruisers *Leander, Carlisle,* destroyers *Kandahar, Kingston,* sloops *Shoreham* and HMIS *Chakdina.* To give early warning, HMAS *Hobart* patrolled near Abu Ail, *Ceres* patrolled the Bab el Mandeb Straits, and *Kimberley* stationed near Perim was radioing Aden W/T that she'd just survived six near misses.

Thick haze restricted visibility as the convoy passed within 3 miles of Haycock Island in the Hanish Group, 180 miles from Massawa. By noon we were 140 miles south-east of Massawa and *Carlisle's* radar wasn't functioning; it rarely did, no other ship had yet been fitted so everyone topsides unofficially assisted the ship's lookouts. Throughout the forenoon Khormaksar Blenheims had been trying to find us and when one did an hour before midday, it began an air-search vigil, relieved four-hourly until dusk when we completed a lengthy zig to within sight of Zubair, then zagged the convoy and escorts north-westward into the night. At dawn we were 120 miles north-east of Massawa, by nightfall 214, having had Port Sudan-based Wellesley A/S patrols over the widespread ships since noon; and during the Middle Watch were swapping signals with *Grimsby* who'd brought a string of empties down from Tewfik and Suez. Many aboard *Leander* slept through the exchange of convoys and awoke in daylight to find our escorts now disposed ahead, astern, and on each beam of a southbound convoy in three extensive columns:

Bulmouth	Khandalla	Almenara
British Colonel	Zamzam	Hersteid
British Commodore	Cogra	Garrymedes
Orwell	Ganges	Egyptian Prince
Athelmere	Clifton Hall	Brouxville
Arabistan	Ross	Khosrou

Six for Aden, the rest to be released to their next escort 300 miles further east.

By mid-1940 Aden was a busy pit stop, and when re-entering on 16 July *Leander* passed between lines of allied and neutral ships awaiting routing instructions, also the Italians *Monte Piano* and *Esquilino* awaiting a decision on their future. Stan Roy and I were among our Main W/T liberty men in the first boat, finding a photography outlet to equip the 'firm' we'd recently started in the Auxiliary W/T Office, then hiring a taxi to explore further afield. A stop at Mala to snap Yemenese prostitutes in various contortions, and a walk around the busy foreshore where the clock went back a thousand years. Here were Arab craftsmen adzing dhow ribs from gnarled branches, shaping planks to be affixed by wooden pegs; creating beautiful vessels to carry Arabian slaves across the Red Sea to the Sultans of Africa, contraband livestock and smuggled weapons for Italian agents in Sudan, Somaliland and Ethiopia, and our naval patrol boats would intercept only a few of them. Our taxi driver grinned incomprehension to everything we asked him but drove out past Aden's salt industry – acres of low-walled pans floodgated at high tide then closed off to evaporate over days, after which the crusted salt was gathered and processed in Dutch-type windmills sited everywhere. Inside them wooden gears operated wooden pumps creaking eerily, salt encrusted with crystalline stalactites hanging under wooden boardwalks. Bare-legged skinny Arabs walked about the pans, poking holes with sticks to allow underlying water to evaporate, and many piles of excavated salt dotted the area, glistening white, older ones yellowed by the frequent sandstorms. Away again to Sheik Othman, the filthiest habitation yet, air thick with flies, goats and camels drinking from slime-coated waterholes, dusty shop-shelves displaying Birmingham scissors, faded packets of cigarettes and bedraggled oddments. We left for Solomon's Well, drove for miles till 'Ahab' stopped near a rusting shed and exclaimed 'Well!' We peered through an unglazed opening at a rheumatic diesel pump, turned to our guide and queried 'Christ mate, is this supposed to be Solomon's Well?' to which he grinned 'Well' the only word of English he'd uttered so far. This artesian source of water was apparently one of a network piped to Aden, and surrounding it were unhappy looking trees, probably the only vegetation in the Protectorate, providing shade for a Punjabi Regiment whose horses were grazing on paddocks of stunted grass. The Punjabis spoke English well enough to say they'd been brought from India in one of the ships in BN3, the convoy we'd taken on up the Red Sea.

We stopped next at Khormaksar's No 8 Squadron East Camp, endless three-storey barracks either side of the road, officers' quarters, mess halls and cookhouses north side; hangars, admin buildings and workshops on the south with runways networked over wasteland everywhere. Aircraft camouflaged desert brown with darker blotches taxied about with motors idling, others streamed dust, props rising to a deafening pitch as they lifted off and disappeared north-westward. An RAF Sergeant took us inside one hangar to see a Marchetti Savoia S–81 recently damaged and forced to land nearby. A Blenheim had been parked under one of its wings for comparison. The huge Italian bomber had fittings for two torpedoes, racks for twenty-eight 50-lb or fourteen 100-lb bombs, a swivel twin .5″ turret above with another below, more machine guns in its wings, and a 1,200 miles range.

Back to the taxi with ample time for a look at Crater City; via Main Pass cut through sheer rock as a massive arch; right through the brown-rock buildings and houses and on up a valley road, this time convinced we were to see Solomon's Wells. Up flights of hewn stone steps past landings, right to the top stone-block lined tank which when filled to its million gallon capacity would overflow down into the next, then the next etcetera. Alongside the brim of No 2 stood a magnificent old mango tree whose branches umbrellaed its reinforced-concrete slab cover, and a manhole through which we peered down 200 feet. Down the steps again past No 3 to No 4, by far the largest into which we dropped a stone and waited seconds for the splash; said to hold four million gallons, in 1940 it had only 8-feet depth of water. Each tank had been excavated out of living rock, but by whom? None knew. There were eight in lower sequence, each designed to overflow into the next down, each with a wooden pulley to drop and raise leather buckets on endless ropes. We wound one up, tasted its lukewarm content and spat it out. A nearby museum contained alabaster curios discovered by an RN geologist with the nineteenth-century fleet which seized Aden. His curiosity led to the ancient debris-covered wells being unearthed and cleaned out over ensuing years; among the earth and rubbish were cuneiform lettered slabs referring to the Queen of Sheba, Assyrian coins and artifacts, and an almost obliterated parchment map of Aden showing it as one vast city among vegetated hills. Back at Post Office Quay we found 'Ahab' to be an economist if not a linguist, and as we negotiated Leander's sea gangway 200 yards offshore, his voice still clearly invented the curse of Allah on us for underpayment, unintentional as we'd given him all of our Arabian rupees and annas.

However, our remorse soon evaporated, the first mail since leaving New Zealand had been craned inboard and sorted into messdeck bundles. Leander was non-combatant and everywhere men had beamed down to their hometowns, their parents or their wives and children. Men stacked their letters in priority and took them topside to be scanned again and again more deeply; no need yet to answer them, before that they would be discussed with understanding mates. But right now Kimberley was easing alongside, dozens of welded patches showing where German bomb fragments had peppered her sides off Norway, killing five of her crew. Our freshwater showers were made available, and having enjoyed them her complement relaxed about our scrubbed wooden upperdecks, later returning to their steel-decked destroyer with arms full of pictorial Auckland weeklies, freelances, newspapers from every New Zealand town or city. Several cables distant Ceres' funnels were belching smoke, Shoreham and Hindustan were also raising steam, and at 1600 our Marine band on X-turret deck played us out to sea, this time to meet a twenty-one ship convoy entering the eastern Arabian Sea.

Abreast of Aden some detached to enter while others emerged signalling their destinations as Perim, Abu Ail, Port Sudan, mostly Tewfik for the Canal transit. *Ceres, Shoreham* and *Hindustan* had been relieved by the cruiser *Carlisle*, destroyers *Kandahar, Kimberley*, sloops *Auckland* and *Flamingo*, and that night we passed through Bab el Mandeb Straits without detection – assisted by that seasonal mist which enabled Mala's dhows to cross to Ethiopia. *Carlisle*'s radar was detecting enemy aircraft in all directions, but they seemed unaware of our presence, and as some may have been our own from Khormaksar all ships held their fire. The convoy speed was determined by our slowest 6-knot decrepit Greek and as we passed Massawa at midnight, Navi pencilled another cross on his chart to indicate the day's 150 miles covered. Hours later in brilliant sunshine, we looked at ships sans smoke to every horizon, 'painted ships upon a painted ocean', we leaned outboard to contemplate the Red Sea drifting idly by; paused to hear a logistician remark that *Leander* had now escorted a million tons of shipping without loss; then resumed our fascination with the waterline. Between watches we processed the Aden films, displayed them for sale in the Canteen Flat, then ditched those of Mala's prostitutes due to a quirk of conscience, 'no porn shots in future'; this reformation of ideals perhaps inclining Allah in our favour, as our southbound string of empties were dispersed their separate ways well south of Aden. But a few hours back in harbour soon dispelled that sort of conjecture.

Warships' bugles blared gun-crews to repel aircraft, sirens ashore were wailing everyone to seek shelter, and interspersed among the general banging and concussion of ships' and shore A/A gun posts, dull thuds were heard as ack-ack shells burst among silvery specks high overhead. A nearby building blew apart and crumbled in dust as we fled the foc'sle, stumbling in a queue making aft through the crowded starboard passage when a stick of near misses strained *Leander* against her moorings. The raid ended abruptly, leaving dead and injured to be extricated from civil and military ruins, and that night Radio Roma saying: 'Our bombers today raided Aden, destroying air force and military installations within the area, and damaging cruisers and destroyers in the inner harbour.' Next day four more raids sent everyone to his anti-aircraft station, and again there were no direct hits or serious casualties on our warships; but not so ashore where RAF establishments were razed and airmen died; so in retaliation Khormaksar intensified its assaults on Massawa's and its outlying islands' defences.

Meantime several new names were appearing in the preambles of W/T messages on the naval network, among them the battleship *Royal Sovereign* and cruiser *Neptune* in addition to large troopers and hospital ships, this adding weight to rumours that the Italian Army was on the outskirts of Berbera in British Somaliland just across the Gulf of Aden. But there wasn't time for conjecture; more convoys were approaching from India, others from Britain around the Cape; so *Leander* sped eastward to relieve their Indian Ocean escorts and shepherd them westward, back and forth across 6- to 8-knot relics crammed with Desert Army material, our ship's company tormented by sweat rash and infested by crabs originating in the Seamen's Heads. Then in mid-August we picked up a faster convoy believed to be transporting a complete Indian Army Division with its armament and provisions aboard the big troopships and fast freighters: *Devonshire, Lancashire, Dilwara, City of Keelung, Khandalla, Raby Castle, Rohna, Rajula, Talamba, Takliwa, Khedive Ismail, Ethiopia, Acadia, Malayan Prince, Egra, British Pride, British Fusilier, Jessmore,* and *Ellenga.* Captain Horan disposed them into two long columns surrounded by every available Red Sea Force destroyer and escort vessel, and ordered maximum submarine surveillance for the full moon Perim passage. Early daylight saw Khormaksar fighters downing a formation of enemy bombers, unfortunate to be returning from an Aden raid as our escort reorganised the convoy into four columns; and in the Main W/T we unofficially read confidential messages detailing the overall worsening situation.

Between 16 and 19 August many warships and merchantmen had assisted in the evacuation of Berbera to Aden, Mombasa and Bombay. All war material and civilian transport was marshalled dockside to be disabled, then *Royal Sovereign's* 15″ and the cruisers' and destroyers' smaller gunnery shelled the whole area before retiring; but now Benito Mussolini had airfields only 200 miles south of Aden. Djibouti and other French Somaliland ports had already been overthrown, so Italy virtually occupied half the Red Sea coast of Africa, all the Somali coast of the Gulf of Aden, and the Indian Ocean coast right down to Kenya. Il Duce needed only to neutralise Aden to block all Red Sea shipping supplying Britain's 8th Army in North Africa. On arrival in port we would be assigned outer harbour anchorages for better searchlight and A/A concentration over the town at night, Khormaksar having no night-fighters. There were continual night bombings and hours-long anti-aircraft gunnery retaliations, then daylight's widespread palls of dust and smoke still hanging heavy if one got ashore to find many buildings and shops damaged, their Arab occupants long since gone inland. From whatever source those days there was only bad news: the Dunkirk saga; France's capitulation; the Royal Navy's bombardment of Oran's French warships; intense bombing of British Isles' cities; German raiders and U-boats decimating Allied shipping. We lost the straggler *Atlas* to an Italian submarine's torpedo just north of Perim, then almost lost the British freighter *Bhima* when she took a bomb aft and began to settle stern first in the same locality; but 'Crash' Horan had other ideas, ordered our machine-gunners to open fire on the Lascar crew's lifeboats if they refused to go back onboard and save her. They did. She was then towed back to Aden, repaired, and came north in a later convoy with her holds still full of ammunition and her deck cargo of tanks and tracked vehicles intact. We were now bombed frequently en route north and south, convoy after convoy, but our A/A gunnery excelled and the enemy flew higher with less accuracy. In late September SNORS warned of an expected night surface attack off Massawa; it didn't eventuate and six of the transports took 20,000 troops into Port Sudan, said to be part of General Cunningham's counter-offensive about to move against the Eyeties in Ethiopia and the Somalilands.

Maybe Italy knew it, so *Leander* wore more rifling out of her 4″ guns, manoeuvred drastically to avoid sticks of well-aimed bombs, then re-ammunitioned again in Aden preparatory to our next northbound bunch of transports, low-Plimsolled freighters and tankers. Several days later we were firing at more silver specks just below the troposphere, once in fact at Venus which could be seen in daylight, each time radioing SNORS an attack was imminent and at 'Cease Fire' transmitting him the result; on Sunday 20 October three attacks and summaries before nightfall took us through to Monday, Trafalgar Day, 1940.

An empty sky throughout the forenoon, afternoon, and dog watches. Then sometime in the First, an alert lookout reported phosphorescent torpedo trails. Asdics probed the depths without an echo. Revitalised lookouts scanned the dark area until doubt prevailed. Midnight came and went; *Leander* relaxed and off-duty watchkeepers slept. Suddenly at 0220 strident alarms urged men from their hammocks, raced them to their action stations where earlier arrivals had already seen nearby ships silhouetted against bursts of gunfire. HMAS *Yarra* had combed torpedoes down either side, and another sloop, HMS *Auckland*, was reporting high-speed enemy destroyers firing at the troopships' Commodore. Starshells were already turning night to blue-white day, exposing two destroyers still firing as they fled, hidden by dense smoke screens. *Leander's* salvoes were being aimed at the densest centre of smoke and a bright flash indicated at least one hit; but she hadn't yet worked up to maximum power, marine growth was retarding speed, and after an abortive chase 'Crash' sent *Kimberley* on alone; his overall responsibility was the convoy safety so we returned to forestall the possibility of an enemy ruse.

At 0320 Kimberley transmitted: 5PS v 8BQ – O = 2DR 336 – 7 – 14 – 113 ZZ 19 = 0320 AR which in self-evident code read: '*Leander* from *Kimberley* Emergency Two enemy destroyers bearing 336 degrees 7 miles from me, their speed 14 knots, my position 113 degrees 19 miles from position ZZ on the squared chart. Time of sighting 3.20 a.m.' That report

prefaced a running commentary in Fleet Code saying one destroyer appeared to be damaged and was under tow. Immediately *Kimberley* attacked,
the tow was dropped and a brief encounter resulted in the Italian being
hit so often she ran herself aground on Harmil Island, where *Kimberley*
was trying to finish her off with torpedoes, one spread going wide and
the next evidently hitting near a magazine which exploded just forward
of her bridge. Nearby gun-site searchlights were now illuminating her and
she was engaging the shore battery. A subsequent message said she'd been
disabled by a hit in her boiler room, she'd silenced some of the enemy
guns but was still under fire while effecting repairs; she would appreciate
assistance and suggested that Khormaksar aircraft be asked to deal with
the other crippled destroyer.

Captain Horan replied that we were coming, asked Commander (E) for
revs for 30 knots, then told all departmental officers to prepare for ship-
to-shore action and whatever might develop practically on Massawa's
doorstep. Men on exposed decks leaned against our self-made rush of wind,
peering ahead at daybreak as if to out-see the crow's nest lookout. At the
first flash of *Kimberley*'s masthead signal lamp 'Action Stations' cleared all
upper decks, but the little destroyer had placed a collision mat over the
shell hole in her side, and repaired her power plant sufficiently to withdraw
out of range of Harmil Island's shore batteries. Reversing slowly stern to
bows, a Warrant Shipwright and two ERAs were transferred, her injured
were passed across on stretchers, then with *Kimberley* cutting our wake on
a long towline we started back to the convoy, now covered by Aden's
fighter-bombers who'd finished off the first crippled destroyer then demolished fifteen enemy aircraft on a nearby field. A subsequent confidential
signal said the destroyer torpedoed by *Kimberley* was *Francesco Nullo*, the
one sunk by RAF bombers was *Leone*, but *Pantera* and *Sauro* which had
been part of the four-destroyer night attack may have got back to Massawa;
then a further Confidential message informed our Captain that six A/A
cruisers fitted with radar-controlled high-angle guns were now at Aden to
escort future Red Sea convoys.

Leander took two more full ones north and brought previous convoys
back empty, before regretfully saying goodbye to Captain H.E. Horan DSC
(First World War), a man who had relinquished his posts as Commodore
NZ Station, Chief of Naval Staff, and First Naval Member, to take *Leander*
overseas as her Captain. Barges eased alongside for eight lengthy crates to
be craned inboard, containing replacements for the 4″ A/A guns worn out
defending 2,750,000 tons of Red Sea convoys, and next evening, Thursday,
28 November, Captain R.H. Bevan, another First World War veteran, took
us out of Aden with a shore bombardment to be done en route to Bombay.

Arriving next forenoon off Banda Alula on Cape Guardaful at the eastern tip of Italian Somaliland, we told Alula Marine Radio to have its D/F Station near the hospital evacuated, also the canning and fish-oil factory we were about to eliminate. The Italian operator morsed acknowledgement, appended a polite 'Gracias', then called Crispi Radio for help: 'aeronautics maritime entende bombardimenti ... Bretagne croriatori.' and so on in agitated morse. Captain Bevan allowed the factory workers and local residents ample time to quit the area, time to quit all of north-east Africa according to our new skipper's critics, then after circling its target, the previously catapulted Walrus dived steeply to release two 250-lb bombs and two incendiaries onto the whitewashed building centred among an array of aerials. An expanding pall of dirty smoke erupted long seconds before we heard the muffled explosions, and Alula W/T's transmission ceased abruptly. Now the Walrus was over the factory area, signalling readiness to spot for Leander's fall of shot. Ninety-six rounds of 6" reduced the huge concrete structure and its storage tanks to twisted metal and four-storey rubble; we swept an expanse of still water for the amphibian's landing, craned it onto its cradle, then steamed eastward while learning from an Italian broadcast that Leander and Liverpool were sunk off Massawa on 25 November. Radio Roma had now sunk Leander twice within two months, and Radio Berlin sank three heavily escorted troopships off Massawa on Trafalgar Day, 26 November. However as at that date we were S.O. Escort to the only convoy near Massawa, and it reached Tewfik undamaged, our appreciation of Axis newscasts was being given lessening credence.

At Bombay we were out of the War for a month, lost interest in it when crowding into buses alongside King George Dock for a five-mile drive to Dyatalawa Rest Camp: 'Sleep in the camp or sleep in brothels if you have the inclination, and the money; but be bloody certain you're on each morning's 0700 bus, or onboard when it arrives at the ship. That's all.' Three of our watch took beautiful Seychelle Island hostesses to the races one Saturday and won enough to pay for the whole day, and night; we visited the Hanging Gardens, Balcan's Tower, Gateway to India, Zoo, Apollo Club, and Julie's. And for all who so wished, there was hospitality. Several Christchurch ratings and a youthful Lieutenant were invited to a rich Parsee's marble mansion in an elite Malabar Hills suburb, driven there in glossy black limousines chauffeured by tall white-frock-coated and turbaned Indians. Our host went annually to Christchurch to arrange shipments of Canterbury lamb carcasses, and we were lavishly entertained throughout a Christmas dinner at his ornate table hidden under crystal bowls of fruit, carafes of wine, and a bewildering assortment of heavy silver cutlery. We drank from the delicate crystal finger-washing goblets and ate with the wrong utensils, but our genial host covered our ignorance by doing likewise, brought his family with us in a cavalcade of limousines around Bombays' outlying beach resorts, then after a convivial evening supper on his lantern-lit immaculate courtyard, returned us to our ship.

Repairs and alterations had proceeded quickly, the entire ship's company returned aboard on 26 December 1940 to a *Leander* degaussed against magnetic mines, her bridge structure altered to accommodate new equipment, the recently near-miss-distorted rudder re-aligned, and our new 4″ guns installed. The ship was ready for sea, now camouflaged dark grey with much darker segments and triangles and, as the lights of Bombay's Salsette Island disappeared far astern, the month's layers of dockyard filth were hosed and broomed overboard. Next day red-leaded partitions received grey enamel, while gunners fine-tuned their recent modifications, coxswains proved the new rudder-settings, and we came topside to find *Leander* escorting three 12-knot Indian troopships westward. The BBC said a Med Fleet destroyer had entered Bardia at night, put a boarding party aboard an Italian freighter and sailed it out, meanwhile sinking an anchored troopship by torpedoing it before departing at speed; then Cunningham's battle fleet had dumped 150 tons of 15″ demolition shells among Bardia's defences, and a poised Australian Army Division stormed in to capture its 25,000 Axis defenders.

But here were we back on the old grind. How much longer would SNORS punish the ship for some of its larrikins pinching his lousy gin? We refuelled in Aden at 0630 on 2 January 1941, emerged at 1300 with twenty-nine more ships for the Red Sea transit, and three days later heard that the 8th Army supported by Med Fleet bombardments had taken Tobruk and another 20,000 prisoners; two-thirds of Italy's North African Army now languished behind barbed wire, or were dead.

We consoled ourselves that those millions of tons of arms, ammunition, beer and bully-beef, were essential to the army's advance, and that the strings of southbound empties were required back quick at their sources of supply. So, off Abu Ail HMAS *Paramatta* detached to sink some floating mines, we went to 'AIR ALERT' off Perim until assured approaching bombers were ours heading for an attack on Asmara, then to prove our pessimists right there was no mail for us in Aden, nor were there any cruisers or destroyers; the reason becoming clear when Admiral Murray addressed our crowded quarterdeck to say goodbye. German raiders were operating in the Indian Ocean and C-in-C East Indies required *Leander* in the force searching for them. From scraps of evidence deduced from victims' final transmissions, he continued, we could be looking for the 8″ heavy cruiser *Prinz Eugen*, the pocket battleship *Admiral Scheer*, or possibly the Reich's 32-knot, 40 aircraft, 18 × 6″ gunned carrier *Graf Zeppelin*. (Under construction during the Second World War *Graf Zeppelin* did not see service and was scrapped. But in 1940/41 we did not know this.)

We left Aden expecting to meet all three in the Gulf, grew less apprehensive as the days passed until 21 January, when we entered Colombo shortly after the arrival of HMAS *Canberra* and the armed merchant cruiser *Hector*. Friday the 24th dawned with them gone, and *Leander* awaiting her Walrus about to get airborne after landing on a central Ceylon lake with engine problems; but it crashed on lift-off and caught fire, there were no casualties but we sailed sans amphibian. The British ship *Mandasar* 300 miles north-east of Seychelle Island had reported being bombed by a German floatplane; a different-toned transmitter cancelled the report using *Mandasar*'s callsign, so Aden Marine Radio receipted the cancellation as if it was genuine. Two days later Seychelles', Hawsea England's, and Bombay's shortwave D/F stations cross-fixed a German naval transmission to the north of Mauritius; and subsequent South African, Indian, and United Kingdom H/F D/F fixes gave daily positions estimated within a few thousand square miles triangle. C-in-C's hunting force comprised the cruisers *Dorsetshire, Shropshire, Australia, Canberra, Glasgow, Enterprise, Emerald, Leander, Hawkins, Caledon*, the carrier *Hermes* and her crash-boat *Kandahar*; but there were millions of square miles of Indian Ocean to cover.

We refuelled from RFA *Appleleaf* at Addu Atoll in the Maldives, returned to Colombo for a replacement Walrus, then commenced a triangular search deep below Ceylon, punctuated by refuelling visits, and a brief change on

Photographed from her Walrus aircraft, *Leander* in the Indian Ocean with new camouflage 1940/41.

20 February when we took Convoy US9 over from *Canberra* near the Equator. We cheered the 4th Reinforcements of the 2nd NZEF aboard *Aquitania*, *Mauretania* and *Nieuw Amsterdam*, and they returned the greeting as we drew abreast of each ship in turn. But having shepherded them into Bombay we oiled and left immediately; SS *Tekoa's* RRRR report had been cut short, followed hours after by another unfortunate vessel's last transmission: 'RRRR de GSTL = SS *Canadian Cruiser* – 036E 009 S – being chased by battlecruiser'.

This placed the call south-west of the Seychelles some 3,000 miles from Bombay; futile to hurry, and we had orders to see if Axis ships known to have left Kismayu were in neutral Goa. Our Walrus initiated a Portuguese protest as it flew over their harbour on India's west coast, it came back with a nil report, and *Leander* continued south-west until Wednesday, 26 February when ordered to search due west along the Equator, everyone onboard despondent. Our cat Minnie, recently mated to *Kimberley's* Tom, received ship's company affection; several times a day her pregnant body was dunked in a bucket of cooling water and she loved it. About noon as she lay dreaming, a flying fish flopped down beside her then flapped itself overboard again. Instinctively alerted she leapt after it, bobbing atop successive bow waves sweeping her astern until lost to straining eyes. Men looked up at the bridge willing Captain Bevan to reverse course, but he had implicit orders and could not stop for her.

Someone with knowledge had issued those orders, and near 1100 next forenoon the foremast lookout picked up mast tips on the horizon; 'ACTION STATIONS' sounded as *Leander* trembled with increasing speed, but an hour elapsed before Chief Gunner's Mate Harold Firth at the DCT rangefinder, reported a possible gun-mount on her foc'sle, and as we didn't appear to be closing the gap fast enough, Commander Vereker rang the Plot for an estimation of the still-distant ship's speed. Schoolmaster Stan Hermans who'd been plotting her position said it appeared to be twenty knots, but was told not to be so wet as merchant ships couldn't do that. More revs were asked for and the gap closed, sufficiently for Chief Yeoman 'Yum' Ackerley to say that although she was wearing the Red Duster she didn't look like a British ship; so *Leander* was taken closer, beam-on to within 3,000 yards where she made the 'Secret Challenge'. All sorts of replies came back including the signal letters for *Gromont Castle*; then in the midst of this quiz session her Red Ensign flew down to be replaced by the Italian flag; midship flaps and camouflage screens on her poop deck and foc'sle dropped and she got away twenty-four rounds of 4.7″, one blasting a 12″ jagged hole in our funnel and the rest whining overhead, or landing part-way to richochet over our foc'sle, gaps between the funnel and cradled Walrus, and the quarterdeck.

Heard above the enemy fusillade our Gunnery Officer was roaring 'OPEN FIIRRE!' in response to Bevan's request for 'a shot across her bows'; and *Leander*'s turret crews with their guns already trained on the suspicious vessel's waterline now within a mile, had already taken the initiative. Five salvoes at mini-second intervals saw the Italian flag struck quickly in surrender. Expecting to engage a German warship, *Leander*'s magazine crews were feeding the turrets armour-piercing ammunition which penetrated deep inside before detonating; so the results of our gunnery weren't evident about the several thousand-ton streamlined vessel, lying peacefully some three cables to port. But lowered boats were pulling frantically away from her, men were diving overboard and swimming away fast, and as our boarding party's power boats surged to within hundreds of feet, a mass of erupting after-deck reared high above the ship. Its shockwave and roar buffeted our ears; Italian swimmers were plucked from the water in haste as the boats were recalled, and before they came alongside our davit falls several internal explosions were visibly shaking the raider. Minutes later a midship magazine blew in a flash of flame and smoke, then a deep muffled explosion tore her bows apart. Dishevelled prisoners were now assembled on our quarterdeck, watching her fore-deck disappear among expelling air, watching the Indian Ocean climbing up her bridgeworks, stern and dead propellers high above the surface, unwilling to go down. Finally the top half of her stern somersaulted upward, torn from the remainder of the ship. Prisoners and *Leander*'s crew hit the deck face down as the shockwave thudded against our cruiser, simultaneously with a drawn-out BAAANNNGG; and when we looked again there was only smoke, a rising black column seared by flames until all the gases were consumed, leaving discoloured vapours drifting wide-spread into the distance.

We had sunk *RAMB–1*, a 22-knot motor vessel of Italy's Royal Associated Monopoly of the Banana trade, recently converted in Massawa to be an armed raider; and at sunset men of the New Zealand Division of the Royal Navy stood to attention alongside men of the Italian Navy and their still quivering fox terrier, all paying last respects as two Italian bodies in weighted hammocks slid to their watery graves, their injuries beyond repair in our Sick Bay.

Back at Addu Atoll *Leander* refuelled from RFA *Pearleaf*, transferred the prisoners to her, then escorted her part-way to Colombo until radioed to rendezvous with *Canberra*. Both cruisers hove-to while senior officers boarded for a briefing, there learning that *Glasgow*'s plane had identified *Admiral Scheer* south of the Seychelles on 22 February but lost contact in bad conditions; so from dawn to dusk in four-hour relays each cruiser's Walrus searched far and wide, maintaining W/T silence as we steamed fifty miles apart on long zigzags, our mean course south-westward toward

Smoke after the 3rd & final big explosion. *RAMB-1*, Italian Raider sunk in Indian Ocean.

the Sayha de Malha Shallows. C-in-C East Indies' intelligence department had surmised the area to be a refuelling possibility for *Scheer* and they were right. *Canberra* endeavoured to stop the Norwegian tanker *Ketty Brovig* from being scuttled by its German captors, while *Leander* raced after the now distant Reich Navy Supply Ship *Koburg*, but when we located and approached her it was too late, she was almost under and we embarked forty-six German Reserve officers and ratings, five Norwegians and another fox terrier from their lifeboats. Arriving back at the shallows we were treated to a spectacular display of dusk-to-dark firing as *Canberra* put the sinking *Ketty Brovig* under, meantime learning from our Norwegian embarkees that *Koburg* and *Ketty Brovig* had two days earlier refuelled and stored a pocket battleship or a heavy cruiser, maybe both.

Next afternoon in the Auxiliary W/T Office my hair stood on end when *Canberra*'s aircraft broke silence to report the pocket battleship in sight. The given position placed her close to our hourly updated one, and immediately I phoned this to the bridge *Leander* shuddered as her propellers thrashed for increased speed; alarms and bugles blaring men to 'ACTION STATIONS AT THE DOUBLE!' Already *Canberra*'s powerful H/F transmitter was informing the C-in-C that we would shadow the enemy until sunset when we could be up-sun of him. Ensuing coded messages were being broadcast around the East Indies naval network, but still our lookouts hadn't found the enemy's mastheads with their powerful glasses and telescopes, nor had the DCT's rangefinder. Then *Canberra*'s embarrassed Walrus radioed its mistake. *Leander*'s single funnel profile had deceived the observer and the pocket battleship *was Leander*. The Australian cruiser's red-faced Captain dictated explanations for transmission to GZH Colombo, and the Bombay-Aden-Mauritius naval network quietened considerably.

Post-war research indicates that the sinking of *Ketty Brovig* and *Koburg*, together with a Vichy French tanker captured at that time by *Shropshire* and prize-crewed to Durban, effectively terminated *Admiral Scheer*'s Indian Ocean activity. In addition *Shropshire* had sunk a German raider two weeks earlier, but although sustaining considerable damage herself, the County Class cruiser remained at sea. And after a pit stop at Port Louis, Mauritius, *Leander* captured the Vichy French freighter *Charles L.D.* while looking for Vichy France's liner *Verdun de Ville* reported to be en route for Madagascar from Siam with Axis 'high brass' onboard. But *Charles L.D.*'s 'am being boarded by a British cruiser' radioed to Madagascar's Tananarive Marine Radio enabled our more important quarry to take evasive action, so we tumbled about in rough seas between Madagascar and Mozambique until everything except the ship's cockroaches was eaten, challenged nothing but our own tanker *Trocus*, the Q-ship HMS *Port Durban*, and RFA *Olcades*; then on 29 March after a day in Port Louis we sailed for Colombo, learning en route on 2 April that Asmara, the capital of Eritrea, had been retaken from the Italians and our army was advancing on Massawa. But the sun hadn't yet broken through the Allied clouds of doom and despair; German and Italian armour had retaken Benghazi; German panzer divisions were invading Greece and Yugoslavia; and in Egypt the name 'Rommel' was being ominously repeated as the depleted 8th Army retreated from Libya, its seasoned desert troops having been ordered to Greece by Churchill.

We read some of this in Colombo newspapers while refilling *Leander*'s chill-rooms. We sped to Madras to escort the troopships *Devonshire*, *Cynthia*, *Talma*, and *Neuralia*'s Pathan Regiment to Singapore; but when only 300 miles outbound, handed them over to the D-class cruiser *Danae* and increased speed to Trincomalee. Due to critical losses, long-range cruisers were in demand, and having refuelled we were churning water en route the Persian Gulf. But don't bet on it. Another signal redirected us to Colombo for the C-in-C and his staff. No waiting, minimal formalities, 29 knots up India's west coast while impersonating Colombo Navy W/T Station, GZH, continually transmitting the Admiral's long cyphered messages. Intelligence had reported Iraq's Rashid Ali to be welcoming German military aircraft onto Iraqi airfields, so we were going to Basra to change his mind. Bayonets were being honed on Blackie's grinding wheel; Vickers machine guns and .303 carbines were being issued to marine and seamen landing parties; but on arrival in the Shatt el Arab estuary of the Euphrates River on 18 April 1941, the Admiral transferred to *Seabelle* which continued upriver accompanied by *Falmouth* and *Yarra*, all three escort vessels smothered with khaki-clad troops and marines.

Whether it was the show of force or the Royal Navy's inherent diplomacy which swayed Iraq's Regent, who knows? But without firing a shot, *Seabelle* returned the Admiral after five days wherein we stood-by off Kuwait. *Leander* then cruised slowly past Muscat wearing huge flags to impress the Sultan of Oman, our cruiser scrubbed and polished befitting its role as Flagship of C-in-C East Indies Station, Vice-Admiral R. Leatham CB RN, until 29 April when he disembarked back in Colombo. But Regent Rashid Ali changed his mind again, and while once more a unit of our widespread Force V searching for raiders, we learned that his air force had attacked the RAF airfield at Habanniyah, which lost him more than half of Iraq's military aircraft and brought Britain into a semblance of war against his country.

Right now *Leander*'s aircraft was covering thousands of square miles daily, airborne continually except for gas-ups from dawn to dusk, searching for the raider which sank *Clan Buchanan* a few hundred miles west of the Maldives. Nothing. So, back to Colombo on 6 May to escort New Zealand's 6,000-strong 5th Reinforcements westward at 20 knots aboard *Mauretania*, *Aquitania*, and *Ile de France*; then when still in the Arabian Sea, handing them over to *Canberra* and detaching at 25 knots when the raider struck again. *British Emperor*'s interrupted *RRRR* appeal placed her about 350 miles south-east of Cape Guadafui, and this time the wasp had trespassed inside a tight web converged on by *Glasgow*, *Liverpool*, *Cornwall*, *Ceres*, and *Hector*; but should the predator escape eastwards there was a chance that she would run head on into *Leander*. At 0707 on 8 May one of *Cornwall*'s two aircraft sighted a suspicious ship which hoisted the Norwegian signal letters for *Tamerlane*. This motor vessel was not in the area's daily list of expected ships so *Cornwall* increased speed to close the 65 miles separation. Contact was lost while the aircraft returned for fuel, but regained shortly after midday after the plane again catapulted off. At 1609 *Cornwall*'s DCT had the ship in sight, but it refused to heave-to even when warning shots were fired; so the cat and mouse charade continued until 1718. Now at a range of 12,000 yards the raider opened fire and the result was inevitable, although disabling *Cornwall*'s forward steering position with a direct 5.9″ hit, an 8″ salvo penetrated the raider's midship magazine and she blew up. Survivors identified her as Schiffe No 33, *Pinguin*, but only 25 Britishers and 58 Germans were rescued from her 350 naval complement and 180 prisoners, one of the officers having in his possession a water-damaged list of *Pinguin*'s victims and some of her early operations.

In October 1940 she had converted the captured Norwegian tanker *Storstad* to a minelayer, then together they had laid minefields in the Bass Strait and in the approaches to Adelaide, Hobart and Sydney, these sinking several British freighters and the American *City of Rayville*. This information continued in tabulated form: [sic]

Date	Type	Name	Tonnage	Result
7–10–40	Norg tankr	*Storstad*		versenkt
20–11–40	Engl dampfer	*Maimoa*	10,123	versenkt
21–11–40	Engl motorschiff	*Port Brisbane*	8,739	versenkt
29–11–40	Engl dampfer	*Port Wellington*	10,065	versenkt
30–11–40	Engl dampfer	*Nowshera*	7,920	versenkt
14–1–41	Norg whalr	*Ole Wegger*	12,200	priz
14–1–41	Norg whalr	*Pelagos*	12,383	priz
14–1–41	Norg supply	*Solglimt*	12,246	priz
14–1–41	Norg chasrs	11 whale chasers each about 1,000 ton–priz		

[All of this captured whaling fleet was prize crewed to a French Atlantic port for Germany].

25–1–41	Engl dampfer	*Empire Light*	6,950	versenkt
26–1–41	Engl dampfer	*Clan Buchanan*		versenkt
7–5–41	Engl dampfer	*British Emperor*	3,663	versenkt

Now no longer required in the north-east Indian Ocean, *Leander* continued her search pattern south-eastward into mid-May, then returned to Colombo for a complete change of duties. On 23 May our Prime Minister Peter Fraser, currently in Cairo, agreed to *Leander*'s transfer to the Med Fleet for the evacuation of Crete. We sailed expecting to be at Alexandria in five days, but heavy seas reduced our speed to 18 knots, then 12 with conditions worsening hourly as the barometer plummeted; the heat below was intense but all exposed decks were declared closed, too dangerous throughout the majority of those six days just to Aden. Meantime the wily Hun had parachuted 20-foot-long magnetic and acoustic mines into the Suez Canal, intended to prevent warships coming through while they occupied Crete; so more delays kept *Leander* in Tewfik awaiting permission to proceed, then a cautious transit ensued past the remains of deep-laden freighters blown apart when they had attempted the passage.

Open-wounded warships and merchantmen floated awry in Suez, Tewfik, Ismailia, and Port Said; and in Alexandria as *Leander* glided to her buoy near the ancient Greek battleship *Georges Averoff* we saw more queued for attention. In the dry-dock *Naiad*'s damage was marked by sputtering torches and welding rods. Anchored nearby, *Formidable* nursed a distorted nose. Showers of sparks outlined workmen cutting away *Warspite*'s, *Valiant*'s and *Barham*'s bomb-wrenched metal; and the stench of death drifted over us from our sister-ship *Orion*, alongside an upwind wharf, many of her crew's and evacuated soldiers' bodies not yet recovered from her mangled lower decks, her B-turret guns curved upward by the blast from a 1,000-lb bomb which penetrated deep between A- and B-turrets before exploding. The evacuation had cost Cunningham's Med Fleet dearly: three battleships and a carrier damaged; the cruisers *Calcutta*, *Fiji*, *Gloucester*, sunk, *Ajax*, *Carlisle*, *Coventry*, *Dido*, *Naiad*, *Orion*, *Perth*, damaged; the destroyers *Diamond*, *Greyhound*, *Hereward*, *Imperial*, *Janus*, *Kashmir*, *Kelly*, *Wryneck*, sunk, *Decoy*, *Griffin*, *Havock*, *Jaguar*, *Jervis*, *Kelvin*, *Kingston*, *Kipling*, *Nubian*, damaged; the fast assault ships *Glenearn* and *Glenroy* damaged; 2,261 navy personnel killed or listed as missing.

We drank beer in tree-shaded hotel gardens until dark when we drank whisky-flavoured meths in Stanley Bay's Kit Kat and Acteon cabarets, we danced with fair-skinned Egyptian hostesses employed to elicit information in the rowdy but happy din, then near 10 p.m. when we should have already been onboard, we found our way in the dark to be pinnaced aboard anticipating sleep. Sleep? This wasn't the Indian Ocean, and hardly had we dispersed to various messdecks when 'AIR ALERT YELLOW' sounded. 'RED' followed before all *Leander*'s stations were manned, and already the harbour pulsated as the guns on sixty ships crashed and recoiled in one thunderous roar. Our new A/A barrels grew warm then hot as we in the RCO relayed *Valiant*'s morsed directives. She, *Warspite* and *Queen Elizabeth* rippled end to end in smoke-haloed silhouette, upperworks starkly exposed, gunfire concentrating aft for seconds then racing forward to leave their after-structures invisible. Again our sector letters and figures were morsed and *Leander*'s gun-muzzles jetted flame in unison with unexpectedly illuminated warships everywhere one looked. Our 4″ fired methodically, lighting the underbelly of a torpedo-bomber gliding low over our bridge, then gone. Immediately to seaward a tremendous gush of flame erupted as it flew into the harbour's high sea-wall. Throughout those long night hours spent shrapnel clanged against our structure. We wore the headphones in relays, ran to the Remote Torpedo Firing Platforms port and starboard in time to see parachute-bombs descending into the city centre, then watched dazzling flashes outshine everything; but in that night's general crescendo those brilliant explosions hadn't registered.

Momentarily all went quiet then it started up again, *Leander*'s guns cracking and banging, multi-barrelled machine-gun tracers curving in low trajectory, *Georges Averoff*'s antiquated 11″ blasting shockwaves against our bridge as she fired her old guns; then! Searchlights sweeping the fleet from ashore! 'What for Christ's sake are the stupid bastards up to?' They were manned by Egyptian militia, 'bluudy British infidels in our bluudy cuuntry.' At least they could speak English.

Men went to the galley for thick corned-beef sandwiches and fannies of thick cocoa, took them to their action station mates. On and on it went until sheer monotony kept us in our RCO, taking turns at long naps under operators' desks. Finally, daylight, local fighters airborne and the enemy gone. We found dark corners in which to drop befuddled.

The attack had been pressed home from 2300 to 0500 without respite; *Leander* fired 200-plus fused 4″ up into her vector, countless close-barrage tracer at barely visible torpedo-bombers. Every other ship and shore battery had done the same or more. A square mile of the Sister Street and cool-storage area lay in smoking ruins, two men from *Leander* and several hundred civilians and servicemen died, hundreds more were being extricated from collapsed multi-storey rubble, and a large-scale evacuation to Cairo was underway. Taxis were commandeered as ambulances and trams stood where their power had failed. We wandered through cordoned-off streets, boarded a berthed freighter when hearing cries for help, and brought the injured off on makeshift stretchers to be taken elsewhere. It was nearing sunset, time to go to Stanley Bay's Acteon where we fought among ourselves when stupid on firewater. Tables and chairs were flung about

Air Raid over Alexandria, 1940.

and we came off drunk, in the rattle for being hours adrift; but charges were dropped when our names were telephoned to *Leander* from the skipper of the bomb-damaged freighter we'd boarded.

No raids, no duty, we snored right through the forenoon then went topside to see the fleet readjusting. Three destroyers towed *Formidable* from her berth and an hour later, *Leander* a quarter mile distant, shuddered when a delayed action mine exploded on the harbour bed where the carrier had been. Meanwhile divers were below salvaging ammunition crates from an ammunition ship submerged to her upperworks two berths from ours. It was dicey for them and for us as, with time-fused mines possible in our vicinity, the work aided by some of our crew proceeded quickly. The total explosion of her cargo could have devastated much of Alexandria, so we weren't sorry to awaken next morning at sea heading for Port Said. There our catapult and Walrus were removed, two multiple pom-poms were mounted on the vacant space, and an Italian Breda gun was bolted down port-side aft on the quarterdeck, this with boxes of ammunition thenceforth becoming TGM George Cameron's Air Action Station. Forty-eight hours after leaving Alexandria we were back there sending and receiving many signals, one of them on 12 June 1941 dispatching *Leander* ahead of the destroyers *Hasty* and *Jervis* to the Lebanon coast.

German forces now occupied airfields in Iraq, and Syria was encouraging them by the Vichy French attitude in Beirut. Australian, British and Free French troops advancing along the coast road to Sidon were impeded by Vichy French 75mm batteries covering the route, so *Leander* and her escorts were joining cruisers and destroyers supporting the Allied columns. Watching through binoculars we saw enemy vehicles retreating in clouds of dust, visible for minutes then disappearing in cuttings. Inshore destroyers ranged on the downhill end of those defiles and fired salvo after salvo as the leading trucks emerged. They leapt upward in shell-bursts, others tumbled sideways over road edges onto rocks a hundred feet below, greyish puffs along the clifftops indicated enemy retaliation, and when the shells landed close our destroyers retired laying smoke screens.

A few visual signals from *Phoebe* and it was our turn. All along the ridges, upheavals of dust and debris blended into one wide pattern of destruction until we were signalled 'Cease Firing'. Now *Phoebe*, already fitted with radar, was transmitting to Haifa Airbase: GN5R v L6M – O-A = 6AC – 11 – etc etc; and within minutes both cruisers and destroyers were hammering at six German Stuka dive-bombers hurtling down almost vertically. Pompoms thumped in harmony with Cameron's Breda, and through the din we heard the sound Nazi dive-bombers had terrified Europe with – sirens fitted to instil fear – and right now they were succeeding. But their bombs missed as did those of their Axis partners in the Red Sea, so we realised the Nazi could also make mistakes. He made one right now by staying too long, vainly tried to elude Haifa's Hurricanes, but lost three in sight of *Leander* as the others fled with our fighters in pursuit. Shortly our guns swung to face more planes, only to find them our Hurricanes returning in a long surface-top victory roll. We'd been on the Lebanon coast three hours when Rear Admiral E.L.S. King flashed: 'Glad to have you in my suicide squad. We will be busy for a bit, so we will drink to your good health later in Haifa.'

Captain Bevan replied: 'Thank you for the warm reception. Your kind offer accepted. We will try to work up a suitable thirst.'

Day by day King's force answered calls from Army Sigs requiring treatment of Vichy 75s obstructing the advance. Men below were kept informed on the results of our bombardments, the mounting tally of downed Stukas, Junkers 88s, and Vichy Glen Martins, even the crippling of our destroyers *Isis* and *Ilex*; dive-bombed within an hour of each other. Given heavy anti-aircraft cover as our cruisers and destroyers circled them American Indian-style to drive off attackers bent on their destruction, they were later dispatched under tow to Haifa. *Leander* chased Vichy destroyers towards Beirut and hurried them in with a salvo of 6"; we became Senior Officer 15th Cruiser Squadron while *Phoebe* was away in Alexandria; then one night we followed her relief *Naiad* right into Beirut Bay, where we sank two Vichy destroyers, probably *Guepard* and *Chevalier Paul*, by point-blank gunfire and launched torpedoes at indistinct warships further inshore. We retired at speed with searchlights on us and shore batteries putting some short and some over, we fought off angry aircraft attacks against our two cruisers and several destroyers on the run home in daylight, were given an umbrella of Hurricanes across the Bay of Acre, then entered Haifa with no damage or casualties. To give authencity to our action in Beirut Harbour, Admiral Cunningham's congratulation message from Alexandria said: 'Well done *Naiad*. Well done *Leander*.' Our gunnery or torpedoes must have done something to get that butterfly on the hand; but before leave was piped that day Captain Bevan cleared lower-deck and warned the ship's company against mentioning the event ashore or in our mail, concluding: 'Vichy France has not been declared an official enemy.'

Next day Padre Noakes took busloads of us to the Sea of Galilei, stopping at Nazareth to visit The Carpenter's Shop and Jacob's Tomb down hewn stone stairs under the Church of the Holy Family. I'm not overly religious but my skin tingled in the gloomy biblical atmosphere of the huge cavern, and the aura lingered when we emerged into sunlight to stand around the Virgin's Well. At Tiberias where Jesus fed the multitude with a loaf, five fish, and wine transformed from water, we remained unfed, re-entering our buses due to a telephoned message for our Padre to return post haste.

So 70 m.p.h. all the way back, *Leander* was waiting for us and we sailed on arrival near 8 p.m. *Kimberley, Jaguar* and *Jackal*, whose Crete-bombed backside now repaired and red-leaded looked more like a baboon, cut our boiling wake to the coast north of Beirut, where a massive concrete structure awaited Army Command attention. And while the destroyers exchanged shells with shore batteries, *Leander's* 6″ salvoes blasted great chunks out of the suspected German Intelligence Headquarters, before shifting target to a bivouac area for military vehicles and guns recce-photographed in adjacent woods. This was given a half-hour's patterned firing, then we raced for Haifa with *Kimberley* astern, *Jaguar* to starboard, and the sun's first rays glinting on *Jackal's* raked mast abeam to port. For three more nights we were given up-coast targets, the last near Damour, and on return to base it seemed that General Dentz, French High Commissioner to Syria, was contemplating Armistice terms, and Admiral Andrew Browne

Leander's Radio Branch 1940/41.

Left to right, Back Row: Tim Cooley (Petty Officer), Ralph Greentier, Rex Randall, ? Frew, Pete Illsley, Bill Bailey, 'Shiner' Wright, Stan Roy.

Left to right, Centre Row: Duff Mayer (Petty Officer), Jack Harker (Petty Officer) Lieutenant Luard (Signals Officer), Joe Crouch (Chief), Cappy Harris (Petty Officer), Tom Sawyer (Petty Officer).

Left to right, Front Row: Sap Ryder, Jim Roberts, Archibald 'Haggis' Craig, Joe Taylor, Charles Beasy.

Absent: Rocky Princep, Lofty Durham.

Cunningham, known widely as 'ABC', wanted the 15th CS and its destroyer flotilla back in Alex.

Oberkommando der Wermacht, Field Marshal Wilhelm Keitel, had overrun the Balkan States with his ruthless *panzergruppes* and the *Luftwaffe's flieger-korps*; Field Marshal Erwin Rommel's *Afrika Korps* had halted Wavell's 8th Army advance in Cyrenacia, then shoved it right back onto the Egyptian border; Germany signed a ten-year friendship pact with Turkey on 18 June, and on the 22nd Hitler invaded Russia along an 1,800-mile front from the Arctic to the Black Sea, hurling 3,000,000 troops, 600,000 vehicles, 750,000 horses, 3,600 tanks, and 2,000 aircraft across the Soviet border. He needed oil and there was plenty of it in Arabia and Persia. But Britain wanted it too, and presently held access to it, even though 'things looked mighty touchy' especially with America's 'sit on the fence' attitude. Yet we still held the Canal, the 8th Army was licking its wounds but now reconstructing under General Sir Claude Auchinleck, and although being bombed nightly in Alexandria our Mediterranean Fleet still packed a powerful wallop.

Two thousand miles west at Gibraltar, Vice Admiral Sir James Somerville's fleet covered the Central Atlantic and Western Mediterranean, giving support to convoys endeavouring to supply beleaguered Malta; but having occupied Greece and Crete, Keitel might make another step into Cyprus, so this needed forestalling. Hence the arrival of *Leander* and *Jervis* in Port Said on 20 July. Wharf-compounds of Bombay-bloomered Geordies and Jocks spread everywhere one looked, the advance guard of many more to be embarked and rushed to Cyprus. We stowed them wherever sitting room could be found about the ship, sped north fast at noon, fed them meals which drew thankful comment, and at midnight stealthily entered Famagusta Bay, shuttled our passengers ashore aboard *Jervis* whose draft enabled access to a wharf too shallow for *Leander's*, then hastened south to Haifa.

Meanwhile 'Operation Substance', a large convoy which had left the Clyde on 11 July for Malta, was leaving Gibraltar on its last leg escorted by Somerville's Force H. Heavy Italian naval units at Taranto, Catania and Messina were to be contained or sunk by Cunningham's Eastern Med Fleet if they tried to interfere, and as the force left Alexandria on 23 July, *Leander* arrived to take her place in Vice Admiral H.D. Pridham-Wippell's 7th CS – *Ajax* (Flag), *Neptune*, *Leander*, *Hobart* – in line-ahead formation disposed to port of Cunningham's battleship *Valiant* ahead of *Queen Elizabeth* – and on the other flank, Rear Admiral King's 15th CS – *Phoebe* (Flag), *Naiad*, *Carlisle*, and the superfast 3,000-ton minelayers *Abdiel* and *Latona*; all screened by the destroyers *Hasty, Havock, Jaguar, Jackal, Kimberley, Kingston, Maori, Nizam, Nubian*. As we steamed north-westward reports filtered through about 'Operation Substance' now approaching Skerki Channel to the west of Malta; *Manchester* and the destroyer *Fearless* struck by aerial torpedoes and retiring; *Firedrake* also torpedoed and ordered by Somerville to have her crew taken aboard another destroyer which then sank her. Just before dark *Leander* and *Neptune* put up a well-judged barrage of 4″ which burst right among enemy recce intruders who fled trailing smoke, after which our 7th CS was ordered miles ahead of the battle fleet as night scouts. During the Middle Watch one of the fast freighters, *Sydney Star*, known pre-war on the NZ/UK refrigerated meat run, radioed Malta that she'd been torpedoed, was down to 40 feet in the bows but could manage 14 knots at danger to her bulkheads, and would require immediate docking or beaching on arrival.

At dawn our fleet was patrolling the southern Ionian Sea searching for surface enemies; all six relief ships of 'Substance' had arrived in Grand Harbour, so 'Operation Guillotine', the securing of Cyprus now had priority, and *Leander* was detached with *Latona* and *Jaguar* for a fast 24-hour dash to Port Said. Not in company or visible, *Neptune*, *Abdiel* and *Kimberley* were also heading for Port Said, as were *Hobart*, *Latona*, *Jaguar* and *Kipling*, there finding the two RAN sloops *Flamingo* and *Parramatta* already loading.

Spread in an almost static khaki-coloured mass, one saw battalions and regiments of the 8th Army 50th Division, milling among the RAF 259 Wing; troops of the Green Howards, the Cheshire Regiment, the Durham Light Infantry, all Anglo-Saxonising their impression of Headquarters' Snafu as they streamed down gangways onto immense pontoons and up ships' gangways, to be dispersed throughout tween-deck messes, then squeezed into every crevice topsides. Dockside cranes were waving robot arms everywhere, loading several grey-painted merchantmen with tracked vehicles, tanks, field guns, crated RAF stores and parts, motorbikes, staff cars, and all manner of ammunition. A thousand troops and airmen covered *Leander's* upper decks and crammed all messdecks and flats, as we sped north thirteen hours to a midnight Famagusta arrival, there in shielded lighting transferring them to *Latona* and *Jaguar* who'd already disembarked their troops alongside shallow quays. Days later with the 50th Division and 259 Wing ashore in Cyprus we sped south, this time for a dusk arrival at Alexandria.

Displayed on our Canteen Flat noticeboard were two new documents: one, Admiralty Fleet Order, AFO–1033, reading:

> The Admiralty has agreed with the New Zealand Government to gradually man a Leander Class Cruiser, probably HMS *Neptune*, with a New Zealand ship's company. New Zealand officers and ratings serving on Defensively Equipped Merchant Ships and His Majesty's Ships and Shore Establishments, will be appropriated to HMS *Drake* with their papers, as reliefs are made available. When convenient they will be drafted to HMS *Neptune*.

The second, a memorandum from Captain Bevan's Secretary, invited volunteers for transfer to *Neptune* to see the Regulating Office regarding such a draft. Necks entwined to peruse and talk about this important memo. There were rumours that *Neptune* was about to take our place in the 7th CS. Then a fast trip to Port Said to have the Breda and pom-poms replaced by our catapult and Walrus gave substance to the rumour, so with the prospect of a return to New Zealand paramount, few knocked at the Regulating Office door. We returned to Alexandria where Vice Admiral Andrew Browne Cunningham came aboard from *Valiant* to say farewell, we received goodbye signals from CS7 and CS15, and one from *Kimberley* who in Aden had loaned us her tomcat when Minnie yowled on heat; who had come alongside at an invitation to use our freshwater showers; who had escorted us during bombing raids in the Red Sea, and on the Lebanon coast.

Leander's ship's company dressed part-of-ship decks as we glided through the Mediterranean Fleet, our Marine Band on X-turret playing 'Now is the hour', en route Suez Canal and New Zealand.

Leander Convoys January 1940 to January 1941

2nd NZEF, 1st Echelon, Wellington-Sydney, Sat 6 January 1940

Dunera	*Strathaird*	*Empress of Canada*	*Rangitata*	*Sobieski*

2nd NZEF 2nd Echelon 2nd AIF, Tues, 2 May 1940, Ex Wgton & Sydney

Empress of Britain	42,348	*Queen Mary*	81,236
Mauretania	34,000	*Empress of Japan*	26,032
Andes	26,000	*Empress of Canada*	21,517
Aquitania	45,647		
		7 ships, total tonnage	266,779

BN1 Indian Ocean to Port Sudan & Suez, Tues, 2 July 1940

Beacon Street	7,432	*Anna Odland*	4,890
Akbar	4,043	*Svenor*	7,616
British Architect	7,388	*William Strachan*	6,157
British Hope	6,951	*Tubor*	4,782
Drava	3,566	Plum Leaf (RFA)	5,916
		10 ships, total tonnage	58,741

Escort: *Leander, Carlisle, Kandahar, Kingston, Shoreham, Flamingo*

BS1 North of Port Sudan, Wed, 10 July to South of Aden, 15 July 1940

Bullmouth	7,519	British Commodore	6,999
British Colonel	6,365	Athelmere	5,568
Arbistan	5,874	Khandalla	7,019
Cogra	5,190	Ganges	6,246
Ross	3,066	Almenara	1,851
Egyptian Prince	3,490	Khosrou	4,043
Clifton Hall	5,026	Orwell	7,968
Hersteid	5,100	Brouxville	4,553
Zam Zam	8,039	Garymede	2,682
		18 ships, total tonnage	97,107

Escort: *Leander, Carlisle, Kandahar, Kimberley, Auckland, Flamingo*

BN2 Indian Ocean from AMCs Westralia & Cathay, 26 July to N of Port Sudan

Vanseva	4,701	Jehangin	3,566
Cornwall	11,288	Hawal	5,430
Longwood	9,463	Ranee	5,060
Ellenga	5,196	Jaharashui	4,449
Allula	5,282	Haegh Hoed	9,351
Olivia	6,207	Daveikin	2,922
Vil	2,993	Suena	8,117
Izarau	4,791	Peshawar	7,934
Beacon Street	7,432	British Judge	6,735
Hatchiwa	8,890	Necudees	2,276
		20 ships, total tonnage	122,083

Escort: *Leander, Carlisle, Kandahar, Kimberley, Auckland, Flamingo*

BS2 N of Port Sudan to SE of Aden, 2 August to 8 August

Hasiral	6,578	Westbank	5,060
Havasli	3,204	William Strachan	6,157
Suvla	6,256	Tweed	2,697
African Prince	5,119	Esuali	1,931
Hanaqui	2,802	Hope Castle	5,178
Anna Odland	4,980	Traganus	1,712
Akleau	4,043		
		13 ships, total tonnage	55,717

Escort: *Leander, Carlisle, Kingston, Kimberley, Grimsby, Parrametta*

BN3 Indian Ocean to N of Port Sudan, 15 August to 21 August

Talamba	8,018	Takliwa	7,936
Khandalla	7,018	Devonshire	11,275
Dilware	11,080	Egra	5,108
Lancashire	9,557	Khedive Ismail	7,290
Acadia	5,002	Rajula	8,478
Rohna	8,602	Ethiopia	5,574
British Fusilier	6,943	Elmdene	4,853
Jessmore	4,099	City of Keelung	5,186
Malayan Prince	8,593	Raby Castle	4,996
British Pride	7,106		
		19 ships, total tonnage	136,714

Escort: *Leander, Kingston, Kimberley, Hindustan, Auckland, Grimsby, Parramatta*

BS3 N of Port Sudan to SE of Aden, 21 August to 25 August

President Doumer	11,898	Grena	8,117
Jaharashui	4,449	Dorysoa	4,790
Ranee	5,060	Talma	10,000
Nawal	5,430	Olivia	6,307
Steama Romani	5,311	Anna Odland	4,980
Oltenia	6,394	El Nil	7,690
Sardinian Prince	3,491	Egyptian	2,868
Rahmani	5,463	Halka	3,471
Brux Jarl	1,890	Daviken	2,922
El Amin	746		
		19 ships, total tonnage	101,277

Escort: *Leander, Kandahar, Kimberley, Hindustan, Auckland*

BN4 Indian Ocean to N of Port Sudan, 1 September to 8 September

Nizam	5,322	Rajput	5,497
Khosrou	4,043	Erinpura	5,143
Amra	8,314	Nevassa	9,213
Ismali	5,897	Varsova	4,701
El Madina	3,962	Varela	4,651
Subadar	5,424	Karagola	7,053
Ekma	5,108	Jalavihar	5,330
Bankura	3,185	Jaladuta	4,966
Jalakrishna	4,991	Nurmahal	5,491
Jelamoham	5,100	Rezivani	5,448
Bahadur	5,424	Northmoor	4,392
Baron Erskine	3,657	Davonia	8,129
Vaeport	6,774	Ilanwern	6,000
Brittdah	4,968	El Amin	746

Westbury	4,712	Tomislav	5,387
Polyktor	4,077	Star of Cairo	4,579
Jalapdna	3,935	Warlady	4,876
Trevarrack	5,270	Dramatist	5,443
Ayamonte	845	Atlas	7,058
El Hak	1,022		
		39 ships, total tonnage	196,088

Escort: *Leander, Auckland, Shoreham, Yarra, Kandahar*

During this convoy at least 36 bombs were dropped at *Leander* and nearby ships between 1200 and 1530 on 6 September. Five aircraft were confirmed shot down.

BS4 N of Port Sudan to SE of Aden, 8 September to 13 September

British Fusilier	6,943	City of Keelung	5,186
Palestinian Prince	1,960	Beacon Street	7,432
British Union	6,987	Captain A.F. Lucas (US)	4,188
Planter	5,887	Mathura	8,890
Felix Roussel (Fr)	17,083		
		9 ships, total tonnage	64,556

Escort: *Leander, Kingston, Hindustan, Yarra*

BN5 Heavy night raid on convoy in Aden. Sailed up Red Sea, 0600 19 September

Aniylus	8,017	Jalaganga	4,981
Santhia	7,754	Bhima	5,280
Akbar	4,043	Westralia	4,568
British Emperor	3,663	Cyclops	9,076
Sindo	3,921	Protector	562
Karoa	7,009	City of Christiana	4,940
Pellicula	6,254	Shamlea	4,252
Heron	5,540	Tremminara	4,694
Theseus	6,527	Nils Moller	6,647
Clearpool	5,404	Tomislav	5,387
Westbury	3,901	Ovington Court	6,195
		22 ships, total tonnage	118,615

Escort: *Leander, Auckland, Shoreham, Parramatta*

At 1030 bomb hit aft on *Bhima*, crew abandoned ship, ordered back aboard by *Leander*'s Captain Horan. Ship saved and towed back to Aden by *Westbury*. Several enemy aircraft downed by A/A gunfire.

BS5 N of Port Sudan, 23 September to SE of Aden, 28 September

Ekma	5,168	Georgiston	5,888
Myrtlebank	5,450	Galavihar	5,330
Rizwani	5,448	Varvosa	4,701
Subadar	5,424	Malayan Prince	8,593
Helen Moller	5,259	Davonia	8,129
Velho	1,089	El Madina	3,962
Peshawar	7,934	Germa	5,282
Vacport	6,774	Acadia	5,002
Nurmahal	5,419	Kawsar	7,778
British Judge	6,735	Iris	1,851
Salamohan	5,100	Panaghiotis	3,577
Islami	5,897		
		23 ships, total tonnage	125,809

Escort: *Leander, Auckland, Shoreham, Parramatta*

BN6 Sailed Aden 3 October to N of Port Sudan, 8 September

Dilwarra	11,080	Devonshire	11,275
President Doumer	11,898	Lancashire	9,549
Rajala	8,578	Marisa	8,029
Rhona	8,602	Talamba	8,018
Elsegundo	3,663	Egra	5,108
Rajput	5,497	Lisa	5,932
Jahangir	3,566	Lukrigathan	3,564
El Amin	746	Recorder	5,982
Robert L Holt (US)	2,918	Takliwa	7,936
Helka	3,471	Star of Alexandria	4,329
Ranee	5,060	City of Singapore	6,555
Borgestad	3,924	Boncruachim	5,920
Umberleigh	4,950	Ascot	1,323
Khandalla	7,018	Clan Ross	5,897
Sarmuha	5,254	British Captain	6,968
Cyprian Prince	3,071	Devis	6,054
Elphis	3,651	Soli	5,834
Shirala	7,841	Strix	6,219
Naringa	6,607	Ayamonte	854
Therese Moller	3,930	Helen Moller	5,259
Pundit	5,305	Quiloa	7,766
Jalaputra	4,856	Jhelum	403
Nizam	5,322		
		45 ships, total tonnage	259,217

Escort: *Leander, Auckland, Hindustan, Yarra, Kandahar*

Bombed on 5, 6, 7 October, aircraft driven off by ships' A/A gunnery no damage.

BS6 N of Port Sudan 8 October to SE of Aden, 13 October

Phoenix	5,907	Charlbury	4,900
Star of Mexico	3,350	Raby Castle	4,996
Duffield	8,516	Jessmore	4,099
British Pride	7,106	Hydroussa	2,038
Jalapundma	3,935	Baron Erskine	3,657
Bahadur	5,424	Khandalla	7,018
Trevarrack	5,270		
		13 ships, total tonnage	66,216

Escort: *Leander, Auckland, Hindustan, Yarra*

No air attacks, storm conditions throughout trip.

BN7 SE of Aden 16 October to N of Port Sudan, 23 October

Felix Roussel	17,053	Tyndarcus	11,361
Nevassa	9,213	Empire Advocate	9,515
Nurmahal	5,419	Inviken	4,171
Cranfield	5,332	Australind	5,020
Ethiopia	3,574	Egra	7,590
Subadar	5,424	Ascot	1,323
Hatarana	7,522	Jalarishma	4,991
Nyholm	5,843	King Arthur	5,224
Karagola	7,053	Kurdistan	5,844
Ekma	5,108	Mandalay	5,529
British Colonel	6,999	Marcella	4,592
Nyco	1,345	Hannah Moller	2,931
Varsova	4,701	Olive Moller	5,080
Kingswood	5,163	Marion Moller	4,986
Margot	4,543	Arundo	3,827
Myrtlebank	5,150		
		31 ships, total tonnage	195,258

Escort: *Leander, Auckland, Yarra, Parramatta, Kingston, Kimberley, Derby, Huntly*

Bombed on 19, 20 Oct, A/C driven off by A/A gunfire. Night attack 21 Oct, convoy shelled by Italian destroyers *Leone, Pantera, Nullo* and *Sauro*, damaging one ship; torpedoes fired at *Yarra* but no hits. *Leander* fired 129 rounds of 6″ and damaged one destroyer as they retired under smoke screens. *Kimberley* chased, gunned and torpedoed *Nullo* near Massawa's Harmil Island, leaving her grounded and wrecked. Shore batteries damaged *Kimberley*, *Leander* took her in tow at daylight, heavily bombed, severe buffeting by near misses, retained tow; A/C again driven off by A/A gunfire. Took *Kimberley* back to convoy, *Kingston* then towed her to Port Sudan.

BS7 N of Port Sudan 23 October to SE of Aden, 28 October

President Doumer	11,898	Dilwarra	11,080
El Segundo	3,663	Naringa	6,607
Ancylus	8,017	Nizam	5,322
Rajula	8,478	Tomislav	5,387
Theseus	6,357	Shirala	7,841
Sanganger	7,616	Brittdal	6,547
Svenor	9,525	Treminand	4,694
Egra	5,108	Ovington Court	6,095
City of Christiana	4,940	Hilda Moller	5,289
Jalaganga	4,981	Alavi	3,566
Marissa	8,029	Narpalycus	4,107
		22 ships, total tonnage	145,917

Escort: *Leander, Carlisle, Kingston, Yarra, Auckland*

BN9 Assembled at Aden and left 18 November to N of Port Sudan, 22 November

British Endurance	8,406	Beacon Street	7,402
Wayfarer	5,068	Jaladuta	4,966
Jalavihar	5,330	Luna	662
British Loyalty	6,993	Traganus	1,712
Desmoulea	8,120	Marie Maersk	8,271
Ayamonte	8,120	Kate	6,825
British Judge	6,735	Velho	1,098
Stan Park	5,103	City of Florence	6,862
Pericles	8,327	Helen Moller	5,259
El Hak	1,022	Iris	1,881
Sandown Castle	7,607	City of Christchurch	6,009
		22 ships, total tonnage	114,533

Escort: *Leander, Auckland, Parramatta, Kingston, Hindustan*

Off Perim on 18th, passed by *Shropshire* and *Carlisle* escorting 11 fast troopships north.

BS9 N of Port Sudan 22 November to S of Aden, 26 November

Australind	5,020	Bahadur	5,424
Arundo	5,163	Recorder	5,982
Clan Campbell	7,255	Serbino	4,099
Subadar	5,424	Myrtlebank	5,150
Konistra	3,527	Elphis	3,651
Nyco	1,345	King Arthur	5,224
Erica	5,112	Kingswood	5,080
Jalarishna	4,991	Ascot	1,323

Daisy Moller	4,087	*Katie Moller*	3,100
Inviken	4,171		
		19 ships, total tonnage	86,028

Escort: *Leander, Carlisle, Auckland, Kingston, Hindustan*

24 November, enemy A/C driven off by *Carlisle* mass A/A gunfire on outer screen. 28 November 1940 *Leander* dispatched to bombard Italian D/F Station and fish canning factory at Ras Alula on Cape Guadafui, Italian Somaliland (NE Africa), then operated with Indian Ocean cruisers searching for enemy raiders, until 2 January 1941.

BN12 Joined Ex-Bombay Convoy off Aden 2 Jan, took it N of Port Sudan 6 Jan

Drupa	8,102	*Eugenia S Emburicos*	4,882
Egra	5,108	*Bahadur*	5,424
Sandara	5,281	*Nordanger*	3,297
El Amin	746	*El Nil*	7,690
Jeanette Skinner	5,800	*Harmattan*	4,558
Takliwa	7,936	*Arundo*	5,163
Levernbank	5,150	*Kyriaki*	4,130
Christos Marketos	5,209	*Thermoplyae*	6,655
Andreas	6,566	*British Motorist*	6,891
Condylis	4,439	*Torstad*	3,246
Varsova	4,701	*Fram*	2,930
Peebles	4,982	*Therese Moller*	3,930
Jalapadma	3,935	*Istria*	5,416
Ovula	6,256	*Fred*	4,043
Nicolaou Georgis	4,108	*Teti*	2,747
Maro	3,549	*Ada*	2,595
		32 ships, total tonnage	

Escort: *Leander, Hindustan, Amber, Flamingo, Kimberley*

BS12 N of Port Sudan 6 January to SE of Aden, 11 January

Nirvana	6,044	*City of Dunkirk*	5,861
Jhelum	4,038	*British Chemist*	5,060
Sygna	3,881	*Elizabeth Moller*	5,863
Hatarana	7,522	*Silver Maple*	6,997
Sarmula	5,254	*Sazana*	4,353
Jalavihar	5,330	*Naringa*	5,313
Athelstan	8,782	*Talma*	10,000
Jaladuta	4,966	*Addington Court*	6,607
Tanfield	4,538	*City of Auckland*	8,336
Velma	9,720	*Egra*	5,108
Sandown Castle	7,607	*Islami*	5,879

Trentbank	5,060	*Octavian*	1,345
		24 ships, total tonnage	142,622

Escort: *Leander, Amber, Hindustan*

9 January off Centre Peak Island roughest seas met yet in Red Sea. 10 January headwind easing through Perim Straits. 11 January dispersed convoy. 1830 arrived Aden before midnight. To date, escorted 446 ships in Red Sea totalling 2,512,965 registered tonnage. Cargo tonnage probably 2 to 3 times that.

This ended *Leander*'s Red Sea convoys. Only one ship lost, a straggler which was torpedoed and sunk.

CHAPTER XII

Almost HMNZS Neptune

WELLINGTON IN LATE AUTUMN 1940 was cold; and windswept sleet enshrouded HMAS *Canberra* on Wednesday, 1 May as the heavy cruiser's stern faded around Massey Memorial, en route Lyttelton for the South Island's 2nd NZEF 2nd Echelon contingent aboard Poland's liner *Sobieski*. They would join the North Island ships in Cook Strait.

And next day with Governor General Sir George Galway's intended farewell visits cancelled due to driving rain, the troopships *Andes, Empress of Britain, Empress of Japan* and *Aquitania* moved down Wellington harbour escorted by *Leander* and *Australia*. Already Galway's talks had been replaced by harangues from loud-mouthed sergeants and petty officers, informing their khaki-clad thousands and navy-blue hundreds about specific abandon-ship stations, and the shipboard routine to be observed over this long voyage to England. There, these high-spirited weekend sailors from New Zealand's four provincial RNVR headquarters would be drafted to every class of Royal Naval vessel from battleship down to minesweeper. Then in 1941, further to NZNB's advice that sufficient ratings were now available from Motuihe Island's *Tamaki* Training Establishment, and from accelerated enrolment through *Philomel*, to man a 3rd NZ cruiser preferably similar to *Achilles* and *Leander*, Admiralty was so informed and AFO–1033 was circu-lated to all Royal Naval Ships and Establishments to be displayed ASAP.

Within days men were fronting noticeboards, some to make uninterested remarks and wander off but others to become excited as they read:

Admiralty has agreed with the New Zealand Government to gradually man a Leander Class cruiser, probably *Neptune*, with a New Zealand crew. All New Zealand ratings and officers serving on Defensively Equipped Merchant Ships and His Majesty's Ships and Establishments will be appropriated to HMS *Drake* with their papers, as reliefs are made available.

Meantime the Colony Class cruiser *Nigeria*, battlecruiser *Hood* plus other light and heavy units, were standing 300 miles south-west of Brest antici-pating a clash with Germany's capital ships *Scharnhorst, Gneisenau* and several destroyer flotillas should they emerge; whilst in Whitehall, War Minister Churchill was grumbling through a cigar to his First Sea Lord Sir Dudley Pound: 'If they come out my navy will be waiting, but if they don't my air force will undoubtedly destroy them anyway,' an observation disproved months later when the bomb-damaged ships were repaired sufficiently to make an epic 'Channel dash' to temporary safety in Norway.

But back to the Brest blockade force constantly updated by morsed W/T broadcasts from GYC, amidst which one signal detached *Nigeria* two days south to reinforce a round-the-Cape north-bound convoy, twenty-one ageing freighters escorted by two corvettes and a sloop from Gibraltar which elicited a messdeck tactician's observation: 'Why doesn't Churchill just give the bloody ships to Hitler? No flippin wonder we're losin the poor bastards quickerin we can build newuns!'

Hood's flashed farewell message was receipted and reciprocated in calm warm weather, so placid that glistening blue Atlantic swells caressed ships' bows then undulated aft to marry into lazy wakes; but over the next forty-eight hours an ominous low worked north and overtook the distant 6-knot convoy, also the approaching cruiser whose catapulted Osprey made contact then returned just in time to be retrieved. Over ensuing days and nights *Nigeria*'s Captain Ransome rarely closed his eyes; nor did the twenty-five New Zealanders among his ship's company. Force 7 to 9 hurricanes hurled mountainous seas over quarterdecks and poops, a man washed overboard at night from one tramp was almost rescued by a shipmate who threw a lifebelt, tied a line round his waist then dived in after him. He struggled towards the lifebelt light as it topped succeeding crests, but breaking waves forced him under. He surfaced coughing salt water and the line dragged. He was yards off that unattainable belt when the First Mate ordered crewmen to haul him back aboard. They watched that light crest huge swells and disappear, time and again until it was lost forever.

In Scapa Flow on Easter Friday 1941 rumours persisted around the 10th Cruiser Squadron that *Nigeria* would shortly depart 'On loan' to New Zealand as were *Achilles* and *Leander*. *Nigeria*, now motionless on a single cable in the Orkney's sun-drenched tide, was washing down salt-encrusted paintwork after her harrowing experience across the Bay of Biscay. For the cruiser and her charges it had been a several-day nightmare, constantly urging the twenty-one tramps to extract more revolutions from their antiquated reciprocal engines, ever on the alert for telltale periscopes in that sub-infested tiger country. But perhaps those relentless hurricanes had kept Doenitz's U-boats submerged; perhaps the convoy was just lucky; so all made it safely to their respective Liverpool or Belfast approaches, where *Nigeria* made appropriate visual signals then increased speed north through the Irish Sea. It was now known that it would not be *Nigeria*, but the Leander Class cruiser *Neptune* upon which Admiralty and the New Zealand Government had agreed; so 'Down unders' on many ships of the Home Fleet were queuing at Regulating Offices to be directed to Captains' Offices for their cards to be checked and draft chits authorised.

For a pre-Second World War period *Neptune* had been attached to the South Africa Station, on which at the eve of war she intercepted and sank the German freighter *Innsbruck* from which *bruck* had been deleted and her port of registry altered to a neutral country. Shifting north *Neptune* operated as a unit of C-in-C West Africa's powerful Anglo-French force based at Freetown and Dakar, until late April 1940 when Mussolini became grandiloquent at conferences with Hitler. Admiralty ordered the Royal Navy to base a Mediterranean Fleet at Alexandria, France immediately agreed to transfer some of her Western Mediterranean battleships and cruisers to the Egyptian harbour, and French Admiral Godfroy accepted his long-term friend Admiral Cunningham to be the Anglo-French fleet's C-in-C.

(Andrew Browne Cunningham, aged 14 in 1897, entered the Royal Navy and was dubbed '*ABC*' by his classmates, a tab which remained throughout his naval career. As a middie on the cruiser *Doris* he won recognition during Boer War landings; then years later at Gallipoli in command of the destroyer *Scorpion* his exploits earned him the DSO. Back in home waters as SO Dover Patrol Destroyers whilst blockading Zeebrugge he was awarded the Belgian Croix de Guerre and a bar to his DSO, and post-First World War he merited a second bar when commanding the destroyer *Seafire* during Baltic operations against the Bolsheviks. Between the First and Second World Wars promotions raised him from Flag Captain America & West Indies Station, to CO HMS *Rodney*, Home Fleet, Rear Admiral Med Fleet Destroyers, then Vice Admiral Commanding Med Fleet with his flag on the battlecruiser *Hood*).

In mid-May 1940 at Malta several of *Neptune's* cabin occupants were downsized to lesser cabins, when ABC's flag graced the cruiser's foremast peak and his senior staff came aboard for a fast transfer to Alexandria. Having arrived in the strategic Egyptian harbour he shifted his flag ashore, or onto *Warspite* when at sea. And now with Captain Rory O'Conor on the bridge in place of Captain Tony Morse, *Neptune* took station astern of Rear Admiral Tovey's 25th CS flagship *Orion* when Cunningham led his Anglo-French battlefleet to sea for exercises in gale-strength Mediterranean gusts. There in two columns at 20 knots, *Warspite*, *Malaya* and *Royal Sovereign* smashed through white-capped rollers, mere cables abreast of *Lorraine*, *Bretagne* and *Provence* – ponderous great gun-platforms torrenting angry seas across their foredecks. Disposed line ahead to port were the heavy cruisers *Duquesne*, *Duquay Troin*, *Tourville* and *Suffren*; and to starboard the RN's *Orion*, *Neptune* and the ageing D-Class cruisers *Dragon* and *Delhi*, all van-and-outer-screened by Tricolour and White Ensign destroyer flotillas.

When if ever had such an Anglo-French battle fleet taken to the high seas? So, now convinced that he was ready should Italy enter the War as an enemy and, satisfied that he and Admiral Godfroy could operate in unison, ABC ordered a course for the return to harbour.

Over the years from 1911 Italy had gradually colonised Libya and her armed forces now threatened Egypt from the west. A blacksmith, Benito Mussolini entered Italy's political arena as its fascist leader in 1922, invaded Abyssinia with 200,000 troops in the mid-1930s and now posed a southern threat to Egypt, and Britain's Red Sea traffic. The Suez Canal and vast Sinai Desert provided a modicum of comfort on Egypt's eastern front and, although Italy had 6 battleships, 19 cruisers, 45 destroyers, 120 submarines, and numerous MTBs etc., Cunningham was confident his Mediterranean Fleet would rule the waves lapping Egypt's northern coast.

At this stage Hitler was concentrating his war in Europe, leaving Mussolini's powerful land, sea and air forces to take care of the Mediterranean and its northern countries. This, and the evacuation of Britain's army from Dunkirk, allowed Churchill to amass a Desert Army in Egypt, intended to secure all of North Africa, the Lebanon, and the Middle East oilfields; one of its early intentions being the occupation of Bardia, a Libyan seaport fortress 250 miles west of the Egyptian border. This would be attempted immediately after Cunningham's agreed naval bombardment.

On Wednesday afternoon 19 June the cruisers *Orion*, *Neptune* and *Sydney*, accompanied by *Lorraine* and four destroyers left Alexandria, arriving seaward of Bardia at dawn and shortly signalling readiness to their individually catapulted spotting planes. Gun ready lights in each director tower and on each bridge told gunnery officers they could fire when indicated by the synchronised signal. Seconds ticked by ... then ... 'Tinng Tinng' on *Neptune*'s bridge. That dazzling muzzle-lit rolling powder cloud; gun-recoil concussion from each turret, ear-thumping WHHHOOMMPHH and almost instantaneous shockwave against superstructures from *Lorraine*'s 13.4″ salvo only cables abreast ... 'Tinng Tinng' ... a second sheet of man-made lightning, rolling booms, decks and bulkheads trembling ... 'Tinng Tinng' ... another thunder crash, again, again and again until men below were breathing cordite fumes and punkalouvre dust.

Right from the opening salvo spotting aircraft were signalling straddles and direct hits on the ships' 12,000 yard distant targets, all along the 300-feet-high escarpment, flame streaked upheavals, gun-site debris thrown hundreds of feet skyward, twisted metal and blast-torn bodies, diminishing retaliation by Italian coastal batteries until there was none at 0615 when CS7, Rear Admiral Tovey on *Orion*, signalled cease firing.

Lorraine had suffered casualties and superficial damage when a near-miss 9″ shell hurled shrapnel and large fragments inboard, and now in daylight as the force retired it was set upon by Fiat fighters and fighter-bombers, one putting a burst through *Sydney*'s Walrus which managed to crash-land at Mersa Matruh, while the remaining British and French spotters kept out of the way until the Italian planes were driven off by intense A/A fire. Only then could *Lorraine* and the cruisers sweep a swathe of still water for them to land and be retrieved.

At midnight the ships were back in Alexandria, repelling reprisals by Libyan-based Italian bombers and torpedo-bombers – terrific explosions erupting among the fleets' cruiser squadrons and major ship anchorages; searchlights intertwining about the overhead, locking on to Marchetti Savoias and lesser aircraft, A/A crews ramming, loading, firing, ramming, loading, firing, ejected brass cylinders clanging on steel decking, spent machine-gun ammunition and shell fragments peppering the harbour and rattling onto ships' upper decks and structures; while determined torpedo-bombers skimmed low over masts to drop their missiles then roar seaward followed by converging tracer. Suddenly it seemed, there was quiet, downed aircraft burned and crackled momentarily until they sank, some flamed furiously where they'd crashed ashore, and oil tanks billowed flame-lit rolling smoke. Then Alexandria became another nightmare, with wailing sirens as new waves arrived, some brought down, caught in the glare of searchlights and torn apart when shells burst around them. Hour after hour the overhead brilliance of bursting shells, curving tracer, search-light beams, dockside buildings flaring when hit, then crumpling. Men gradually became inured to the bedlam of that night's engulfing cacophony. Ships were thumped by near misses, rocked and pitched then stabilised. Alarm etched on the faces of those below deck, turned to nervous laughter then confidence at a Cockney's sudden outburst: 'Strike me flippin pink. Didn't think the fookin wops were that bloody good!'

Pre-war years of training now turned the attack into another exercise, tension eased, some slept until offsiders shook them to take over for a spell, then it was over. Growing daylight saw the last attacker disappear hotly pursued by RAF Hurricanes. Tired men sought places to sleep, uninterested in other ships' fates, uninterested in the pall of smoke hanging over Alexandria.

Two days later ABC took his flag aboard *Warspite* then summoned the fleets' senior officers to a briefing, and when back on *Neptune* Captain O'Conor asked his department officers to meet in his cabin where he spoke on the C-in-C's intentions: 'Admiral Cunningham is taking the fleet on the offensive into Italian waters to draw them out of harbour. We will leave together and remain so until beyond night-glass range before dividing into four groups, each with separate orders after which we will rendezvous at the entrance to the Adriatic. We and *Sydney* will be with *Warspite* escorted by *Nubian*, *Mohawk*, *Defender* and *Decoy* for a sweep south of Crete to the Sicily coast.' He paused, looked momentarily at each officer and continued:

'We and *Sydney* will then detach and patrol north of Messina Straits to draw the Messina based battlefleet onto *Royal Sovereign* and *Ramillies* who will have been joined by *Warspite*. Should we and *Sydney* encounter enemy cruisers before rejoining we will engage. Meanwhile *Eagle's* bombers and torpedo-bombers will attack Port Augusta which will then be bombarded by *Warspite*, *Royal Sovereign* and *Ramillies*. At the same time *Orion*, *Liverpool* and *Gloucester* will search the Dodecanese, then between Greece and Crete and across to the Messina Straits. And to the south, *Duquesne*, *Duquay Trouin*, *Tourville*, *Suffron* and four French destroyers will be going west along the Libyan coast. So ... in some shape or form we can expect to engage the enemy within the next forty-eight hours. Any questions?'

At 2200 on Saturday, 22 June the fleet left harbour and steamed steadily north, but shortly before ABC's four-part strategy was to be put into operation the whole fleet reversed course and returned to harbour. Due to the worsening French situation Admiralty had ordered Cunningham back to Alexandria without delay. Days passed with French and British liberty men allowed ashore until 2200, but only the fleet's RN cruisers and destroyers were sent out on convoy missions. Then shortly after 'Colours' on Saturday, 6 July ... panic ... men racing to their action stations ... someone yelling: 'Raus Raus. The bloody Frogs are going to break out!'

Neptune's Lieutenant Commander Armstrong brandishing a sword and pistol, urged his armed boarding party down the quarterdeck gangway into a waiting pinnace, then leapt aboard as its motor revved when shoving off. But hours passed awaiting further orders as he and other boats lay off French cruisers and destroyers. Midnight came and went, then alarms sounded and bugles blared on all men-of-war – but not for an Anglo/French confrontation – for another Italian air raid, an opportune one welding both sides together, once again fighting side by side. Cruisers' boats drifted away from gangways empty as men scrambled aboard to their A/A posts. The screech of bombs was lost in a bedlam of gunfire, detonations from near misses between anchored ships, clang of fragments on steel, shriek of men torn by shrapnel, some killed, others wounded. And at dawn when the enemy departed, French and RN matelots waved intership; camaraderie returned.

Alexandria's papers headlined Somerville's Gibraltar-based fleet's attack on France's fleet in Mers-el-Kebir and Oran; said Churchill ordered it to stop Germany getting them when France fell; then reported Godfroy's consideration of fighting his Alexandria-based fleet out to sea, and the air raid which decided him against the attempt.

Meantime Cunningham had drawn up proposals to be put to Godfroy, the French admiral was piped aboard *Warspite*, warmly invited into the C-in-C's ornate and spacious quarters, and there on Sunday, 7 July 1940 deliberated a draft agreement which both admirals subsequently signed item by item:

1. French warships in Alexandria shall not be scuttled and will be maintained in existing condition.

2. French ships in Alexandria shall not be seized by the Royal Navy.

3. French naval personnel will be reduced to an agreed complement; men released from duty will be repatriated.

4. French naval personnel remaining aboard French ships will not attempt to leave Alexandria or engage in hostilities against the British.

5. The Royal Navy will ensure adequate fuel, rations, medical supplies and clothing to the French ships.

6. This agreement will be revised if French ships in Alexandria are to be seized by the Axis powers.

Cunningham now revised his recently cancelled foray into Mussolini's 'Mare Nostrum', although he no longer had the French fleet at his disposal, and Intelligence informed him that five Italian troopships left Naples for Benghazi on 6 July, escorted by the battleships *Guilio Cesare*, *Conte de Cavour*, six 8″ heavy cruisers, twelve 6″ light cruisers, thirty-two destroyers, and a number of submarines stationed along the route. Regia Aeronautica would be providing them air cover from Sicily and Cyrenaica.

By coincidence two British convoys were about to depart Malta for Alexandria; the first, three ships transporting Maltese evacuees; the second, five fast freighters from the UK with arms and supplies for the Desert Army.

Late into the First Watch on 7 July the Med Fleet cleared Alexandria's boom and diverted in three groups: (1) the carrier *Eagle*, battleships *Malaya*, *Royal Sovereign*, and two destroyer flotillas heading for Sicily to attack Port Augusta; (2) *Warspite* with destroyers escorting her on a westerly course south of group one; (3) Admiral Tovey on *Orion* following further to the south with *Neptune*, *Sydney* and four Australian destroyers. After the Port Augusta assault, unless the enemy had been intercepted en route to Benghazi, Cunningham's three forces would combine and cover the eastbound British convoys. *Neptune*'s lookouts scanned the empty horizon through powerful night glasses, men not yet turned in watched phosphorescent bow waves, looked up where gently swaying mastheads scribed arcs across a star-studded black sky, filled their lungs with crisp night air then went below.

An hour after daybreak *Gloucester* radioed she was under air attack, a direct hit had killed her Captain Garside, her Gunnery Officer, the

Commander and fifteen ratings. Then *Neptune*'s bugler raced men to 'Repel Aircraft Stations'; high-level bombers were already being fired at, and 4″ shells fused to activate at their height were exploding among the big Savoias as Rory O'Conor demanded more speed and an urgent turn to starboard. Bombs shook *Neptune* as they erupted close astern; one bomber trailing black smoke and flame gyrated seaward; twin 4″ muzzles still blasted rolling smoke rings at the departing aircraft and as suddenly as it had started, the action ended.

In her van position several miles ahead, *Neptune*'s lookouts scanned the hazy horizon continually but it remained empty. Up in the DCT Lieutenant Mountfield pressed his cheekbones against the rangefinder's soft rubber eyepads, adjusted the focus and concentrated on an indistinct blip, swung gently off it to another, then a third, fourth, more, definitely mastheads as he buzzed the bridge and shouted: 'ENEMY IN SIGHT. IT'S THE WHOLE BLOODY EYTIE FLEET. THE HORIZON'S THICK WITH THE BAS-TARDS!'

Orion's RCO telegraphist was copying *Neptune*'s Fleet Wave enemy report, relaying it to the bridge. Admiral Tovey was ordering 28 knots for his cruisers, telling them to engage opposite numbers when in range. Cunningham on *Warspite* miles behind the cruisers was asking his Engineer Commander for maximum speed and Rory O'Conor was asking his Navi to turn *Neptune* toward the enemy when they opened fire; a requirement immediately obeyed as distant flashes indicated the Italian battle fleet had engaged from 28,000 yards. Seconds became minutes, then the air vibrated as huge shells rumbled over to explode hundreds of yards past as massive geyser upheavals.

Neptune's rangetaker shouted out the closures. '27,500 … 27,000 … 26,500 … down each 500 until … 22,000.' All this time the computer table decks below had been fed relative information, wind direction and speed, air temperature, ship's speed and head, estimated enemy speed range and course, plus a diversity of details to be ingested in that era of gunnery technology. A and B turrets trained slightly right, slightly left, steadied, their guns elevated and depressed as directed, gun-ready lights glowed and at 22,000 yards *Neptune* opened fire on the Italian lead cruiser, now identified as the 8″ heavy cruiser *Bolzano*.

Orion, *Sydney* and *Liverpool* were firing at the next three in line, 12.7″ and 8″ enemy salvoes were falling short, going over, sometimes straddling, so, considering the odds to be unacceptable at this stage, Tovey ordered a general 'Cease Fire' and retired out of range while awaiting *Warspite*. Soon after 1700 she was in company with the enemy in sight, her eight massive 15″ guns elevated, then flame and burnt cordite clouded her stem to stern. Her targets were identified as Admiral Campioni's flag battleship *Cesare* and her sister-ship *Conte de Cavour*, but when debris-laden shafts speared high from *Cesare* both battleships sped westward under heavy smoke screens.

As an incentive for the Italian departure, *Neptune* closed to 12,000 yards and obtained direct hits on *Bolzano*. The chase developed into a 'Tally Ho' with *Eagle*'s aircraft launching torpedoes in an attempt to slow the fleeing enemy. Out of the dense smoke screen there were sporadic enemy destroyer attacks, and inaccurate bombing by high-level aircraft, but the British-named 'Skirmish off Calabria', or Italian-recorded 'Battilio di Punta Stilo', decidedly went to Cunningham. The Italian battle fleet would not again challenge his supremacy in the Mediterranean, but there would be individual feats of bravery, continued night air raids over Alexandria, and submarine attacks which would in future be devastating to Malta convoys and major naval vessels.

Over the next several months *Neptune* would share the tasks of all cruisers, and following is an abbreviated record of her operations after the Calabria clash:

13.7.40   In Alex. Duty cruiser 1 hour's notice to sail. No leave.

19.7.40   With *Orion* to Libya coast to intercept 2 Iti cruisers seen en route Tobruk by *Sydney*. *Sydney* sank *Bartholomeo Colleoni*, rescued 500 survivors.

21. 7. 40   With *Malaya, Royal Sovereign, Warspite, Eagle* & 10 drs, Steamed SW of Crete to cover Greece-bound convoy.

23. to 27.7   With *Sydney* and drs to Sth of Dardanelles, cover for *Orion* with Sth bnd convoy, on 27th *Neptune* intercepted and sank enemy tanker *Hermione*.

15. 8. 40   Sent from Med to Sth Africa Station for 11 weeks raider hunting.

7. 11. 40   Depart Capetown for Lagos, flag of V-Adml John Cunningham (ABC's brother) transferred from *Devonshire*.

19. 11. 40   To Gulf of Guinea, 'Showing the Flag' off Libreville, Port Gentil and other French possessions to support General de Gaulle during his French Equatorial Africa tour.

14. 12. 40   With *Dorsetshire* searching for French steamer *Duquesa* which sent an RRRR message in posn midway from Brazil to NW Africa.

Xmas 40   Still at sea, cruisers *Berwick, Bonaventure, Dorchestershire, Hawkins, Cumberland, Newcastle, Enterprise, Dragon*, AMCs *Pretoria*

Castle and *Esperance Bay*, carrier *Hermes* searching mid to sth Atlantic for *Scheer* and raider *Thor*.

28. 12. 40   In Freetown transferring V-Adml John Cunningham to liner *Orontes* for passage to UK as 4th Sea Lord. New V-Adml Raike now flying flag on AMC *Edinburgh Castle*.

1. 1. 41   With *Delhi* & corvette *Milford* escorting Fr troopers *Cap des Palmes* and *Toureg* nth. Detached to search for German ship near Ascension Is.

7. 1. 41   Refuel in Lagos.Then escort with *Delhi* & drs *Isis & Encounter*, for carrier *Furious* flying off 40 Hurricanes & 9 Fulmars to Lagos for overland flight via Lake Chad – Khartoum – to Cairo for Desert War.

12. 1. 41   In Freetown, refuel, 'No mail for *Neptune*. It was on-posted to England.' Loud cheers!

20–27. 1. 41In Gibraltar. Hearing about home folk from *Sheffield* & other W/S arriving from UK.

28. 1. 41   Left Gib. 4–2–41 at Scapa. 9–2–41 left for Chatham and LONG LEAVE.

Chatham in February 1941 was cold and wet, but inside pubs the open-fired warm atmosphere pulsed with conviviality and naval jargon, even New Zealand RNVRs who'd done months on all manner of RN ships were adept in Scouse, Jordie, Glasgie and other British Isles' dialects; but now the topic focused on *Neptune*. They'd come to Chatham Barracks to await her emergence from dock, where for three months naval experts and dockyard maties had replaced her single sticks with slender tripods festooned by all manner of radar and VHF gadgetry; updated her A/A capability; cut away steel partitions to make room for smaller compartments housing the latest technologies and the men to operate them.

Came the day when hundreds of draft-chitted 'Rockies' and 'Regulars' queued at *Neptune*'s port-waist gangway; stepped aboard, faced aft and saluted, then found their way to the Regulating Office for their Commissioning Cards – Ben Riley NZD999 joined *Philomel* late 1920s from Coromandel; LTO Doug Harvey NZD1158 joined *Philly* 1932 from New Plymouth, both Petty Officers; Auckland RNVR Signalman Ken Button; Otago Div 'Hud' Biggs; Wellington Div Alan Burt, Ian Brackenridge, Norm Andrew, Ces Rickard-Simms; an endless blue chain, some quipping the Marine Corporal and RPO as they boarded and went forward. Leaving the Reg Office later with cards indicating messdeck; locker number; boat station; G,T, or UA regarding rum issue; watch and part of watch plus other etceteras, men made their way up, down, or straight through to allocated messdecks, stowed their hammocks in the nettings then unloaded kit-bags into individual spacious lockers.

On Wednesday, 7 May 1941 *Neptune*, having completed a two-month refit and ingested some 750 complement, departed Chatham for the short Medway River transit to Sheerness, there next day being visited by New Zealand's High Commissioner, Bill Jordan, who told his 167 countrymen they might be home for winter where, he said, a large proportion of the ship's RN complement would be replaced by similar NZD ranks and ratings.

By Friday *Neptune* was provisioned, ammunitioned and fuelled to capacity; that night's liberty men were warned the ship was under sailing orders, and about mid-forenoon Saturday, with the last gangway craned ashore, Captain O'Conor issued quiet but distinct orders from his bridge, easing *Neptune* gently ahead against a taut spring as an outboard propeller eddied muddy water. The gap between stern and wharf widened slowly; coir fenders squealed somewhere for'ard and both engine-room repeaters jangled as their pointers swung to 'SLOW ASTERN'. Foc'sle Party men ran in the last headline as it splashed from a wharfside bollard; and *Neptune* slid stern first into open water, siren whooping manoeuvring warnings as she stopped, then, accompanied by the destroyer *Cottesmore*, she picked up headway toward the Medway-Thames confluence en route for Scapa.

Born 1903 into a landed Irish family with naval heritage, Rory O'Conor was enrolled in an Officer Training College. He served at sea in the latter

HMS *Neptune*, Leander Class Cruiser, at Scapa after her 1941 refit. Preparing to transfer to NZ Navy, note tripod masts etc.

years of the First World War, later attained Commander rank aboard *Hood*
on which he wrote *Running a Big Ship*, published by the RN as an Executive
Officer's bible; and during shore periods he came under Winston Churchill's
notice in Whitehall's Plans Division. And on 24 May 1940 he was appointed
Captain of *Neptune*, soon becoming 'father' to wardroom *and* messdeck
because of his obvious ability and his Daily Bulletins when clear of land,
these disclosing the ship's restricted information as he intended the complement to be 'intelligent and informed', not mere disciplined servants. Day
and night evolutions on the way north soon increased the ship's efficiency
to such an extent that following on Sunday's Quarterdeck Service in Scapa,
Rory's only reproach referred to his A/A gunners' inability to get off a
single round at the ME110 which plummeted from cloud on the second
day out from Sheerness, near-missed the ship either side with bombs, then
disappeared east at sea level undetected throughout by *Neptune*'s radar
operators. He emphasised the necessity for alertness in every department
then commended everyone for their evident intent to make this cruiser
'Crack ship of any squadron in which she might serve'.

Currently the 1941 war wasn't going Britain's way. May 20 – Crete
invaded by German paratroops; May 24 – *Hood* sunk by *Bismarck*; late May
– cruiser after cruiser being sunk or severely damaged in the Med. Disheart-
ening. But the more *Neptune*'s New Zealanders, new Imperials, and South
Africans learned about their captain from retained men of her previous
commission, the more confidence they felt in him; especially when hearing
old hands say they'd go through anything with him on the bridge. And
right now Churchill was desperate for a victory, anywhere but preferably
in North Africa, so he told the Navy to give his 8th Army Desert Generals
the tools and the men to achieve one over Rommel's Afrika Korps threatening Egypt from Libya.

Several thousand troops vied for grandstands about the liner *Duchess of
Bedford* as she steamed down the Clyde on 1 May 1941, short cables ahead
of the fast freighter *Port Wyndham* whose holds and decks were crammed
with tanks, mobile guns, tracked vehicles, ammunition and everything
available from British factories. Cleaving her wake came one of New
Zealand's refrigeration ships, M/V *Waiwera*, well below her Plimsoll line
with beef, mutton and yes, mutton birds for the Maori Battalion. Next
morning's Coastal Command Hudsons flashed greetings as they droned
close to identify and log this WS8X 'Winnie Express' escorted in the van
position by SO(D) *Legion*, with *Wild Swan, Vansittart, Wyvern, Suquanay*, as
the port leg and *Brighton, Piorun, St Mary, Sherwood*, angled out to starboard
of an arrowhead screen.

Inside this formation came *Port Wyndham, Duchess of Bedford*, then the
armed merchant cruiser *Esperance Bay* followed by *Waiwera*; and a mile

astern of her the carrier *Victorious* flanked by *Neptune* and the County Class cruiser *Norfolk*.

'Nine destroyers, a carrier, armed merchant cruiser and two cruisers for three flamin merchants!' a Hudson's Australian pilot drawled to his navigator. 'Must be the flippin crown jewels on their way to Canbruh!'

'Where the hell's that, Oz?'

'Our capital for Geez sake, Freddie boy. Thought you navis knew geography.'

When not closed up for action exercises, off-watch *Neptunians* stripped to the short hairs and lay about the foc'sle and boom decks imbibing sunrays; some leaned on guardrails discussing *Victorious*'s Blackburn Skuas lifting off to reconnoitre far from the convoy, saw previous scouts queuing to land back on. Occasionally a thud and distant upheaval would indicate an outer-screen destroyer's depth-charge in those sub-infested waters. But when well west of the 'Rock' the destroyers flashed farewell messages and left for Gibraltar. WS8X zigzagged south.

Auckland Rockie Ldg Tel Dave Watson had been talking with Able Seaman John Ross RNVR about their summers at Mission Bay, when he rose to brush off the seat of his shorts and went below for his 1st Dog in the Main W/T. John Ross did likewise and wandered aft to relieve his offsider on P2 A/A gun. Hours later men waxed poetic about the splendorous golden red sunset then sought their nearest gangway hatch. Coding Office punkalouvres blew more heat into the fetid air as Dave Watson stuffed the message he'd just decoded into a cartridge, slotted it into the SDO tube and pulled the handle to blast it topside. In moments Rory O'Conor was reading: '*Victorious* from Admiralty – Emergency = *Esperance Bay* reports unknown enemy vessel in posn 4332 N 2346W Detach cruiser for necessary action = 0835Z.

Neptune got the nod, worked up to 28 knots and was signalled by a Skua there were two enemy vessels 30 miles directly ahead. Half an hour later with the ship at Action Stations, *Neptune*'s masthead lookout was reporting masts on the horizon, 'Possible Hipper Class cruiser.' Then: 'Could be pocket battleship.'

Whichever, Captain O'Conor was already briefing bridge officers on his intention to identify the target, then remain out of range until *Victorious*'s torpedo-bombers made their attacks, thereafter he and *Norfolk* would close for the kill.

The distant enemy was turning broadside to engage, her profile showed flush deck stem to stern, three triple turrets all forward, none aft, squarish superstructure, small single funnel. No pocket battleship could disguise herself as *Nelson* so *Neptune* turned broadside on for easy identification. Messages flashed intership as *Nelson* signalled the enemy's position, said

she'd put a secondary armament 6" across her bows to make her heave
to, finished with 'Am busy please take over.'

Neptune's boarding party found the 8,000-ton German supply ship Gonzenheim burning below where she'd been sabotaged, red-hot bulkheads
warping and groaning as water flooded through opened seacocks. All codes
and confidential documents had been disposed of in weighted bags, leaving
only personal letters to be gathered from cabins and crew quarters for
later scrutiny. It seemed she had departed Brest three weeks earlier to
rendezvous with Bismarck near the Azores. Sixty-eight came up Neptune's
Jacob's ladders from German lifeboats, thirty-two of them naval personnel,
after which O'Conor ordered A- and B- turrets to put the doomed vessel
under; but when she still floated evenly after several rounds he told his
Torpedo Officer, Lieutenant Woodward, to try his luck. Minutes ticked
off over the 3,000-yard run, then Gonzenheim started like a spurred stallion,
her after-magazine erupted in an almighty mushroom belching flame,
rolling smoke and debris, high over her bridge. Britons and Germans
looked in awe as the shockwave rebounded off Neptune's upperworks, and
a group of kriegsmariners saluted at attention, lustily singing their naval
anthem until boiling waters subsided, leaving flotsam over their foundered
home.

Discharging her prisoners in Gibraltar and refuelling, Neptune sped after
the 15-knot convoy, caught up with it just before WS8X became embroiled
in one of the Atlantic's worst tropical storms and remained in Sierra Leone
two days until it abated sufficiently to proceed on 16 June. Without
ceremony they crossed the Line, lifting the hearts of South African officers
and ratings who soon would be with their wives and families, also the
nostalgia of New Zealanders on discovering their Southern Cross low in
the south-eastern night sky.

WS8X entered Cape Town on Monday, 23 June 1941, refuelled, took on
craneloads of beef, spuds and greens for two days and departed under RSAN
escort; but Neptune had gone through False Bay to berth in Simonstown,
Rory O'Conor had postponed all outstanding punishment until back at sea
and everyone not essential to the ship's security was to have the maximum
of liberty, so that they did. But on leaving harbour tempers soured among
those who'd once more farewelled wives or sweethearts, and among those
who'd come off with pulsating heads, yet there was more to come off Cape
Agulhas when Neptune barged right into an Indian Ocean/South Atlantic
confrontation, testing every rivet as she contorted through white-water
atop hill-sized swells torn by Force–9 southerly busters.

For the first time Captain O'Conor's temperament seemed similarly
affected and he demanded every evolution in the book as well as some of
his own. They were again with WS8X and Waiwera was now an enemy

cruiser who'd hit *Neptune* repeatedly; messenger boys came up to purpose-fully clamped bulkhead doors and searched darkened passages for ways to reach officers they'd been sent to find; damage control and first-aid parties did their best to fight imaginary fires and render aid to injured; fuel was theoretically pumped port tanks to starboard to correct listing; and internal buzzer lines morsed enemy reports followed by codes and cyphers about the action. A day, a night and hours later 'Father' expressed satisfaction and the ship reverted to 'cruising stations'.

Officers only were allowed ashore in Kilindini, this raising tempers in the already overheated tropical temperature where sullen messmates dis-cussed pigs and asked how many r's there were in bastards. But even when given leave days later in Aden it was unusual to find anyone who answered civilly. The questions revolved about *Neptune*'s future movements – 'south-east to Australia then New Zealand?' – 'come under C-in-C East Indies for convoy escorting and raider searching?'

Red Sea charts on Navi's table ended the suppositions; cable party men in the duty whaler slipped their buoy off Stanley Point, 2nd Part of Starboard along the boom deck manned their falls to hoist the whaler and secure it ready for emergency; and again the convoy moved north with its sorely awaited reinforcements; out through Aden's mined channel into Aden Gulf, through Perim Straits and up the Red Sea in pleasure-cruise conditions, then the 200-mile-long, 20-mile-wide Gulf of Suez to re-enter the war as WS8X anchored off Tewfik at night. The 30,000-ton liner *Georgic* lay beached and burning, bombed hours earlier in a night raid still in progress; A/A gun crews remained closed up until the 'all clear' sometime after midnight, relaxed until daybreak but remanned their guns when high-level flights returned to bomb Suez and the inner harbour.

Proceeding alone on Thursday, 18 July *Neptune* steamed slowly through the first 300-feet-wide, tens-of-miles stretch of canal, increased speed across Bitter Lake's vast expanse, slowed again to transit the centre miles of artificial waterway, then crossed Lake Timsah to stop briefly at Ishmailia and, at daybreak entered Suez Canal's stop-banked 60-mile cut across the un-navigable shallows of Lake Menzaleh, to anchor offshore of Port Said's Navy Office. There on 18 July Indian Ocean and Red Sea charts were exchanged for more appropriate ones covering the Mediterranean and its adjoining seas; the Walrus was flown ashore; her catapult was lifted off by a floating crane to be replaced by port and starboard multi-pom-pom mounts, while Oerlikons and four-barrelled point–5s were positioned in many vacant spaces.

Next day, immediately after ABC's flagship *Valiant* led *Queen Elizabeth* and *Barham* inside Alexandria through the opened boom, followed by the carrier *Formidable*, cruisers *Ajax*, *Sydney* and two destroyer flotillas, the gate was towed shut. And hours later it opened again to admit *Neptune* with her pennants hoist in forenoon sunshine, negotiating avenues of destroyers and cruisers toward her buoy among the 7th Cruiser Squadron, New Zealanders scanning the harbour for their sister-ship *Leander*. But right then *Leander* and the destroyer *Jarvis*, as units of 'Operation Guillotine', were entering Port Said to embark WS8X troops railed north from Suez for urgent transport to Cyprus.

To *Neptune*'s last-commission men still aboard, the eleven-month absence from Alexandria seemed mere weeks. In the Main W/T Chief Tel Caleb Brough was perusing a week's old Med Fleet List including *Barham*, *Royal Sovereign*, *Malaya*, *Queen Elizabeth*, *Ramillies*, *Valiant* and *Warspite*, deleting those off-station after Greece and Crete and now under bomb and torpedo repair in India, South Africa and America; but the French battleship *Lorraine* and four cruisers were still at anchor minus their main armaments' mechanisms; and all berths appeared to be occupied by the same squadrons and flotillas.

Alexandria's airspace was now an immense cube composed of smaller cubes; each ship was allocated one of these cubes, its guns would elevate and align to the altitude and bearing denoted by morsed letters and numbers, its A/A shells were fused to detonate at the given altitude and, during almost nightly air raids, *Valiant* as central control would morse each sector being approached by the enemy. Immediately, that cube would be a mass of impenetrable explosions, then the adjoining one, and the next until each successive ship was signalled to cease fire. In massed attacks the whole of Alexandria became an awesome pyrotechnics display and only the intrepid airman or the fool ran that gauntlet. Few survived.

Code-named 'Operation Substance' six 15-knot supply vessels escorted by the battleship *Nelson*, cruisers *Arethusa*, *Edinburgh*, *Manchester* and several destroyers, departed the Clyde on 11 July 1941 bound for Malta. Refuelling at Gibraltar they proceeded into the Western Mediterranean; and that same day Cunningham's fleet left Alexandria to engage the Italian fleet if it left base to attack the escorts and supply ships from Gibraltar.

Neptune and *Jarvis* had been ordered from their Port Said-Cyprus ferry service to join outside Alexandria, and the force cruised steadily north-west, *Queen Elizabeth* ploughing through *Valiant*'s glistening wake; CS7 Vice Admiral Pridham-Wippel's flagship *Ajax* out to port ahead of *Neptune*, *Leander*, *Hobart*; CS15 Vice-Admiral E.L.S. King's *Phoebe* disposed to starboard leading the A/A cruiser *Carlisle* and the 3,000-ton 40-knot minelayers *Latona* and *Abdiel*; all screened ahead, to port, to starboard, and half a mile astern, by the destroyers *Jackal*, *Jaguar*, *Jarvis*, *Kandahar*, *Kingston*, *Kimberley* *Maori*, *Nizam*, *Nubian*, *Hasty*, *Havock* and others of earlier vintage. Espionage reports from Taranto, Palermo and Messina had indicated Italian fleet preparations for sailing in strength, so with night approaching, Cunningham signalled the cruisers to screen 20 miles ahead of the main body where just before dark *Neptune's* radar detected enemy aircraft high overhead, no bombs were dropped and immediately *Neptune's* and *Leander's* accurate 4″ barrage exploded around them they fled.

Near midnight a coded message from the fast refrigerated ship *Sydney Star* to Malta W/T said she'd been mined or torpedoed in the Skerki Channel, was down to 40 feet for'ard and 30 feet aft, still making 14 knots at danger to her bulkheads and would require docking or beaching on arrival. Other signals intercepted from the Gibraltar to Malta convoy indicated that *Manchester* and *Firedrake* had retired damaged by aerial torpedoes, the destroyer *Fearless* being damaged more drastically was ordered by Admiral Somerville to be sunk; and he, now at the approaches to Skerki Channel, would retire his heavies to Gibraltar, leaving Admiral Syfret's cruisers and destroyers as convoy escort over the remaining miles.

Italian and German aircraft, submarines and MTBs constantly assailed the relief ships but all of them got through. Grand Admiral Iachino's Italian battlefleet remained in harbour throughout, and although not the most lauded Malta relief epic, *Substance's* co-ordinated operations gave Malta

Neptune, on the catapult platform.

the means: (1) to counter Axis attempts at subjugation; (2) to launch an offensive by air and sea against Tripoli- and Benghazi-bound Italian convoys.

With German armies occupying Greece and Crete, urgency dictated the need to hasten Operation Guillotine's transportation of troops from Port Said to Cyprus, the obvious Axis stepping stone to Syria. So *Neptune*, *Kimberley* and *Abdiel* crammed their decks and messdecks with men of the Cheshire Regiment – fast run up to Famagusta; fast return for more; back and forth over four days during which *Leander*, *Hobart*, *Latona*, *Jaguar*, *Kipling* and the Australian escort vessels *Parramatta* and *Flamingo*, worked in tandem until the 8th Army's 50th Division and RAF 259 Wing were ashore with their mobile guns, A/A weapons, ammunition, vehicles, food, fighter-bombers and aviation fuel.

Together in Port Said on Thursday, 31 July 1941, *Neptune* saw *Leander*'s multi-pom-pom mounts craned off, her catapult and Walrus being reshipped, and evident signs that she was preparing to leave the Med. *Neptunians* visiting mates on *Leander* read the Canteen Flat notice inviting volunteers to transfer in accordance with AFO–1033. Some entered the Regulating Office then the Captain's Office for draft chits, but most who'd experienced those bombing raids on Alexandria from midnight to daybreak, week after nerve-racking week, muttered caustic remarks: '*Baksheesh ana muskeen marfesh faloosh, effendi?*' 'I'll be glad to hear people talking English again mate. You want it? It's all yours!' as they made off to their messdecks.

PO Tel Harker stood with others of his radio branch, looking back at *Neptune* who'd now assumed *Leander*'s role in Vice Admiral Pridham-Wipple's 7th CS. Port Said's Navy Office, then the Suez Canal Offices intervened as Captain Butler asked for port wheel to head south into Egypt's strategic waterway. It was the last time they would see their sister-ship.

Next in priority after Malta and Cyprus was Tobruk, under siege by Rommel's Afrika Korps since April when the 8th Army retreated from Libya. By mid-August Cyprus was deemed self-sufficient and the cruisers were withdrawn from their Port Said ferry service; and a Polish Brigade embarking on destroyers at Alexandria was to relieve Tobruk's Australian garrison.

'Operation Treacle' got under way at 0830 Saturday, 16 August 1941, *Ajax* and *Neptune* as A/S and A/A cover; *Latona*, *Kipling*, *Kandahar*, and HMAS *Nizam*, crammed with khaki-clad soldiers pointing skyward, gabbling unintelligibly about the day-long umbrella of Hurricanes. At 2330 the exchange inside Tobruk took place without enemy interference; but while leaving Tobruk Channel at daylight *Nizam* shuddered to a standstill, blasted by a near miss 40 feet from her engine-room. Towed offshore by *Kipling*, the damaged Australian destroyer was encircled at speed, all ships covering her with a thunderous barrage until signalled to cease firing by arriving Hurricanes. Almost instantly a JU–87 corkscrewed down with smoke trailing till it splashed, then another Junkers dive-bomber and a Focke Wulf FW190 before the attackers withdrew under angry pursuit.

Eventually *Nizam*'s mechanicians repaired the damage sufficiently to provide steam for 20 knots, but that night the force's tired men were again repelling high-level bombers aiming at the head of fluorescent wakes, right through till dawn off Alexandria when the RAF reappeared. Rory O'Conor's noticeboard bulletin described the operation as a complete success and suggested all should take the maximum of shore leave ... 'the ship will soon be doing much more sea-time'.

One of the more red-eyed perusers voiced the opinion of many: 'What does the dozy bastard think we've been doing up till now, for Christ's sake!' And instead of taking Rory's advice after that day's Sunday Rounds, 'Piiipe Dowwn' over the SRE saw bodies laid out on mess tables, stools, contorted over hammocks stowed erect in nettings, inert on every deck-space available. Dog-tired, *Neptune* slept; *Naiad*, *Phoebe* and accompanying destroyers were doing the second transfer, then *Ajax* and *Neptune*'s turn again, and again until days hence when 'Operation Treacle' had ferried 19,568 relief troops to besieged Tobruk and brought out 18,865 tired Aussies; much credit being due to the Hurricanes, Martlets, Tomahawks and Spitfires which gave them overhead protection throughout.

On 16 September *Ajax*, *Hobart*, and *Neptune* escorted more destroyers to Tobruk with relief troops and supplies, and on the 18th *Neptune* eased alongside a wharf in Beirut to embark soldiers from one of the Queen's Own Regiments, very hungry swaddies who loudly voiced their appreciation of *Neptune*'s cooks when disembarking at Alexandria's Quai 35 after their 36-hour run south. But depleted cool stores needed replenishing, men were humping hundredweight bags up gangways and down hatchways, rushing crates of tinned everything from crane slings to dry-goods store-rooms and readying the ship for urgent departure on another Tobruk run. The Captain's sea-time prediction was already evident, and *Neptune* re-turned with the destroyers whose decks were sardined by weary troops, only to find herself assigned to Cunningham's battle fleet anxious to sail. An RAF reconnaissance aircraft over Italian waters on 26 September had morsed its Malta base in 'Self Evident Code': G5R v 8MJ2 – O = 2BS 5CR 12DR – 035 – 18 – 141XX13 = 0628.

Within minutes of decoding, Admiral Cunningham was reading the relayed enemy report: 'Emergency. 2 battleships 5 cruisers 12 destroyers steaming 035 degrees at 18 knots in position 141 degrees 13 miles from XX on the squared chart at 0628.'

ABC immediately boarded *Valiant* and passed through the boom gate ahead of *Queen Elizabeth* screened by *Ajax*, *Hobart*, *Naiad*, *Neptune* and nine destroyers, steaming north-west at 21 knots, until late next night when south-west of Crete the fleet reversed course and arrived back at Alexandria on 30 September; intercepted Italian scout-planes' messages had reported the approaching British fleet and Iachino's ships were back in Sardinia's minefield-protected harbours.

It was time for *Neptune* to enter Alexandria's floating dock for bottom cleaning and repairs to items on departmental officers' 'Defect Lists'; liberty men were given all-night leave and the 'dinkum grif' was rife throughout the ship.

'Didga know *Galatea* was bombed and crippled last week in the Red Sea? Yep, Cookie, right from the Cypher Office, we're going there to take over.'

'Sure, Brackie, ship's under Navy Office Wellington now. We're getting our NZ cap ribbons in a day or so, then, *Haere mai Rangitoto!*'

Hanging over the foc'sle rails discussing their selection as commission candidates, Ian Brackenbridge, Norm Cook, Wynn Denny and Alan Burt mulled these rumours over, gave them dubious reflection then sauntered below to supper. After twenty-four days in dockyard hands *Neptune* again nuzzled a buoy in the cruiser berth, now under the command of *Ajax*'s CS7 Rear Admiral Bernard Rawlings who'd been called to *Valiant* for briefing on Cunningham's plans to bombard Bardia.

At sunset on Friday, 23 October ABC led his battle fleet out of Alexandria, steered north until beyond prying telescopes, then changed course west-ward up the Libyan coast with Rory O'Conor's voice informing every compartment below decks:

'I take it that you all know we are going to bombard specific targets at Bardia. First the Fleet Air Arm and Royal Air Force will bomb known ammunition dumps and fuel depots. Then it will be our turn. This operation should be of valuable assistance to the 'big push' everyone in Alex and Cairo has been talking about. I am sure the enemy must have heard about it by now, so give it your best, and good luck.'

A click then momentary silence as the fleet pounded westward at 2nd Degree of Readiness until near midnight when strident bugle calls alerted men to their action stations.

A solitary flare outlining a ridge topping Bardia's shoreline cliffs, another, then parachuted flares all along the target area. *Neptune* wrenched violently as black-ringed stabs of flame momentarily floodlit her port side accompa-nied by an ear-shuddering BAAANNNGGG, long seconds then another jolting BAAANNNGGG and the stench of cordite, concussions from nearby cruisers thumping *Neptune*'s bridgework, brilliant thunderclaps as the bat-tleships' 15″ shells rumbled overhead from further seaward, inshore destroyers silhouetting indistinctly against billowing fireballs when muni-tion dumps and fuel tanks erupted. Enemy shells were landing short and over, one landing between *Neptune* and *Hobart* now only 400 yards ahead.

After a seeming eternity ABC signalled the ceasefire and retired his fleet at speed to Alexandria to refuel, re-ammunition, and prepare for a second Bardia bombardment, this time joined by *Latona* who would seal the harbour off with mines.

The general feeling was that Bardia wouldn't be caught unawares a second time and, although the whole area was ablaze from aerial bombing, more flak indicated an increase in mobile A/A sites. But this time two or more ships concentrated on each target, and shortly after firing commenced an orange firestorm welled high over Bardia's defences followed shortly by the shockwave of a violent explosion. There were more fiery explosions, some from bomb blasts, some from naval shells, yet when the ceasefire bells clanged there was still desultry retaliation from shore batteries.

Dawn saw the ships in single file formation entering harbour but where were the destroyer *Hero* and minelayer *Latona*? *Hero* was already inside, nursed back during the night after damage control parties warped anti-flood mats over a great shell hole on her waterline. *Latona* tragically had been attacked by Italian torpedo-bombers while laying mines across the harbour entrance, a hit midships had exploded mines working aft along their rails, and her final message said she was abandoning ship as it foundered. But the mines laid by *Latona*, plus the air and sea attacks, had rendered Bardia useless to Rommel as a forward supply base, his Afrika Korps materials and reinforcements would now have to be routed through Tripoli or further east at Benghazi.

Although Malta-based aircraft and submarines were sinking enemy shipping, 70 per cent was arriving in Tripolitanian harbours, so on 21 October the cruisers *Aurora*, *Penelope*, and destroyers *Lance* and *Lively* entered Valetta to assist. Designated Force K they operated with the island's RAF, FAA and submarines so successfully that now only 23 per cent of Rommel's needs reached Tripoli, and on 24 November when Taranto agents reported two enemy convoys leaving en route Benghazi, ABC ordered the 7th CS, 15th CS, and a destroyer flotilla to intercept them, immediately to be followed by *Queen Elizabeth* accompanied by *Barham*, *Valiant* and escorting destroyers.

Had this been an enemy ruse?

Having scoured the eastern Mediterranean day and night by air and sea for thirty-six hours Cunningham ordered his search groups back to base. RSAN Paymaster Lieutenant Dixie Dean, recently appointed from *Neptune* to *Queen Elizabeth*, was talking aft on the rumbling quarterdeck to Reuter's war correspondent Massey Anderson embarked for the operation. They were discussing the role of battleships in air-to-sea warfare, casually looking back at *Barham* surging astern in the flagship's turbulent wake when Anderson yelled: 'CHRIST ALMIGHTY!'

A shaft of blackened water speared up *Barham's* port side midships, an explosive thud smote men's ears as they looked back from *Queen Elizabeth*, unbelieving. Telltale white smoke was rising from the deck of *Barham's* after-structure as the old dreadnought slewed out of line, heeling uncontrollably with men grasping her guardrails for support, clambering over them to slither en masse into the cauldron along her waterline. Then absolute catastrophe as her after magazines blew, blasting bodies high into the eruption of After-Control, Officers' Galley, turrets and gunmounts cartwheeling amongst rolling smoke and hungry flames. In this instant of eternity terrible thunderclaps had wrenched *Barham* apart, inundating her capsized forepart and dragging it below. And already as main ships of the fleet increased speed to nearby Alexandria, destroyers were extricating survivors from the oil-covered debris while others asdic-searched for the undetected submarine; but only 296 of *Barham's* 1,268 complement were rescued.

Three NZ RNVRs, Ces Goding, Bill Moore and Alan Burt, had been drafted off *Neptune* for interim commission courses at Alexandria's *Canopus* Barracks; but the courses had been cancelled and on fronting the Marine Sentry at Quai 32 they were told *Neptune* was two hours at sea steaming west: 'You'd better go back to *Canopus*, maties. I think the last tram to Malta has just gone.' They unknowingly were among those fortunate to have been drafted off her over the past few months.

But back to *Neptune* now steaming astern of Rear Admiral Rawlings' *Ajax* accompanied by the destroyers *Kimberley* and *Kingston*, en route Malta to reinforce Captain William G. Agnew CB's Force K cruisers *Aurora*, *Penelope*, and the destroyers *Lance* and *Lively*. In keeping with his habit at sea of informing the ship's company about current policy, Captain O'Conor had blown into the SRE mike to ensure it was working, then said the squadron was now designated Force B, he was delighted at the prospect of working with Force K, he was sure all would understand the more spartan conditions to be expected at Malta, and there would be much more sea-time and action.

And this prediction soon became a reality, typified by RNVR Ldg Seaman R.S. Percival W/3420 in a censored letter to his Wellington parents:

HMS xxxxxxx
12 Mess
C/- NOWgn

My dear family   11/12/41

This is the first opportunity I have had to write you a letter for a considerable time. The trouble is we have been at sea very nearly every day and only coming into port for fuel and ammunition then out again. For the most part during our time at sea we are closed up in the first degree of readiness during the day to ward off enemy aircraft and in the night to encounter enemy surface craft, consequently we get very little sleep and when one has any time to oneself it is always spent in sleep. For a couple of days enemy planes harassed us and every now and again they would attack us, but fortunately none of their bombs hit us although a couple of them were too close for comfort. It is not the explosion that puts the wind up one, it is the sound of the things coming down that makes one want to duck and hide. I managed to get a photo of a couple that dropped quite close to us but you will have to wait till I get home before you see them. xxxxxxxxx be prepared to get my mail in spasms, perhaps not for weeks on end. xxxxxxxxxxxx endeavouring to get out into the Pacific now that Japan is in xxxxxxxxxxxxxxxxx hope at present xxxxxxxxxxxx needed here. Does xxxxxxxxxx have a blackout xxxxxxx tasted our worst spell of weather high wind and rain don't go well when doing high speed xxxxxxxxxxx won't be able to see Pat when he comes out of the desert, at least for xxxxxxxxx months, he's with the xxxxxxxx doing the big push into Libya.

My love to you all and Myna you tell Sylvia I've written to her by surface mail.

Stan XXXX

Latest buzz. The ship is going to xxxxxxxxxxxxxxxxxxxxxxxxxx. Love. S.

XX

Excerpts from a 'World Ship Society' *Neptune* 1941 diary, abridge the ship's operations during this period:

27.11.41   Left Alex with *Ajax, Kimberley, Kingston* for Malta. Escorted part way by *Euryalus, Naiad, Griffin* & *Hotspur*. Met Force K 28th. Malta 29th.

30.11.41   Left with Force K, *Neptune* in Force B, found nothing, back in Malta 1st December.

3.12.41   With *Ajax, Kimberley, Kingston, Lively*, escorting tanker *Breconshire* to Malta. *Kimberley* & *Kingston* relieved by *Jaguar* & *Kandahar*.

Attacked from air. Arrived Malta 8th Dec.

9.12.41   Left with *Aurora, Penelope. Jaguar, Kandahar*, to intercept reported sth bnd enemy convoy. Attacked from air. Found nothing. Returned Malta 14th Dec.

17.12.41   Left with *Jaguar* & *Kandahar*, joined *Breconshire's* escort late pm.

Detached with *Aurora, Penelope, Kandahar, Lance, Lively, Havock* to intercept enemy convoy bnd Tripoli. Destroyers fuel low, all returned Malta pm 18th Dec.

About 8 Dec *Ajax* developed engine problems which put her into dockyard hands and upped Captain O'Conor to SNO Afloat, so now on 18 December no sooner had *Neptune* berthed than Captain O'Conor was summoned to Naval Operations Room to be greeted by Vice Admiral Malta Ralph Leatham CB, Rear Admiral Bernard Rawlings (Flagship *Ajax*) Force K, Chief of Naval Staff Captain G.W. Wadham, plus a few senior FAA and RAF officers.

Handed an envelope marked SECRET he broke it open and read the contents in silence:

SECRET	SECRET
Para 7. Malta 00786/4 14 Dec 1941 Memorandum on co-operation be- tween Air and Surface Units operating from Malta (Short title S.A.M)	VA Malta Signal 1730/18B Dec 1941 *Neptune, Aurora, Penelope, Kandahar, Lance, Lively, Havock,* & 830 Squadron, 828 Squadron, Special Wellington.
7. General	Relative to para 7 (S.A.M)
(A) Composition of own surface units.	(A) Ships addressed.
(B) Expected composition of enemy.	(B) 3CR 6″, 8DR, 3MV.
(C) Possible intention of enemy.	(C) Enter Tripoli about 0200/19B.
(D) Pos'le enemy psn, course, speed.	(D) 3308N 1600E – 270 – 13 at 1515.
(E) Our air attack Before or After our surface attack?	(E) Before.
(F) Posn our ships at our air attack?	(F) Not used.
(G) Policy our ships after surface attack.	(G) Leave for Malta by 0400119 unless still in contact.
(H) Route of return to Malta.	(H) South East Channel.
(I) Safeguard against air attack on own surface units by RAF.	(I) RAF attack not later than 2300/18.
(J) Latest time our ships arrive Malta.	(J) Not used.
(K) Spare.	(K) Our ships route & speed going. 195 deg 27 kts after safe channel.
(L) Spare.	(L) Not used.
Air Striking Force	Air Striking Force
(M) Expected composition.	(M) Not used.
(N) Latest time of air attacks.	(N) 2300/18
(O) Latest ETD Air Strike Force.	(O) 1900/18
(P) Spare.	(P) Not used.

Air to Surface Vessels	Air to Surface Vessels
(Q) Posn ASV will start search.	(Q) 3308N 1500E
(R) ETA ASV in target area.	(R) 2100/18
(S) Is ASV to use V/S or W/T for 1st sighting report?	(S) V/S to surface forces.
(T) Is ASV to continue with V/S or W/T?	(T) V/S
(U) If no ASV link from target, is ASV to REMAIN over target or CLOSE our ships to obtain link?	(U) CLOSE
(V) Need for Enemy Reports: (i) When in ASV touch. (ii) When not in ASV touch.	(V) (i) As requisite. (ii) W/T report after FAA attack.
(W) When should ASV drop flares?	(W) For FAA attack then only if required.
(X) When should ASV make a possible 'No sighting report'?	(X) 0400/19
(Y) ETD ASV to base?	(Y) 0400/19
(Z) Will second ASV be available?	(Z) Yes. T.O.O. 1730/18

Having read the memorandum, O'Conor remarked that it made no reference to enemy minefields, saying that although he and his navigator were up to date on 'Q' data, that might not be so on all Malta-based ships. Vice Admiral Leatham thanked him for pointing out the omission, then penned a handwritten note on all copies: 'Attention of Surface Forces is invited to QB10 & QB11'.

But what could not be made known was the field laid in June by Admiral Casardi's and Admiral Giovanola's minelayers after *Barham*'s bombardment of Tripoli. Only the enemy knew of its existence.

It was imperative that the interception force get under way; Rory O'Conor ran down Strada Real's long flight of stone steps to his boat back to *Neptune*, each ship's captain was speedily delivered V-A Malta's 1730/18 document and *Neptune* passed through the breakwater at 1821, then came *Aurora* at 1828, *Penelope* at 1830 and *Kandahar* at 1835 followed closely by *Lance*, *Lively* and *Havock*. Once clear of the South East Channel Captain O'Conor signalled down the single file ships for a 195-degree course, 30 knots, paravanes to be strung; this needing revolution adjustments according to their drag and that of each hull's marine growth; and at 2200 he signalled all ships to action stations.

An asdic operator, twenty-year-old John Walton P/SSX26921, had joined *Neptune* at Alexandria six weeks past, right now a Force 7 sou'wester was rolling each ship as it climbed up oblique seas then down into deep troughs, and he was thinking how much colder it must be for his mum in Smaleswell, North Tyne. The SRE system livened, someone blow-tested its mike then:

'This is your captain speaking. We are now 40 miles from the Tripoli coast and will shortly alter course eastward in line abreast formation. We can expect to intercept an enemy convoy escorted by cruisers and destroyers between 0200 and 0400. Flares were seen a short time ago by aircraft from Malta which are also searching. They will assist in our attack. That is all.'

Chief Tel Caleb Brough in the Main W/T coding office was jubilantly showing PO Tel Walter Baker the latest FAA report to Malta: 'two crippled destroyers and two towing them. Four from eight makes four Wally; piece of cake, matey,' as he stuffed the cartridge into its pneumatic tube and blasted it up to the SDO.

'That's if we find them Cal.'

'Gord Wal, you always look on the pessimistic side.'

There wasn't time for a rejoinder to that one. In the 2nd W/T Office O'Conor's turning signal lay on Telegraphist Jim Leckie's Fleet Wave desk where PO Tel John Carty had placed it, awaiting the bridge order for transmission. A loud jolting WHOOMMPHH hurled John hard against the panelled bulkhead; Leckie's earphones flew across the office together with signal pads and pencils which they scrambled around in darkness trying to find. Bridge officers and men staggered as *Neptune* lifted for'ard, foc'sle momentarily illuminated by a massive orange flame rearing mast high among an acrid black cloud of explosives, salt water steam, and scorched paint. The flame was gone in an instant to leave blind darkness topside, steering unaffected, tween-decks' lighting and electrical circuits coming back on.

'Obey Telegraphs' rang far below as both pointers swung to 'Full Astern'; chief stokers whirled turbine throttles open, and above the overall roar in boiler-rooms, Chiefs handsignalled for more sprayers to be flashed to maintain steam pressure. With the helm midships O'Conor had the ship's four propellers thundering in reverse, everything vibrating violently with the drastic engine and turbine manipulations necessary to bring *Neptune* to a standstill. Damage Control parties were already assessing damage, rushing baulk timbers below to strengthen buckled bulkheads, stemming water gushing in through sprung plates, and extinguishing flames in the paint shop. Then disaster.

Where before, the ship's forward momentum had been thrusting water away from her hull, and the mine which exploded had been against a paravane, now her propellers were racing astern and the suction was attracting mines in. Two crashing explosions wrecked her propellers and steerage, blew off large parts of her stern together with first aid parties and others stationed aft, flooded compartment after compartment and left her powerless, at the mercy of that wild night's elements.

No need now to keep men at gun stations. Every man uninjured searched wrecked areas for torn and broken wounded, endeavoured to prise open distorted bulkhead doors to reach men entrapped. Their cries for help grew fainter; ceased when rising water rose to deckheads. On the bridge Rory O'Conor received damage control reports: boiler-rooms flooding, generators failing as pipe-glands parted and jetted flesh-stripping steam, but even though down several feet aft *Neptune* still floated with only a slight list and foc'sle parties were busy preparing her for towing; it was 0116.

Speeding half a mile astern in *Neptune*'s wake *Aurora* had seen the initial violent flash and minutes later the two which crippled her. Captain Agnew ordered starboard 25 to steer clear, ordered the wheel midships for moments then port 15, and almost instantly *Aurora* jarred throughout as a mine detonated on her port paravane. Severely damaged below she began to lose power but managed to retain steering and revolutions for 10 knots.

Penelope, three cables astern of *Aurora*, saw the explosions on *Neptune* then one on *Aurora*, so thinking they were under submarine attack Captain Nicholl helmed hard starboard to comb torpedoes; but at 0110 an explosion buffeted his ship port side abreast the bridge, lifting generators off their mounts and cutting power to all turrets. Now realising they were all in an extensive minefield, and being told by Senior (E) that *Penelope*'s main turbines seemed to be undamaged he brought her head north to get clear, and seeing *Aurora* doing likewise he eased down to 10 knots while taking station astern of her.

Over the next half hour *Neptune*, *Aurora*, *Penelope* and the destroyers exchanged V/S signals about the predicament and the best means of solving it, but at 0143 Captain Agnew's damage reports made it clear *Aurora* could not assist further. He signalled *Penelope* to do what was possible for *Neptune*, ordered *Havock* and *Lance* to escort him back to Malta and unwillingly departed. Then throughout the next two hours successive attempts were made by *Penelope*, *Kandahar* and *Lively* to close the crippled cruiser and take her in tow; but when *Kandahar* tried again at 0318 she too had her stern blown off and now drifted helpless in those heavy seas.

This left *Penelope* and *Lively* with decisions to be made about the fate of *Neptune*'s and *Kandahar*'s hapless crews only twenty miles from enemy territory with daylight rapidly approaching. At 0335 *Kandahar* signalled *Penelope*: 'My ship is flooded aft of the engineroom bulkhead, could be towed but realise this is impossible.' To which Captain Nicholl replied: 'Regret I must keep clear.' And a minute later when *Lively* made an attempt, *Kandahar* ordered her out of the field.

As those with night glasses topside on *Neptune* saw *Lively* obeying

Kandahar's emphatic order, their cruiser drifted onto a fourth mine port side abaft the funnel, this one ripping an immense hole below sea level and delivering the coup de grace. On the foc'sle John Walton was attaching a chain strop to a tow wire when the blast whipped the anchor cable onto his shin, breaking his leg. Christchurch RNVR Duncan Munro and Ron Quinn from Lower Hutt tried to assist him but they were swept down the slanted deck and leapt overboard. Unable to stand, John slid to the guardrail, climbed over it and was washed clear on the crest of a surging wave. He struggled towards a Carley float surrounded by some thirty survivors and was dragged aboard.

Neptune lay wallowing on her side with men trying to maintain foot and hand grips, but one by one they were torn off by seas crashing over her oil-covered underbelly. It was obvious she was foundering and by inherent impulse the Asdic Officer led men in pathetic cheering. In the dark it was neither epic nor spectacular, *Neptune* just heaved a long-drawn out sigh and disappeared, leaving men vomiting in a stinking mess of oil, trying to grasp slippery debris but losing their grip and mercifully drowning. Someone on the Carley float shone a torch on Captain O'Conor clinging to an anchor buoy; men swam over and shouldered him onto a raft tethered to the float's lifeline.

Meantime *Kandahar*'s Commander Robson had signalled *Penelope*: 'Suggest you go. Consider sending a submarine for survivors.' There were more flashed messages, one from *Lively* begging permission to remain in the area to rescue both ships' survivors; to which *Penelope* replied 'Regret *not* (R) *not* approved. Follow me. G20,' at which speed both ships left for Malta.

In the few hours before dawn many of the thirty on or clinging to *Neptune*'s only known float and its tethered raft perished; others suffering from hyperthermia died during that first day and were given naval rites when their rigid bodies were slipped below. Still others showed increasing depression, especially after an RAF plane droned overhead and disappeared without seeing them. As the float crested high atop swells men saw *Kandahar* far to the north-east but there were no means of communication, and as the day wore on Commissioned Gunner Laban and the Asdic Officer decided to swim to her for help, an heroic sacrifice as neither was seen again.

On the second day when Rory O'Conor estimated they should be within 5 miles of the coast, attempts were made with a broken oar to paddle southward but opposing seas soon discouraged the few who tried. Able Seaman Quinn died on the third day and men were succumbing one after another until only the captain and three ratings remained alive; and at sunrise Christmas Eve 1941 John Walton woke to find Rory O'Conor and one of the seamen dead, with his last companion Able Seaman Albert Price close to death. John too wavered between oblivion and hazy recollections of life; he dimly perceived an Italian aircraft circling low overhead; drifted off to semi-consciousness; then hours later peered with failing eyes as an Italian destroyer marked CP on her bows edged close and threw a heaving line. Totally weakened and practically blind he groped for the line, eased himself off the float to be pulled slowly to the destroyer's stern, and just managed to drape himself over its outjutting propeller guard where he collapsed unconscious.

On coming-to days hence in a Tripoli hospital he was blind, his broken leg had turned gangrene, and an English-speaking Italian doctor told him that Price had died when being lifted out of the float. Walton's sight gradually returned but as his leg didn't heal, German doctors had him flown to southern Italy for consultative treatment in Bari Hospital, where the compound fractures and gangrenous infection eventually responded, and weeks of physiotherapy had him walking without the sign of a limp. On being declared fit he spent fifteen months in a POW camp until 13 March 1943 when he and other repatriates embarked on the Italian Hospital Ship *Gradiska* for an exchange of prisoners through the Turkish port, Mersin. From there he was shipped aboard HM Hospital Ship *Talma* to Alexandria where Admiral Cunningham questioned him in hospital, listened intently to the able seaman, then closed *Neptune*'s 'Final Inquiry' by saying: 'Well, John Walton, you have either one hell of a constitution, or you were bloody lucky. I think that both apply.'

Survivors still on board *Kandahar* during the approaching daylight hours of 20 December 1941, swam to *Jaguar* who'd raced down from Malta, and as attempts to scuttle by opened seacocks were wasting drastic hours *Kandahar* was sunk by *Jaguar*'s torpedoes before she quit the area so close to Tripoli.

Aurora's, *Penelope*'s, *Hotspur*'s, *Lance*'s, *Lively*'s, *Kandahar*'s Commanding and Senior Officers plus a host of other Service Chiefs, gave evidence as they recalled it at the 'Board of Inquiry', convened aboard *Ajax* in Malta during the last few days of 1941 and early months of 1942 into the loss of *Neptune* and *Kandahar*. But had John Walton not survived that tragic night and the subsequent two years and three months in enemy hospitals and prison camps, only the bare facts recorded during that Board of Inquiry would have remained in history.

CHAPTER XIII

Achilles *Back on the NZ Station*

A chilles' 23 FEBRUARY 1940 triumphant return from the 'Plate' was now a three-month-old memory, recruiting drives throughout both New Zealand islands completed; ship's company returned from weeks of long leave; their cruiser minus its H/A and 6″ DCT, torpedo mounts, catapult; and boiler tubes cluttering the dockside; while her crew kept in touch with the War by listening to 1YA and 1ZB newscasts or reading Auckland's daily papers. But gradually everything jigsawed back together, and mid-June found the ship doing Hauraki Gulf trials, anchoring for the night of Tuesday, 11th in Great Barrier Island's Port Fitzroy, then securing nightly throughout the 12th, 13th and 14th alongside Devonport Naval Base's Calliope Wharf; those on duty and those ashore sleeping peacefully unaware that a German raider had mined Auckland approaches during the evening and night of the 13th.

Built in 1930 in Hamburg as the 7,000-ton 17-knot turbine-driven freighter *Kurmark*, her strengthened gun-emplacements and 4,000-ton oil-fuel capacity betokened her future use; but listed only as *Schiff No 36*, her *Kapitan zur See* Kurt Weyher renamed her *Orion* when leaving Kiel on 8 April 1940 to test her six 5.9″ and several HA/LA guns, two triple torpedo mounts, Arado float-plane, and the rail mechanism for launching 230 mines to be carried in her after holds. When given a satisfactory clearance she sailed south-west across the Atlantic, sank the British tramp *Haxby* on Monday, 22 April near Bermuda, and pushed deep into the South Atlantic where off South Georgia Islands, the German auxiliary *Winnetou* waited to refuel her for the long Pacific crossing to New Zealand.

At dusk on Wednesday, 13 June, *Orion* ran mines along their rails to splash over her stern into the sea between Great Mercury and Cuvier Islands; in the clear evening she laid more between Cuvier and Great Barrier Islands; she then continued with a long traverse from Great Barrier Island, past Moko Hinau Island and six miles seaward of the Hen and Chickens Group to finish somewhere off Whangarei Heads, thus covering all entrances to Hauraki Gulf. During his seven-hour operation Weyher had kept the crew at Action Stations, closely observing several ships passing in or out of Auckland, but none showed interest and on completion of the mission at 0230 he stood his ship's company down and headed north.

Five days elapsed with ships arriving and departing regularly, one of them the Union Steamship Company's 13,500-ton liner *Niagara* inbound from Sydney; but pre-dawn on Wednesday, 19 June on her way out for Suva and Vancouver with 136 passengers, £2,500,000 sterling of South African gold for America, and half of New Zealand's small-bore ammunition donated to Britain as part replacement of her Dunkirk losses, she struck one or more of Weyher's mines laid near the Hen and Chickens. Her initial transmission: CQ de GNRL = *Niagara* 0344. Explosion No 2 hold. Position Maro Tiri 270 degrees 6 miles = AR was read by Wellington Marine Radio ZLW and acknowledged. But the situation deteriorated rapidly as her next message indicated: SOS SOS SOS de GNRL 0352 = Engines disabled. No 2 hold full of water. Vessel going down by head. Putting into boats. Heading towards Hen and Chickens = AR. Having received these messages by telephone Commodore Parry left Auckland aboard *Achilles* at 0523, ordered the converted Sanford Fisheries' trawlers *James Cosgrove* and *Thomas Currell* to sweep near the Hen and Chickens, then streamed PVs when off Rangitoto and increased speed to 30 knots. *Niagara*'s lifeboats were sighted at 0812 and Huddart Parker's liner *Wanganella* arriving from Sydney was asked to assist with her boats, but to stand off in case she too hit a mine. Meanwhile Lieutenant Commander Washbourn with *Achilles'* pinnace and two motorboats, supervised the overall transfer of *Niagara*'s passengers and crew to the incoming coaster *Kapiti*, which then offloaded them onto *Wanganella* who had major facilities for tending to those requiring treatment. By 2.15 p.m. the rescue operations were completed, extensive sweeps of all approaches had been ordered, and before *Achilles* secured again at Calliope Wharf, SO 15th M/S Flotilla was receiving reports of mines being located and destroyed.

Long monotonous search patrols now lay ahead of *Achilles* assisted by RNZAF offshore reconnaissance, and for some weeks by the armed merchant cruiser *Hector* until Admiralty ordered her to the Indian Ocean; but more problems arose for Navy Board Wellington as an aftermath of France's capitulation. The unfortunate Royal Navy 3 July action against the French Fleet at Oran and Mers-el-Kebir, and on 8 July against its uncompleted battleship *Richelieu* at French West Africa's Dakar naval base, soured many French naval minds against their recent ally. There were French possessions in Polynesia; hopefully their political and military leaders might go Free French De Gaullist; but they might go the way of Pétain; they had to choose, and Britain exhorted New Zealand Chiefs of Staff to ensure this was done with alacrity.

The French liner *Commissaire Ramel* crossing the Pacific to report to Admiral Robert at Martinique in the West Indies, entered Suva where Fiji's Governor promptly requisitioned her and asked for New Zealand assistance to escort her to Sydney. So, on Saturday, 20 July Parry greeted the Chief of General Staff and the Chief of Air Staff onboard for the passage north and, four days later, while the three top New Zealand service chiefs discussed Pacific defence strategy in Fiji's Government House, Lieutenant Commander C.R. Carlyon RNZNR and Warrant Engineer C.H.J. Stone RN boarded the impounded French liner with an eighteen-man guard, all single filing up the three-stage sea gangway while ensuring free access to the .45 Colts swinging at their hips. The enmity seen when looking up deepened on the face of every Frenchman as an interpreter repeated the penalties laid down in the Royal Navy's *King's Rules and Admiralty Instructions* which would be implemented in the event of obstruction or attempts at seizure during the voyage to Sydney. On the way to their allocated cabin Mervyn St Clare was saying to his offsider Harcourt Cleave: 'What do you reckon about these Froggies, Harkie? They look as if they'd take over, given the chance.'

'Just thinking the same Merv, s'pose we'd feel the same if the boot was on the other foot.'

So, as *Commissaire Ramel* sailed toward the New Hebrides for disembarkation of Noumea-bound passengers onto Free French vessels awaiting them in Vila, the liner's French helmsmen were checked continually to see they stayed on courses set by Lt Cdr Carlyon; Charlie Stone's stokers went below with loaded pistols to guard against boiler or engine mishandling; and PO Tel Adrian Bywater-Lutman kept unauthorised Frenchmen out of the ship's commandeered wireless office. When off watch the prize crew ate well in the huge dining saloon, being befriended more and more each day, sleeping with pistols under their pillows, and fortunately overhearing a plot to set the ship afire before arrival in Sydney. But the plot was forestalled and *Commissaire Ramel* arrived safely on 5 August, having been lucky to have sailed unseen through the area at that time patrolled by Kapitan Weyher's raider *Orion*. *Ramel*'s crew was interchanged with British seamen and officers, she loaded wool and general cargo at successive Australian ports, then on 20 September in the Indian Ocean on her way to Cape Town she was intercepted and sunk by Kapitan Rogge's raider *Atlantis*.

Before returning to Auckland with the New Zealand service chiefs, *Achilles* searched as wide an expanse of the South Pacific as her Walrus could cover in daylight, entered Nukualofa for high-level defence talks with Queen Salote and her advisers, then continued the search pattern southward to a 31 July Auckland arrival for degaussing. A German scientist had devised a mechanism to trigger mines moored at depths below those swept by paravanes – they would detonate when activated by the inherent magnetic field surrounding ships' metal hulls; but British scientists soon overcame this by ringmaining ships with cables carrying depolarising currents of equal but opposing intensity. The idea worked. *Achilles*' cables were fitted and tested by 13 August when the ship's company was warned the ship was under sailing orders for next day. A German raider, or group of raiders, was suspected of being near New Zealand, and *Achilles* sped down North Island's wintry coast, men shivering in turrets or huddled in whatever shelter might be found at exposed quarters, thankful when relieved to seek the warmth of mess-deck hammocks, and sleep.

In Cook Strait the fast trooper *Mauretania* surged past Barrett's Reef, leaving a turbulent wake through which *Achilles* trailed her into Wellington on 16 August. Four days later *Orcades* and *Empress of Japan* arrived to complete the convoy embarking New Zealand's 3rd Echelon; but that evening *Orcades* departed alone to Lyttelton for the South Island contingent, and only hours after her departure *Achilles'* siren echoed off the capital's hills as a 'GENERAL RECALL' for all liberty men. Recall messages were flashed on every cinema screen throughout Wellington and all but fifty-three men had returned aboard by 2135, when their ship sped to a position 290 miles north-west of Cape Egmont, where the freighter *Turakina* had keyed a transmission saying she was being approached by a suspicious vessel, then an unfinished one saying she was being shelled by a raider. Although assisted by the TEAL flying boat *Awarua* nothing was found to indicate the 10,000-ton cargo vessel's fate; *Awarua* signalled by flash lamp that she would search the mid-Tasman area, but after a dawn-to-dusk south-west search *Achilles* was again approached by the big amphibian to say she'd seen no sign of the raider.

Days of high-speed coverage from the Three Kings to Campbell Island were broken only by a brief Auckland visit for fuel, then a hares-and-hounds dash south in pursuance of Navy Office reports of short-wave D/F bearings on a German ship near Stewart Island, but which Admiralty considered to have originated north of Scotland. Navy Office then relayed reports of gunfire off North Cape which had *Achilles* racing up-coast for hours, until a 'most immediate' message from Navy Office reported gunfire off Napier. More 180-degree swathes turned the cruiser north, then south, before negating signals dropped the revs for 25 knots to those giving fifteen; then in Wellington Commodore Parry banged a lot of oversized heads together on 27 August, stressing the need to sift information, the need to use correct priority prefixes, the need to establish the reliability of unconfirmed reports; and when Parry took *Achilles* south to rendezvous with *Orcades* off Lyttelton, he left many pink ears in Wellington.

At daybreak on 28 August *Orcades* and *Achilles* were joined in Cook Strait by *Mauretania*, *Empress of Japan*, and an umbrella of Airspeed Oxfords, Lockheeds, and Vickers Vildebeestes, droning overhead until a magnificent sunset which presaged a fast and uneventful Tasman crossing. Outside Sydney the 3rd Echelon transports turned south, now accompanied by

HMAS *Canberra* and the troopship *Aquitania*, but when entering Bass Strait HMAS *Perth* closed while signalling *Achilles* to heave-to and receive Rear Admiral J.N. Grace; then with the transfer completed *Perth* made off back towards Sydney while *Achilles* increased speed to Port Philip, there disembarking Parry and Grace for top-level discussions at Navy Office Melbourne, a three-day meeting with Australian Commonwealth Naval Board members, interrupted by Navy Office Wellington who wanted *Achilles* back home, and quick. Three Kings loomed to port at rum-up on 5 September, those who'd suffered the after-effects of Aussie beer during the ship's 25-knot crashing through head seas had recovered, and at 2245 when *Achilles* berthed at Calliope Wharf with liberty men in their No 1s ready to step ashore, the stage was set for mild panic in many homes. Lights went on as men paid taxi drivers then knocked on sleeping doors, kettles sang on gas burners, and drowsy wives tried to restore beauty as they talked into the morning hours. Then a lightening of Auckland's eastern horizon, dog-tired men dressing to run for first trams to Queen Street, Admiralty Steps a mass of white caps cramming aboard the pinnace for the Waitemata Harbour crossing.

By 1030 *Achilles* was rounding North Head on her way to Tahiti with the Secretary of External Affairs Mr C.A. Berensden, who as Permanent Head of the Prime Minister's Department had been commissioned by England's Home Office to tender British Commonwealth assistance to the Provisional French Oceanic pro-De Gaulle Government, it having recently deposed Tahiti's Vichy-minded Governor.

It was cold about exposed decks, good to be below in 'A' and 'B' boiler rooms providing steam for 20 knots as *Achilles* sped through the 'Mist Ocean' where cold southern currents clashed with those from the warmer north. But within days men were emerging in shorts and sandals to enjoy the tropical sun, hanging their Persil whites to freshen on anything available, making up fours to toss their ukkers dice, or just draping themselves over guardrails to get a suntan while watching startled flying fish glide away off bow waves, albatrosses winging lazily over the wake in search of edible gash. Tuesday, 10 September saw the ship at Action Stations off Faaa Point, guns trained on military targets around Papeete while awaiting the new Governor's boat; then as he, his ADC, and the British Consul were piped aboard, *Achilles*' SRE speakers cancelled Action Stations, and ordered: 'EVERYONE OUT OF THE RIG OF THE DAY OFF ALL UPPERDECKS. CLEAR LOWER DECK FOR ENTERING HARBOUR. ATTT THERR DOUBBLE!'

Tahitian festivities were already well advanced in honour of fifteen chiefs visiting from Papetoa and Hoapiti on Moorea: Papenoo, Faaone, Taravao, Paea, Vairoa and Puniaauia from Tahiti-nui and its adjoining Tahiti–iti; and from smaller unpronounceable settlements on nearby islands. Everybody went ashore. Most succumbed to the intoxicating hospitality, the intoxicating beauty of friendly vahines, or just the straight out intoxication of French wines and Manuia beer. Then on Thursday, 12 September four platoons of seamen, all of the 'Royals' and their marine band, marched through throngs of Tahitians and French civilians lining Quai Bir Hakeim and up through Rue Jeanne D'Arc to the palm-surrounded Cenotaph, where in the presence of Papeete's small 'Corps du Defense' and a French Naval Detachment, Achilles' landing party presented arms while Free French Governor Monsieur M. Mansard laid a wreath at the Great War Memorial, then stood saluting alongside Britain's Consul Mr Edmunds in similar stance while Commodore Sir Edward Parry stepped forward to lay his wreath. The overall ceremony, clapped and cheered during the band's easy martial swing back to the landing steps, ended with a 'Grande Finale' when a stern-sheetsman fell off the back of his pinnace in front of the whole appreciative Polynesian assembly.

Achilles' boats now plied back and forth with the fifteen chiefs according to Tahitian rank; sideboys piped them onto the awning-covered quarterdeck to be received with naval courtesy; and interpreters conveyed speeches and replies referring to the entente cordiale experienced back to and beyond the eras of Bligh and Cook. And in response to many invitations, hundreds went in open buses to outlying villages for feasting and entertainment previously only dreamed about. It was evident that the Friendly Isles' Polynesians had affection for the British Navy; this having been woven into their traditional songs and dances which continued late into that moonlit romantic night. Then next day the Union Steamship Coy's motor-vessel Limerick, just arrived from Auckland, embarked Tahiti's deposed Governor, some Vichy naval officers, thirty Americans awaiting passage to the States, and on 14 September departed for Vancouver. Meantime Lt Cdr Carlyon, who'd been OIC prize crew on Commissaire Ramel when it left Suva on 26 July for the Fiji-Vila-Sydney trip, now took twenty specialist guards aboard the Messageries Maritimes 7,000-ton steamer Ville d'Amiens on 15 September and, as the ship's pro-Vichy captain and officers had been disembarked for security, Carlyon later sailed the ship to Auckland as its master, arriving there on 27 September 1940.

Hours after transferring the armed guard to Ville d'Amiens, Achilles cleared Papeete's reefs which were thronged with happy waving locals of European and Polynesian extraction, intent on farewelling the warship they'd entertained over the past five days. A brief visit in his barge to Raratonga's VIPs while Achilles rolled gently on lazy Pacific swells, then directly to Auckland from where Commodore Parry flew to Wellington. He had more representations to make as Naval Adviser to the Government:

Almost a complete reshuffle of Navy Office Staff; Operations and Intelligence must be separated from technical matters. The duties of CNS were not compatible with command of a cruiser. He could not be dealing with top-level matters in Wellington, and at the same time making decisions concerning his ship perhaps in Auckland and, he must attend all War Cabinet meetings.

Commodore Parry's views were accepted by Government and concurred with by Admiralty. As Chief of Naval Staff he would be stationed in Wellington; his command of *Achilles* would be assumed by Captain H.M. Barnes RN whose position as Commanding Officer *Philomel* would go to Lieutenant Commander D.A. Bingley RN; and the rank of Commodore Commanding NZ Squadron would be abolished.

During the first half of October *Achilles* exercised in Hauraki Gulf with the 17-knot Union Steamship Coy's liner *Monowai*, recently appropriated by Navy Board and converted to an eight 6″ gunned armed merchant cruiser commanded by a very popular Captain H.V.P. McClintock RN; these exercises so close to home creating minimal inconvenience for *Achilles'* complement, as she had just been placed in two weeks' quarantine due to Lieutenant Stephenson's diagnosed *cerebro spinal meningitis*.

On her 15 October arrival back at Calliope Wharf Captain Barnes embarked as Commanding Officer, and at 1530 after Wardroom farewells and a '*Clear Lower Deck*' speech, Commodore Parry left the ship with full VIP ceremony; then two days later six bus loads of *Achilles'* men drove to Waikumete Cemetery to enact another naval ceremony, this one for Lieutenant Stephenson who had died in Auckland Hospital on Tuesday, 16 October 1940.

Now began a long period of sea-time, months with scant respite as *Achilles* and *Monowai* escorted troopships or freighters within the vast South Pacific and Tasman areas of New Zealand's naval responsibility. Throughout fruitless days they covered thousands of square miles searching for the raider which occasioned *Karitane's RRRR* report; then one night an *Achilles* lookout detected a 21-knot vessel off North Cape, but after shadowing it till dawn it was seen to be the Tasman ribbon-holder *Awatea* inbound for Auckland. There were the 1st Section 4th Reinforcements on Poland's liner *Batory* and the Union Steamship Coy *Maunganui* to be escorted in severe gale conditions to Sydney, rather embarrassing when Captain Barnes shepherded them into Botany Bay on 12 November in dense fog, and later in Sydney took two hours forty minutes to moor at a Farm Cove buoy in remnants of the gale; all this after the cruiser's crane-driver had been on the mat for clobbering the main-top-mast, and duty hands were mustered in dark driving rain to secure it for that night's departure from Wellington.

Four days after departing Sydney with a new main-top fitted, heavy seas off Auckland Island's storm-battered cliffs did their best to dislodge it again, while men at General Quarters shivered in sub-zero temperatures, preparing to engage a secretly reported enemy in Carnley Harbour. Nothing. Nothing in Campbell Island's Perseverance Inlet away south next day; followed by a leisurely cruise in the faintest of early summer breezes, en route Port Chalmers until diverted fast to Lyttelton for oil-fuel when *Maimoa RRRR'd* her final plea; but it was shortly reported to have come from west of Fremantle. While in Lyttelton's nor'wester heat, Milton (Pusser) Hill and Claude Brash were lounging in Bert Herdman's open-windowed sitting-room, looking across to tranquil Diamond Harbour, entertained by their host at his centuries-old upright piano with Austrian masterpieces, Vienna compositions, moderns and the blues. Bert Herdman's coaster *Holmwood* was in Chatham Island's Waitangi Harbour loading wool bales and passengers for the return trip to Lyttelton where Bert would rejoin her; *Achilles'* South Islanders were packing their gear to go on long leave next day.

But daylight found the cruiser churning north through Pegasus Bay at 25 knots, speeding to a position 300 miles east of East Cape signalled by NZ Shipping Coy's 17,000-ton liner *Rangitane*. Surely the raider couldn't get away from this one; TEAL's flying boats *Awarua* and *Aotearoa* were already searching the area; there were RNZAF long-range aircraft at Gisborne and other nearby fields; the 900-ton Anchor Line motor vessel *Puriri* converting to a minesweeper in Auckland had been dispatched instantly; *Monowai* would refuel at Suva and search southward; *Achilles* would be on site soon with her Auckland University-designed radar apparatus operating. Not one, but three enemy vessels operating in company escaped undetected: *Orion, Komet,* and their supply tender *Kulmerland,* had come south from near Fiji in the first days of November. En route they had intercepted the US freighter *City of Ellwood* and let her proceed with the promise that as a neutral she would not report them. She didn't. Three weeks passed without a sighting on the NZ-UK shipping routes east of the Chathams, then when several hundred miles south-east of Lyttelton wherein *Achilles* awaited instructions, the trio turned north with Nauru and Ocean Islands' phosphate installations in mind.

In line abreast at crow's nest vision they scanned a 100-mile wide pattern; passing a few hundred miles east of Lyttelton, and at dawn on 25 November sighted smoke. Within hours hundreds of sheep, tons of produce, twenty-five passengers and the crew of Bert Herdman's *Holmwood* were transferred to *Komet* who then sank the small coaster by gunfire. Two days later and again in daylight the raiders intercepted *Rangitane* who immediately made a QQQQ report and endeavoured to escape at full speed. As soon as his ship came under fire Captain H.L. Upton DSC ADC RNR ordered his Chief

Radio Operator N. J. Hallett to make a full *RRRR* signal, and it wasn't until *Orion* and *Komet* were signalled the presence of women and children, that they ceased firing. Two stewardesses, three engine-room hands, two male and three women passengers were killed and many were wounded, one so badly that she died next day aboard *Orion*. But unable to sink the liner by gunnery she was sent below by *Komet*'s torpedoes.

It has been established post-war that the raiders sighted TEAL's big amphibians while steaming northward from the area, but only those who have experienced the difficulty of seeing surface vessels among whitecapped waves some thousands of feet below, or detecting them by radar in its infancy, will understand. After sinking *Rangitane* the raiders vanished, anchoring off the Kermadecs while formulating their plans regarding Nauru and Ocean Islands' phosphates works, W/T station, and possible shipping – 185 *kriegsmarines* would land and destroy the plant, then specialist crews would man vessels captured at anchor. They weighed at dusk and steamed northward into the night.

The Union Steamship Coy's 4,000-ton *Komata* was lying off Nauru's loading gantry and Captain W.W. Fish was asking Chief Officer T.A. Mack what he made of the muffled rumble they'd just heard.

'Can't be anything unusual, Skip, must be thunder.'

'You hear anything on 500, Eddie?' as he poked his head in E.H. Ward's radio shack.

'No, Tom, might pay to move out to sea if the wind's rising, eh?'

Eddie emerged from his radio room and was asiding to the 2nd Mate: 'Hey John, feel like uncorking a few from the fridge?'

'Looks like you'll have to ask that question later, Ed, we've got visitors—'

Eddie didn't hear the last bit, he'd dived back inside his shack and swung the generator handle to power his transmitter: QQQQ QQQQ QQQQ de ZMVS ZMVS ZMVS = *Komata* Nauru = 1013 AR. *Komet*'s more powerful transmitter was blanketing his signal. He changed the prefix to *RRRRs*, kept on keying his message until a shell burst on the bridge and brought down his aerial. Another crashed the foremast overboard, rigging trailing. Tom Mack lay bloodied and dead among the carnage, near to John Hughes who'd crumpled mortally wounded as he reached for the engine telegraph; he wouldn't uncork any more from the fridge for his bridge-mates. Skipper Fish fought against nausea and fainting spells as he tended the wounded man, ignoring the red stains spreading through his own white shirt. Shells continued to explode about the upperdecks and waterline, letting in thousands of tons of unrelenting Pacific which sent *Komata* to the bottom.

The Norwegian motor vessel *Vinni* had been drifting off Nauru awaiting her turn at the gantry, and the thunder heard by *Komata* came from German demolition charges detonated deep in *Vinni* after her thirty-two crew were taken off. The British Phosphate Commission's 4,500-ton steamer *Triona* was torpedoed with the loss of 3 crew, then her 61 surviving crew together with 8 women and 3 male passengers were transferred to the German ships; and while *Komata* was being shelled, *Orion*'s boats were rescuing survivors from the British Phosphate Coy's 6,000 tonners *Triadic* and *Triaster* which she'd sunk by torpedoes. Rising seas had made landings impossible, there were 265 seamen prisoners on *Orion*, 153 on *Komet*, and 199 men, 52 women, and 6 children aboard *Kulmerland*, so the raiders negotiated the Marshal Islands' reefs and atolls, steamed a thousand miles west to the Carolines, then south-east to Bismarck Archipelago where 343 Europeans and 171 Asians were disembarked ashore at Emirau Island on 21 December 1940. After refuelling from *Kulmerland* which then departed to Japan, *Orion* returned to the Carolines where she captured Norway's tanker *Ole Jacob*, before an arranged rendezvous with the German auxiliary *Regensberg* bringing required engine parts from Yokohama. During the past 288 days *Orion* had steamed 65,327 miles without an engine shutdown, so she now began its long-overdue maintenance. *Komet* went back to Nauru on 27 December to shell the island's fuel tanks, phosphate works and cantilever loading assembly, leaving a mess of twisted corrugated-iron buildings and distorted girders before laying a course to the Marshals and Gilberts.

Nauru at that time produced New Zealand's and Australia's basic fertiliser without which their meat and agriculture exports to Britain would have declined. *Achilles* couldn't be spared to guard the phosphate islands. Although Britain said it was an ANZAC problem, garrisoning hadn't yet been officially contemplated, and even with *Monowai* to share the burden, both ships were at sea on other duties most days of each month. So Commodore Parry banged his drum louder in Wellington, requiring the Pacific movements of all merchantmen and warships no matter who owned them. NZNB and the War Cabinet paid heed, as did the Intelligence Departments of Australia, Singapore, Ottawa and South America. Wellington laments were brushed aside:

> Resign from your damned golf clubs. Get your wives and daughters to mow your lawns. NO! NO! I want you in your office day and night, and weekends! [then in reply to one braver than the others] No sir. If you wish to complain, I'll arrange for you to do so before my boys on *Achilles* and *Monowai*. Now hear this well. Shipping reports will be on my desk immediately they arrive by teleprinter or whatever. There will be constant and prompt distribution to Chief of Air Staff. A twenty-four hour plot will henceforth be manned.

Parry cabled Admiralty on 24 April 1941 for the appointment of a Staff Officer Intelligence for New Zealand and Royal Navy interests. Lieutenant Commander F.M. Beasley RN came out of retirement to do the job, and right from inception there were results. No longer did the 'WS'-taped transmission from Tinakori Hill's ZLP multi-channel naval broadcast contain a preponderance of dummy messages; cypher staff in Navy Office filled signal pads with shipping information funnelled in from overseas headquarters. *Achilles* and *Monowai* could now escort convoys or single ships while being prepared to aid other ships now known to be in their area. It probably accounted for the fall-off of raider sinkings. Kapitan Robert Eyessen's fiery little *Komet* cruised the mid-Pacific for the first three months of 1941 without success, tried near Pitcairn, the Marquesas and Tuomotos, the Panama-NZ route, the Chathams again, got stuck in ice while seeking whalers near the Balleny Islands, met *Pinguin, Alstertor*, and *Adjutant* at an arranged Kerguelen rendezvous: 'Not er godverdamt ting.' And within this period *Monowai* and *Achilles* escorted ships in every direction as catalogued below for those chaperoned by *Achilles*:

Date	Port Departure	Ship (Nearest 1,000 tons)		Limit of Escort
20 Dec 40	Wellington	2nd Sectn 4th Reinforcements		
		Dominion Monarch	26	Sydney
		Empress of Russia	30	Sydney
30 Dec 40	Sydney	*Empress of Russia*	30	Cape Brett
		Port Chalmers	14	Cape Brett
		Maunganui	12	Cape Brett
2 Jan 41	Mid-Tasman	*Akaroa*	13	Auckland
8 Jan 41	Auckland	*Empress of Russia*	30	Suva
10 Jan 41	Suva	*Empress of Russia*	30	350 mls North of Equator
7 Feb 41	Auckland	*Suffolk*	14	450 mls E of Chat
12 Feb 41	Wellington	*Awatea* joined 14th by *Wairangi* from W'gton	9	
			13	Sydney
18 Feb 41	Sydney	*California Star*	13	Cape Maria van Dieman
26 Feb 41	Napier	*Dunedin Star*	14	450 mls E of Chat
3 Mar 41	Wellington	*Trojan Star*	9	300 mls E of Chat
		Mahana	11	300 mls E of Chat
9 Mar 41	Wellington	*City of Canberra*	13	450 mls E of Chat
17 Mar 41	Wellington	*Port Jackson*	12	400 mls E of Chat
23 Mar 41	Mid-Tasman	*Aorangi*	13	Auckland

Date	Port Departure	Ship (Nearest 1,000 tons)		Limit of Escort
27 Mar 41	Auckland	Aorangi	13	to Monowai off Three Kings
29 Mar 41	Auckland	Port Fairey	13	400 mls E of East Cape
2 Apr 41	Auckland	Tongariro	14	400 mls E of E.C.
		Kent	12	400 mls E of E.C.
7 Apr 41	Wgton with HMAS Australia and Hobart	5th Reinforcements		
		Mauretania	34	S of Sydney
		Nieuw Amsterdam	36	S of Sydney
10 Apr 4	Jervis Bay	Queen Mary (at anchor)	84	Guardship
11 Apr 41	Jervis Bay	Queen Mary	84	To join Mid East
		Queen Elizabeth	86	convoy south of
		Ile de France	45	Sydney
		Nieuw Amsterdam	36	with 8th Army
		Mauretania	34	reinforcements
19 Apr 41	Auckland	Tamaroa	12	E of Gt Barrier Is defective PVs return Auckland.
21 Apr 41	Hauraki Gulf	Tamaroa	12	500 mls E of E.C.
29 Apr 41	Auckland	Awatea	9	Suva
3 May 41	Suva	Awatea	9	100 mls N of Eqtr
21 May 41	Auckland	Rangatira	7	Suva
23 May 41	Suva	Rangatira	7	Auckland
26 May 41	Auckland	Rangatira	7	Suva
29 May 41	Suva	Rangatira	7	Wellington

On her way back to Auckland after taking *Awatea* north from Suva on 3 May, *Achilles* had exchanged greetings off Cape Brett on 14 May with the converted minesweepers *Gale* and *Puriri*. They said they were heading for the fishing launch *Pearline*. A mine had surfaced in its net which the skipper buoyed and cut loose; then without radio he'd made for Sub Lt Bruton's naval patrol boat *Rawea* for the incident to be reported by R/T to North Head. Subbie Bruton ordered some thirty feet of the net to be hauled in until the mine appeared twenty feet down, whereupon he secured the net to another buoy.

Gale and *Puriri* arrived at dusk, decided to deal with the mine next morning, and *Puriri* was told by the S/O on *Gale* to patrol northward from Bream Head and rejoin at daybreak. But next morning the seas had heightened, they couldn't find their marker, and just as *Puriri*'s skipper Lieutenant D.W. Blacklaws was taking a sight on Maro Tiri a thundering explosion heaved the ship's bows skyward. Evidently hitting the mine they were looking for, it detonated *Puriri*'s magazine, killing Lt Blacklaws, Stoker PO B.A. Mattson, Able Seaman L. Purkin, and Stewards J. Richardson and G. Hobley, while five others were seriously injured. *Puriri* foundered almost instantly and her twenty-six survivors were rescued by *Gale*'s boats.

Such tragic events in New Zealand waters were fortunately rare and the fighting war was brought to our navy at sea by radio broadcasts: the battlecruiser *Hood*, pride of Britain's Royal Navy, sunk in the Denmark Strait by Germany's new mammoth battleship *Bismarck* on 24 May 1941; *Bismarck* shadowed and attacked by destroyers, carrier aircraft, heavy cruiser gunfire, and battleship gunnery over the next three days until she went down only a few hundred miles from Brest; Germany's First World War 'Kaiser Bill' died on 4 June; severe Med Fleet losses especially while evacuating remnants of our Empire's 8th Army from Crete; Atlantic convoy losses causing drastic food and clothes rationing in war-ravaged Britain.

Many of *Achilles*' long-service men had gone to *Monowai* when she commissioned, others to New Zealand's converted trawlers; new trainees had replaced them, found their sea legs over the past weeks when ferrying *Rangitira* back and forth to Suva, and were now about to experience the southern latitudes' roaring forties. HMAS *Australia*'s familiar County Class outline materialised from lifting mist as she rounded Massey Memorial on 9 June ahead of *Largs Bay* and *Thermistocles*, two ancient liners being used as troopships and both emitting dense smoke as they came to their Wellington berths. Within hours every pub in the capital bulged with khaki-clad Aussies on their way to England, then next day they too were introduced to the Pacific's fortieth latitude. *Achilles* wallowed eastward with the two old relics still belching unburned coal-dust, all three striving to remain stern-on to huge following seas raging unimpeded from Antarctica's icy wastes. Suitcases crashed off lockers onto unsuspecting heads to invent new nautical terms; plates and cups rose strangely from racks to pause mid-air before shattering when the deck came up to meet them; while greenfaced men clasped hands over bulging cheeks and tried to make it topsides. On the third day out with *Achilles* a shuddering waterlogged shambles, lookouts and bridge staff watched *Largs Bay* and *Thermistocles* rolling eastward still shrouded in funnel pollution, momentarily atop mountainous gale-torn swells then disappearing completely in their vast cavernous troughs.

It was now a 9-knot slog back against those massive rollers 300 miles south-east of the Chathams, this time veering slightly to be nearer *Port Melbourne* known to have departed Wellington for Britain, but keeping an intent watch for *Brisbane Star* already on her way from Lyttelton to be met and escorted 300 miles east of the Chathams; that done there was the 11,000-ton refrigerated motor vessel *Otaio* east-bound from Napier to be similarly protected against possible raider attack; her 20,000-ton cargo of frozen carcasses were going to the UK via the Panama Canal. There were more: *Wairangi* lapping her plimsolls with 20,000 tons for hungry Britons; 13,000-ton *Dorset* from Napier with another 20,000 tons; then the Dutch tanker *Andersjake*. Sheer continuously wet monotony. But the War wasn't as far away as had been thought.

Komet was cruising off the Chathams in late June in search of the train of NZ-UK shipping *Achilles* had been protecting, but having intercepted none of them she transferred some of her mines onto a recently captured 350-ton Norwegian whale chaser *Pol–1X*, changed its name to *Adjutant* and sent it off to lay ten magnetic mines across Godley Heads at the entrance to Lyttelton in the early hours of 25 June, then another ten across Wellington Heads at midnight on 26 June, just six hours before *Achilles* passed over them on her way in. Probably defective or not correctly activated, they were intended to float at a depth calculated to be triggered by ships over 5,000 tons; however, thousands of such vessels have passed over them without effect and they're possibly still there on the bottom. Two days after they were laid *Achilles* escorted 4,000 troops of the 6th Reinforcements from Wellington to Sydney aboard *Aquitania*, continued as part escort for *Aquitania*, *Queen Mary* and *Queen Elizabeth* to Bass Strait where she released them to *Australia*, then brought *Dominion Monarch* back to New Zealand.

It was now that the punishment taken in *Achilles'* excursions 'Down the Gut' to the east of Chatham Islands was recognised; rivets in her bows had been sprung as she warped and crashed through head seas when returning westward, other damage required attention so she entered Calliope Dock for a month during which her complement went on two watches of long leave; in the interim her escort duties being shared between *Monowai*, Canada's armed merchant cruiser *Prince Robert*, and whatever Australian cruiser or AMC might be available.

Meanwhile what of *Leander*? Her Lebanon coast operations had concluded when an armistice agreement was signed at Acre on 14 July 1941; she had been a unit of 'Operation Guillotine', the cruisers and destroyers ferrying RAF and army contingents from Port Said to Cyprus to forestall German occupation of the strategic island; and she had joined Cunningham's battle fleet at sea off Alexandria for a sweep into the Ionian Sea, to contain the Italian Fleet while a relief convoy fought its way from Gibraltar to Malta. Then on 26 July after another deckload of Geordies to Famagusta, she had entered Alexandria for farewells to Sister Street, the Acteon and Kit Kat Cafes, CS7, CS15, C-in-C Admiral Cunningham, and finally her mates who had volunteered for *Neptune*. At Port Said she exchanged all the Navy's Mediterranean charts for the return of her Walrus and its catapult before entering the Suez Canal. Some of the twenty-foot-long German mines dropped by parachute into the Canal were still there awaiting victims, and although they were pinpointed by red buoys, to warn ships to stop engines and everything liable to cause vibration while gliding over them, it was still a hair-raising experience to know some were activated magnetically against which most ships were now degaussed, while others were triggered acoustically against which there was yet no counter. Their tripping mechanism was also staggered but *Leander* wasn't the loser of that day's Russian roulette, and swarms of convalescing New Zealand servicemen paddled all manner of floatation out to her night-long Ismailia anchorage.

Their boats and other strange craft queued at the sea gangway, and before long the messdecks and wardroom were noisy with walking wounded seeking relations, giving them uncensored letters for wives, Mums, Dads, and sweethearts back home; right through from late afternoon till they were piped back ashore near 2200 when an imminent air raid was warned from local HQs. Bombs were dropped and A/A posts retaliated. Next day near Tewfik, men saw the burnt-out liner *Georgic* aground and listing; liberty men streamed ashore to swap their Egyptian £1 notes for pockets full of New Zealand coins, crammed trains to Suez, came back aboard at 2300 to find new faces in their messdecks, new entries just arrived as passengers on the massive liner *Queen Elizabeth*. On again through the Red Sea heat to Aden where Britain's modern battleship *King George V* lay broad-beamed and imposing in the bay, until men learned they were looking at the old gunnery target battleship *Centurion*, now mounting wooden quadruple turrets, fighting-top and funnels reconstructed to look like *KG-V* as she slipped in and out of Middle East harbours to deceive Axis agents.

At Colombo *Leander* waited for the A/A cruiser *Ceres* to come out of dock, then took her place on the chocks while men entered open carriages to rattle 6,000 feet uphill to Djyatalawa Rest Camp's brisk air – three days away from bugle calls and gunfire – just clear streams and open country interspersed by tea plantations, and burrows in clay banks into which laughing men poked long sticks to pull out and antagonise angry cobras. At Fremantle from 20 to 22 August the ship's patrol Lieutenants were kept busy bailing miscreants out of jail, dozens came off adrift hours after midnight, suffering from Perth's unstinted hospitality, fatigued after hours in Fremantle's licenced hostess bedrooms, unconcerned about the OOW's admonishments. Then onward in fair seas escorting the liner *Ceramic* to Adelaide's approaches where *Leander* said 'Bon Voyage' and carried on to Sydney.

Meantime *Achilles* had completed her refit and Gulf trials by 27 August, met *Rimutaka* near Cape Brett on the 31st for the Chathams run, repeated it for the Federal Company's *Cornwall*, and on the way back to Wellington, cleaned ship for a Governor General inspection ruined by driving rain when Sir Cyril Newall was piped aboard at Aotea Quay; but next night Sunday, 7 September 1941 at 2230, the ship's SRE broadcast in every messdeck and department: 'This is your Captain speaking.' A pause for attention then: 'I have been informed that *Leander* is due in at 0600 tomorrow from the Mediterranean. She will berth ahead of us and we will cheer ship as she passes. That is all.'

That is all? It was momentous! All were topsides in the cold frosty dawn hours for first glimpses of Sis. 'THERE SHE IS!' as her camouflaged hull and upperworks rounded Massey Memorial. Now bows on for the approach, funnel vapour white before it evaporated. Movietone newsmen whirred film from atop *Achille*'s bridge-roof while one with a microphone straddled the 6" DCT. She was gliding past at hailing distance, her ship's company at 'Entering Harbour Stations' mirroring *Achilles*' division by division, *Leander*'s bearded or suntanned.

In the still air Captain Barnes spoke into a loud-hailer: '*ACHILLES*! THREE CHEERS FOR *LEANDER*! HIP-HIP ...'

'HOOOO RAYYYY' as up at arms length went 700 white caps.

'HIP-HIP ...'

'HOOOO RAYYYY,' as up went the caps again.

'HIP-HIP ...'

'HOOOORRRAAYYYY,' caps waving till the loud applause subsided.

Then from across the narrow gap Captain Bevan's reply:

'*LEANDER*! THREE CHEERS FOR *ACHILLES*! HIP-HIP ...'

'HUUURRRAAAHHH!' 760 shipmates' shouts echoing the loud triple salute as the sister-ships came funnel to funnel, superstructures momentarily imaged.

While the last roaring salutation died away, the harbour boiled around *Leander*'s stern, eddies widening when her port and starboard propellors thrashed in opposition to force the bows in. Muddied foam swirled with each engine-room demand. Mooring lines snaked across the surface to be hauled up onto bollards, for'ard ones already singing taut as steel fairleads smoked. More telegraphed orders, fenders squealing as her whole length pressed gently alongside. Finally Captain Bevan saying into the engine-room phone: 'Finished with engines.'

That afternoon *Leander* marched through Wellington's crowded streets, a man hearing his proud father's voice above the appreciative tumult, chests swelling with emotion as they entered the Town Hall for a dinner reception lorded over by the capital's dignitaries, some talking on, boring and stuffy.

The parade marched back aboard, but soon South Islanders were lining bars preparatory to their crowded *Rangatira* trip to Lyttelton. At 1700 *Leander* departed for Auckland, there in Wednesday, 10 September's brilliant sunshine, marching up a happy Queen Street, bandsmen's brass glinting, side and base drums beating the step, Aucklanders several deep either side cheering, constantly urged back by horse-mounted, grinning police along the whole confetti-showered route. Men were yelled to by name but the male and female calls were drowned in that undulating roar of welcome as the parade swung by, ticker tape and streamers wafting in the light breeze to settle on marching men's shoulders. From a raised and flagged dais fronting the Town Hall, Mayor Allum said it was a day of rejoicing; CNS Commodore Parry commended the ship and its men; then other VIPs spoke, concluding with the Minister of Agriculture, Mr Barclay, who said; 'When Walter Nash addressed you in Wellington, one of you yelled "Make it snappy" – I fully agree with that man and you won't have to say it to me – "WELL DONE LEANDER!"' whereupon he sat down to appreciative laughter and applause.

Captain Bevan thanked New Zealand for the welcome at Wellington, and Auckland in particular for its warmth and sunshine, continuing that the day held special significance for New Zealand's naval forces. 'You will read in tonight's paper that His Majesty has today approved the title of "His Majesty's New Zealand Ship" to ships and establishments of the now "Royal New Zealand Navy".' There was more applause amid which officers and men streamed inside to sit at profusely laden tables, beneath a gallery and upper circle of relatives and intimate friends. Mr Allum announced amid laughter: 'The next of kin are not expected to remain silent, AND ... there will be no speeches.' After grace he called for glasses to be raised for the Loyal Toast. At Captain Bevan's call, officers and men gave three cheers for the Mayor and Citizens of Auckland; then with the dinner concluded there followed a Master at Arm's request for organised dispersal. Within minutes happy reunions were taking place outside the now deserted Town Hall; Queen Street reverted to its usual busy activities, and soon there were white caps predominant among tram and bus passengers heading for suburban homes.

To date, apart from liners taking air force trainees north to Canada, and the recent ferry service of troops and airmen to Fiji, the preponderance of shipping went east-about with food and raw materials for beleaguered Britain, or westward with reinforcements and supplies for the North African Desert 8th Army; so *Achilles* waited a week in Wellington, until 15 September when the 7th Reinforcements embarked on *Aquitania* and *Johann van Oldenbarnevelt*, a Dutch vessel built big to display its name. South of Sydney *Achilles* relinquished them to Australia's antiquated cruiser *Adelaide*, which confounded messdeck gamblers who'd put money on going right through to the Med in place of *Leander*, then they were more confused when they went topside to see America's white-hulled Matson liner *Monterey* abreast to starboard, punching into heavy seas and maintaining station at 17 knots en route Auckland. 'What in hell are we escorting goddam Yanks for?' they grumbled. 'The bastards aren't even in the bloody war!' To cap it all the big liner asked by signal lamp if *Achilles* wanted less speed. Skip's face changed from wind-chafed tan to deep purple: 'What bloody sauce. Yeoman! Make to *Monterey*: We can give you another fifteen if you want them,' a deterrent to the American's solicitude for our New Zealand cruisers in future rough weather.

From Auckland she was escorted to Suva; Suva to Pago Pago; Pago to the Equator where she was exchanged for her sister-ship *Mariposa* on the run south. It seemed that America *was* doing a bit for our Empire, its twin liners were transporting large numbers of New Zealand and Australian airmen to Vancouver for Canada's fighter and bomber pilot training scheme. And in Suva there was evidence of other pro-Allies assistance; five Dutch freighters and a Dutch naval tanker had just been escorted from Cairns by the Netherlands East Indies cruiser *Java*, the Cross-of-Lorraine's armed merchant cruiser *Cap des Palmes* and destroyer *Le Triomphant*. So the warships of Australia, New Zealand, French Oceania, and the Netherlands East Indies were actively committed to assisting the UK's war in Europe, while preparing their Pacific bases for a much closer fists-up against the Rising Sun. *Leander*'s minor refit had been completed, she had done Gulf trials from 12 to 15 November, then sailed on the 17th with *Monterey* for Suva, Pago Pago, then Canton Island, a British possession ceded to the US under its Lend Lease Agreement. There while awaiting *Mariposa*, *Leander* anchored close to the US destroyer *Selfridge* and supply ship *Antares*, both stationed at Canton while Seebees constructed an American Air Force base; then on the run south the US liner and *Leander* were joined by *Achilles* for combined exercises all the way to Auckland.

It was there on 3 December that the *Herald* reported HMAS *Sydney* lost days previously off north-west Australia without a sound or trace, but months would elapse before it was learned that the cruiser renowned for her Mediterranean actions had fallen into a trap set by Germany's raider *Kormorant* sailing under disguise. *Sydney* had approached too close while querying the stranger, and the German's opening salvoes were accurate, exploding in *Sydney*'s magazines and creating havoc as she retired to engage from a safer range. Although mortally crippled and sinking, the Australian cruiser's gunnery damaged *Kormorant* so critically that she also foundered; her German naval survivors arriving by their ship's boats in Indonesia, said they saw *Sydney* blow up at a great distance. Although they searched the area they could find no Australian survivors.

It was also in Auckland that news of Japan's 7 December 1941 attack on Pearl Harbour shattered any complacency about New Zealand's remoteness from aggression.

CHAPTER XIV

War in the Pacific, Pearl Harbour, Singapore, Coral Sea

SINCE US ADMIRAL PERRY'S 1853 expeditionary squadron introduced a Western influence to Japan, the Rising Sun's Shogunate had gradually given way to a form of Imperial Government whose leaders cast their eyes on neighbouring territory, declaring war on China in 1894, and under the 1895 Shimonoseki Treaty inheriting Formosa and expanding into Korea. Forming an alliance with Britain on 30 January 1902 Japan learned much from the RN, also the British Army whose General Younghusband occupied Tibet's capital Lhasa on 3 August 1904 and signed an Anglo-Tibet Treaty on 7 September. Japan had declared war against Russia on 8 February 1904, then captured Port Arthur on 3 January 1905 after which her Admiral Togo annihilated Admiral Rozhdestvenski's fleet, the same year that New Zealand was content to invade Britain with her All Blacks who came home victorious. Short wars were the 'In-thing'; everyone had one, cartographed new boundaries, donned splendid military regalia and signed treaties of equally short duration, the Portsmouth-USA Treaty in late 1905 ending Japan's conflict with Russia. Post First World War as an ally of Britain and the USA, Japan gained many footholds in Asia and the north-west Pacific islands, now becoming a powerful voice; but her militant industrial strength depended on raw materials and oil imported from Arabian, Asian, and Netherlands East Indies sources, virtually controlled by British, American and Dutch organisations subject to their governments.

In 1931 Japan's long tentacles enwrapped Manchuria into her Manchukuon puppet state; the League of Nations 'tut-tutted' adequately to the bombing and callous bloodshed featured in picture-theatre newsreels; but Britain and America profited from their supply of war materials aiding Japan's armed invasion of China, and from their supply of oil, rubber, iron and other raw commodities to Japan's home foundries and factories. Meantime China's provincial lords were fighting each other, her navy often had its pay cheque stolen by defecting admirals, and with little opposition Japan's 10,000-strong Kwantung Army of 1931 grew to 165,000 troops plus 200 war planes in 1935; then too late on 7 July 1937, due to a Japanese 'dirty-trick' artillery and infantry assault on Peking's 'Marco Polo Bridge' over the Hun River while tentative peace talks were in progress, China's

Communist Leader Chou En-Lai agreed with National China's General Chiang Kai-Shek to make a concerted stand against their common enemy; a full-scale Sino-Japan war developed, and Japan's Prime Minister, Prince Fumimaru Konoye, ordered another 150,000 Kwantung, Korean, and home-land troops into the conflict.

Japan's military strength in China in July 1937 now numbered 470,000 regular army with 4 million reservists on call at home. Her air strength totalled 3,000 fighters and bombers. Her Navy was kept secret. Throughout 1937–38–39 the carnage increased; periodic League of Nations appeals for peace received unconcealed contempt; American and British gunboats were purposefully bombed then given a polite apology; and now instead of rubbing their hands at the flow of yen and sen into their coffers, the UK and USA realised they'd fostered an evil genie.

Pre-Second World War Britain and France had formulated a Joint Naval War Policy in which:

(1) The Royal Navy would be responsible for the North Sea and the North Atlantic; also Eastern Mediterranean.

(2) *La Marine Nationale* would look after the Western Mediterranean.

(3) Both navies would share responsibility for the Central Atlantic, and assist each other in (1) and (2) when necessary.

(4) Should Japan show definite signs of becoming an Axis partner, *La Marine Nationale* would assume responsibility for all of the Mediterranean, and the British Mediterranean Fleet would transfer to the Indian and Pacific Oceans, allowing three months for it to be based in Colombo, Trincomalee and Singapore.

No thought had been given to the collapse of either nation so, when France capitulated on 21 June 1940 Admiralty had to develop a totally new naval strategy. With her European involvement paramount Britain stopped her aid to Japan, and in September 1940 America applied an iron and steel embargo on all combatant nations, then several months later cut off all aid to Japan and froze her assets in the USA, so that 80 per cent of Japan's oil and petrol, and a massive amount of her raw materials, ceased to arrive. She might yet send her freighters and tankers to Netherlands East Indies sources, but Singapore and the Philippines stood either side of the narrow sea route there and back, America had a considerable strength of her overall fleet based in the Hawaiian Islands, and although the Royal Navy was fully committed in the Atlantic and Mediterranean, attempts were being made to send a battle fleet to the Indian Ocean and Singapore.

Meantime Japan knew the Rising Sun in China would set ignominiously if its war machines ground to a halt, its politicians tried in vain to alter

America's stance on supplies and its war lords argued successive proposi-
tions. 'War is the only solution!' The Emperor's quiet opposition was
politely overruled, so was that of C-in-C Admiral Isoroku Yamamoto who
warned of America's industrial might, also that of moderate premier Prince
Konoye who was replaced by irascible General Hideki Tojo.

On 3 November Yamamoto stopped arguing, and devised a plan to
eliminate the US Pacific Fleet by an air strike. It received approval.

On 26 November Admiral Nagumo's carrier fleet, maintaining total W/T
silence, departed Tankan Bay in the Kuriles for a refuelling rendezvous half
way to Honolulu. Dummy W/T communications were made in all Japan's
naval bases to give the impression their fleet was still dispersed about the
homeland islands. The Strike Force would await the signal: 'Niitaka Yama
Nobore' (Climb Mount Niitaka). If it *wasn't* made, the Japanese diplomats
in Washington would have gained concessions from the USA and the fleet
would return to Japan. If it *was* made, the fleet would move to a point 500
miles north-west of Honolulu and Admiral Nagumo would attack Pearl
Harbour as so often rehearsed.

Transmitted in Japan's strange *katikana* morse, *Niitaka Yama Nobore*
screamed through a flagship operator's headphone's in 1 December's early
hours. Then having received it Admiral Nagumo ordered all ships to
replenish their tanks, and on 3 December he moved his battleship and
cruiser supported Strike Force – six carriers paired in three groups –
south-east three days to the launching point, constantly aware that any
lessening in America's political stand on embargoes would be signalled to
him and the operation would be cancelled. But the US remained adamant,
he got the final nod, and shortly after 0600 on 7 December 1941 local time,
'TORO TORO TORO!' resounded about *Akagi*'s flight-deck, repeated on
Kaga, *Hiryu* and *Soryu*, *Shokaku* and *Zuikaku* when they saw the late Admiral
Togo's 1905 Tsushima battle-flag hoisted on Nagumo's flagship and relayed
carrier to carrier.

Propellers screamed to an ear-piercing pitch as throttles opened, droned
down to an erratic stutter while plane after plane was handled into position,
rose again to a shuddering crescendo when chocks were whipped away
and bombers, dive-bombers, torpedo-bombers, and fighters rumbled forward, increasing speed to lift-off and climb high above into flight formation.
First Wave: 51 Nakajima B5N2 'Kate' bombers carrying 1,500-lb bombs,
59 Nakajima B5N2 'Kate' torpedo-bombers armed with special fin-fitted
shallow-water 24" diameter torpedos; 30 Aichi D3A2 dive-bombers carrying
800-lb bombs, 43 Mitsubishi A6M2 'Zero-sen' fighters armed with two
20mm cannons and two 8mm machine guns. Second Wave: 78 bombers
and dive-bombers: 54 torpedo-bombers: 35 escort fighters.

As the first wave approached Oahu, radar operators reporting them were told they'd be aircraft returning from *Enterprise* and *Lexington* who'd been ferrying planes to Wake and Midway Islands: 'Don't worry Buddy, see yuh in the Canteen after Church.' It was Sunday. Civilians looking up at the increasing roar thought it was an exercise. But just before 8 o'clock Colours, wave after wave of enemy aircraft swept down on the peaceful fleet, blasting great torpedo holes and bomb destruction in the battleships *Arizona*, *California*, *Oklahoma*, *Utah*, and the minelayer *Oglala* which all foundered; and severely damaging the battleships *Maryland*, *Nevada*, *Pennsylvania*, *Tennessee*, the cruisers *Helena*, *Honolulu*, *Raleigh*; the destroyers *Cassin*, *Shaw*, *Downes*; seaplane tender *Curtiss*; and the repair ship *Vestal*.

While the fleet was being savaged, other aircraft were ripping apart American aircraft parked on tarmacs about Navy, Army, and Marine airfields; leaving Pearl Harbour and its military environs a blazing smoke-enshrouded battlefield, its fleet a shambles of listing, upturned, and deck-lapped wreckage; entombing in *Arizona* alone more than 1,100 dead including Rear Admiral Isaac C. Kidd, last seen manning and firing a machine gun before his battleship blew up and also entombed him.

The second wave arrived later to be met by stiffer opposition, creating more devastation but losing a large number of its aircraft. There would be Top Brass American excuses to be written and documented. Stars of rank would be stripped from Navy, Army and Marine uniforms. There would be demotions and promotions. And now after little more than twenty years, the whole American nation was totally involved in a second world war from which its government had tried to remain aloof – this one, it might be said in retrospect, a confrontation for which she was partly responsible.

And how did this momentous event affect New Zealand? Even though Japan had bombed Pearl harbour we hailed it as the first Axis error, for it had brought America into the War. Our naval code books were being updated with the names of yet-unlaunched British battleships, carriers, cruisers and destroyer flotillas; and in our eyes the Royal Navy still 'Ruled the Waves'. Why had Japan risked such a confrontation? 'Holy cow, man, the stupid bastards must be committing hari kiri!' And apart from sympathy for our RN messmates whose relatives were still being subjected to intensive Nazi bombing, we now considered the European conflict to be secondary. But where was the Far Eastern Fleet promised pre-war for just this emergency? On 7 December 1941 NZ CNS Commodore Parry was in Singapore discussing the imminence of war with Japan; and with the need to find cruisers for an Eastern Fleet he had volunteered *Achilles*. Our War Cabinet concurred and *Achilles*, right then escorting *Wahine* to Fiji, was told to 'rush things along, refuel at Suva, proceed with despatch to Port Moresby, then Singapore'. She reached Port Moresby on 11 December but already *Prince of Wales* and *Repulse* had been sunk; the possibility of a British Fleet based on Singapore was abandoned; and *Achilles* arrived back in Auckland on 16 December 1941, just three days before our expected third Leander Class cruiser *Neptune* would be lost to mines off Mediterranean Tripoli.

However, Admiralty had put together a considerable, if ageing, battle fleet destined for the Indian Ocean under the command of Admiral Sir James Somerville, and from different directions *Warspite* (Flag), *Queen Elizabeth, Resolution, Revenge, Ramillies, Royal Sovereign,* the carriers *Formidable, Hermes,* the heavy cruisers *Dorsetshire, Cornwall,* and two destroyer flotillas, were converging on Ceylon to be based at Colombo and Trincomalee. Throughout January 1942 seven troopships took five Army Divisions to Malaya without loss, seven fighter squadrons were transferred to the Dutch East Indies, and late in January the repaired carrier *Indomitable* flew fifty Hurricanes onto Javanese airfields. Also in January an Allied naval force designated ABDA was assembling in Java and Sumatra: it comprised the US cruisers *Marblehead, Houston,* destroyers *Pope, Alden, Paul Jones, John D Ford, John D Edwards;* the British cruisers *Exeter, Dragon, Danae,* HMAS *Perth, Hobart,* HMNZS *Achilles;* RN destroyers *Electra, Encounter, Jupiter:* Dutch cruisers *De Ruyter* (Flagship of Dutch Adml Doorman), *Java,* and destroyers *Kortenar, Witte de With, Eversten.*

But back nine months on 10 March 1941, with little option, French authorities had granted Japan military use of French Indo-China's ports and Saigon's airfields, and four months later General Tomoyuki Yamashita's armies occupied the country to stand poised, awaiting the order to seize Thailand's Gulf of Siam harbours, then march down through Malaya to Singapore.

British agents had reported all this yet Whitehall still considered Singapore impregnable, its air force capable of repelling any seaborne assault, its army able to mop up any landed forces which may not have been destroyed at sea. And due to Britain's deteriorating position in Europe and North Africa, Churchill opposed attempts to move additional strength to the area, but the Chiefs of Staff insistence did result in the arrival of some English, Indian, Canadian and Scots army units. However, Britain's politicians downright vetoed suggestions of occupying Thailand before they were convinced of a Japanese invasion, and to top it all they considered that Japan, in recently becoming a Germany-Italy-Japan tripartite member, was preparing for war against Russia, not the Western nations in South-East Asia. So right up to late November 1941, Singapore's high-ranking Army, Navy, and Air Force wallahs yawned, sank deep into Raffles Hotel's soft-leather armchairs and dozed. Debated idly. 'Oh come along, Captain. Get an army through that bally jungle? Preposterous! One couldn't lead one's platoon through it single file. Chin chin; care for another?'

'Not now, Major, have to see who's responsible for those crated

Hurricanes down at the wharf.' Then at the door: 'By the way I hear some battleships are arriving tomorrow.'

'Ohh. Must see that. Are you taking Merle to the ball tonight?'

It was hot outside, cool within, gin and bitters were plentiful so eyelids tended to droop. Then true to that captain's rumour, next morning 2 December, Captain John Leach conned Admiral Sir Thomas S.V. Phillips' flagship *Prince of Wales* into harbour, ahead of the battlecruiser *Repulse* and their escorting destroyers HMS *Electra*, *Express*, *Tenedos* and HMAS *Vampire*. The modern 40,000-ton carrier *Indomitable* with its numerous squadrons of fighters and fighter-bombers was meant to be part of this embryo fleet, but an accidental grounding near Jamaica had put her into an Atlantic dock so Phillips' force was without naval air-cover. On 6 December a Hudson reconnaissance plane reported heavily escorted transports heading into the Gulf of Siam; on the 8th, messages cut short during transmission told of landings on the Thai coast at Prachuab, Chumphon, Bandon, Patani, Singora, and at Kota Bharu just inside the Malayan border.

Discussions at British Malayan HQs about sending the two capital ships north without adequate air support concluded p.m. on 8 December; at 1735 the boom gates opened and *Prince of Wales*, *Repulse*, *Electra*, *Express*, *Tenedos* and *Vampire* passed through. Before leaving harbour Admiral Phillips had asked for fighter protection to be overhead at the time he expected to be in place for the expected enemy landing at Kota Bharu; but next day his Chief of Staff, Rear Admiral A.F.E. Palliser, sent a signal regretting this protection was unavailable, and that strong forces of enemy bombers were being reported in southern Indo-China. Having next day sighted an enemy reconnaissance aircraft and being aware that it would have reported his presence, Phillips now turned south for Singapore to await more naval reinforcements, then that night a priority signal reported: 'Enemy landings Kuantan Lat 3 deg 50 min.' This was near his return course, 400 miles from the nearest enemy airfield. He ordered complete W/T silence to effect surprise and asked for increased revolutions; but at dawn off Kuantan there were no enemy transports; it was obviously a ruse, probably initiated by Japanese HQs when one of their submarines reported the British ships steaming north the previous day. Flights of long-range bombers were sent south in search of Phillips' squadron and fate was about to overtake the British ships.

Most of the trip north and return had been made in drifting mist and intermittent rain, obscuring Force Z from the enemy bombers which had searched right down the coast almost to Singapore, then started on their long flight back to French Indo-China. By mere chance one of the aircraft saw the ships' wash through a widening gap in the clearing mist. As if by a giant hand the whole curtain was dragged aside, and there in that late forenoon's sunlit blue sea was the group of British warships heading south. Without fighter protection they stood no chance when the eighty aircraft attacked. *Repulse* had worked up to only part of her evasion speed when hit by a bomb; then while struggling for speed *Prince of Wales* staggered from two tremendous detonations as torpedo-bombers drove in through a literal blizzard of death to launch their missiles. Although out of control and coming to a standstill, the flagship still continued to send her assailants cartwheeling down in flames, adding to the mass of seething short-barrage machine-gun tracer, rhythmic thump of multi-barrelled pom-poms and reverberating crash of triple-mounted 4″ gunfire through which the bombers, torpedo-bombers and dive-bombers swept to release more death and fly off seemingly indestructible.

Near midday the attackers disappeared and at 1214 *Repulse*, whose evasive actions had taken her well south, signalled Phillips: 'Thanks to Providence we have dodged 19 torpedoes so far.' But the interlude was brief; and as Tennant closed the obviously crippled battleship, new waves of approaching enemy aircraft were detected. Again the sky was filled with short-barrage tracer, bursting A/A shells, the death throes of torn-apart, plummeting attackers; yet some came through, rending *Prince of Wales'* hull with four more torpedoes exploding on opposite sides. Her list appeared to correct but she now lay low with water lapping her quarterdeck. *Repulse* could do nothing to assist as she too was under fierce attack from several directions, unable to evade this onslaught of torpedo-bombers. One torpedo struck directly under the after funnel port side, then three more along the port side and one to starboard. Immediately *Repulse* listed heavily. Tennant knew she was finished and ordered: 'Prepare to abandon ship'. Men attempting to dive from her fighting-tops misjudged, crashed to their death on her slanting decks; others lost their balance and slithered down her hull to disappear through jagged holes imploded in her side; a number of Marines dived off her quarterdeck and the water bloodied as they were sucked into the still revolving propellors and butchered. At 1233, only half an hour after the first attack, *Repulse* slipped stern-first below the oil-covered surface in which men vomited, lost their grip on fuel-smeared debris and drowned.

Prince of Wales' portside 'A' bracket had been wrenched inward, the still driving propeller sliced through her stern plates and, gradually filling through the several great rends about her hull she thrust forward water-logged, sinking but again and again being bombed while her upperworks were strafed without respite. At 1300 Captain Leach signalled *Express* alongside to receive some 1,500 men who jumped aboard, scrambled down nets slung from her rails, slid down ropes draped from outswung davits; and near 1320 right after *Express* cast off from under the heeling overhang,

Prince of Wales rolled slowly to port, wallowed keel up for an eternity of seconds then disappeared in a vast cauldron of expelling air.

Of *Repulse's* complement, 796 including Captain Tennant were rescued by her escorting destroyers; also 1,285 of *Prince of Wales'* 1,612, but unfortunately Admiral Tom Phillips and his flagship's commanding officer, Captain Leach, were not among the survivors.

To make matters worse, in late 1941 when Singapore had been expecting the build-up of a sizable Pacific Fleet to deter Japanese aspirations, the Royal Navy was experiencing unsustainable losses in the Western and Eastern Mediterranean. On 14 November the carrier *Ark Royal* was torpedoed and sunk near Gibraltar by U–81, the carrier *Indomitable* was seriously damaged when going aground off Jamaica on her way to the Pacific, battleship *Barham* on 25 November was torpedoed and blown up outside Alexandria by U–331, the cruiser *Galatea* on 14 December was torpedoed and sunk outside Alexandria by U–557, the cruiser *Neptune* and destroyer *Kandahar* on 19 December was sunk off Libyan Tripoli in a minefield which also damaged the cruisers *Aurora* and *Penelope*, and the battleships *Valiant* and *Queen Elizabeth* on 20 December were put on the shallow bottom of Alexandria Harbour by Italian frogmen, refloated and repaired months later. In the two years of war so far, the Royal Navy had lost so many capital ships sunk or severely damaged that a British Pacific Fleet was temporarily out of the question.

Now without assistance from *Prince of Wales* and *Repulse*, emergency messages were arriving at Singapore Military Headquarters from British Army units around Kota Bharu and westward along the Thai-Malay border. Position after position was taken during fierce fighting and heavy losses on both sides, but the Japanese had back-up and the 8th Infantry Brigade didn't. Its Baluch, Dogras, and Frontier Force Rifles initially supported by the 21st Mountain Battery fought until they fell, constantly shelled by Japanese light field artillery, strafed and bombed by enemy air support. It rained as never before. While retreating to rear lines vehicles and guns got bogged down and were left undamaged, drums of fuel intact, ammunition awaiting use by Yamashita's advancing troops as the invaders' morale soared. The 11th Indian Division gradually tired and over successive days of relentless attack became disorganised. By 10 December three-quarters of the 15th Brigade were dead, 700 of the 28th Brigade killed. Wavell was flown to Singapore on 8 January but any decision at this point seemed hopeless against the Japanese momentum.

The 8th Australian Division and 9th Indian Division were moved up from Singapore, and although they had initial success in stemming the advance, Kuala Lumpur fell to Yamashita's 5th Division on 11 January, but on putting the question Wavell was told there had been no plans made for an organised withdrawal to Singapore Island: 'No sir, it is impossible to adapt the fortress guns to train inland.'

'Have you erected obstructions at potential landing sites along the Johore Straits?'

'No sir.'

'No sir, we haven't arranged machine-gun units … ', and so on and on in negative answer to every query.

Wavell took a signal handed to him by Percival. It was from Churchill: 'I want to make it absolutely clear that I expect every inch of ground to be defended, every scrap of material for defences to be blown to pieces to prevent capture by the enemy, and no question of surrender to be entertained until after protracted fighting among the ruins of Singapore City.'

Had Wavell and Percival known that Yamashita was having similar problems the outcome may have been different. On 1 January Yamashita had written in his diary: 'I suspect that Tojo plans to kill me when my task is over. I can't rely on communications with Terauchi and the Southern Army. It is bad that Japan has no one in high places who can be relied on. Most abuse their power.' On 5 January he continued: 'These men pressed into national service are seldom any good in a crisis. I shall have to watch them.' He then mentioned his military adversary Nishimura: 'He has wasted a week by disobeying my orders. I ordered General Matsui and the 5th Division to carry out a flanking movement and so trap and crush the enemy. But my orders weren't obeyed. I am disgusted with the lack of training and inferior quality of my commanders.' On the 8th he wrote: 'The battalion commanders and troops lack fighting spirit. They have no idea how to crush the enemy That bloody Terauchi. He's living in luxury in Saigon, with a comfortable bed, good food, and playing chess.'

But whatever Yamashita's problems, there was no way of halting his army's advance. On 10 February Wavell flew to Singapore for the last time, flew back to Java and signalled Churchill: 'Battle for Singapore not going well. Morale not good. I have categorically ordered no thought of surrender.' It was too late. At 1100 on 15 February a white-flagged British Army car from the besieged city approached Japan's 25th Army Staff Officer Lieutenant Colonel Sugita, and announced the British party had come to discuss terms of surrender. They were escorted through the enemy lines and faced Yamashita at 1400. Yamashita ordered them to tell Percival to come in person, which he did at 1715 with Major Wild as interpreter. Face to face in a room at Bukit Timah's Ford Factory where the Japanese interpreter, Hishikari, introduced the two opposing generals, they shook hands then sat facing each other across a table at which the interpreted conversation was recorded, first with Yamashita's question:

'Answer me briefly. Do you wish to surrender unconditionally?'

'Yes, we do.'

'Have you any Japanese prisoners of war?'

'None at all.'

'Have you any Japanese civilians?'

'No. They have all been sent to India.'

'Very well, you will please sign this document of surrender.'

Reading half of it carefully, Percival asked if it could wait till next morning, at which Yamashita's eyes narrowed as he hissed: 'If you don't sign right now we shall continue fighting. Do you surrender unconditionally or do you not?'

Percival demurred, frowned as he spoke quietly to his interpreter; but Yamashita was angered, pointed a finger at Percival and half rising from his seat shouted: 'YES! OR NO?'

Percival told Major Wild to say 'Yes'.

'Very well,' as Yamashita resumed his seat, 'We shall cease hostilities at 10 p.m. Japanese time.'

There followed discussions about the treatment of service and civilian prisoners, the many varied matters ensuing; then the terms of surrender were signed and countersigned at 1810, making official Britain's worst ever military disaster, a 73-day debacle. And within weeks the ABDA Force – apart from HMNZS *Achilles* which had been detained at the outset by NZNB, and HMS *Dragon* and *Danae* which had both been required elsewhere – was further weakened by USS *Marblehead*'s damage in a skirmish with Japanese heavy cruisers which necessitated her return to the States. Then came the destruction of Dutch Admiral Doorman's ABDA Squadron at the Java Sea Battle, 26 to 29 February 1942, from which only the US destroyers *Alden*, *Paul Jones*, *John D Ford* and *John D Edwards* survived to reach Australia. Following fast on the heels of this catastrophe, and to emphasise the power of naval aircraft, Japanese Admiral Nagumo's Fast Carrier Force drove eastward into the Bay of Bengal and north-east Indian Ocean, bombing Colombo and Trincomalee, sinking numerous Allied merchantmen, and on 5 April sinking *Dorsetshire* and *Cornwall*, then next day the carrier *Hermes*, destroyers HMAS *Vampire*, HMS *Hollyhock*, and two RFA tankers.

To say the least Japan's crushing blows had left the Pacific allies reeling in these initial rounds, particularly when Singapore surrendered, the Dutch East Indies were overwhelmed, and Darwin on 19 February was bombed by 180 Japanese aircraft into long months of uselessness. But Britain's defiant stand against Goering's relentless bombing, her Merchant Marine's persistence in braving the terrors of Doenitz's Atlantic wolf-packs to sustain their beleaguered isles, and the inability of Germany and Italy to starve Malta into submission, had inured the Allies to reversals. Now the RAF was gaining strength, the 8th Army was holding against Rommel's onslaughts in Libya, and even though the Royal Navy was stretched from Murmansk right round the world to the Pacific, we sensed that the pendulum was about to swing against Hitler's, Mussolini's, and Tojo's Axis aggressions. So, while British, American, and Japanese Chiefs of Naval Staffs pondered the most effective dispositions of their Indian and Pacific Ocean fleets, *Achilles, Leander* and *Monowai* escorted more and more troops and material about the South Pacific – NZ Army and RNZAF personnel with bulldozers and guns aboard *Rangatira, Wahine, Matua,* and *Port Montreal* to establish bases, runways, A/A and coastal gun emplacements in Fiji – then RNZN craft to lay minefields against enemy underwater or surface intrusion.

While in Auckland awaiting the next convoy, we took our wives or sweethearts to the Civic Theatre where film stars of the period enthralled their fans; to local North Shore theatres where one needn't cram into buses and go by ferry; or maybe stayed home by the lounge fire listening to that night's episode of *Easy Aces, Randy Stone, Dad and Dave, Office Wife* or *Tusi Tala Teller of Tales.* We had brought back silk stockings and many New Zealand unobtainables; single men stayed in the Albion, the 'Vic' or perhaps Fred Gleeson's for two-bob bed and breakfast; they ate steak and massive Bluff oysters at Cook's Restaurant, served on immaculately starched white table covers by immaculately uniformed polite waitresses; and at 0700 they queued at Admiralty Steps to learn that one of *Monowai*'s 6″ guns had back-flashed during a Gulf shoot. Three men were dead and six badly injured. But three days later *Monowai* sailed with *Leander* as escort for *Wahine* and *Matua* to Fiji with more troops and material.

On the next trip north *Achilles* and *Leander* were joined by *Australia* and *Perth*, an impressive escort appreciated by the swarms of khaki-clad servicemen seen waving from *Rangatira, Port Montreal* and *Wahine* on the three-day trip to Suva. But without time for fraternising ashore, the four cruisers refuelled on arrival and within hours were back at sea exercising en route Sydney. Nothing new. We'd done all this pre-war, and already understood our Oz neighbours' eccentricities sufficiently to avoid night-exercise collisions as we sped south-westward. My Morning Watch telegraphists came topside to find *Leander* cleaving *Perth*'s swirling wake. Beyond her lazily swaying upperworks we could see *Australia* distorting through *Perth*'s bluish funnel haze, but where was *Achilles*? She'd been recalled to Auckland last night and on our starboard horizon we could make out the low-lying sun-scorched Australian coast. We went below for Kornies and Ideal milk, got plates of 'rashes and red lead' from our messdeck watchkeepers' warmers, then showered and shaved before heading for the Signal Bridge. Now close to starboard Sydney Head's 'Lovers Leap' was passing, its sheer cliffs sun-drenched, its base rock-shelves pounded by

Tasman swells as always. We'd been identified as friendly by the boom defence vessel and she'd opened the gate. Manly ferry sirens welcomed the three cruisers as we coursed up harbour, to separate, to secure at our allocated berths. *Leander*'s was at a lower harbour buoy serviced by passing ferries. I was tired, unfolded my low metal-framed camp stretcher in the darkened 3rd W/T Office and was soon fast asleep. Others were thumbing pocket books for familiar phone numbers, forgetting the War as they went ashore to the enticements of Australia's most entertaining city.

Apart from a shoot outside with *Australia* and *Perth*, *Leander* remained at anchor for her eight days in Sydney, enjoying Bondi Beach's tepid surf, King's Cross's carefree nightlife, the search for opened pubs as each closed due to rationing. Meantime US, NZ, UK, and Oz Service Chiefs planned their combined Pacific strategy – a chain of defended islands reaching from New Guinea to Fiji, some already garrisoned, all to have airstrips from which to detect enemy vessels venturing south; lookout posts and radar posts to be established on smaller islands. Fiji and Pago Pago were now regarded as able to withstand attack. New Caledonia would be next, then the New Hebrides. 'Right gentlemen. Now howsabout we call our combined naval task force the ANZAC FORCE? And the operation zone the ANZAC ZONE?' This was discussed by the Australian, American, and New Zealand VIPs. Eventually they settled on the ANZAC SQUADRON and the ANZAC AREA. These TOP SECRET agreements were priority coded and rushed to designated commanders, four star downward, in sequence. Captain Bevan received his sealed orders and on 27 January 1942 *Leander* sailed in company with *Australia*, *Perth* and *Adelaide*, course generally north-eastward.

Only two weeks earlier *Monowai* had earned the distinction of being New Zealand's first Second World War warship to engage a Japanese opponent. Having accompanied the 4,300-ton fast steamer *Taroona* up from Auckland, both carrying troops for Fiji, the two ships on 16 January were only miles out of harbour on their return trip, when two loud explosions and high columns of water were heard and seen 200 yards off *Monowai*'s port beam. Thinking his ship was under air attack Captain G.R. Deverell immediately ordered evasive manoeuvres, made the AAAA signal on 500 kc/s and sounded Action Stations; but within moments he ordered the SSSS warning to be transmitted as her four portside 6″ guns trained on a surfaced submarine several thousand yards off the port bow. *Monowai* shuddered throughout when she opened fire, breeches flashing open to receive new shells and charges, slamming shut to be triggered, guns recoiling as their charges blasted smoke, flame, and projectiles at the now crash-diving enemy. But the safety of his converted liner and his troopship were Deverell's major concern. It was time to quit the area and avoid

possible torpedoes so, signalling *Taroona* to follow, they increased speed
and escaped through Mbengga Passage when *Monowai*'s navigator, Lieutenant G.H. Edwards VRD RNZNR, declared confidence in being able to
negotiate the reef and rock-strewn waterway used only by Fiji's most
experienced coastal skippers.

By this time American troopships were being escorted by US cruisers to
the ANZAC boundary, where RAN and RNZN cruisers rendezvoused to
take them on to Melbourne, Sydney or Brisbane. *Perth* and *Hobart* had
already been assigned to Doorman's ABDA Squadron, and in our Main
W/T Office there hung a sheet of names depicting the ANZAC Squadron:

Aircraft Carrier:	HMS *Hermes*
Cruisers:	HMAS *Australia, Canberra, Adelaide*, USS *Chicago*, HMNZS *Achilles, Leander*
AMCs:	HMAS *Kanimbla, Manoora, Westralia*, HMNZS *Monowai*
Destroyers:	HMAS *Stuart, Voyager*, USS *Lamson, Perkins*

Dramatic events had outdated this document and some of the names
were already erased before the remainder arrived within hours of each
other at Suva on 12 February. US Task Force 11 was on its way to bomb
and bombard Japanese ships and shore establishments at recently occupied

US invasion ships in Wellington, 1942; note landing barges slung outboard.

Rabaul, and our ANZAC Squadron was to cover the area between Fiji and New Caledonia as they passed through. This was something positive after months of escort duties. As we cleared Navula Passage astern of *Achilles* and the Australian cruisers, Captain Bevan spoke over *Leander*'s SRE to brief the ship's company on our operation. And once more one sensed that atmosphere of calm expectancy among *Leander*'s war-seasoned crew, heard the comfortable rumble of her propellers growling as our stern dipped, the slight revving as it lifted on the Pacific swells.

We negotiated the blue-lit portside passage to our Main W/T Office for the First Watch, transited it again for the Morning, then after breakfast came topside to rid our lungs of the punkalouvered semi-stagnant air below, to give tin-fish-men at their torpedo mounts the latest gen, then lean on guardrails to look at nearby cruisers rolling gently to show their red-leaded undersides, their bows slicing through white caps to spit warm spray against A-turret. Later on that 16 February forenoon men made for vantage points, Stan Roy and others with cameras. There converging from all points of the starboard horizon was Task Force 11: the big flat-top *Lexington* whose scout planes had earlier interrogated our squadron; the 8″ heavy cruisers *San Francisco* and *Indianapolis*, screened ahead, to either side and astern by destroyers; and now coming into sight two more cruisers with their

US landing barges Wellington, in Oriental Bay yacht basin. *Rangatira* at Aotea Quay, July 1942.

destroyer escorts. Then as we watched, *Australia* closed the carrier for Admiral Grace to be taken by boat for a brief conference, after which our ANZAC Squadron was ordered back to Suva. Evidently someone had forgotten the 20,000-ton US tanker *Platte*, and when we returned to the refuelling area well eastward of Rabaul with her, it seemed the assault on Rabaul had been cancelled. Japanese reconnaissance aircraft had alerted the enemy to TF–11's presence, long-range bombers had attacked *Lexington* but her fighters had downed most of them, and now short of fuel the Task Force had withdrawn so once more we headed back to Suva.

Fuel was a major consideration in planning any naval operation, even the New Zealand cruisers' minor participation when one digests the Engineer Commander's monthly mileage return for each ship:

Leander	24 days at sea	7,546 miles steamed
Achilles	21 days at sea	6,703 miles steamed
Monowai	21 days at sea	7,588 miles steamed

And most of this was done at an average 20 knots which soon emptied fuel tanks, however, for the last two days of February *Leander* and *Achilles* were stationary in Suva, and the only seatime being done was that of their Communication Department's Maori War Canoe race around the anchored cruisers, enacted in whalers urged on by hakas, blood-curdling chants, and daubed pakeha warriors wielding carley-float paddles to the incredulity of nearby USN and RAN spectators.

This may or may not have decided Admiral Grace to quit harbour before his ships were attacked, but within hours *Australia*, *Chicago*, *Lamson* and *Perkins* weighed anchor and departed, leaving the two 'Shaky Isles' cruisers to dwell two days on *Leander*'s win, before steaming east for the ANZAC boundary to relieve USS *Portland* of a three-ship convoy she'd escorted from San Francisco. Signal flags ran up and down halyards; US and NZ bridge officers spoke inter-ship without restraint on TBS; then as the American heavy cruisers' mastheads dipped below our eastern horizon, *Achilles* and *Leander* sped escort-stationed either side of the Matson liners *Monterey*, *Mormacsea* and *Matsonia*, doing 20 knots towards a red-slashed golden sunset. Next day on an unruffled blue Pacific, both cruisers treated their American audience to an accurate fused-6″ H/A shoot at smoke bursts from 4″ shells lobbed high to port and starboard. Two days later the GIs and Marines watched a reduced-charge full-calibre 6″ throw-off shoot, where each cruiser in turn raised water columns the determined hundreds of yards from its adversary; but that night, Friday, 6 March 1942, when west of New Caledonia, the weather turned sour. Before daybreak all ships were wallowing in an old man blow; all day Saturday and into the night; safety lines rigged in the waists, water sloshing sickeningly in messdecks and flats, nil visibility causing concern over the possibility of collision.

Sunday dawned through the still-raging storm to see *Matsonia* and *Mormacsea* corkscrewing spectacularly to starboard; but where were *Achilles* and *Monterey*? We were to have entered harbour about noon but *Matsonia* signalled her intention to carry on southward, her deck-cargo was in danger of breaking loose if she steered crosswind, but late that afternoon we came under the lee of a promontory sufficient for our two liners to come about safely. *Leander* came round Fisherman Islands' South Point into Moreton Bay to find *Achilles* there without *Monterey*, and as she left to find the missing troopship we carried on up the Brisbane River with ours to Hamilton Wharf. Few wanted to go ashore, we just wanted sleep, and next morning *Monterey* crept past our berth, rust streaked, lifeboats hanging awry; she also had been unable to alter course for fear of capsizing in those mast-head seas which were still lashing the Queensland coast. Vivid lightning illuminated the dark underbelly of pregnant low cloud; spasmodic rain squalls deluged the city, thunderclaps shook nearby buildings continually until Wednesday afternoon, so our hammocks and camp stretchers were preferable to some of South Brisbane's doss-houses, and there weren't many heartbreaks when 'Special Sea Dutymen' was piped on Thursday, 12 March.

Achilles and *Leander* cleared Moreton Bay on a breathless blue sea reflecting the blue sky, there wasn't a cloud between Australia and New Caledonia, but there was an official military one over Noumea. There'd been fighting ashore between US sailors, GIs and Marines; RAN sailors had aligned themselves with the Yankee matelots; and to prevent additional broken heads all warship liberty had been curtailed; then when the restriction was lifted a curfew was placed on the town's liquor outlets. We anchored near HMAS *Westralia*, *Australia*, USS *Chicago*, a brood of Yankee tin-cans, and a Brooklyn Class cruiser recently arrived from the States; we refuelled and watered from harbour barges and relaxed into a low category of air defence for which the warships were requested. The cruisers' Walruses and other types of reconnaissance amphibians maintained air patrols over Noumea approaches, which irritated sleepy W/T operators looking for an after-watch head-down, but instead being told to take over on one of the fleet channels for another four hours. 'Goddam bloody war!'

My watch's run ashore was brief; GIs and Marines were sleeping all over the jacaranda-shaded grass square, sitting on town pavements playing crap and arguing; buildings and lattice-shuttered shops were long neglected, blue and red paint flaking, especially those unkempt backyard loos with doors ajar to reveal trousers-down or skirts-up occupants mindful of 'Dad and Dave' cartoons. We sought the landing and awaited its 1800 liberty barge, resigned to be returning to a clean messdeck where a ninepenny bottle of beer per man was issued daily due to pub closures.

At the end of ten days during which the transports gradually emptied and sailed, it seemed the Squadron's A/A defence was no longer needed; US shore batteries had been established and we departed in single file, out past Amedee Lighthouse to negotiate Noumea's safe passage, between Allied minefields in which the masts and funnel of an erring merchantman emphasised the need for caution. The Pacific had again turned dirty and the cruisers took another pummeling while looking for three US troopers accompanied by destroyers, then escorting them to Vila in the New Hebrides. This accomplished, we remained in harbour as A/A protection, each cruiser's plane in turn winging a hundred-mile perimeter from pre-dawn to dusk while the American advance party disembarked. Bulldozers, massive concrete mixers, trucks and building materials were offloaded and work commenced on a 5,000-yard runway; but there were tens of thousands of US servicemen on their way to base camps in New Zealand, Australia, Fiji, New Caledonia, and few cruisers to escort them. So, while *Achilles* was taking over USS *Chester*'s San Francisco to Sydney convoy consisting of *Mariposa*, *President Coolidge*, and Britain's 84,000-ton liner *Queen Elizabeth*, *Leander* was relieving USS *New Orleans* of her 10,000- to 20,000-ton Americans *Santa Clara*, *Santa Lucia*, *Santa Paula*, *General J Parker*, and *Uruguay* en route New York to Australia via the Panama Canal.

Monowai having just escorted *Rangatira* from Napier to Suva then down to Auckland, was now south of Tonga waiting to take *Uruguay* and *Santa Paula* from *Leander*. They were short of fresh water so *Monowai* escorted them to Auckland for it, then on to Melbourne, while we continued with the remainder to Brisbane. Meanwhile *Achilles* who'd rushed ahead of her Sydney-bound convoy, with *Queen Elizabeth* which could enter only an hour each side of high tide, then remained two weeks in Cockatoo Dockyard being fitted with mounts for several Oerlikons at present in boxes aboard *Leander* a long way north. And while in Sydney *Achilles*' Captain C.A.L. Mansergh DSO (First World War) RN, released his cabin to Captain H.M. Barnes RN who'd also served throughout the Great War.

Monowai, while still bound for Fremantle from Melbourne with *City of London* and *City of Paris*, had clocked up 7,831 sea miles for the month ended midnight, 30 April 1942. Throughout the next twelve months she would traverse many more thousands of miles as escort for troopers and supply ships, then on 24 April 1943 she would depart the Pacific for a dockyard in Scotland to be converted from our HMNZ Armed Merchant Cruiser to His Majesty's Troopship. Since being appropriated from New Zealand's Union Steam Ship Company as a trans-Pacific liner, she'd become

HMNZS *Monowai* and had engaged a large Japanese submarine which broke off their gunnery duel and crash-dived to escape, she had transported and/or escorted multi-thousands of NZ, US, and Australian servicemen to forward Pacific strongholds, and in so doing she had steamed 149,629 sea miles without requiring major dockyard maintenance, a salute to her builders, her engine and boiler-room stokers, and her mechanicians. In his publication *Our Navy at War*, US Admiral King stated: 'The establishment of those bases in large measure were responsible for our ability to stand off the Japanese in their advance toward New Zealand and Australia. Without them we should have been at such a disadvantage that it is doubtful if the enemy could have been checked.'

But back in Noumea in mid-April 1942 the War seemed remote, only *Australia*, *Lamson*, and a few store ships swung with the tide, and ashore the Americans had gone to remote New Caledonian camps. *Chicago* and *Perkins* arrived by themselves, then next day the ageing *Adelaide* and four-funnelled US relic *John G Edwards*. Our watch had gone shoreside to celebrate coder Nicholson's 21st birthday; we'd sewn ourselves up on French plonk, and done the long boat trip back to *Leander* with every indication of a prolonged pulsating head, an indication which materialised and remained throughout next day's Forenoon Watch as *Leander* departed for Suva. The occasional rush topside to a lee guardrail, lungs replenished with fresh air, stomachs readjusted to the ship's menus, and Nicholson's 21st now a days-old memory as we refuelled at Suva then sailed with *Lamson* for Tutuila Island, American Samoa's long-established Pago Pago naval base, outside which *Leander* loitered as the US destroyer received permission to pass through the boom gate.

Hours later *Helm* and *Henley* emerged from the picturesque winding harbour with its cloud-tipped 'Rainmaker', followed by *Lamson* and *Achilles* to be disposed as an integral group steaming eastward for a rendezvous with USS *Honolulu*, three more American destroyers and an eleven-ship convoy. The ANZAC Squadron no longer existed, nor did the ANZAC Area. New Zealand and Australian ships now operated under the orders of US C-in-C Pacific Fleet, Admiral Chester Nimitz; our present squadron was designated Task Group 12.2 of RN Admiral Grace's Task Force 12, we were copying fast morse from NPM Pearl Harbour and NPU Tutuila US Navy broadcasts and it was obvious something big was about to happen. There were warnings of Japanese carrier and battleship groups in the area we were traversing on our way to the New Hebrides. Lookouts were relieved hourly so as to remain alert while scanning the surface for possible enemy periscopes; and at dusk when the cruisers' aircraft were retrieved, additional lookouts were posted with powerful night-glasses to detect surface intervention. The transports were urged to find more knots, and on arrival at Efate Island they were hastened inside Vila Harbour while *Achilles* and *Leander* patrolled offshore.

Later in the day we were allowed inside so that *Achilles* could come alongside for her crated Oerlikons, ours having been installed weeks previously and tested; but the first time *Achilles'* were fired there was pandemonium. The Oz dockyard hadn't considered restriction rails to raise muzzles over the bridge when traversing; 20mm shells penetrated or ricochetted off steel upperworks as the mounts tracked inboard with startling results, but fortunately there were no injuries except to the Gunnery Officer's pride when Captain Barnes blasted his efficiency. 'Blackie' Payne copied the preventative rails around *Leander*'s Oerlikons, and the two cruisers alternated day and night patrols about Vila's horizon, comforted on each daytime occasion when returning US Catalinas signalled 'Nil Reports' of the Japanese carrier group thought to be approaching Efate Island; US minelayers laid protective minefields either side of a narrow safe channel into Vila, and then laid mines across all of Efate's beaches and possible landing sites.

One forenoon *Achilles* and a destroyer idled astern across harbour to attach tow lines to the hulk of a grounded schooner, *Star of Russia*, which although weather-beaten and firmly gripped by coral sand appeared to be in reasonable condition. Vila's US Naval Commandant wanted her for a jetty and, when both ships took the strain she budged, the tow lines sang as they tautened, milky coral sludge loosed its grip, then with more power applied, great whirlpools raged around the swaying schooner as she glided free, later to be pumped out and used for storing ammunition. Meantime *Leander*'s Walrus had been severely damaged in a crane snafu when lifting it off its cradle, and without it we felt blinded when our range of search was reduced to visual distance, but there came salvation in the form of the Australian AMC *Westralia*'s amphibian, and she departed for Suva with ours as a CER arrangement years before its NZ-Aust conception. Very soon it was our turn to do the decent act when a Kingfisher recce plane force-landed 70 miles west of Vila and *Leander* raced out at 30 knots in time to salvage it and its appreciative crew; but a more unfortunate patrolling Swordfish radioed that his amphibian was under attack by a four-engined Japanese aircraft, those being the last words he uttered.

All this time we wondered why *Achilles* and *Leander* were ordered by Nimitz to maintain steam for high-speed departure when so required. We weren't so required by the US C-in-C, and although a flood of emergency signals on the LOTE circuit, and a rash of 'Yellow' alerts indicated something momentous taking place nearby, we didn't then know that a major naval battle was in progress only hundreds of miles west in the Coral Sea. America's replication of the Axis 'ULTRA' coding device had enabled

Washington to anticipate some of the enemy's strategy, and the basics of Japan's 'Phase Two' consolidation plan had been revealed. Japan was preparing to neutralise or occupy Port Moresby, New Caledonia, the Solomon Islands, Fiji and Samoa in the South, and Wake Island, Midway Island, and some of the Aleutian Chain in the North from where she could fly bombers to neutralise Hawaii.

Nimitz ordered Rear Admiral Fitch aboard *Lexington* to take Task Force 11 south from Pearl Harbour, and join Rear Admiral Fletcher's Task Force 17 carrier *Yorktown* and its support ships. Rear Admiral Grace's Task Force 44 would rendezvous with them on 4 May in the Coral Sea. Over the period 1 to 8 May, Japanese and American carrier-planes made and lost contact with each other's warships, at times seen steaming under clear sky, other times hidden under low cloud, but always separated by hundreds of miles. General MacArthur's South-West Pacific Command land-based reconnaissance planes sighted Japanese units in the Solomon Sea on 2 May, but little credence was given to the report until 3 May when enemy transports were observed discharging troops and material onto Tulagi just offshore of Guadacanal. *Yorktown* sped north and on 4 May launched a dawn strike, followed by two more dive-bomber and torpedo-bomber attacks as her aircraft refuelled and re-armed. Three US planes were lost, and the remainder when debriefed reported crippled and destroyed enemy ships and massive damage inflicted ashore; but these were the excited reports of inexperienced pilots and in fact only one destroyer and three minesweepers had been sunk, and five anchored seaplanes set on fire.

Task Forces 11, 17 and 44 spent most of 5 May refuelling from the US tanker *Neosho*, this being completed on the 6th, then Fletcher detached Grace's *Australia*, *Chicago*, *Hobart* and a destroyer escort to intercept the enemy's Port Moresby invasion force expected to be southing through Jomard Passage. Incorrect reports from both sides' scout planes had strike flights going on wild goose chases, except for the unlucky US tanker *Neosho* and escorting destroyer *Sims* who were reported as an American aircraft carrier and a heavy cruiser – 60 Japanese dive-bombers and 18 Zeke fighters overwhelmed and sank them before help could be given.

Shortly after this, *Lexington*'s attack group, airborne in rolling cloud and rain squalls near the Louisiade Archipelago, broke out into clear sunshine and sighted distant enemy warships. Recognising them as the auxiliary carrier *Shoho* supported by cruisers and destroyers, the Doubtless dive-bombers concentrated on *Shoho* from several directions, down through a barrage of exploding H/A shells and streams of concentrated tracer from all the enemy ships, down determinedly to bomb-drop height and away up in curving arcs, engines screaming and propellers grasping tropical air in a bid to distance their bombers from those Japanese gunners. Wildcats were tangling with *Shoho*'s fighters desperately trying to intercept Devastator torpedo-bombers skimming in at low altitude. Bomb bursts were seen on *Shoho*, then eruptions at sea level as torpedoes slammed home; and as *Lexington*'s aircraft withdrew, *Yorktown*'s resumed the attack. In all, thirteen bombs and seven torpedoes sent *Shoho* under for the loss of only three US aircraft.

When informed of Admiral Fletcher's success, and the presence of Admiral Grace's heavy cruisers near Jomard Passage, Admiral Inouye aboard his light cruiser *Kashima* at Rabaul, ordered his Port Moresby Invasion Force to retire, until the threat from Grace's cruisers could be eliminated by land-based dive-bombers and torpedo-bombers now on their way. Strike after strike from 1400 till dusk was averted by the high-speed weaving ships, with paint burning off their funnels, off their high-angled guns, and off the fuselage of three US Army fighters escaping from a barrage thrown up at them by mistake. Then further north a late-afternoon attack by *Shokaku*'s and *Zuikaku*'s aircraft was beaten off by *Lexington*'s Wildcats already overhead in anticipation, and by *Yorktown*'s waiting combat air patrols. No hits were registered on the big carriers, two Wildcats were shot down, but the Japanese attackers lost a Val, eight Kates, and numerous unconfirmed Zekes.

Friday, 8 May dawned cloud driven and squally, and Dauntless scouts peering through a momentary break made the day's first enemy sighting, remaining concealed while directing *Yorktown*'s Devastators onto the un-suspecting *Shokaku* for a torpedo attack. About 0930 the approaching nine torpedo-bombers, twenty-four dive-bombers and their fighter escorts, were spotted by Zekes of the Japanese carrier's combat patrol who were imme-diately pounced on and destroyed. *Shokaku* now alerted increased speed. Her intense barrage and that of her cruisers and destroyers unnerved the low-flying Devastator pilots and she came through the torpedo attack unhit, but not so from the dive-bombers who had damaged her flight deck and started fires below. By now the cloud ceiling had lowered considerably and most of *Lexington*'s strike flights were turning back without a sighting, only one dive-bomber managing to land his bomb on the crippled carrier. But it and those earlier from *Yorktown*'s attack were sufficient to put *Shokaku* out of action; when last seen she was low in the water, on fire and creeping north. She made it back to a homeland dockyard.

Meanwhile on 8 May *Zuikaku* had been unobserved beneath virtual sea-level tropical cloud, aware of *Shokaku*'s predicament and receiving position reports of Fletcher's carriers. Flights of Vals, Kates, and supporting Zekes were on their way and although detected and tracked by radar, the Japanese bombers approached unopposed by American fighters who were busy dog-fighting their escorts; the barrage through which they attacked was more spectacular than effective and *Lexington* unwieldy at the best of times, was trapped in the maze of criss-crossing torpedo trails. Two of the missiles caved great implosions on her waterline, two bombs penetrated her flight-deck and exploded deep below, and near-miss heavies buffeted her almost to a standstill. *Yorktown* had been more fortunate, managing to turn and comb eight torpedoes launched at her port side; fires started four decks down by an 800-lb bomb explosion were quickly contained, and even though her aircraft hoists were rendered inoperative, they had jammed at deck level and her returning planes with some from *Lexington* were landed back on.

Many had been killed and wounded on both American carriers, but Damage Control parties had gradually fought *Lexington*'s lower deck fires until most of them were extinguished, then just as her engineers had brought her back from a seven-degree list, a devastating explosion of ignited petrol fumes shot hatches, bodies, aircraft and all kinds of debris whirling high above her fighting tops. More deep-seated explosions sent a mushroom of flame-ridden smoke hundreds of feet overhead and she listed heavily while settling by the bows. All hope of saving her had gone so the order was given to abandon ship, and hours later when she still floated as a smoking wreck, the destroyer *Whelp* sent her below with five torpedoes.

So ended the Coral Sea Battle, on paper perhaps to critics a Japanese victory with a US fleet carrier, a destroyer, and a navy tanker sunk; as opposed to one auxiliary carrier. But to historians only thirty-five quickly replaceable US planes were lost, compared to three times that number of enemy aircraft whose losses kept the undamaged *Zuikaku* out of Japan's Phase Two plans for many weeks. Add to this the months required to repair *Shokaku*, and Admiral Inouye's cancelling of the seaborne invasion of Port Moresby. Now the pendulum tends to swing in favour of the United States. Would these Japanese naval setbacks stop her execution of 'Phase Two'? Unlikely. She still had more carriers, battleships, and heavy cruisers than America, and two of those battleships, *Musashi* and *Yamato*, displaced 70,000 tons and mounted eight 18.1″ guns each, way beyond the power and range of any other battleship in the world.

CHAPTER XV

Midway, Early Guadalcanal

IT WAS NOW 20 May 1942, survivors of the Coral Sea battle were licking their wounds in distant dockyards, and with Efate Island's airstrips and gun sites established it was time to move further up through the New Hebrides. During the forenoon *Achilles* had departed for Suva to refuel, embark forty-two new ship's company awaiting her arrival, drag bags of mail up the gangway, then leave next morning, 24 May, for Pago Pago where she was joined by the US destroyer *O'Brien*, the 3,000-ton US survey ship *Sumner*, and the US seaplane tender *Swan*, all transporting an echelon of GIs to Wallis Island some 400 miles west of Tutuila. On arrival *Sumner* and *Swan* were escorted in by the Free French patrol vessel *Chevreuil* while *Achilles* and *O'Brien* patrolled outside until dusk, then sped back to Pago Pago for a much larger American contingent to Wallis Island aboard two troopships.

This time *Achilles* entered to remain two weeks as A/A guardship, while *O'Brien* ferried more and more transports and store-ships to the French archipelago from American Samoa.

Meanwhile *Leander* had been busy back and forth between New Caledonia, Fiji, and the New Hebrides, escorting converted US liners and Kaiser Shipyard Liberty ships to garrison and fortify Espiritu Santo, 200 miles north of Vila. C-in-C Pacific, Admiral Chester Nimitz, now considered the South Pacific zone to be adequately secure and both New Zealand cruisers were assigned to his SOUWESPAC Force; we weren't expecting to come face to face with Japan's main battle fleet, but this inclusion in the US Pacific Fleet's forward operational zone gave *Achilles'* and *Leander's* ships' companies an anticipation of something better than endless convoys.

Unknown to us Admiral Yamamoto's fleet was converging on Midway Island at the western extremity of the Hawaiian Chain, only 2,000 miles east of southern Japan. As a feint Attu and Kiska Islands in the western Aleutians would be invaded, the carriers *Ryujo* and *Junyo* with supporting heavy cruisers would bomb and bombard Dutch Harbour, and four battleships escorted by cruisers and destroyers would be positioned halfway from Honolulu to the Aleutians, to ambush the task force expected to be rushed north.

A large convoy of Japanese troopships under heavy escort would be nearing Midway while Admiral Nagumo's Fast Carrier Force, *Akagi* (Flag),

Hiryu, *Kaga*, and *Soryu*, softened-up Midway's defences. Admiral Kondo's four battleships with heavy cruisers and destroyers would then be arriving in support of the invasion fleet; and in all, dozens of capital ships, carriers, submarines, store-ships and tankers were right now dispersing about the North Pacific Ocean in preparation. Except for America's foreknowledge of the operation, Japan may well have gained air and naval bases to the north and west of Hawaii, thus rendering Pearl Harbour and other North Pacific bases untenable. But US scientists had made replicas of Germany's 'ENIGMA' cypher machines which Japan was using for top-level communications, so the enemy plan was no secret.

The US Navy knew its own deficiencies – its battleships assembling off the American Pacific Coast, 3,000 miles away from Midway and too slow to be of use, *Yorktown* still repairing at Pearl Harbour, only *Hornet* and *Enterprise* available. Dockyard officials were told to get *Yorktown* to sea, fast! She came out of dock operational if not comfortable, and the three carriers with their escort groups rendezvoused north-east of Midway on 2 June 1942.

In the Aleutians away to the east at daybreak on the 3rd, Admiral Kikuta's carrier aircraft wrought destruction on Dutch Harbour's oil tanks, installations and administrations. This air assault was repeated next day but Nimitz was not sidetracked, even by the American public outcry when Attu and Kiska were occupied by Japanese troops; and hour after hour he paced his Pearl Harbour Headquarters awaiting news from Midway. Then his patience was rewarded. In the early hours of 3 June a reconnaissance Catalina 700 miles west of Midway reported Japanese carriers and capital ships, although subsequent reports by other Catalinas corrected the initial sighting to be troopships and support vessels of the expected Japanese invasion fleet. Land-based bombers from the tiny island took off for the radioed position, but their airmen were inexperienced and only one tanker was damaged while most of the American high-level and torpedo-bombers were shot out of the sky.

By now Admiral Fletcher had positioned his three carriers half an hour's flying time north of Midway, from where he flew scout planes south-west in search of the Japanese carriers while, with the intention of assuring himself there were no American warships in the area, Nagumo's scouts were aloft from *Akagi* and *Kaga* together with float-planes from the heavy cruisers *Tone* and *Chikuma*, searching the areas south and east of Midway. Nothing. It was time to soften up the island's defences.

Shortly after 0445, 36 Kate bombers, 36 Val dive-bombers and 36 Zeke fighters assembled over the Japanese carriers and Nagumu's first strike headed for Midway, being detected by the island's radar at 0553. Brewster Buffaloes scrambling to intercept them were no match for the experienced enemy fighter pilots, 17 being shot down and 7 severely mauled as the strike overran them in formation to destroy fuel storage dumps, hangars, buildings and power-plants; while of 10 torpedo-bombers sent out to attack Nagumo's fleet only 3 survived. None scored a hit on the Japanese carriers and only a few Kate bombers were downed. At 0728 *Tone's* amphibian sighted Fletcher's force some 200 miles north-east of Midway, but it didn't identify the type of ships in the enemy report so Nagumo still wasn't aware of the American carriers, even at 0820 when his strike flight returned, some damaged and being given priority landing, all short of fuel and needing to be rearmed. This refuelling operation was still continuing at 0920 when outer-screen destroyers reported approaching American aircraft, but Nagumo's luck was temporarily with him and Fletcher's counter-strike searched the cloud-covered area without a sighting, continuing south-east until their fuel gauges indicated time to return to *Hornet*, while some who had almost expended their flying time refuelled at Midway, although a few of the escorting fighters weren't so fortunate, ditching far from land when their engines sputtered and died.

Airborne again at 1015 with the Japanese fleet now visible below scattered cloud, all three US carriers' torpedo-bombers attacked without fighter escort, but one after another the unwieldy Devastators were splashed or blown to bits in the wall of close barrage. And although some had launched their torpedoes before being hit, those missiles which struck a target were faulty and didn't explode. Flight after flight suffered similar fates in the impenetrable gunfire, or were shot down by swarms of Zeros protecting the big carriers whose decks were still covered by the refuelling bombers. Yet more aircraft were down in hangars having bombs mounted as their torpedoes were removed, but this is where Nagumo's luck ran out.

Eighteen dive-bombers from *Enterprise* and seventeen from *Yorktown* were high over *Akagi* and *Kaga* as Nagumo was turning them into the wind for launching, and even though only three Hell-divers had sighted *Akagi* their undetected perpendicular dive was accurate. One bomb crashed through the flight-deck and exploded among aircraft being re-armed, detonating their torpedoes, rupturing the hangar's fuel lines and spewing high octane over the conflagration. A second bomb burst among Kates topside with their engines revving for take-off, spreading carnage and creating an inferno as their fuel tanks and bombs erupted. Nagumo's flagship was obviously doomed so he transferred by boat to the light cruiser *Nagara*; *Kaga* had momentarily emerged from drifting low cloud and thirty-four dive-bombers interwove down at her, near-misses punching in plates below her waterline, enveloping her in great geysers of blackened ocean. Then four bombs smashed through her steel decks and almost instantly she blazed from stem to stern, torn apart internally as magazines and fuel tanks disintegrated with shattering destruction.

Now Captain Ryusaku Yanaginato's carrier *Soryu* was pounced on by *Yorktown*'s dive-bombers, deluged by 1000-lb bombs, some landing in her curving wake as she helmed to port and starboard, others exploding in her bow waves to rupture oil tanks and open her hull to the Pacific; one also burst in her hangar and threw the lift platform up against her bridge structure. Yet more bombs burst among topside aircraft to engulf the surrounding deck and upperworks in flames, and soon after the initial 1030 attack three of Nagumo's feared carriers were reduced to blazing wrecks. But where was the fourth? Fletcher ordered a widespread search without result, then his own carrier came under attack. *Yorktown*'s radar was detecting approaching bandits; 'FLASH YELLOW' closed men to the alert stage, additional Wildcats roared off into the wind as CAP reinforcements, then 'FLASH RED' sounded as screening cruisers' and destroyers' A/A bursts smudged clear patches between low cloud. Now the gunners were ranging on visible enemy aircraft – eighteen dive-bombers arcing down with their fighter support, ten torpedo-bombers coming in low with more fighters' wing-guns spitting flame. These, all from *Hiryu*, were being savaged by Wildcats who splashed ten of them from the overhead melee. Two were blown apart by screen cruisers' gunnery, then six got through to Fletcher's flagship, and men died at their gun-blisters when bomb-blasts wrecked steel structures and tore splintered chasms in the wooden flight-deck.

A resounding detonation inside *Yorktown*'s multi-cored funnel-casing blasted destruction down into her boiler rooms; another bomb went through three deck levels to burst and threaten magazines. Those fires were brought under control, but with his ship now unmanageable, Fletcher transferred his flag to the cruiser *Astoria* and ordered *Portland* to take the crippled carrier in tow; but while this was being done *Yorktown*'s mechanicians managed to raise steam for 17 knots and *Portland* resumed her screening disposition, barely in time to put up a thundering barrage as more waves of enemy aircraft arrived. Torpedo-bombers flattened out hundreds of yards from the American carrier and launched missiles which were impossible to avoid, opening her double bottom to an inrushing flood which listed her almost to the capsize degree; all power failed and at 1500 she was abandoned.

Shortly after this, *Hornet*'s and *Enterprise*'s dive-bombers located *Hiryu* 164 miles north-east and attacked, leaving her a hopeless hulk wreathed in flames and billowing smoke; by 2130 she was wallowing powerless, and at 0230 next morning she was finished off by torpedoes from her own escorting destroyers. Then at daybreak Nagumo ordered his still blazing flagship *Akagi* to be sunk.

On 4 June Admiral Kondo was hurrying north to assist with his two battleships, four heavy cruisers, the light-carrier *Zuiho* and a flock of destroyers, as was Admiral Yamamoto from the deep south aboard the leviathan *Yamato*, accompanied by the modernised battleships *Nagato* and *Mutsu* under cruiser and destroyer escort. Japanese search planes were scouring the seas around Midway, endeavouring to locate and shadow the American carriers for Nagumo to exact revenge and save face. But Spruance and Fletcher had retired eastward awaiting daylight to again release their fired-up bomber and fighter pilots. However this engagement between Japanese battleships and American carrier-borne aircraft was not to eventuate; Yamamoto realising a night fight was not possible and that his fleet now needed refuelling, abandoned the Midway invasion and ordered a general withdrawal; but that night more salt was rubbed into his wounds. Admiral Kurita's heavy cruisers *Kumano*, *Suzuya*, *Mikuma*, and *Mogami*, in line ahead formation on their way to bombard Midway, were ordered onto another course, but *Mogami* missed the turning signal and plowed full speed into *Mikuma*. Both ships were so badly damaged that they were left in tow by two destroyers; they were sighted by a Midway dawn patrol, dive-bombers directed to the reported position followed *Mikuma*'s oil slick

US aircraft raid on Japanese-held positions in the Guadacanal/Tulagi areas immediately before the 7 August 1942 American landings.

and put her under at 0805, but *Mogami* who had caused the collision could not be found, was mistakenly reported as sunk, yet somehow survived and days later limped into Truk.

In the forenoon hours of 5 June American technicians decided that *Yorktown* might still be saved, salvage teams boarded her and the long tow to Pearl Harbour started, only to end when Yamamoto alerted his submarines lying east to search for her, and at sunrise on 7 June I–168 penetrated the anti-submarine screen and sank her with two torpedoes. So ended the Battle of Midway. Losing the four big carriers which had swept like a forest fire through the Indian Ocean was an abrupt set-back for Japan's naval tacticians, as was Yamamoto's roundly criticised decision to abandon his Midway invasion. 'Ahh Soh,' they said with shaking heads; 'Soh sad. Not to worry.' Japan still had bases in the Aleutians; her footholds in the Solomons seemed secure; after their Coral Sea reversals *Shokaku's* and *Zuikaku's* hangars were again full of combat aircraft, pilots eager to die for the Emperor, and his armies throughout Indonesia, Eastern and Southern Asia and along the Burma-India border were intact, campaign hardened.

Rear Admiral Frederick Carl Sherman, in command of the task force, gets good news from Commander Joe Cliftea, Commander of the fighter group in raid on Rabaul.

While in north-east India there were dissident forces willing to assist in overthrowing the British imperialist regime.

But on *Achilles* and *Leander* thousands of miles south, this meant little as we continued day by day, night after night with USN and RAN units escorting American troopships north to stronghold islands, right through to 17 August 1942 when *Leander* entered Calliope Dock for five days' bottom scraping and anti-fouling; on 8 September *Achilles* completed 200,000 miles since launching and the Dockyard Commander took her from Captain Mansergh for a six-week overhaul.

Before this *Leander* had reversed out of dock on 22 August and a few days later was slicing through unruffled blue Pacific seas, en route Pago Pago with *Cummings* to escort a large convoy to Noumea, in 2nd degree alert until 1 September when the boom gate opened and we filed in through Amedee Channel. There, everywhere one looked about the cluttered harbour were drab Liberty ships, transports with landing barges outswung on massive davits, minesweepers *Gale*, *Kiwi*, and cruiser *Achilles* ingesting fuel on the starboard side of *Rising Sun*, a rugby-field sized USN tanker against whose portside fenders *Leander* pressed astern of an American destroyer. Later at our down-harbour mooring we watched Task Groups of American and Australian cruisers and destroyers arriving, others including *Achilles* on her way to Auckland leaving. Our Paymaster had signed for all manner of American victuals from the US supply ship *Merker's* several-deck supermarket, and obtained an unedited 'SERVICES ONLY' film for that night's upperdeck screening. Then next day, back in reality, men draped over guardrails, commented on *Wasp* as she glided past ahead of one of the USN's latest battleships, *Mississippi*, followed by triple-turreted, storm-bowed cruisers and rakish destroyers flaunting their colourful ensign, some with submarine kills painted on their funnels.

Hours later men were absorbed in mail from home, post-dated yesterday and flown up in the Catalina seen furrowing the harbour as it settled deeper and surged towards a nearby mooring. We got another mail next morning, Sunday, 6 September before moving to a berth near Noumea's boom gate, close to a deep-laden monster tanker mounting twin 6″ turrets fore and aft. Carrier aircraft droned low overhead on their way beyond our horizon, relieving dawn patrols now returning in the safe corridor outside of which they would be shot down; and on the nearest carrier's flight-deck, combat aircraft aligned in scramble positions were revving their engines to a high crescendo, then throttling them down to a propeller kick-back stop.

Now out of the harbour's unending activity came a wide-beamed bum-boat, to solidly thump *Leander's* sea gangway while tossing lines inboard to be caught and secured. Crates labelled 'US NAVY – ELECTRIC CODING MACHINE – TOP SECRET' for all to see, were followed by Ensign Paul

Sinking of the USS *Wasp*, 15 September 1942.

Clark and 3rd Class Radioman (Smoky) Erwin Jene, all on loan to our Communication Department. And as another Uncle Sam service, the ship's liberty men went ashore and back in one of the invasion ship *McCawley*'s landing barges. 8 September lightened to the bustle of a Task Force preparing for sea, saw the boom gate towed aside to exit impatient destroyers, men shading their eyes against low sun-glare to see *Wasp*'s CAP fighters lifting off as she glided past, massively impressive, barely a ripple along her waterline, gun blisters protruding outboard of her flight-deck, dual and triple mounts bristling in the open spaces below. Next came the big cruisers *Salt Lake City* and *San Francisco* at a walking pace as *Leander* eased into station astern, then a chevron of destroyers followed by *McCawley* with landing barges hanging from heavy davits, and finally *Rising Sun*, the 30,000-ton armed tanker riding deep. On the second day out *Leander* detached with *Cummings* and *McCawley*, arriving in Espiritu Santo on the 10th to an anchorage crammed with transports, store ships, the cruiser *Boise*, and in a secluded arm some forty Catalinas at anchor near their large tender.

Four days later *Minneapolis* arrived with ten more transports and several destroyers, plus the news that the new battleship *North Carolina* had been torpedoed and was on her way to Pearl Harbour. *Wasp*, which was

Brisbane Maru
Japanese ship run ashore on Guadalcanal and sunk by bombing.

torpedoed at the same time, had sunk. And to make matters worse, we now learned that the cruisers *Astoria*, *Quincy*, *Vincennes* and HMAS *Canberra* were attacked and sunk near Savo Island in the dark hours of 9 August, mere miles north-west of Guadalcanal's Henderson Airfield, a month-old secret just released. As soon as *Minneapolis* refuelled we sailed with her, *Boise* and four destroyers, being told over the SRE that the ships would rendezvous about noon next day with a reinforcement convoy expected off Henderson at 0600 Wednesday, 16 September 1942.

Japanese troops had occupied Guadalcanal and nearby Florida Island in early May, and they had just completed an airfield on 7 August when the first US invasion force surged ashore against minimal opposition from the Japanese construction workers. In memory of one of the US heroes of Midway the captured Guadalcanal airfield was named Henderson, and it was hotly contested by the Japanese who wanted it back. Half of US General Vandegrift's 1st Marine Corps Division had previously exercised on New Zealand's Hawkes Bay beaches, also either side of Cook Strait, wherever considered to be similar to Tulagi's and Guadalcanal's landing sites. Other major units had exercised at New Caledonia and Hawaii. From 26 to 30 July the entire force assembled for a final exercise on Fiji's Koro Island before sailing en-masse for the Solomons. There, unopposed, they landed at Tenaru and Taivu on northern Guadalcanal; but those going ashore 20 miles across the straits at Tulagi, Gavutu, and Tanambogo Islet met fanatical resistance as both armies attacked and counter-attacked.

From Radio Tokyo in English, 'Tokyo Rose' announced in seductive undertones that the Emperor's superior warships were annihilating the American, Australian and New Zealand navies; that the poorly equipped American 'Joes' on Guadalcanal were moths in the night, about to die in the flame of Japan's invincible army; and that those silly GIs who had wives in America could be comforted by the assurance that their male neighbours were comforting the lonely young women in bed.

Only the US 1st Marine Division units who fought at Tenaru River on 21 August can recall the ferocity of Colonel Ichiki's Regiment, can recall the blood-soaked battlefield strewn with Japanese bodies mangled under the tracks of Vandegrift's light tanks, can recall those unwise GIs who tried to help wounded enemy soldiers, only to be blasted to bits with them when they pulled the pin from hidden grenades. With but a few survivors Colonel Ichiki escaped across the Ilu Stream, then tore his regimental colours to shreds and committed ceremonial *seppuka*. Meanwhile none of these previous engagement details were known on *Leander* as our task force steamed north, constantly on the alert for air or surface action, in 2nd Degree on 15 September as the cruisers took station about six heavily armed transports escorted by three destroyers. The SRE said we would probably be off the beachhead next dawn; then Henderson Airfield radioed their inability to provide air support and a Japanese battleship force was approaching from 180 miles north-west of Lunga Point.

Right now our Task Force 64 was 200 miles south-west and it seemed we'd be in action within twenty-four hours. Working parties were ripping wooden panelling from the wardroom and officers' cabins, heaving it overboard. *Leander* was now at 1st Degree, taking catnaps at action stations, being fed man-size corned beef and pickle sandwiches and fannies of thick hot ki brought from the galley. Sometime during the Middle Watch of 16 September US Admiral Turner on his command ship *McCawley* decided the situation was too uncertain: enemy forces in the vicinity hadn't been sufficiently identified or pinpointed; the loss of *Wasp*'s air cover and *North Caroline*'s big-gun support gave the Japanese an advantage; so dawn found us steaming south, on a course maintained all day till dusk when Turner manoeuvred the whole force 180 degrees back for another approach, this time with a Henderson offshore 0500/18/9 ETA. That night we slept fitfully, comforted by the constant drone of powerful turbines, steady rumble of our four propellers, and muted roar of *Leander*'s boiler-rooms' forced-draught intake. In the Main W/T men copied the continual stream of Pearl Harbour's fast high-pitched morse; in lesser offices the drawl of American voices from TBS receivers. One at a time since 0300 an RCO W/T operator had gone port or starboard to the Torpedo Firing Platforms to view the situation, and shortly after 0430 Stan Roy came back with news: 'We're close offshore – looks like a Gyppo harbour – power boats everywhere. The transports are still moving with Yanks scrambling down nets like ants.'

There wasn't time for him to say more as we brushed past. He was right. Half a mile off the jungle-fringed coral beach, fully kitted Marines were clambering down draped nets, rifles and scatter-guns over their shoulders, roughly assisted into barges bumping heavily alongside to be drenched as their blunt bows thumped the moving transports' wash. Helmeted occupants yelled for their buddies to let go and jump, grasped outstretched hands and pulled hard as they leapt; then no sooner had the barges loaded and cast off than more moved alongside. *Leander*, *Boise* and *Minneapolis* circled individual areas seaward of the unloading transports and store-ships; destroyers searched for submarines further out; and now in full daylight five Wildcats provided Henderson Field's remaining air cover. On the inshore traverse we passed near transports swinging tank-landing-craft outboard, saw them splash heavily and surge shoreward, watched returning empties being grappled and hoisted inboard to receive more tracked ve-hicles with engines running awaiting their turn. Amphibious tanks were being lowered from massive davits to splash alongside and swim ashore under their own power; and right throughout that day thousands of 'leathernecks' with rifles held aloft, leapt from barges to wade through hip-high surf, scramble up the beach and disappear in dense undergrowth under coconut palms. We anticipated enemy air action but the only A/A fired was from a *McCawley* gunner who brought down a Wildcat. Hender-son now had four.

No enemy aircraft, no opposing battleships, just the sound of naval gunfire three miles west of Alligator Creek, where two destroyers off Lunga Point were bombarding Japanese positions near Kokumbona Village and light artillery retaliated briefly, but even that ceased as 5″ shells threw up debris and black smoke over the target area.

It still drifted over Lunga Point as our TF–64 withdrew with the empties, now including three more late arrivals who'd quickly offloaded drums of diesel and aviation spirit. And late that night as Admiral Turner urged the convoy south to Espiritu Santo, he was informed by SO Guadalcanal that the Marine beachhead was under a heavy naval bombardment. Two days later we were swinging at our moorings in Santo's picturesque Luganville Bay, refuelled, ships' boats taking men ashore to swim or laze about the beaches. The 18 September operation may not have been one of the Pacific War's memorable events, yet it had successfully put thousands of Marine reinforcements ashore, it had given Henderson's defenders their first decent feed in weeks, and it had supplied a month's fuel for the replacement bombers and fighters now being flown in from southern bases. And now America and Japan were realising the advantage of transporting troops and material by stripped-down destroyers – the US Navy's being classified ADP 'Attack Destroyer Personnel', the Japanese ones rushing reinforcements from Truk to Guadalcanal being nicknamed 'Tokyo Express' due to their regular arrivals and departures.

General Hyakutake's 17th Army unit skirmishes on Guadalcanal were becoming more fanatical, bloodier as *'Banzai!'* attackers broke out of thickets to be torn apart by the Marines' mortar blasts, machine-gun bursts and thrown grenades. Counter-attacks drove them back from Henderson's outer defences, but there was minimal respite before they came yelling through again, time after suicidal time. Offshore, both sides claimed victory in the 23/24 August 'Eastern Solomons' naval engagements; declared superiority in the 11/12 October 'Cape Esperance' battle; did likewise after the 24 to 26 October clashes off Santa Cruz; all fought in late 1942 when because of the dozens of cruisers and destroyers sunk in battle, 'Iron Bottom Sound' was appended to an area not much greater than that from our Whangarei Heads, down through Hauraki Gulf and across the Firth of Thames to the tip of Coromandel Peninsula.

America's shipyards and aircraft factories could readily replace her losses but, as Admiral Yamamoto had warned the mid-41 War Council, Japan who lost sixty-five combat ships and 847 aircraft around Guadalcanal between early August and mid-December, could not. The starving remnants of her 17th Army had dwindled to some 11,000 and on 31 December 1942 Emperor Hirohito approved their evacuation to Bougainville and nearby Japanese-occupied islands.

About now *Leander*'s Engineer Commander reported salinity in one of the fuel tanks, so the ship was withdrawn from Rear Admiral Tisdale's TG16.6 about to be sent north by Admiral 'Bull' Halsey to intercept a Tokyo Express seen leaving Truk; perhaps fortunate for *Leander* when cracks found in her side kept her out of the 30 November 1942 'Battle of Tassafaronga'.

Although detected at night as they came south past the Shortland Islands, Admiral Tanaka's destroyers and destroyer-transports sank the US cruiser *Northampton* with torpedoes, in addition damaging *New Orleans*, *Minneapolis* and *Pensacola* so severely that they remained in US repair yards for almost a year, only *Honolulu* of the task group coming out of that night action undamaged. Hit by 8″ shells, Tanaka's destroyer-flagship *Naganami* continued firing in retaliation and managed to retire to Truk with his destroyers and the 'Express' intact; and instead of a hero's welcome for his lopsided victory, Tanaka was relieved of his command for not putting the reinforcement troops ashore. He was transferred to Singapore, then Burma.

Meantime after *Leander*'s arrival in Auckland, her fuel-tank problem, hull cracks and updating programme kept her out of service until March 1943.

From the outset, while New Zealand's cruisers were overseas, NZNB appropriated and converted fishing trawlers which by November 1940 were organised as the minesweeping groups scheduled below:

1st M/S Flotilla	*Matai* (SO), *Rata, Gale, Puriri; Coastguard* (Danlayer)
1st M/S Group (Auckland)	*Wakakura, Humphrey, Duchess*
2nd M/S Group (W'gton)	*South Sea, Futurist*
3rd M/S Group	*James Cosgrove, Thomas Currell*

As required, additional vessels were requisitioned, many with their skippers and crews given naval status for the duration, others being manned by RNZNVR officers with permanent-service Chiefs, POs and specialist ratings to oversee and instruct 'Rockie' call-up crews. Then with Japan's anticipated declaration, anti-submarine patrols were needed, so existing minesweepers capable of extended service outside New Zealand waters were fitted with A/S apparatus, and selected ratings were trained to operate it. But it became apparent that specifically designed naval craft were necessary and, after prolonged NZNB, NB-Melbourne, Admiralty discussions seven such ships were allocated, all 12-knot, armed with a 4″ gun and lighter weapons, equipped for asdic and minesweeping duties, four of them coal-burning Scottish Isles Class minesweepers, and three oil-fuelled 600-ton corvettes launched and commissioned as shown below:

HMNZS *Moa* (Lt Cmdr P.G. Connolly DSC RNZNVR born Dunedin 14 Nov 1899) was launched at Leith on 15 April 1941 by Lady Fergusson (wife of New Zealand's 1924–1930 Governor General Sir Charles Fergusson) and departed Greenock on 1 November 1941 as part escort for a Newfoundland-bound convoy, and continued via Panama Canal to Suva where, with Japan now an aggressor, she did a month's A/S patrol before her 10 April 1942 Auckland arrival.

HMNZS *Kiwi* (Lt Cmdr Gordon Bridson DSO DSC RNZNVR born Auckland 2 Dec 1909) was launched 7 July 1941 by Lady Galway (wife of New Zealand's April 1935 to February 1941 Governor General Viscount Sir George Vere Arundell Moncton-Arundell Galway DSO OBE etc etc) left Greenock on 1 January 1942 with another North Atlantic convoy to St John's Newfoundland, then traversed *Moa*'s route for a 21 May 1942 Auckland arrival.

HMNZS *Tui* (Lt Cmdr J.G. Hilliard DSC RNZNVR born Auckland 15 January 1908) was launched on 26 August 1941 by Countess Jellicoe (widow of New Zealand's 1920–24 Governor General, Admiral of the Fleet Lord Jellicoe of Jutland) was commissioned 26 November 1941 at Leith and went to Greenock to join the four other A/S vessels purchased from Admiralty by NZNB on 27 January 1942.

With *Inchkeith* (Lt Cmdr H.A. Dunnet RNR born NZ 8 January 1907), *Killegray* (Lt Cmdr A.A. Bell RNZNVR born Auckland April 1907), *Scarba* (Lt Cmdr Peter Phipps DSC RNZNVR born Milton 7 June 1907), *Sanda* (Lt Cmdr N.L. Mackie RNR born Scotland July 1901) *Tui* departed the Clyde on 15 March 1942 as escorts for convoy ON S–76 en route St John's, after which they steamed south to Bermuda where they waited from 8 to 20 April while panel beaters realigned *Inchkeith* and *Killegray*, and the two skippers scripted excuses for their mid-journey collision. On again in company to spend a week in the Canal Zone, then a few weeks in San Pedro before joining two US escort vessels and ten laden tankers en route Pearl Harbour. Leaving Honolulu on 6 July without *Killegray* the NZ warships shepherded America's transport *Majaba* to Suva, then during their last leg *Sanda* and *Scarba* ran short of coal and had to be taken in tow by *Tui* and *Inchkeith*, finally reaching Auckland on 4 August to complete their five-month delivery. Because of insufficient coal in Pearl Harbour for all four coal-burners, *Killegray* remained there until 29 August whence she was towed by the Dutch motor vessel *Japara* to Suva, there coaling and reaching Auckland on 16 September 1942.

No submarine sightings were confirmed off the New Zealand coast although several adamant reports indicated their presence, especially when numerous Auckland residents insisted they'd seen a small Japanese-marked float-plane flying westward up the length of Waitemata Harbour, and a fishing boat skipper swore he saw its mother-submarine in north-east Coromandel Peninsula's Waikawau Bay. So, asdic- and radar-equipped RNZN corvettes and sweepers were released to Norfolk Island, Fiji, New Caledonia, the New Hebrides, and lastly the Solomons.

A/B Torpedoman 'Bill' Yates had joined the NZD in the 1920s; he was in one of *Diomede*'s landing party operations during Samoa's Maumau uprisings against NZ imposed taxation; he landed with *Diomede* men to assist at Napier's disastrous 3 February 1931 earthquake; he was on *Diomede* in 1935 when we were dispatched to be a unit of the East Indies Fleet protecting Red Sea British interests during Mussolini's Abyssinian campaign; and after being among the first twenty of us to board our new cruiser *Achilles* at Sheerness on that cold wintry Tuesday, 31 March 1936, he was my shore-going oppo in 1938 aboard the old *Wakakura*.

Then in 1940, having done six months on *Muritai*, he was drafted to the converted government lighthouse tender cum Governor-General Pacific cruise steam yacht *Matai*. Lt Cmdr A.D. Holden RNZNR, a 38-year-old merchant marine officer who'd been Chief Officer of the Government's MV *Maui Pomare* from 1933 to 1939, occupied *Matai*'s main stateroom as

SO 25th M/S Flotilla, Lieutenant John O'Connor Ross occupied a lesser one as her Executive Officer, and the remaining guest cabins and luxurious crew quarters were occupied seniority-down by her naval officers and crew. She was an efficient and happy ship whose atmosphere soon permeated all of the little flotilla, as it swept Cook Strait preparatory to the 2nd NZEF 1st and 2nd Echelon departures in January and May 1940, during later sweeps off other main ports, and while sweeping Hauraki Gulf after *Niagara* sank in a German-laid minefield.

One night in Great Barrier Island's Tryphena Harbour as a *Matai* seaman watched moonlit water gently rippling past his anchored ship, he was startled from his reverie by the sight of an ominous black sphere, almost submerged as it approached with the tide. He raised the alarm but it was too late to move *Matai* out of danger as the mine veered perilously close. Water pressure on the hull pushed it away on two occasions, then all the transfixed watchers relaxed as it drifted away astern, now being followed at a safe distance by a demolition party in the ship's dinghy, until dawn when they cautiously stranded it on a beach for disarming at low tide. Later their 25th M/S Flotilla – *Matai* (SO), *Kiwi*, *Moa* and *Tui* – was dispatched to Fiji for escort and anti-submarine duties, these being interspersed with surveying operations off Nandi for a projected seaplane base. Soon the Pacific War began moving north and, after a spell back in Auckland for dockyard maintenance the flotilla departed for Noumea, then Espiritu Santo, and finally Tulagi where on 15 December 1942 they commenced asdic and escort duties in co-operation with groups of US Navy PT-boats, one of which was commanded by US Lieutenant John Kennedy, America's future president, at that time only one of the GOBs and generally addressed as: 'Say, Jack ... '

The New Zealanders' efficiency and their easy-going bonhomie soon warmed US top staff and individual PT-boats' crews to the little ships' 'Kiwi limeys' who 'were good for a tot when visiting'. This hospitality was returned by invites to film evenings during quiet nights, and by gifts of anything unobtainable in the NZ flotilla's stores. However, water was scarce, even rationed from the US torpedo-boats' supply ship, so Bill Yates and Ted Andrews solved their profitable 'Dobey Firm' problem by funnelling rain water off awnings into empty petrol drums. Right about now the 'Tokyo Express' was arriving almost nightly to evacuate northern Guadalcanal's hard-pressed Japanese troops; heavy allied naval units weren't available, and *Matai* on her rounds of US tenders was cadging oil-fuel when an American voice by TBS said: 'Say youse Kiwis, if the goddam Nips arrive, beach your boat, burn the goldurned thing and beat it for the bush!'

The Nips didn't arrive, but next day adjacent waters were covered by collapsible boats the Japanese had left Guadalcanal in to reach their waiting destroyers. Some yet occupied were being rounded up by PT-boats, and not far from *Matai* a large Japanese landing barge drifted. Yates rowed over to it in the skiff and clambered up its side, ready to dive back overboard if confronted. It had been vacated but still contained large quantities of stores and medical supplies; US Corsairs were becoming inquisitive on seeing Bill moving about its deck so he returned with a White Ensign and spread it out on the well deck, while 'his prize' went under tow by power boat to Tulagi.

Then days later *Matai* was ordered to the south side of Guadalcanal to embark a Japanese army captain required at Henderson Field for questioning by American intelligence staff. Captain Shino Chugi, a married tailor's cutter in civilian life, had three children whose photograph he showed to Yates who'd been put in charge of the prisoner. At first he begged Yates to bayonet him to death, shoot him, give him a knife so he could gut himself for having been captured. 'No way man! You now prisoner New Zealand Navy. You Japanese Captain. New Zealand Articles of War say – you be treated as officer.' Shino Chugi's eyes brightened. 'Ooooh ahh NOO Zillin – Noo Zillin number wun country!' A big beaming smile as he wrote A-U-C-K-L-A-N-D by finger in dust on the bench in Chippy's workshop where he was being held. 'Ooooh *arigato, arigato*' he bowed in thanks for the proffered cigarette. Then next morning when he was taken topside for a breather, *Matai*'s 4th Engineer Bill Wylie was asking him the Japanese words for different things when Lt Cmdr Holden appeared. On hearing Wylie address Holden as Sir, the Japanese prisoner asked; 'You Number Wun man, ah so?' and stood erect saluting. *Matai*'s skipper repressed a grin and returned the salute.

When it was time to hand him over Shino Chugi begged to be kept as a New Zealand Navy prisoner. Impossible. A guard of hefty 1st Division Marines hustled him unceremoniously down the gangway, and Yates reflected that they'd probably entice from him the information required. Almost every night high-level Japanese aircraft bombed Henderson from 25 to 30,000 feet, then they would be expected over Tulagi as Guadalcanal's A/A guns ceased firing, week after week until it became routine, with one of the regular early arrivals being nicknamed 'Sewing Machine Charlie' due to the noise similarity of its engine. So 1942 dragged to an inconclusive three years of worldwide warfare. The Solomons' 1943 was ushered in with famed American entertainers giving a shore-side concert at Tulagi. Comedian Joe E. Brown mounted the open-air stage and announced: 'I've come here so you guys can have a good look at my kisser,' and went 'Woooooow' with his world-renowned mouth widely agape. Thousands of Marines yelled and shrill-whistled applause at each of his jokes; also for Johnny Marvin's guitar-accompanied songs of home; but 'FLASH RED' cut him short as entertainers and Marines fled for foxholes while RNZN boat crews raced for the wharf.

That week the PT boat tender with which they'd been good mates was relieved by USS *Niagara*, originally the much-married Tommy Manville's 2,000-ton steam yacht. Its crew was anything except friendly, even with the PT-boats' crews, the situation deteriorated rapidly and a good-natured southern state US Navy signalman attached to *Matai*, having imbibed more tots than his own, yelled from the flag deck: 'Hey thure youse pack of Yankee bassturds, Ise comin over to fight thu whole goddam lot of yuh!' an uncompleted challenge as he was dragged below to stop him being shot by *Niagara*'s trigger-happy crew. Nothing further eventuated from the incident and at dusk *Matai* slipped out on her A/S night patrol up the Slot towards Kolombangara. Near 0200 American PT-boat voices were heard talking ship to ship over the TBS: 'Say, Wilbur, there's something screwy out thair on yurh port side, can yuh see it?'

'Yeah, just pickin it up now.'

The rest was overtalked by the first boat's sudden warning: 'Hey man, that thing's sure screwy! For geez sake, Wilbur, give it a fish, NOW!'

A searchlight stabbed the night followed by a brilliant rumbling flash then total darkness and: 'Good fishin, buddie boy.'

Another night off Lunga Point a PT-boat had been badly shot up and abandoned; Japanese boats were seen towing it inshore, so *Matai* directed another US torpedo boat to within a few miles, from where it powered in intent on destroying both, but its Engineer and several crew were injured by retaliatory gunfire and it retired at speed. *Matai* was now asked if she could destroy the PT-boat under tow; the job was handed over to Jack Ross the Gunnery Officer whose first 4″ shell ricocheted short and whined away inland, but his second and third landed smack on both targets to destroy them in dazzling blasts. Lieutenant Ross now had the urge and when lights were observed moving about onshore he shelled the area so accurately that next day arriving Americans reported well over a hundred Japanese bodies among *Matai*'s shell craters.

Then weeks later an incident highlighted poor recognition and communication between early US and NZ occupation units. An RNZAF P–40 pilot who'd got away from Zeros on his tail over Rabaul, was fired on by American fighters as he approached home base. Evading them also he was so infuriated that he buzzed Henderson Field's outer airstrip with all guns blazing while yelling over the R/T: 'What's wrong with you Yankee bastards, come out of your foxholes and remember what a Kiwi bloody Corsair looks like!' His CO sympathised at the inevitable inquiry, then grounded him, it being an isolated occurrence in the generally good New Zealand-American relations. Within a day or so Bill Yates as a permanent navy torpedoman was loaned to *Kiwi* when it investigated a large USN Auxiliary half submerged and abandoned. There might be salvageable electrical gear for 25th M/S Flotilla spares? No. Everything except an undamaged Oerlikon had been destroyed before her crew left; so *Kiwi*'s pirates 'borrowed' the gun, mounted it on the forecastle, and in time it was to be of immense value to the 650-ton A/S corvette.

CHAPTER XVI

Achilles' *X-turret Destroyed* at Guadalcanal

SHORTLY AFTER *Leander's* late November 1942 arrival in Auckland she docked for a lengthy period to repair hull cracks which were letting salt water into her fuel tanks.

About now *Achilles* was nearing the end of her three-month refit, a considerable number of *Leander's'* ship's company were drafted to her and within days she was en route Wellington where, on Saturday forenoon 12 December she departed as escort for *Aquitania* transporting the 2nd NZEF 8th Reinforcements to Egypt.

However, sea battles for Guadalcanal supremacy over the past four months were entailing too much damage and loss of cruisers and capital ships: 8/9 August, the cruisers HMAS *Canberra*, USS *Vincennes*, *Quincy*, *Astoria* sunk, *Chicago* damaged and sent to Pearl Harbour; 15 August the carrier *Wasp* torpedoed and sunk, battleship *North Carolina* torpedoed and sent to Pearl Harbour; 31 August, the carrier *Saratoga* torpedoed and off to Pearl; 11 October, the cruisers *Salt Lake City* and *Boise* limping away north-east; 26 October, carrier *Hornet* sunk, carrier *Enterprise*, battleship *South Dakota*, cruiser *San Juan* damaged; 12/13 November, cruisers *Atlanta*, *Juneau* sunk, *San Francisco*, *Portland*, *Helena*, damaged; 30 November, cruisers *Minneapolis*, *New Orleans*, *Pensacola*, *Northampton*, damaged; all these damaged ships needing weeks or months in repair yards.

This attrition of US Admiral Halsey's task forces was causing him concern, he considered the disposition of available warships in the South Pacific area and immediately asked for *Achilles*. Captain Barnes, then near Tasmania, received instructions to hand *Aquitania* over to HMAS *Adelaide*, refuel *Achilles* at Port Phillip, then proceed 'with despatch' to join Task Force 65 in Noumea.

Although some enemy-occupied islands along the route to Japan were ordered by US tacticians to be bypassed, 'The Solomons' was not on their 'ignore list', and it wasn't yet 31 December 1942 when Emperor Hirohito would sanction the withdrawal of Japanese troops from Guadalcanal. General Hyakutake's 17th Army was still being supplied and reinforced, and to do this General Maruyama's 2nd Infantry Brigade was being transferred from the aborted Port Moresby campaign, together with General

Kawaguchi's 35th Brigade from Hong Kong, and the 38th Division from Indonesia. So, as soon as Halsey's damaged ships were repaired they were flung back past 'Torpedo Junction', down the 'Slot' to 'Ironbottom Sound', place names already commonly used around Guadalcanal.

Achilles arrived in Noumea on Monday, 21 December and anchored near heavily armed cruisers, battleships, a fleet carrier, three 'Woolworths', numerous destroyers and many back-up vessels. This was a fleet preparing for action, not escort for another convoy. Tuesday dawned over mist veils lifting off vegetated hills, chimneys emitting lazy smoke as workers ate, before going to local mines producing nickel and other valuable ores. Men came off watch to shower and shave prior to breakfast, then within hours stood before Vice Admiral Halsey on *Achilles*' quarterdeck. In his mid-fifties, slicked back short hair, tanned square-jawed features with deep-set humorous eyes below bushy brows and broad forehead, he faced 'March of Time' American cameras and boomed: 'Pleased to meet you Noo Zillinders – my buddies, that's what we call our friends. I've bin told you call them silly bastards. Waal, seeing as how I'm your friend I expect I'm a silly bastard. Anyways, here on I'm your commander, and I want you to know we're fightin' a beast who gives no quarter.' Raising his arms in expression he continued louder, 'So we do the same. We sink Jap ships. And when we sink some ... we'll sink some more, AND ... when those are sunk we'll sink more still!' He paused for effect. There wasn't a movement from him or from his audience. 'Also,' he said quietly, 'we kill Japs. And when we've killed some, we'll kill more yet.' Another silent pause, then quietly insistent as he leaned forward. 'And by that time the war in the Pacific will just about be over. I wish you boys a Merry Christmas. God bless you. And good hunting.' His emphasising arms dropped. His wide mouth lifted at the corners in a real friendly grin as he waved to each corner of the packed quarterdeck; then with applause ringing in his ears he disappeared before the scrambling battery of newsmen.

Later that day men were over the side on painting stages, pausing brush in hand to watch *Saratoga* entering harbour, earlier damage no longer evident, flight-deck a mass of aircraft with their hingewings vertical at the stub, others positioned ready to scramble. Two lengths astern of each other the battleships *Washington*, *Alabama* and *Indiana* blocked out the sun in passing, fighting tops from their rangefinders downward a mystery of radar gadgets and electronics, nests of multi-barrelled barrage weapons on every projection. Astern of them came heavy cruisers, deadly, followed by throngs of destroyers – playful teenagers of every fleet.

At 1145 on Christmas Day Captain Barnes trailed *Achilles*' youngest member through messdeck after messdeck in RN tradition; greetings were exchanged; the usual polite jests were accepted; as the retinue passed, Christmas Dinner was brought into festooned quarters from the galley:

Tomato soup.
Turkey, green peas, cabbage, roast potatoes, cranberry sauce.
Brandy-laced Xmas Pudding with white sauce.
Mixed nuts and dried fruit, an apple and an orange per man. Ice cream
and Xmas Cake.

Then an upperdeck of men relaxing, walking in conversational pairs about the foc'sle and boom decks, the A/A gun-decks, the covered waists, torpedo-mount and crane spaces, officers doing likewise on the quarter deck; right through to the 1900 supper of ox-tongues, pickles and salad; canned peaches and cream; a bottle each of chilled beer; and finally in the starboard waist the film *College Swing*.

Two days later *Achilles* was hundreds of miles north of New Caledonia in company with *St Louis* and four US destroyers, supporting two Wool-worths, *Nassau* and *Altamaha* whose scouts winged all horizons in search of the enemy, returning successively with nil reports until the ships entered Espiritu Santo in single file – only 15 degrees below the Equator, another hot harbour, American warships everywhere one looked. *Minneapolis* rode at anchor with fifty feet of her bows missing, not far from *Pensacola* who lay low in the water with scorched upperworks, both 8″ cruisers having been torpedoed in a recent Solomons encounter.

Now assigned to Task Force 67, *Achilles* refuelled before anchoring near *Helena* who soon became her chummy ship, handing out and accepting all manner of sports challenges followed by invites aboard the US cruiser and return invites to *Achilles*; leaving later with 'bubbly-warmed' praise for those 'hospitable goddam Kiwi limeys'. On board *Helena* Chief TGI Colin Malcolm drank his first glass of iced Cola laced with something strong, but the US Chief beside him cautioned against a second refill: 'It's aircraft alcohol they blame on leakage, buddy, sends guys nuts.' And that's what it did to some of the unwise who had to be assisted in and out of the host cruiser's power boat back to *Achilles*. Men looked about an unreal tropical setting of tall coconut plantations right to the water's edge, cows grazing unconcerned at the roar from Catalinas departing low overhead or returning from patrols.

The US 1st Marine Division still on Guadalcanal was about to be relieved, and US 25th Army Division transports were arriving from Noumea, awaiting the order to be taken north. No longer an idyllic tropical paradise, Santo projected the activity of a fleet readying for sea, bustling escorts shepherding transports and supply ships into some semblance of organisation, stately cruisers turning to the thrust of opposing screws pointing their bows at the entrance. Rear Admiral W.L. Ainsworth's flag preceded that of Rear Admiral M.S. Tisdale on the way out through Santo's boom, followed by the 6″ cruisers and finally *Louisville*, the only 8″ cruiser of TF67. Outside, each ship assumed its signalled two-division disposition – 1st Div, Ainsworth's flagship *Nashville* ahead of *Helena, St Louis*, and the destroyers *O'Bannon, Fletcher*; 2nd Div, Tisdale's *Honolulu, Achilles, Columbia, Louisville*, and the destroyers *Drayton, Lamson, Nicholas*; all cruising northward in two watches throughout the day and night until 0530 dawn stand-to. At 0900 lookouts reported mastheads and signal lamps chattered, greeting and deploying about six US destroyers escorting seven large transports 250 miles south-east of Guadalcanal. Next night the whole force steamed slowly through intense rain squalls, except for an hour's clear after dawn when land was seen while passing San Cristobal, and Captain Barnes blew into the SRE then said: 'The transports will now be nearing Henderson Field's Lunga Roads. Rear Admiral Ainsworth's First Division has detached to bombard New Georgia's Munda airfield, and our task group will remain in support of the relief operation. Ahum, that is all.'

The day passed without incident and at daybreak Tuesday, 5 January 1943, Division 2 rendezvoused 12 miles west of Cape Esperance with Ainsworth's returning cruisers and destroyers. On arrival off Munda he sent the destroyers in close, manoeuvred his cruisers seaward of them and immediately commenced the bombardment, an ear-jarring nightmare of gun-lit thunder, long muzzle-flames spearing at a low trajectory through illuminated palls of billowing cordite fumes, conflagrations rearing ashore then dying, flaring again to reflect in still offshore waters. Firing over their destroyers, the cruisers' ripple firing and that of the tin-cans demolished hangars and supply structures, disrupted runways and gutted administration buildings, poured 4,500 rounds of 6″ and 5.5s into the Japanese base. And now once more combined in two columns steaming east at 15 knots, Admiral Ainsworth's 1st Division cruisers in the northern line were screened further seaward by *O'Bannon* and *Fletcher*. Several miles off Cape Hunter with the sun beating down through vast gaps between four-tenths cloud, Rear Admiral Tisdale paced port to starboard on *Honolulu*'s bridge, cap under arm, conversing with his flag captain and stopping periodically to look back beyond *Achilles* to *Columbia* and *Louisville*, sometimes focusing his telescope shoreside on the destroyers *Drayton, Lamson* and *Nicholas*.

The scene was peaceful, reassuring; off-duty stokers and tween-deck watchkeepers were relaxing topside smoking. At 0925 four aircraft flying at 12,000 feet were reported by the flagship as Grumman Wildcats providing CAP from Henderson. Moments later Able Seaman Jim Thurston at his lookout position on *Achilles'* bridge yelled: 'FOUR ENEMY AIRCRAFT OVERHEAD, SIR!'

Grabbing a TBS mike the OOW warned *Honolulu*: 'Four hostile aircraft overhead!' but a laconic voice through the bridge loudspeaker replied: 'Take no notice, *Achilles*, they're ours.'

Clarrie Johnson, enjoying the sun at his lower bridge starboard Oerlikon, heard the Air Defence Officer's warning, the commotion as other lookouts now confirmed the aircraft were enemy, AND hostile. He needed no direct order, scrambled into the gun harness and activated its safety catch. Close on the starboard bow he saw an aircraft diving on *Honolulu*, swung his gun at it in readiness and allowed 300 knots on the cartwheel sight. Already it had dropped its bomb, just missing *Honolulu*'s stern as the pilot lifted low across her quarterdeck towards *Achilles*, wing-guns spitting flames. Desperately attempting to track the rapidly approaching dive-bomber Clarrie got off thirteen rounds, saw them ripping chunks out of its tail, then had to stop firing to avoid hitting *Honolulu*: 'If only I'd allowed for another ten knots,' he still berates himself, 'I'd have got that bastard.'

Eddie Buckler's cruising station was on S2 4″ A/A mount; his action station was in Y-turret on the quarterdeck and, immediately on being relieved at S2 he sped aft right behind Roy Honeyfield, one of the turret's rammers. Men were running in all directions to their action stations, and just as Eddie was passing the Captain's Cabin all hell broke loose. An almighty 'BAANNNGGG'. One side of X-turret hurtled overhead. Roy Honeyfield was thrown down the Officers' Cabin Flat hatch by the blast. In the wrecked turret Lofty Andrews was looking down at his blood-covered legs. A moment earlier and the shrapnel which wounded Andrews would have killed Eddie as it crashed onto his gun-position. In a fleeting glimpse engraved forever in his memory as he ran aft, he had seen the dive-bomber levelling out of its dive, flashing so close along the ship's side that its pilot's and observer's oriental faces remain photographically imprinted.

Had the aircraft not veered sharply to avoid crashing inboard, its wing-guns would have wreaked carnage among the mass of men clearing *Achilles*' foc'sle, waist, and quarterdeck, squeezing through Rec' Space doors, down hatches, taking cover as bullets ricocheted off the ship's side. Some looking upward saw the bomb release from another diving aircraft's belly, saw it dip and explode in X-turret. It penetrated the roof and burst on the 'right-gun' chase, somersaulting the roof and its top-mounted Oerlikon onto *Achilles*' quarterdeck. The Oerlikon gun's crew Bernie Grice and his handler weren't seen again. The turret's right wall crashed upright against the Captain's quarters; and fortunately for *Achilles* the bomb had detonated on the starboard gun breech-block, only feet from an ammunition hoist down which it would have gone to the handling rooms and magazine.

Leading Torpedoman Bert Rogers' action station was normally in Y-turret, but his opposite number LTO Hessey from X-turret was somewhere for'ard and Bert was about to take his place, climbing up through its overhang-deck manhole when the bomb exploded, killing him and eleven Royal Marines outright. A Marine making for the turret misfooted and knocked himself out on the bottom of the turret wall; and his following mate was decapitated by a piece of bomb-blasted metal. Another Marine's legs still in his boots were found below his hair-raised silhouette on an inside-turret wall; and a Marine sergeant entering the turret door was hurled back against the Officers' Galley bulkhead to slump apparently unconscious – but every bone in his dead body was broken.

It was learned later that the four enemy aircraft were all that remained from ten bombers and fifteen fighters which raided Henderson Field after Ainsworth's Munda bombardment. Three had spiralled down on *Honolulu*, one of their bombs near-missing her starboard bow, another exploding 25 yards off her starboard beam, and a third deluging her quarterdeck when it burst near her starboard quarter. Within seconds of the alarm *Achilles'* Oerlikons were pumping rounds away, some at the aircraft diving on *Honolulu* whose close barrage was throwing up a fiery mesh of converging tracer. An enemy bomber was seen trailing smoke and flame in its curving death plunge beyond the weaving flagship; another whirled crazily as a mass of burning debris showered into her wake and as unexpected as it began the attack finished with no one sure who had brought down the aircraft seen splashing, or whether either of the other two had survived, but *Columbia* claimed a third dive-bomber she said she'd blown to eternity while firing over *Achilles'* masts.

Men were astounded that after all their Solomons engagements the Americans could be so casual about *Achilles'* hostile-aircraft warning. Ainsworth's and Tisdale's sympathy messages for the New Zealand casualties smoothed many ruffled feathers; then the job of clearing wreckage began, while Henderson Field provided an umbrella of Corsairs which relaxed taut nerves for the remaining daylight hours. Only eight of the dead were given traditional sea burials at 1600 that afternoon. The remaining dismembered bodies were being identified before burial. And two critically wounded in the Sick Bay were failing hourly.

All next day TF67's radars detected snoopers shadowing from a distance as surveillance off Lunga Roads continued; Wildcats and Corsairs deterred further interference as the last of America's 1st Marine Division embarked on their relieving US Army 25th Division's emptied transports; then after another night offshore at constant alert, both TF67's Task Groups deployed about the south-bound convoy. Even now it was hard to relax so soon after *Achilles'* damage. Shortly after 0900, when more identified remains and the bodies of the two critically injured who'd died were given their funeral rites, the alarm sounded and men rushed to their action stations,

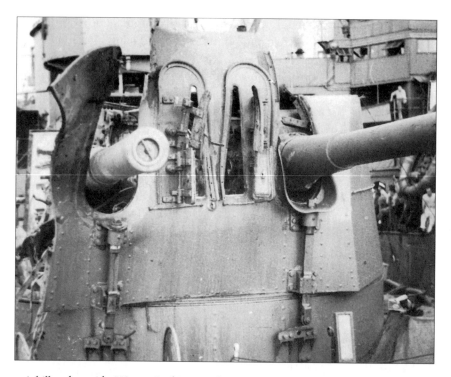

Achilles alongside US repair ship *Vestal*, January 1943, "X" Turret blown apart
by Japanese bomb at Guadalcanal.

remaining there for half an hour until 'All Clear' allowed the service to be
completed. Next morning, Friday, 8 January 1943, on arrival at Santo
Achilles queued for her turn alongside a US tanker, then made for the US
repair ship *Vestal* in heavy rain which possibly impaired Captain Barnes'
judgement. *Achilles'* wartime 9,000 tons screeched loudly as she tore a long
gash in the repair ship's side, sending men scampering to safety as the
signal deck bent upward, then surged away sideways to leave American
and New Zealand matelots staring speechless across the thirty-foot gap.
That is, until an *Achilles'* loudmouth bellowed through the silence: 'SAY
YOU GUYS! IS THIS THE REPAIR SHIP?'

'SURE AS HELL IS, LIMEY!'

'WELL HOW ABOUT PATCHING UP THAT HOLE IN YOUR SIDE,
SAILOR!' He'd acted his part and disappeared off-stage with a Crusher in
pursuit.

For the three weeks it took to reroof and rewall X-turret with light plate
to make it weatherproof, there were inter-ship boxing matches against *St
Louis*, and against *Honolulu* who'd been nicknamed USS *Hollywood* because
of her captain, the film star Robert Montgomery. Yanks and Kiwis sought

footholds and perches about *Vestal's* and *Achilles'* upper structures to applaud their favourite contestants, some winning and some losing. Then in wildly acclaimed three-minute bouts, *Columbia's* ex-world middleweight champion Fred Apostolle, gave exhibition rounds against *Achilles'* Stoker Tommy Dunn, Clubs Heath and Leading Seaman Nobby Grant.

With her X-turret weatherproofed *Achilles* moved away to anchor throughout the remainder of January, frustrated at watching the task force move out on Friday the 22nd to return four days later signalling a successful operation. So she vented her anger each night when firing at intruders over Santo's airstrips, when matching her boxers against those from *Chicago*, the carrier *Enterprise*, seaplane-tender *Curtiss*, and bow-less cruiser *Minneapolis*.

TF67 steamed out on 28 January with *Enterprise*, and returned on Sunday, 1 February minus the heavy cruiser *Chicago*, it soon being learned that, while approaching Lunga Roads with their four-transport convoy, they'd undergone a night attack which disabled *Chicago* who was hit twice by torpedoes, and although taken in tow throughout the dark hours, she had to be cast adrift in early daylight when Japanese torpedo-bombers arrived in force. This time hit by four torpedoes the helpless cruiser could not be saved.

Task Force 67's daily bulletin, brought to *Achilles* as she was clearing lower deck preparatory to departing Santo for Auckland that Sunday, went on to say that American troops on Guadalcanal had pushed north without opposition, finding only a handful of emaciated remnants from General Hyakutake's 17th Army. From the few prisoners taken, it seemed that without supplies its brigades and divisions had survived on grass roots and jungle vegetation, even those who'd been evacuated by some sixty destroyers being in poor condition from malaria and dysentery. It was probable that the determined air-attacks against TF67 were a distraction, launched to keep *Enterprise* and the cruisers and destroyers away while Hyakutake's army was being extricated.

But Japanese forces weren't the only enemy as Bill Yates vividly remembered. *Matal* and *Tui* were asdic and radar searching north of Tulagi for a big submarine known to have left Truk to pick up high-ranking Japanese officers. An American dive-bomber chased away from Rabaul by Zeros, still had his bomb and wanted to drop it on something. So, sighting *Matai* and *Tui* steaming in line abreast he ignored their flashed British recognition signals, buzzed *Matai* with his wing-guns, wrecking her crow's-nest, came in again firing bursts across the well deck, raked her stern before spiralling up for a dive-bombing attack, then almost brought her to a standstill when his bomb threw up a thousand-ton Pacific eruption only a cable ahead. Fortunately there were no casualties, and although the pilot was later invited aboard in Tulagi he didn't arrive.

Meanwhile two other ships of New Zealand's Tulagi-based 25th M/S,

Kiwi and *Moa*, were also sub-hunting off north-east Guadalcanal, unaware that 'the Boss' and *Tui* were saying rude things about their American allies. Dusk faded away to nightfall, then darkness illuminated by shafts of phosphorescence glinting on the corvettes' bow-waves and curling wash; a Kamimbo Bay headland looming blacker than the black hills beyond. Leading Signalman Buchanan passed his night-glasses to Ernie Barton who'd come up on the flag-deck for a breather: 'Seems quiet tonight, Ernie.'

'Yeah, Chas, sure does.'

But right now 22-year-old asdic operator Eddie McVinnie, a pre-war refrigerator mechanic from the Bay of Islands, was about to shatter their tranquility, busy on his voice pipe to the bridge reporting a definite contact. Alarm rattlers hustled men to their action stations. *Kiwi*'s engine-room repeater demanded full speed and Lt Cmdr Bridson brought her onto an attack course while *Moa* stood off, maintaining asdic contact. Men at *Kiwi*'s port and starboard throwers had inserted pistols and screwed detonators in place for hydrostatic firing at given depths; others at the stern racks were ready to roll their charges overboard when ordered. Closer … closer. Contact lost as *Kiwi*'s depth-charges hurtled outboard to splash 50 yards either side, to roll off their rack and disappear in her 12-knot wake, soon to activate a hundred feet down in almighty upheavals around the enemy submarine's phosphorescent outline, seen clearly as *Kiwi* passed close over-head. With contact regained Bridson sped his corvette in for another attempt, but aborted it when contact was lost too early. When regained he altered course for a third run-in, this one a successful six-charge attack which saw the I-boat surfacing in a swirling cauldron and attempting to escape on her loud-thumping diesels. If he could elude his attackers under cover of Guadalcanal's dark background, his greater surface speed would outrun the two smaller vessels, his 125mm shells passing over each attacker as his gunners ranged on them. But a direct 4″ hit aimed at his searchlight-and-star-shell-illuminated hull reduced his speed and swung him side on.

Now only hundreds of yards away and closing fast, Bridson prepared to ram while *Moa*'s 4″ gunners lobbed more and more starshells over *Kiwi*'s target. And this is where that Oerlikon 'pirated' weeks ago from the abandoned US auxiliary now played a vital role, sweeping the enemy's 5.9″ gunners overboard as *Kiwi* approached at speed, crunching over the rolling submarine's deck aft of her conning tower, scattering fully-equipped Japanese soldiers attempting to launch landing barges secured to her spacious deck. Ordering emergency power, Bridson reversed his awkwardly angled vessel off to clear water, then as all *Kiwi*'s weaponry created more unhappiness for the Japanese commanding officer, he surged in for a second ramming well aft in a glancing blow which tore off the submarine's port hydroplane and wrecked its port propeller. Spasmodic rifle fire still came from enemy soldiers not yet dislodged off the damaged submarine, this being returned by *Kiwi*'s machine guns, foc'sle-mounted 4″ and the Oerlikon as Bridson rammed her onto the I-boat a third time. Oil fuel now streamed from a great gash in the hull up which *Kiwi* mounted in a grinding collision, hurling the remaining Japanese to their doom. Below in the corvette's boiler room, stokers and mechanicians were thrown about on slippery foot-plates with each ramming, fought for extra power when reversing off the battered hulk. Still the 2,500-ton submarine was not beaten, so, with his ship's stem badly distorted and flooding, asdics no longer functioning, Lt Cmdr Bridson hauled her clear to give *Moa* an unrestricted target as it gathered headway in a final bid to escape. But tonight wasn't its most auspicious evening, it had only one propeller shaft operable, it couldn't dive, and after weaving constantly to avoid *Moa*'s accurate gunnery it ran at 13 knots onto an inshore reef.

There were more incidents as daylight revealed the submarine's stern protruding acutely skyward; only one survivor was plucked from the sea protesting profusely, then *Moa* had to retire when shore-based artillery lobbed shells perilously close. Days later an inspection by *Matal* revealed that the submarine, *I–1*, had been transporting troops and supplies to Kamimbo Bay, her great size made her capable of deck-loading landing barges, and her forward mounted 125mm gun together with 20 knots surface speed, made her a formidable opponent for New Zealand's two little 12-knot corvettes.

During the night encounter Leading Signalman Charles H. Buchanan RNZNVR from Port Chalmers, although critically wounded by *I–1*'s machine-gun fire, continued to direct *Kiwi*'s searchlight onto the submarine, until late in the action when someone reported his predicament and he was relieved at his post. For his gallantry he was 'Mentioned in Despatches' by the Royal New Zealand Navy, and awarded the United States Navy Cross by the US Navy. But his wounds were beyond recovery and he died in Tulagi US Military Hospital on Sunday, 31 January 1943.

The night he died his ship *Kiwi* was being prepared for the long haul back to Auckland for docking, and her sister-ships *Tui* and *Moa* were off Cape Esperance hotly engaging successive Japanese landing barges illuminated by their searchlights. In the running melee, *Moa* damaged one large craft before a machine-gun bullet ignited a 4″ cordite charge which enveloped the gun platform in searing flames; men not wearing flash-hoods and adequate dress staggered about yelling in flesh-stripped agony, some were also injured by metal fragments; all received first aid by Ernest Barton RN the ship's steward, who ignored his own wounds for over an hour until he collapsed and was taken below. Having already been 'Mentioned in Despatches' for gallantry in the *I–1* action, he was now awarded the

Distinguished Service Medal for his devotion to duty in this latter action, during which *Moa* and *Tui* sank or crippled most of the landing barges encountered.

Whether true or otherwise, the buzz was going round the 25th M/S that when ramming *I-1*, Bridson had said to his First Lieutenant on the initial impact: 'That's got us back to Santo.' As he side-swiped the submarine on his second ramming: 'That should get us to Noumea.' And as he drove *Kiwi* high up among landing barges secured aft of *I-1*'s conning tower: 'That, Number One, has got us back to Auckland.' He was right.

On its broader spectrum, Naval Board Wellington had authorised plans for *Achilles* and *Leander* to refit in England where the latest technology would be available; each in turn would go there as convenient; but now that *Achilles* was short of X-turret the 'Who first?' question had been answered. When detached from Task Force 67 and clearing Espiritu Santo on Monday, 1 February 1943, men at their 'Leaving Harbour Stations' waved to Yankee matelots leaning on the guardrails of four damaged cruisers, stood to attention as other TF67 warships cheered her down harbour. There were lots of acquainted buddies on those cruisers and destroyers, and as a final tribute Santo's airbase gave Corsair cover right through till nightfall, by which time *Achilles'* 27-knot phosphorescent wash stretched miles astern on the unruffled Pacific, downhill four days all the way home, not even a pit-stop for oil, only the news as a reminder that the world was still at war.

Gannets dived on surface-shattered schools of yellow-tail off Cape Brett on Monday the 3rd near midday as *Achilles* sped south, streaming paravanes on entering Hauraki Gulf but retrieving them again abreast of Rangitoto Beacon, liberty men already in their No 1s to step ashore on Calliope Wharf at 1900. *Leander's* masts and upper-structures could be seen above the Harbour Board Shed south-side of Calliope Dock, where the cruiser's cracked fuel-tank plating was being repaired. Captain 'Pinocchio' Bevan had left her on 27 November 1942 when ill health necessitated his return to England; and the 'Black Mamba', Commander Stephen Wentworth Roskill RN, having been up-ranked to Acting Captain, temporarily occupied the vacated cabin. And when *Achilles'* ship's company returned from long leave in remote New Zealand towns they found there'd been more re-shuffles – *Achilles'* Captain Mansergh had been assigned to *Leander*, and Commander Gronow Davis DSC RN now wore four rings on his sleeves, having been shifted from his Commander's Cabin into that just vacated by Captain Mansergh.

On Friday, 19 February Gronow eased *Achilles* away from the Cruiser Wharf, saluted *Philomel* in passing, then after rounding North Head asked for more revolutions throughout a fast trip via Bora Bora, Panama Canal and Bermuda to Plymouth. But mass bombings had devastated the city and *Achilles* was redirected to Portsmouth – a cautious Channel navigation in pea-soup fog, punctuated by raucus epithets describing the Captain as his ship's wash dramatically rolled small craft he'd narrowly missed. The Isle of Wight peered bleakly through a patch of clear, evoking a nostalgic RN rating's poetry: 'Gor blimey Scouse,' he romanticised to his mate, 'I've pined for this flamin' wevver for five long bloody yures.' It was Monday, 22 March as *Achilles* arrived with arms-length defect lists.

We return here to late 1941 when the NZDRN was short of a chaplain for one of its two cruisers. Bishop Holland of Wellington, whilst in conversation with Chief of Staff, Commodore Parry, mentioned a parson who'd been a year with the NZ Mounted Rifles Regiment which was right then being disbanded: 'Yes, Commodore, entirely suitable man for your navy, I would say. You should talk to him.' Outcome? Temporary Chaplain RNZNVR Claude Francis Webster, born Yorkshire, Friday, 2 September 1910; educated Cambridge University where his ungainly tall frame and unhandsome features earned him the nickname 'Gargoyle of Trinity'; he entered the priesthood at Westcott House, then after coming to New Zealand, preached the gospel in remote parishes before becoming Chaplain to the rough-riding Mounted Rifles; and now was about to be appointed an RNZN padre: 'Best of luck, Padre,' as he picked up his papers from Navy Office Wellington, 'HMNZS *Leander*, Captain R.H. Bevan Royal Navy; you'll find her in the Naval Base dock at Devonport. These are your meal tickets, that's your train ticket. There'll be a navy car at the Auckland station for you.'

Although a six-foot outdoor man who found difficulty in contorting his angular physique into his twelve-by-eight cabin, he managed somehow to amass books, games, correspondence files and his clerical gear onto his bunk and wherever he found inches of previously undiscovered space; all this for the benefit of his nautical flock to whom the door was ever open, only a drawn curtain should a troubled member wish to speak in privacy. *Leander* according to the Black Mamba, Commander Stephen Wentworth Roskill RN, who'd just taken over from Commander Vereker, was going through a bad patch after her return from the Middle East and Mediterranean. 'New entries have replaced men drafted off with tuberculosis and yellow jaundice; she needs working up to her overseas standard again, and I feel my task will be made easier by your appointment.'

Here was a man at ease with hardened army horsemen, men with whom he'd spent months in New Zealand's roughest terrain, downed his beer with them in remote high-country pubs, those same men who'd grown to accept his no-nonsense insistence on a daily Christian Service. Captain Bevan took an instant like to the new chaplain, so did Commander Roskill, and more gradually the ship's company.

Meanwhile *Leander*'s leaking hull had been made watertight, dockyard maties relinquished their temporary messdeck residence to the ship's naval occupants, and on 2 March Captain Mansergh took his cruiser out for Gulf trials, in which many newcomers would learn the practical applications of their training at *Tamaki* Naval Barracks on Auckland's Motuihe Island. One such trainee, Ordinary Seaman Cliff Dawe NZ5924, born Sumner, 14 May 1923, schooled at Sumner Primary, Christchurch Boys' High, and Christ's College, before becoming a Union Steamship Company purser, an Army 1st Canterbury Regiment inductee, then on 24 September 1942 a Service transferee to an Ordinary Seaman entry at *Tamaki*.

On *Leander* he soon accustomed to shipboard routine, meals in a heaving and rolling messdeck, night watchkeeping at the end of which one quietly located one's relief's hammock in the dark, dawn stand-to when you'd just got your head down and, that first experience of a full-calibre, full-charge, all guns salvo. There were leisure hours when one joined throngs purchasing toiletries and nutty bars from the Sick Bay Flat canteen; Sunday Service on the quarterdeck by a tall padre who spoke loud and comfortably rather than preached; then Cliff's first time as crow's-nest lookout. That unnerving climb up an unsteady runged ladder as *Leander* swayed, the sense of safety in the crow's nest, and that magnificent Hauraki Gulf vista of sunset painting Whangaparaoa's barren headland gold and red, the ship's wash disappearing far astern as darkness fell, star-clouds building the Milky Way's immense overhead arch, and a huge orange moon rising resplendent over the Coromandels. But where was his relief? *Tamaki* had insisted during training that a man remains at his post till relieved. In desperation he blew down the voice pipe to activate its whistle on the bridge, and was told to come down immediately; down those swaying rungs to be admonished for not descending at dusk. 'Oh well.'

A brief return to Auckland, long enough for married couples to recognise each other in bedrooms oppressive with citronella mosquito repellant, long enough to make arrangements for wives' return to their parents, early morning farewells; the 0645 tram to Queen Street, bleary-eyed matelots down Admiralty Steps into the 0730 powered pinnace; then away north for a 13 March arrival alongside Espiritu Santo's US tanker *Sapine*; there to scan the harbour for chummy ships. Sure, familiar names remained on the SDO fleet list – carrier *Enterprise*, cruisers *Honolulu*, *St Louis*, destroyers *Ralph Talbot*, *Sterrett*, *Strong*; but deletion lines had been drawn through many – *Minneapolis*, *San Francisco*, *Salt Lake City*, *Chicago*, also *Portland*, *Pensacola*, *Northampton*, *Achilles*, *Kiwi*, *Moa*; some sunk and others away in busy yards. Those days one expected casualties and name changes engendered minimal interest.

There were invitations to films in *Enterprise*'s vast hangars, on one occasion a dinner followed by *My Sister Eileen*; then several days abreast of the big flat-top, sweeping south, west, and north of the Solomons as her aircraft searched beyond horizons for Japanese surface forces. Only a placid Pacific, sans enemy ships, sans enemy aircraft, until Task Force 15 re-entered Santo and refuelled. Com-TF15, Rear Admiral W.L. Ainsworth USN came aboard on 28 March, said to the crowded quarterdeck that he remembered *Achilles* on the day she was bombed, recalled New Zealand's loss of *Neptune* in the Mediterranean, and *Leander*'s past operations under RN Admiral Cunningham whom he knew as a personal friend. He continued that he was proud to have New Zealand's remaining cruiser in his Task Force; was sure she would do as well for him as she had done for other Admirals of the Royal, and the United States, Navies.

Sunday, 4 April saw boatloads of 'down-unders' attending church on *Helena*, heard them thanking donors for gifts of Chesterfield cigarette packs, and being thanked for the small bottles of neaters smuggled aboard. Later Claude Webster encouraged Commander Roskill when he repeated a *Life* magazine reporter's remarks after being shown around *Leander*: 'Yuh-know-Padre, I've just realised the different attitudes between your ship and ours. On yours all the guys are busy, debatin' groups, boxin', fencin', that singalong in your recreation room up front. They look so doggon' happy. Our boys are always askin' – When'll we be home? When's the next mail or the next movie? They don't organise anything for themselves. I dunno.'

Maybe it was the newsman's off-day. Maybe he was of the evolving breed who go public before in-depth research. There were American Army-organised track events ashore, picnic parties where everyone, US or NZ, enjoyed the cool freshwater streams and tropical fruit. Padre Webster joined wholeheartedly in these diversions, his boundless energy and laughter spreading like an epidemic throughout both nations' recreation parties; and onboard he would find time to help officer-teams censoring personal letters awaiting postage. That is, apart from those written by the ship's four Fijians whose problem was solved by Able Seaman 'Tungi' Brewis. Born of European parents in Lautoka, Frank had joined the training ship *Philomel* mid-1930s as a happy-natured lad, and when asked by one of his classmates what the Fijian word was for 'happy', Frank replied 'tungi' which thereafter he remained known as throughout the New Zealand Navy. Up in the Pacific his fluency with the Fijian language was put to use, when only he could interpret the Fijian's letters which had to be censored before release. So he was paid one shilling per letter on a quarterly basis; and when it was paid Tungi Brewis, Timo Paumau, Savu Naulamatua, and Napoleon Wara, had sumptuous runs ashore. Another interpretation duty involved official correspondence mailed aboard from a Fijian Commando unit operating on Guadalcanal, but even with this essential assignment additional to his seaman duties, NZNB reduced his interpreter's increment to five pounds a quarter: 'In order to avoid the accounting involved'.

One Sunday forenoon in Santo when Tungi was goalie for his side's water polo match alongside, Surgeon Lt Cmdr E.S. (Doc) McPhail leaned outboard and hollered: 'I say, Brewis, your Fijian boys aren't writing home very often these days!' to which while treading water Tungi looked up and laughed when replying: 'What does the Naval Board expect for a fiver a quarter, sir?' His laughter always infected everyone including officers, and Doc chuckling to himself went off to repeat their conversation in the wardroom. Then that afternoon during a rumbling rainstorm, a legendary Norse deity hurled his shaft of lightning down *Leander's* foremast to phizz off its lightning conductor and split the outswung starboard boom.

Two days later on 7 April TF15 left Santo for a sweep up the Slot, *Leander*, *San Diego* and six destroyers escorting *Enterprise* while some of her Corsairs reconnoitred far afield and others maintained overhead CAP. On past Guadalcanal where 17,000 Japanese soldiers lay mouldering in the steaming jungle near the bodies of GIs and Marines; on over Iron Bottom Sound where mutilated warships almost side by side were already the tombs for thousands of Allied and Japanese naval men, confounding the oft-quoted dictum that East is East, West is West, and never the twain shall meet; then a rendezvous with TF19's *Denver*, *Columbia*, *Montpelier* who said two of their escorts, *Strong* and *O'Bannon*, had sunk two Japanese submarine-transports. When off San Cristobal Island *Leander* detached to join TF18's *Honolulu*, *Helena*, *St Louis* for the sweep south, and at the end of another week the three task forces were again at anchor in Santo.

Here it was learned that HMNZS *Moa*, the US tanker *Kanawa* and destroyer *Aaron Ward* had been sunk in Tulagi, but forty-five years were to pass before Bill Yates unfolded some events of that day. He recalled the time when *Matai* was working near Vella Lavella and anchored off Green Island which had just been occupied by troops of New Zealand's 3rd Division. *Matai* had escorted a supply ship to the beachhead then remained offshore as A/A and A/S guardship, slipping out to sea each night on asdic patrol. One day her Exec Officer, Jack Ross (later Rear Admiral) sent for Yates and said: 'Say Bill, there's someone to see you.' It was his Napier home-town cousin Sergeant Ray Yates coming up the sea-gangway from an army boat; and in Bill's cabin where they were retracing old times, the door opened to admit a dozen beers – 'For you Bill, courtesy of Skip' perhaps an unwise inter-service gesture as at 1700 when *Matai* prepared for her night patrol, Sergeant Yates lay out to the world on rum and beer, his boat hadn't returned for him, so he remained onboard right through the night-search for enemy submarines or motor-torpedo-boats.

Next forenoon back at anchor, *Matai's* cooks baked piles of buns to be taken ashore with a carton of New Zealand butter, and Bill was given permission to accompany his cousin ashore along with crates of chilled beer and bags of dry goods from the ship's victual store, a godsend for the troops' mess-tent where they'd been rationed Yankee hard tack and 'axle grease'. Upward of thirty Kiwis a day were invited aboard for dinner and a bottle of cold beer per man whenever *Matai* came to anchor off Green Island – and it happened again off Lunga Point after Bill's brother came out to the ship. In the course of their liquified conversation, RNZAF Warrant Officer Ralph Yates, a Ventura air-gunner, said it was common knowledge the American mobile A/A batteries concealed among coconut palms shot first and answered questions later: 'That's right, Bill, they're bringing down planes at about four Lightnings to every eleven Zeros.'

On Wednesday, 7 April when TF15 was heading up the Slot, Ainsworth was warned that some seventy bombers and a hundred fighters were on their way from Munda Airfield to bomb and strafe Henderson and Tulagi so, altering course out of their path he warned US and NZ units of the impending attack but it was too late for the small ships anchored in Tulagi to break out to sea. Right then *Matai, Gale* and *Tui* were sub-hunting near Cape Esperance, but *Moa* wasn't so fortunate and when the attack developed she was still refuelling from the US auxiliary. Hit by a large bomb which exploded in her bowels she heeled and sank within minutes, barely having time to launch a boat to rescue survivors. Telegraphist Duncan, Able Seaman Bailey, Leading Seaman Moffat, Leading Stoker Crawford and Stoker Buckeridge died; others including Lt Cmdr Peter Phipps were wounded; and deeds of bravery ensured that the critically injured were found and assisted to safety.

Two days later when *Matai* anchored in Tulagi some of *Moa's* survivors came out for 'tots and dinner' and Dolly Gray with his arm still in a sling and his head bandaged, told Bill he was downing his bubbly when the bomb exploded. When he recovered from being hurled against the deck-head he was heard to say: 'By God, Wilson, what in hell did you put in my bloody rum?' That evening Tug Wilson and Dolly Gray clambered down a Jacob's ladder into the inflatable raft they'd paddled out in, shoved off in an eddying tide to be whirled round and round, both full of squirt and beer, yelling advice at each other, as Dolly with one arm and Wilson with two, disappeared in the gloom on their circuitous way shoreward.

About now the Allied Air Force Chiefs received information that several Japanese naval VIPs would be flying from Rabaul to Bougainville on Sunday, 18 April. Subsequent intelligence messages pinpointed the airfield as Kahili near Buin, even the ETA. Then US HQs seethed with excitement when another message named two of the VIPs as Japan's Combined Fleet C-in-C, Admiral Isoroku Yamamoto and his deputy, Vice Admiral Ugichi.

P–38 fighters from Henderson arrived as the Japanese fighter-escorted transports approached and, leaving the escorts to be dealt with by designated US pilots, the others blasted both obvious VIP bombers out of the sky. And even though this must have been a major set-back for Japan's War Cabinet, it amazed US Intelligence that Japan didn't now realise their top secret codes had been broken. No effort was made to change the code and America continued to be handed vital enemy information on a plate.

But back to the War as it affected the RNZN. Since mid-1941 England's Ministry of Troop Transport had been unsuccessfully trying to entice our government to relinquish *Monowai*: 'We want her for a fast transport. Yes we understand your predicament, but we'll give you something slower for your Pacific escorting responsibilities.'

'Nothing doing. Call us again if America becomes an ally. Right now we need her as an auxiliary cruiser while you have *Achilles* or *Leander* overseas.'

NZNB's sphere of Pacific responsibility was vast; *as it still is*; Admiralty had agreed to *Neptune* becoming our third 'Leander Class' cruiser on station, but had diverted her from her delivery voyage back into the Med where she went down in a minefield off Tripoli; nineteen days before 'Pearl Harbour' brought America into the Pacific War. Now with Uncle Sam becoming more the benevolent relation than John Bull, the Pacific was becoming a stamping ground for the USN and *Monowai*'s role lapsed significantly. She was too slow as an aircraft-carrier escort, so a further request from Britain's Transport Minister saw her departing Auckland 24 April 1943 for Greenock, there in a Clyde shipyard to be converted for British troop transporting.

At this date *Achilles* rested on a Portsmouth dry-dock's chocks being repaired and updated; so *Leander* as our only remaining cruiser did three excursions up the Slot with TF15 and TF18 in March/April; but even her input was about to terminate, leaving the 25th M/S Flotilla and a flotilla of A/S power boats to shoulder New Zealand's naval operations in the Solomons campaign.

On Wednesday, 28 April *Leander* and the US destroyer *Cory* left Santo, to rendezvous with the troopship *Fuller* being escorted to Hawaii by *Smith* and *Lamson*. There were the usual hiccups associated with destroyer-re-fuelling under way in rough weather, especially when *Smith* rolled dangerously close while still ingesting, and gave *Leander*'s pipeline party and the bridge staff heart palpitations; but all other intership evolutions concluded with minimal concern. Then came the morning when off-watch men massed starboard side, commenting on Diamond Head, the Pacific's Rock of Gibraltar, standing proud beyond an expanse of mirrored blue unruffled ocean through which the ships steamed without a tremor. Not a cloud disturbed pre-war memories of visits aboard *Dunedin*, *Diomede*,

Achilles, the Royal Hawaiian Hotel gleaming white among tall palms to dominate Waikiki Beach. Someone at the crowded foc'sle rail was saying: 'Shirley Temple sang and danced for us there in '34.' And through binoculars one could see the Hawaiian Flag, Union Jack instead of stars in a top corner of the red and white striped ensign.

'CLEAR LOWER DECK FOR ENTERING HARBOUR. ALL HANDS OUT OF THE RIG OF THE DAY – OFF THE UPPER DECK.' Years of experience had taught old salts where to avoid the Jaunty while still able to observe the vista of foreign harbours; but this time instead of berthing city-centre as anticipated, *Leander* followed the American ships to Pearl Harbour. The Stars and Stripes still draped lazily at *Arizona's* masthead where she lay submerged, and intense dockyard activity spelt bad news for Japan as torn parts of damaged warships were incised and craned away. Prefabricated components were being swung into place and welded. Rivet guns stuttered, oxy-welding guns spat showers of white-hot sparks, metal clanged on metal, and finishing teams could be seen working on the latest of electronics and short barrage weaponry; while restored destroyers and cruisers moved out for trials before being sent back south-west. For the ten days in Hawaii *Leander's* liberty men enjoyed Oahu, saw the cliff over which King Kemehameha drove an opposing Polynesian army to their death, surfed at internationally famous Waikiki, drew straws for a night in the Royal Hawaiian, or looked about surreptiously before entering Honolulu's 'other Hotels', where 'US contracted hostesses' lounged in see-through-pyjamas awaiting them.

Meantime there were convoys awaiting escorts, so *Leander* sailed to the mystic strains of 'Aloha – Aloha Hawaii, throne of King Kemehameha, Conqueror of the Islands – Islands of Romance – Islands of near forgotten Polynesian mythology – Aloha'.

That evening as clouds mantled the peaks of Oahu's mountains and mists swirled inland from the warm Pacific, the grey above deepened, stars emerged to brighten and flash, facetted jewels on an immense overhead black velvet cloth, shimmering just beyond reach. Men went below to eat, to sleep, to go on watch. *Leander* shepherded three troopships and two destroyers to Noumea, refuelled and provisioned. Took empties part-way to the States, turned them over to US cruisers off Bora Bora and refuelled. Took more ships to Suva and refuelled. Everywhere she went she refuelled. Again at Noumea. Then to Espiritu Santo in late June 1943, this time to anchor in familiar surroundings, and await Rear Admiral Ainsworth's assignment to one of his Task Groups intercepting Tokyo Expresses en route Bougainville and Kolombangara with reinforcements.

Leander was about to rejoin.

CHAPTER XVII

Leander *Torpedoed at Kolombangara*

CAPTAIN (RETD) STEPHEN WENTWORTH ROSKILL CBE DSC RN. Fellow of the Royal Historic Society (FR His S) Fellow of Churchill College Canterbury 1961; Life Fellow of Churchill College Cambridge 1970; MA Canterbury Litt D 1971; SBA 1971.

Born 1903 as the son of an eminent QC, Stephen aged 13 entered HM Naval Officer School, *Osborne*, finished his training at *Dartmouth*, then served on the China, Med, and West Indies Stations; being promoted to Gunnery Officer on various ships including *Eagle* and *Warspite*. He did the first two years of WW2 on Naval Staff Admiralty and in late 1941 became HMNZS *Leander*'s Exec Officer, her Acting Captain from November 1942 to February 1943, then her Captain from November 1943 to June 1944 when *Leander* reverted to the RN. In August 1944 he was appointed to Washington as a member of the British Naval Mission; and in 1946 the US Naval Board invited him to be Britain's Senior Naval Observer at America's Bikini Atoll nuclear bomb tests. He then officiated as Deputy Director of RN Intelligence from 1947 to 1949 when he was invalided from the Royal Navy and appointed Author of Britain's Official Naval History, *The War at Sea 1939–1945*. Subsequently he wrote several books and numerous articles on naval and maritime history, and in 1961 he delivered the Lees-Knowles Lectures at Cambridge University. At the inauguration of New Zealand's Ex-*Leander* Association, Captain Roskill was made a member, and he corresponded regularly until his Thursday, 4 November 1982 death in England, when respects for his international faculty memberships were expressed in the Obituary Notices of leading periodicals and newspapers including England's *Times*, *Guardian* and *Telegraph*.

Tall dark and aristocratic, Commander Roskill during his early years aboard *Leander* was not her most popular officer. An inherent *hiss* when addressing defaulters at Commander's Report quickly established his 'Black Mamba' nickname; and his insistence on strict observance of every minor detail during Damage Control, Fire Drill and First Aid exercises, became a messdeck-aired source of annoyance, but without a doubt those

ingrained procedures were instrumental in saving the ship at Kolombangara.

After her early 1943 Auckland fuel-tank repairs, *Leander* arrived back in
Santo to a south-west Pacific war-zone period of near stalemate. General
MacArthur was insisting on his 'Fight island by island to the Philippines;
then somehow to Japan' strategy. Japan's warlords were concentrating naval
and air groups to contest superiority in the northern Solomons; so April
closed without *Leander*'s guns being fired except to blow the moths out
and awaken her turret crews. Where was this Japanese Navy? True, task
groups had limped back into Santo with ships missing or damaged, but
both forays involving *Leander* had seen nothing except empty sea and sky.
Before and since her Middle East and Mediterranean operations, she'd
shepherded big and small ships here there and elsewhere: '*Leander* – Convoys'. Every nationality imaginable: Arabian, British, Czechoslovakian,
Dutch, Egyptian, French, Greek – Greek, rusty, smoky, slow; always with
a list – on through the alphabet to Turks, Uncle-Sams, Venezuelans, Welsh,
Xanthians, Yugoslavs, even one registered in Zurich. If High Command
wanted a gaggle of worn-out derelicts taken somewhere unpronounceable
its Transport Clerk would scrutinise the list of available cruisers, page after
page until: 'Ahh, ahaah! *Le–an–der*,' with malice aforethought. 'I'll send that
New Zealand so and so.' Even in the Pacific, north, south, east, west, and
every direction in between until now, at anchor back in Espiritu Santo on
30 June 1943.

Away north, US Rear Admiral Turner's Amphibious Task Group 31
had landed thousands of GIs and Marines on Rendova Island, with the
intention of their being ferried five miles across Blanche Passage at night
to a beachhead on Japanese-held New Georgia. There at Munda Airfield
and twenty miles north on Kolombangara, Japan had two army divisions.
The struggle for New Georgia was mounting as both sides rushed in
reinforcements, and the first naval clash, termed the Battle of Kula Gulf,
began on Monday night, 5 July. The previous night Rear Admiral Ainsworth's cruisers *Honolulu* (Flag) *St Louis*, *Helena*, and the destroyers
Jenkins, *Nicholas*, *O'Bannon*, *Radford*, *Strong* were in support when *Strong*
was torpedoed and sunk, presumably by a submarine. Then later while
returning to Tulagi Ainswoth was ordered back to Kula Gulf, but quick:
'There's two Tokyo Expresses and a pile of destroyers headin' hell-bent
for Kolombangara!'

At 0147 on Tuesday, 6 July Ainsworth's force made contact. Seven of
the ten Japanese transports were converted destroyers, preparing to disembark as Rear Admiral Akiyama skirted Kolombangara coast in Kula Gulf,
across which the US task group was doing 25 knots when a van destroyer's
radar detected the enemy. Akiyama had detached his 1st Transport Group

to their destination, and was about to dispatch Group 2 in its wake when lookouts sighted the American ships silhouetted against a clear northern horizon. He recalled both groups just as the leading US 6″ cruisers were ranging on them by radar control, and for some reason Ainsworth ordered all their guns to concentrate on Akiyama's light cruiser flagship *Nizuki* then 6,800 yards on his port beam, leaving her a pulverised wreck after only the first few minutes ripple-firing. In retrospect an unwise decision as it left *Suzukaze* and *Tanikaze* undamaged, with an unrestricted range to launch sixteen Long Lance torpedoes at the line of US cruisers, then more at Ainsworth's destroyers awaiting permission to launch their torpedoes, an order which came far too late for their missiles to be effective. Thinking by the dense pall of smoke from *Nizuki* that his ships had knocked out the opposition, Ainsworth ordered a 180-degree 'turn-in-succession to the right' with *Honolulu* leading; but before *Helena* next in line commenced the turn she was struck by three torpedoes, the first tearing away her bows and the other two ripping open her hull amidships. Within six minutes she foundered, leaving her bows still afloat.

There were unco-ordinated skirmishes over the ensuing two hours but the only additional damage inflicted was on *Amigiri*; while at the far end of Kula Gulf both Japanese destroyer-transport groups disembarked their reinforcements anxiously but undisturbed.

Here with *Helena's* demise, *Leander's* unwanted status in Espiritu Santo came to an end. Halsey's SOUWESPAC HQs were informed of another 'Express' about to depart Rabaul for Kula Gulf, and *Leander*, who'd been chafing at the bit, was eager to be in the punch-up, especially when a departing cruiser's loudmouth hollered: 'When're youse Kiwi yokels comin' out to do some fightin'?' Moments of silence elapsed, then a stentorian answer roared: 'As soon as you Yankee Rookies finish your bloody shakedown!' This incident was out of keeping with the intership bonhomie normally experienced; friendly waves from following cruisers re-established cordiality and no more was said; and that night *Leander* sped north to refuel in Tulagi before moving across the expansive bay to anchor in Port Purvis at four hours notice for steam, there to up-anchor at daybreak on Sunday, 11 July and depart en route Savo Island off where Task Force 18 awaited her.

Within hours mastheads then warships' upperworks were sighted. *Honolulu's* bridge lamp flashed a welcome from the American admiral, and Captain Mansergh replied: 'Com Task Group 36.1 from *Leander* = Glad to be in your command. Hope to help you avenge the loss of *Helena* and *Strong*.' This message was passed and receipted as *Leander* slewed into the gap opened up for her between *Honolulu* and *St Louis*, while Desron 21's destroyers, *Nicholas* (McInerney, Capt D), *O'Bannon*, *Taylor*, *Radford*, *Jenkins*, screened ahead and abeam for the remainder of the day and all night; everyone at 1st Degree stations as the task group patrolled across and north of Kula Gulf to cover another landing of Marines and their equipment at Rice Anchorage, then retired to Tulagi for fuel before resuming the northern vigil.

Five hundred miles north-west of Tulagi, native agents at Rabaul had reported Rear Admiral Shungi Izaki's light cruiser *Jintsu* and the destroyers *Mikazuki, Hamakaze, Yukikaze, Ayanami, Yugure*, leaving harbour as escort for 1,200 troops seen boarding the destroyer-transports *Yunagi, Amatsukaze, Satsuki,* and *Minasuki*. Shortly after leaving Tulagi, Ainsworth's Task Group 36.1 was joined by six additional destroyers, this now creating a powerful strike force driving toward New Georgia under a rising three-quarter moon – *Nicholas, Taylor, Buchanan, Woodworth, Jenkins, Maury*, three miles ahead of *Honolulu, Leander, St Louis*, in line astern disposed a thousand yards apart, then three miles back to the US 12th Destroyer Squadron , 'Desron 12', *Ralph Talbot* (Capt T.J. Ryan, Flag), *O'Bannon, Radford, Smith, Gwin*. The stage was set and at something like 62 miles an hour the opposing warships closed.

Previous Japanese 'Expresses' were handicapped through lack of radar, but Izaki's cruiser *Jintsu* had recently mounted an electronic device capable of detecting the American radar transmissions at twice *their* effective detection range and, now able to accurately record their direction, Izaki was well aware of his opponents' presence as the distance decreased. Then having detached his destroyer-transports to Kolombangara's west coast Sandfly Harbour, he steered unhampered towards Ainsworth's task group, with *Mikazuki* ahead of *Jintsu* and the other four following close astern.

On board *Leander* there'd been an aura of apprehension-tinged elation, intensifying as the long line of destroyers and cruisers sped up the dimly moonlit Slot, San Cristobal's peaks sombre and darkening in the distance to starboard. Tungi Brewis on his way from B-turret to the galley for a fanny of ki, paused to chat with Petty Officer McPike and Able Seaman George Dryland, and quipped: 'Tonight's the night, George, I bet we meet the Tokyo Express.' Dryland and McPike had been discussing just that probability and George's answer seemed strange: 'Yes Tungi, I feel you're right. Quite a few of us won't be on board *Leander* tomorrow.' Matter-of-fact remark, almost psychic as Tungi left the pair to their forebodings.

Some weeks earlier Cliff Dawe's action station had been changed from the 6″ T/S to SI twin 4″ A/A mount, just forward of the starboard seaboat between S1 and S2, and sited above the huge boiler-room air intakes. Directly across-ship were P1 and P2, and now instead of being deep in the ship's bowels breathing foul air when in action, Cliff would be topside inhaling ozone while allocated a ringside view of whatever might eventuate.

It had long been Commander Roskill's directive that men be given alternate action stations to ensure everyone became familiar with departmental parts-of-ship; and right now Lieut (E) Lee-Richards in charge of C boiler-room electrical repair party, had sent Ldg Stoker Brian Boate from the after engine-room to A boiler-room to take over from Ldg Stoker Des Price who was well acquainted with all of *Leander's* power-control electric systems. Des had joined from Palmerston North in August 1938, and after six month's *Philomel* training he was drafted to *Leander* on 4 March 1939. He did a pre-war trip to Sydney, then the Middle East and Mediterranean operations, and now as *Leander* sped astern of *Honolulu* towards Kula Gulf he was reporting by phone to Lee-Richards that he'd assumed Boate's after engine-room duties.

Captain Mansergh ordered his ship to 1st Degree readiness; Divisional Officers reported their particular weapons and communication systems functional. First Aid and Damage Control parties were in their years-re-hearsed stations about the lower decks, and in his 2nd W/T Office off the Stokers' Messdeck PO Tel Jim Craies was telling his operators, some of them boys of sixteen and seventeen to: 'Pack up that card game. It's time to get your act together.' Jim replaced the phone through which he'd been told *Nicolas* in the van screen had reported the enemy on radar: 'distance eight miles, estimated speed thirty knots'.

Over a bridge loudspeaker in broad American, Ainsworth was heard ordering the forward screen to attack by torpedoes. A glance at a clock showed six minutes after 1 a.m. and the destroyers were already turning to starboard to close the range. At 0107 with *Honolulu* giving the range as 10,000 yards, Ainsworth quietly ordered his cruisers to 'Open fire when on your target'.

Gun flashes and rolling thunder from the cruisers' combined thirty-eight 6″ created a holocaust of man-made destruction; great sheets of flame illuminated billowing smoke; seconds for gun-ready lights to glow ... the gun-triggered *ting-ting* ... more short seconds ... then another shuddering 'WHHOOOMMPHH' with *Leander* heeling against her eight-gun salvo, another, and another, until one no longer distinguished her loading pause from *Honolulu's* and *St Louis'* fifteen-gun ripple-firing. Unnoticed in the height of battle, four torpedoes streaked from *Leander's* starboard tubes. It was 0112 and *Honolulu* had ordered the cruisers to 'Turn left one one degrees', slightly south of west to clear the range for Ryan's destroyers' torpedoes. Chief GI Harold Firth aloft in the DCT had focused his range-finder on *Jintsu's* searchlight. So had the other cruisers and within moments it went out under a deluge of bursting shells. Still the firing continued. Cliff Dawe's S1 4″ guns had lobbed starshells over the enemy cruiser; he'd seen her searchlight play on *Honolulu* then almost instantly extinguish, blown to eternity in the cataclysm of converging shells; he saw enemy gun-flashes then a low trajectory of approaching balls of white light, disappearing as their flight ended short.

At about 0120 Ainsworth ordered his force to turn right 180 degrees. His voice came loud and clear over the TBS on *Leander's* bridge. Captain Mansergh awaited the 'Execute' signal. Seconds elapsed and he was still waiting.

'BRIDGE! SHIP DEAD AHEAD! IT'S *HONOLULU* SIRRR!'

'HARD TO PORT, PILOT!'

'ALL GUNS CHECK CHECK CHECK!'

Orders came thick and fast as *Leander* helmed dramatically to avoid colliding. She was now following *St Louis* with *Honolulu* ploughing across their bows and coming in astern. By a million to one mischance *Honolulu's* VHF 'Execute' had been screened by her funnels or upperworks and *Leander* didn't receive it. Nor did *Ralph Talbot* two ships in line astern, throwing the rear destroyers into a frenzy as they zigged and zagged all over the ocean, sirens whooping in the dark to avoid each other.

Cliff and his gun-crew mates had just recovered from the ship's erratic contortions when a booming explosion staggered them against projections. Hit port-side *Leander* heaved upward then sagged; upperworks and foremast momentarily illuminated as she lost speed while rolling back to port, an upheaved torrent raging aft to sweep men from their torpedo mount and cataract them overboard off the quarterdeck. Wounded in both legs, Commander Roskill was saved by seventeen-year-old Seaman Boy Mervyn Kelly's rugby-style tackle from being swept over the side, and although he too was badly injured he continued as the Commander's messenger, neither of them reporting their injuries as the Mamba went into the worst-affected areas checking that everything possible was being done by those in charge.

A lookout after-end of the bridge had been peering through gun smoke, subconsciously comforted by that sound of power coming up A boiler-room air intake. Suddenly a crashing blast hurled heat and steam up the intake, a moment of agonised screams then silence. Cliff Dawe and the starboard A/A gun-crews heard those terrible screams, but not so some of the port-side crew immediately above the impact who were hurled outboard.

Des Price at his electrical repair station in the after engine-room, had been watching an ERA whirling the big polished-steel throttle-wheel as Captain Mansergh ordered those drastic revolution changes to avoid *Honolulu*. Des knew they were hotly engaging an enemy, was wondering how things were progressing with all that gunfire, then grabbed for support when the torpedo struck. Quickly the ship regained an even keel but everything went deathly quiet, pitch black below apart from the beam from his torch as he wormed along a narrow starboard tunnel, unclipping dogs to go through the Breaker Room door, then reclipping it shut before resetting switches giving power to stand-by pumps and emergency lighting in B boiler-room. He had no idea what had happened, made his way in the dark to C boiler-room and found that it was virtually intact, there learning that B boiler-room had been evacuated as its lights had again failed and it was beginning to flood. By now Chief ERA Maurice Buckley had found the bulkhead seams between A and B rooms opened by the explosion – A boiler-room wide open to the sea through a 600 sq-ft chasm in Leander's port side, and B boiler-room in danger of inundating if the weakened bulkhead seams collapsed. Des having restored emergency lighting and reactivated the emergency pumps, now joined volunteers stuffing hammocks into cracks and holes until gradually B room's deck plates emerged and the water level continued to fall.

Volunteering to go to B boiler-room Harry Hutton and Jack Halliday arrived to find it partially flooded, and immediately helped Chief ERA Maurice Buckley who was directing the shoring up of its bulkhead, sledge-hammering timber baulks into place to be wedged secure by shipwrights and stokers. At one period when some idiot passed the word down that Japanese destroyers were approaching for the kill, they almost gave up, but another message said the approaching ships had identified themselves as Radford and Jenkins, detailed by COMDESRON 12 to stand by the crippled New Zealand cruiser. Meantime department after department was reporting its situation to the bridge. Chief Tel Chas Rosbrook had restored power to his Main W/T equipment, checked that although the 2nd W/T Office was wrecked the 3rd W/T Office and RCO were functioning, then, having a direct line to the bridge, rang to say Leander again had a voice and ears. The main switchboard room was flooded, as were the forward dynamo room, low-power room, and the 6″ gunnery control room computer, so turret captains got word through by sound-powered phones that they were in local control. Five fuel tanks were wrecked and two salt-water contaminated; but the Mamba's years of irksome damage control evolutions were now producing results and Leander was responding.

PO TGI Charlie Patchett had been about to launch more torpedoes at identified Japanese destroyers, but each time conditions were right the van destroyers crossed his line of target; then he was struggling to his feet dazed, bruised, shaking his head to clear furious ringing in his ears; helping other torpedomen up where they'd been thrown against a bulkhead by the enemy torpedo's blast. The intense brilliance had temporarily blinded him, and it seemed an eternity before he saw the whole quadruple mount was wrenched several feet aft and dangling outboard. Where were the remainder of his torpedo crew? All but the two he'd been hurled against the wall with had disappeared in the explosion; so having established there was nothing to be

done at his port tubes, he organised his survivors and the starboard torpedomen into electrical repair parties under Chief EA Jones who, on learning
that Commissioned Electrician A. Barlow and his staff were killed in the
main switchboard room, assumed responsibility for the ship's electrical
breakdowns and restored power where vitally essential.

Many compartments below the Stokers' Mess were still flooded; forward
turbo-generator room evacuated; port-side Stokers' Mess decking blasted
up to within two feet of the overhead, killing the Damage Control Party
stationed there. Mechanician Alex Simpson found Les Groves alive, in shock
and about to sink in a swirl of oil-covered water. He managed to prise his
fingers into Grove's mouth and nostrils to drag him clear, then somehow
got him up the ladder to a first aid team.

At midnight Stokers Harry Hutton, Les Gardiner and others of C boiler-
room's Middle Watch under Stoker PO Ray Wade and their watch chief,
Stoker PO 'Lofty' Hughes, had relieved their First Watch offsiders. It was
hot as they settled in for the anticipated four hours through to 0400; but at
0103 the bridge rang down for maximum power, and soon it was obvious
by the ship's excessive vibration and sudden listing accompanied by dull
thuds, that the course alterations and opening broadsides foretold a major
engagement. Tense moments each time the deck-plates canted and vibrated.
Boiler-room now a Devil's Orchestra of howling furnace sprayers and roaring forced-draft air-intake fans; stokers obeying their chief's hand signals to
flash more sprayers, sometimes to dowse them to regulate boiler pressure.
Then that horrific explosion which threw men off their feet, plunged all
compartments into darkness, and blasted A boiler-room out of existence.

Stokers were regaining their feet only to go sliding down the tilted plates,
grasping hand-holds as emergency lighting flickered on and off, seeing steam
pressure bottoming in the gauges. Lofty Hughes was looking for the Watch
Engineer, couldn't find him so assumed the task of getting the port and
starboard furnace sprayers flashed again. Pressure began to register but
steam was jetting dangerously out of distorted glands and ruptured overhead pipes. Arriving ERAs were being assisted by Harry and his mates to
cross-connect undamaged pressure pipes and give steam to the for'ard
engine-room. With water above their ankles men slid on oil-smeared plates,
struggled to manipulate sprayer cocks until first the starboard furnace
sprayers, then those portside were ignited and, although heavily salinated,
those tubes had to have feed water, any sort of water or they'd collapse.
Blow-down valves were opened at intervals to flush out mounting residue
and salt crust from the bottom drums, first one boiler then another as
against every warning in the Admiralty manual they were steaming with
salt-polluted water, getting those shafts turning – 2 knots – 3 – then after
an eternity of desperate nursing – 5.

In his 2nd W/T Office Jim Craies had been transmitting a message when the terrific thump impacted him across the room; all lights failed and it was evident the ship had been torpedoed. In the dim secondary lighting which flickered on and off, he opened the transmitter cage door and found the bulkhead bulging inward, transmitter wrecked, deck buckled upwards and outside the office the Stokers' Mess a shambles; stanchions distorted, lockers and tables smashed, decking buckled and fissured, squashing everything portside up toward the deckhead. You could look down through a gaping hole in the hull and see the gleam on oil and debris surging in and out of A boiler-room. Everywhere in *Leander*'s damaged areas control parties were extricating the ship's wounded, running communication and electric power cables, determining the extent of departmental damage. The thing that registered most was an atmosphere of calm in which men went about their work, so, back in his office Jim got a battery-powered receiver going, retained one operator then dispersed the rest to assist wherever required; but by 0153 some two feet of water and oil had risen and shorted out the batteries. They too abandoned the 2nd W/T Office.

Des Price spent hours with boiler-room staff isolating ruined fuel and steam pipes, breaking joints and cross-connecting to others beyond the ruptures, stuffing more bedding and overcoats into opened bulkhead seams until gushes became trickles, while power-restored pumps lowered the water level enough for B boiler-room's stokers to reflash furnace burners. Now with steam for 12 knots *Leander* began the long limp back towards Tulagi, making hard work of it, groaning and creaking as every wave washed right across-ship through the torpedo-devastated A boiler-room. At any moment it could break apart. B room's footplates lapped bilge water. It receded and rose as the pumps worked beyond expectation. Steam and scalding water jetted through gland packings. Water levels fluctuated in gauge glasses where they should have remained steady. The boilers primed and turbo-fans 'hunted' as stokers turned valve wheels, nursed pumps, fed the boilers saline-contaminated water with no other choice, upsetting all the laws of safe steaming. But with communication lines disrupted, and in semi-darkness, they did their utmost to give constant steam – two sprayers on each boiler, one on each, then three as they fought hour after anxious hour with the blow-down-valves open. And by dawn men were recalling incidents which would remain forever in their memory.

A-turret's crew had heard the order for broadsides, felt the concussion from their furious firing, and the tremendous impact of that Japanese torpedo which left their turret without power, the ship listing frighteningly, then deathly silence pervaded by a persistent blowing noise until secondary lighting revealed its source. It hadn't registered when every man was blowing up his Mae West in anticipation, but Leading Seaman Lake was still puffing steadily when Tungi burst out laughing and broke the tension: 'You won't get any air in that, Slash, you haven't unscrewed the tit.' Up in the RCO immediately under the bridge, early air attacks were being reported over the TBS in American drawl; three successive attempts all being repelled by the reporting ships' concentrated barrage and by Corsairs from nearby Russell Island airstrips.

On S1 gun-deck Cliff Dawe and his mates were welcoming the daybreak, enabling them to see and realise the ship's narrow escape from destruction. But were they out of danger? 'REPEL AIRCRAFT! AT THE DOUBLE! REPEL AIRCRAFT!' All available guns swung onto the distant approaching enemy. *Leander* was an easy target, uncontrollable black funnel-smoke and still listing as she surged slowly down the Slot. Layers and trainers were following directives through their headphones, then, 'CHECK CHECK CHECK!' The aircraft now flashing low overhead had been identified friendly, Corsair pilots giving the 'Thumbs up' greeting, engines droning power as they circled low around *Leander* and her escort *Radford*. But Captain Mansergh had been contacted by *Ralph Talbot*'s Captain Ryan miles back, with *Maury* covering the crippled *Gwin*; there were dogfights nearby against intruders so *Leander*'s umbrella was directed there to assist; and at this juncture *Radford* was interrupting to say: 'I've got me a good submarine contact, *Leander*. I'll drop a couple here and see if I can improve it any.' He dropped them there and no further contact was made.

Down in damaged boiler-room and compartments' dimly lit entangle-ment of hanging wires, gaping ends of twisted fuel and steam pipes, Commander Roskill heard Padre Claude Webster encouraging tired men with whom he'd toiled right throughout the night, sometimes knee or waist deep in swirling water and oil fuel, retching from the acrid stench while rescuing injured crew, or reaching into hazardous corners inundated with each inrush of sea as the ship swayed, struggling to maintain handgrips on bodies and torsos they were trying to recover. Des Price felt something slide across his face, shone his torch up to see a man's entrails hanging from the mess of distorted wiring. This was no time to be squeamish. In every damaged area visited the Mamba recorded similar feats of endurance and bravery, hour after long night hour through which men slaved, at first with that desperate instinct for survival, then when it became evident the ship could be saved, a team effort to overcome those tremendous odds. And among those later awarded for bravery were the youngest Sick Berth Attendant Norman Craven from Whangarei, who toiled ceaselessly night and day in dangerous situations, expertly preparing wounded men for removal to First Aid Centres and Sick Bay; Chief ERA Maurice Buckley who toiled below without respite until led away to rest before going down again; and many others including Commander Roskill and his messenger

Merv Kelly, both eventually collapsing through loss of blood and being escorted, unaware of the extent of their injuries, to the care of Surgeon Lieutenant Commander McPhail.

When passing the wrecked port 4" gun-deck shortly after daybreak Tungi learned that George Dryland's eerie prediction had come true, George being among those lost overboard. He then stopped to talk with Benny Qio, a tall, muscular Fijian whose cheeks were streaming tears, and knowing the language Tungi asked: '*Ko sa bula, Peni?*' ('Are you alright, Benny?')

'*On sa bula venaka Tungi, na ka sara ko Savu sa matei ko Timo sa sali.*' ('I am well, Tungi, but Savu is dead and Timo is lost.')

Seriously injured when a steel ladder fell on him during the explosion, Savu died hours later in the Sick Bay, and Timu was hurled overboard in the same blast. But by mid-forenoon *Leander* was gaining more headway and, as B room's stokers and ERAs coaxed increased power, its boilers priming and being blown-down frequently to avert dangerously built-up density, its evaporators producing reasonably distilled water, and its feed-tanks being allowed to overflow continuously, revolutions for 12 knots were provided and various departments began to get themselves reorganised. There were identified dead to be prepared for sea-burial, and because a badly infected hand prevented the Sailmaker using his leather-palm and needles, *Leander*'s bosun Mr Papworth asked Tungi to take on the unhappy task, each body being sewn into his hammock with a 6" projectile weighted at the feet, then carried ceremoniously onto the still-listing quarterdeck to be laid in rows awaiting burial.

Now in brilliant sunshine, bare-headed men in overalls and all manner of battledress mustered aft to stand in silent tribute. Body after body was lifted onto a low-framed stretcher, an ensign was draped over it, and it was carried to the port-side rail where Padre Webster read the Naval Service; a rifle-guard volley rang out and as the stretcher was upended its cocooned body slid feet first into the sea – a moving ceremony with Claude Webster in his breeze-ruffled robes, quarterdeck covered by men in last night's motley battle garb, and the Mamba in khaki overalls rolled up to his knees with his legs bandaged, looking more like a Kiwi gunner than an aristocratic Commander, standing capless near the Padre in mute harmony with the ship's company until the last man so far identified went to his watery grave.

Meantime Captain Mansergh was concentrating on *Leander*'s preservation; he could have more revolutions but B boiler-room was still off line, volunteers down there were restarting pumps as the water level rose, and another problem had arisen. As each quarter-sea lifted her stern ominous crunchings and groanings grew louder; the ship could break apart across A boiler-room's immense rupture, so haste had to be sacrificed for caution. *Leander* had to be nursed hour by hour, mile by mile throughout that night and day of uncertainty, with Captain Mansergh being informed about the state of his ship's side after each unusual lurch. Not many knew this dangerous situation and it wasn't made public; men remained at their air defence and surface action stations, under escort by *Radford, Jenkins*, and later for some hours by *Taylor* until she was recalled to Desron 12 by Captain Ryan whose flagship *Ralph Talbot*, and *Maury*, remained in the distant vicinity all the way to Tulagi.

And en route it was learned over the TBS that at the height of the action torpedoes were seen everywhere, three passing close ahead of *Honolulu*, one under her bows and two just clearing her stern. Another struck *St Louis'* port bow, slowing her to eight knots and putting her out of the fight, minutes before Ainsworth turned *Honolulu* and had thirty feet of her bows blasted away, leaving the steel foc'sle folded down over her exposed interior. Then as he urged her round to avoid *Gwin*, his flagship was hit in the stern by yet another torpedo which fortunately didn't explode.

These successful attacks were made throughout by *Yugure, Ayanami, Hamakaze*, and *Yukikaze* who in all fired thirty-two 'Long Lance' missiles before withdrawing north-west in search of *Jintsu*, but unable to find her they sped back to Rabaul. *Gwin* also had been torpedoed, jamming her rudder, wrecking her propellers and setting her afire aft. Then while in that night's confusion the US destroyers screened their damaged cruisers, *Buchanan* in manoeuvring to take *Gwin* in tow collided with *Woodworth*, damaging one of her propellers, flooding an after compartment and to make matters worse, shaking a depth charge overboard, this exploding near *Buchanan* and giving her flood-control party a lot of overtime.

Leander perhaps was the last of Rear Admiral Ainsworth's battered task force back through Tulagi's boom, drifting to her anchorage in the early evening accompanied by a motor boat striving to come alongside, someone in the sternsheets shouting that he wished to come aboard; and no sooner had the port jumping-ladder uncoiled on its way down, when that someone ascended nimbly and clambered over the rail while announcing himself to an inquiringly amused quarterdeck officer: 'Good evening, sir, I'm Baddeley RNZNVR Chaplain and Bishop of Melanesia. Glad you made it. I've been kept informed by the American Navy Base Secretary. Could I speak to your Chaplain?' Within minutes their further discussions were interrupted by Claude Webster's arrival, and the job of securing ship for the night proceeded while the two clerics went below to work out their ongoing funeral programme.

Cable parties, seaboat's crew, the blacksmith and duty foc'sle men, were piped for under a moon so bright that colours as well as shapes stood out clear. So clear that after *Leander* had been moored, a service conducted by the two chaplains for the ship's dead and missing needed no artificial lighting, nor for Captain Mansergh when he angled a list of those so far identified to the moon's illumination and read out their names. Only now after this solemn and moving rite was *Leander* piped down; Tulagi was still well within the active war zone, but right now an atmosphere of security lulled the task force's weary men; those on US cruisers and destroyers being asleep the moment they hit their bunks; and the instant *Leander*'s Kiwis and Imperials dropped onto hastily laid out hammock-bedding on the still canted deck, they too were in the arms of Morpheus.

Honolulu and *St Louis*, torpedoed for'ard away from their boiler-rooms and able to steam at a reasonable speed, had arrived several hours earlier; but next morning when Ainsworth advised *Leander* to move closer inshore there was another problem – no steam on the capstan motor. 'Volunteers to man the capstan muster on the foc'sle' had men making their way there, some manhandling long steel-capped spars up from the Capstan Flat stowage and slotting them into square sockets around the capstan head. Then with six men to each of the eight spars, the order was given and forty-eight men laid their weight in treadmill fashion. But little progress ensued in that tropical humidity until the Marine Band arrived and struck up one of Britannia's sea shanties. What a difference! Sagging backs straightened, stamping feet matched the drum-beat tempo, and *Leander*'s cable rattled up through the hawse, along its foc'sle plate, and down noisily through its vertical steel tube into the cable locker, as revitalised men on the rotating spars almost jogged to the lilt of those near-forgotten shanties.

Captain Mansergh steamed his ship gently up to a signalled standing cable, then as soon as the mudhook broke bottom he manoeuvred out of the fairway to another anchorage only a Coston-gun-line from the tree-lined shore, there when hawsers were transferred and secured to large tree-trunks, being winched parallel to the bank, with kedges out seaward from the foc'sle and stern. Finally an endless line was rigged through pulleys ship-to-shore from the sea-gangway, and those with business ashore could pull the tethered dinghy hand over hand there and back.

Some of the more seriously wounded were transferred by power boats to Tulagi Base Hospital, as were more identified bodies and remains to be given a ceremonial burial conducted by the Bishop of Melanesia, Padre Webster, and a twelve-man firing party. And those men interred in that recently formed military cemetery went to their eternal rest alongside hundreds of Allied servicemen, whose wooden crosses already occupied much of the consecrated flatland bulldozed out of the hilly tropical forest. Once back onboard, funeral party men returned their gear and dressed for whatever lay ahead; a large American barge had sidled alongside to deliver hundreds of yards of sand, metal mix, and an enormous concrete mixer to be set up forward of the torpedo tubes where men in swim-shorts worked day and night shifts, sending concrete down hoists to B boiler-room for a massive support across the weakened bulkhead. When this was completed, timber formwork and reinforcing iron was erected and filled with reinforced concrete across the top of the hole in Leander's side. Meanwhile technicians were repairing electrical equipment and circuitry, also the after generators which had blown last night and cut all power just as Leander was negotiating Tulagi's boom gates. The port torpedo tubes were craned back inboard after one unfired missile was defused and carefully withdrawn, W/T receivers and transmitters in all offices except the wrecked 2nd Office were repaired and tested, and the shambles which had been P1 and P2 A/A gun mounts were cleared away by O/As and gunnery rates.

Eventually after isolating ruined steam pipes and cross-feeding those able to withstand pressure, it seemed there was nothing else to be achieved in Tulagi. Repair parties came topside for a well-earned rest, and the first rostered shift went below to the eeriness of silence except for the sound of water dripping from a leaking gland, the muted whirr of a bilge pump, and an oil pump running at minimum revs. But now with watchkeepers at their regular stations one of the forced-draught fans started at slow speed, increasing as the oil-fuel heater brought the temperature up towards its 200-degree fahrenheit flash point. A wad of fuel-saturated waste was ignited and inserted on a long poker into the combustion tube while the manifold valve was opened, and at last a low-key start-up cycle was done per the book, requiring gradual heating of furnace firebricks in harmony with slow expansion of the steel boiler and furnace walling. Steam again hissed from aircocks, also from superheat drain-valves being closed as the pressure reached 5lb/sq''; then when the gauge registered working pressure the lighting-up atomiser was activated in the Normal Unit and B boiler-room's tempo changed dramatically. Those whispering fans were now roaring; the atomiser was bellowing like a giant blow torch; the feed-water pump was screaming at its 5,000 revs; and each stoker atop a boiler to set its safety valve to blow off at 9psi, came down from his essential but unpopular 150 degree fahrenheit job almost dehydrated. The Watch Chief was opening steam and hot water supply valves to bathrooms, ship's company and officers' galleys, and so far there'd been no hiccups. This was reported to the bridge and at Captain Mansergh's request for main engine steam, its stop-valve was opened and, when the second forced-draught fan was activated, one had to experience a boiler-room's overall crescendo to understand why stokers called it the 'Devil's Orchestra'.

Two hours had elapsed since B room's light-up procedure – 48,000 of the ship's 72,000 horsepower was now available. Rear Admiral Ainsworth after saying the usual goodbyes sent Radford along as escort to Espiritu Santos; but before nightfall there were doubts about making Auckland in one piece; those ominous hull groans persisted with each lifting of the bows or stern, and each time *Leander* corkscrewed on a quarter wave the bangs and grinds intensified. In Santo advice was given by American naval engineers, railway tracks were welded to decking above the damaged area, then on Sunday, 25 July ships at anchor cheered *Leander* downstream, past *Australia* whose band had mustered aft to play 'Will ye no come back again' which had the ship's Scots unpocketing handkerchiefs and supposedly wiping their noses: and also many of her Imperials and Kiwis. For a final salute as *Leander* negotiated the opened boom, a flight of RNZAF Wildcats swept low overhead and up in a 'Prince of Wales feathers' display, then plummeted in two single lines to scream down either beam at zero altitude. They were gone as abruptly as they appeared, Santos' forested hills reflected astern on a sun-glazed Pacific mirroring the cloudless deep blue sky, and within hours there was nothing left in the world except *Leander* and her escort *Radford*.

But late that night a soothing breeze drifted over, followed in the Middle Watch by a moderate easterly gradually rising at daybreak to a steady Force–3 which continued to develop. Whitecaps slapped the ship's side and threw warm spray inboard, cumulo-nimbus advanced from the east to cause anxious discussions between Captain Mansergh, the Met Officer and Navi. By mid-afternoon *Leander* groaned and squealed as her ruptures agonised in a Force–6 blow, while *Radford* exposed her red-leaded buttocks atop spume-blown hillocks then hid except for her mast-tops in their troughs several cables upwind. Although she was making hard work of it, *Leander*'s ship's company was comforted in knowing they had a 2,500-ton lifeboat at hand if needed. Her W/T operators were now copying ZLO Waiouru transmissions, among which a priority message for Captain Mansergh warned of a deep low developing near the Kermadecs. However, the Met Officer and Navi had been studying its eastward movement and, in changing course had already skirted its worst threat; but rivets were being sprung in the distorting plates, wild seas were surging in through the chasm in A boiler-room's side, then out as she rolled with that constant *bang*, *bang*, *bang* of her ruptured hull; right down past the Three Kings, down New Zealand's north-east coast, past Bream Head and into Hauraki Gulf.

Home! Had it been mere months since the ship left Auckland with her damaged fuel tank reinforced with concrete? It seemed an eternity and here she was, returning now with recently poured concrete reinforcing her boiler-room bulkheads; everyone topside at 2300 that Thursday night, 29 July, Rangitoto's moonlit silhouette to port, barely visible dim lights sparse about Cheltenham and Takapuna to starboard. The outline of North Head, then essential navigation lights about Waitemata Harbour, especially those appearing on the last Devonport to Auckland ferry when *Leander*'s propellers thrashed madly astern to avoid the now brilliantly illuminated *Makora* whose siren whooped stark alarm. The collision was narrowly averted, *Leander* idled slowly to an anchorage off Western Wharf's oil tanks, and as it was near midnight Captain Mansergh closed his ship down for the night. No leave.

Next morning men massed along guardrails and about the upperworks to see Auckland awakening, until after an early breakfast when the tugs *Te Awhina* and *William C Daldy* nursed *Leander* across harbour and directly into Calliope Dock, much to the surprise of ferry commuters who'd crowded to one side while pointing excitedly at the gaping hole in the cruiser's hull.

Identified bodies and unidentifiable remains were still to be recovered from A boiler-room before dockyard workers agreed to go below. The grisly task was beyond most men, and when one stoker couldn't stick it after several hours Harry Hutton took his place, later being roundly admonished by Cmdr (E) Clayton Green for his unauthorised initiative. Eventually the last of those human remains were brought topside in bags for burial. Four Auckland Bus Company buses arrived for *Leander*'s mourners, pall bearers and firing party; then at West Auckland's Waikumete Cemetery, where even now each Anzac Day ageing ex-*Leanders* muster for a service at the 'Unknown *Leander* Sailors' graveside, those earthly remains were committed to the grave.

Month superseded month until October 1943 when *Leander*'s Gulf Trials indicated that she could be released from Dockyard responsibility. Captain Mansergh had departed for a promotion appointment back in the Royal Navy and Acting Captain Roskill shifted permanently into his cabin with the 'Acting' appendage dropped. It so happened that the Bishop of Melanesia, the Rt Rev. W. H. Baddeley DSO MC, Honorary Chaplain RNZNVR, was visiting Auckland, so our Senior Naval Chaplain George Trevor Robson OBE MC RNZN invited him to consecrate the memorial tablet honouring *Leander*'s 'Killed in her New Zealand Naval war service' about to be dedicated into St Christopher's Base Chapel. Padre Webster on returning to the ship partly recuperated from chronic yellow jaundice, prepared the service which packed the chapel on Wednesday, 3 November 1943; he also chose the Lesson read by Captain Roskill; then the wives and families of those commemorated were invited aboard *Leander* for tea, during which Claude Webster took his Captain and the Bishop from bereaved to bereaved to be introduced individually.

Leander's service in the New Zealand Division of the Royal Navy from 1937 to 1941, then in the Royal New Zealand Navy from 1941 to 1944 was coming to an end. She had rushed New Zealand troops to Fanning Island in 1939 to garrison the mid-Pacific cable station; she then searched our cold

Leander in dock, repairs not yet completed.

sub-Antarctic seas and islands for German vessels en route to their Fatherland; escorted the 2nd NZEF 1st and 2nd Echelons part way overseas; became Rear Admiral A.J.L. Murray DSO RN's Flagship of his Red Sea Force during which she sank an enemy submarine by gunfire and brought

Leander, December 1943, leaving Calliope Wharf, Devonport, Auckland, after temporary repairs for Boston Naval Dockyard.

down numerous enemy aircraft. She wore the rifling out of her A/A guns while operating actively in Red Sea and Mediterranean squadrons; captured enemy freighters and sank an Italian raider in the Indian Ocean; bombarded and left in ruins an oil-producing factory at Italian Somaliland's Cape Guadafui; helped HMAS *Canberra* drive *Admiral Scheer* from the Indian Ocean by eliminating the pocket battleship's store and fuel ships *Ketty Brovig* and *Koburg*. She escorted two-thirds of the Desert Army's material up through the Red Sea at a time when the 8th Army's survival depended on it; operated in Vice Admiral E.L.S. King's 15th CS 'Suicide Squadron' on the Lebanon coast where one night they entered Beirut Harbour and sank two Vichy destroyers at point-blank range; then became part escort for Cunningham's battle fleet containing the Italian Fleet while Operation Substance's supply convoy got through to replenish besieged Malta.

Then back in the Pacific War with Japan she toiled endlessly establishing NZ and US garrisons and airfields on Fiji, New Caledonia, the New Hebrides and the Solomons. Tiring constructionally, her war-torn and torpedoed body could do no more. She steamed her patched-up hull out of Auckland on Tuesday, 30 November 1943, bound via the Panama Canal to Boston for virtual reconstruction at a time when Navy Board Wellington had cruiser crews but no cruisers.

At Kolombangara the Japanese destroyers had once more demonstrated their night-fighting skills, and the tremendous advantage of their 'Long Lance' torpedo, a pre-war revolutionary innovation designed in Japan's torpedo school and kept secret right throughout the Second World War.

In 1933, Rear Admiral Kaneji Kishimoto and Captain Toshihide Asakuma of the Kure Torpedo Institute, perfected the oxygen-driven torpedo which outclassed those of all other seafaring nations.

Categorically this is apparent:

Country	Diameter (Inches)	Speed (Knots)	Range (Yards)	Warhead Charge (Pounds)
Japan	24	49	20,000	1,093
	24	36	36,600	1,093
USA	21	45	6,000	825
	21	35	10,000	825
Britain	21	46	5,750	784
	21	36	10,150	784

CHAPTER XVIII

New Zealand Cruisers Reorganised

To the north and east of New Zealand lies the world's largest tract of water, over which Polynesia's ancestors fled from the Inca chief Cari about 500 AD. According to Peruvian legend, the supreme god-man Kon Tiki provisioned balsa-log rafts and sail-drifted westward on a great oceanic river known today as the Humbolt Current; and it is said some of those rafts grounded on one of the Galapagos Islands where centuries later descendants of the survivors believed most of Kon Tiki's raft-fleet had disappeared westward in the grip of that relentless current and prevailing wind.

And there but for Thor Heyerdahl the legend may have remained among the mid-Pacific's stone statues hidden in jungle. Heyerdahl, a young Norwegian scientist who with his wife were the only whites on Nukuhiva in the Marquesas, was doing field research in the 1930s. He had gained the friendship of a venerated, leathery, centenarian chief, Tei Tetua, who said his ancestor Tiki had come by square-sailed rafts from a big land far beyond the eastern horizon, and that most of the men were white with beards, and ear lobes lengthened to their shoulders by weighty ornaments.

Thor Heyerdahl's research was interrupted by the Second World War during which he flew planes of Free Norway's Air Force in his country's Arctic wastelands; but his post-war reed-boat expeditions from Egypt to Morocco and Easter Island, then his balsa-log journies by drift-sail from Peru to Polynesia to prove Tei Tetua's belief, are well published.

Now steaming eastwards across Tei Tetua's ancestors' westward migration, HMNZS *Leander* in November 1943 was making for Bora Bora in the Society Group to refuel; she would then pass through the Tuamotu Archipelago onto some of which a few of Kon Tiki's rafts had been driven 1,400 years earlier; she would traverse an artificial waterway bisecting an isthmus over which men before Kon Tiki had trodden; then she would enter a warm-water current rivering north-eastward through the Atlantic to its cold reaches, where she would leave it for an American dockyard, there to be repaired and updated in consequence of the damage inflicted in the Solomon Islands by that Japanese 'Long Lance' torpedo.

But those repairs and RN/USN modernisation would use up a lot of

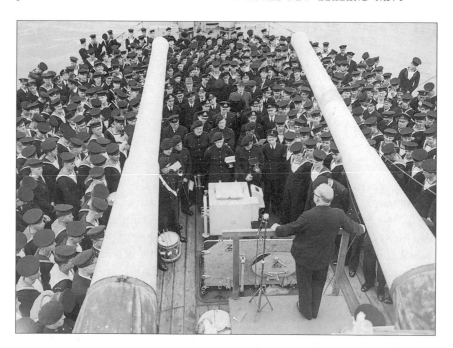

Hon W.J. Jordan, High Commissioner for NZ in UK addressing ship's company *Achilles* at Greenock, Scotland, 18 June 1944. Author is fourth left from Jordan.

war-time. And to exacerbate NZNB's dilemma, a catastrophic internal explosion in *Achilles'* double bottom mere weeks before she was about to be released back into service, now meant that she would spend more months in war-torn England's Portsmouth Dock. Add to this US Admiral Nimitz's declaration that our armed merchant cruiser *Monowai* no longer served a useful purpose in his strategy to defeat the Japanese Navy, and it can be seen that there was no longer reason to oppose British Ministry of Transport representations to Prime Minister Peter Fraser that *Monowai* would suit Britain admirably as a fast troop-transport. NZNB protests diminished, and on Saturday, 24 April 1943 the heavily armed liner departed Auckland for Bora Bora, the Panama Canal and Bermuda en route to Scotland for conversion. So, by mid-1943 New Zealand owned three 6″-gunned warships' experienced crews now rendered non-combatant; however, the Rt Hon Peter had an ace up his Prime Ministerial sleeve in the person of his Government's High Commissioner to England, the Rt Hon W.J. Jordan – known to Kiwis in London as 'Bill'.

Apart from being a fatherly pocket into which moneyless servicemen reached for the 'odd quid or three' to survive in the great metropolis, William Jordan constantly reviewed the standing of his country's military needs and here before him lay a naval problem requiring immediate attention. He must scout around for something more appropriate than naval barracks and naval schools to accommodate some 2,000 restless New Zealand matelots. Yes, what could be better for half of them than this almost brand-new Colony Class cruiser just returned from her initial fifteen months in the Atlantic and Indian Ocean war zones – soon to be in Liverpool ready for the asking?

By teleprinter on Wednesday, 30 June 1943 he informed his Prime Minister that *Gambia* was refitting and could be commissioned into the RNZN about September, concluding with details and recommendations which were to be the catalyst of innumerable pen-to-paper negotiations between NZNB, Government and Admiralty. But such were the verbal deviations and procrastinations among committees at the top and bottom of our globe, that it would be almost twelve months before agreement emerged that NZ Government would supply and maintain *Gambia* as from a.m. Monday, 8 May 1944, at which hour, day and date HMNZS *Leander* at Boston would revert to the Royal Navy.

NZNB understood and agreed the contract would be similar to those negotiated for previous loan cruisers; *Gambia* would remain under the control of Admiralty who anticipated her attachment to Admiral Sir James Somerville KCB KBE DSO RN's British Eastern Fleet, soon to be based at Trincomalee. They further anticipated her transfer to Rear Admiral E.J.P. Brind CB CBE RN's 4th Cruiser Squadron, pencilled-in to Admiral Sir Bruce Fraser GCB KBE RN's British Pacific Fleet, which would be serviced by a fleet train in the north-west Pacific south-east of Japan.

Meantime back in late November 1943 when traversing the south-east Pacific while those negotiations were being aired, *Leander* was enjoying a leisurely cruise toward Panama, through waters remote from the naval actions east and north of New Guinea. Where previously she'd been steaming about the tropical Western Pacific war zone at 16 to 28 knots dependent on urgency, this trip was being done at eleven to conserve fuel, so the ship's company relaxed. Some participated in afternoon sports and other activities; but many leaned on guardrails remarking on the abundance of albacore, bonito and dorado seen harassing schools of flying-fish into hundred-yard glides over the surface. Then at night under an overhead of glittering stars and the eastern aura of a yet unrisen moon, Middle Watch men paced the foc'sle for that cool breather before going below, perhaps contemplating the ship's phosphorescent wash, the unexpected phosphorescent scatter of flying-fish and cuttle-fish, ever hunted as their progenitors had been in the days of Kon Tiki and beyond.

As *Leander* neared the Galapagos Archipelago men rigged a canvas pool in readiness for King Neptune's visit, and two of the ship's complement enjoying the ceremony were the Padre and the Mamba, two big kids chasing the uninitiated and showing no mercy as they pinioned their arms, brought them before the 'Throne' for trial, then helped to administer the 'Royal Penalty' of lathered shaving and ritual dunking no matter what rate or rank. Three days later *Leander* turned north-west off Rey Island, undid knots through Panama Gulf, then idled slowly between Balboa and Panama seaports after embarking a canal pilot for the transit. Considered at its August 1914 opening to be man's most monumental achievement, the 50-mile long 10-mile wide plague-ridden swampland had been denuded of jungle and drained; oil was spread on every vestige of water to kill the death-dealing mosquitoes, after which three-hundred-thousand-million tons of clay and rock were blasted out of hills to align the waterway, and where this was impossible, locks were constructed to lift ships from Atlantic sea-level to the highest point before again lowering them to that of the Pacific, or reverse. So while Captain Roskill relaxed, leaving his ship's navigation to the Canal Pilot, Claude Webster gave an SRE insight to his flock about the Canal's overall history since inception.

There was liberty in Colon, a Munster-Monster's game of patience with the cards dealt over the naked body of a pretty senorita; his lack of interest as he lifted card after card from the cleavage downwards, then each end of the bolt through his neck flashing in the dimly-lit nightclub as he lifted the one covering her vital area. There were brawls initiated by anti-British Panamanians, P/O Tommy Gunderson's shore patrol intervening and shepherding the ship's intended victims to more peaceful night-life; then the early morning drift aboard for departure through the Caribbean Sea.

Because of U-boat operations on the American coast, *Leander* was afforded US destroyer escorts until clear of the Greater Antilles and Bahamas when she carried on alone, driving day by day north-eastward in the warm Gulf Stream's mid-70s fahrenheit air temperature, until east of snow-encrusted Boston. Men were still in tropical khaki shorts and shirts when Navi laid off a course due west. Some were asleep with punkalouvres directing cool air at their bedding; but as night temperatures fell they awakened shivering, closed the apertures and reached for a greatcoat to augment their blanket, later switched on both bars of wall heaters and still shivered. Within hours of leaving the Gulf Stream *Leander* struggled in cold rough seas, right throughout the Middle and Morning watches, all that day until she negotiated Boston's boom with icicles hanging from her guns, rigging and projections, stem shoving aside mini–ice packs, men in Arctic coats hosing ice off ropes and wires in preparation for berthing at sundown on Thursday, 23 December 1943.

Next day being Christmas Eve everyone played his part in decorating messdecks for Christmas Day, when officers and rates crammed the Rec Space to be led by Padre Webster in popular carols, and near midnight many were invited to the decorated Gun Room where he conducted a candle-lit Midnight Celebration. But Christmas Day might be better described in the actual words of Captain Roskill who wrote in his diary:

> On Christmas Day we managed, in spite of the cold, to hold a short service on deck; and then came the traditional naval ceremony of Captain's Mess Deck Rounds with the youngest members of the ship's company playing the parts of the Master at Arms, the Sergeant Major of Marines and so on. I had often told Claude of these time-honoured traditions which the war had forced us to put in cold storage, and he wanted particularly to see how the Navy celebrated Christmas in happier days. He had his wish and thoroughly enjoyed the numerous ceremonials, and the enormous Christmas dinner which followed. Claude then threw himself into the task of helping to make the men's stay at Boston as comfortable as possible.

His biography on Padre Webster continued with the many and varied entertainments this big raw-boned man of God arranged in US Service and Patriotic Organisations ashore; but as soon as the ship's company was issued with 'NEW ZEALAND' shoulder-flashes there was scant need for assistance. Liberty men were literally besieged on trams and buses, or on the snow-packed sidewalks as they looked in wonder at America's festival glitter in brilliantly lit shop windows, looked admiringly at pretty young women in colourful warm street-wear, red coats white fur trimmed at the neck, arms and knee-length hem, calf-length wool-lined red boots with white fur tops, red-riding hoods and ready smile. Men were invited by car to suburban houses, streets of them outlined at night with coloured lamps, roofs, pavements, lawns and trees, snow-covered in a White Christmas previously seen only on Christmas cards.

But the hands of a clock keep turning as do the pages of a calendar, 1943 became 1944 and all too quickly *Leander*'s ship's company thinned out. Men left weekly then almost daily to US-built Landing Craft (Infantry) awaiting crews to sail them to Britain on Lend/Lease Charter; among draftees being the ship's ex-Merchant Marine officers, Lieutenants R.T. (Subby) Hale RNZNR, J.A. Kirk RNZNR, J.R.P. Hopkins RNZNR, and Lt Cmdr F. St Peter Woodhouse RN who would be S/O of their LSI (Landing Ship Infantry) flotilla about to depart 24 January from Norfolk Shipyards en route for twenty-six days to Falmouth. Two weeks earlier Ldg Tel Arthur Stratford, Tels Mick Ryan, Willie Martin, Jimmy Boyland, Coders Tommy Sadler and John Nicholson had gone to Fargo Barracks Boston preparatory to barracks at Bethlehem-Hingham Shipyard, where the new destroyer-escort HMS *Tyler* awaited them; while several others, mostly Writers were drafted to the D/Es HMCS *Sprag* and HMS *Trollope*, and issued with pin-on tunic-breast badges displaying 'UNITED NATIONS SHIPS COMPANY'.

After working up in Casco Bay, Maine the three D/Es departed on Thursday, 17 February 1944 on a ten-day delivery to Londonderry in Northern Ireland where New Zealand communication rates in their crews were shipped to Glen Holt Naval Communications School, Devon, and seaman rates went to gunnery and torpedo schools about Southern England before being drafted to *Achilles*.

PO Tel Jim Craies was one of the fortunates who embarked on the mammoth liner *Queen Mary* at Manhattan Dock's Pier 9 for the Atlantic crossing. She had just disgorged a thousand RNZAF and RAAF recruits en route for Canada for training prior to entering the European air war, also several hundred psychiatric-case American GIs and Marines ex-Pacific. Now she was embarking 17,000 mid-West US troops who had yet to experience any form of water transport, and during the seven-day rough crossing via the North Atlantic's Arctic regions to Greenock they suffered continual seasickness.

It was now nearing the end of the Boston holiday for the majority still on *Leander*, and on Friday, 14 January we left by train to New York Central Station where a cavalcade of buses awaited our night arrival, with the disorganised bustle of wartime metropolis civilians, white-helmeted and gaitered US patrols with long truncheons strapped to their wrists, railway guards' whistles, shouting sergeants, Gunnery POs and distraught lieutenants, and the disorganised bustle of allied servicemen and women, breaking through haphazard queues of near 400 ex-Leanders filling bus after departing bus. Across a glittering Madison Square we saw Carnegie Hall bill-boarding current theatricals and other featured entertainments glimpsed and gone; then on to Pier 9 and alongside the old three-funnelled liner *Ile de France* for slow embarkation while Ldg Tel Syd (Andy) McGill talked to an American wharfie who was saying: 'Say, pally, rather you than me on that Froggie bucket, it's just come back from its second attempt to leave New York.'

'Why was that?'

'They had to put out thirty fires started all over her by those goddam pencil incendiaries. Sabotage pally, goddam sabotage.' There was more but impatient embarkees were urging Andy inside the covered gangway piercing *Ile de France*'s fourth deck down, as 11,000 raw US troops, hundreds of Commonwealth airmen and *Leander*'s big contingent went inboard, along or up her various gangways to be dispersed throughout her many decks – Andy, Chief Tel Chas Rosbrook and a few elite in cabins near to lifeboats, mine a saloon deck filled with corridors of three-tiered metal-tube bunks accommodating GIs loud-mouthing in Italian, Mexican, Negroid and even German accents about their goddam army.

Men clambered from their bunks at dawn to queue for the nearest heads

– 'Shake it up, Limey, I's about to mess mah goddam self' – queued for a bowl of brackish water to clean the teeth – 'Rous-rous thure sailor, uhre not t'only guy with goddam teeth' – queued down companionways three decks a shuffle at a time for two hours, to front up at stainless-steel serving counters near big oil-fired ranges and baking ovens for the first of each day's two meals – 'What in heil's this stuff?' from one GI to another.

'Horsemeat fellah, goddam bloody horsemeat.'

'Get it down youse guys, dere's guys queued to the arse of this goddam bucket waitin tuh eat for godsakes.'

The bits of conversation understood indicated that God had damned everything to do with Americans, even the horse meat, but those eternal queues allowed no time to be particular.

Ile de France smoked her way south-eastward in a long arc to Greenock, unaware she'd been the sitting target for a U-boat which launched a spread of Germany's latest electric-motor-driven torpedoes at her. No result. On return to Germany with one kept for investigation, it was found that the nickel-iron batteries were defective, otherwise *Ile de France* would have taken me among her 13,000 passengers to the bottom.

Greenock in late January displayed drab wet granite quays, wet cobble-stoned, narrow streets bisecting rows of drab wet stone houses with their doors opening directly onto narrow wet flagged footpaths. An ant trail of dispirited Kiwis lugged personal gear to the railway station, there to cram wartime carriages soon skirting the Clyde en route for Glasgow's Souchie-hall Street Station, where massive scones and mugs of steaming tea were handed out at Patriotic Society stalls. Khaki-clad Jocks, black-capped RN sailors and Wrens shouldering gas masks and carrying green 'pusser' suitcases mingled among white-capped ex-*Leanders*, but not a civilian boarded those bulging carriages for the non-stop run to Edinburgh.

Then that fast journey south enjoying the afternoon and evening country-side, the sleep-inducing whirr of wheels on rails, the sound of night air compressed against buildings as the Flying Scotsman flashed past station after station, men stepping over recumbent bodies to the 'Gents' then over them again on the way back, admiring the dimly illuminated curves of a strap-hanging Wren as the express swayed gently on long bends, trying to sleep among passengers with no room to lie or sit. Eventually London to change trains to Portsmouth barracks where an irate Jaunty was awakened to receive 400 Kiwis he didn't want to know about. He dumped us onto a gymnasium floor already partly hidden under new RN entries with dirty feet.

Next day the majority of New Zealanders were entered on *Achilles*' books, but she was still in dock being pushed and pulled into shape after an internal explosion which distorted her 4″ armour belt outward on 22 June

1943, so having deposited their kits and hammocks in allocated messdecks they were billeted ashore or sent to local naval schools for upgrading courses. At Glen Holt Signal School, a pre-war nudist camp appropriated by Admiralty, some became instructors and others learners. Then small drafts went on to HMS *Mercury*, the 12-mile-inland Leydene Castle surrounded by long dormitory and instruction Nissen huts. But one day in May after passing my Higher Standard exams, CPO Tel Stan Keeley, I and a South African Chief Tel were playing snooker when the Jaunty entered in search of a replacement for the Chief Tel on HMCS *Tadoussac*; and I was nearest to him. 'Follow me, Harker,' which I did to the Transport Office. 'Here's your meal coupons and train ticket to Falmouth. Grab your gear and get on that bus quick, it's waiting for you.'

'Thanks a lot, Master'.

The unfortunate S/O Minesweeping Flotilla Chief Tel had killed himself while working on the ship's transmitter, and as soon as I introduced myself to *Tadoussac*'s Captain he led his fleet of A/S sweepers out of Falmouth, and down Channel to continue working those rough waters off the Scilly Isles; day after day sweeping up mines dropped each night by German Heinkels and Dorniers; cutting them adrift and sinking them by Oerlikons; repairing sweep gear snagged on rocks and the remains of numerous wrecks; then going over the same ground daily from dawn to dusk.

On one occasion, the vintage First World War destroyer *Warwick* made her pendants while approaching ahead of lines of invasion ships surging into the Channel from the Irish Sea; and as we discussed them on *Tadoussac*'s bridge, *Warwick* jack-knifed midships. She momentarily displayed her broken red underbelly, then erupted in a ball of flame-lanced black and yellow smoke mushrooming as the shockwave rebounded off our upperworks.

There was dumbfounded silence among all spectators until it was broken by Skip's solitary 'GOOD CHRIST' in broad Canadian; then while his coded message was being transmitted to Lands End Naval W/T for Rear Admiral Southern Sweepers information, the convoy about-turned and fled.

Days later it reappeared en route England's south and east coast invasion ports; Skip sent for me and together we went through code and signal books, brought onboard last time in Falmouth for our imminent transfer to Normandy's heavily mined offshore waters. But the day before *Tadoussac* was to lead the flotilla east, my recall to *Achilles* arrived and Skip wished me well as we shook hands in his cabin.

Achilles was out of dock but far from ready to participate in any invasion, so men remained billeted ashore, those in Southsea's Overseas Club sitting night by night on a third-storey windowsill, watching Luftwaffe attempts to blanket-bomb Portsmouth off the map. The old building shook when near-miss bombs screeched down to blast back-street rows of houses; 'flaming onions' stood the whole area out in a garish orange glow, while the air trembled from continual A/A gunfire and the 'cuurrrmmmph' of near and distant explosions. Then one night I and my mates on the wide sill nearly fell out the window when a blinding yellow flash and an ear-numbing WHHOOOSSSHHH enveloped the whole of an expansive park immediately across the road. At dark the Army had moved in dozens of multi-tube rocket launchers, and when the unsynchronised German bomber engines sounded directly overhead they launched the whole damned lot as one. If they downed any of the raiders it wasn't known, men's eyes retained that all-engulfing flash and their ears sang for days.

Tree-bordered roads fanning miles out from Portsmouth were lined nose-to-tail either side with Allied tanks, armoured tracked vehicles, mobile guns with their ammunition limbers, diesel and petrol tankers, all khaki camouflaged with their crews eating and sleeping nearby. It wouldn't be long now.

However *Achilles* would not be part of the drama, her ship's company embarked in its entirety, then on D-Day minus two, Captain F.J. Butler MBE RN, who'd assumed command ten days previously, received orders to proceed to Greenock for refit completion. Seventeen of her officers were New Zealanders who'd already done war service, barely having time on the way north to become acquainted with their departmental responsibilities and various crew members, 90 per cent of whom were RNZN. *Achilles'* rudder motors weren't working nor were many other essentials, so Captain Butler and his 2i/c, Commander H.B.C. Holmes, relied on Radar Plot guidance as the ship threaded her way north at night, right through unseen convoys steaming south in the Irish Sea.

In almost every department, artificers and senior rates worked alongside dockyard specialists retained to complete their firms' contracts, even during *Achilles'* twenty-seven days in the Clyde, and in some cases from Tuesday, 4 July to Friday 4 August during her Scapa Flow completion and work-up. X-turret had been replaced by four quadruple pom-poms, two each side of the gun-deck; her single 4″ A/A guns were replaced by four twin 4″ dual-purpose HA/LA mounts; eighteen 20mm Oerlikons had been fitted wherever practicable and her original pom-poms were still in place. Instead of single-stick masts, she now had tripods bristling with dipoles, mesh antennae, and dishes for air and surface detection, and for her new radar control gunnery; all of which would be handled by the many strange faces recently instructed in these technologies. But *Achilles* still suffered from earlier actions and damage caused by the recent internal explosion, as her Gunnery Officer, Lt Cmdr Lewis King DSC RNZNVR recalled:

On the way north from Portsmouth I spent more time in overalls with Commander (E) and the Chief O/A trying to rectify a 14' (minute) turret training backlash and other gunnery problems, than I did in the Director. *Achilles* never really recovered, and for the war's last two years she went in and out of dock with A-bracket shaft and bearing troubles – Trincomalee – Bombay – Auckland – Manus twice – then again in Auckland.

Lewis King, who'd been decorated for gallantry and resourcefulness in destroyer operations, reflected the memories of every man involved in that 2 June 1944 'Do it yourself' Admiralty order to refit in the Clyde and the Orkney Isles. Lead-covered power and control leads dangled randomly from overhead channelling throughout the ship, and Chief Tels vied with Chief TGIs and EAs for ownership, cursing when bitten by live innocent-looking bare ends, working into Scapa Flow's after-midnight daylight, but eventually soldering or screwing home the last connection.

The ship's electronic and gunnery technology had been modernised to that era's Pacific War standards and, having missed the Normandy landings *Achilles* was to participate in the imminent 'Operation Dragoon' to be launched on France's Mediterranean coast. For this and for possible similar ship-to-shore and ship-to-aircraft operations, a powerful Type 87 VHF transmitter had been established in a compartment adjoining the Radar Plot directly below the bridge. I spent many day and night hours in Scapa connecting its unfinished wiring yet there hadn't been an opportunity to test it with aircraft, so on *Achilles'* way south after revisiting Greenock it was to be tried with Northern Ireland reconnaissance bombers. First attempt at daybreak, nothing. An anxious hour checking and rechecking circuit by circuit, meters reading correctly, then when it seemed something was irrevocably wrong, a flight-leader's voice answered loud and clear. His flight had just reached the ceiling for direct-line communication, and we in the tiny shack relaxed as *Achilles'* air-controlled bombardment would be assured for the troops who would be surging ashore.

But when leaving Greenock *Achilles* was already a day late. Assisted by heavy naval gunnery and air support on Tuesday, 15 August 1944, the American and De Gaullist forces under Lt Gen Alexander Patch had landed in the Cannes-Toulon area, four days before *Achilles* swept into Gibraltar Bay, and two and a half months after the opening phases of Normandy's 'Operation Overlord'. However there was still a need for troops in North Africa so *Achilles* eased alongside one of The Rock's stone wharves, embarked 300 Pongos and on 20 August proceeded under air cover to Algiers. No beer in the French-Saharan town; wine debauches and secretive ventures into the Casbah's out-of-bounds alleys; then pulsating headaches next morning as men queued to puke and moan in the heads.

Hereabouts *Achilles'* Signals Officer, having seen the wall-map of Europe I updated daily with pins and coloured string in the RCO, asked me to produce a several-page newspaper, which was done by inserting eight thin carbons between nine foolscap sheets and thumping hard on the Underwood. No matter whether ally or enemy, so long as a station was morsing news in English it got whacked on the keyboard to produce a legible ninth copy. Then one morning after a long night's dial search for news, I'd just gone to sleep in the darkened RCO, when some clumsy oaf stumbled over my low-framed camp stretcher to be told all about his lack of wedded parents. And that was where my string of invectives turned to mumbled apologies when Captain Butler thumbed the light switch.

'No, no, Harker, don't get up,' he said. 'If I wait for my cabin copy the bridge tells me all the latest news, and that's not good for a captain.' Thenceforth his copy was clipped just inside the RCO door, and he imparted up-to-the-hour happenings to the bridge's morning watch while I slept undisturbed.

On Wednesday, 23 August as the Allies were recapturing Paris and Marseilles, and as Rumania swapped jerseys to join the winning side, *Achilles* dropped anchor in Valetta Harbour for a three-day Malta stay. Now no screeching bombs blasting stone houses and their occupants. Now no wailing sirens, no fighter pilots scrambling for their Hurricanes to decimate wave upon wave of Axis bombers. Only empty berths. Only the rusting upperworks of merchantmen and destroyers protruding in mute testimony to their gallant end. *Achilles* gave them silent thought while passing down Grand Harbour; looked up at cratered buildings reaching in tiers from the shore to the ramparts' shattered skyline; made her pendants to the Tower when negotiating the moles; then piped cruising stations for the leg to Alexandria. Here too was the aftermath of war; the vibrance of hostilities had moved on to Italy and Southern Europe; buildings were in their first stage of repair, streets were void of laughing troops, and where were those men from Cunningham's Med Fleet who'd vied with soldiers for that flashing eye signal of a blonde, brunette, or red-haired Kit Kat cabaret hostess.

For *Achilles* now entering Suez Canal the war in Europe was an ending chapter. Over the page there would be new chapters involving the Indian Ocean from which Germany, Italy and Japan had been driven; then the north-west Pacific with its fanatical enemy yet to be overwhelmed. But US Admiral Ernest J. King who on Thursday, 26 March 1942 had been promoted Chief of Naval Operations in place of Admiral Harold R. Stark, was now C-in-C US Pacific Fleet, and he openly objected to HMS's presence in 'His' Pacific; didn't think his US Fleet Train should be required to service other than US warships; insisted that the Royal Navy would be better occupied in the eastern Indian Ocean and Dutch East Indies.

At this meeting presided over by Roosevelt, Churchill chewed his cigar to pulp throughout King's anti-British tirade. Then, biding his time until one could hear a pin drop, he rose to give the Admiral a lesson in Bulldog tenacity, reminded him in low rumbling glower about the unstinted aid afforded by Australia and New Zealand to US warships and convoys en route to the Solomons and north-west Pacific, referred likewise to Britain's Japanese-occupied possessions; then after inferring that neither the Japanese nor Admiral King would keep his Navy out of the Pacific War, he nodded to President Roosevelt and resumed his seat.

The President's admonishing look at his Commander-in-Chief forbade further USN discrimination, preparations went ahead throughout 1944 for a Sydney-based British and Dominion fleet of an estimated 400 ships, and *Achilles* having sweated a day and night in Aden departed Monday, 4 September 1944 on a four-day Arabian Sea crossing to Bombay, there effecting repairs to damage caused by a fire in B boiler-room on her way over.

On 13 September she entered Trincomalee to become a unit of Rear Admiral A.D. Reid RN's 4th Cruiser Squadron and anchored near *Gambia* who'd been part of C-in-C Admiral Sir James Somerville RN's Eastern Fleet since 19 January. And in *Achilles'* Signal Distributing Office there hung the list of ships under C-in-C EF:

Battleships & Battlecruisers		Carriers		Submarines
Queen Elizabeth (Flag)		*Illustrious* (R.A. Moody)		*Lucia* (Parent
Valiant				Ship) Various
Richelieu (Fr)		*Saratoga* (US)		of the P, R,
Renown B/C (V.A. Power)				S and T
				Classes
Cruisers		**Destroyers**		**Supply Ship**
Achilles (NZ)	*Ceylon*	*Dunlap* (US)		*Borodino*
Colombo	*Cumberland*	*Cummings* (US)		Many
Gambia (NZ)	*Kenya*	*Fanning* (US)		harbour
Newcastle (CS4)	*London*	*Napier* (Aus)		defence &
Nigeria	*Suffolk*	*Nepal* (Aus)		maintenance
Sussex	*Swiftsure*	*Nizam* (Aus)		ships.
Van Tromp (Dutch)		*Penn*		
		Quadrant	*Quality*	
		Queenborough	*Quiberon*	
		Quilliam	*Racehorse*	
		Rotheram	*Van Galen* (Dutch)	

Day by day the list changed as warships departed and new ones arrived to strengthen this nucleus of Britain's projected Pacific Fleet. *Gambia*'s months with the 4th CS ended on Monday, 16 October 1944, the day her telephone line to *Achilles* was disconnected at the dual anchorage near Borodino Creek, and she moved out to Farewell Buoy expecting a butterfly-on-the-hand from Rear Admiral Brind. Unfortunately Bula the big Fijian liberty-boat coxswain had rammed his loaded boat up a couple of the sea-gangway steps the previous night, the crushed grating and timbers hadn't been repaired so CS4 had to clamber up a jumping-ladder and over the guardrail, much to the chagrin of Captain N.J. William-Powlett and Commander Harper, who were endeavouring to placate their cruiser-squadron Admiral as he wavered on the quarterdeck facing them slightly out of breath.

Perhaps that was why *Achilles* also departed next day, but her lengthy defect list necessitated another nine days in Bombay's King George drydock. That Japanese bomb at Guadalcanal, a German one which nearmissed her and perceptibly lifted her on the chocks in dock at Portsmouth, then the internal explosion which killed numerous dockyard workers at mealbreak in the Stokers' Mess, hadn't done the ship's structure any favours; so her ship's company took in more sightseeing and a lot of Patriotic Society entertainment within India's widespread metropolis.

Back at Trinco there awaited 150 bags of New Zealand and United Kingdom scented letters; but hereabouts a tragedy affecting everyone built up to a climax. In late November *Achilles* was quarantined when men started queuing at the Sick Bay with painful carbuncles, especially USN P/O 2nd Class Radioman 'Smoky Joe' Gene Erwin who'd transferred from *Leander* as a liaison member. A golf-ball sized carbuncle on his upper lip crazed him for days, as did similar-sized malignant tumours about many other victims' sensitive regions. And Padre Claude Webster, who'd been taken to Trincomalee Naval Hospital died there of meningitis – a man amongst men, one who had toiled without respite at Tulagi getting the wounded and dead from *Leander*'s wrecked boiler-room, one whose manful dedication to God had won initially derisive men to his chapel, and now one whose neglect of self had finally left his large body unable to fight the ravages of this Eastern epidemic.

Notwithstanding these medical ailments, *Achilles* extracted congenial admonition from CS4 when he signalled from *Newcastle* during an A/A exercise: 'Will get my plane to tow an Ace of Spades for your gunners,' after they twice severed the drogue tow-wire. And later that day Lewis King's 6″ shoots stood up admirably in comparison to those of *Swiftsure*, *Newcastle*, and *Nigeria* in squadron exercises at sea with *Renown* and three destroyer flotillas, the last being a night encounter on Friday,

1 December after which Captain Butler got his orders to join the British Pacific Fleet.

As *Achilles* left the jungle-surrounded harbour *Kenya* flashed: 'Goodbye and good luck, Kiwis'. *Renown's* signal lamp rattled off: 'Remember us to NZ the next time you are there' and semaphore flags smacked against bunting tossers' legs on other ships to separate their words of farewell, while lamp shutters clacked in response to V/S-morsed adieus until beyond reading distance. Up Ceylon's north-east coast then down through Palk Strait and Mannar Gulf to Colombo, Jim Craies purchasing a beautifully crafted moonstone ring for his wife Ida while others purchased garnets, sapphire pendants, suspect diamonds set in Ceylon's soft-silver filigree for their dream girls; all these gifts being locked in ditty-boxes on 9 December when *Achilles*, *Whelp* and *Wager* sailed as escort for the two Woolworths, *Battler* and *Atheling*.

Twenty-four hours out, men came topside to find the force disposed about Rear Admiral Brind's flag-cruiser *Swiftsure*, in company with two more escort-carriers *Fencer*, *Striker*, and the destroyers *Kempenfelt* (Capt D4), *Wakeful* and *Wessex*. There were deductions and additions to the force on its 3,600-mile south-eastward leg to Fremantle; communication and A/A exercises with and against the carriers' aircraft; destroyers to be refuelled from the two cruisers; then on the 16th a series of V/S signals to the various S/Os to say *Swiftsure* and *Achilles* were detaching and proceeding independently at speed.

A brief interlude at Fremantle where trains were caught to Perth's assured hospitality. Swaying in *Swiftsure's* 25-knot wake across the Great Australian Bight's 2,300 miles, to arrive on Christmas Eve in Hobart for Yuletide and Tasmania's extended New Year celebrations. Then from Tuesday, 9 to Sunday, 14 January 1945, back across the Bight at 21 knots as escort for Australian troops and New Zealand's 14th Reinforcements aboard the fast transports *Empress of Scotland*, *General George M Randall*, and *General William Mitchell*, until off Cape Leeuwin where HMS *London* assumed responsibility, and a few more days were enjoyed renewing acquaintances among Perth's femininity.

It was while in Fremantle on 17 January that the big grain-carrier *Panamanian* caught fire across harbour from *Achilles*. Within hours dense smoke was hampering attempts to extinguish her smouldering cargo and the timbered wharf now set ablaze by the ship's intense heat. The submarine tender HMS *Maidstone* lying at the same wharf, whooped 'going astern' warnings as she drew clear with scorched sides near her torpedo storage. Fremantle's fire brigade had been haphazardly flooding *Panamanian* until she developed a 26-degree list and was in danger of capsizing; then *Achilles'* fire control parties boarded the burning freighter and, under

SS *Panamanian* on fire in Fremantle, 17 January 1945.
Extinguished by *Achilles'* fire control party.

Commander (E)'s directives fought their way to the heart of each fire, gradually gaining control as her list visibly lessened over the next two days, and when *Achilles* retrieved her men and gear before sailing at 0700 on 20 January, *Panamanian*'s fires were out and she sat even keeled on the bottom awaiting salvage.

Once more *Achilles* rolled heavily in the Bight's notorious groundswells, which at night had men tying the legs of their low metal-framed camp stretchers to fixtures for stability. In company with *Quickmatch* and *Quiberon* she was escorting Australia's new Governor General, HRH the Duke of Gloucester and his family to Sydney aboard the NZ Shipping Company's 16,576-ton liner *Rimutaka*.

RAAF reconnaissance bombers remained in the vicinity from dawn to dusk throughout the seven-day journey south around Tasmania and up the New South Wales coast. All manner of antics were executed by the destroyers for His Royal Highness's entertainment. Then in brilliant sunshine on Saturday, 27 January – with *Rimutaka* resplendent under the Duke's Flags, *Achilles'* ship's company at their entering harbour stations in khaki drill shorts and shirts, and the Royal Marine band playing high-spirited traditionals atop Y-turret – the liner followed by its royal escort in naval procession steamed proudly past C-in-C British Pacific Fleet, Admiral Sir Bruce Fraser, standing at attention on his flag-battleship *Howe*'s quarterdeck in sight of Sydney Harbour Bridge.

It seemed there was no war. The harbour was a moth-plague of white sails. Ships' horns howled a symphony of discordant salutations. RAAF aerobatics greeted the Duke and his family from above. And as *Rimutaka* sidled in to her banner-strewn berth, the queues of invited VIPs jostled apologetically for pre-eminence.

Although Sydney pulsed with excitement for O/A 'Aussie' Hawkins and the one or two other Australians in *Achilles'* complement, New Zealand lay just across 'the ditch' and the recent two-week shuttle service Fremantle to Hobart and back, hadn't ingratiated anyone to the armchair tactician who'd sent RAN warships to Wellington for the NZEF's 14th Reinforcements.

'Why not *Achilles*?' men angered, 'What sort of wet-eared nitwits have they got in bloody Navy Office?'

However, the exile ended on Friday, 2 February 1945 when *Achilles*, *Quadrant*, *Quality* and *Queenborough* trailed *Howe* out of Sydney's Port Jackson. It had been hot on crowded Bondi Beach, hot in the big city's crowded streets. And even though the temperature hadn't dropped crossing the Tasman, the seas had, but Sir Bruce Fraser's wide-beamed battleship showed no respect for Moana Kiwa's glistening swells, as it ploughed at speed straight through them with torn white-water foaming over her bows to be smashed against her quadruple 14″ A-turret. In revenge Kiwa grappled with the three destroyers whose propellers thrashed air on the crests of

HMS *Howe*, 1st Battle Squadron BPF, Flag Vice Admiral Rawlings, March 1945.

those mid-Pacific-originated swells, then wrestled them down to mast tip visibility.

Came that surge of innate nostalgia as *Achilles* passed between the Three Kings and Cape Maria van Diemen, before following *Howe* down Northland's East Coast. That mounting enthusiasm as Navi took sights on Bream Head, Mokohinau, and the Needles; Little Barrier looming midway between Cape Rodney and Great Barrier Island; Hauraki Gulf with *Achilles* almost listing to starboard as men pointed at Auckland's North Shore Bays passing in succession, then: 'Clear lower deck for entering harbour!' Many of Auckland's city-side public had gathered to welcome *Howe*, as *William C Daldy* and *Te Awhina* nuzzled the great Royal Navy battleship into her Prince's Wharf berth; but NOCA Commodore W.K.D. Dowding DSC RN had authorised a Dockyard 'open gate' for *Achilles*' Calliope Wharf arrival, and no sooner had the steel-shod brow clanged onto concrete than the Jaunty and Crusher joined that eager ship's company they'd intended to control. They too were swept into the mass of waiting wives and sweethearts by a torrent of carefree matelots each intent on being first ashore.

CHAPTER XIX

Gambia *in the Atlantic and the East Indies*

Gambia, C48, Pdts 48 Colony/Fiji Class Light Cruiser

As built

Displacement:	Designed, 8,000 tons. Wartime full load appx 10,000 tons
Dimensions:	555.5 ft overall. 62 ft beam. 16.5 ft draught
Power Plant:	Parsons geared turbines. 4 shafts. 80,000shp. 32.5 kts
Complement:	700 to 800. Eventual wartime approx 1,000
Armament:	12 × 6″(4 × 3). 8 × 4″(4 × 2). 10 × 2pdr (2 × 4; 2 × 1). 6 × 21″ torps (2 × 3). Depth-charges on quarterdeck. 3 Supermarine Walrus Amphibian A/C. 2 in port and starboard hangars. 1 on telescopic catapult.

BEFORE, DURING, AND AFTER the First World War, Royal Navy ships stationed about the British Empire policed the World's shipping routes; but fleet limits imposed in the 1922 Washington Naval Treaty saw many of Britain's capital ships and cruisers scrapped, and her uncompleted 16″-gunned battleships *Rodney* and *Nelson* redesigned to be only two-thirds of their intended 50,000 tons. Japan and lesser nations however were allocated additional tonnages to their declared naval building programmes.

Endeavouring to retain her international influence Britain hosted the 1931 London Naval Conference, and although Japan walked out of it on 15 January, subsequent political interchanges of views led to the London Naval Treaty circa 25 March 1936 whereat Britain, America, and France approved among other agenda a 35,000-ton limit on battleship displacement.

Italy refused to sign this agreement; Germany defied it by laying down the keels of her 45,000-tonners *Tirpitz* and *Bismarck*; and Japan prepared secretly to construct four 75,000-ton, nine 18.1″-gunned mammoths *Yamato, Musashi, Shinano,* and another on paper as 'No–111', yet to be named. Their shells would have a range of 35 miles and penetrate 16 inches of armour.

These signatory nation limits now introduced a flurry of designs intended to reap whatever benefits might remain – Germany's 10,000-ton, six × 11″-

334

gunned pocket battleships were theoretically counteracted by the RN's 10,000-ton, eight × 8″-gunned County Class cruisers, then when RN ordnance proved that an 8,000-ton cruiser's twelve × 6″ weapons could deliver 3 tons of HE per minute as against the County Class rate of 1 ton per minute, eleven of the smaller type were ordered under the title 'County Class'. They would be *Bermuda*, *Ceylon*, *Fiji*, *Gambia*, *Jamaica*, *Kenya*, *Mauritius*, *Newfoundland*, *Nigeria*, *Trinidad*, *Uganda*; and the alias 'Fiji Class' was appended in 1937 when *Fiji* was the first to be named and launched.

Swan Hunter of Wallsend-on-Tyne won the contract for *Gambia* and the blocks on which her keel would be laid were aligned on Monday, 24 July 1939. She was named and launched by Lady Hilbery on a bleak Saturday, 30 November 1940; then accepted into the Royal Navy in late February 1942 after sea trials conducted by her first commanding officer, Captain M. J. Mansergh DSC (First World War) RN. *Gambia*'s 2i/c, a surly three-ringer reminiscent of the days of sail and iron, hadn't endeared himself to the RN crew. He continually threatened them with dire penalties for minor lapses and shouted at them to double while on the quarterdeck, so that few sympathised one day when he crashed down through the officers' hatch to lay unconscious on the Wardroom Flat, and was transferred ashore to hospital. 'No one' knew who'd removed the hatch cover's securing pin which caused his fall, an inquiry produced no evidence, and his replacement, the short, dapper Commander H. Riley, soon became very popular.

The cruiser's initial commission was a short one – six weeks Orkneys work-up, S/O Escorts as far as Cape Town with a fast 'Winston Special' Suez-bound convoy, a brief spell at the Cape when HMS *Hecla* limped into harbour after being torpedoed, and *Gambia* took her dead to sea for burial, then on again to Kilindini to become a unit of the 4th CS in Admiral Somerville's British Eastern Fleet.

Around the Kenyan harbour as she glided past *Warspite* to her signalled berth, there were the old R-Class battleships *Ramillies*, *Resolution*, *Revenge* and *Royal Sovereign*; the modern carriers *Illustrious* and *Formidable*; cruisers dating back to the veteran *Dragon*; destroyers even older; sloops, submarines in rafts alongside their mothership *Maidstone*, and all the back-up vessels and tenders necessary for this sizable fleet.

That night in the Fleet Club, *Gambia*'s liberty men imparted recent news of home in exchange for information about Japan's 5 April *Akagi* and *Kaga* carrier raid on Colombo, about the sinking of *Dorsetshire* and *Cornwall* who were en route Addu Atoll to join Somerville's fleet, and about the enemy carriers' subsequent 9 April Trincomalee raid, then their sinking in nearby waters of *Hermes*, her attendant destroyer HMAS *Vampire*, corvette HMS *Hollyhock*, and the two RFA tankers they were escorting. But since the fleet shifted to Kilindini there had been more encouraging news, the recent

Navy-supported occupation of Diego Suarez and other Madagascar ports by Royal Marine and Commando forces.

Within the next week *Gambia*'s Marine Captain, 'Big Joe' Killen – because he was big – and his Marine Lieutenant 'Penguin' Whiteby – due to his large splayed feet – landed with their Marine detachment for exercises preparatory to more land assaults, on one occasion when put ashore by *Gambia*'s boats at a Zanzibar Island town, appropriating the Mayor's open-topped Daimler for Big Joe's triumphal seizure of the main street. However, an intended message informing the town's Defence HQ's about the forthcoming exercise hadn't been sent, so ferocious, skinny, native home-guardsmen in khaki shirts, Bombay bloomers, and puttees down to their wide bare feet made a fanatical attempt to recapture the Mayoral conveyance, and instead of an occupation rehearsal, it turned into a bone-crunching knuckle-up, eventually sorted out by frantic whistle-blowing and multilingual blaspheming. Then after dark, when the landing party returned from hours of revelry in a debauched-looking owner's thatch verandahed pub, they were greeted by Jolly Jack's ribald encouragement while struggling up the rolling ship's scrambling nets to be helped over the guardrail.

Gambia then accompanied *Warspite*, *Illustrious*, *Formidable* and several screening destroyers to Colombo on a flag-showing operation intended to reassure Ceylon's population. She spent most of June and July on Indian Ocean convoy escort and trade route patrols and, with the AMC *Worcestershire,* shepherded several big troopships returning the first of Australia's desert forces part-way from Colombo to Fremantle. More patrols, until recalled to Kilindini to be part of another combined services landing.

Admiral Somerville had already occupied bases on northern Madagascar's Indian Ocean coast south from Diego Suarez, but he wanted one on the west coast to launch fast A/S vessels against Japanese submarines operating in the Mozambique Channel. Majunga had been chosen and at daybreak on Thursday, 10 September 1942 he paced *Warspite*'s bridge, awaiting word from *Gambia* that the envoy sent ashore in her speedy R-boat had convinced the Vichy Commandant to accept a peaceful British occupation; but an eruption of shell bursts greeted the boat as it rounded the harbour entrance and it was fortunate to retire without being hit.

Somerville now issued an ultimatum to surrender before midday or be taken by force. He ordered *Gambia* to close the fort and open fire on it if there was no satisfactory answer. The hours elapsed with no sign of communication from Majunga's military commander until … 1155, 1156, 57, 58, 59 – 1200. A muted 'Ting Ting', then 'WHHHOOOOMMMPPHH' and the severe jolt as B- and X-turrets' triple 6″ guns belched flame-pierced rings of gun-cotton fumes. An acrid stench swept the bridge and quarter-deck, 'Ting Ting' and another pause before the roar of A- and Y-turrets shook *Gambia* stem to stern. Smoke and masonry lifted slowly over the distant fort from the first two-turret salvo. Flames and debri-laden smoke billowed from the second, but there would be no third. A white flag could be seen hoisting on the fortress tower and it was all over. *Gambia* had done the heavy-handed bit and the 29th Infantry Brigade was already surging inshore to consolidate. 'Operation Stream' had succeeded with minimal French casualties; *Gambia* remained with the fleet in Diego Suarez as support for forces ashore in Madagascar until mid-November when shaft bearing troubles necessitated docking in Bombay.

Unobtrusively since becoming the ship's replacement upperdeck officer, Commander Riley had planned the cruiser's seatime evolutions and exercises to the point where they achieved a high standard. He had arranged sport and recreation to meet the requirements of individual groups. His 12 November 1942 Daily Orders authorised a 'Beard Contest' to be judged six weeks hence on Christmas Day. No need to apply for permission to discontinue shaving and, after the judging, KR & AIs would be waived for those wishing to recommence shaving; just notify the MAA's Office.

On leaving the big Indian dock after men had enjoyed three weeks in rest camps, *Gambia*'s Walruses winged beyond horizons during daylight without sighting even a whale, just a forsaken ocean until 28 November when convoy OW1 appeared, under escort by the Dutch cruiser *Jacob van Heemskerck* and Australia's veteran *Adelaide* on the northbound leg from Fremantle. This rendezvous was part of Admiralty's world-wide convoy protection, ensuring that escorts' fuel reserves were maintained in case of action or emergency. So while the Dutch and Australian cruisers returned to Fremantle, *Gambia* took convoy OW1 on for the next few thousand miles to Bombay, where they would replenish oil tanks or bunker with coal, to be escorted by other warships across the Arabian Sea for a top-up at Aden.

Meanwhile *Gambia* resumed her search for raiders or blockade runners in the Indian Ocean, working south-west till just before Christmas when she entered Diego Suarez where British Isles mail awaited her arrival. Somehow those bomb-wearied cold families in Britain had found Yuletide gifts to parcel and post, small Xmas puddings made from their meagre rations to remind loved sailors of Scottish snow, of pre-war celebrations when relations had gathered to sing carols around grandparents' pianos in England, Wales and Ireland.

And here from *Gambia* in this north Madagascar harbour, Commander Riley sent a boat party ashore to cut decorative greenery for the Wardroom, Gunroom, Marine Barracks, all for'ard messdecks, and a huge bunch of foliage to be hoisted to her mast-tops while she made out to sea, passing and receiving farewell messages as she departed for Durban. 'Then Home?'

– a week-long buzz on the way south during which Christmas was celebrated, and Commander Riley officiated at the 'Best beard' selection. Yet
after a few days lazing on Durban's beaches with lightly tanned beauties,
the yearning for an English winter dissipated. Now when returning from
daily exercises with local naval units the ship's liberty men were dressed
ready for first liberty call, anticipating those intimate feminine smiles
awaiting them at the wharf gates.

But earthly Paradise is usually temporary and *Gambia* received new
sailing orders, not this time for England but to resume her raider-search
patrols, back on the old grind – speeding along D/F bearings to an empty
horizon, sweating watch by watch in boiler rooms, W/T offices, and other
sweltering compartments deep below the upper deck – then a death which
stunned the whole ship's company. Early one morning Commander Riley's
steward found him in his bunk saturated with blood, diagnosed shortly by
the Surgeon Commander as an hours-old massive internal haemorrhage.
Funeral arrangements in the tropical heat had to be made without delay,
and that evening before sunset all men off watch mustered aft to stand in
reverence throughout the full naval service; rifles volleyed in tribute to the
ship's beloved Commander, then his hammock-cocooned body slid from
the Union Jack-draped board to his final rest.

Back in Durban Captain Mansergh drafted a teleprinter message to
Kilindini for CS4's action, resulting in an instruction to join the escort for
convoy WS20 now just north of Durban. When abreast of Mombasa he
should detach to embark Commander L.E. Moncaster RN who would have
Gambia's sealed orders for her next assignment 'Operation Pamphlet'.

The sun blazed high over a burnished surface to the south-west of Socotra
on Monday, 8 March 1943 when *Gambia* made her Pendants 48 to *Devonshire*.
The County Class cruiser was aware of this rendezvous and she now
detached six Aden-based destroyers back to harbour. Each cruiser took
station port and starboard of the huge grey painted liners *Queen Mary*,
Aquitania, *Ile de France*, *Nieuw Amsterdam* and *Queen of Bermuda*, transporting
the remainder of Australia's 9th Division home from North Africa whence
they'd been recalled to fight in New Guinea; and after a refuelling stop for
all ships at Addu Atoll they sped onward south to Fremantle. There and in
Perth, men from *Gambia* were drowned in hospitality, fourteen days of it
from 9th Divvy Aussies in pubs, and from West Australians in their homes.

Weeks later back in Durban *Gambia* flew the flag of CS4 Rear Admiral
W.G. Tennant, kept him aboard for a month while again searching the
Indian Ocean for enemy vessels, then set him ashore in Colombo after his
speech farewelling the ship from his 4th Cruiser Squadron – the usual
rehearsed flannel, but the unrehearsed ending of 'Give our love to all at
home'.

Gambia needed no urging this time, made a beeline for Cape Town to refuel and cast off on Friday, 28 May before CS4 changed his mind, made a pit-stop at Bathurst in their name colony, and on leaving asked for a lot of knots to outwit U-boats known to be working off north-west Africa, the Portuguese coast and in the Bay of Biscay. It was well into June and Allied armies had won the North African campaign though not so in Europe, yet war was far from the RN crew's thoughts that summer's day as the cliffs and paddocks of Holyhead drifted by to become the green pastures of Anglesey, and soon the coast of Lancashire to port with Cheshire close off the starboard beam, smiling at *Gambia* as she negotiated shipping in the Mersey's busy waterway. Barrage balloons. Torn hulls of merchantmen and warships rusting at anchor awaiting repair. Shipyard smog so dense it muted the clang of steel. 'Lease lend' cargo being craned from freighters' holds. And hanging heavy at the end of a jib filament, the distorted upperworks of a bombed destroyer as *Gambia* sidled to her adjacent berth.

Liverpool was as they had left it fifteen months ago; now it seemed like fifteen days. They came alongside without fanfare, stepped ashore with leave passes authorising three weeks among loved ones, some with travel warrants to distant towns and cities, all with ration coupons and foreign presents for mums, wives and female relatives; illegal tins of 'Ticklers' and skilfully concealed bottles of 'Neaters' for Dads.

And when the ship recommissioned it would be as an HMNZS.

Freddie Connew had originated in New Zealand's West Coast mining town of Stockton in 1918, and at 14 he started work several hundred feet underground at the coal face, but his 1934 application to join the NZDRN's immobile training cruiser *Philomel* was accepted, and in September 1935 his Class 18 Seaman Boys were drafted to the Station Flagship HMS *Dunedin*. In 1937 after accelerated advancement from Boy to Ordinary Seaman and on to Seaman, Fred joined *Achilles* on which, apart from a Leading Seaman course in Melbourne's HMAS *Cerberus* Naval School, he remained pre-war and at the River Plate Battle where he merited a Mentioned in Despatches award. Later on temporary draft to *Philomel* he stood before Commander 'Long John' Elworthy to be told there was no immediate vacancy for his request to become a PTI: 'Perhaps later when one dies.' At the MAA's Office Fred was asked if he had ever considered the Regulating Branch: 'What! Be a Crusher? Unthinkable.' Two weeks passed and the badge on his right sleeve set him apart from those with whom he'd joined and messed, even back aboard his beloved *Achilles* in the Regulating Office – convoys to 400 miles past the Chathams; to the Great Australian Bight with 2nd NZEF Reinforcements en route North Africa; to the South Pacific with NZ and US troopships after 'Pearl' – and now *Achilles* was under repair in a Portsmouth dry-dock after her 5 January 1943 bomb damage at Guadalcanal.

All except a small maintenance and fire party had been dispersed to Naval Schools and camps pending the ship's return to service. But on Tuesday, 22 June 1944 the MAA Jackie Cameron who'd gone earlier than usual to the ship, rang P Hut to tell the working party not to come: 'There's been a bloody great explosion somewhere below!'

The accidental blast which killed many dockyard workers left the ship a shambles. A wide gash had been opened right across the Stokers' Messdeck. Mangled components and debris erupted up through the jagged rip. Torn bodies were heaved up on the deck now only two feet from the deckhead. Bulkheads and the ship's side were ruptured and distorted.

Almost internationally a quick-sketch bald head with one curled hair, large ears and a large inverted question-mark nose graffitied 'FOO WAS HERE' wherever something underhand or unsolved occurred. It had been chalked on various parts of Achilles until some idiot chalked on a bulkhead opposite the gangway head for all to see: 'FOO HAS STRUCK'. This was the limit according to the dockyard maties who downed tools. Captain W.G. Davis cleared lower deck and sternly admonished the naval maintenance party: 'FOO,' he said, 'has been given a draft chit. He will NOT return to my ship – EVER!' And he didn't.

Gambia in Liverpool now awaited her Achilles complement, so MAA Cameron went ahead to Liverpool to arrange their embarkation, leaving Fred Connew as Senior RPO to organise the main draft assembling in Portsmouth. 'Piece of cake,' Fred thought to himself, but what a headache he inherited: a sixteen-carriage train emitting repressed steam, hundreds of inebriated matelots crowding into the first few carriages and being ordered out as they were reserved for officers, the officers in a nearby pub wishing their gin-sobbing sweethearts goodbye, and an irate Rail Transport Official yelling at RPO Connew: 'For God's sake Petty Officer get this bloody train moving!'

Fred entered the hotel lounge and on announcing: 'Come on, ladies and gentlemen, I've got to get this train away!' he was confronted by the ship's newly appointed Paymaster who demanded: 'WHO, are you? What do you think you are doing here, Petty Officer? What is your name?'

'I'm Achilles' Senior Regulating Petty Officer Connew, sir. I have to ensure everyone gets to Gambia and, sir, you all have to leave here now.'

'Don't you tell me what I have to do! I'll see you in the morning!'

'There's no doubt about that, sir. I will see you in front of the Captain, because, sir, you are stopping this train's departure for Liverpool.'

There was no reply but as Fred departed, the lounge quickly emptied and within long minutes, well-wishers and bewildered bystanders were making their way back to Portsmouth pubs as the last 'Gambia Special' carriage snaked out of sight. A mid-afternoon stop at some name-obliterated station for stale buns and tepid tea, wailing horn-blasts when speeding past expressionless faces on more unknown platforms, a church spire rising out of trees in the descending dusk, an indistinct glimpse of unlit rows of stone or brick tenements, then the haunting sounds of Britain's wartime railroads at night.

Daybreak. Men awakening and stretching cramped limbs. Cheshire's farmlands flashing by in panorama, the train jolting when brakes were applied in Liverpool's outer suburbs, steel wheels screeching on curved rails as the train shunted onto Gladstone Dock's branch line; the final jolt and hiss of released steam as carriage after carriage gently rammed its predecessor on the stone wharf alongside *Gambia*.

Over past months her superstructure had swarmed with maties wielding cutting torches and welding guns, removing the catapult, the three Walruses and one of the port and starboard retrieval cranes. The other had been resited centreline, one hangar had been transformed into mezzanine messdecks for A/A gunners and radar operators, and its opposite one was now a recreation space cum 'Odeon' cinema. VHF dipoles and radar antennae sprouted from the ship's masts and yards, essential for automatic aiming and firing the rash of new-technology small-bore weaponry evident on every flat space and projection.

Many Admiralty marked crates still lay nearby, some for *Gambia*, and one stencilled 'Cinematograph Equipment – Ascania', which attracted Chief TGM Ron Ansley's attention. Ron had run *Achilles'* projector, knew the time wasted rewinding reels before inserting others in sequence. He also knew that the armed merchant cruiser *Ascania* had been decommissioned and wouldn't now be needing a projector. The temptation was too great, so that night he and some of his tin-fish pirates manhandled the crate inboard to the 'Odeon', and *Gambia* would henceforth be the only Royal Navy cruiser to show uninterrupted films. Explanations could be dreamt up in due course.

Within days of occupying their new home, men had broomed messdeck filth into buckets and tipped it into dockside carts while others scrubbed the flooring until cortisene appeared, punkalouvres were breathing fresh air into below-deck offices and compartments; soft-soap and hot water revealed enamelled bulkheads, and foc'sle debris was hosed over the side when upperdeck officers were absent.

Meantime individual RNZN officers and men were being checked aboard from RN ships and establishments, one an ex-Wellington AMP Society clerk, John Smith, who in 1939 transferred from the NZ Territorial Army to the RNZAF, then after several months to the NZDRN as Ordinary Seaman NZD3851 on passage to the UK as a Commission Candidate. He passed successively through *Ganges*, *Drake*, and *St Christopher*; did Subbie time on the Channel Flotilla destroyer *Attack*, a shore course on Fighter Direction, back to sea as FDO on *Activity* and *Phoebe*, and now to *Gambia* with a Lieutenant promotion. (John ended his naval career as a Captain.)

Another Wellingtonian, Shipwright Clark, had left the Salvation Army and a swimming future in 1939 to do a Joinery Trade Test on *Philomel* before transfer to the RN. Four years later as a shipwright on the ancient harbour-bound French battleship *Paris*, in use as an RN repair ship, he applied for and received a draft to *Gambia* where, on entering the starboard hangar 'Chippies Mess' he was christened 'Nobby' by two of his messmates, 'Blackie' Ron Payne, the ex-*Achilles* Blacksmith, and 'Joins' Tony Dodds an ex-*Achilles* Shipwright.

At the start of the Second World War, Christchurch-born Arthur Cecil Poll was an Able Seaman on Shell Company's tanker *Paua* when his application to join the Navy was accepted. He enlisted at Wellington's *Philomel II* HQ and after training was drafted in January 1941 to our AMC *Monowai*. Meanwhile Army HQs had been posting 'Call-ups' to his home address, and although his wife explained to Buckle Street Recruiting Office that he was in the Navy somewhere in the Pacific aboard HMS *Monowai*, they gazetted him as an army deserter. But after receiving a scathing telegram from *Monowai*'s Commanding Officer via Navy Office, Army HQs conceded defeat and the Minister of Defence, Mr Jones, signed a letter of apology. Arthur Poll's deserter status was eradicated from gazettes and he remained on *Monowai* until June 1943 when she paid off from the RNZN in Liverpool.

At that stage 'Bill' Jordan's *Gambia* negotiations were incomplete, so along with many others Arthur experienced air raids, first at *Drake* barracks in Plymouth, then at *Raleigh* Naval School, Cornwall, where he did night sentry duties because the CO suspected German spy infiltration by parachutes. One night when furtive steps were heard on a tree-lined gravel path, Poll recognised the shadowy figure as the School CO and, intending to show that he was alert, had advanced one leg from the sentry-box while hefting his bayonetted rifle from the stand-easy stance when there was an overhead thud. His bayonet had pierced the wooden door-frame and he stood transfixed in the dark, being chastised for not carrying out the correct challenge procedure. Then as the CO melted into the night Arthur retrieved the bayonet, thankful that neither his misadventure nor his red face had been noticed.

His application for submarine service – assuming that a vessel designed to sink was safer than one that wasn't – reached the MAA's Office too late and he paraded with *Monowai*'s main draft to *Gambia*. As he entered Mess 33 and rendered 'Poll' for the Leading Hand to record, some witty tin-fishman loudly appended 'Totem' by which he was thereafter known. Another rating announcing his name as 'Glew' immediately got 'Sticky'. Men surnamed White became 'Knocker' in ages-past tradition, and throughout the ship such nicknames common to the Navy were apportioned.

Gambia's previous owner, Captain Mansergh, had been succeeded during the refit by Captain N.J.W. William-Powlett DSC RN who'd been a Subbie on *Tipperary* at Jutland in 1916, and whose brother had captained *Dunedin* on the NZ Station in the 1930s when 90 per cent of his crew were Imperials on loan. But NJW now had a shipload of RNZN officers and men supplemented by a Royal Marine Detachment and a sprinkling of RN specialists. It was time to re-enter the War and anyone anticipating a tropical island cruise was hallucinating. *Gambia* completed her initial work-up in sight of the Clyde's Ailsa Craig and Mull of Kintyre, then she surf-rode off the Orkney's Old Man of Hoy where one man who'd done the Plate Battle on *Achilles*, and rammed projectiles up the breech against Jap aircraft off Guadalcanal, complained: 'What! More bloody gunnery exercises?'

'Bet your tot on it, Sunshine,' from his gun captain, 'Why'd you think God put Scapa Flow here?'

So the ship corkscrewed sickeningly in seas raging down from the Arctic, exercised every evolution conceived by torpedo and gunnery sadists back through history, cursed the cruiser's designers for the Colony Class top-heaviness, then went back inside for what was a 'one-day-was-enough' run ashore experience.

On Saturday, 14 October 1939, Unterseeboot Kapitan-Leutnant Gunther Prien had entered Scapa Flow to sink the old battleship *Royal Oak* with 833 of her crew, and escaped undetected as proof of the Flow's vulnerability. But its fleet anchorages were also vulnerable to North-east Atlantic and North Sea storms which made life miserable, and hazardous. Blackie Payne, Nobby Clark, Joins Dodds and a host of *Gambia's* 1st XV supporters had ventured ashore after tot-time and lunch to cheer their team to victory under a bleak sun; then late that afternoon while they were celebrating in the quanset-hut Fleet Club, dark pregnant clouds gathered overhead for an evening assault. Lightning flashes illuminated frozen men cowering back-to-wind, pelted with driving sleet and enormous hailstones while angry gusts thumped the fleet's liberty lighter against truck tyres draped along the wet granite steps, as men judged their hesitant leap aboard.

Spume-driven seas punched the wide bows and drenched all but those in shelter on the way out to *Gambia* who strained at her cable; it was a personal triumph for every man who made a flying leap and clambered up the lee-side gangway. Then in the warm messdeck during supper Blackie asked: 'Where's Nobby?' Somewhere between those wet granite steps and his ship, Shipwright Clark had been lost overboard. Daily searches were made, but his body was not found.

Eventually CS1 released *Gambia* from his training schedule, graded each department highly and farewelled her from the Flow.

'En route New Zealand?' from a super-optimist later in the mess.

'You'd be bloody joking!'

On *Gambia*'s arrival at Plymouth, C-in-C Western Approaches, Vice-Admiral Horton, commandeered her for 'Operation Stonewall', his force of cruisers blockading the Atlantic approaches to German-occupied French ports.

Each night Plymouth's harbour and city was bombed but England was long since inured to Goering's attempts at demoralisation; buildings not yet destroyed were sandbagged up their outside walls, and 'Open for business' was displayed throughout in typical British stoicism. Without all-night leave *Gambia*'s liberty men came off bawdily drunk on scrumpy – a fiery apple cider with a mean head punch – which didn't improve the 2300 lighter trip down Plymouth Sound in rain. On one occasion they were loudly singing the Red Flag much to Captain William-Powlett's indignation as he turned to the OOW: 'Blasted Bolsheviks! Officer of the Watch – stand that boat off until they quieten down.'

'Aye aye, sir' while reaching for a loud-hailer.

The lighter lay to in a downpour, but shortly when signalled to approach, angry voices were yelling: 'Send our bloody ship home you stupid Pommie bastards. We've got a war on with the Japs. We don't want yours!' There was more, some worse, so the sea-gangway was raised and the duty watch was mustered to drop a scrambling net. Eventually the most dissident were silenced by their saturated mates and they clambered inboard. And although the wet-through duty watch had plenty to say to that night's revellers nothing official eventuated; the Royal Navy had its own methods of bringing men to their senses. C-in-C Western Approaches endorsed CS1's Scapa commendation and within days *Gambia* steamed southward to be S/O of 'Operation Stonewall'. But there were headaches of another sort in the for'ard engine-room: electrolysis corrosion had created finger-sized holes in bilge plates; escaping oil congealed into pitch-like lumps unable to pass through bilge pump filters, and a bucket chain had to be formed to pass it hand to hand up the engine-room hatch, along the starboard passage, up more hatches and over the side. Spillage made transit hazardous as Mechanician Ron Kirkwood found when he made the attempt, skidded shins-first against a steel door-sill and spent days in Sick Bay for a painful infection in his legs which even in 2001 still trouble him.

Many who went ashore in Horta came off mildly bellicose from Fayal's wines and spirits, making hard work of the gangway especially for Chief Tiffy Chas Foster who misfooted with a yell that ejected his top and bottom dentures when he hit the water and disappeared. Fortunately Ernie Jackson the Canteen Manager grabbed his hair as he surfaced, and heaved him onto the grating seconds before the motor-cutter lurched back against the lower platform. MAA Cameron sent him and other rowdies forward without comment, except for one loudmouth who was escorted to cells where the duty MO came to decide if he should remain there. Even this didn't silence the drunk who loudly accused the MO of 'sheltering behind your gold braid instead of raising your fists like a bloody man!'

'Oh, RPO, would you please leave us for a while?' from Surgeon Lieutenant Walton.

Outside the cells Chuffy Blair heard the sound of blows and on re-entering saw the now subdued man being assisted off the deck.

'Release him when he comes to, RPO. I don't consider him sufficiently intoxicated for further confinement. Uhmm, I will handle the necessary paperwork.'

Whether or not the engine-room pitting had been accelerated by a severe whallop felt throughout *Gambia*, when an amatol-explosive depth-charge dropped for an earlier exercise exploded too soon, is now immaterial; she soon recovered her full power. And it is a pity she was several hundred miles west at the extent of her blockade patrol on 28 December 1944, when a long-range Sunderland reported German destroyers 250 miles north-west of Cape Finistere. Captain William-Powlett as S/O of Force 3 (*Gambia, Glasgow, Enterprise, Penelope*) ordered *Glasgow* and *Enterprise* who were only 45 miles from the enemy to attack, and in the rough-sea skirmish which followed they found themselves confronted by more opposition than anticipated. Both cruisers were straddled by 5.9″ and 4.1″ shells as the Narvik and Elbing Class destroyers tried to encircle them, but rough weather severely restricted this strategem and although *Glasgow* took a direct hit which killed and wounded many men, both RN cruisers' accurate gunnery turned the German strategy into a mauled retreat.

8th DD Flag Captain Erdmenger and his Commander Gunther Schultz went down with *Z27*, as did Commander V. Gartzen with his *T25*, and Lt Cmdr Quedenfeldt with *T26*; *Z38* also went down and others received near-miss and direct-hit damage while retiring. *Z24*, *T23*, *T24*, and *T27* reached Brest; *Z32* and *Z37* the Gironde; and *Z23* with *T22* arrived in St Jean de Luz.

> Under the circumstances [William-Powlett ruefully recorded in his diary], I as SNO of the force could merely play the part of an eavesdropper. *Glasgow* and *Enterprise* took *Ariadne* with them to Plymouth. *Penelope* returned to Gibraltar. But with more blockade runners expected I returned to the outer cruiser patrol, north of the Azores, now partnered by our sister-ship *Mauritius* who'd been dispatched from Gibraltar.

The German destroyers had been sent from French ports to escort the fast freighter *Alsterufer* arriving from Bangkok and *Orsono* from the Far East; but *Alsterufer* was located by a Liberator of No 311 Czechoslovakian Bomber Squadron on 27 December, set ablaze and sunk by rockets; and although *Orsono* had been sighted and bombed on 24 December, her fate wasn't disclosed until the 28th when reconnaissance photos of Le Verdun Harbour revealed her aground there being unloaded into lighters.

Admiralty now decided it was more economic to intercept and attack future blockade runners by air; on 2 January 1944 senior naval captains were called to a formal conference at Whitehall, the nucleus of a British Eastern Fleet to be based at Trincomalee being on the agenda, with an underlying accent on compilation of a British Pacific Fleet to be based at Sydney. All senior officers must ensure that their ships' companies were well drilled in A/A defence.

So, having had her electrolysis problem rectified back in Plymouth, *Gambia* on 30 January sailed alone for the 'Rock' and spent much of each day brushing up on A/A gunnery of every description. Pom-pom crews left their weapons on half cock in order to have all four barrels thumping heartily at the proverbial 'REPEL AIRCRAFT' hat-drop. Drills became automatic and one evening after 'CEASE FIRING' someone triggered off a couple of rounds. Nothing was said, but next daybreak when P1 thumped off a few more its gun captain Jim Howell was required on the bridge. There he explained the need for test-firing, lack of last commission maintenance, sea air corrosion, and hard-to-get-at gun parts sticking due to solidified grease.

'Yes, I understand, Howell. Lieutenant Commander Horan, would you check the gun and report back to me?'

Down at P1 platform Horan stood between the four barrels and told Jim to explain.

'Well sir, see that corrosion on the interrupter, and that congealed grease away down in there, and that old paint—'

'Yes, yes,' impatiently as he leaned closer. 'Which trigger gives the trouble?'

'This one here ...' but the unintended touch blasted off four rounds only inches from the ADO who was now staggering about holding his head and shouting: 'GOOD GOD, HOWELL, ARE YOU TRYING TO SHOOT ME?'

All gun captains were severely cautioned and Jim laid more stress on his 'Trigger Happy Club's' indiscriminate gun play.

Gambia's buccaneers downed the usual excess of firewater in Gibraltar's tavernas, made their way to off-limit *casa de tratos*, and came back sullen tempered, much to the disgust of their opposite watch next morning when there was no leave. Instead, both watches sweated all afternoon and evening stowing and securing 300 torpedo warheads for Eastern Fleet submarines. Then next forenoon, in lieu of a look around the famous Royal Navy bastion, they were steaming east through Gibraltar Straits on the way to Alexandria, under long-range fighter protection provided by Malta and successive North African airfields. The Wehrmacht still occupied parts of Italy although Admiral John Cunningham (Brother of ABC) commanded the Tyrrhenian Sea allied fleet, supporting troops fighting around Anzio, Salerno and Casino. Germany's Luftwaffe still threatened from its bases on Crete, and it had parachuted troops and guns onto Cos and Leros in the Levant. But *Gambia* transited Mussolini's Mare Nostrum unmolested to enter Alexandria, with a warning from Captain William-Powlett who seemed to be mastering the Kiwi language: 'There's no need to advertise that you are a New Zealand ship on the way east; see if for once you can keep your traps shut!'

Among the first ashore, Clarrie Johnson was immediately greeted with 'Hullo Mister Kiwi – welcome to Alexandria.' He wore nothing distinctive, hadn't uttered a word, yet here he was, bailed up by this scrawny little shoeshine urchin crouched at his feet, the tip of a knife against the calf of his leg: 'If I don't shine your shoes I stick this in your leg, Kiwi.' Hearing from Clarrie's profanity that he hadn't made a friend, the skinny Egyptian entrepeneur produced a small round tin from his *kalibu* and smeared its contents over his reluctant customer's footwear – and stink? It was over-ripe excrement, maybe animal, so a deal was verbally agreed and when his shoes no longer stank but shone, Clarrie goodheartedly paid extra for the experience.

And that night with returning liberty men sewn up on *Zibbib*, MAA Cameron took charge of the *felucca* they were coming off in. He steered it all about the moonlit harbour as its irate owner scaled the mast in an attempt to drop the sail, while someone yanked at his trousers with the boathook trying to entice him down; but at last they banged hard against *Gambia*'s sea gangway, a couple fell overboard while checking the boat's momentum, and the OOW looked elsewhere. Thus they continued – 10 February through the Canal, 11th and 12th down the Red Sea with sweat floating each word off the paper they were writing home on, 13th refuelling in Aden; then arrival on the 19th at Trinco, into the 4th CS after saluting Admiral Sir James Somerville KCB KBE DSO RN's flag hanging listlessly at his battleship *Queen Elizabeth*'s forepeak.

While at anchor there were the usual bleats, grizzles about the 'Pommie bloody ref' who awarded a knock-on try to *Renown*'s rugby team which gave them an 11–9 victory over *Gambia*'s previously unbeaten 1st XV; heat-induced protests about slavery when humping 'bloody great' Yak carcasses through flats and down hatches to the depleted fridge; moans about the dearth of liberty boats by impatient men waiting at the wrong steps; then an uplift of souls on 22 February when *Gambia* trailed *Illustrious* for an Indian Ocean sweep named 'Operation Sleuth', accompanied by the destroyers HMS *Rotherham* and NNF *Tjerke Hiddes*. The blockade runners expected near Cocos Island were a myth as was anything else apart from water; but the ship's telegraphists, signalmen and Flight Direction officers, rapidly understood the English language voicing from VHF receivers in RN College, RNZN, RAN, and NNF accents; then on 28 February HMAS *Sussex* arrived to relieve *Gambia* who'd been ordered to refuel in Perth ready to escort a ten-ship convoy north on 7 March.

Eight days among hospitable West Australians! What more could one wish for? It was the next thing to being home except that those days of bliss fled fast. The convoy was taken to Colombo without incident and two days later *Gambia* was back in Trinco, being belatedly welcomed by the C-in-C whose quarterdeck speech hinted at the arrival of more powerful ships, after which 'your cruiser might move closer to your homeland. But first I have something in mind for you within my Eastern Fleet. This will become evident very shortly.'

Under the pseudonym 'Diplomat', Somerville's fleet filed out through Trinco's boom after local sweepers had ensured safe passage; first ten destroyers composed of the RAN's 'N' boats, the RN's 'Q's and the NNFs *Van Galen*, *Tromp* and *Tjerke Hiddes*; next *Queen Elizabeth* ahead of *Valiant* and *Renown*; then the heavy cruisers *London*, *Cumberland*, and finally the light cruisers *Gambia* and *Ceylon*. Navy Office Colombo had been informed that an allied freighter near Cocos Island mentioned three Japanese cruisers in its unfinished appeal for help. Somerville would be met 850 miles south of Ceylon by RFA tankers, then he would rendezvous with US Task Force 58.5 – the carrier *Saratoga* with her destroyers *Dunlap*, *Cummings*, *Fanning* – assuming that on their way north from Fremantle they didn't intercept the enemy cruisers; or that 'Diplomat' hadn't intercepted them on the way south.

Neither interception eventuated and on 2 April 1944 'Diplomat' re-entered harbour, now reinforced by the USN ships. Top-level phone discussions had been prioritised between Allied C-in-C East Asia Admiral Lord Louis Mountbatten at his Colombo HQ, and US Chief of Naval Operations, Admiral E.J. King at Washington. US Pacific Fleet Admiral Chester Nimitz proposed an assault against Hollandia and Aitape on New Guinea's north coast; and in tripartite telephone link-ups Admiralty agreed to a diversionary attack on Sabang Island by Somerville's Fleet Air Arm, supported by his battle fleet in anticipation of surface retaliation.

'Operation Cockpit' started out from Trincomalee on 16 April as two groups: Force 69 comprising *Queen Elizabeth*, *Valiant*, France's modern battleship *Richelieu*, screened by five cruisers and eight destroyers; Force 70 being the carriers *Illustrious*, *Saratoga*, one cruiser and six destroyers; but when two days out from base, *Gambia* and *Ceylon* were detached from Force 69 to strengthen Force 70, and that's how both groups remained offshore throughout the raid as forty-six bombers and twenty-seven fighters raged down on Sabang and Lho Nga airfields. Twenty-four parked Japanese aircraft were certified destroyed and others claimed; fuel dumps and storage tanks exploded into flames; a power station, W/T network and several admin buildings and barracks were left in smoking ruins; and specified runways were heavily cratered. Other Allied aircraft simultaneously bombed and strafed freighters and warships about the harbour; and the whole operation succeeded beyond expectation for the loss of one US plane although its pilot was rescued a mile offshore by the RN submarine *Tactician*.

Several hours later *Tactician* resurfaced to report huge fires and spasmodic detonations, with Japanese troops running helter skelter in obvious confusion well into the night. Meantime while the fleet retired, radar-detected enemy aircraft met a concentrated barrage, a brilliant display of intertwining multi-coloured tracer tracking low-flying targets which evoked an unmistakable American reprimand: 'Say you Limeys, howsabout a slight elevation, your tracers are bouncin' off the surface and goin' between our goddam smokestacks!'

'Cockpit' ended on 24 April when the two Forces anchored back in Trincomalee. There were more link-calls with Colombo, London and Washington as Somerville, Mountbatten, Churchill, and Pentagon strategists detailed requirements to coincide with US Admiral King's next West Pacific operation.

Designated Force 65 and Force 66 the combined Eastern Fleet left harbour on 6 May for 'Operation Transom', refuelled in north-west Australia's Exmouth Gulf from RFA tankers escorted there by *London* and *Suffolk*, then sailed at sundown on the 15th to be in their strike position at dawn on Wednesday, 17 May. This time with Surabaya the target, a 10,000-foot mountain range had to be crossed by the bombers, torpedo-bombers and fighters; and again the Japanese were caught with their kimonos up. Ten ships at anchor were sunk or left sinking; an oil refinery, power station and engineering works were demolished; the naval base and two floating docks were deluged by 500-lb and 1,000-lb bombs; storage tanks and warehouses were set ablaze; and nineteen grounded aircraft disintegrated when strafed while the only two Zeros to get airborne were immediately downed. Runways were cratered and associated buildings rocketed and strafed with incendiary bullets; then that night as the fleet withdrew, US Superforts flew a thousand miles from SW Pacific bases, timed to arrive shortly after some from Ceylon to give the bewildered enemy more headaches. Guided by the still burning harbour they offloaded strings of heavies and thousands of small incendiaries.

Over the following two months *Gambia* and a flotilla of destroyers trailed *Illustrious* and the Woolworth *Atheling* about the Bay of Bengal, launching airborne forays against Japanese positions to keep enemy aircraft in the area while American Pacific forces invaded the Marianas. The NZ cruiser did a solo trip to Madras to embark Burma-wounded FAA and RAAF personnel and take them to Colombo; she then had nine days R & R at Djyatalawa Camp high in the cool Ceylonese mountain air; and returned to Trinco in time for Somerville's next operation, this one a naval bombardment code-named 'Operation Crimson'.

Saratoga and her three US destroyers had by now been replaced by *Victorious* and her crash-boats; but scrutiny of aerial photographs taken after 'Cockpit' and 'Transom' indicated that the bombing hadn't been as effective as first thought, so Somerville was determined to carry out the type of naval assault he remembered from his youthful Great War days. Admiral Moody's carriers would be confined to ensuring that Japanese aircraft didn't get off Lho Nga, Kota Raja and Sabang airfields, after which they would unfold an umbrella over the battle fleet. Rescue submarines had been dispatched a day early to be in place before sun-up on Friday, 25 July, when FAA pilots including many from New Zealand lifted off *Victorious* and *Illustrious*.

The first rays of an Indonesian sun were filtering through gaps in bamboo blinds covering the windows of Japanese barracks, military bugles were rousing soldiers and airmen from deep sleep to rub their eyes and scratch their torsos; then there was panic. Sirens wailing and strident calls sent pilots racing half naked to their Zeros. Tree-top Seafires screaming over the compound triggering their wing-guns and rockets. Steams of bullets scything wild-eyed running soldiers. Incendiaries leaving rows of blazing buildings surrounding airstrips being reduced to burning aircraft. But this was only the beginning. At 0655 when nine miles offshore, *Queen Elizabeth*, *Renown*, *Valiant* and *Richelieu* illuminated and shimmered surrounding water with a rolling thunderclap, as the combined thirty-two heavy-gun salvo literally moved the battle line sideways.

A second 15″ and 14″ reverberation trembled *Gambia*'s bridge miles away, as she with *Ceylon* and *Kenya* rounded a headland to knock out known batteries and A/A emplacements. Spotting aircraft were radioing corrections to the battleships' individually coloured shell explosions. On and on, salvo after air-shaking salvo, whole concrete structures uprooted and hurled through nearby buildings, in which those sheltering were smashed against walls and torn apart in the immediate vacuum.

Gambia and her sister-cruisers were steaming back and forth across Sabang Harbour entrance, firing steadily at designated and newly detected targets. A hillside moved when one of *Gambia*'s 6″ shells penetrated a magazine ventilation shaft, then the whole area erupted. An eternity elapsed before they heard the battleships' last shells rumbling over. The cruisers now covered Captain Onslow's destroyers *Quality, Quilliam, Queenborough* and *Tromp* as they raced past on their way inside to complete the day's operations.

Inner-harbour gun-emplacements were engaged and destroyed. Two RAN gunners were killed and several RN crew lay injured when *Quality* and *Quilliam* sustained damage but remained in action. A New Zealander on one destroyer died when his anti-flash gear tangled in the breech and the gun recoiled; and a newsreel cameraman filming his destroyer's fight was seen spreadeagling outboard with the film trailing when a shell exploded at his feet. A floating dock and several freighters were torpedoed and sunk; harbour installations were wrecked by gunnery; and on the way out while engaging batteries not yet silenced, *Tromp* took four dud shells which caused minor damage but no casualties.

None of Somerville's force was lost, and right on sunset *Victorious* and *Illustrious* turned up-wind to recover their returning spotters and CAPs. Then apart from a few night intruders who were splashed or driven off in a spectacular barrage, 'Operation Crimson' concluded successfully when the fleet entered Trincomalee on Wednesday, 27 July 1944, with Admiral Somerville beaming proudly as *Queen Elizabeth*'s and following ships' Royal Marine Bands played old-time victory marches.

This was *Gambia*'s last major operation in the British Eastern Fleet. She participated in a seven-day exercise with the 4th CS in August and a two-day series of evolutions in mock opposition to *Cumberland, London,* the newly arrived ten × 14″-gunned *Howe*, and her caprice of unpredictable destroyers.

She then did four weeks in a Colombo dock before returning on 6 October 1944 to Trinco's Borodino Creek, where days later *Achilles* unadvisedly secured to the next buoy ahead. It transpired that the New Zealand cruisers' antipodean escapades were a bit heavy for C-in-C British Eastern Fleet, and for Supreme Commander Allied Forces South East Asia, Admiral Lord Louis Mountbatten, who addressed both ships' companies to impart memories of the antics he and his cousin Lieutenant Prince Edward got up to when they visited New Zealand aboard *Renown* in April/May 1924: 'There she is,' he pointed down harbour to the beautifully streamlined old battlecruiser, 'but,' he warned with an amused frown, 'unless you too suffer from Royal blood, you may not be excused as we were.'

Whichever of the two top admirals was responsible, both agreed that the New Zealand cruisers behaved better when separated, so *Gambia* sailed on 16 October with service passengers embarked for Australia, some disembarking at Fremantle and the remainder at Melbourne's Port Philip, whence she departed on 1 November for a few days' stay in Wellington, then onward, minus her South Islanders and southern North Islanders who were sent on overseas leave, to her Wednesday, 8 November 1944 ticker-tape arrival home in Auckland.

Back in mid-December 1939 schoolboys throughout New Zealand heard the news of *Achilles'* exploits at the River Plate Battle, and it fired their enthusiasm for the Navy, but it could be years before some of their enrolment applications were rendered. Those of age who persisted received call-ups and transport vouchers to Auckland, there at *Philomel* being issued uniforms, service numbers and all the accessories, then ferried perhaps on *Duchess* to Motuihe Island's *Tamaki* Naval School for months of training preparatory to sea service. Some went to coastal patrol launches such as *Lady Margaret*, others humped their gear aboard the Scottish Isles Class 590-ton sweeper *Killegray*, currently clearing our own Hauraki Gulf mine-fields now considered a menace rather than a protection. And while so occupied some saw this magnificent White Ensigned cruiser inbound to Auckland that sundrenched Sunday, 8 November 1944.

'That's *Gambia*!' one man with knowledge was yelling at those without; and within minutes *Killegray*'s Skipper (a personification of James Cagney as Hollywood's 'Rusty Bucket' Mr Roberts) was ranting and raving at his 'rebellious crew' who now wanted a draft to *Gambia*. But his threats fell on deaf ears and when their dream cruiser departed Auckland on its 'Get to know you' New Zealand circuit, many of those Gulf pirates were on her Complement List.

And in late November 1944 while *Gambia*'s liberty men entered Wellington's matelot-frequented pubs, events of dire naval significance for Japan were looming off the coast of Honshu.

Two years previously when Admiral Nagumo lost his carriers *Akagi*, *Hiryu*, *Kaga* and *Soryu* at Midway, Grand Admiral Isoroku Yamamoto ordered construction of the 'secret' battleship *Shinano* to be suspended while plans for her conversion to a 75,000-ton aircraft carrier were approved; but the War was turning sour for Hirohito's warlords. American B–29 Superforts were devastating Tokyo and major cities, while *Shinano*'s completed sister-ship mammoth *Musashi* had been sunk by relentless bombing in the Philippines' naval battles. And now that battleships seemed to be so vulnerable, *Shinano*'s conversion was accelerated in her lair behind towering corrugated-steel walls at Yokosuka, entirely unknown to the Allies and to all but a few authorised Japanese – 18,000 tons of Kamaishi steel went into her flight-deck as bomb protection; she was made safe against torpedo attack by the addition of 'Blisters' along her waterline; then on

Tuesday, 28 November 1944 when partly commissioned, she steamed south on the 500-mile route towards her finishing yards in Kure. There it was intended she would embark the rest of her crew, hundreds of airmen and flight upon flight of attack-aircraft.

But for the perseverance of US submarine *Archerfish*'s skipper, Commander Joe Enright, right then solo patrolling seaward of Tokyo for downed US aircrew, *Shinano*'s multi-scores of fighter-bombers and torpedo-bombers might have assisted the gigantic battleship *Yamato*, when five months later it sailed on an abortive suicide mission against Okinawa's American invaders.

Archerfish's radar was playing up the night *Shinano* departed Yokosuka, and while Enright's navigator visually checked radar bearings of known islands called out from below, one of the dark masses was seen to be moving. Simultaneously the radar operator confirmed Navi's assertion: 'Yeah, Skip, sure as hell is, about twenty knots I'd say.'

This was *Archerfish*'s top surface speed, but due to a glitch in *Shinano*'s engines, her Captain Toshio Abe had to reduce speed although aware that enemy radar had been detected.

And now convinced that he was stalking a massive enemy vessel, Commander Enright tracked it by radar and periscope night and day until fortune placed him in ideal range at 0315 on 29 November 1944 when he ordered: 'FIRE ONE!' Fortune stayed with him, and a succession of his 10-second interval torpedoes were felt and seen to be blasting great chasms in the enemy carrier. Already, inrushing seas were smashing through her distorted internal bulkheads until near mid-forenoon when *Archerfish* returned to periscope depth to see her dangerously listed without power, her destroyers closing to take off survivors. He dived again and stopped engines for safety, then shortly after midday his hydrophone operator heard unmistakable sounds of the huge carrier foundering, expelled air bellowing, metal grinding as bulkheads collapsed, depth charges detonating at random far away where destroyers were attempting to bring their assailant to the surface.

Down at 400 feet lying quiet, *Archerfish*'s crew counted off those exploratory explosions and relaxed as the concussions decreased. Then that night Commander Enright surfaced, crept miles off to a safe distance, engaged his diesels and powered away to make a cyphered report before resuming his rescue-submarine assignment.

But back at Guam a fortnight later he found his report getting cynical scrutiny: 'Big carrier, Joe?' from a Senior. 'Hell man, our bombers haven't seen a carrier near Tokyo in months. There just isn't one like you claim. Sorry, Commander but Intelligence won't wear your report.'

Then later when Enright produced the sketches he'd made during

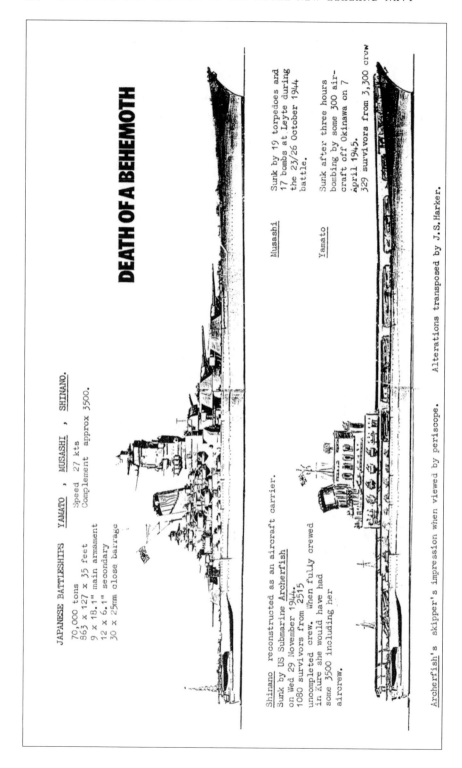

DEATH OF A BEHEMOTH

JAPANESE BATTLESHIPS   YAMATO , MUSASHI , SHINANO.

70,000 tons
863 x 127 x 35 feet
9 x 18.1" main armament
12 x 6.1" secondary
30 x 25mm close barrage

Speed   27 kts
Complement approx 3500.

Shinano reconstructed as an aircraft carrier.
Sunk by US Submarine Archerfish
on Wed 29 November 1944.
1080 survivors from 2515
uncompleted crew. When fully crewed
in Kure she would have had
some 3500 including her
aircrew.

Musashi   Sunk by 19 torpedoes and
             17 bombs at Leyte during
             the 23/26 October 1944
             battle.

Yamato   Sunk after three hours
             bombing by some 300 air-
             craft off Okinawa on 7
             April 1945.
             329 survivors from 3,300 crew

Archerfish's skipper's impression when viewed by periscope.   Alterations transposed by J.S.Harker.

periscope examinations while shadowing his huge quarry, a young Intelligence officer exclaimed: 'Goddam! That submarine guy's not wrong. That sonofabitch carrier's been adapted from the Yamato Class battlewagon our agents have been lookin' for since 19 f..kin' 37.'

So, 'For the relentless pursuit and sinking of Shinano', Commander Joseph Enright USN was awarded the United States Navy Cross by Secretary of the USN, James Forrestal, on Monday, 5 March 1945.

CHAPTER XX

Union Coy's MV Hauraki Captured by Japs. Gambia in the BPF

BORN IN 1891 in Stockholm, Sweden, Martin Hedlund entered the merchant service as a lad of thirteen to spend his next fifty-two years at sea, apart from Sept 1918 to Sept 1924 when he worked for the Christchurch Metropolitan Electricity Department, and mid-July 1942 to the end of the Second World War during which period he was a Japanese POW.

At Auckland on a sunny Monday, 9 March 1925 Martin left the Union Steamship Company Office, with registration papers showing him to be their three-year-old diesel-powered freighter MV *Hauraki*'s electrician. A modern 7,113-ton 14-knot motor vessel, she plied Pacific trade routes unheralded except for her arrival and departure mentions in newspaper shipping columns until, in dense fog on Sunday, 6 August 1935 she grounded off Tararata Point near Brown's Bay, Auckland, there to be a source of interest for reporters and sightseers until the USSC's steamer *Waipiata* and a brace of enthusiastic tugs refloated her a week later.

Five more years drifted past an apathetic British Empire which wakened abruptly on 1 September 1939 when Hitler invaded Poland and 3″-headlined the world's 3 September newspapers: 'BRITAIN AND FRANCE DECLARE WAR ON GERMANY'.

Early in 1940 the British Ministry of War Transport registered *Hauraki* to carry troops and war material if required; she had an ancient 4″ gun, two Vickers and two nameless machine guns fitted, some RNZNVR gunners were embarked extra to her usual thirty-five mercantile crew and, so armed as a Defensively Equipped Merchant Ship she defied the Axis powers for two years.

On Boxing Day 1941, when outbound past Takapuna Beach, Martin Hedlund came topside into the sun, remarking to Jack Thompson the 3rd Engineer that Japan's entrance into the War hadn't kept North Shore bathers out of the water; then they both joined in conversation with nearby civilians, mostly Australian schoolteachers evacuated from Norfolk Island for the passage home. At Melbourne the ship's Captain and Chief Engineer were replaced by Captain Albert Creece and Chief Engineer Bill Falconer, but the remaining officers remained unaltered – Bill Todd, 1st Mate; Mac MacIntyre, 2nd Mate; Wally Wallace, 3rd Mate; Jock Lindsay, Chief W/T Op; McInley, 2nd W/T Op; Watt, 3rd W/T Op; Martin Hedlund, Electrician; and the ship's engineers: Jock Thompson 2nd; Bill Hall 3rd; Charlie Hurley 4th; Harry Brodie 5th; Bill Porteous 6th; Jim Innes 7th; Gordon Hutton 8th; Bluey Meredith 9th; D. Scott 10th.

After discharging general cargo at Port Phillip a manifest of goods was checked into the holds for Sydney. There a return load was taken aboard for Melbourne, after which she carried on westward to complete at Fremantle for Egypt and Palestine; but because of a Japanese carrier-force threat in the eastern Indian Ocean *Hauraki*'s sailing instructions took her away from the normal shipping route via Colombo. Instead she was directed to go south of Chagos Archipelago and north-north-west around Socotra into the Gulf of Aden, hearing on the way that Singapore had surrendered on 15 February 1942; the Red Sea, hot on deck and sweltering below while checking the big diesel motor; Suez and Port Tewfik where she was loaned a barrage balloon to tether at her foremast as protection against enemy aircraft throughout the Canal transit; Port Said where Martin and his mates mingled in its infamous night clubs with British officers off the captured Italian *Ramb III*, now converted to a hospital ship; Haifa, clean, busy with an ant trail of humans offloading a thousand tons of 200-lb bags of flour down perilously angled gang-planks.

Two months later on 31 May *Hauraki* approached Sydney, unaware she was passing between the Japanese submarines *I–21*, *I–22*, *I–24* and *I–27*, lying submerged 3 miles apart awaiting the return of three midget subs sent inside to torpedo allied warships known to be at anchor. Through mere chance, or more likely because the assault on Sydney's warships demanded secrecy, she entered harbour unmolested by the semicircle of submarines.

This operation had been planned by Japanese High Command several weeks earlier. Captain Hankyu Sasaki on *1–21* which housed a small observation aircraft would command the attack force assembled at Truk, where *I–22*, *I–24*, *I–27* and *I–28* each had secured to its deck a two-man battery-powered midget submarine armed with two 18″ torpedoes. But in the early hours of 17 May, shortly after their departure south, an American submarine saw *I–28* on the surface and sank her with torpedoes. So, near dark on 31 May, *I–22*, *I–24* and *I–27* launched their manned midgets seven miles off Sydney Heads then waited at periscope depth for their return.

Lieutenant Chuma crossed the indicator loop at 2001, became enmeshed in an A/S net at about 2230 and was reported as a drifting mine. And at 2235 when the patrol boat *Lolita* arrived to investigate, Chuma, unable to extricate his midget, detonated both torpedoes and died in the explosion.

Sub Lieutenant Ban's mini-sub crossed the loop at 2048, cut through the net but was sighted by USS *Chicago* who exposed her with searchlights and opened fire as she dived. Twenty minutes later the launch *Nestor* narrowly missed her offshore of Fort Deniston; then it is thought she was detected passing outward over the indicator loop at 0157, and possibly due to flat batteries sank in deep water off the coast.

Off Bradley Head at about 2330 HMAS *Geelong* put her searchlight on *I–24*'s midget and opened fire without making a hit; then Sub Lt Ban launched his two torpedoes at *Chicago* but they ran under her and exploded on the harbour bed, directly under the converted 2,100-passenger harbour ferry *Kuttabul*, at that time designated HMAS as a navy accommodation vessel. Twenty-one RAN engine-room and seamen rates died as *Kuttabul*'s hull opened in the blast and she settled deck-awash on the bottom.

Meantime *I–22*'s midget, manned by Lieutenant Matsuo and Petty Officer Tsuzuku, was sighted near the entrance at 2253 by HMAS *Yandra*, but she lost contact for a quarter of an hour until it was made again near Hornby Light where depth charges were dropped. These apparently did no damage and it is thought Matsuo lay doggo until, on her way out to sea at 0300, *Chicago* saw the midget's conning tower moving toward the entrance and alerted all harbour defences. At daybreak HMAS *Goonambee* made contact in Taylor Bay; the patrol launches *Yarroma*, *Steady Hour* and *Sea Mist* dropped depth-charges and later that day divers found the wrecked mini-sub, its crew still inside having committed suicide by shooting themselves in the head.

Six weeks elapsed and *Hauraki*, now battling an Antarctic-born storm in the Great Australian Bight, was being whipped by great sheets of frothed green ocean torn from the crests of mountainous swells, into which her bows plunged as the stern rose with propellers racing, water deluging down engine-room air intakes to stop her port motor then the starboard which left her wallowing dangerously. All hands slaved desperately to secure hatch covers, and to dry the motors sufficiently for power to be restored; but even so she lay in Fremantle dockyard hands for days until released to Captain Creece on Tuesday, 7 July to depart for Colombo. But something more than the usual regret at leaving sweethearts waving from the dockside pervaded the ship this time.

A sixth sense of unease prevailed day and night, especially a week out when Bill Todd insisted he'd heard an aeroplane above low cloud in the Force–6 semi-gale. That afternoon McInley triggered the key of his Aldis at a distant vessel but it altered course away without answering. Then half way through the First Watch *Hauraki*'s klaxons hurried men to their emergency stations, hand-shading their eyes against the glare of searchlights from two ships, one on each quarter at a thousand yards. Although signalled

to stop, Captain Creece ordered maximum revolutions in a bid to escape
but several shellbursts off the bows decided him to heave-to; and within
long minutes a large Japanese boarding party of naval officers and men had
taken control of his bridge, radio shack and engine-room. However there'd
been time to dump weighted bags of secret mail for Colombo overboard
together with the ship's route instructions and confidential codes, before
Captain Goto asked Captain Creece in perfect English: 'What is the nationality of your ship?'

'British.'

'Have you any objection to your ship being declared a prize of war?'

'What difference would it make if I had?'

Captain Goto then stated: 'I declare this ship, on behalf of His Japanese
Imperial Majesty's Navy, to be a prize of war. You are now ordered to
haul down the British flag.'

This was done under searchlight, the Japanese flag was raised, and
Hauraki's assembled crew was told that under the rules of maritime warfare
normal duties were mandatory until arrival at a port where a Prize Court
could deliberate. A heavy guard under Naval Reserve Lieutenant Sakomoto
descended to the engine-room and *Hauraki*'s shafts again revolved.

Initially the guards were nervous and trigger-happy, but within days they
relaxed, even allowing the ship's officers to retain their usual seats at meals
and telling the Chief Steward to prepare his regular menus: 'We will get
used to your food much easier than you will get used to rice.'

En route to Penang it was learned the two armed merchantmen in
company were the fast 12,600-ton liners *Itoku Maru* and *Hotoku Maru*, each
crewed by 450 naval men and mounting eight 6″ guns and eight torpedo
tubes. They were escorting three large submarines back to Singapore from
their operations in South Africa's Mozambique Channel, and the enemy
warships stayed in company until *Hauraki* anchored in Penang. During
heavy rain the second night after capture the guards had sought shelter,
thus enabling MacIntyre and two seamen to remove eleven more bags of
Colombo mail from a strongroom and slide them overboard. MacIntyre
and Hedlund now dropped two activated flares down a ventilator shaft but
next day found their charred handles feet from the wool bales meant to
be ignited.

As time passed some of the Japanese officers sought conversation in
English, and one, Yoshiharu Mizuta, occasionally reminisced with Martin
Hedlund about their diverse boyhood lives in Japan and Sweden, however
this friendly approach was far from normal. Without regular maintenance
the diesels deteriorated until *Hauraki* barely managed 6 knots; the engineers
were threatened but not punished, and at Penang Mr MacIntyre was taken
ashore for interrogation about engine-room sabotage, being told he would

be shot if he failed to reveal Allied sailing routes from Fremantle to Colombo: 'You have till 6 p.m. to make a choice!' The ultimatum time passed; MacIntyre remained doggedly silent, he was given a cigarette and taken back aboard.

Hauraki now proceeded to Singapore and anchored off Sereta naval base where only the top of a floating dock protruded at low tide; and the crew of a tanker coming alongside with diesel fuel was composed mainly of dejected survivors from *Repulse* and *Prince of Wales*, under the watchful eyes of Japanese armed guards.

Hauraki's first attempt to depart for Japan failed when she grounded outside Johore Straits, there to remain a day until refloated at high tide under her own power, but the strain on her neglected motors caused damage to a starboard compressor and back in Singapore its piston and liner were sent ashore for repair. This entailed a long delay with the result that only Martin Hedlund and a few essential officers were kept on board, the remainder being marched off to Changi Jail and, except for Lieutenant Yoshiharu Mizuta the rest of HIJMS *Hotoku Maru*'s prize crew was relieved by an army guard before the armed merchant cruiser departed.

Mizuta went to Sereta Dockyard to supervise the piston repairs, and when informed that Hedlund was ill in hospital he visited daily to ensure the maximum care possible. In a post-war letter to Mrs Hedlund he wrote:

> On account of some trouble of engine I was at Sereta about four months to repair it. Mr Martin was in hospital and I took care for him. But because it was my duty I couldn't take care enough. I was a warrant officer and he a prisoner of war. And he recovered well and we had friendly relations.
>
> Because after that I broke with him to be appointed to embark a warship to Newginia and Solomon. If the war came to an end, we could meet with again and he gave me that photo. I got back in 1946 and I'm well now.
>
> Yours sincerely.
> Yoshiharu Mizuta. August.

But back to 1942 those still aboard *Hauraki* were mustered by the Commandant and his interpreter who yelled: 'You are prisoners of war! Try to escape you will be shot! Disobedience will be punished publicly at the whipping post ashore. You will each sign this paper promising not to escape, but in the event of being caught trying to escape you will not object to being shot!'

Each man came forward in turn to sign, and those who showed reluctance were roughly manhandled and slapped vigorously about the face. It was obvious the lenience shown by Japanese Navy men would not be repeated by their army counterparts. Meals were now eaten in the greasers' quarters aft and army guards took their place in the saloon. The Japs pillaged everything portable, and what was more confusing, a guard would one day invite someone to help himself from a broached crate, then next day punch and slap the same man when finding him eating tinned Oxford sausages that they'd pilfered together.

While at anchor barges secured alongside for the whole of *Hauraki's* cargo to be discharged, only a few hundred bales of wool and a quantity of copper ingots being left in one hold. Then in October 1942 shortly after Captain Creece, the Chief Officer, Chief Wireless Operator, Chief Engineer and four passengers were returned to the ship from Changi Jail they were again transferred, this time to the steamer *Tokio Maru* for passage to Japan; and several weeks later *Hauraki* departed Singapore in convoy to Indo-China, one night experiencing a thunder of gunfire which brought everyone topside. Brilliant flashes away to starboard were followed by frightening shellbursts among the slow-moving ships. Was this a chance for freedom? Would all the convoy go down under the shells of American cruisers? Now the Japanese escorts were retaliating. Then the whole action stopped abruptly. It was another Japanese convoy southbound and neither had understood the other's recognition challenge.

Next morning at 'tyso' it was excessively hot and men turned out in their singlets, much to the anger of the Japanese Captain. 'Animals!' he screamed, 'Animals! No shirt!' as he bashed and punched all he confronted. But that afternoon as he conned the ship 46 miles upriver he was again inscrutable, pointing to paddy fields either side and calmly explaining: 'That is what we coming for here to Saigon.'

Hauraki secured to a buoy near a French naval base across river from the Harbour Board Office; and even though each day a Vichy French frigate passed there was no sign of friendliness from any of its crew, nor from the emaciated British POWs and Indo-Chinese staggering aboard day and night with 200-lb sacks of rice, ox hides and containers of tallow, week after week until the holds were filled. Saigon's flowering trees belied the misery of its Asian inhabitants, and when subtle enquiries got the answer that it would be more than foolhardy to attempt an escape, the few yet aboard *Hauraki* deemed it wiser to remain and before anyone made the bid for freedom it was too late. With 6,000 tons of rice and hundreds of tons of drummed aviation fuel as the major items loaded, the ship now renamed *Horagi Maru* joined a convoy of derelict 5-knot tramps on Wednesday, 16 December 1942 and arrived Christmas Eve at Moji, a bustling seaport on the extreme northern tip of Kyushu at the western entrance to Japan's Inland Sea.

By now the men's main diet was rice, the weather was miserably cold and it blew hard continually during their three days at Moji, also during the two-day trip to Osaka where the ship's remaining cargo went ashore to be replaced by army huts destined for Tokyo.

On 15 January 1943 Martin Hedlund looked back with misgivings at *Hauraki* as he was hustled roughly into a truck for transfer to Dispatch Camp No–1 at Yokohama, being warned on arrival that the Commandant and his interpreter 'Claude' were renowned for thrashing anyone at their merest whim.

One of *Hauraki*'s passengers, RAN Lieutenant 'Aussie' Warner, had been sent to Ofuna Camp well up Mt Fujiyama where he complained of the cold. The whole camp was immediately mustered to run round and round its perimeter for an hour, and when some collapsed through emaciated weakness they were savagely beaten to their feet, Aussie Warner being given an extra beating each time he fell until he remained down unconscious; and another who received similar thrashings was his shipmate RN Commander Packard. Together with *Hauraki*'s Captain Creece they had arrived in Yokohama's Camp D–1 obviously nervous and in poor condition, having already been subjected to endless and brutal interrogation about shipping routes and major refuelling sites.

Camp D–1 was housed in cargo sheds along the waterfront, initially accommodating officers and men including USN prisoners taken during the Japanese raid on Kiska in the Aleutians at the time of Pearl Harbour, their Senior Officer, Charlie House, having escaped into the hills and lived on grass roots until he gave himself up. Another American, Turner, knew the Japs liked dogs as pets so he cleaned out a guard-dog's dish and put a morsel of his meagre rations in it, which the dog immediately ate while the Jap guard looked on. The guard then went to the galley and replenished the dish, but as soon as his back was turned Turner gobbled the lot except for a bit kept for future guard bait. Those fortunate enough to be assigned work in factories were spared some of Yokohama's winter rigours; there was heat from massive tallow smelters, and one day when a Japanese upset a cauldron of molten fat which burst into flames, Jack Thompson and his mates managed to extinguish the conflagration, thus saving many Japanese lives and later being apportioned two paddle crabs instead of one for that evening meal. On another occasion an American, Marshall, found some rotting whale meat ignored even by Jap dogs; it was washed then cooked and eaten within minutes and even though they suffered gastronomically in their emaciated state it was by such means that some of the men survived.

One end of the camp had been partitioned off as a hospital and officers' quarters, a few pot-belly stoves were issued with next to no wood or coal, and even throughout each winter the fires were restricted to two hours between 5 and 7 a.m., then between 5 and 7 p.m. So American, Dutch, English, Australian and New Zealand servicemen's health quickly deteriorated, and it was a miracle that any of Camp D–1's original 530 survived on their 300 grams per day of semi-cooked grain in a mug of soup strained from green leaves and a dash of soy sauce. If sick, the Jap doctor put the patient on half rations; if working, men received five cigarettes a day but that was soon reduced to one, then none. On rare occasions a coarse bread was issued in small portions, but in order to stay alive it became essential to pilfer from the Jap stores and risk savagery or death if caught; especially when the USAF started bombing and all pretence of Japanese humanity immediately ceased.

The Mitsubishi Dockyard where Martin Hedlund worked ten-hour shifts had tried to operate a POWs' canteen where their 10-sen per day wages could be saved to buy cigarettes at 23-sen for a ten-pack until this too was prohibited by the Military Commandant. And if it hadn't been so painful there might have been humour in the treatment meted out to guards and POWs alike for not saluting the Commandant. He would bash the nearest Jap sergeant who would attack the closest sentry, then the sentry would rush amongst the rows of tiered bunks and turn everyone out to salute *him*; anyone slow in obeying would be bashed about his head with a rifle butt. This sometimes led to a hospital visit where there were no medicines, only the treatment of half rations, so with experience men preferred to nurse their own injuries. In consequence of a neutral Swiss inspection of the camp during which access to POWs wasn't permitted, a 'Dockyard Dental' was promulgated, but again because of the unhygienic and painful experiments made on toothache patients, men suffered unless driven by pain to allowing extraction by one of their mates. Arduous toil, lack of food, and camp epidemics began to tell, then increasingly year by year men died, mainly from pneumonia occasioned by malnutrition.

One man caught eavesdropping on a partially understandable discussion by Japanese guards about the trend of war, received thrashings until unconscious when he was dragged to a post and tied in a sitting position to be left in the snow for hours. Yet the men planned and carried out shipyard sabotage – as Japanese inspectors disappeared after chalk-marking loose rivets for removal and reriveting in new ships' hulls, the markings were erased and good rivets were chalked for treatment. There came the day when a newly launched vessel filled and sank to deck level over the next forty-eight hours during which the Japs searched for pump blockages. Martin Hedlund who'd purposefully rewired every dockyard pump incorrectly, kept well out of sight throughout all this activity, but eventually suspicion fell on him, and even though he couldn't be identified as the culprit he received an overdose of bashings at the inquiries.

That evening really small loaves of bread as hard as stone and covered in mould were issued, with a warning that if not eaten they would be collected and reissued for breakfast. They were eaten. So weeks became months, all guards and POWs went through a delousing tub bi-weekly, and as each was doused fully clothed, the liquid thickened and fouled until men crawled with lice throughout winter and were savaged by fleas and bed-bugs during summer. At all sorts of inconvenient night hours, roll calls were inflicted without warning to ensure that none had escaped, and woe betide the man arriving late. Dysentery was rife and one night Bill Falconer and Bill Hall who'd been unable to rise from the 'banjo' because of stomach gripes, crept along the rear line to their vacant spaces, but they were spotted and called out for punishment. 'Combi San the Mad Nip' drew a circle with a knobbed cane while indicating calmly for the Chief to step into it. When in Bill Falconer looked down to ensure his feet were inside and got a swinging bash with the knob which sent him reeling; then when Bill Hall stepped in he collected a haymaker to raise an emu egg behind his ear which spurted blood. The camp light was turned off and guards bullied each man into his quarters. But day-calls were being abandoned more and more when air-raid sirens sent the Japs scurrying for cover, and the POWs looked skyward to see 'Photographic Joe', a US bomber now becoming a regular event as he flew over around each noon at 30,000 feet. Christmas 1944 was approaching and a rumour spread that Japanese cities were taking a pounding.

Meanwhile in November 1944 HMNZS *Gambia* was being introduced to New Zealand's public. In sequence she visited our Windy City capital; Lyttelton for a parade through Christchurch, the City of the Plains; Dunedin for the Hoots Mon inhabitants to come aboard in droves, envious lads just out of school but yet too young to be in uniform, meeting recently joined schoolmates who'd trained at *Tamaki* and received draft chits to the big New Zealand cruiser; new girlfriends for each city's civic dance; finally back to Auckland for Gulf exercises with C-in-C Pacific Fleet's modern battleship *Howe* in company with his escorting destroyers *Quality* and *Queenborough*. During daylight thousands of Aucklanders gathered excitedly on Hauraki Gulf vantage points as *Howe*'s ten 14″-gunned salvoes concussed the air and trembled the ground on which they stood. Then in November's warm moonlight they thrilled equally when *Gambia*'s twelve 6″ illuminated offshore waters: 'Are those shockwaves from the battleship, Mummy?'

'No dear they're from Daddy's ship I took you to yesterday!'

One of *Gambia*'s new entries from *Tamaki*, Wally Nielsen, had as a Taranaki schoolboy heard the news of *Achilles*' exploits at the 'River Plate'; he'd since then determined to join the Navy when of age; and when Admiral Bruce Fraser's flagship led the way back over Moana Kiwa in mid-February 1945, Wally was one of the lads being dovetailed into *Gambia*'s ship routine and action stations. Already in three months they had been absorbed into the almost one thousand ship's company, learned the harmony of discipline, and were now topside discussing a surface bloom of red ash on the placid Tasman. Fierce New South Wales bush fires and awesome heatwave whirlwinds were lifting Eastern Australia's red topsoil and its gum-tree ash to be dusted onto the Tasman Sea and much of New Zealand; but of more interest was their first sight of Sydney Heads, then 'the Bridge' after *Gambia*'s proud entrance astern of *Howe*.

In Auckland Wally and his mates had been accustomed to Queen Street's US Marines, GOBs and GIs, shops displaying the Stars and Stripes, and a harbour full of US transports, liberty-ships, and warships waiting to escort them north. But Sydney was different. Here were the nuclei of a British Pacific Fleet: modern battleships, carriers, cruisers and destroyer flotillas, all wearing the White Ensign aft, and either the Union Flag or an individual Dominion Ensign for'ard. Shops and buildings ashore displayed the Empire's flags, and to maintain this growing BPF when it too moved north to crush the Rising Sun, there were the tail-enders of a vast fleet train of escort carriers and every type of naval auxiliary which had already departed to its North Pacific position. Pitt Street, George Street, Kings Cross, every city street, rail station and quay was thronged with RN, RAN, RCN, and RNZN uniforms wending their varied ways about the BPF base.

Gambia had anchored in Rose Bay then shifted to Woolloomoolloo, from where her liberty men passed through the fleet while making ashore to pubs time-structured due to beer rationing. Then on Thursday, 1 March 1945: 'Do you hear there. Cable party muster on the foc'sle. Clear lower decks for leaving harbour.'

Previous calls had seen all the ship's boats hoisted and secured for sea. Other calls had sent watchkeeping stokers and ERAs below to man additional boiler-rooms. All bridge officers and personnel were at their appointed stations and, with the bugler answering lesser ships' salutes, Captain Edwards conned his cruiser out through Sydney Heads to turn north in the wake of Admiral Rawlings' CS4 flagship *Swiftsure*. Again astern somewhere in a turmoil of gale force cross seas were the DCTs and funnel tops of *Argonaut*, *Black Prince* and *Euryalus*, at times their foc'sles uprooting the angry Tasman and slamming it over their for'ard turrets to smash against the bridge.

Gambia rolled and pitched sickeningly as the ships plunged northward up Australia's east coast, making life miserable for men below on greasy boiler-room foot-plates, also for those in the stifling Plot Office where Surgeon Lieutenant Pat Dunn puked turn for turn, in or at a bucket materialised to the Plot by one of his seamen team. Captain Edwards was being blamed for the ship's endless interdepartmental exercises regardless of increasing heat and Queensland's sub-tropical storms; but he had no option as the whole BPF had been ordered to prepare itself for whatever Admiral Yamamoto might have in mind as a much hotter reception. Then came the dawn stand-to when there were no distressing rollers, not even a wave or breath of wind, just heat with Navi's yeoman saying; 'No wonder the Papuans are all so bloody black, sir.'

'Yes, Wright, I agree. Pass that jug of lime juice will you.'

And this heat intensified as the ships progressed up through the Coral Sea, beyond the eastern tip of New Guinea where Australian and Japanese bodies rotted side by side along the Kokoda Trail, on across the Solomon Sea and through Dampier Strait into the Bismarck Sea, which led the 4th CS to Manus Anchorage in the Admiralty Islands.

Corked deckheads dripped condensation onto off-watch men at their messdeck meals, but they were becoming inured to this tropical environment only two degrees below the Equator. They participated in boat races against whalers, gigs and cutters from battleships who'd challenged; they watched occasional duffed landings which left carrier pilots crippled or burnt beyond recovery in their wrecked Corsairs and Seafires; then they enjoyed that artificial breeze as *Gambia* cut *Illustrious*'s wake during the BPF's shift north to Ulithi Atoll in the Carolines, to be designated Task Force 57. The calendar displayed Sunday, 18 March 1945.

To every point of the compass there were warships apparently anchored in mid-ocean, but they were all within the atoll's barely covered reef, a haven for an Allied fleet so vast that merely the tips of neighbouring battleships' mastheads showed above the eastern horizon. No leave. No need for leave as there seemed nowhere to go; but *Gambia* experienced her first Pacific War alert when a 'YELLOW' alarm chased everyone to his 'ACTION-AIR' station. 'Green' alarm relaxed men to a 'Second Degree' preparedness, then further VHF messages stood all but 'Third Degree' A/A gun-crews down. If there'd been an attack it must have been on US ships over the horizon where they stretched for another twenty miles; but there were no more alerts for the three days spent refuelling to capacity and cramming stores and ammunition into every nook and cranny.

Already Japan was reading the writing on the wall. On 22 January Stilwell's construction teams pushed his Burma Road through to China and days later when supplies began to arrive General Chiang Kai-Shek renamed it the Stilwell Road. So, now more adequately armed Chinese troops began to take a toll on the forward lines of Japan's China Expeditionary Army on 25 January, compelling Tojo to order its retreat to defend occupied Manchuria and the coast. Meantime Japanese freighters were being sunk by mines dropped into the Yangtse by India-based B–24s, while blockade runners were increasingly becoming casualties to mines dropped by B–29s in the approaches to Singapore, Penang, Saigon, and Japanese homeland harbours. On 10 February a major earthquake shook Tokyo onto which some ninety B–29s rained incendiaries to increase its devastation; then two days later General Slim's tentacles closed around Lieutenant General Hei-taro Kimura's army in the Mandalay area, while the 20th Indian Division crossed the Irrawaddy River and advanced on the vital Burmese city.

The Pacific War was now gaining impetus with successes day by day – 16 February US paratroops landing on Corregidor as a spearhead for the sea-borne US 34th Div infantrymen, a surprise operation which cost Japan 4,000 dead for the loss of only 140 GIs; 19 February, the landings on Iwo Jima which developed into a bitter four-week battle involving 30,000 young US Marines whose first ashore had been given to understand it would be a picnic; 9/10 March, 280 B–29s dropping 1,700 tons of napalm bombs on Tokyo and leaving 84,000 dead and 40,000 injured among the resultant inferno; 19 March, US Task Force 58 beginning a five-day bombardment of intended Okinawan landing sites.

Meanwhile away to the south-east one huge attack group of America's 5th Fleet had been escorting hundreds of landing ships full of US Marines and equipment north-westward from the Solomons since 8 March; another had departed Leyte on the 21st; and now on Friday 23 March the BPF as TF57 stood out to sea from Ulithi for a pit stop 400 miles east of Luzon, there to be replenished by its RN Fleet Train before continuing onward to arrive off Sakishima Gunto by 26 March. That day, 'Operation Iceberg' (America's invasion of Okinawa) was scheduled to start immediately Ad-miral Marc Mitcher's carrier force withdrew from its softening-up of Kerama Retto beachhead.

Bad weather had hampered TF57's fuelling operations by parting hoses as the ships rolled out of phase with their RFA tankers, but with the evolution completed Admiral Rawlings's flagship *King George V* arrived at the carrier's flying-off destination, 150 miles south of Okinawa as the eastern sky lightened. From his bridge Rawlings looked back at the dark bulk of his other battleship, *Howe*, then he focused his telescope on *Gambia* cruising quietly astern of *Illustrious*; *Euryalus* moving slowly through an easy slick left by *Indefatigable*; further eastward *Black Prince* bringing up a bow-wave as she and *Victorious* manoeuvred into position; as did Rear-Admiral Brind's cruiser flagship *Swiftsure* taking off knots astern of Admiral Vian's 1st Carrier Squadron flagship *Indomitable*. Already the cruiser *Argonaut* had been dis-patched to her advanced warning position 50 miles offshore of Ishigaki Airfield, halfway from the intended target and Vian's airstrike force.

Rawlings' field was now almost in place for the first delivery – the 4th Destroyer Flotilla: *Quickmatch* (Capt-D4), *Quality*, *Queenborough*, *Quiberon*; the 25th DF: *Grenville* (Capt-D25), *Ulster*, *Ulysses*, *Undaunted*, *Undine*, *Urania*, *Urchin*; and the 27th DF: *Kempenfelt* (Capt-D27), *Wager*, *Wakeful*, *Wessex*,

Whelp, Whirlwind; all were assuming their A/S and A/A screens as a vast circle around the main force in American fashion. And similarly in American fashion the airwaves were a hubbub of coded and plain language inter-fleet talk between Flag Rank and their S/Os; between CAP Control Officers and Combat Air Patrols airborne since dawn to take care of enemy intruders; and between Flight Control Officers and their Avengers, Corsairs, Hellcats, Seafires and Fireflies according to which carrier had been modified to handle the type of aircraft borne.

Gambia's action alarms had sounded as had those in every ship, and the day's events were being logged:

0600	General action stations. Bring everything to the action state.
0605	General: Four Corsairs flown off to protect *Argonaut*, four CAPs up, eight Seafires snooping bogies.
0620	Fleet turning upwind; flying off Corsairs.
0636	Flying off Strike Able, 48 Hellcats and Corsairs, 8 more CAPs, some Avengers for Fleet patrol.
0649	Bogey bearing 295, 14 miles, 2,000 ft.
0652	*Victorious* considers bogey to be *Argonaut* CAP opening out.
0658	General: Fighter strike nearly formed up. One section of Fleet CAP now at 12,000 ft.
0705	General: Small bogey group closing astern. 0708, Now reported friendly.
0715	Fighter strike going away, only CAP and medium-level patrols remain.
0743	Fighter strike estimated over target, they will be over target about half an hour.
0755	First strike completed. Pilots asking permission for re-run to use remaining ammunition. Approx 100 miles away.
0806	A/C over target in 3 groups. Pilots reporting a few A/C undamaged at NE corner of airfield. They're having another go.
0813	Pilots report heavy attack launched. Group of small ships strafed.
0827	Strike Able making one more run before reforming to return.
0900	Strike Able returning, one A/C ditched but Air Sea Rescue on way to pick up pilot.
0909	First wave approaching, nearest A/C has wounded pilot.

Indomitable's 1839 Fighter Squadron had formed up above the carrier and droned inshore where its leader Lieut (A) MacRae RNZNVR talked them onto their nominated targets at Ishigaki Airfield. Grounded planes were strafed, admin buildings set ablaze with incendiaries, and information was recorded for subsequent strikes; but not all their ammunition had been expended and, as he was leading his squadron in for a final assault his plane rocked when a 20mm shell exploded in the cockpit. Blood was streaming down his right leg from a severe wound in his thigh. On the way back he began to feel drowsy from self-injected morphine. He was flying alone; fifty miles off-course when *Indom*'s FDO gave him homing instructions. Thoughts of his mother in Pahiatua where he'd been a clerk befuddled the FDO's bearings. He concentrated on the compass. Would that unfinished letter to his fiancée ever reach her? There in blurred outline was his carrier but an indistinct voice was telling him to ditch or bale out. He didn't have the strength to do either. *Indomitable*'s stern rose and fell uneasily and he just managed to veer away before hurtling into the gun-deck below the tail of her flight deck. He came round for another try but that blasted voice was telling him his undercarriage wasn't down. He tried to lower it but the hydraulics weren't working and what did it matter as the voice droned on? 'Up right wing a bit. That's right now. Steady ... steady.'

Indom's stern was going down as her fan flashed underneath; there was a bone-jarring thump before he hurdled the first tripwire and was dragged to a sudden stop on the emergency barrier. Fire parties were racing there with their gear, arriving right behind the crash gang. First aid men were easing MacRae out of the blood-stained ruins of his cockpit but he didn't see them. He was unconscious as they hastened him by stretcher to the sick bay. His fighter was dragged out of the flight path to a parking space as landing-on resumed. As soon as possible Strike Baker would be on its way to destroy more Japanese aircraft, to strafe, bomb and launch rockets at installations. Runways had to be cratered to stop enemy aircraft refuelling on their way up from Formosa to participate in Japan's defence of Okinawa; VHF waves were still a vibrance of reports and orders heard and recorded:

1028	Strike Baker Avengers aborting reserve tanks and going in to bomb.
1104	Strike Baker 1st report, runways cratered.
1140	Firefly wants emergency landing, one rocket stuck up. 1143, making landing now. Landed safely.
1220	Strike Charlie flying off; 8 Hellcats, 4 Fireflies, 18 Avengers, 16 Corsairs. General: Strike Baker reports: 1st strike – 12 A/C on ground destroyed; meagre flak. 2nd strike – 12 single-engined, 1 four-engined on ground destroyed; 10 damaged.

1346	Walrus back with ditched pilot, has landed on *Victorious*.
1749	Strike Dog landing on. *Queenborough* depth-charging contact.
1850	'CEASE FIRING' from flagship, 'Target was a Liberator' – 'Friendly?' – 'Not now!'
1900	'Flash White'. Relax damage control parties. Darken ship. Up spirits!
2032	Assume 3rd state damage control readiness.

The time gaps shown above hadn't been idle, all VHF channels were busy throughout the day, but now it seemed there'd be enough relaxation to drink the day's tot, grab a shower then get back topside for your normal watch. Those not due till midnight were unlashing hammocks to get an hour's sleep, and their eyes had barely closed before it was time for Middle Watchmen to take over; 'Lucky bloody First Watch, four hours head-down every night.' Not this night however:

'REPEL AIRCRAFT! AT THE DOUBLE! REPEL AIRCRAFT!'

'Quarter to three, Slinger!' as men swung up and out of their slung hammocks. 'What's wrong with the dozey bastards?' But already the Plot was giving a running commentary:

0257	Bogey 5 miles *Gambia*'s beam. 'Which bloody beam?' 'Port– Sorry.' 'Wakey wakey, mate!'
0301	Bogey now a bandit.
0303	Bandit probably two-engined.
0310	*Euryalus* dispatched from fleet to open fire when well clear.
0314	*Euryalus* now firing.
0319	Bandit 13 miles south, opening.
0325	Now astern 20 miles.
0330	Still astern 35 miles.
0350	Bandits closing astern. *Indom* flying off night interceptor.
0358	Night fighter being homed by control ship, 6 miles port quarter.
0402	Bandits now red 45, 10 miles.
0406	Bandits now red 45, 17 miles opening, interceptor still looking.
0408	'Tally Ho! Two bandits, closing for attack!'
0428	Interceptor recalled, he claims hits but lost contact.
0430	'Assume 2nd state damage control readiness.'

'What's the use of crashing me swede now, Slinger? An hour and we'll be up on the pom-poms all bloody day.' He was right, and so would everyone else be at his action station, minimal spells to eat, wait for a relief before going to the heads. 'Dhobeying? Me locker's starting to stink with it, mate!'

Shortly before daylight the fleet CAPs were airborne – F6F Hellcats and adapted Corsairs at high altitude; F111 Seafires covering medium airspace; and L111 Seafires flying at a lower level but keeping clear of the day's first bomber strike protected by detachable-tank fighters. From here on there'd be a repetition of yesterday's operations, apart from the mini-drama when *Undine* raced inshore to haul 857 Squadron Leader Lt Cmdr (A) Stuart RNVR and his Avenger crew out of their ditched aircraft; then fortuitously for an American pilot she rescued him too after he'd dunked 24 hours previously. Minutes later when the US submarine *Kingfish* surfaced nearby, her skip was asked to keep a good lookout for downed British airmen, but he said he'd have to ask his boss about that. However 'his boss' must have given the okay as *Kingfish* broke silence to say he'd picked up Lt Cmdr (A) Fred Nottingham RSANVR and his Avenger crew from *Illustrious*.

This common use of R/T channels by both fleets provided light-hearted diversion as well as serious cooperation. An *Illustrious* Corsair flight led by Lt Cmdr (A) Norman Hansen RN had been flying CAP over TF57 for three hours and his flight was hungry, expecting their 1230 recall. Instead, their FDO said: 'Make it 1330, there's a good chap – Out.' Hansen's No 3 interjected, 'I say, Norman, what do we do about lunch?' and an American drawl from far to the north above Okinawa chipped in: 'Don't worry, Limey, they'll send it up to you – What else!'

Then that evening in atrocious conditions with low cloud darkening the carrier, *Indomitable*'s FDO told a returning Hellcat flight to switch on navigation lights to assist the batman. Some of the new boys hadn't done night landings, hadn't accustomed themselves to their aircrafts' light panels, and one lad queried on air: 'I say, FDO, which is the bloody light switch?' Calmly his ship's Group Commander took the mike and replied in aristocratic Oxford: 'Buggered if I know either, son. Put the bloody lot on and f..k the expense.' Immediately a Christmas tree appeared astern of *Indomitable* and the Hellcat came in with its wingtip lights, navigation lights, searchlights, the lot, illuminating the carrier's slowly heaving stern, her foaming wash, and the upperworks of every warship in considerable proximity.

Next day as a diversion TF57's battleships and cruisers were to move inshore for a bombardment; an air of excitement ran through *Gambia*, Canada's sister-ship *Uganda*, the RN's cruisers and the battleships, but well into the First Watch derisive comments preceded boredom on hearing Vice Admiral Rawlings' signal read throughout each ship: 'In view of the success of our aircraft the scheduled bombardment will not, repeat not, take place tomorrow. I am sorry to disappointment ships' companies, but further opportunities will not long be delayed.'

Three military airfields had been attacked on each of Sakishima Gunto's main islands: Hegina, Ishigaki, Miyara, on Ishigaki Shima; Sukhuma, Hirara, Nobara, on Miyako Shima. Some 600 sorties were made on aircraft and shipping; a hundred 1,000-lb and two hundred 500-lb bombs were dropped on vital targets; hundreds of rockets were fired, and thousands of 20mm cannon rounds and 12mm incendiaries left buildings and grounded aircraft ablaze in the two day's initial attacks. Numerous aircraft kills were claimed by fighter pilots escorting the fleet's bombers, but substantiation was not promulgated straight away; only our own losses as seventeen downed by flak over the target areas, and some by lift-off and landing mishaps in the inhospitable conditions offshore. Nine aircrew so far had been rescued.

Fleet meteorological officers were predicting typhoons, as were long-range US meteorological aircraft flying off the coasts of Southern Japan, Okinawa and the chain of islands right down to the Philippines, and as this placed the Sakishimas fairly central, TF57 withdrew to a few hundred miles north-east of Luzon for a rendezvous with TF112, Rear Admiral Fisher's refuelling and reammunitioning train. Meanwhile US Admiral Mitcher's carriers and the US 7th Fleet heavies were about to conclude their mass bombing and continual bombardment of Okinawa defences; and Vice Admiral Rawlings needed his task force to be fully equipped to meet a main Japanese counter-offensive off the Sakishimas, expected to coincide with the imminent invasion by massed US Marine Divisions now approaching their intended Okinawa beachhead. He wasn't wrong.

At daybreak on 18 March *Gambia's* Plot was reporting a blur of bogeys at Red 033, 40 miles; the fleet CAPs were up, fighters were being directed towards the intercept area, and the ship's loudspeakers were intoning the alert: 'General action state. Surface and air.' Calm but firm. 'Yuh hear there. Bring all quarters to the action state. Surface and air.'

They'd rehearsed it time and time again; gun crews around their mounts expectant; A/A weapons training and elevating automatically by DCT. The bogeys were now bandits, the main group at 35 miles closing; some at 22 miles, 8,000 feet, starboard beam; others at 18 miles, 6,000 feet, port quarter; more at 12 miles, 9,500 feet, astern. FDOs were homing Seafires onto this group in high cloud. They emerged from cover, identified as 20 Zekes and Oscars breaking formation as *Indefatigable's* fighters attacked. Two were plummeting, bits of fuselage trailing as they corkscrewed out of control. Sub Lt (A) Dick Reynolds RNVR said he was lining up a Zeke diving on *Indefatigable*; got off a burst then stopped firing to avoid hitting his carrier. Men were dropping at their gun blisters, blasted by the Zeke's wing-guns as it raked the port side. Reynolds' world rolled crazily, sea and sky cartwheeling, his sights flicking on and off the weaving enemy, his thumbs triggering burst after intermittent burst until his adversary's starboard wing ripped away, just before the Zero erupted in a ball of flame and bluish smoke at the base of *Indefatigable*'s island.

Unable to avoid the conflagration Reynolds hurtled his Seafire right through it and streaked at 400-plus mere feet above the flight deck in a simulated take-off. A massive saucer was punched deep into the steel decking; the island walling buckled inward, paint burning; arrestor wires and crash barriers vanished. Below in the hangar damage and fire parties were gaining control of blazing high-octane lines, extinguishing ignited fighters and bombers to be sent topside and ditched overboard along with the burnt-out Zero. At the point of impact mobile mixers were churning out quick-set concrete to fill and screed-off the massive dent; fourteen identified A/A gunners' bodies were laid out in rows; sixteen wounded lay in Sick Bay beds and, within half an hour returning aircraft were being flagged back onto *Indefatigable*'s repaired flight deck. And Reynolds? Miles away from the carrier he was exultantly claiming another kill onto which he'd been directed as it prepared to kamikaze the destroyer *Ulster*. This time he wrecked the enemy's controls so effectively that it thrashed into *Ulster*'s wash amidships, bringing her to a standstill when the Japanese underslung 16" shell exploded. Again Reynolds wasn't there to witness the result; he'd been homed onto a third fighter-bomber which disintegrated as a fireball viewed by destroyers on the outer screen – a hat-trick which cost him dearly that night at 887 Seafire Squadron's bar aboard their damaged but now fully operational carrier.

During the heat of this early morning fighter and kamikaze onslaught *Indomitable* lost one man killed and six wounded when a Zero strafed her upperworks then veered sharply through a blizzard of close barrage tracer and raced down the length of *King George V* with its guns triggered.

By 0820 those enemy planes not accounted for had fled; CAPs and fighters still airborne were identified, and Admiral Rawlings, who had predicted this attempt on TF57, now signalled Admiral Vian to launch the day's first strike on Ishigaki and Hirara airfields. 'Flash White' relaxed ships to the 3rd Degree state and at 0837 *Gambia* sent hands to breakfast in relays, a quick meal interrupted when 'Special Sea Dutymen' were piped to get out the towing gear. *Gambia* had been ordered to take *Ulster* to the Philippines, 'Geez, Bruce, that's 800 flamin' miles.'

Twenty minutes later Bruce Williams stood near the stern looking across at the little destroyer riding uneasily in a considerable swell. He'd been selected by Petty Officer Taffy Reece to go over the side, had the bowline-on-the-bight adjusted around his midriff, and now waited to be lowered away with a heavy shackle and pin. Men had grabbed *Ulster*'s Coston gun line and brought it back in through an after fairlead before hauling the attached hawser as close as safety would permit. Communication between the quarterdeck and bridge ensured that *Gambia*'s stern didn't collide with the destroyer's heaving bows. The huge eye of *Gambia*'s towline surfaced and submerged uncomfortably as Bruce struggled to attach the shackle and when the cruiser's stern went down he was neck deep in swirling water, then as it rose he dangled ominously near a slowly turning propeller, a never-again seven minutes until he at last coupled it to *Ulster*'s tow-line and yelled to be hauled back inboard.

There were other problems en route south at seven knots in the persisting heavy swell: *Ulster*'s towing bollard carried away to call on more manoeuvring skills while rearranging things on her foc'sle, just when the Radar Plot detected aircraft at 28 miles and sent both ships to 1st Degree Air Alert. Nothing developed and after long hours the tow continued. Then *Ulster* signalled a shortage of drinking water, distilling plant unserviceable, down to half a pint per man per day, 'And it's dastardly hot with no punkalouvres working. I'm issuing two bottles of beer per man per day in lieu.'

Some wit on the signal bridge flashed back, 'You sure get all the tough luck,' and disappeared. Three days out *Gambia* floated kegs of drinking water back to the destroyer, then sealed containers of food as that also was deteriorating and in short supply; and next day two badly worn links in the destroyer's cable parted, taking them five hours to wind it in by hand and more precious hours to pass a 6″ wire from *Gambia* and again shackle the tow together. This time a flap occurred when what looked like two unusual destroyers' fighting tops appeared, but evidently the bridge was expecting the two RAN escort vessels *Ballarat* and *Lismore* who thenceforth remained in company.

That night a flat calm made better towing conditions, the Philippine's northern tip showed on radar screens and men in the DCT could see distant flashes before hearing the low rumble of gunfire; it seemed there were yet pockets of Japanese to be emptied; but *Gambia* was dealing with men reporting to the Sick Bay in droves, not as a result of the distant fighting but because of a mumps epidemic. Forty-five had already been housed in a temporary isolation compartment, a signal to SMO Leyte got immediate reaction, at dusk an American naval tug relieved *Gambia* of her crippled destroyer, and now free to proceed at speed she arrived alongside a tanker in San Pedro Bay at 0900 on Friday, 6 April. Thirty-seven ratings and two engineer officers were transferred to the British hospital ship *Oxfordshire*, and a Lieutenant (E) was embarked from the escort carrier *Unicorn*.

Leyte appeared to be about the size of Hauraki Gulf, although being too far out in the bay and with only six hours allowed to onload disposable fuel tanks for TF57's fighters *Gambia* saw nothing of the town; and at 1400 she sailed in company with HMCS *Uganda* plus the destroyers HMS *Ursa* and *Urchin*, all travelling north at high speed and taking only thirty-six hours to cover what had been a five-day slog south.

Meantime Rawlings' fleet had relentlessly attacked Ishigaki and Miyako airfields to prevent their use as aircraft pit-stops midway Formosa to Okinawa. Kamikaze raids, regular fighter-bomber and torpedo-bomber attempts had been countered with minimal damage, and this good fortune stayed with the BPF task force's siege of Sakishima Gunto right through April, May and the first three weeks of June 1945 – almost when Martin Hedlund and his MV *Hauraki* shipmates were being shifted from Camp D–1 at Yokohama.

Martin's hidden notes showed that two years nine months had elapsed since their ship was captured in the Indian Ocean. Somehow many of the crew had survived Japan's rigorous winters, survived the plagues of disease-spreading vermin, and they no longer exclaimed in pain when struck repeatedly by sadistic guards bereft of humanity. Rumours were gaining intensity of a shift from Yokohama's central waterfront, probably due to increased American bombing. One day they counted 168 B29s flying high over the camp and soon they learned that Tokyo's extensive Mitsubishi Aircraft Works had been demolished. Later that afternoon the sky became pockmarked with A/A bursts as US dive-bombers attacked and sank a newly commissioned light carrier while it tried to exit the Mitsubishi breakwater. Then that night the sky lit up as 50 square miles of Tokyo City was flattened and incinerated by the heaviest concentration of bombers to date – 87,000 died in that carnage but it merely heralded the devastation to follow. Japan no longer kept their losses secret.

On 8 May Germany's capitulation filtered through to the POWs, a week after Berlin had announced Hitler's death, and now there were rumours that Tokyo was to be largely evacuated and Camp D–1's occupants were to be transferred to a town north-east of the capital.

Martin stood among the first hundred being herded into rail wagons at daylight on Saturday, 11 May. Inscrutable stone-faced Asians spat at the train windows as it creaked slowly towards an underground platform at Tokyo Central, and there with a hundred more POWs from Ofuna shoe-horned into already crowded wagons, they waited all day for a break in the bombing. Asians again spat at the barred openings in their wagons as the train jolted out, and at Marioka where they shuffled across the tracks into another train more Asians spat at them when they were given two riceballs each – the first food since leaving Yokohama – the only food issued throughout their two and a half days' journey the 350 miles to Kamaishi, a cold, dirty, steel town of 27,000 population among mountain ranges, at the head of a long narrow reach with a breakwater harbour and skinny wharf to handle incoming coal and outgoing steel.

Having arrived at night after a slow drag over the mountains they were marched forty-five minutes to their new camp and manhandled roughly into the sleeping quarters – 27″-wide pigeon-holes on bare boards arranged in tiers. 'So this is Kamaishi,' Martin Hedlund asided quietly. 'From the ashes to the fire,' he added dispiritedly to no one in particular. No one replied. Two hundred Dutch East Indiamen already in camp refused to believe the newcomers stories of massed US bombing of Japanese cities and Germany's capitulation. 'All bluidy imagination,' they insisted; then their consternation deepened when told: 'You'll see about bluidy imagination. Won't be long before this place cops it too.' But weeks dragged by with *Hauraki*'s crew awakening daily to more forced labour in the steelworks; bossed by little Asians whose ages were secreted by layers of foundry grime; merciless floggings at night in the guardhouse of a culprit who asked to see a doctor, ensuring his death rather than his inability to perform the next day's work satisfactorily.

Martin staggered to his bed-slats from one savage lashing inflicted after he overheated the CO's bath. He'd been chased around the camp while being whipped by the oath-screaming official, then sentenced to a guardhouse flogging.

Several hundred miles south at sunrise on Thursday, 21 June 1945, Okinawa's overall commander Lieutenant General Mitsuru Ushijima spoke reverently to his illustrious ancestors as he sat cross-legged, the ends of his robes tucked firmly beneath his buttocks on a ceremonial quilt. He apologised for his inability to repel the American invasion. He slowly incised a razor-sharp ceremonial knife under his ribs and attempted to draw it across his abdomen. His hands wavered. His face distorted in pain. He bowed his head.

Now seeing by this gesture that the General was in difficulty, his appointed aide upraised the family's bejewelled sword and slashed it down across the exposed neck. The Commander-in-Chief went to meet his Samurai predecessors honourably attoned.

Having stood impassive throughout the ritual, Ushijima's 2i/c Lieutenant General Cho ordered removal of his superior's bloodstained body and paraphernalia, then he supervised preparations for his own final act. Calmly seating himself in the traditional erect stance he accepted the seppuka knife, declared all resistance to cease immediately upon his demise, then without a flinch he slowly disembowelled himself.

The 81-day battle for Okinawa was over. The Japanese Navy lost some 180 vessels including their leviathan battleship *Yamato*; almost 8,000 aircraft of every type from conventional to kamikaze were destroyed; 131,000 defenders had died; and on General Cho's last command the remaining 7,500 laid down their arms. But America also paid a premium – 12,500 GIs and Marines killed, 36,800 wounded, 36 assault ships sunk and others severely damaged, 4,907 navymen dead or missing, and 793 combat aircraft shot down or lost by accident, all involving the loss of experienced airmen. But these losses in no way hindered US Admiral 'Bull' Halsey who having replenished his fleet at Leyte, sailed his TF38 on Sunday, 1 July 1945 for Japan's home waters; soon to be joined by Rawling's BPF under the new designation Task Force 37 to which New Zealand's cruisers *Achilles*, *Gambia* and the combined fleet radio repair corvette *Arabis* were attached.

Flying his flag on *Missouri*, Halsey's task forces comprised 8 new battleships, 16 fleet carriers, 18 powerful cruisers and 62 destroyers on 9 July when they deployed only 170 miles seaward of Tokyo.

Without delay he launched a thousand fighter-bombers against targets adjacent to the capital, and next day while Tokyo still reeled from that onslaught he hit again with 2,000 sorties aided by B–29s from Iwo Jima in the Bonins and repaired airstrips on Okinawa. The destruction was beyond imagination but Halsey intended Japan to know there would be no limit, so he rushed a task group 350 miles north to bombard Kamaishi steelworks before continuing another 250 miles to pound similar installations at Mururan and Hokkaido.

Air-raid sirens had wailed near midday at the Kamaishi foundry and men looked up to see light aircraft circling in light smog at several thousand feet. Then within seconds A/A gunfire resounded off hillsides as heavy explosions scurried everyone into a tunnel, there to sit crouched side by side as the ground shook. Word came through of a naval bombardment. The shelling intensified and both Japanese and POWs lay face down in trepidation when direct hits filled the air with dust and loosened mortar. A terrific thud at the tunnel entrance was followed by a blinding explosion and chaos. Jock Thomson semi-conciously heard Bill Falconer calling his name, but Jock's scalp hung down the nape of his neck dripping blood and dirt as two Dutchmen carried him outside and down into an immense shell crater. Still in the tunnel Martin Hedlund and others were removing debris in an attempt to extricate Bill Falconer from chest-high rubble, finding it difficult due to a mangled body among the reinforcing iron around his legs. Ground-shaking explosions were bringing down masonry and tunnel lining onto those assisting the badly injured shelterers; and during a lull the POWs were ordered from the tunnel. They yanked Bill outside cursing in pain, only minutes before the shelling resumed and all the Japanese inside were killed by another direct hit blast at the tunnel mouth.

Witnesses from hillside safety were amazed at the bombardment's

Achilles refuelling DR *Tenacious* with BPF, 1945.

accuracy, its shelling directed along the works' front by spotting planes, then to its distant rear and lastly throughout its central factories. Lulls in the firing may have been for more precise observation, before it resumed in frightening intensity, over and over again. Men wondered why some clusters exploded red and others billowed green, blue, yellow, white, until a naval gunner explained how the spotter observers identified individual ship's fall of shot for radioed corrections when necessary.

Eventually the firing ceased, the aircraft disappeared, those able to walk began the gruesome task of digging out injured men and women trapped under fallen concrete and twisted reinforcing. Captain Creece accompanied by Thomson with his scalp held in place by a dirty bandage, found Falconer attending to Harry Brodie's badly burned head, then because their quarters had been blasted away they slept that night under dislodged sheets of roofing iron. Daybreak awakened them to a valley shrouded in lifting smog, revealing ruined structures standing in the steelworks' confines. It was evident the output had been drastically curtailed, and in many of the stark remains there were smouldering coke ovens leaning awry, distorted, some totally wrecked; cauldrons with their spilled molten metal red-hot and solidifying; teams of Japanese and POWs working together while extricating the dead and injured beneath gaunt framing, grotesque in that pall of lowering dust, steam, blackened smoke and acrid fumes.

Yet over ensuing weeks some of the less-damaged works were repaired sufficiently to fire-up their furnaces, rail lines were replaced for arriving wagons of ore and coal, and POWs initially removed to temporary camps up the valley were returned to their partly renovated quarters. But it was obvious because of increased air reconnaissance that Kamaishi hadn't been ignored.

It hadn't been, and next time one of the bombardment force would be HMNZS *Gambia*.

CHAPTER XXI

Achilles *Goes North and Joins the BPF*

Gambia HAD BEEN WITH TF57's 4th Cruiser Squadron in the north-west Pacific since March 1945; but what of *Achilles* after her fourteen months in Pompey Docks since 22 March 1943. On Tuesday, 23 May 1944 Captain F.J. Butler MBE RN commissioned her with a 90 per cent RNZN ship's company, a large proportion from *Leander* which had been left in Boston; 400 'Defect List' items were yet uncompleted but Butler had notice to quit Portsmouth whose berths were urgently required for invasion ships daily swelling the harbour's cross-Channel armada. These defects were largely self-doctored but she missed the Normandy landings, missed the South of France Mediterranean landings and worked her way via the Suez Canal, Bombay, Colombo, Trincomalee, Fremantle, Hobart, to a Monday, 5 February 1945 Auckland arrival, several days after *Gambia*'s departure for Sydney and the Pacific War. It would be another ten weeks before *Achilles* followed, and to realise what lay ahead for her we will recount the changing pattern of naval warfare since 'Pearl Harbour'.

Immediately after much of the USN's Pacific Fleet was decimated at its Hawaiian base, Japan's Imperial Navy Command dispatched its fast carrier force on a sequence of operations intended to gain mastery over the waters of Burma, the Dutch East Indies, North Australia and the North-west and Central Pacific. When this was accomplished Japan would consolidate before further expansion. But in the ensuing five months her big 27-knot, multi-plane carriers *Akagi*, *Hiryu*, *Kaga*, *Shokaku*, *Soryu* and *Zuikaku*, which had devastated British, Dutch and American strongholds in the Pacific and Indian Oceans, suffered damage and the loss of irreplaceable aircraft, and more drastically their experienced pilots in combat and by accident; perhaps not then a decisive factor, but one which denied the Japanese Navy its use of *Akagi*, *Hiryu* and *Soryu* in its attempted early May 1942 Port Moresby invasion. Only its hastily repaired *Shokaku*, *Zuikaku* and the light carrier *Shoho* were available for Rear Admiral Hara when he led the assault force from Rabaul.

Per 'Enigma' American cryptologists kept C-in-C Pacific, Chester Nimitz, aware of Admiral Shigeyoshi Inouye's complex plan involving navy, army and air groups from Rabaul, Tulagi and Truk. Nimitz disposed the carriers *Lexington*, *Yorktown*, and the cruisers USS *Chicago*, HMAS *Australia* and

Hobart in intercept positions south-east of San Cristobal Island around which he expected the Japanese to enter the Coral Sea; and he put HMNZS *Achilles* and *Leander* on stand-by in Vila where they were supporting US Marine garrison forces occupying New Hebridean islands.

In the four-day Coral Sea battle none of the opposing ships sighted each other: the Allies lost *Lexington* to bomb damage so intensive she had to be sent down by US destroyer *Phelps'* torpedoes; Japan lost *Shoho*; *Shokaku* retired ablaze and low in the water, unable to retrieve her aircraft; and *Zuikako* left the area undamaged but minus all *her* aircraft.

Without air support the Moresby attempt was cancelled and Japan's warlords reorganised their strike groups to neutralise then occupy Midway, another fiasco in which Japan lost the carriers *Hiryu*, *Kaga*, *Akagi* and *Soryu*. America lost *Yorktown* but, thinking there were more than the three US carriers involved Admiral Yamamoto aborted the entire operation. Henceforth America's ability to outbuild Japan in every type of ship or aircraft would ensure Allied success in the Pacific; statistics rather than heroics or fanaticism would decide the outcome. But still in control of French Indo-China, the Malay Peninsula, Borneo and the Dutch East Indies, Japan tried again to reach Port Moresby, this time by landing near Buna on northern Papua then crossing the Owen Stanley Range. Again they were unsuccessful, being repulsed in fierce hand-to-hand jungle fighting by relentless Australian troops who asked for no mercy and gave none.

Japan now had no alternative than the abandonment of her planned invasion of New Caledonia, Samoa and Fiji; it was time to consolidate on Guadalcanal; Truk and Rabaul would be their strategic bases. And opposing these enemy plans, US Joint Chiefs of Staff were intensifying their northward advance, initially onto Santa Cruz, then Tulagi, Guadalcanal and onward to Bougainville. But both powers had underestimated each other's determination and it took two years for the Allies to wrest the Solomons from their fanatical occupiers, a feat emblazoned in Pacific history by successive naval engagements:

'Savo Island'	9 August 1942	'Cape Esperance'	11–12 October 1942
'Santa Cruz'	26 October 1942	'Savo Island'	12–13 and 14–15 Nov 1942
'Kula Gulf'	5–6 July 1943	'Kolombangara'	12–13 and 14–15 July 1943
'Vella Gulf'	6–7 August 1943	'Empress Augusta Bay'	1–2 November 1943

There were others perhaps not so well documented during those night surface encounters and daylight air assaults giving birth to place-names: *Henderson Field*, *The Slot*, *Torpedo Junction*, *Iron Bottom Sound*. Surrounding seas became the graveyard of battleships, carriers, cruisers, destroyers, troopships and supply vessels of all combatants; and there would have been more in the immediate aftermath of Empress Augusta Bay, if Vice Admiral

Takeo Kurita's six heavy cruisers and mass of destroyers hadn't been reported entering Rabaul to refuel en route to redress Japan's setback.

Having no battleships or heavy cruisers right then at his disposal, Halsey told Rear Admiral Fred Sherman to get there quick with the carriers *Saratoga* and *Princeton*; they arrived 200 miles south-east of Rabaul on Wednesday, 5 November, launched strikes of Corsairs, SBD dive-bombers, Avenger torpedo-bombers, and fighter escorts, which so severely damaged five of Kurita's six cruisers that they just made it back to Truk.

Placed under Japanese mandate after the First World War, the Caroline Islands' 549 volcanic upthrusts and coral atolls stretch along the West Central Pacific's 5 to 9 degree North parallel, with Yap at its western extremity only 800 miles east of Leyte in the Philippines; 1,400 miles east of Yap, Ponape marks the Carolines' eastern extent, and coming back 400 miles we find Japan's strategic Truk Archipelago. Volcanic activity had created a low 1,400-feet peak looking across 50 square miles of rich alluvium, now blanketed by coconut plantations punctuated with Micronesian villages, adjacent to military airfields interconnected by paved roads leading to Truk City's sizable population. Millions of years of coral growth had encompassed this tiny archipelago within a 30-mile diameter reef, penetrable only through four narrow gaps; a natural haven in flying distance to other island groups around the compass.

From the stratosphere we look down at this sunbathed tropical paradise, its coral halo glistening white when lapped by swells coursing down from the East Mariana and Philippine Geological Basins; its islands Dublon, Moen, Tol, Udot, Uman and lesser jewels set green within their crown of crystal-clear security. Probably pre-war, in those idyllic days of peace, Japan had named four of them Natsu (Summer), Aki (Autumn), Fuyu (Winter), Haru (Spring).

But now we focus on a straggle of damaged cruisers and destroyers negotiating a boom-defended entrance, dispersing to allocated berths. Foam spreads astern as each takes off way. Anchors splash and they ease back to run out their cables. Oilers sidle close to replenish tanks, then water barges, ammunition lighters, storeships; each in turn as night edges away the sun's last rays, blacks out the town and its anchorages. The Japanese Combined Fleet lies secure inside Truk's closed boom-gate, and at daybreak surrounding seas will be under surveillance by Dublon's long-range flying boats, then Truk's airfields will become hives of anticipatory activity.

It was from here in November 1940 that Lieutenant Michiharu Shinya sailed as Torpedo Officer of the destroyer *Akatsuki*, a unit of the screen for Vice Admiral Hiroaki Abe's battleships *Hiei* and *Kirishima* which, supported by the carriers *Junyo*, *Hiyo*, and large cruisers of the 2nd Fleet under Vice Admiral Nabutake Kondo, were to give Guadalcanal's Henderson Field a concentrated bombing and bombardment. But Lieutenant Shinya would not see the outcome of this operation; his destroyer came under fire shortly after midnight 13 November off Savo Island. Hit and sunk by 8″ cruiser shells *Akatsuki* left dozens clinging to whatever floated, but next day only a few were found and dragged protesting weakly aboard an American landing craft. Eventually shipped down to New Zealand's Featherston Camp, Michiharu Shinya described the mass shooting incident of 25 February 1943 without bias. Whilst in camp he turned to Christianity, in later years graduating from Chicago's McCormick Theological College and, in 1979 becoming Principal of the Japan Biblical Seminary. His translated book *The Path from Guadalcana* provides an insight to the minds of those Japanese naval and construction-gang POWs at Featherston.

It was also from Truk that the Zero which attacked *Achilles* off Guadalcanal's Cape Esperance on 5 January 1943 had flown with pit stops en route. And here it might be relevant to emphasise the two-year swing of naval strength in America's favour. We will compare opposing forces on 26 October 1942 at Santa Cruz to those on 26 October 1944 at *Leyte Gulf.*

The Battle of Santa Cruz (Solomons) 26 October 1942

United States Navy C-in-C South Pacific Admiral W. Halsey

TF16 Adml T. Kincaid	TF17 RAdml R. Spruance	TF64 RAdml W.A. Lee
Carrier *Enterprise* (Flg)	Carrier *Hornet* (Flg)	Btlshp *Washington* (Flg)
Btlship *South Dakota*	Cruiser *Northampton*	Crs *Atlanta, Helena, San*
Crsr *San Juan*		*Fransisco*
Screen 9 destroyers	Screen 6 destroyers	Screen 6 destroyers

Japanese Imperial Navy Combined Fleet Cmdr Adml Isoroku Yamamoto

Advance Force		Vanguard Force		Strike Force	
Adml Nabutake Kondo		Adml Hiroaki Abe		Adml Chuichi Nagumo	
Btlships	*Kongo*	Btlships	*Kirishima*	Carriers	*Shokaku* (Flag)
	Haruna		*Hiei*		*Zuikaku*
Lt Crsr	*Sendai*	Hvy Crs	*Chikuma*		*Zuiho*
Screen	12 drs		*Suzuya*	Lt Crsr	*Kumano*
Carrier	*Junyo*		*Tone*	Screen	8 drs
Escort	2 drs	Lt Crsr	*Nagara*		
Hvy Crs	*Atago*	Screen	12 drs		
	Takao				
Screen	5 drs				

USN Total = 30 Warships	Japanese Total = 55 Warships

Battle of Leyte Gulf (Philippines) 23–26 October 1944

USN Third Fleet Adml W. Halsey

TF38 Carriers Adml Marc Mitscher

TG38.1 Adml J. McCain		TG38.2 Adml G. Bogan		TG38.3 Adml F. Sherman	
Carriers	Wasp II	Carriers	Independence	Carriers	Langley
	Hornet II		Intrepid		Princeton
	Hancock		Cabot		Lexington
	Cowpens	Btlshps	Iowa	Screen	10 dstrs
	Monterey		New Jersey		
Cruisers	Chester	Cruisers	Biloxi	TG38.4 Adml R. Davisen	
	Oakland		Miami	Carriers	Enterprise
	Pensacola		Vincennes	Belleau Wood	Franklin
	Salt Lake City	Screen	16 dstrs		San Jacinto
	San Diego			Cruisers	New Orleans
Screen	13 destroyers				Wichita
				Screen	13 destroyers

USN Seventh Fleet Adml T. C. Kincaid

TG77.2 Adml J. Oldendorf		TG77.3 Adml R. Berkey		TG77.4.1 Adml T. Sprague	
Btlshps	Mississippi	Crsrs	Boise	Esct Carriers	Sangamon
	California		HMAS Shropshire	Chenango	Suwannee
	Maryland		Phoenix	Saginaw Bay	Santee
	Tennessee	Screen	5 US drs and		Petrov Bay
	Pennsylvania		HMAS Arunta	Screen	6 destroyers
	West Virginia				
Screen	16 destroyers			TG77.4.2 Adml F. Stump	
Cruisers	Columbia			Esct Carriers	Natona Bay / Manila Bay
	Denver				Marcus Island / Kadashan Bay
	Louisville				Savo Island / Omnamey Bay
	Minneapolis			Screen	8 destroyers
	Portland				
Screen	11 destroyers			TG77.4.3 Adml C.A.F. Sprague	
				Esct Carriers	Fanshaw Bay / St Lo
					Kalinin Bay / Kitkun Bay
					Gambier Bay / White Plains
				Screen	7 destroyers

Japanese Imperial Navy Combined Fleet Adml Soemu Toyoda					
Carrier Force		Force A		Force C	
V Adml J. Ozawa		V Adml T. Kurita		V Adml S. Nishimura	
Carriers	Zuikaku	Btlshps	Yamato	Btlshps	Yamishiro
	Chitose		Kongo		Fuso
	Chiyoda		Haruna	Cruiser	Mogami
	Zuiho	Cruisers	Atago	Screen	4 dstrs
Lt Crsrs	Isuzu		Haguro	Chikuma	
	Oyoda		Chokai	Kumano	2nd Strike Force
	Tama		Myoko	Takao	V Adml K. Shima
Screen	8 dstrs		Tone	Suzuya	Cruisers	Abukuma
			Maya	Noshiro	Ashigara	Nachi
				Yahagi	Screen	4 destroyers
		Screen	15 dstrs		

USN Total	Japan Total
8 battleships	7 battleships
15 carriers	4 carriers
18 escort carriers	19 cruisers
18 cruisers	31 destroyers
106 destroyers	61 warships
165 warships	

After the Allied land, air, and sea successes in the Central and Western Pacific and Asia, General Douglas MacArthur plugged hard for an all-out blitz to repossess the Philippines. Admiral Chester Nimitz opposed this proposal and in mid-1943 convinced the US Joint Chiefs of Staff that his campaign-tested surface, air and amphibian forces should now be launched against Japan's outer perimeter bases. His 5th Fleet (US Central Pacific Force) operating as three separate but cohesive units – TF52 (Northern Amphibious Force), amassing in Hawaii for an assault on Makin in the Japanese-occupied Gilbert and Ellice Islands; TF53 (Southern Amphibious Force), assembling in Wellington New Zealand, and Efate in the New Hebrides, with its target Tarawa; and TF50 (Fast Carrier Force), divided into three groups of modern battleships, carriers, heavy and light cruisers, and destroyer desrons, each in support of the landings. Another force, TF57, comprising land-based flying boats and heavy bombers including a hundred-plus Liberators under Rear Admiral John H. Hoover, would soften up intended beachheads, then as required give support from their bases in Samoa and the restored Solomons and New Hebrides airfields.

One of the coincidences of life appears hereabouts by the similarity of top-brass surnames in North Africa and the Pacific:

Admiral Sir Andrew Browne Cunningham (C-in-C Med till 1943)

Admiral Sir John H.D. Cunningham (C-in-C Med after his brother)

Lt Gen Sir Alan Cunningham (Commanded drive into Italian Somaliland)

Now back to the Pacific in 1943 where three top US commanders share a name during the Marshall Islands campaign:

Maj Gen Holland M. Smith USMC (5th Amphibious Corps – overall CO)

Maj Gen Julian C. Smith USMC (2nd Marine Div – Target Tarawa)

Maj Gen Ralph C. Smith US Army (27th Infantry Division – Target Makin).

On Monday, 10 November 1943 Com 5th Fleet, Vice Admiral Raymond Spruance hoisted the 'LET'S GO' for his 200-ship, 1,000-aircraft assaults. To make the enemy divide any major counter, both Tarawa and Makin were timed to be struck at daylight on Thursday, 20 November and, although defended to the death of virtually every Japanese, Makin first, then Tarawa, fell to the US Army and Marine assailants within four days.

Within two months airstrips and facilities were repaired and adapted; strike and assault groups were reorganised for C-in-C Admiral Nimitz's Marshall Islands offensive. On Saturday, 29 January 1944 Admiral Hoover's Tarawa-based aircraft mass-bombed Jaluit's and Mili's defences, while Wotje and Maloelap were given similar treatment by one group of the carriers involved. The remainder concentrated on Kwajalein, the main objective, and some of the fifteen battleship and eighteen heavy cruiser armada closed inshore to bombard Eniwetok with 16″ and 8″ shells, all day and night without pause on the 30th; then in the first glimmer of dawn 53,000 GIs and Leathernecks poured ashore from troopships discharging and immediately getting out of the way of successive arrivals.

By Friday, 4 February the Stars and Stripes were flaunting atop Japanese flagpoles throughout the Marshall Islands; 177 Americans were dead and under a thousand were wounded, against 8,000-plus Japanese killed and only a few hundred wounded and taken prisoner of war.

TF50's aircraft carriers now pounded Truk on 16–17 February 1944, destroying 270 aircraft, razing depots and administration complexes, sinking 2 cruisers, 4 destroyers, numerous lesser naval craft and 30 merchant vessels – one of them the Union Steamship Company's motor vessel

Hauraki captured in July 1942 in the Indian Ocean, renamed *Horagi Maru* and for many months used by the Japanese as a fast troop transport.

The Rising Sun had initially scorched the pants off America's and Britain's slumbering Pacific admirals and generals, but within two years their successors were tugging hard on the halyards of the Emperor's ensign. C-in-C Japan's Combined Fleet, Admiral Isoroku Yamamoto was ambushed and killed by Guadalcanal-based P–38s sent to intercept his plane known to be flying him to Bougainville's Kahili airfield on Sunday, 18 April 1943; his successor, Admiral Mineichi Koga, experienced ten months of setbacks culminating in the 16–17 February 1944 devastation of his Truk Headquarters; he shifted what remained of his Combined Fleet to Palau but when deciding to transfer it further to Cebu in the Philippines, he and his top Navy execs died in a night storm on Friday, 31 March when their flying boat crashed and disintegrated on landing.

The stage was now rearranged for Japan's Navy swansong, Yokosuka Base Commander, Vice Admiral Soyamu Toyoda, being given the leading role; his theatre would have its opening night in Leyte Gulf but the credits would not headline him as that year's star. America declared 'The Battle of Leyte Gulf – 23–26 October 1944' to have been the greatest naval engagement in history, perhaps a bit aggrandising, but it cost Japan a lot of ships and face. During the various gunnery, torpedo, and air engagements their Mobile Fleet lost the 75,000-ton 18″-gunned battleship *Musashi;* 30,000-ton battleships *Fuso, Yamashiro;* heavy cruisers *Atago, Chikuma, Maya, Myoko, Suzuya;* light cruisers *Abukuma, Noshiro, Tama;* fleet carrier *Zuikaku;* light carriers *Chitose, Chiyoda, Zuiho;* and the destroyers *Asagumo, Hatsuyuki, Isokaze, Kasumi, Michishio, Sugi, Usho, Urukaze, Yamagumo.*

America lost her light carrier *Princeton;* escort carriers *Gambier Bay, St Lo;* destroyers *Hoel, Johnston,* and escort destroyer *Samuel B. Roberts,* an overwhelming victory which left the US Pacific Fleet an unrestricted passport to go almost wherever it might be dispatched. But one of the battle's more ferocious episodes deserves its place in written history.

US Rear Admiral Clifton A.F. Sprague's Northern Carrier Group 77.4.31 – escort carriers *Fanshaw Bay* (Flag), *Kalinin Bay, St Lo, White Plains* – Group 77.4.32 – escort carriers *Kitkun Bay, Gambier Bay,* their destroyers *Hoel, Heerman, Johnston;* and the escort destroyers *Dennis, John C Butler, Raymond* and *Samuel B Roberts* – were giving support to the 25 October 1944 US landings on Leyte, when Catalina pilot Ensign Jansen on his A/S reconnaissance at daybreak reported four enemy battleships, eight cruisers and a number of destroyers only 20 miles from Sprague's carriers, on a closing course. Relief was 300 miles away, escape for the 18-knot 'Woolworths' impossible from the monster battleship *Yamato,* her conventional battleships *Kongo, Haruna, Nagato,* together with the modern Atago Class 8″ cruisers and their destroyer flotillas approaching and now in sight. But Admiral Kurita, having the previous day witnessed the loss of his sister-leviathan *Musashi* to aerial bombing and torpedoing, was over cautious and reversed course with torpedo trails to port and starboard hurrying him away from the action.

There'd been bedlam as Sprague's three destroyers and lightly armed escort destroyers raced in and out of their smoke screens, closing to point-blank range to launch their torpedoes and fire their 5″ guns. Commander Ernest Evans ran his destroyer *Johnston* full speed at the heavy cruiser *Kumano*, scoring hits about her high-rise fighting top and launching ten torpedoes while turning to retire. Regaining the shelter of his smoke-screen he heard two underwater detonations and emerged to see *Kumano* ablaze forward, crippled beyond further participation; but two enemy salvoes had knocked out his after boiler and engine-room, killing many of his crew including three bridge officers, stripping him topless and blasting off two fingers.

Again and again some of the enemy battlefleet tried to close and destroy Sprague's escort carriers, only to be turned away by determined US destroyer counter-attacks until all their torpedoes were expended. *White Plains* shook three separate times as 14″ salvoes straddled her; then *Hoel* was hit when turning to launch torpedoes at *Kumano*, came to a sudden stop with her guns still blazing, but took merciless punishment and had to be abandoned at 0835. *Kalinin Bay* took thirteen direct 8″ hits in the hour from 0750 but somehow remained operative; *Fanshaw Bay* and *White Plains* were hit although not seriously; *Gambier Bay* came under the enemy 8″ cruisers' range at 0810 and was left listing, on fire and being hit continually until *Heerman*, and *Johnston* with only three guns serviceable, both engaged *Chikuma* at 6,000 yards. Now *Raymond* and *Samuel B Roberts* emerged from smoke screens to divert *Chikuma*'s 8″ gunnery off the crippled carrier, then *John C Butler* arrived ahead of *Dennis* to initiate a 'David and Goliath' enactment against the heavy cruisers *Chikuma*, *Haguro*, *Chokai* and *Tone*.

Shortly, with her guns destroyed by direct hits and all her torpedoes launched *Dennis* had to retire, just as *Samuel B Roberts* was smothered stem to stern by 8″ shells and a salvo of 14″ which wrenched her apart, a distorted mess of abandoned metal hissing steam as she foundered. Survivors in the water watched in dismay as *Hoel* capsized and sank. Then it seemed the imminent end for *Gambier Bay*, but right when the destroyer *Yahagi* manoeuvred to launch torpedoes, Commander Evans urged his battered *Johnston* across the line of sight and forced *Yahagi* away with several 5″ hits. Now sandwiched between Japanese cruisers and a squadron of enemy destroyers, Evans' ship was doomed; large and small shells wrecked the remaining engine-room, brought her to a standstill drastically listed among a ring of hyenas circling for the kill. Evans died when an explosion evaporated his submerging bridge. He did not witness the final torpedo strike which sank his destroyer; nor did he see the Japanese Captain who launched that missile, now facing outboard as his destroyer swept by, standing at attention and saluting in honour of a gallant opponent. But one of *Johnston*'s few survivors saw that act of recognition and later placed it on record.

Commander Evans' determination did not save *Gambier Bay* which went down at 0825, nor did the other destroyers and destroyer escorts save *St Lo* which possibly rated the distinction of being the first warship sunk by a Kamikaze pilot who crashed his adapted Zero almost vertically down through her flight-deck. *St Lo* would not however be the last, and many USN and RN warships would be subjected to this Japanese innovation in the long months to follow.

So to cope, Allied ships bristled with radar-controlled A/A weaponry and *Achilles* was no exception. The removal of her X-turret may have instilled nightmares in gunners who'd sweated throughout the heat of 'River Plate', but the change from four single 4″ to four twin 4″ A/A mounts, plus a mass of pom-poms and other multiple-barrelled close-barrage automatics, meant that when she departed Auckland via Sydney for the war zone on Thursday, 26 April 1945 she stood proud alongside most modern light cruisers.

Whilst in Calliope Dockyard the usual complement changes took place, some being drafted to shore establishments as newcomers arrived, one being a 1923-born pre-war Dunedin bike shop mechanic James Alec Flash Mac McGregor. Mac served in the 1942 13th call-up ballot, transferred in June 1944 to a *Tamaki* Stoker Class until drafted to HMNZS *Cook*'s Base Party, then in April 1944 shouldered his bag and hammock up *Achilles*' gangway and into Mess 39 – Service number NZ9884, 'G' for grog, action station Damage Control Party Wardroom Flat, watch station 'A' Boiler Room: 'Report to the Stoker's RPO.'

Born in Hastings on 15 December 1923 David Eric Comin schooled at Mahora Primary then for four years at Wellington's Scot's College, until 1940 when he started as a clerk for Hastings 'Loan & Merc'. Whilst there he received an army call-up in 1944, but was exonerated when the Wellington Loan & Mercantile office required his expertise. His application for the RNZN's Scheme 'B' was declined due to impaired eyesight, but before he completed a private wireless telegraphy course the Navy enrolled him in its Supply Branch, with a draft to Shelly Bay, Wellington where he celebrated his 21st birthday. 'Celebrated? Bloody near Obliterated! My messmates almost pickled me in bubbly, then hid me during Rounds on a shelf so high that an intoxicated fall could have killed me.' But he didn't fall and moments before *Achilles* departed Auckland for the BPF, Stores Assistant D.E. Comin deposited his gear in Mess 6 starboard side aft of the Canteen Flat, directly under S1 twin 4″ A/A mount. Action Station – 'B'-turret cordite magazine, work place Engineer's Store, abandon ship station etc. etc. etc.

Thus they came aboard day by day, singly from small ships, in groups from Motuihe Island's *Tamaki*, from everywhere and anywhere until a late one was left scratching his head on Calliope Wharf, gear at his feet as the last line splashed overboard. On rounding North Head, Captain Butler asked for more revs en route for Sydney with expectations of a pit stop before speeding north.

'No, no, no, *Achilles*; you've got to teach your new lads how to handle all that latest technology. Then you can go.'

So the ship worked up in Jervis Bay throughout early May, learning on the 9th that the war in Europe had ended; a cause for excess rum dissipation by RNs still on *Achilles'* books, but something of an anti-climax for RNZNs who'd done their bit on that side of the world and were now keen to bloody Hirohito's nose. Each day A/A gunnery improved, fire drills ended quicker, so did damage control exercises plus towing evolutions and other situations dreamt up by Commander Roskill, until he reported the ship ready to proceed, this occurring a.m. on Friday, 11 May 1945 in execution of the contents of Captain Butler's 'Sealed Envelope'.

Meanwhile a hundred miles east of Sakishima Gunto TF57 hadn't been having things all its own way. Fighter-bombers were coming up against intensified flak over the target areas, resulting in increasing casualties; rocket-firing Fireflies streaking at roof level over airfield buildings to launch their missiles straight into caves sheltering enemy aircraft, were sometimes misjudging their escape and crashing into cliffs; and bad weather was creating difficulties in replenishing the dwindling number of available aircraft, so on 23 April the BPF had gone a thousand miles south to the Philippines' San Pedro Bay. *Gambia* berthed close inshore, close to banana plantations, thatched houses among coconut palms and luxuriantly flowering trees, all inaccessible due to her yellow quarantine flag. Bad mumps cases were again transferred to HMNZHS *Maunganui* and Admiral Rawlings authorised a beer issue to *Gambia* due to her plight. Then on Sunday, 29 April Captain William-Powlett said a moving farewell after quarterdeck church, before introducing his successor Captain R.A.B. Edwards CBE, a 44-year-old RN officer who'd been a 'snottie' on the battleship *Tiger* from 1917 to 1919, ranked Captain at Naval Staff Admiralty in 1939, then in 1941 a VIP member of C-in-C Eastern Fleet's staff until his *Gambia* appointment. Meantime aboard *KG V*, Admiral Sir Bernard Rawlings was conferring with USN C-in-C Admiral Chester Nimitz, countering a clique of US VIPs who wished to use TF57 in their Borneo operations, a proposal rejected by Nimitz who insisted the BPF air-strikes against the Sakishimas were vital to the success of the Okinawa campaign. B–29s from Iwo Jima, and US 5th Fleet bombers were softening up Japan's homeland islands, Kyushu, Shikoku, Honshu; and all means possible must be fully exploited to prevent enemy assistance from the south: 'How's about one of your naval bombardments, Bernard?'

'Thought you'd never ask.'

The BPF moved out of San Pedro Bay on Tuesday, 1 May, exercised all manner of A/A firing at towed drogues, and arrived two days later at the Fleet Train for fuel preparatory to a bombardment of Miyako and Ishigaki airfields now reported to be fully operational; and at 1006 while moving inshore, the gunnery forces were detached as two divisions: *KG V* and *Howe* accompanied by *Uganda* to bombard southern targets: *Swiftsure*, *Gambia*, *Euryalus*, *Black Prince*, those to the north.

By mid-day Ishigaki and Miyako were in sight at several miles from the ships' DCTs, lush green and flat, pleasant countryside; but *Gambia's* tourists were being otherwise entertained: 'Hear this,' over the speakers. 'The ship will remain at the alert from now until we are cleared after the bombardment. Ratings at upperdeck positions keep your eyes open for any enemy surface device that may be sent against the task force.'

To the south black smoke could be seen billowing from the battleships' salvoes, moments later followed by their thunderclap; but now the 4th CS's gunnery was drowning out all but their own as *Euryalus* and *Black Prince* shelled Nobara field's shore batteries and A/A emplacements, while *Swiftsure's* and *Gambia's* salvoes tore house-sized craters into the length and breadth of spotter-plane indicated runways. All ships cruised at a mean range of 18,000 yds offshore, turned 180 degrees in single file at the end of their run, turrets revolving and long barrels waving independently until corrected for elevation, declination and deviation. Then fire gongs rang again, heavy jolts broke messdeck crockery and filled compartments with fumes, and a spotter reported that a W/T complex that was, wasn't. Two high-rise chimneys wavered then collapsed into a vast pall of dust-laden smog, and so it continued until Admiral Vian's carriers 100 miles seaward radioed for A/A assistance.

While TF57's battleships, cruisers and destroyers were busy shoreside, enemy fighter-bombers and suicide planes had approached the carriers undetected at wave-top level, streaking skyward to get plummeting velocity before diving. Some of these were 'Tally Hoed' and splashed by CAP fighters, but one got through *Formidable's* desperate barrage as she turned and counter-turned at speed. Hit repeatedly it glanced off the superstructure and exploded 100 feet clear on striking the surface. Attempts were made on Rawlings' fast returning bombardment force but night closed in to end the day's events.

More attempts to break through defensive CAPs on Monday, 7 May ended with Zeke after Zeke being splashed, or blown to bits when the fleet's intense barrage detonated the Kamikaze's attached missile. But near 1130 one careered down onto *Formidable* midships, disintegrating in a flaming explosion which punched a massive saucer with a central puncture in her steel flight-deck. A bomb fragment penetrated several decks to an engine-room, causing damage which drastically reduced her speed. Parked aircraft and others about to fly off were wrecked, eight crew died and forty-seven received terrible injuries when hurled against nearby super-structure; with debris searing skyward in a pillar of rolling smoke Captain Ruck-Keene exclaimed: 'Little yellow bastard!' over his TBS mike. Then his face creased in a wry grin when Rear Admiral Vian replied from *Indomitable*: 'Are you addressing me, Ruck?' But an attack on Vian's flagship terminated their frivolity as a Kamikaze crashed obliquely onto the flight-deck and hurtled overboard leaving death and twisted Seafires to be dealt with.

Throughout that afternoon more Kamikazes spiralled seaward, shot out of the sky by Corsairs, Fireflies and Seafires, the last three being downed at dusk by 887 Squadron Seafire pilots Sub Lt (A) Charlich, Netherlands Navy, CPO (A) Bird RN and Lt (A) MacCleod RNZNVR.

Impossible flying conditions for the Japanese and British made the 8th a rest day; then 9 May came in with a vengeance; Avengers, Corsairs, Fireflies swept inshore, strike after strike throughout the forenoon, their participation and results being continually voiced and logged by pencil or typewriter according to the ability of ships' VHF telegraphists. Then it seemed to be Japan's innings when *Victorious* became the target for two Zekes only minutes apart. On and on the first one swept through the carrier's concentrated Oerlikons, pom-poms, multi-barrelled .5s and short-fused 4.5″ barrage, banging down on the flight-deck and slithering forward in a ball of flame to damage the catapult and forward lift. And no sooner had fire parties and damage control teams arrived than the second suicide plane roared in, already on fire from the wall of small arms destruction encountered, veering wildly as its port wing boomeranged into space, then whirling, engine still revving among Corsairs now ablaze on the after park. A pom-pom gunner turned to see his mate clambering over the blister's protective steel skirt, blood pumping from where his face had been. He tried to reach him but the lad leapt for a swifter death in the carrier's thrashing screws.

Formidable's gunners were now unleashing a frenzy of tracered ack-ack, thumping Oerlikons, rhythmic pom-poms through which a Kamikaze bore down to explode among eighteen Avengers and Corsairs massed on deck. Others below in a hangar burst into flames when high octane lines ruptured and sprayed blazing fuel; yet as with previous suicide attacks the conflagration was brought under control and FDOs authorised returning aircraft to queue for landing on.

Over the past weeks five BPF carriers had been kamikazied, *Formidable* and *Indomitable* twice, but their armoured-steel flight-decks were designed for maximum protection and all five remained operational. Guncrews with experience gained off Norway, off Malta, and in the Taranto raid, now earned Admiral Vian's written commendation:

> With suicide aircraft screaming straight down at them, seemingly intent on crashing among them, our gun crews served their guns undeterred.
>
> Without their steadfastness more kamikazes would have made direct hits. On *Indomitable* their coolness filled me with admiration, and other ships in my squadron have told the same story.

Bad weather dogged TF57's final series of strikes against the Sakishimas; reluctantly Admiral Rawlings dispatched *Formidable* south from the replenishment area when Corsair guns accidently fired in their hangar, starting a series of ammunition explosions and uncontrollable fuel ignitions which destroyed twenty-three Corsairs and numerous Avengers. This occurred on Tuesday, 22 May shortly after *Achilles'* arrival at the 'Cootie' train, just

Formidable: Kamikazied but operational in an hour.

in time for TF57's 12th and final assault on Ishigaki, Hegina, Miyara, Sukhuma, Hirara and Nobara airfields. She cruised a thousand yards abeam of the remaining three carriers, listening to a war she couldn't see. It was being waged a hundred miles west beyond the heavy seas into which *Indefatigable, Indomitable* and *Victorious* plunged. Through lookout glasses and telescopes men watched brave pilots lifting off when their carrier's nose came up, saw their aircraft small at that distance, clawing for flying statistics sometimes through the remnants of angry spray.

Then later throughout the forenoon, other men saw the bombers and fighters return in strict formation along the fleet's 'safe path' outside of which they'd be fired at. Most made it when called-in astern over the heaving tail; but there were some whose luck had deserted them, when their carrier rolled or pitched unexpectedly and they crashed in her wake. Lt Cmdr (A) J.B. Edmundsen RN as CO of *Victorious*'s 1836 Squadron, ditched after an attack on a Miyako airfield but couldn't get out when his Corsair disappeared below. Another Corsair given clearance for an emergency landing ripped out the arrestor wires and smashed through barrier after barrier before skidding overboard in flames with his propeller still screaming. The pilot, Sub Lt (A) Hardiman RNVR and several deck handlers on *Victorious* were killed, and waiting aircraft were directed onto *Indefatigable* while temporary arrestors and barriers were erected.

One top-level report said aircraft losses during Operation Iceberg (the Sakishimas assaults) were so heavy that TF57 could not have continued its strikes but for the Fleet Train's CVEs *Chaser, Ruler, Slinger* and *Speaker* who had transported seventy aircraft at a time from Australia. With only an eight-day break at Leyte the BPF had remained two months at sea to date, and the experience would be of benefit in its impending operations off Japan.

Now however with the US Admiral signalling TF58 successes offshore of Okinawa in support of American Army and Marine divisions already in control, TF57 retired to Manus at the end of May, then apart from the newly arrived *Implacable* and several cruisers including *Achilles*, the BPF steamed south to repair, replenish and indulge Sydney's unrestrained hospitality. *Achilles*' 'A'-bracket bearings were giving Commander (E) repeated migraines and right here in Manus was perhaps the world's largest floating dock, an American destroyer already inside at its distant extremity, the battleship *Iowa* being edged to within feet of it, and room aplenty for *Achilles* now centring over the yet deeply submerged chocks. By mid-afternoon the three warships rode high and dry, and away below their upper-decks American dockies were emerging from hatchways leading to living quarters below the dock bottom.

All this was being observed by Mick Wright, the Navi's yeoman. Born

King George V bombarding Hirara airfield.

and christened Malcolm Wright in April 1922 at Riversdale Southland, he learned the rudiments of life behind Riversdale Primary's playshed, and in farm and dairy factory work reaching two years into the War as an essential industry. Declared unfit for overseas service by an army doctor, Mick joined the NZDRN mid-41 and trained in Radar Direction Finding at *Philomel*. Given identity as NZD3897 he did time at Tairoa Heads RDF Station whose DSIR manufactured equipment was activated by a scanning device manually rotated when wind conditions permitted, then he shifted north to Cape Brett's more sophisticated set-up prior to an early 1943 draft to *Leander* in time to be torpedoed at Kolombangara. Boston for Christmas, *Queen Mary* across the Atlantic, an RDF course at Chatham and finally *Achilles* – popular Senior Hand and Rum Bosun of his Radar Operators' Mess, action station Chronometer Room alongside PO Tel Jim Craies' 2nd W/T Office by the Stokers' Messdeck. Mick's 6-foot good-natured bulk endeared him to all he fraternised or worked with, and now in this colossal USN floating dock, towed sectionally from the States and assembled in Manus, he was thoughtfully watching those enlisted dockies pouring up out of their virtual submarine city for the day's work. One skirt-surrounded hatch lay immediately below a convenient porthole; each day for weeks he had poured unwanted two-water-rum down the scuppers, and here could be the birth of a NZ/US trade agreement.

So it came to pass: bottles supplied by cooks and stewards; an inauguration chat with interested US delegates who queried: 'Say Limey, how can we get some goddam rum from youse guys?' Then Mick and a couple of nightwatchmen were in business. The whispered 'All clear, Mick'; fanny full of bottled grog lowered on a long line through the porthole. US currency exchanged and hauled up carefully. This nocturnal trade lasted for a week, until raucus hilarity emanated from the American quarters and official questions were being asked, on one occasion by Lt Cmdr Boyack who entered the Chronometer Room unexpectedly: 'What are all these, Wright? There are more empty bottles than charts in my racks.'

Then he left the embarrassed yeoman, obviously unconvinced by his incoherent explanation; but fortunately that day's excess rum hadn't arrived for bottling, and *Achilles* eased out of dock with the empties slipped overboard undetected before the transactions were tracked down by a very suspicious Crusher. Sobriety returned to the predominantly negroid dockies, and Mick delved among his disarranged charts for the large-scale one concerning Truk. But Mick hadn't been the only matelot liaising with the USN. A much senior entrepeneur was *Implacable*'s CO (Air), Commander Charles Evans RN, who'd arranged a wardroom deal with the Captain of an Aussie destroyer about to sail for New Guinea. Two cases of Johnnie Walker went aboard before the destroyer left Manus, one for the Skip, and one to be traded for American P–40 drop-tanks known to be ideal in extending the time Seafires could remain airborne. Sure as hell, back came the destroyer laden with so many that they were stowed everywhere handy in the carrier, even some in CO (Air)'s cabin. On another occasion a BPF destroyer short of radar spares, drew alongside a US can and suggested a 'Scotch for Spares' swap. Over the loudhailer came the answer: 'Jasus man, for a crate of Black Horse you can have my whole goldurned boat.' Another quest, for Hellcat spares, succeeded in a truckload arriving alongside from a nearby US Army Air Base for a carton of White Horse. 'One thing's for sure, Mac,' the American quipped to his 888 Squadron RN counterpart, 'those spares ain't gonna win any wars gathering cobwebs in my outfit.' Even Admiral Fraser, it's been reliably quoted, wasn't averse to the trade of Scotch for complete Avengers.

Truk at this stage of the Pacific War was largely ignored due to its isolation, so 'Operation Inmate' under the command of Rear Admiral Brind RN as CS4 with his flag on *Implacable*, was intended to give new BPF units up-to-date battle experience prior to the impending assault on Japan's home islands.

After being relieved at 0400 on Tuesday, 12 June 1945, Middle Watchmen came topsides to rid their lungs of fetid air inhaled on decks down in *Achilles'* W/T offices, telephone exchange, engine- and boiler-rooms and the honeycomb of other manned compartments. They emerged on deck to a moonless night drowsy under a myriad pulsating stars reflecting on Manus's dark surface. There, a few cables to starboard, stood *Implacable*, shapeless, blacker than the black tropical background. Between her and the distant shore's obscurity one could distinguish the silhouette of *Swiftsure*, then *Newfoundland* and destroyers blending into pre-dawn invisibility. The guardrails were wet with dew, comparatively cold to touch. It was time to push back through the two canvas light-traps and make your way along deserted blue-lit passages, then down to musty sleeping messdecks to find your particular niche and catch that hour of somnolence before daybreak roused the ship.

Morning Watchkeepers above on the signal deck, and on the bridge where preparations for departure were being made, were joined by running men hastened by bugle calls to their dawn action stations. Communication and gunnery circuits were tested and reported to departmental officers on the bridge. A faint luminance depicted the eastern horizon. As minutes lengthened, tentative sunrays touched a stretch of low cloud, red-streaked grey pinkening to bluish grey, then the blue of daybreak above rust-bloomed hulls of the task force. Bugle calls relaxed men now fully alerted and cursing the 'rotten bloody Andrew', sent some back to their hammocks and others to their uncompleted Morning Watch, as visual signals ensured fleet readiness to hoist all seaboats preparatory to weighing anchor.

Achilles' power boats had been craned inboard and stropped onto their cradles, while 2nd part of Port Watch stood in two long ranks along the port boom-deck, ropes in hand awaiting the two-ringer leaning outboard looking down. Suddenly he yelled 'MAN THE FALLS ... HAUL TAUT SINGLY.' Each line came rigid. 'MARRY ... HOOIISST AWAY.' Both lines came together and whistled through their blocks as the men ran forward. 'WAALLKK ... HIIIGH ENOUGH.' The whaler now hung close up dripping water. 'SEPARATE THE FALLS ... SHIP'S SIDE HOIST ... HOIIIST ... HIGH ENOUGH!!' When hand-signalled that the sea-boat was hanging level and shackled, he yelled: 'MARRY ... EASE TO THE LIFELINES ... LIE TO.' Then to the boat's coxswain, 'That'll do, Cox. Secure for sea.' Now he watched as each line was wound onto its drum on the Rec Space bulkhead with its canvas hood laced into place. Satisfied, he left, as those not required dispersed, soon to be running to their leaving harbour stations being piped throughout the task force.

The destroyers *Teaser*, *Tenacious*, *Termagant*, *Terpsichore* and *Troubridge* were easing seaward untidily, wisping blue funnel haze as they accelerated and straightened their line. Some of Lt Cmdr (A) Jewer's 801 Squadron Seafires and a flight of Lt Cmdr (A) Crosley's 880 Squadron were overhead as CAP for *Implacable*, the escort carrier *Ruler*, and the cruisers *Swiftsure*, *Newfoundland*, *Uganda* and *Achilles*, negotiating the opened gate and taking station for the estimated 36 hours to be off Truk. And in formation at 19 knots with shearwater sluicing up bows to whip aft in feathered spray, TF111.2 exercised gun drill individually, each ship's commanding officer and his staff having been briefed about 'Inmate' by Rear Admiral Brind aboard his carrier at Manus. Captain Butler broadcast by SRE what *Achilles* might expect off Truk, then he cut the switch and headed for his day cabin just below the bridge.

Everywhere, men were intertwining en route their forenoon watch, or if day-men, to their department office to be assigned a job. ERA Jimmy Rothwell was asked to check A boiler-room then the for'ard engine-room; Jim, NZD4664, born 1921 in Whangarei from where he'd joined the Rockies as a seaman in 1938, went overseas early in the War and changed to an ERA in *Guz* before joining *Leander* in 1942. After Kolombangara and Boston's Christmas holiday he crossed in *Queen Mary* to the Clyde, then by train to *Achilles* in Portsmouth. But right now he had negotiated the air-lock doors, descended the steel ladder onto A boiler-room's steel decking and was cupping his ear to hear what a Stoker PO was shouting in it through the roar of forced-draught fans. Jim checked the suspect nuts on a steampipe flange and went on to his next day-man assignment. Other ERAs were doing the same in B and C rooms, and in the after engine-rooms; minor problems were put right and logged; more serious ones might need local shut-downs, and some considered beyond staff attention were scheduled in priority on Commander (E)'s Defect List for dockyard treatment.

Similar maintenance applied in every department, but with my draft to *Gambia* pending, PO Tel Paddy Boyle was responsible for the latest VHF equipment I'd assembled and operated successfully since Greenock, Scapa Flow, Trincomalee, and now schooled him in. Chief Tel Artie Hay in his Main W/T Office would be contemplating the array of tobacco pipes racked above his desk, each serving its purpose according to peaceful periods or during the heat of action. And numerous new entries would right now be anticipating their reactions if the ship came under air or surface attack. There was expectancy throughout TF111.2 as it swept through late afternoon into the evening and night. The barometer had been dropping slightly, unseen waves were slopping broken tops onto foc'sles, and the occasional one thumped *Achilles'* starboard bow to send a shudder aft. Around their guns, their lookout stations, on the bridge, at damage control sites, everywhere, watchkeepers changed and those relieved sought brief sleep in the sweltering heat below.

Thursday, 14 June dawned unfriendly and hot, eight-tenths cloud scudding low overhead. To every direction there were warships almost to the horizon as A/A and A/S screens for the two carriers 80 miles south-west of Truk. Rain squalls driven by angry gusts hampered strike-launching shortly after CAPs went up at 0540; but Avenger bombers, rocket-firing Fireflies, and Seafires adapted as fighter-bombers eventually lifted off to attack Moen Island airstrips, shipping within the reef, Dublon Island's seaplane complex, and a network of W/T and radar stations dispersed among nearby islands and atolls. Sub Lt (A) Payne died when his Seafire took a burst of flak over Moen; Sub Lt (A) Scholefield went down inside his Avenger when its engine failed on lift-off, but his observer and air-gunner were picked up by *Terpsichore*; and even during excessive squall conditions which occasionally blanketed *Implacable*, *Ruler* proved her worth by landing-on some of the big carrier's returning aircraft.

Throughout the first two days illicit P–40 drop-tank-fitted Seafires protected by Lt Cmdr (A) Bill MacWhirter's 1771 Squadron Fireflies sought and destroyed targets, 12 of these Fireflies plus 48 Seafires and 21 Avenger torpedo-bombers being *Implacable*'s 81 attack planes.

Brind then decided that his cruisers should exercise their armament as three separate groups – *Newfoundland* escorted by *Troubridge*, *Achilles* and *Uganda* by *Tenacious*, *Swiftsure* by *Teazer* – and 20 miles offshore the carriers as a back-up trailed by *Termagant* and *Terpsichore*.

Max Mains NZ10138 had been an eleven-year-old schoolboy when Dunedin newspapers emblazoned *Achilles'* 'River Plate' participation. This fired his imagination, especially as the Navy had been in his blood since the early 1930s when *Dunedin* and *Diomede* invited families onboard. Kids had slithered down foc'sle-rigged shutes, enjoyed the parties put on by laughing matelots, then stood wide-eyed on the corner of Moray Place and Stuart Street as the ship's company band passed by, big drum booming, side drums rattling, and a variety of instruments doing their best with traditional navy marches, en route to a Town Hall festivity. And, here he now was, a sprog Seaman Boy lookout aft on *Achilles'* bridge at the age of sixteen and a half. Through his powerful binoculars he could just make out shimmering buildings topping an intervening curtain of tropical trees and palms. Sweat rivuleted down his neck from the uncomfortable heat inside his shoulder-length asbestos anti-flash hood topped by a mandatory tin hat. *Achilles* paralleled the distant reef over which breakers creamed in sullen anger. Max heard the muted ting of the 6″ DCT firing bell, experienced a lull before that reverberating BAAANNNGGG when A-, B-, and Y-turrets shook the bridge, then he inhaled those acrid fumes sweeping aft in dispersing clouds. Below in the Compressor Room ERA Rothwell staggered slightly, regained composure as the concussion momentarily dimmed lights and brought down dust, checked his gauges to ensure they still registered 600 psi, waited for the next salvo when his compressor's blasts of air would clear residual gases from all 6″ guns, then assured the Chief ERA by phone that all was okay his end.

Further aft in 'A' boiler-room Mac McGregor and his new stoker mates had been warned by old hands to stand back from the furnaces' inspection flaps. Sprayers could be observed through these, but gunfire could flush tongues of flame through them to seriously injure the unwary. Fume-contaminated salvo smoke was being brought down by the roaring air-intake and pressurising fans, smarting eyes and irritating throats, but this was happening in all ventilated compartments until many shut their punka-louvre outlets. The rise in heat was preferable, even away below in Dave Comin's B-turret cordite room action station which was partly responsible for those fumes, salvo after salvo in an interminable succession of heavy jolts, as he and his mates shoved the heavy charges onto intricate hoists to turret gunners awaiting their arrival.

Bombardment shells from *Achilles* and *Uganda* were wreaking havoc within Dublon flying-boat base 20,000 yards distant, until shortly after midday when Brind said: 'Right, that will be enough.' But at that moment *Achilles*, at the end of her run, was turning with A- and B-turrets training aft to starboard, nearing their maximum bearing when WHHOOMMPPHH and Max Mains' tin hat whipped off his head to be slammed against an Aldis lamp box on the bulkhead, smashing its door, damaging the Aldis, and getting Max a blast from the Chief Yeoman which he considered worse than that from the for'ard turrets. *Achilles'* 6″ gunners had got away 180 rounds, but now all twin–4″ able to bear were banging off fused shells at two aircraft descending out of high cloud.

'CEASE FIRING. CHECK CHECK CHECK! CEASE BLOODY FIRING!'

Extremely rude VHF exclamations were emanating from bridge loud-speakers when Avenger pilots identified themselves as friendly, but only just.

So that climaxed a TF111.2 bombardment not given much credit by top brass back at Manus. *Achilles* again entered dock with shaft and bracket bearing problems, also for more surreptitious barter of bubbly for US tropical shorts and shirts which seemed to please the dock commander. Just as *Achilles* eased out after a week he yelled through a loudhailer: 'I'm mighty happy to see the end of you Kiwi Limeys, you've emptied my goddam PX store!' It was Wednesday, 4 July, Independence Day, two days before the BPF back from Sydney and now designated Task Force 37, departed Manus to join Halsey's US TF38 in Japan's offshore waters.

CHAPTER XXII

BPF TF37 Joins US TF38 off Japan. Gambia *Bombards Kamaichi*

EVEN THOUGH in its three-month defence of Okinawa, Japan sank and damaged numerous US warships by conventional and Kamikaze bombing, the island fell on Thursday, 21 June 1945. But weeks earlier US Admiral Halsey had been instructed to retire his battle fleet and carrier groups to Leyte, in preparation for a massive sea and air assault on Emperor Hirohito's home islands. And with the BPF's containment of Sakishima Gunto no longer necessary, Vice Admiral Rawlings had been invited to US COMPAC HQ Guam in late May for talks on further involvement. He agreed to his British Pacific Fleet becoming an individual Task Force under United States Naval overall control, was cordially thanked for his unassuming acceptance of that role, and briefed on a tentative date for the combined fleet's opening phase. Back in the mid-ocean replenishment area he dispatched many of his ships to Manus, then he arranged a final R&R trip down to Sydney before the 'big push'.

At this time the BPF, designated TF57, was being strengthened by the arrival of more RN warships as they became available, many with RNZN men onboard, and one of those being Ian 'Snow' Hyde-Hills NZ6760, born in Auckland on Friday, 26 October 1923. Ian schooled at Sacred Heart College before working on a sheep station at Cape Runaway near Gisborne until November 1942, when he entered *Tamaki's* Class 35 as an O/D Seaman. After minesweeping on *Sanda* in the Hauraki Gulf during 1944, he joined 200 other ratings as passengers aboard the US troopship *Torrens* en route via San Francisco and Panama Canal to Plymouth, there qualifying QR3 at a Guz gunnery school. Returning on *Dominion Monarch* to Sydney's Warwick Farm *Golden Hind* navy transit camp in February 1945, he romanced around city night spots until 8 May when he departed, draft-chit in hand, to RN Lt Cmdr P.C. Hopkins' 2,500-ton destroyer HMS *Quadrant* – 'G' for grog, sleeping billet under the for'ard torpedo mount, Action Station 'A' 4.7″ QF gun, 'Abandon Ship Station?' from the Buffer, 'Don't ask wet bloody questions!'

Refuelling in Manus on 13 May and again at Leyte on the 17th, *Quadrant* left two days later with the carrier *Indomitable* and three other destroyers to join TF57 in its last strikes against the Sakishimas. Having brought mail up to Manus from Sydney, Lt Cmdr Hopkins ran *Quadrant* close enough alongside each ship for the canvas bags to be heaved aboard, but apart from bags of mail for *Gambia*, *Quadrant* was also to refuel from her. Stationed aft on the destroyer's bridge, Ian Hyde-Hills watched the refuelling procedures while looking about the New Zealand cruiser for a familiar face. *There* was Des Lena, talking disinterestedly to Jack Goldsworthy and Dougall West until they spotted Ian who'd been a *Tamaki* classmate – fatal: 'HEY, SNOW' one of them bawled through cupped hands, 'WATCHA DOIN' ON THAT POMMIE BASTARD? ISN'T A KIWI SHIP GOOD ENOUGH FOR YOU?' Under the glare of *Quadrant*'s skipper and bridge staff, Snow could only pretend the questions were aimed at someone else, as he dipped below the bridge screen and moved to a less vulnerable site midships to swap yarns with his noisy countrymen.

There was jubilation among those ships informed about their forthcoming R&R excursion down to Australia, an appropriate film *Seven Days Ashore* in *Gambia*'s 'Odeon Theatre', swimming over the side to relieve the unbearable heat below decks; then chicken, greens and dehydrated spuds for supper followed by canned fruit salad and a bottle of chilled beer with cigars also enjoyed by visitors from *Achilles*.

Intermittent downpours added to the anticipated pleasure at 1330 Thursday, 31 May when anchors rattled inboard on *Indomitable*, *Indefatigable*, *Victorious*, *Implacable*, the cruisers *Gambia*, *Euryalus*, *Black Prince*, and a flurry of destroyers already making for the opened boom – 'Downhill all the way to Oz, matey. Whacko Kings Cross!' But on Saturday while surfing atop big following seas *Implacable* flashed; 'Goodbye you lucky B's,' then rolled dramatically when turning back for Manus under orders to participate in the Truk bombardment. These semi-gale conditions prevailed right through the Bismarck Sea, through the Coral Sea and down the Queensland coast – high winds but clearing skies, growing colder and invigorating after the debilitating heat up north – everyone rummaging through his locker for No 1s, damp and musty due to weeks of messdeck humidity. Then topside near Sydney Heads on Tuesday, 5 June, men muffled in all available warm gear were expressing genuine feelings for the Corsair pilot who'd just ditched and gone down behind his carrier: 'Poor bastard,' men who'd seen it happen sympathised, 'what a bloody day to do that.'

But the moment passed as more gathered at the rails, concentrating their glasses on Lovers' Leap with Tasman curlers roaring up its sheer face. There were the usual finger gestures and ribald backchat aimed at Aussie matelots on the boom defence guardship as *Gambia* slid past; millionaires' Mediterranean-type residences above cliff-side stairways down to private jetties; the *Dee-Why* and other ferries steering close so their passengers could wave and cheer the long line of rust-streaked White Ensigned warships, entering an hour ahead of *King George V* and her destroyers *Tenacious, Termagant, Terpsichore*, who'd raced down from Guam so that Vice Admiral Rawlings would be among those ashore on day one.

Most of Sydney's pubs were dry but there were sources of liquor for the adventurous to discover, Circular Quay's fruit stalls from which to gorge oneself, digs in the British Centre to start Starboard Watch's four days leave in; then the hunt for something more appropriate like the warm bed of a girl known since the mid-30s; something similar but less personal such as the elegant Vauxhall Inn at Parramatta for Brian White and his mates who slept in daily till called for lunch: 'Glorious,' they said. *Gambia*'s wardroom golfers teed off on exclusive club links then sank into padded leather chairs in front of huge open fires. Sightseers crossed the Bridge or ferried across to Taronga Park, but finally for all there came the last-minute shopping rush for shoes, sandals, singlets and underpants seldom available aboard after weeks at sea; then the return to *Gambia* which had been shifted from Woolloomoolloo to Cockatoo Yard's Sutherland Dock.

It was cold with the boilers dead and the dockside covered with boiler tubes being decalcified; and it was cold with the thought of Port Watch now enjoying what Starboard Watch had experienced over the past four days, especially the lothario rumoured to be sleeping with the girl of my dreams. But soon his dreams too were shattered and both watches again lived on board on Wednesday, 20 June when men saw water flooding Sutherland Dock's concrete floor, saw it boiling out of opened vents, up over the chocks to creep up the hull until *Gambia* once again floated, became vibrant and warm between decks.

A thousand men's ears attuned to the murmur and heartbeat of her dynamos and generators, the muted crescendo of boiler-room intake fans and whining turbines. The caisson drew aside into its own small dock and *Gambia* eased out stern-first to be secured at a buoy past Garden Island. Over the next two days she coursed about Jervis Bay for gunnery exercises, back inside for a memorable last night ashore and a pulsating head back aboard, then on Thursday, 28 June 1945 with Rear Admiral Brind's CS4 flag at the peak, 'Farewell Sydney' with the ship slewing uncomfortably in the slick between *KG V*'s gale-distorted wash, registering a 20-degree roll which sent off-duty sufferers staggering topside with eyes and cheeks distended, attempting to make a guardrail before throwing up. *Black Prince* signalled that she'd done a dangerous 25-degree roll, and throughout that New South Wales storm the battleship, cruisers and destroyers wallowed and corkscrewed until a general signal warned all but necessary watchkeepers off exposed decks, then late at night a furtive signal lamp informed CS4 that *Euryalus* was now in company.

Next morning with the sea back to normal *Newfoundland* made her pendants on joining; a flying fox was rigged tween-ships as she rode close abreast, then CS4 and his staff transferred by breeches buoy as *Gambia* relinquished his flag – possibly because Captain Edwards had been discharged ashore in Sydney with heart problems, the popular Commander C.M. Jacob RN went up a rank to Acting Captain, and now *Newfoundland*'s owner became the Squadron's senior captain.

Days later on passing New Guinea the whole force disposed in single line formation for the narrow passages through Admiralty Archipelago, and early on Wednesday, 4 July *Gambia* lay starboard-side-to alongside the fleet oiler *Rapidol*, across ship from HMCS *Uganda*. 'Hot?' a man in briefs only rejoindered, 'The sweat's giving me crutch a flaming dhoby rash!' And he wasn't the only victim queuing at the Sick Bay for relief.

When refuelled, *Gambia* anchored close to *Achilles* who'd been awaiting the Squadron's arrival. Same old Manus barely distinguishable in the distance; *KG V* nearby with one of A-turret's quadruple 14″ guns angled down from the other three, her modern superstructure alive with A/A gunners servicing close-barrage weapons; *Uganda* anchoring a cable from *Newfoundland*; *Euryalus* and *Black Prince* moving slowly over to their berths near *Swiftsure*; and flotillas of hull-numbered destroyers named on an SDO 'Fleet List': *Barfleur* D61, *Grenville* D11, *Quadrant* D17, *Quality* D18, *Queenborough* D19, *Quiberon* D20, *Quickmatch* D21, *Quilliam* D22, *Teazer* D45, *Tenacious* D46, *Termagant* D47, *Terpsichore* D48, *Troubridge* D49, *Ulysses* D24, *Undaunted* D25, *Undine* D26, *Urania* D27. *Quiberon* and *Quickmatch* were wearing the Australian Ensign, but it was time to give the nearby signalman back his telescope as some of *Gambia*'s junior bridge officers and the Chief Yeoman were arriving to establish communications for leaving harbour.

Days later in clement conditions, Commander T.C. Robinson RN ran his destroyer *Undine* close to starboard where his deck-hands plucked *Gambia*'s Coston gun line from the air, foc'sle hands on both ships prepared a spaced-tag Distance Line between their forward guardrails, a crane-suspended hose was coupled to the destroyer's deck fitting and refuelling began. When topped-up and gone, her place was taken by Commander White RN's *Terpsichore*, then Lt Cmdr Becker RAN's *Quickmatch* which swapped the expected bit of cross-Tasman pleasantry.

Throughout the previous night CPO Cook Joe Dobbin's bakery staff had been doing overtime making huge loaves of bread to be flying-foxed over to each destroyer, sufficient for several days. Similar refuelling and provisioning had been performed by the battleship and each cruiser throughout the day; and by this means every three days when weather permitted, the little ships remained with the fleet when away from its back-up train; then whilst still working north towards Halsey's US fleet already in Japanese waters, the BPF was joined by Vice Admiral Vian's carriers *Formidable* (Flag), *Indefatigable*, *Victorious*, and their anti-Kamikaze destroyers *Urchin* D28, *Wager* D30 and *Wakeful* D31. Now in addition to gunnery exercises suffered day and night, there were stringent aircraft recognition classes for the fleet's A/A gunners and lookouts, briefing-room films and models of Japanese onshore targets for strike pilots and crews, and an urgency in Admiral Rawlings' circulated instructions that gunners should shoot first and answer questions later:

TF37 from C.P.F =

1. It is evident that ships can make better use of the gunnery equipment with which they have been provided, particularly the heavier weapons.

2. On past occasions of successful enemy attack their aircraft have penetrated the fleet without being brought under fire until much too late. This may be due to a desire for visual recognition before opening fire.

3. It is important that all air defence officers in all ships are kept right up to date whether friendly fighters are with the enemy once the latter are in the F.A.O.

4. The fleet may be assured that this information will be passed continuously by the Fighter Direction Ship, and except when General Green is in force, fire is never to be withheld on a target because it cannot be visually identified.

5. Past results obtained by close barrage weapons have been quite good but it is clear we must hit harder yet. All 40mm guns will be exercised continuously and a vast improvement in long range HA gunnery is essential.

6. Expected forms of attack will present difficult and new problems. We will meet them (A) by making still better use of our guns and control, (B) by ensuring that Fighter Direction Officers and gunners operate with clear understandings of each others difficulties = 0350/6/6/45

Obviously and understandably a condolence letter to the next of kin of an allied airman shot down by mistake would be preferable to several hundred such letters or airgrams mailed to the relatives of a bombed-under ship's company.

Gradually catching up to the BPF, the fourth carrier *Implacable* was buffeting into sour weather, with her crash boat *Quadrant* dodging as much as possible by knifing into the swirling wake, so close that Ian Hyde-Hills could see right inside her open after-deck. The destroyer's cooks hadn't been able to bake bread and one day the hungry crew looked aghast at great soggy loaves tossing by in the wake to either side. Skipper Hopkins could also see men on the gaping deck emptying baskets of presumably stale loaves off the carrier's stern. Out came his Commanding Officers' Bible and in minutes his Yeoman was wanking the signal-lamp handle with a message for *Implacable*'s Captain G.C. Hughes-Hallet CBE RN: '*Implacable* from *Quadrant* = Ecclesiastes XI Verses 1 and 2 = 0727.'

Hughes-Hallet sent for the carrier's Bible, thumbed through to page 737 of the Old Testament and read:

1. Cast thy bread not upon the waters; for thou shalt find it after many days.

2. Give a portion to seven, yea, even unto eight; for thou knowest not what evil shall be upon the earth.

He signalled acknowledgement, sent for his baker who got a real bollocking, had a flying-fox rigged lee side and *Quadrant*'s supplication from the wilderness was answered by her implacable deity.

At 0300 on Friday, 13 July 1945 the BPF, already designated TF37, swapped recognition signals with Admiral D.B. Fisher RN's Fleet Train Command Ship *Montclare*, port watch answered its call and all ships commenced refuelling and victualling; *Ulysses* came alongside to borrow one of *Gambia*'s aircraft recognition officers long term; securing lines and fenders were readied to ensure that confidential mail was swapped without accident when the duty mailboat *Quickmatch* approached and, to impress on *Black Prince* that a Friday 13th *is* unlucky, the right-hand gun in her A-turret back-flashed, killing three gunners and injuring others. Then to start next day in semi-darkness, *Quadrant* went astern to heave a bag of confidential mail onto *Gambia*'s quarterdeck and almost immediately powered back alongside to retrieve it – 'SORRY, SIR,' to the puzzled OOW, 'WRONG BLOODY SHIP. IT'S FOR CS4'.

As that day's duty boat she came back at intervals to exchange canvas mailbags; other destroyers came and went constantly among TF37's big ships, and even later at sea while maintaining precise station when refuelling under-way astern of the London-registered fleet tanker *San Amado*, *Ulysses* sidled close enough to pick up a rating she'd previously put in *Gambia*'s Sick Bay; and so did *Undine* for her skipper who'd boarded earlier. At 1315 *San Amado*'s long stern hose was disconnected and retrieved, and at 1530 the R2 Oerlikon gunners had Acting Captain Jacobs grinning appreciation when they sank a drifting mine with their initial burst.

Either en route north, with the Fleet Train, or going south to refill emptied tanks, at this period there were many oil tankers, perhaps half of them Royal Navy or Royal Fleet Auxiliary: *Arndale, Aase Maersk, Bishopdale, Brown Ranger, Carelia, Cedardale, Darst Creek, Eaglesdale, Green Ranger, Golden Meadow, Iere, Loma Nova, Olna, Rapidol, San Amado, San Ambrosio, San Adolpho, Serbol, Seven Sisters, Wave Emperor, Wave King, Wave Governor, Wave Monarch*; all necessary to refuel TF37's front-line ships as well as the Train's own vessels: the Command Ship, 2 dan layers, 2 boom carriers, 2 landing ships, 2 accommodation ships, 10 repair ships, 3 aircraft maintenance ships, 2 aircraft store ships, 2 water-carrier ships, 2 water-distilling ships, 1 net layer, 3 salvage ships, 6 hospital ships, 31 general store ships, 3 submarine depot ships, 26 'S' and 'T' Class submarines, 32 minesweepers, 9 escort carriers, 41 destroyers and 32 frigates and corvettes, all gulping oil. The logistics for Admiral Fisher's back-up fleet alone must have been a nightmare, so what must his staff have gone through when ensuring sufficient fuel, victuals, ammunition and replacement aircraft for the existing TF37, and for the battleship *Anson*, carriers *Colossus, Glory, Venerable*, plus the cruisers and destroyer flotillas known to be heading for the BPF after Germany's collapse.

But if that concerned men still in their hammocks at 0700 on Monday, 16 July 1945 as the present TF37 arrived 100 miles seaward of Honshu, a surprise awaited them when amazed mates shook their hammocks: 'Hey, Pusser, for godsakes come up and have a dekko at the bloody Yank fleet!'

Still rubbing his eyes Milton Hill came topside, and there covering the North-west Pacific Ocean everywhere he looked lay task forces of the mighty American 3rd Fleet, a never-to-be-forgotten sight. Misting into distant obscurity he could see at least ten modern battleships and two battlecruisers, sixteen aircraft carriers and an armada of cruisers with destroyer desrons; the closer fifteen-gunned cruisers looking like battleships; passing destroyers were seen to be mounting twin 5.5″ turrets similar to our Dido Class cruisers. 'How far does this lot stretch to, Bungy?' he asked Ted Williams who was standing next at the guardrail looking through binoculars. 'God knows, Pusser: in the SDO they reckon the most distant are about thirty miles.'

Months earlier US Supreme Commander, Admiral Nimitz, had echoed Admiral King's aversion to a Royal Navy Pacific involvement. Nimitz had cautioned Halsey to keep the BPF out of the forefront, emphasizing: 'This is our goddam pitch, you understand.' But 'Bull' Halsey was the wrong man to talk that way to; he'd met RAN and RNZN ships in the Solomons, fraternised pre-war with high-rank RN and he recognised ability above prejudice. At Guam he'd invited the BPF commander aboard to 'straighten out bends'. And when *Quadrant* powered like a speedboat alongside the storm-bowed rakish *Missouri*'s sea gangway, Halsey's grin of welcome broadened as he took Admirals Vian and Rawlings through a sea of blue-jeaned US sailors and officers to lounge chairs in his stateroom, straight-off setting three options before them to peruse:

1. TF37 to remain in close company as a Task Group of the US 3rd Fleet. It would receive direct orders from Admiral Halsey only, and it would be privy to his orders to the US 3rd Fleet.

2. TF37 to operate independently outside a 30-mile limit from the US 3rd Fleet.

3. TF37 to be allocated ancillary Japanese targets to attack independently.

The two RN admirals scanned their options quickly, consulted together briefly, then without hesitation Admiral Rawlings accepted the first proposal; and at the head of 'Mighty Mo's' white-roped sea gangway the parting handshakes were warm in eye-to-eye camaraderie; photographed by a USN aide who recorded Halsey's comment as *Quadrant* accelerated along the length of American guardrail spectators: 'My admiration for those Brits grew taller at that decision.'

Ex-Surgeon Lieutenant Pat Dunn RNZNVR recalled the BPF's adoption of the USN circular fleet disposition, *Gambia* selected as 'Fleet Center' with the big RN carriers and at times *KG V* and *Howe* around her at 2,000 yards, cruisers disposed ahead and astern, a close-screen ring of twenty A/A and A/S destroyers, and further afield more RAN and RN destroyers – an inspiring sight as the whole task force zigzagged in unison, at times turning en masse at 25 knots into the wind for aircraft operations; much of the time in easy flying distance of Japan for the heavily laden bombers, which during uncomfortable seas got airborne as the carriers' bows lifted over oncoming swells. Navi's yeoman, Brian White, recorded in his diary:

Monday 16 July. Contacted Yank 3rd Fleet near Jap coast. BPF stationed on left flank as the 4th and smallest group. We are 'Unit Guide' or 'Pivot Ship'. We're well out to sea off Tokyo. We go to 'Repel A/C Stations' at 0315.

Tuesday 17 July. 0330 R/A Stations. No bogeys on Plot. 120 miles – 3/4 hour flying time – off coast. WX low ceiling, dull. 0700 Strikes airborne. Report: Damaged Matsushima & Koriyama airfields 150 mls NE of Tokyo. Heavy flak, many Jap A/C destroyed or damaged. Lots of our A/C hit. 2 ditched but crews rescued. Yanks striking Tokyo. Flash Blue at 1200. No attack.

Wednesday 18 July. 0340 R/A Stations. 0700 3rd degree readiness. Filthy WX. 1230 – 120 mls E of coast. Recce fighters reporting bad WX over targets. Strike Able shot down 6 'Tojos' [Nakajima – heavy interceptor fighters], and a 'Jill' [Yokosuka – navy recce bomber], but lost a Corsair to flak. RN & US fleets withdrawing tonight due to an approaching typhoon.

Thurs/Fri/Sat 19/20/21 July. In BPF oiling area. Yanks in theirs. The 'Colonials' *Uganda, Achilles, Gambia* been sent to Yank Train to oil from Tanker-'83'. US can '850' oiling other side of '83'. Destroyer has three twin 5.5″ turrets, 10 tubes, small bore everywhere; top heavy with painted Jap flags signifying kills. Lot of 'bull' more likely. Their carriers on closer inspection not as big as ours. *Indom* heaviest in combined fleets. Oil-pipe burst all over crane, boat deck vege screen and galley flat; what a mess, and sticky. Revictualled ship with veges, carcasses, flour etc from storeship USS *Fort Providence.*

This time it hadn't been easy in the refuelling area, just outside the typhoon's path; and although it had curtailed TF37's and TF38's operations, there were reports of intense damage wrought ashore on cities and factories in its overland sweep. Frequent squalls and confused seas had made it almost impossible to keep station on the tankers whose fuel lines parted continually. And this was the reason that Admiral Halsey and his staff, who'd been invited to *KG V* for consultations, remained aboard from July 21 to 24, a period in which they witnessed her bombardment of selected targets in the Hitachi Engineering compound 50 miles north of Tokyo. In separate shellings 300 tons of 14″ put three enemy works out of operation, leaving a tangle of smouldering ruins in the wake of a night bombardment of Tacha Engineering Plant which had been turning out 25 per cent of Japan's heavy electrical machinery.

It had been agreed in the recent talks that the BPF would concentrate on Inland Sea targets, and when Halsey went back to *Missouri*, TF37 moved down to the Shikoku coast where its strikes hammered military installations near Kobe, Kure, Saka, and Shimonoeski at the Inland Sea's western entrance; but not Hiroshima just miles west of Kure; both Halsey and Rawlings had instructions to keep their itchy fingers off Hiroshima. So the four BPF carriers, some of the US 3rd Fleet carriers, and airfields at Okinawa and Iwo Jima, launched a non-stop 2,000 light and heavy bomber 24-hour assault on naval bases, shipping, airfields, and enemy warships wherever located.

Gambia's Surgeon Lieutenant, Pat Dunn.

The 31,000 ton battleship *Haruna*'s 14″ guns angled high and thundered defiance at waves of approaching aircraft; a US Devastator flight leader's aircraft disintegrated in a fused shell's terrific explosion while his right-wing torpedo-bomber spiralled seaward out of control, its crew unable to avoid their certain death. The remainder of his flight bucketed crazily in the violent turbulence, shouted obscenities through their intercoms then concentrated on the mission. Flak enveloped the planes as observers and pilots checked Shikoku's coastline, dived steep to confuse enemy gunners then roared feet above treetops, farmhouses, villages and churches en route to their Inland Sea objectives. They found the remainder of Admiral Ugaki's Imperial Combined Fleet at anchor as predicted, drove in through a wall of seemingly impenetrable tracer and launched their torpedoes. In the co-ordinated attack Dauntless dive-bombers hurtled down from all directions, a pilot yelling: 'HERE'S ONE WITH LOVE FROM PEARL, YOU YELLOW BASTARDS!' 1,000-lb bombs were released then the dive-bomber throttles were thrust forward for altitude on the way back to their carriers for more.

The attack was reminiscent of Pearl Harbour; first *Haruna* torn by heavy bomb blasts, ruptured by airborne torpedoes and enshrouded in billowing smoke and flames, as her tall fighting-top levered her over to float bottom up before sinking, followed in quick succession by *Ise* and *Hyuga* who'd recently been converted from battleships to aircraft carriers. The USN and RN airmen now sought out *Amagi* and *Kaiyo*, two 40-plane carriers previously beached with their flight-decks almost awash. Torpedoes and bombs put an end to their future, as did the missiles of more and more attackers driving in to finish off the already sinking or overturning cruisers *Aoba*, *Tone*, *Oyoda*, *Iwate* and *Izumo*; while under way but not ignored were the 20,000 ton carrier *Karsuragi* and lesser warships hopelessly endeavouring to escape.

As units of the attack group, *Achilles* and *Gambia* were keeping station abeam of the big flat-tops, alerting to Flash Blues then relaxing on Flash Whites, right throughout the day until 1745 when a mist-obscured aircraft just reported 'Friendly' plummeted in flames. Coming down fast behind it and trailing an unopened parachute, the pilot of a Myrt-II hit by a Corsair's cannon fire right above *Gambia*, frantically trod air. An hour later ships' radar screens crazed when enemy aircraft filled the sky with metallic strips and aluminium coated balloons, confusing ADOs but not the CAP Seafires which accounted for almost all of three groups of Vals, Kates, and Judys escorted by numerous Zekes. Then that night specially trained US night-fighter pilots from their newly equipped carrier *Bonhomme Richard* downed or chased off two more groups of bandits; while the destroyer investigating a ditched flare found it to be lanyard-attached to an unconscious Seafire pilot heard earlier baling out at 30,000 feet. His lungs had collapsed and he died aboard the destroyer.

In the last week of July 1945 *Achilles*, *Gambia*, *Newfoundland*, and *Uganda* close-supported the BPF carriers whose CAPs dealt with snoopers trying to locate the ships hidden under low cloud, making A/A gunnery a hazard rather than an assistance when additional fighters scrambled to intercept approaching bandits. You could hear outer-screen ships firing but seldom those of the fighter-protected inner ring. *Argonaut*, who'd been AWOL in Sydney for some weeks, rejoined on Thursday, 26 July, telling *Gambia* she'd brought Captain Edwards up from hospital to resume command, and she had 'Admiral Surveys' and his experts who wished to start their BPF ships inspection on *Gambia*. 'Please have all department defect lists available when they come aboard.' So Acting Captain Jacob's private gear was shifted back to his Commander's Cabin, Captain Edwards was handed back the key, the defect inspection went through with minimum delay and they were back in the Train refuelling from *Wave Emperor* while *Newfoundland* topped up on the other side. Admiral Brind and Admiral Rawlings came aboard for transport to *Missouri*, but when in sight of Halsey's flagship they transferred to the US destroyer *DD477* for onward passage to another RN/USN VIP conference.

It was generally known that 'Bull Halsey' and 'Twice a k-night Fraser' were naval friends of long standing, also Admiral Rawlings who at this stage of the War had more direct dealings with USN TF38's overall commander. It was known too that something of great importance was lurking in the wings, hence the rash of 'Top Brass' meetings on Mighty Mo. Halsey's battle wagons were going in close to bombard industrial sites with literally thousands of 16″ shell, racing north to blast the Muroran works on southern Hokkaido; racing back to heave destruction at Hitachi; being joined a 100 miles south of Tokyo at night on 29 July by *KG V* to rain battleship salvoes on military and industrial factories near Hamamatsu; while all the time in daylight devastating Kure, Kobe, Nagoya and every city within range of the BPF and USN carriers' bombers, and rocket-firing fighter-bombers. Add to this the terror being wrought on cities by long-range heavy bombers from Iwo Jima, Okinawa and airfields recently lengthened in China; and the countless casualties among terrified Japanese city dwellers already reduced to a sub-human diet deficiency.

Japan's political and military leaders were warned on 29 July that eight cities would be levelled it they didn't surrender. They didn't. So two days passed then B–29s unloaded 7,000 tons of bombs on selected cities, obliterating inner Toyama, adding to the chaos already apparent by napalm bombing of Tokyo and increasing the total of deaths currently estimated at a million plus twice that number injured throughout Japan. The Emperor's warlords were warned via Japanese agents at Potsdam that this was merely the start, but they demurred, played for time, expecting Russia to intercede on their behalf. Raids on northern Honshu airfields were intensified to eliminate aircraft known to be massing there; US and BPF carrier-based bombers launched massive strikes, losing 34 planes to ack-ack but destroying 400 enemy aircraft and damaging 300-plus in the one-day assault.

Hirohito's advisers wanted the War to continue and, although many of their front-line Divisions were still in occupied Burma, Siam, French and Dutch Indo-China, Malaya and the by-passed Pacific islands, and Russian armies were poising along the Manchurian border while Koreans were ambushing Japanese troops abandoned in the peninsula, they still had millions under arms in the Japanese home islands.

Harry Truman's advisers wanted the war terminated, but quick; America had the means of accomplishing it; the combined US/RN fleets and waves of land-based heavy bombers were doing their best to subdue the enemy but: 'Our losses in taking Okinawa, Mr President; goddam, sir: what will the losses of men be in invading Japan itself?' President Truman didn't need reminding about those Okinawa losses, yet he hesitated. 'It's your decision, sir: our Nevada tests exceeded all our expectations, and Little Boy is sitting in Enola Gay on Tinian awaiting your nod.'

He was well aware of that too. It had been giving him sleepless nights. But if the War went into 1946, his statisticians forecast 'upside of seven million Nips are sure as hell going to die from starvation. You want our update on the number of our boys who will be killed?'

Truman removed his spectacles and wiped them, frowned and replaced them: 'I'll give that more thought. Let you know real soon.'

On Tinian Island's North Field Runway in the Marianas, Paul Tibbets' aircrew were alerted on Monday, 6 August. They crossed the tarmac through excited ground staff to take up their months-rehearsed positions in 'Enola Gay' the name of Tibbets' mother. As they mounted the portable steps their names were checked against a list: Colonel Paul Tibbets, CO 509 Group and pilot; Captain Robert Lewis, co-pilot; Captain Theodore Van Kirk, navigator; Major Tom Ferebee, bombardier; USN Captain Bill Parsons and Army Air Corps Lieutenant Morris Jeppson, ordnance officers; Lieutenant Jacob Beser, radar-counter-measure officer; Sergeant Joe Stiborik, radar operator; Sergeant Geo Caron, tail gunner; Private Rick Nelson, radio operator; Snr-Sergeant Wyatt Duzenbury, flight engineer; Sergeant Bob Shumard, assistant engineer. Long-range meteorological reconnaissance aircraft had reported reasonable weather over southern Honshu so the three B–29s of Flight Group 509 were warming up, propellers whining to a full-pitched scream then throttling back to a steady roar. Thumbs-up indicated readiness, chocks were dragged clear and Tibbets' bomber rolled onto the mile-long runway and gained lift-off momentum followed by his two recording Superforts: Chuck Sweeney's 'Great Artiste' which would release three transmitting monitors to record radioactivity etcetera; while Major Marquardt's 'No 91' photographed.

Hours later at 30,000 feet, Captain Parsons edged aft to the 11,000-pound black and orange monster cradled in its bomb bay; he inserted cordite charges each end of the bomb's two U–235 containers, set the necessary relay switches and resumed his seat. When activated by atmospheric pressure at its design altitude, one container would be hurled at the other and a new sun would be born 1,900 feet above the ground.

At 0730 Japan appeared under widespread cloud drifts; restrained excitement permeated each of Group 509's Superfortresses. Paul Tibbets looked at the dashboard clock, checked it against his watch, 0815, looked down at a city miniatured away below and shouted above the din to his co-pilot: 'IT'S HIROSHIMA, BOB!' Captain Lewis already knew, grinned understanding as he and other crewmen glanced down through pressurised windows then concentrated on their instruments. Colonel Tibbets thumb-signalled Captain Parsons to drop the bomb.

At 0817 one of the crew yelled; 'BOMB'S AWAY!' 'Enola Gay' side-slid in a much-practised 60-degree bank, and every member of the three-plane mission busied himself with recording and photographing or whatever other duty he'd been selected to do.

Hiroshima in 1945 was a busy industrial city of 250,000 residents predominantly engaged at Mitsubishi's factories and shipyards, the Eba heavy industry plant, Tokyo machine works, Ujina dockyard, Nippon steel, Saka electrics, and numerous other projects attuned to Japan's war requirements. The city covered several square miles of delta land interwoven by tributaries fanning out from Ohta River, hence its name Hiro (broad) Shima (island). Sited on south-west Honshu it had been chosen as a nuclear bomb target, and in order to assess the full extent of such damage it had been strictly 'off-bounds' to conventional bombing.

Shortly after sun-up Matsu Naga left for work at the Mitsubishi shipyards. His wife Kikuko had gone without her share of a fish they'd been given; it was Matsu's birthday and she wished him to be pleasantly surprised with the large jar of marinated whole carp. He would eat it with the rice balls and bottle of saki she'd included.

Their young son Yasushi had stayed up after seeing his father to the gate and wishing him a happy birthday, then he shouted for his sister Kiyoko to come out in the early morning sunshine. Two years his senior she was visiting from Prefectural Girls' High School before being evacuated to a temple at Fukugi hamlet in Asa County. The war had escalated in recent weeks and it was rumoured that 300 B–29s had razed Tokyo's north-eastern suburbs; refugees arriving from the capital talked of frenzied victims being trampled to death in a mad scramble over Sumida River's inadequate bridges, thousands rushing into the river terribly burned by napalm bombing, clogging the shallows while trying to cross to an illusion of safety but drowning as more and more pressed them from muddy insecurity into floundering depths. One big raid had destroyed 250,000 houses and caused 100,000 casualties, so city authorities were evacuating children into country districts: 'Yes, yes Kiyoko, you will have to go, also young Yasushi. No, your mother and father will stay here and work to win the war. Now that's enough questions, go outside with your brother.'

Kiyoko joined her brother as an undulating 'Air Clear' siren signified the big bombers detected overhead must have been friendly. As the sound of their engines returned they screened their eyes against the sun and peered up at three planes glinting as they turned, small silver specks at extreme height.

Yasushi's keen eyes soon picked up a small object falling from the leading aircraft. He pointed it out to his sister who called their mother. All three gazed skyward, excitedly commenting to emerging neighbours until they lost sight of the falling object in the long seconds this had taken to occur. A blinding blue-edged flash of orange brilliance absorbed the northern sky. An unearthly blast smote the upward-staring spectators. A terrifying roaring WHHOOOSSSHHH accompanying a madly expanding fireball was heard by Kiyoko. It wasn't heard by her mother; she was dead. It wasn't heard by her brother who died instantly. Kiyoko's mouth felt as if it was full of dry sand; her lips were stiff and parched; her throat burned as she struggled with the horizontal door of their flattened smouldering house. The raw flesh of her arms and fingers glared red as she tore the door up to reveal her mother – face, arms, neck, legs and naked torso a black unrecognisable mess. Only little Yasushi's legs protruded, burned skin flayed and hanging from blackened flesh.

She staggered across collapsed walls along their flattened street, into further streets of flattened houses. Power lines lay entangled among smoking devastation. Flames crackled in the wreckage from which plaintive cries emanated. Crazed semblances of humanity stumbled within burning, collapsed residences; tearing at broken framework with hands from which a black lace of skin fluttered at the end of red-raw arms; wailing piteously for someone to help rescue loved ones underneath. None stopped to help.

Kiyoko Naga lurched on dazed, seeking someone, anyone, a familiar face from whom to beg assistance. She saw something which stopped her in her tracks; it appeared to be a woman, not a hair on its head, body and limbs swollen grotesquely. The thing made moaning sounds as it grovelled in the smoking ashes of a flattened house. Kiyoko edged past and made her way toward the Mitsubishi shipyards to find her father; he would make everything right; it was his birthday and she hadn't kissed him before he left home.

Streetcars full of death stood welded by that man-made sunspot, stood mute in a smouldering city of tumbled rubble and tangled girders. Kiyoko felt indescribable nausea and retched up coagulated blood, wavered bewildered as her raw fingers touched her dry scalp to find the hair and skin gone, only hardened dry patches on her skull. She touched her face to find it dry as parchment, looked down to see her legs and feet scarlet, turning brown and black; tried in vain to open her mouth to move her dry swollen tongue. Faint from dehydration she tried unsuccessfully to drink from a scum-crusted drum of stinking water. She sank to the foot of a burned-naked tree, sat on a patch of moist grass sheltered by its gnarled trunk; sat with unblinking eyes staring from her wasted body, asking an unanswerable question as she sat in death.

Aboard USS *Augusta*, a cruiser returning to the States from Potsdam, Harry Truman scanned a dispatch which read: 'Little Boy dropped Hiroshima 0817/6/8 EST. Complete success apparent.'

If success were to be metered in annihilation, then the little boy had done a man-size job. His relatively minor 13,500-ton yield of nuclear energy placed him in the kilo-ton category, but he'd just erased a city instantaneously and killed tens of thousands of its inhabitants outright. As his column of dust and debris ascended under its expanding vivid mushroom, those not protected were seared beyond all chance of survival; thousands more were the city's walking dead, stupefied, awaiting oblivion. Thousands again showed no sign of injury, had been sheltered from direct exposure but were unknowingly irradiated; severe nausea could precede their terminal illness and death. But 'Little Boy's' eventual total would await posterity, become evident by deformity of mind and body in children yet to be born.

Even after the direct result of this one small bomb Japan refused to surrender and 'Fat Man' took his seat in 'Bock's Car'. The target would be Kokura, a northern Honshu industrial town; flight height 31,000 feet and bomb-drop restricted to visual instrumental aim. As the crew climbed aboard their Superfort they edged cautiously past the menacing 11 feet long, 5 feet diameter black teardrop resting in its bomb bay. If successful it was anticipated to outdo 'Little Boy's' achievement.

But on arrival over Kokura on Thursday, 9 August there were ten-tenths cloud under which inhabitants talked about the dreaded sound of '*Binijuku*' high overhead, wondered why these B–29s spent so much time circling without dropping their bombs, then relaxed as the 'All Clear' wailed. Chuck Sweeney had conferred with his crew and let Kokura off while considering other targets:

'Tokyo? Could do but bit dicey, officially off bounds too.'

'How's about Niigata you reckon?'

'Too far, one hell of a long haul back to North Field.' Then to another suggestion concerning the clouded over cities: 'Shit man; NO; capital N goddam O, we're not dumping this baby in the Pacific.'

The dice was cast when a long-range 'met recce bomber' reported breaks in the cloud over Nagasaki. Gasoline was now imperative: 'Might have to drop by radar against orders.'

Finally as morning hours wasted fuel, all voted in favour of dropping the bomb on Nagasaki, a bomb which by itself could end the War. The town emerged on their screens, a lightish centre in darker surrounds indicating hills which coincided with previous briefings. Far below, 200,000 citizens went about their work, not aware that a few Americans 31,000 feet above were focusing the natural X of Nagasaki's valleys on a luminous faded-blue picture before them, aim point slightly south-east of the X. Then mini-seconds before release by radar aim a break opened out in the cloud. Visual aim took precedence and the cross-wires registered perfectly; but there was no time to correlate wind-drift and other conditions against the plane's adjusted speed.

'Fat Man' overended as the B–29 lifted suddenly. The pear-shaped monster gained straight-line plummeting velocity, its mechanisms performing as designed, auto switches flicking open to prevent early triggering, barometric relays closing with diminishing altitude. Inbuilt radar registered precise heights until the pre-destined 1,540 feet when firing contacts clicked and high-voltage accumulators discharged, detonating the cordite charges which rammed both nuclear containers together. Beryllium elements irradiated the plutonium with a stream of neutrons and man's second artificial sunspot glowed brilliantly over the bustling Urakami Valley, just north-east of its intended target.

More thousands of people withered instantly, some innocent, many perhaps not; then without sufficient fuel to make the Marianas, 'Bock's Car' turned south for Okinawa where one motor cut out over the runway and the others sputtered to a safe but hair-raising thump-down.

Now sensing a Japanese collapse inflicted entirely by the Western Powers, Russia invaded Manchuria and Tojo's hopes of Russian intervention on Japan's behalf vanished. Emperor Hirohito summoned his top-level advisers to the Command Room and sat in silence during their political and military tirades. Then he rose. There was abject silence as he intoned quietly about the Pacific War from its Pearl Harbour inception, methodically placing blame on department after department, decisively impressing the futility of further conflict, and concluding that the time had come for acceptance of Allied surrender terms with one exception. The Imperial Throne should be preserved.

Without an invitation to reply he left a room of stunned silence; a room where all wrangling had ceased; a room from which the heads of government and military organisations shuffled out into unseen sunlight as automatons sentenced to death; a sentence not to be self-inflicted until fulfilment of their Emperor's demand. To them the War was over apart from those individual responsibilities. They would play their role in the final act, cross the stage without applause and in most cases a ceremonial knife would atone for their ineptitude.

But back to Tuesday, 7 August when reconnaissance and intelligence reports assured the American President, and Admiral Nimitz, that the Hiroshima bomb didn't initiate a nuclear chain reaction. Its photographed effects were terrible although they appeared to be limited to a smaller radius than anticipated; there were signs of considerable activity beyond its perimeter, and increasing human movement within. So Halsey got the green light to continue his attacks; the Allied Combined Fleet had been withdrawn to refuel and re-ammunition on the 6th; and on the 7th when *Gambia*'s Navi told his yeoman Brian White to get out the charts showing Kamaishis's coast, Brian asked; 'Where's Kamaishi, sir?' and he was told:

'You'll find it about three hundred miles north of Tokyo, and mum's the word. By the way, you might start thinking about Auckland fairly soon, AND, that's not from me, the ship's already full of blasted buzzes.'

Next day however there was no need for questions on any of the US or British ships; they now knew why they'd been retired off-coast twenty-four hours previously; an atom bomb had been dropped on Hiroshima: 'And hey, Russia's just declared war on Japan too.' With Russia's Army about to clear the Nips out of Manchuria and the Sakhalin Island: 'Things are lookin' pretty good,' seemed to be the day's catchphrase.

But not so in Martin Hedlund's Kamaishi POW camp. As soon as the 14 July fleet bombardment ended, prisoners and guards searched the ruins for injured and trapped survivors, taking serious cases to the Camp Hospital where there were bare wire mattresses, no medicines, and only bandages removed from dead patients to be reused without washing or disinfecting. Martin found his *Hauraki* 2nd Engineer Jack Thompson a sorry mess, head punctured twelve times by shrapnel, swollen and bruised when the Dutchman who'd brought him in, shaved away the hair, then sutured the worst gashes with gauze threads from doubtful bandages while washing away the blood with urine. Ignoring protestations he said in Dutch-English, 'It vill gill doze bluidy germ tings you'll zee I tell you.' And it did.

Those not injured were marched at dawn to dig out the dead and clear smouldering rubble from machinery considered salvable, then when smoke again poured from coke oven stacks the initial leniency disappeared. Kamaishi Camp's Nip 2i/c, a short burly sadist, reappeared in American

gear stolen from US patriotic parcels, strutting bandy legged into restored
POW quarters to bash anyone slow at standing erect and saluting. The
Riot Act promising public beatings, hangings or beheadings, was reread at
each muster; and guardhouse whippings were reintroduced as atonement
for being party to the bombing and bombarding of the Emperor's realm.

All POWs had been infected by disease brought from other camps:
dysentery, lung disorders, fevers, malnutrition and beri-beri's paralysing
effects, many having died since *Hauraki*'s July 1942 capture. On arrival in
Japan they'd been stripped and issued Japanese military garb, generally
undersized and obviously 2nd or 3rd ownership bereft of TLC, unwashed
as were the smelly odd-sized canvas shoes exchanged for their leather
footwear. The issue included underpants and a shirt also recycled, with the
guarantee that these garments would be exchanged every six months; but
at the first half-yearly muster the filthy underclothes were reissued still
lousy with vermin. Any comment was noted by an English-speaking guard
who instantly rough-handled the unfortunate outside to be thrashed and
punched insensible.

At the next muster Martin Hedlund took a beating for having discarded
his dilapidated canvas shoes weeks earlier, substituting them with a pair of
hand-made wooden soles to which he'd tacked heavy canvas pouches for
uppers. He'd lost one in mud at the bottom of the shell crater into which
he'd been dragged injured in the recent bombardment, later recovering it
by an elbow-deep search. The pouch upper had become detached, he had
no tacks to reattach it, so he hobbled about awkwardly until a *Hauraki*
shipmate slipped him a pair of worn-out boots taken off the feet of a dead
Dutch Indonesian. Originally the POWs had shown aversion to that sort
of thing, but three years privation convinced them that warmth prevailed
over human niceties.

Not all the Japs were insensitive, one or two having been pre-war in
Hawaii or the States where they'd mastered the English tongue and could
foresee the War's outcome. Some surreptitiously passed on brief items of
factual news and, after one day of evident discomfit among the camp
guards, one said Hiroshima had suffered a horrendous calamity, tens of
thousands dead, atomic blast responsible.

'What in Hell's a goddam atomic blast,' a tall skinny Texan queried
audibly before being told to shut his flippin trap. 'You'll have Combi San
parading us all bloody night to find out what we know, you daft Yankee
bastard!'

'Okay Limey,' in lowered voice. 'But what's an atomic f..king blast fer
Christ sakes?'

He with his buddies captured at Corregidor in May 1942 were beaten
more often than other POWs, and his ability to laugh at adversity had long

endeared him to every prisoner. It was now almost a month since the US fleet bombardment, a large percentage of the works again functioned, and day by day more rail wagons were bringing coal and iron ore 12 miles down from the Ohase Valley mines. But recce aircraft were returning as evidenced by an increase in local A/A gunfire, deepening Martin Hedlund's and his mates' anticipation of another bombardment or bombing. That night at dusk Martin looked at their home-made calendar which displayed Wednesday, 8 August 1945. He wedged his frail body into the 28″ wide slatted rack between those cocooned either side, adjusted his frayed cover where possible and slept, unaware that right now a cruiser from his adopted New Zealand was coming up-coast to enact their forebodings.

At 0330 *Gambia* sounded Dawn Stand-to, checked each man's action station and the ship's internal communications, then relaxed to 2nd Degree alert in grey daylight when the Radar Plot reported clear screens. Those not rostered for the Morning Watch dispersed to shower before breakfast, then made their way topside to once more see the bombardment force they'd come north with from Shikoku. On the SDO noticeboard hung a list of the ships taking part: USN Rear Admiral Shaforth's Task Group 38.4 battleships *South Dakota*, *Indiana*, *Massachusetts*; cruisers *Boston*, *Chicago*, *St Paul*, *Quincy II*; Desron 48.2's seven destroyers; and RN Admiral Brind's Task Unit 37.1.8, *Newfoundland* (Flag), *Gambia*, and the destroyers *Tenacious*, *Termagant*, *Terpsichore*; impressive on the SDO wall, but even more so outside at 0900 when Shaforth asked for 25 knots, and the two forces were disposed in separate single line-ahead formations with Admiral Brind's on the Americans' north flank. Action stations hadn't yet sounded so Doc Hamlin and Pat Dunn stood among spectators seeing the Kamaichi coast loom rugged under sullen cloud; then when the bugle blared they paused a moment to see the ship's biggest New Zealand ensign breaking out atop the foremast peak: 'LOOK AT THAT, PAT!' Reg Hamlin yelled before scampering below. 'WONDERFUL ISN'T IT!' But his Surgeon Lieutenant mate was already running for'ard to his first aid post in the Petty Officers' Mess, there checking his team and their casualty gear before cautioning them to sit if the ship came under attack: 'Blast upheaval has been known to damage men's os calsis,' he warned; then added, 'Heel bones, not your masculinity,' at which their looks of concern changed to expressions of relief.

Bow waves crept up each ship until literally multi-ton seas crashed onto the battleships' foc'sles as they drove straight through oncoming whitecaps; similarly on *Gambia* whose boiler-room air-intake fans, turbo-feed pumps and powerful turbines were creating a devil's orchestra for those below. On reaching an after boiler-room, Chief Mechanician Ron Kirkwood heard the massive steel hatch covers clanging shut, denying escape should the ship be vitally damaged, but assuring buoyancy due to the cruiser's sealed compartment design. The thought of scalding by dry steam spitting unseen from defective gland packing; the stories of agonising death suffered when steam pipes burst and boilers disintegrated, flashed through his mind. Each stoker or mechanician at some time had experienced those momentary concerns but thrust them aside and concentrated on his assignment. Ron checked his engine-room log, noted the time that minor defects had been given attention, ensured that orders for revolution changes had been registered and timed, that every item in his engine-room was functioning correctly, then he relaxed with a huge cup of ki.

Officers, petty officers and leading hands throughout the ship had done likewise, and when several miles offshore, flag-hoists and VHF commands turned both columns 90 degrees to port, this bringing all ships into a single line ahead disposition at 15 knots preparatory to opening fire. At 1255 when communications were established with spotting aircraft off the battleships, each cruiser's turret captain awaited last-minute corrections from his DCT. Target ranges and bearings had been received, turrets had swung as their long barrels elevated or depressed, then eased and steadied: 'LAYER ON!'

'TRAINER ON!'

Gun-ready lights glowed red in sequence up in the Control Tower and on each turret's repeat panel on the bridge. The order was given, men heard the trigger-activated firing bells, then tensed for that ear-smiting BAANNNGGG. Muzzle flames lanced through immense cordite smoke rings and rolling fume. *Gambia*'s superstructure shook at her own gunfire, vibrated when slapped by the shockwave from *South Dakota* a thousand yards ahead. The three US battleships were ripple firing, their 16″ guns elevated high, the huge ships visibly wallowing sideways at each thundering broadside. *Gambia* was told to 'Lift 'em up a fraction' by her Seahawk spotter. 'That's spot on, keep 'em there, Buddy!' in response to the corrected salvo. All ships were now on their given targets; rubber ear plugs were partially muting the discordant gunnery, but that acrid vapour blown down from the battleships was burning nasal tracts. No rhythm now, just a constant rumble interspersed with solid thumps as *Gambia*'s twelve 6″ fired, and the sharper BANG when her twin 4″ mounts ranged on selected targets. Meantime further inshore, RN and US destroyers were knocking out located shore batteries and sinking coasters inwardbound with coal and ore.

Senior Surgeon Derek Symes RN was a stickler for discipline, and he wouldn't grant Surgeon Lieutenant Hamlin's request to have a look at what could well be the swansong for battleships: 'No, I'm sorry, but no one will leave the Sick Bay unless we are ordered to abandon ship.' Whereas not so rigid, Pat Dunn in the POs' Mess First Aid post, kept his men ready until he was convinced there was no retaliation to *Gambia*'s continual firing, then let his team on deck in brief relays.

As *Gambia* passed the harbour entrance Kamaichi town came into telescope view and, further up the long fiord shell-bursts could be seen among smokestacks rising above smoke and dust engulfing the steelworks. At the end of the run *South Dakota* ordered a 180-degree about-face and each ship pivoted in the whirlpool left by its predecessor, turrets rolled around onto their new bearings and the firing recommenced.

That morning at daybreak Martin Hedlund and those in the partly restored quarters were bullied from their sleeping racks and marched off to work, but Allied recce planes flying lower than usual were making the POWs nervous, especially when Combi San screamed them into a roadside ditch as A/A fire erupted close by. Then four Zeros roared overhead hotly pursued by cannon-firing fighters displaying US stars, and in a flash both flights swept up over hilltops. Rockets streaked down from new arrivals to incinerate Japanese gunners at A/A sites, and heavy explosions near the town and its foundries indicated that gun-sites there were being targeted by fighter-bombers.

After a period of quiet the prisoners were reassembled, and soon the incident seemed unreal as work resumed on production, or for many their ongoing task of clearing previous debris to get more plant into operation.

But almost without warning a heavy naval bombardment had men running for shelter. As in the past month's shelling it started along the front of the steelworks, lifted to the rear for a time, then concentrated the next sequence of vari-coloured shell-bursts throughout the steel-making complex in between. By now it was known to be coming from close offshore destroyers and a line of battleships and cruisers not many miles further out. Small observation planes were seen circling near the top of a hill obscuring them from the few remaining Japanese A/A batteries. Martin saw a bridge near his camp demolished, moments before he staggered to his feet dazed by the blinding eruption of a nearby ammunition dump; other men were rising drunkenly from the rubble and dust, striving for balance, falling and trying again, some not making it.

Someone grabbed his arms and dragged him into a shell hole by the riverbank. He saw Jack Thompson's hands dripping blood, skin burnt from his arms. Thompson and two mates had fought through flames to get out of a foundry. His mates had dropped through inhaling hot air devoid of oxygen. He got help and went back to haul them outside but one was dead so they left him and rescued the other.

The shelling continued hour by hour, reducing to twisted girders and useless machinery whatever had escaped the first bombardment. Sometime later when the Navy had gone, *Hauraki*'s surviving POWs looked for their

Chief and found him emerging from a pile of logs where he'd taken cover. He pointed to a length of jagged metal protruding from both sides of a log mere inches from where he'd been lying. Remembering the Dutchman's substitute for disinfectant, Thompson washed Hedlund's worst cuts with urine and bound them with strips of his months-old shirt, while others suffering deep gashes received similar aid. He then went with Hedlund to the harbour into which they'd been told an Italian-American had jumped clothes afire; and there the poor man stood neck-deep, his swollen head pitifully burnt, so they hauled him out but could do nothing for him and he died. There were numerous men in that river badly burnt and injured. Some including Harry Brodie, their 5th Engineer, died during the night, and at daylight after eating bits of a burnt pig and scorched grain found in its smouldering pen, men fit enough placed a long plank across the blasted-away gap in a bridge, and by this means they transported most of the injured across on makeshift litters, just in time to take shelter when Allied fighter-bombers streaked down the valley and blew up the plant's chemical laboratory together with undamaged A/A sites previously missed.

The sites had been abandoned, but an American ex-Corregidor Marine named Walsh was inside inspecting one of them when a 500-lb bomb landed close, blowing a huge slice of rock into the air. It crashed down through the gun-site roof and cut Walsh almost in half, the last man at Kamaishi to be killed by direct action although many died later from their injuries.

The night passed without camp guard interference, and that afternoon the POWs were told to go to the hills as the Navy had been reported on its way back to shell the works again, but halfway up a road leading to a mine shaft they were overtaken by a messenger, sent to bring them back because the fleet was still on its way south.

Something was afoot: 'The Nips are having special drills and they're bowing to the sunrise, then towards Tokyo,' Martin Hedlund said. 'I think its the start of an armistice!' It was.

CHAPTER XXIII

Victory in the Pacific

O N 8 AUGUST 1945 Task Force 37 was riding over typhoon-threatened swells 83 miles east of Tokyo, still launching fighter ramrods whenever reconnaissance aircraft reported unclouded targets. But later that day a sea-fog drifted inland and, as recalled by Admiral Vian (of *Cossack* fame), the entire US 3rd Fleet was withdrawing seaward when he took *Implacable* right inside Tokyo Bay in an attempt to recover fog-bound flights of Seafires. Aboard her crash-boat destroyer *Quadrant*, 'Snow' Hyde-Hills was being physically restrained from diving overboard to assist exhausted airmen unable to maintain their grip on thrown lines. He swore at those ordered to hold him back, cursed the two-ringer who'd given the order, and swore louder on hearing the desperate cries of pilots and aircrew as, unable to climb the rolling destroyer's scrambling net they let go to be lost astern in the impenetrable fog. Some were hauled aboard, cared for in *Quadrant*'s cramped messdecks, then later returned by breeches buoy to their carrier.

Hours earlier south of Kamaishi in similar conditions, four Corsairs of US Navy Flt Lt Marshall Lloyd's VBF–6 Division had powered off the big carrier *Hancock*, formed overhead with other fighter-bomber groups and flown inland to the distant steelworks. Arriving over the partly clouded town they sought out local airfields and destroyed parked aircraft in addition to blasting others attempting to get airborne. They then strafed and bombed A/A gun sites, hangars, administration blocks, radar and radio networks, before returning south to each group's individual flat-top, on the way signalling identity as they flew low past north-bound battleships, cruisers and destroyers, including the New Zealand cruiser *Gambia* which Marshall Lloyd remembered from an occasion south of Okinawa when he'd flown CAP for the RN force attacking Sakishima.

Two hours after landing on, VBF–6 was again flying north to Kamaishi where this time they encountered heavier flak. Lloyd's Corsair lurched and shuddered on the fringe of a shellburst as he dived through a barrage to release a bomb smack on a gun-site, before streaking full throttle over a hilltop now buffeted by a shockwave as the emplacement erupted. It was time to reform his division and go but a glance at his fuel gauge indicated a ruptured tank. Fortunately the bombardment force was still strung out miles offshore and he crash-landed near a destroyer to be hauled onboard as his aircraft sank, so for the remainder of that Thursday, 9 August he viewed the Kamaishi naval assault as a guest on *DD468*'s bridge.

About mid-afternoon with dense smoke and a sea fog rolling in to obscure the town and steelworks, the American spotter planes were alighting on slicks swept by their battleships and cruisers; then immediately they were craned inboard and secured, Rear Admiral Shaforth signalled a line-abreast formation and the entire force steamed seaward. But not all the enemy aircraft had been destroyed; a low-flying bandit was detected by radar as it approached. Down in his First Aid Post Surgeon Lt Pat Dunn heard the sharp crack of *Gambia*'s twin–4″ mounts, the rhythmic thud of her multiple pom-poms, and the staccato of her Oerlikons. Gunnery Lieutenant Brian Turner (Later Commodore Auckland), in his starboard 4″ A/A Director saw the enemy torpedo-bomber flying low towards *South Dakota*, saw it turn in a storm of bursting close barrage to disappear across *Gambia*'s stern tracked by converging streams of the cruiser's starboard tracer. Wally Nielsen on the Starboard Pom-poms Director saw the aircraft low in a blizzard of *South Dakota*'s small-bore gunfire, wavering in the concussion of bursting shells, veering unsteadily toward *Gambia* whose close-barrage gunners were following it as it roared past the stern, pumping tracer at it until all firing stopped to avoid hitting *Newfoundland*, over which it staggered trailing smoke and flames, before splashing in an upheaval of wreckage and angry white water just beyond a weaving destroyer.

Wally Nielsen saw a torpedo trail crossing *Gambia*'s stern, others have no recollection, and not reported to the bridge there was no avoiding action, but Brian White's diary reads:

> 1500. Went on deck and saw a huge pall over the fiord city despite dense fog. We fired 402 rounds of 6″, cleared the last one after cease fire with Shaforth's okay. Later a Judy broke out of low cloud launching a fish which missed us. Then two more planes; our 4″ put a pattern round them and they turned fast – they were Hellcats! Our favourites! We heard the Japs had attacked the carriers in our absence. One kamikazied a Yank can's bridge and killed the officers; another crash-hit a picket ship. During our bombardment some of the destroyers breached Kamishi's boom and sank ships inside. Russia has invaded Manchuria. An atom bomb has been dropped on Nagasaki.

That casual mention of clearing an unfired round wrote a small sentence into history. The gun fired and *Gambia* was credited with firing the final naval shell against Hirohito's homeland.

It had been a long 9 August for both the United States and British ships involved; they'd been in two watches since 0330 the previous day, supporting carriers anticipating a break in the fog to resume strikes, a state of alert throughout the night, then action stations since dawn in preparation for the Kamaishi bombardment. And now with dark descending over the retiring force, men on USN ships were forming chow lines for their first substantial meal as RN and RNZN men drank tots in their messdecks while awaiting the arrival of a hot dinner. *Gambia* rode uneasy swells, bows lifting over some and slicing down through the troughs of others, her screws racing as the stern rose clear, then grumbling when they burrowed deep to send a shudder throughout the ship while it corkscrewed in the cross sea.

Men slung their hammocks, inserted nettle spreaders and, reaching overhead for rails to swing up and in, were soon sound asleep for the few hours left before their next watch.

In many Allied HQs top naval decisions were leap-frogging each other in rapid succession since the Hiroshima and Nagasaki nuclear bombings. Admiralty Lords were rising bemused from the depths of their leather lounge chairs, chorusing: 'Good God, Attlee, what does one do now, bai Jove?' It had been intended to retire the BPF to Sydney starting 10 August. There it would have been reinforced by the Royal Navy's 2nd Battle Squadron comprising *Anson, Howe, Duke of York*, and possibly *Nelson*; the 11th Carrier Squadron, *Colossus, Venerable, Vengeance*, and the refitted *Indomitable* together with a flooding steam of escort carriers, cruisers and destroyers already coming east after Germany's defeat. Then, accompanied by a much larger and efficient Fleet Train this mighty British Pacific Fleet would have gone north, totally adequate to fight alongside America's 3rd Fleet in 'Operation Olympic', the invasion of Hirohito's home islands fortress.

Now however the plot had changed entirely. A third Kamaishi bombardment, this time by *King George V, Newfoundland, Argonaut, Gambia*, and several destroyers was cancelled. On 10 August Japan announced her willingness to talk surrender provided the Emperor's status remained unchanged, but Halsey replied with a relentless US/BPF carrier-based attack on northern Honshu airfields, destroying some 400 and damaging 300 aircraft being readied against the imminent Allied invasion; and the White House told Japanese agents that their Emperor *would* be subjected to Allied authority. Next day Soviet troops invaded Sakhalin Island, Russian armour poured over the North Korean border on 12 August, and the Mongolian Peoples' Republic rose against its Japanese oppressors, slaying in pent-up fury whilst declaring war against the Japanese Empire.

During this international turmoil Admiral Halsey had been intensifying his carrier assaults and, when invited to a conference aboard *Missouri*, Admiral Rawlings agreed to retain a token force to be designated Task Group 38.5 which would become the US 3rd Fleet's most northerly unit. Comprising *KG V, Indefatigable, Newfoundland, Gambia* and the destroyers

Barfleur, Napier, Nizam, Teazer, Termagant, Troubridge, Wakeful and *Wrangler,* they were maintained by Halsey's supply train, a spectacular sight for Fox Movietone News, theatre-goers seeing HMS *King George V* and USS *Missouri* refuelling on opposite sides of the big US tanker *Sabine*. But right now *Gambia's* HODs were busy assigning landing party men their duties in response to a general signal just received:

TG38/5 from CTG 38.5 = NR78 =

1. Ships are to be prepared to land maximum numbers for whom machine guns or rifles are available.

2. Leading organisations must allow for half A.A. armament being manned in two watches.

3. Cruisers and above report by signal: (A) Number of Royal Marines: (B) Number of other ratings available consistent with 1 above.

4. Destroyers report in accordance with para 3 (B).

5. Cruisers and above be prepared to land one demolition party each.

6. Details of landing organisation will be signalled later = T.O.O. 120800

Gambia replied:

Your 120800 = (A) Number of Royal Marines 70. (B) Number of other ratings 110 in three platoons of seamen and one platoon of stokers = T.O.O. 120903.

Sadly in light of their arduous participation off the Sakishimas in support of America's Okinawa invasion, and their later assistance in Japanese offshore waters, the carriers *Formidable, Implacable, Victorious,* the cruisers *Achilles, Argonaut, Euryalus,* and the bulk of TF37's destroyers had refuelled from the remnants of Rear Admiral Fisher's TF112 train and were already southbound to await further orders at Manus. But C-in-C BPF, Admiral Fraser, who'd been conferring with US C-in-C Nimitz at Guam, was now pounding north aboard his flagship *Duke of York* to be in at the kill.

On 13 August the Allies launched their most concentrated air assault – 1,600 carrier aircraft demolition bombing, incendiary bombing, strafing and rocketing Tokyo, while B–29 Superfortresses dropped millions of leaflets on other Japanese cities, detailing in their language the Potsdam Declaration calling for their High Command to: 'follow the path of reason or face utter devastation'.

Multi-millions of Japanese listening where possible to Radio Tokyo on Tuesday, 14 August were astounded to hear the voice of their deity; it was tantamount to Christians hearing the voice of their Almighty. Without elaboration Hirohito intoned an order for his subjects to lay down their arms. There followed minutes of reverent silence, then an announcer declared that Japan had agreed to the Allied demand for unconditional surrender.

Laconically, Brian White had been writing up his diary as he saw or heard events:

Sun. 12 Aug. AM Sent off ship's mail but got none. PM. Much of BPF left for Manus. As part of Yank TG38/5 we're doing a strike tomorrow.

Mon. 13 Aug. 0330 Dawn R/A. Nothing doing so 3rd Degree. Yanks splashed 6 Japs, we saw nothing. 1630, radar detected bogeys everywhere, two waves of 7, and others. Saw a dogfight between Fireflies and Jap 'Nicks', columns of smoke marked the Jap graves. Still nothing near *Gambia*. 1815 more bogeys, none came near; our fighters claimed 3 Myrts while attacking targets near Tokyo. Yanks took on a Jap twin engined bomber until they saw it was a B–29.

Tue. 14 Aug. In oiling grounds alongside Yank No 52 from 1400 to 1540. Been cleaning and painting all day to look spruce for Tokyo. 2 platoons of landing party brushing up on rusty drill. I'm in No 3 if it's required. We're getting in to peace routine. Possible strike tomorrow.

WED. 15 AUG. VICTORY PACIFIC DAY

0345 R/A stations then 3rd Degree. 0800 Japan has accepted unconditional surrender; war as good as over, we go to 4th Degree. Strike Able attacked naval installations in Tokyo Bay. Strike Baker recalled. 1115 our yards are covered with flags – HOSTILITIES NOW CEASED AGAINST JAPAN –
1120 Straight above us a Judy dived on *Indefat*, three Seafires followed him pouring in bursts of fire; 1000 feet above us his tail and one wing blew off; then the plane exploded and splashed 500 yards ahead as a flaming wreck. Pilot ejected but chute didn't open and he hit hard. Landing parties practising on the quarterdeck scrambled. I was scraping crab-fat off a bridge voice pipe when parts of the fuselage landed on us and Captain Edwards got one piece from the bridge.

This aerial attack had gone unnoticed by below-deck watchkeepers. Since 0800 they'd considered the War over and late that forenoon they were anticipating their tot. Out of the strike zone rum was issued at 1130, three-water to Leading Rates and below, neat rum to Chiefs and Petty Officers; it being customary but not official for messmates to take the tot down to men in remote parts of the ship, or for them to be relieved so that they also could enjoy the day's issue. With his 'neaters' in mind, Chief Mechanician Ron Kirkwood thanked his temporary relief on the starboard-after-turbine then scaled an engine-room ladder. Negotiating a couple of flats he stepped out into bright daylight on *Gambia*'s starboard waist, just in time to be met by a blast from the exploding Japanese aircraft and the lesser concussions of its pursuing fighters' cannon fire. He staggered in the unsuspected shockwaves, ears ringing and stars swimming across his eyes as he groped for support, urged forward by sadistic tinfishmen yelling: 'PISSED AGAIN, CHIEF?'

There have been diverse accounts of *Gambia*'s and *Indefatigable*'s near-miss attack; the correct one being written to me in late 1989 by US Navy Commander (Retd) Marshall Othman Lloyd, the VBF–6 Corsair Division Leader then on USS *Hancock* who stated:

> For the five days following my dunking off Kamaishi on 9 August, I led my division in bombing and strafing strikes on Nagano and other targets, until that momentous surrender announcement. We had been airborne since dawn on 15 August and were awaiting our relief division's arrival. On my right was my wingman Ensign Curtis A. Weaver, then Lieutenant (Jnr Grade) R.S. Farnsworth, and past him his wingman Rex A. Benedict. Shortly after 1100 a general recall confirmed earlier indications that Japan was ready to concede defeat, and our Task Force Director relayed a 3rd Fleet order: 'Cease all offensive operations against Japanese forces. I repeat. Cease all offensive operations against Japanese forces.' During a break in the mayhem on TBS, and on VHF channels the Director vectored me to a 'Bogey' above HMS *Indefatigable*, and there was no doubt when he came in sight, a single engined Nakajima 'Kate' going into a dive over the British Task Group. Signalling my division to follow I made a hot pursuit down through broken cloud. The A/C seemed to be targeting *Indefatigable* and when he broke from cloud I fired my six wing guns in an initial overhead pass, and seeing bits of wing shredding before I pulled out in a wide arc to clear the target. Subsequent passes by my VBF–6 division destroyed it in time to avoid tragedy to the British carrier, and as we swept by the shattered plane it exploded and strewed fuselage over an old acquaintance, HMNZS *Gambia*.

There had been long gaps in *Gambia*'s action-state announcements, and next time the SRE speakers hummed, they drew everyone's attention to a TBS link-up for Admiral Halsey's broadcast speech; but he'd got no further than: 'THE WAR IS NOW OVER. WE'VE BEATEN THE ENEMY TO HIS KNEES—' when his voice was overridden by familiar alarms, then a later announcement that more intruders had been splashed by outer screen CAPs. And for the majority who'd been closed up on Flash Blue, a transcript of the US 3rd Fleet Commander's oratory appeared on every noticeboard:

COM T.G.38.5 from COM T.G.38.1 =

ADMIRAL HALSEY'S SPEECH.

This war is now over. We have beaten the enemy to his knees. It has been a Victory of Good over the Forces of Evil. I thank the Third Fleet for its part in the Victory, and I can not stress sufficiently how great that part has been. I congratulate all Air and Surface Forces on their great achievements. I would have liked to thank every Man and Officer individually, but due to the great size and commitments of the Fleet this was impossible. I thank all those in hospital, and those who have been crippled; and I thank all the Mothers, Wives, and the Families of Those who have made the Supreme Sacrifice. It is up to us now to see that this Sacrifice has not been made in vain, and we must see that the task is properly finished. Many will be returning to civil life, and they must keep the Torch burning. And You who will be remaining in the Service must Keep Your Swords Sharp. One of our main tasks is to uphold the morale of the Occupying Forces, and steps have already been taken to provide sport and recreation.

I am very proud to have had ships of the Royal Navy serving with us, and under my command. Those who have known the British Navy of old knew what to expect, and these expectations have been fully justified. The British Pacific Fleet has shown every great readiness to co-operate to the fullest extent. And the manner in which they have adapted themselves to American tactics and American methods has been remarkable. I thank them for the work they have done, for they were not a separate unit but part of a big team – THE TEAM THAT HAS WON – Again and again I say: 'GOD BLESS YOU ALL, THANK YOU, AND WELL DONE!'

This speech was delivered by Intership Telephone about 100 miles east of Tokyo to all ships of the US 3rd Fleet, and ships of the British Pacific Fleet, standing by to sail in to Tokyo Harbour at the cessation of hostilities; but owing to an air attack in progress at the time, only a few were privileged to hear our famous Admiral speak.

Signed T.L. SPRAGUE
Commander Task Group 38.1 US 3rd Fleet

On Thursday 16 August after dawn stand-to and relaxation to 4th Degree Alert, men topside watched Admiral Fraser's flagship *Duke of York* taking station ahead of *King George V*, to lead Task Group 38.5 in its appointed position amidst this colossal Allied armada standing off the Japanese capital. No matter where one looked there were warships, rust-streaked hulls but clean from their decks up, some British within cables and the majority American reaching over horizons to the north, east and south. Now passing a mile abreast with their impressive storm-bows shearing water were the modern 16″ 56,000-ton battleships *Missouri, Iowa, New Jersey, Wisconsin*; 45,000-ton 16″ *Washington* and *North Carolina* followed by older modernised ones mounting 14″ guns. Yet their impression of total power was already passing into history, made redundant apart from use as coastal bombardment platforms. Henceforth technology would decree that aircraft carriers would be the 'gun' of the future, able to strike far inland with devastating accuracy and able in the future to carry aircraft capable of delivering nuclear bombs instead of conventional. But right now, here to show Japan and the world that the Allies once more ruled the Pacific; although much of the US 3rd Fleet and most of the BPF had been detached to eastern US bases and southern RN bases, there were still 14 battleships, 24 fleet-carriers, 22 cruisers, 130 destroyers and frigates, together with 200 support vessels, a proud and victorious Allied ceremonial of massed-fleet manoeuvres being recorded on camera by overhead newsmen, all Task Groups turning together under brilliant sunshine, leaving long white scimitars of glistening turbulence on those many square miles of blue north-west Pacific. Then next day all ships were faced into the wind for 1,200 aircraft to fly over in history's greatest naval air pageant ever seen.

It could be said that US Admiral 'Bull' Halsey was the Second World

TF38 Combined Fleet display off Tokyo, 17 August 1945 – photographed by plane from US Carrier *Shangrila*.

War's most swashbuckling seaman, he having impressed this on Japanese naval commanders from Guadalcanal to Tokyo, and now parading his victorious Allied fleet across the screens of every picture-theatre throughout the world. Yes, his superior, Admiral Chester Nimitz had been Commander-in-Chief Pacific, but 'Halsey' would remain on the tips of naval tongues for generations if not centuries, alongside America's War of Independence John Paul Jones, and Britain's 'Twice a K-night' Bruce Fraser, Med Fleet's 'ABC' Cunningham, Jutland's Earl Jellicoe, and seventeenth-century Spanish Armada destroyer Sir Francis Drake. Admiral Bruce Fraser had been given a royal instruction, a commitment obeyed at the first opportunity to bestow on US Admiral William F. Halsey aboard the BPF flagship, a British Knight Commander of the Bath, after which the US-KCB spoke over HMS *Duke of York*'s BBC link-up to the British Commonwealth. Having survived thunderous applause from the crowded X-turret deck and quarterdeck, Honorary Sir William Halsey retired with Admiral Fraser to more informal talks in the British C-in-C's ornate apartment, prior to being piped away in *Missouri*'s Admiral's barge.

Day by day after the 17 August mass air display a growing state of boredom became evident aboard *Gambia*; seamen and stokers were issued rust scrapers, buckets of diluted caustic, wire scrubbers, paint brushes and

US 3rd Fleet – Massed fly-over, 23 August 1945.

pots of red lead, then a final coat of Pacific grey to transform the cruiser's tarnished upperworks. There'd been no New Zealand mail for a month and even the Victory Dinner on Sunday evening, 19 August, lacked spontaneity, except for moments of light banter when Commander Jacob then Captain Edwards visited each mess. But although *Gambia* steamed under navigation lights and parts of her decks were illuminated, she still exercised a low category of action alert, those at A/A and A/S posts had to be systematically relieved, so some left unfinished meals to take over their turn with night glasses.

Men strolled about the foc'sle under a bright quarter moon and starstrewn overhead; joined groups leaning in conversation on guardrails; drifted below to sling hammocks or wait until messdecks quietened and their bed spaces became available on tables, mess-stools or the deck, to sleep, perchance to dream before that irritating bugle call to Dawn Action Stations. But there was now no visible enemy, just a through-dawn easy swell with *Indefatigable*'s first flight lifting off on its way inland in search of unplotted POW camps. Not a Geneva Convention signatory, Japan hadn't notified the location of these camps, and many were purposefully sited close to shipyards and strategic military or industrial areas. Till now, where camps were known or suspected to be, pilots had been briefed to bomb elsewhere; but henceforth they were sighing off the remaining BPF carrier to locate such camps as targets, targets on which to drop huge canvas bags of food and medical supplies.

Born in Auckland on Wednesday, 26 November 1919, Gwynne Woodroffe trained overseas during the Second World War to become a Fleet Air Arm pilot, eventually being attached to *Indefatigable*'s 820 Avenger Squadron in which he merited the DSC for 'Determination and dash on operations'. Now having been decorated in the war against Japan, Gwynne, or 'Woody' as the wardroom knew him, was waiting, engine revving in a queue of eight Avengers about to be catapulted off, each laden with 300 lb of provisions for the hundreds of men in a camp located by drop-tank Fireflies. This camp on Ise Wan inlet near Yokkaichi south of Nagoya, had been marked by big POW letters recently painted on the roofs of four buildings. All day and night the carrier's decks were hives of industry, with seamen and ground crew becoming sailmakers, cooks and bakers slaving to provide extra bread, and stores assistants denuding shelves of everything considered necessary for those starving inmates awaiting relief.

These huge canvas containers manipulated inside Avenger bomb-bays were attached to parachutes and bomb-release mechanisms. But due to a loosely anchored load Woody's Avenger skidded and lumbered its personal way off *Indefat* as he fought the controls for flying statistics throughout his one-hour flight. Apparently no longer restricted, the POWs had constructed a Union Jack on the 10-metre-wide beachfront, and white-lettered US 195 BR 25 DU 75 on the ground. So as to ensure a safe drop and not into the sea, Woody' first release was made at minimal speed at about 400 feet, but the chute didn't open fully and its load smashed through a shed roof. All subsequent drops were made 200 feet higher and the containers were seen being dragged to safety by the waving POWs. This was so different from previous flights over Japan: no flak, no enemy intercepters, only a leisurely scenic excursion 1,000 feet above villages, small townships, two aerodromes, trains already running through a peaceful countryside. The Japanese authorities had been ordered to line all aircraft up on runways, propellers removed, and on each of the two airfields there stood about fifty; apparently hundreds of planes had been previously hidden in sheds, barns, even in churches and schools all over the country for counter-attacks against the expected American November/December 'Olympic' invasion.

And what was being done by *Indefatigable*'s airmen was also being done by US airmen from the numerous big carriers of TG38.1, TG38.2, TG38.3 and TG38.4 in an immense drive to locate and relieve Allied POWs. In Kamaishi Camp a Canadian had built from purloined Japanese bits and pieces a tiny radio which he'd hidden in the back of a desk made by POWs for the Camp CO. As night cleaner of the CO's office he had gleaned news items for his mates, but now the radio was out in the open, astounding the Japanese Commandant who'd never dreamt that those he had absolute power over would dare to hide anything so forbidden in the very desk at which he sat. But now American planes were flying low overhead dropping parcels, white material strips with notes telling them to form large letters on the ground indicating what was most needed; other notes told them to: 'Hang in there buddies. Medications and victuals are on the way.'

Hours later planes came over at about 2,000 feet dropping drums of canned food, chocolate, medicated bandages, antibiotics, everything considered essential, some of the drums breaking away from their parachutes to hurtle down alarmingly, one smashing through timber beams close to where Jock Tomson had dived for shelter and showering Martin Hedlund with splintered wood as roofing iron flew close over his head. Just then an American flew out of the *banjo* (heads) when a drum screeched down into the sewage trench at his back and covered him with excrement; but now with food arriving regularly from above, the burst drum's contents of slab chocolate were not salvaged.

The recent naval shelling of Kamaichi town and steelworks had killed and injured thousands, leaving an overpowering stench of decomposing and burnt flesh as the corpses were extricated from wreckage to be incinerated. And soon Allied relief teams were arriving, first an Australian group to tally the number of surviving prisoners and the identity of those who had died; then in order to issue repatriation instructions, US Colonel Simpson, who had been the Duchess of Windsor, Mrs Wallace Simpson's previous husband.

Each day POWs were driven by truck to the wharf, filing aboard the US Hospital Ship *Rescue* to be registered, showered, disinfected and issued with American clothing, unbelievably clean underwear, shirts, outer garments, socks and shoes which fitted. Then through a regiment of specialist doctors and finally, sitting at tables with gleaming white covers, bread and ANCHOR New Zealand butter – Livingstone Thomson couldn't recall the main course, but he would never forget that first taste of American bread and New Zealand butter. *Rescue* being American was returning to the States, so Australians, Britishers and New Zealanders were transferred to the British Hospital Ship *Vasna* just arrived from Wellington and serving them fresh mutton, toheroa soup and Red Band beer. At Yokohama Thomson and some of the walking repatriates were whisked off to Yokohama Airport for a night flight to Okinawa with its mass of city lights, but with daylight the city dematerialised; what they had seen below when coming in to land was miles upon miles of ships not now required for the 'Invasion', fully illuminated, no longer subject to black-outs.

On again in a huge C46 for an uncomfortable flight to Manila with its harbour littered by 252 sunken vessels, embarkation on HMS *Formidable* to be allocated cabins once occupied by flying officers, to be shown through her boiler and engine rooms en route to Sydney for a celebrity entrance, with everyone in two lines right round her flight deck as the carrier passed hundreds of flag-decorated ships and pleasure craft displaying WELCOME HOME banners, and the names of Australian men they were seeking. Days later they were bussing all the way to Melbourne in a journey made slower by it becoming a several hundred-mile pub crawl. It was over a month since they'd left Kamaishi, two months since the Japanese surrender, and more weeks dragged by before their last-leg liner *Andes* berthed in Wellington, those from *Hauraki* being welcomed home by the Union Steamship Company's Superintendent Engineer, all on board being delayed by a Prime Minister Peter Fraser speech; then that long dreamt wharfside reunion with loved ones.

Martin Hedlund had been among those considered unfit to walk, doing the sea journey from Yokohama to Manila in USS *Monitor*'s sick quarters, fourteen days at anchor before a transfer to the escort-carrier HMS *Speaker* en route Sydney, train to Melbourne's Port Philip to be reunited with his *Hauraki* shipmates aboard *Andes* to Wellington, then Lyttelton and home in Christchurch.

But the privations suffered since *Hauraki*'s 11 p.m. Sunday, 12 July 1942 capture now left him generally incapacitated and although he tried a spell back at sea it proved beyond him. Martin Hedlund died in the third week of December 1956, aged 64. His ashes were given to the sea off Godley Heads from the inter-island ferry *Hinemoa* at 9.15 p.m. on Saturday, 22 December 1956, by his old *Hauraki* shipmate, 3rd Engineer William (Bill) Hall whose eulogy concluded: 'I was through a great deal with Martin. He was a shipmate in the truest sense, and a gentleman always.'

Martin was of course his wife Margaret's husband, and to expose the lack of respect accorded him, and others, by post-war authority, I have included a copy of the letter to Margaret after her husband's death, in which Martin is referred to as her son.

P.M. 91/4/24/6

DEPARTMENT OF EXTERNAL AFFAIRS
WELLINGTON

Mrs M.T. Hedlund,
31 Target Street,
Pt. Chevalier,
AUCKLAND   29 November 1957

Dear Madam,

The Government recently received compensation from the Japanese Government for various sums of currency confiscated from members of the crew of the "Hauraki' while they were in a prisoner of war camp in Japan.

According to the receipt issued by the Japanese aurthorities, £1.10.0 in Australian currency was confiscated from your son, the late Mr M. Hedlund. Since the war Australian currency has been devalued, and the amount confiscated from your son is now worth only £1.4.0.

I understand that you were named as your son's next-of-kin, and I am therefore enclosing a cheque in your favour for £1.4.0.

Yours faithfully,
Secretary of External Affairs

But back to August 1945 when it was intended that the Combined Fleet would proceed in to Sagami Wan on Sunday the 26th. Met reports predicted typhoon conditions so Halsey postponed the event pending suitable weather for his triumphal entry; also, there were enemy forts to be occupied along the vast bay's shores, and American minesweepers were still busy ensuring a safe passage through the narrow neck of water connecting Sagami Wan to Tokyo Bay; so, with landing party preparations completing on all ships, the US 3rd Fleet and its invited International warships marked time a hundred miles offshore.

Chas 'Bogey' Harris had been a professional cyclist and bowling-green keeper until Friday, 5 May 1933 when he joined the NZDRN as a Stoker

2nd Class in training on *Philomel*. All Harris personnel since pre-Trafalgar had been nicknamed 'Bogey'. Why? I don't know. He served on the cruisers *Diomede*, *Dunedin*, *Achilles*, *Leander*, *Gambia*, *Black Prince*, *Bellona*, *Royalist*, then the corvette *Stawell*, and during a pre-war three-year interchange to the RN, on the destroyer *Delight*. He at some period changed to the Regulating Branch and as MAA on *Gambia* became Commander Jacob's Assistant and Gofer – 'Gofer this, gofer that' – a friendly appointment to the extent that he cajoled the Commander into adding him to the ship's initial Occupation Party, the only non-gunnery type to embark on USS *Pavlic* with *Gambia*'s 'Turkeys' and No 4 Seaman Platoon.

A festering dislike between the Torpedo Officer Lt Cmdr Davis-Goff and the Gunnery Officer Lt Cmdr John Wilkinson, had erupted in a wardroom knuckle-up; but as they held equal rank Captain Edwards asked Commander Jacob to sort it out, which he did with a mouthful of very audible Anglo-Saxon before sweeping it all *under* the mat. Then because of a bias toward Davis-Goff, he side-stepped Wilkinson's insistence that MAA Harris should not be in the landing party, so Bogey boarded *Pavlic* fully accoutered while No 4 Platoon crossed by barge in a boisterous sea to USS *Barr*, a similar 3,000-ton invasion ship; seamen berthed in three-tier drop-down bunks either side of two wide passages running fore and aft; officers accommodated in the ships' sizable wardrooms. Having flat bottoms these four ships, *Pavlic*, *Barr*, *Simms* and *Patterson* had to run before a typhoon for days, thus delaying them till Monday, 27 August when they entered Sagami Wan near Arasaki, eight miles south of *Gambia* at anchor a few hundred yards off a beach lined by interested Japanese spectators close to three big coastal guns, these each having hoisted white surrender flags.

There were full battledress rehearsals using invasion ships instead of beaches; there were Company Commander conferences on board *Simms*; and there was consternation as Surg Lt Pat Dunn distastefully handled the Webley six-shooter the Royal Marine officer of his party insisted he wear: 'Probably anti my Hippocratic Oath to drill holes in someone,' he inwardly conjectured, 'then have to patch him up again.' But there couldn't be chances taken with an enemy known for its ruthless barbarity.

At 0500 on Thursday, 30 August the four invasion ships weighed and proceeded into Tokyo Bay, passing gun emplacements displaying white flags, passing the burnt-out wreck of Japan's battleship *Nagato*, then to disperse – *Simms* to Yokosuka Harbour, *Pavlic* to land two *Newfoundland* platoons and one from *Gambia* to secure Fort No 2, then cross by land to investigate Fort Surashima before rejoining in the Dockyard anchorage. Each landing ship carried several landing barges slung outboard on massive derricks. Filled with seamen and Royal Marines in battledress and tin hats, they were lowered to surge shoreward, most of their coxswains sheltered by metal plate except for their helmeted heads, apart from one *Gambia* cox who languished atop the housing, dressed only in matelot's jeans, white cap flat-aback while he chewed on a huge cigar.

All over Tokyo Bay similar crafts' blunt bows buffeted waves, sheeting spray aft as group commanders shouted their men to be ready for the impact on grounding: 'Half cock your weapons when the ramps drop!' Wide-eyed Royals and seamen hit the beach immediately the ramp banged down from Davis-Goff's grounded ship, keen to overpower all or any resistance encountered. Jack Stuart was yelled at to guard the first inter-section. He looked up at a Japanese face three floors above, brought his Lanchester to the ready and saw the face disappear. Others surrounded the building, automatics now cocked, fingers caressing triggers for instant pressure as men moved cautiously from room to room. Nearby buildings were searched similarly until one near the front gate was found to be the Administration Block, occupied by eleven Japanese officers and forty guides with interpreters. Keys and plans of the dockyard were handed over, enabling the British Landing Force area to be more quickly covered, buildings searched, sentries placed, and eventually the Research Laboratory being commandeered for Company Headquarters with the White Ensign and New Zealand Flag hoisted.

Near sunset all landing parties were ashore, the last platoon bringing in fourteen suspects who were interrogated and released. *Gambia*'s Royals had landed on Azuma Peninsula which they secured by nightfall, just before which David-Goff ordered all sentry posts to be relieved every two hours. Japanese military and civil authorities given temporary control showed total obsequiousness, even abject fright, but not so the Emperor's mosquitoes and varied creepies which plagued men on or off duty throughout that first night. According to calendars and dated documents the dockyard had been evacuated since Sunday, 22 July and the vacuum cleaner hadn't been used before vacating. It was worse than your cruiser after a long Pompey Dockyard refit, absolute filth.

All hands turned to at daybreak on 31 August, piling paper and rubbish in the yard for incineration, sweeping debris and dust outside, covering drains and reservoirs with oil from drums found in a tunnel, and congratulating the man who located a storeroom full of mosquito netting. Meanwhile although it was late summer, and hot, all were cautioned against drinking local water, instead being rationed from the meagre supply landed in drums from *Simms*.

And here the inclusion of MAA Harris, ex-stoker, proved his worth. Being naturally inquisitive he'd scrutinised a dubious naval boiler, traced its steam pipes to various machines, ignored its unintelligible Japanese instructions, flashed it up and PRESTO! Its pressure gauge flickered then swung hard over before falling to a steady #^//X#*#*><.

This possibly being normal pounds per square inch as it hissed and burbled from a relief valve, Bogey opened the valve to a generator and its rotor started to whine as the lights came on, another valve and entrapped air spat from an immense washing machine then hot water flowed reassuringly; another valve, another machine, and before long the Kiwi camp had all the amenities of home. But that wasn't enough for Master Bogey, he tried key after key in the locks of every door until ... here was Aladdin's Cave ... a spacious storeroom with its shelves crammed with articles still wrapped as they had been brought from Hong Kong when it fell: priceless oil paintings; embossed silverware and cutlery from Manila; gilded crockery, unused typewriters, sporting guns, German Mausers, Winchester rifles, everything in pristine condition.

Meanwhile *Gambia*'s bandits had discovered a cellar filled with crated Japanese beer, which Davis-Goff wouldn't let anyone touch until he tried one to ensure it wasn't poisoned. In front of the lads he upended a bottle and grimaced; 'OOUUCCHHH,' he uttered, 'this stuff is ... BLOODY TERRIFIC!' Seeing that he'd ordered a NO-NO on local water he put Bogey in control of the beer distribution in lieu, a situation long remembered by Jack Stuart who recently reminded his old MAA: 'You, Bogey, were a real bastard. There were lots who complained of an invented thirst. But when I came off sentry watch with a parched throat you refused me too.'

As the days progressed, Royal Naval occupation companies established control of strategic areas, on one occasion creating a VIP International impasse at the main gate, when a *Gambia* sentry cross-chested his bayoneted rifle to an American Colonel who refused to show his identity, a contretemps which inflamed the red-faced Yankee more when the Guard Officer also denied him admission, until between expostulations the identity card was produced. Wheels burned rubber and spat bitumen as the jeep accelerated through, but no more was heard of the incident aside from the OOG's: 'She's right, Kiwi,' as with an assuring grin he went back inside the guardhouse.

On Monday, 3 September C-in-C BPF Admiral Fraser complimented B Company Guard paraded in smart naval khaki at the landing for his afternoon visit; and next day US Admiral Badger inspected the zone, then warmly complimented the assembled British Occupation Force before his US Marines relieved the RN sentries at 1400 and assumed responsibility.

But prior to the BPF force's general evacuation at 0530 on Wednesday, 5 September, Lt Cmdr Davis-Goff allowed each of his *Gambia* contingent in to 'Aladdin's Cave' to souvenir items small enough to be rabbited onboard unseen; then at 0700 the RNZN men embarked on Australia's destroyer *Napier* for transfer at 1300 back up their cruiser's sea-gangway.

Back in their messdecks they learned that the whole combined fleet had entered Sagami Wan on 27 August with everyone at his action station, main and secondary armament trained on known gun sites, hundreds of fighters providing CAP while fighter-bombers reconnoitred anything nearby resembling an enemy airstrip. Although as a precondition, white flags had been flown over everything considered military, there was to be no loophole for a repeat Pearl Harbour and, on Wednesday, 29 August when satisfied the moment was favourable, Halsey ordered all Task Group Commanders to ready their ships for the grand naval procession into Tokyo Bay. Flags and VHF communications gave the word for which captains and lesser skippers had been waiting since sun-up; anchor cables rattled along steel decking and down into rusty lockers; steam vented as sirens signalled intentions; then in single line each astern of his senior officer, battleships down to frigates negotiated the Uraga Strait narrows all that day. By late afternoon each group or individual ship had anchored according to a previously circulated harbour layout, with *Gambia* only cables abreast of America's 3rd Fleet flagship.

Aboard the USS *Missouri*. Japanese Foreign Minister, Mr Mamoru Shigemitsu, signing the Surrender Instrument on behalf of Emperor Hirohito and his Government.

Supreme Allied Commander, General Douglas MacArthur, addressing Japan's envoys at the 2 September Surrender Ceremony on USS *Missouri* in Tokyo Bay. *Front row*: Allied representatives, *left to right*: General Hau Yung-chang (China); Admiral Sir Bruce Fraser RN (United Kingdom); Lieutenant General K. Derevyanko (Russia); General Thomas Bailey (Australia); Colonel L Moore-Cosgrove (Canada), obscured by MacArthur; General Jaques Leclerc (France); Admiral C.E.L. Helfrich (Netherlands); Air Vice-Marshal Sir Leonard Isitt (NZ); behind him his ADC, HMNZS *Gambia*'s Lieutenant Jack Allingham RNZNVR.

There now followed three days of conferences ashore and on *Missouri* between allied nation representatives and Japanese surrender officials; protocol rehearsals for the formalities about to be dramatized; then the tedium of waiting, broken momentarily on *Gambia*'s quarterdeck by the appearance of her Captain of Marines, Joseph Killen, just promoted to Major. Pat Dunn nudged Doc Hamlin on observing that Joe was wearing spurs, not even a seahorse within miles. But Joe being of Irish aristocracy and a Royal Marine to the marrow, proclaimed to the grinning colonial irreverents grouped nearby; 'Majority, you antipodean heathens, is field rank. And the propah dress for a Major is spurs!' He clanked further aft to gaze haughtily seaward while the 'down-unders' continued grinning until cautioned by Captain Edwards' icy glare.

Dawn broke peacefully on Sunday, 2 September 1945, not a ripple on the expansive bay, away in the distance Nippon's capital backgrounded by snow-capped Fujiyama. The day's first zephyrs played with ships'

Air Vice-Marshal L.M. Isitt signs the Japanese surrender on behalf of New Zealand on board USS *Missouri* in Tokyo Bay, 2 September 1945. General Douglas MacArthur at the microphone looks on. *Gambia*'s Lt Jack Allingham RNZNVR in white shorts behind Isitt.

commissioning pennons, while here and there sea-breeze shimmers dulled patches of the harbour's glassy surface, then spread. And after 'EIGHT O'CLOCK, SIRRH!' when American and British bugles had accompanied flags creeping up ensign and jack staffs, a harbour chop was developing to the discomfort of high-ranking dignitaries converging on *Missouri* to be piped aboard. At 0900 the Supreme Allied Commander, General Douglas MacArthur, stood facing an array of microphones, surrender documents in hand as he addressed the Japanese envoys summoned onboard. Behind him stood four rows of Allied witnesses, the front row, from left to right being: General Hsu Yung-Chang (China), Admiral Sir Bruce Fraser (United Kingdom), Lieutenant General K. Derevyanko (Soviet Union), General Thomas Blamey (Australia), Colonel Moore-Cosgrove (Canada), General Jacques Leclerc (France), Admiral C.E.L. Helfrich (Netherlands), Air Vice-Marshal Sir Leonard M. Isitt (New Zealand) and immediately behind him his ADC, *Gambia*'s Lieutenant John Allingham, the only official smiling.

Immaculately tailored in top hat and tails, Mr Mamoru Shigemitsu came forward in the role of Minister of Foreign Affairs in Japan's new cabinet, bowing profoundly to General MacArthur across the table before signing on behalf of his Emperor and government.

Next to approach, bow low to his conqueror then sign as Head of Imperial General Staff, was General Yoshijiro, his signature legalising Japan's acknowledgement of the 'Instrument'.

Later, General Douglas MacArthur signed for the Allied Forces, then Admiral Nimitz for America, followed in priority by the front row National Representatives already named; thus concluding in mere minutes a war which had raged throughout much of the Pacific Ocean and its north and western lands since the infamous Sunday, 7 December 1941 Pearl Harbour attack.

On that day aboard USS *Arizona*, the then US Pacific Fleet Commander, Admiral Isaac Kidd, was last seen firing a machine gun at diving aircraft when his flagship's magazines exploded, and his body still lies with many of the 1,103 killed, entombed in *Arizona*'s hull as an underwater shrine to her dead.

Back in Tokyo Bay when signatures were being appended to the 'Instrument of Surrender' documents on Sunday, 2 September 1945 men were looking up at an unusual ensign at *Missouri*'s masthead, which had thirty-one stars not forty-eight, and was the ensign flown by US Navy Commodore Perry in 1843 when his trade mission anchored off the Nipponese capital. But soon *Missouri*'s spectators were looking toward Uraga Strait where the first of forty-two US transports emerged, landing craft outboard below huge derricks, decks an ant-hill of camouflaged khaki GI and Marine occupation troops preparing to disembark.

All throughout the forenoon Perry's 102-year-old ensign stood stiff in a strong breeze which died away mid-afternoon, encouraging *Gambians* topside to the early autumn warmth, to comment on nearby troopships wending their way inshore between anchored warships. Some whooped angry manoeuvre blasts at unheeding mailboat destroyers doing their eternal rounds of the fleet; meanwhile an Admiral Fraser signal was instructing BPF cruisers and above to dispatch their Royal Marine Bands to *Duke of York* for a ceremonial 'sunset'. So Bandmaster-Sergeant Norman 'Dolly' Gray was busy ensuring his musicians were *au fait* with this seldom-rendered Royal Naval traditional. Dolly with his trim moustache reminded me of the film star Don Ameche; his grandfather had been a Royal Marine in the mid-1800, so had his father in the 1890s and during the First World War; and now Norman Gray, born in 1919 in Portsmouth, was carrying on his family heritage, proud of his bandsmen as he marched them to *Gambia*'s gangway to be barged across to the BPF flagship. On her vast holystoned quarterdeck US Admiral Halsey sat centre-stage on a white-covered chair beside RN Admiral Fraser, in laughing conversation just aft of the massive 4-abreast 14″-gunned 'Y'-turret. Facing aft beyond the seated rows of invited VIPs were the colourful uniformed bands of *Duke of York*, *King George V*, *Newfoundland* and *Gambia*, instruments and white-helmeted brass badges glinting as bandsmen moved while standing at ease, some blowing moisture from flutes, cornets, clarinets, saxophones and trombones as the flagship's 'Bandie' motioned them to the ready. Five minutes to sunset the 'Preparative Flag' had broken out on *Duke of York*'s upper yard, furling and unfurling in light evening airs, being watched through telescopes by yeomen on all Allied ships. Right on the dot it whipped down and signalmen at foc'sle and stern staffs bawled 'SUNSET, SIIHHRRR!' The 'Still' sounded, facing everyone aft at attention, then the opening bars of 'Abide With Me', drifting soulfully across the fleet from the massed bands on *Duke of York*'s after-deck, emotional, slow, interspersed and at times blending with the clear notes of a bugler's Royal Naval 'Sunset'; a never-to-be-forgotten musical rendition over the now peaceful waters of Tokyo Bay; Fujiyama silhouetting against the sun's last rays, golden, fading to red-streaked orange, then russet gradually through grey to the dark of another star-studded velvet canopy.

Boats sidled alongside the battleship's floodlit sea-gangway, taking away ships' officers, among them *Gambia*'s Captain Edwards with his secretary Lieutenant Tom McFlinn, the heads of departments and finally, Dolly's C-in-C complimented musicians.

Signed at TOKYO BAY, JAPAN at 09 04 I

on the _____ SECOND _____ day of _____ SEPTEMBER _____, 1945.

重 光 葵

By Command and in behalf of the Emperor of Japan and the Japanese Government.

梅 津 美 治 郎

By Command and in behalf of the Japanese Imperial General Headquarters.

Accepted at TOKYO BAY, JAPAN at 0908 I

on the _____ SECOND _____ day of _____ SEPTEMBER _____, 1945, for the United States, Republic of China, United Kingdom and the Union of Soviet Socialist Republics, and in the interests of the other United Nations at war with Japan.

Supreme Commander for the Allied Powers.

United States Representative

Republic of China Representative

United Kingdom Representative

Union of Soviet Socialist Republics Representative

Commonwealth of Australia Representative

Dominion of Canada Representative

Provisional Government of the French Republic Representative

Kingdom of the Netherlands Representative

Dominion of New Zealand Representative

CHAPTER XXIV

Repossession of Japanese-Occupied British-Asian Interests

M ENTION 'PEARL HARBOUR' at a Second World War naval reunion and
you will recall those Sunday, 7 December 1941 exclamations of elation
when Japan precipitated America into the worldwide conflict. Then mention 'Hiroshima' and opinions will predominantly support US President
Harry Truman's 7 August 1945 decision to authorise the ultimate deterrent.

Those two paramount events bracket the intervening four years' se-
quence of major Pacific Ocean clashes, to quote: 'Pearl', 'Singapore' and
Malaya', 'Java Sea', 'Coral Sea', 'Solomons', 'Midway', 'Philippines', 'Maria-
nas', 'Bonins', 'Ryukus', then Japan with the coup de grace delivered on
Nagasaki to terminate that trail of death and exultation leading to VJ Day
– for adherents to 'Our Empire' the 15th of August 1945 when 'CEASE
HOSTILITIES' rang throughout the Combined Fleet standing off Sagami
Wan – for America the 2nd of September 1945 when Japan signed the
'INSTRUMENT OF SURRENDER' aboard USS *Missouri* in Tokyo Bay.

Even after 'Nagasaki' Japan did not concede defeat, although it was
assumed she would within days, so Britain's War Department initiated
demobilisation procedures: 'Cancel all unstarted contracts. Retrench where
possible all sea, land and air forces. No more fuel to be shipped to BPF
ships immediately off Japan. Only those ships already designated are to
participate in the Tokyo Bay surrender formalities.'

The majority were dispatched south under Rear Admiral M.M. Denny
CB CBE aboard the carrier *Victorious* and, unless directed elsewhere, detailed instructions would await his arrival in Manus. Meanwhile, battleships
down to support vessels in the east-bound stream from Britain should refuel
at the nearest allied port and await further orders.

At times pitching heavily in Force–6 gusts on the fringe of a typhoon,
the cruisers *Achilles*, *Argonaut* and *Euryalus* rode easier than the cumbersome
flat-tops *Victorious*, *Implacable*, *Formidable* and the eight destroyers in company, en route some 3,000 miles south from Honshu waters to Manus in
the Bismarck Archipelago. Admiral Denny's meteorologist and his navigator
had advised an east-about diversion to avoid the typhoon's intensity as it
raged toward Japan so, with time now of less consequence, their advice
was taken. On 13 August Captain Butler announced by SRE that HMNZS

Gambia was still in action against Japanese homeland targets, and that night *Achilles'* newspaper prepared and distributed by PO Tel Jim Craies' 2nd WT Office, indicated on page 1 that Halsey's 3rd US Fleet including *Gambia* and other BPF units had bombarded targets near Tokyo. Simultaneously the fleet's carriers had continued their massed aircraft assaults on railways, bridges, airfields and industrial complexes, accounting for scores of enemy aircraft for the loss of seven US fighter-bombers and two from *Indefatigable*. Then on 15 August Captain Butler took the bridge mike to say the War was ended: and Vice Admiral Rawlings had ordered the British Pacific Fleet to SPLICE THE MAINBRACE!'

This was an order not to be disobeyed; not only was it received with vociferous acclaim but with an endeavour to exceed the Admiral's expectations. (UA) Under Age personnel were excluded by KR & AIs; (T) Temperance personnel were exempt by preference; (NE) Not Entitled Defaulters and Men Under Punishment had had their tot stopped; but the bulk of the ship's company including officers who were not issued rum, were entitled to two servings on such occasions.

Illicit hoards of bubbly appeared from men's lockers as the hilarity heightened, until it became difficult to find a man sober enough to relieve his opposite watchkeeper; *Achilles* was now the acme of Rank to Rate relations and, when acquainted with an unusual caprice on the foc'sle, 'Father' merely bellowed through a loudhailer: 'Someone down there get that man below before he goes over the side!' Mick Wright, the Navigator's hefty yeoman who'd been prancing unclad beyond A-turret, was led from the foc'sle unprotesting, intoxicated but happy; and the ships, veiled in rum fumes, zigzagged their merry way south.

Just six days steaming brought the detached fleet down from Japan's cold autumn conditions to the Equatorial heat at Manus where bags and bags of New Zealand mail awaited in Pitiylu Post Office; also where the US floating dock Commander downright refused entry for *Achilles'* shaft bearings to be doctored once more: 'No! Noohhh!' he groaned. 'Not that sonofabitch Kiwi cruiser again. They emptied my PX store. They got my dockmen drunk on rum. Take that goddam ship out of my nightmares, anywheres but here,' he pleaded. Captain Butler being kindly disposed toward the distraught man stayed with the carriers throughout 18/19 August, then nursed his much-maligned cruiser onward via the Bismarck, Coral, and Tasman Seas in company with Admiral Denny's fleet to Sydney. But here too there were problems: no immediate dock vacancy. 'What about Auckland?' So while this was being debated top level, men saved their pay whilst in harbour, did subs for lotharios intent on Sydney's night life, and awoke off Rangitoto with money to be lavished on wives and sweethearts on Friday, 31 August.

That same day, Sydney turned out en masse for its colossal Victory Parade in which the Fleet Air Arm off *Implacable, Formidable, Victorious*; and the battleships, cruisers and destroyers ships' companies marched in participation, bands blaring, drums booming, all of New South Wales' femininity shrieking hour upon hour as their army, air force and navy gladiators paraded past eight-abreast in an endless ticker-tape and confetti-showered column. This was Australia's day of celebration, a celebration of the end to human history's worst world-encompassing conflict.

Achilles had occasioned New Zealand's first Second World War victory march on Friday, 23 February 1940 when she returned from her decisive December 1939 role in the River Plate Battle. Auckland had turned out en masse to glorify her in that march up Queen Street; but the city hadn't waited for her to participate in its VJ-Day knees-up so she entered Calliope Dock without fanfare to have the lignum vitae bearings replaced on their shaft supports.

Back up north Admiral Denny's carriers and cruisers had anchored in Manus or gone alongside tankers to refuel, a few including *Quadrant* then being dispatched to Hong Kong at the same time that Admiral C.H.J. Harcourt CB CBE, aboard the cruiser *Swiftsure*, was making 24 knots there from Sydney. British Intelligence, being aware of General Chiang Kai-shek's aversion to Western reoccupation of Hong Kong and Shanghai, had empowered Harcourt to command a strong naval force to be based at Hong Kong, so on *Swiftsure*'s 31 August arrival he transferred his flag to the carrier *Venerable*. Already her 1851 Squadron Corsairs, 814 Squadron Barracudas together with *Indomitable*'s 857 Squadron Avengers and 899 Squadron Hellcats, were dive-bombing and strafing 20-foot wooden, Mitsubishi-engined, suicide craft which hadn't yet surrendered; also innocent-looking junks reported to be delivering ammunition and torpedo warheads for installation in the speedboats' bows. Straightaway the destroyers *Whirlwind* and *Quadrant* were ordered down to a Picnic Bay depot where the suicide launches were being prepared, en route drilling landing parties who would round up Japanese and Korean army and naval personnel for transportation back to confinement.

'What steps, Conway,' *Quadrant*'s Gunnery Officer queried a tall Liverpudlian, 'would you take if you were confronted by a sword-swinging Samurai?'

'Big Bastards, sir!'

'Right Conway,' without a change of tone, 'let me see you demonstrating them round the upper deck till I tell you to stop. Now the rest of you pay attention to me.'

On negotiating the narrow channel which opened out to an expansive bay, *Quadrant*'s two embarked interpreters worded a signal made in

Mandarin and Japanese to a small naval base as the two destroyers steamed past on a circular course at about 20 knots. Observers on Quadrant's bridge concentrated their glasses on the depot signal tower, but there was no answer to the demand for a 'Parley Truce', only indications of aggression from troops lining the foreshore.

Lt Cmdr Hopkins now ordered both destroyers to fire five rounds each from their A- and X-turrets into the hills immediately behind the naval establishment. A white flag ran up the signal tower halyard, after which Quadrant and Whirlwind remained stationary, guns trained on the enemy headquarters while a negotiating party landed. Shortly the Japanese flag was lowered, a White Ensign took its place atop the tower and with the situation defused, the destroyers' Gunnery and Torpedo Officers took their landing parties ashore to disarm and disable the suicide launches, ship many of the depot officers and officials aboard and return with them to Kowloon.

At some stage of her Pacific operations the destroyer Ursa was leaving Tokyo Bay on her way south. George Robinson's action station in the after cordite magazine hadn't given him much opportunity to see what was going on up top, but during this early-morning departure he stood with mates on X-gundeck, almost spellbound as sunrays caught Mount Fuji's snow-capped peak, casting a bright orange glow which slowly washed down the slopes in those intense minutes of nature's artistic creation. Refuelling in Hong Kong and for a period engaging in occupation duties, Ursa was dispatched to Taipeh to embark some of Formosa's naval POWs for repatriation to Australia, one being so thin even his Aussie mates called him a pipe-cleaner. But hours out of harbour in mid-forenoon daylight a Flying Fortress passed low overhead on its way south; then that afternoon what appeared to be another until it signalled that it was the same one in trouble and about to ditch as close as possible. Eleven aircrew baled out over Ursa then its motors cut and it threw up an eruption of whitewater and somersaulting fuselage before sinking in mere seconds, leaving debris everywhere. Ursa's boats were already fighting their way over wind-buffeted swells, searching for those bobbing heads near their parachutes, being directed from aboard by lookouts with binoculars until the last US airman was dragged over a gunwale.

In this kaleidoscope of confused events the new battleship Anson, en route with the carrier Vengeance to take back Singapore, had been redirected with lesser units to bolster Harcourt's Hong Kong fleet which within days comprised:

Battleship	Cruisers	Submarines
Anson (R Adml Daniel)	*Swiftsure*	*Sea Scout*
	Euryalus	*Scotsman*
Carriers	*Black Prince*	*Selene*
Colossus	HMCS *Prince Robert*	*Sidon*
Indomitable		*Supreme*
Venerable	Destroyers	*Solent*
Vengeance	*Kempenfelt*	*Spearhead*
	Quadrant	*Sleuth*
Hospital Ship	*Ursa*	
Oxfordshire	*Whirlwind*	S/M Depot Ship
		Maidstone
A Mini-Train of Supply Ships, Tankers etc.,		
		RAN M/S A/S Corvettes
These vessels carried medical supplies and additional naval personnel to man the port and restore it to full operation		*Bathurst*
		Broome
		Fremantle
		Castlemain
		Mildura
		Strahan
		Wagga

Harcourt's big ones with adequate A/S protection had been moored off the main city, Victoria, while the remainder were busy disarming enemy forces and placing them in prisons recently incarcerating captured Allied servicemen and interned civilians. After neutralising the Picnic Bay base *Quadrant* sped down to Formosa's main port, Taipeh, to embark Australian, British and American POWs awaiting repatriation, pathetic men suffering the ravages of starvation and brutal treatment, many with gangrenous sores, anthrax, untreated dislocations, unable to walk and clad in lice-infested rags. Over two days and nights Ian Hyde-Hills worked in teams assisting these wretched men to temporary delousing tents, having to pick-a-back many who couldn't even stand, and in so doing becoming infested themselves but ignoring their discomfort until the maximum for each trip were treated and embarked. Throughout these operations *Quadrant's* seamen and stokers messed together so that the rescued POWs could be shoe-horned into the seamen's quarters; many had crabs and earned typical Cockney accusations by the destroyer's Tiffy who reckoned the parasites were Japanese: 'See,' he showed the victim he'd tweezered one off, 'they've got thu flippin Rising

Hong Kong: Japanese Vice Admiral Ruitaro Fujita; R.M. Escort to
Government House.

Sun on their bums.' Being light in colour their blood-filled veins formed a perfect Japanese flag.

Skippered by Lyttelton-born Lieutenant Nigel Blair, the 925-ton corvette HMNZS *Arbutus* left the BPF Train on 8 August as escort for empties to Manus, where she refuelled and took in stores and NZ mail. Days later she escorted full tankers up to Hong Kong, arriving in time to witness the surrender at Government House. There in full dress to represent the C-in-C at this public ceremony, Rear Admiral Cecil Halliday Jepson Harcourt CB CBE, accepted the unconditional surrender of Major General Umekichi Okada, Vice Admiral Ruitaro Fujita, and all the area's Japanese and Korean forces. Asian and British signatures were appended to the 'INSTRUMENT OF SURRENDER' and, on Sunday, 16 September 1945, Hong Kong and Kowloon reverted to being a British Crown Colony leased until 1997.

It was also an important day for Ian Hyde-Hills who returned aboard *Quadrant* from the event and subsequent buffoonery with his shipmates in Victoria's hot spots, to be required at the Buffer's Office where a draft to *Arbutus* awaited him. No longer would he hear the eccentricities of his Pommie messmates; no longer would he man the whaler to rescue ditched carrier pilots and aircrew who'd dunked; he was back among Kiwis for the return trip via Manus and Sydney to the corvette's Monday, 1 October arrival in Auckland. Many short-service men were being offered a further three-year enlistment with a draft to *Achilles* about to sail for Japan to relieve *Gambia*; but Ian along with others nearing their original term opted for discharge, went through *Philomel*'s demobilisation routine and walked out the 'Gate' in February 1946 to resume their civilian life.

Ross Todd was a Thursday, 26 July 1923 Dunedin product who finished his schooling at Auckland Grammar, and later aged 18 enrolled as NZ3503 in a 1941 *Tamaki* seaman class. Thereafter he crewed on *Rata*, a requisitioned 974-ton coaster adapted for minesweeping in New Zealand waters; then a draft to *ML 404* an 80-ton lightly armed Fairmile in the Solomon Islands' RNZN A/S Flotilla. In 1944 Ross passengered on the US troopship *Torrens* via Panama to Plymouth, qualifying AA3 at Guz, back on *Dominion Monarch* to Sydney's *Golden Hind* transit camp, then onto *Quilliam* to be *Indomitable*'s crash boat off Sakishima. There while trailing her on a fog-bound Sunday, 20 May 1945 dawn, *Quilliam*'s skipper Lieutenant J.R. Stevens RN wasn't aware that *Indom* had drastically reduced speed, so he rammed her right between the cheeks which barely affected the carrier's posterior but completely crumpled the destroyer's stem. With the destroyer *Norman* standing by, *Black Prince* began a stern-first tow to Leyte but the distorted bow acted as an uncontrollable rudder; the tow was bestowed on an American tug *Turkey* which, assisted by HM Tug *Weasel*, eventually reached Leyte and, after being fitted with an ersatz bow *Quilliam* steamed cautiously down to Sydney where she was given to the RAN. Ross Todd and his ex-*Quilliam* Kiwi mates were billeted at Manly but Sydney's naval drafting office soon ferreted them out, their idyllic sojourn among the resort's patriotic beauties terminated abruptly, and they humped their gear aboard the carrier *Venerable*.

As Admiral Harcourt's flagship she moored off Hong Kong's capital and next day Todd's landing party awakened to the basics of Kowloon's Bay View Hotel. Once grand, it had been neglected entirely during its Japanese tenancy, until now when the Royal Navy appropriated it 'As is', filth, starvation, vermin ridden. Immediately at the hands of Todd's mates the hotel staff experienced an about-face: scrubbers, soft soap, brooms and cleaning cloths were introduced for Asian use; harsh words and a modicum of physical encouragement established hygiene; then the arrival of naval rations set aside all Oriental opposition, especially when a blind eye ignored the influx of staff relatives near meal hours. The poor wretches rummaged through gash buckets for anything edible, even cramming handfuls of soggy tea-leaves into their mouths while trying to catch rats attracted by the smell of cooking.

Another New Zealander, Ernie Healy, born in Auckland on 4 March 1921, registered NZ6800 in *Tamaki*'s 1944 Class 38. He then served on the 290-ton sweeper *Pahau* in Wellington's 95th Auxiliary M/S Group, until February 1945 when he reclined on the liner *Ruahine* via Panama to Halifax. There she joined an Atlantic convoy bound Liverpool, one evening witnessing one of those wolf-pack attacks during which a nearby tanker erupted in a roaring column of smoke-blackened flame. Visible for hours as night encroached, the oil-fed pyre marked her crew's grave, then vanished miles astern as she foundered. Ernie went on a week's leave, did a Gunnery School course, then scrutinised his Commissioning Card at *Devonshire*'s Regulating Office before being directed to the County Class cruiser's Mess 28, en route via Gibraltar, Suez, Aden, Colombo, Fremantle, to Sydney. On passage during an initial Atlantic bollocking *Devonshire* recorded dangerous rolls and Ernie, who'd wedged himself in a funnel niche for warmth, was looking up apprehensively at some metal equipment strapped in place above his head, right when the cruiser lurched heavily to port, catapulting him from his perch together with the big metal object which he glimpsed smashing overboard through the guardrails. He would have followed it but he struck his head on a partly submerged stanchion, then fortunately a Royal Marine struggling aft, just managed to grab Ernie's unconscious body and drag him out of the receding deluge.

At Sydney Ernie transited in *Golden Hind* until an August 1945 draft put him in *Colossus*'s Mess 55. Originally with the 11th Carrier Squadron on its way to the BPF, *Colossus* now flew the flag of Rear Admiral R.M. Servaes who had orders to proceed 'with dispatch' via Manus, Leyte and Manila to reoccupy Shanghai. But almost by the day, top-level orders were countermanding top-level orders regarding the rapidly changing political situation, most urgent being the reoccupation of enemy-held British possessions, and there were other vital considerations.

Lease-Lend terminated on 21 August, America didn't want war materials loaned to Britain returned, so aircraft just assembled near Sydney were flown aboard British carriers to be taken beyond Australia's Continental Shelf and dumped; but as with some carrier COs, *Colossus*'s Captain G.H. Strokes CB DSC was told to fly off his Corsairs to the nearest forward base, then prepare the hangars to accommodate repatriated POWs, a task well remembered by Ernie Healy and his accomplices who hand-scrubbed the vacated space prior to setting out hundreds of camp stretchers.

In Manila *Colossus* manoeuvred around submerged warships and merchantmen, whose upperworks protruded as a reminder of those savage air and sea battles for the Philippines; then having replenished and refuelled she sailed in company with the cruisers *Bermuda*, *Argonaut*, and the destroyers *Tumult*, *Tuscan*, *Tyrian* and *Quiberon* for Shanghai. Here as her remaining fighters flew overhead in squadron formation, Rear Admiral Servaes accepted Japanese military commanders' swords at the surrender-signing procedure; he then transferred his Flag to a lesser Shanghai-stationed vessel, and Captain Strokes had his gear shifted back into the 'Master Suite' as *Colossus* departed south to Keelung, a Formosan port where hundreds of emaciated captives awaited repatriation. It brought lumps to the throats of hardened men assisting them aboard, a few making it unaided, many stumbling as they attempted the carrier's gangways, others on stretchers managing a skull-like appreciative grin, yet all responding to the naval marches and heart-stirring Empire glories played continuously by the ship's Royal Marine band.

In every enemy-occupied British interest throughout Asia and the sphere of Pacific intrusion there were surrender formalities. Admiral Walker with his East Indies Command Flag at *Nelson*'s masthead off Penang, received local Japanese commandants aboard and prepared them for their impending surrender at Singapore on Wednesday, 12 September 1945, to the Supreme Allied Commander South-East Asai, Admiral Lord Louis Mountbatten.

On the way up-coast from Sydney in the first few days of September, the carrier *Glory* was assigned a navigational duty relating back to Captain James Cook. His surveyed information still featured largely on Admiralty Charts of the area and as *Glory*'s course lay through adjacent waters, Lieutenant Commander (A) Martin's 837 Squadron Barracudas reconnoitred ahead plotting unknown reefs for Admiralty's cartographers. Then with the Australian sloops *Hart* and *Amethyst* in company and her aircraft up on A/A and A/S patrols in case of Japanese treachery, *Glory* entered St George's Channel near Rabaul for Australia's 1st Army Corps Commander, Lieutenant General V.A.T. Sturdee, to oversee the surrender of all Japanese forces throughout New Guinea, New Britain, and the Solomons. The first was carried out on *Glory's* flight-deck where General Hitoshi Imamura and Vice Admiral Jinichi Kusaka laid their samurai swords on a wardroom table brought topside, then after scrutinizing the Japanese translation, they brushed their signatures on both versions of the Instrument of Surrender.

Similar functions were enacted at New Britain's Jacquinot Bay; New Guinea's Wewak; Bougainville's Torokina; and at Nauru where the local commandant was brought aboard the RAN frigate *Diamantina* to surrender his 3,200 Japanese and 500 Korean troops to Australia's Brigadier Stevenson, and New Zealand's Captain Peter Phipps DSC & bar, VRD, US Navy Cross. This occurred on Thursday, 13 September 1945 while talks between US Chiefs of Staff and British, Australian and New Zealand government officials established future control of the phosphate islands. Lying in the sphere of US War Operations they were technically under US jurisdiction, but lengthy demands by Sir Albert Ellis (NZ Rep. British Phosphate Commission) and Mr Bissett (NZ Manager of the Commission) that production recommence immediately to maintain agricultural aid to Europe, won the debate, and perhaps the final surrender took place at Ocean Island on Monday 1 October 1945 when Lieutenant Commander Suzuki signed over the garrison's 500 Japanese.

So the War was ended, the shouting had reverberated around a thankful world, and now came the aftermath which we might view through the experiences of HMNZS *Gambia's* ship's company, a close-knit family sharing its hilarities and its worries, respecting members for their attributes and in some cases for their failings. This camaraderie reaching beyond the junior rates messdecks to the POs' Mess, CPOs' Mess, the Marine Barracks, Gun Room and Wardroom to the Sick Bay for normal or sometimes embarrassing medical treatment; perhaps the Regulation Office to be booked for Commander's Report, or maybe 'OFF CAP' before the Captain and detention in Sydney while more circumspect mates dressed for shore.

And it wasn't only the lower deck who saw Captain Edwards for a ruling on behaviour. One recalls the punch-up between Lt Cmdr George Raymond Davis-Goff and Lt Cmdr John Wilkinson, which had brewed in the Wardroom and erupted on the quarterdeck outside the Captain's Cabin. Then another incident involving John Wilkinson's attitude to New Zealanders, when he made a derogatory remark to Lieutenant Tom (Mack) McFlinn RNZNVR, and got a hefty smack on the chin for it. Being Captain's Secretary, Mack was given a 'fatherly' admonition in the circumstances, John was advised to think before he spoke on 'Colonial' matters, and

Commander Harper was told to sweep *that one* under the carpet also. It was unfortunate that John Wilkinson incurred the wrath of his Kiwi wardroom occupants, because it would have been hard to find a gunnery officer throughout the BPF with equal efficiency.

For idle entertainment the NZ warships had always received bundles of hometown newspapers, *Auckland Weekly* with its central photographic pages, *NZ Womens Weekly* with its Pen Pal column; and that's where some goon got a bright idea. He wrote stressing his loneliness and would a similarly lonely twenty-year-old girl reply enclosing a recent photograph. Address: Able Seaman Ray Goddard, Hangar Mess, HMNZS *Gambia* on Active Service. Ray knew nothing of this. But weeks later when a duty mail destroyer ran alongside with NZ mail-bags bulging, it seemed there were many lonely young women. Messmen stood around the Rec Space as bags disgorged letters from home while Postie and his helpers flipped letters in appropriate directions; 'Goddard, Hangar Mess.' Several to men awaiting their messdeck's mail. 'Goddard, Hangar Mess.' And so the pile diminished until one man stood with arms full of letters for Ray Goddard; some 300 fervent females had responded with their promise of eternal love, love anyway. All that night on watch at the Damage Control Switchboard, Ray with Ian Boyes, Johnny Lomas and Dick Hunt, sorted out a few worth further investigation before passing the rest around ad lib, and some of that bogus correspondence resulted in deeper relationships than had been originally envisaged.

Monday, 3 September 1945 dawned bleak across Tokyo Bay, for the poetic recalling Kipling's nineteenth-century portrayal of the British Flotilla across Mandalay Bay, but for the mundane majority this twentieth-century Allied Fleet with men scrubbing and squeegeeing its decks, as had their predecessors 119 years ago in Burma. Now however *Gambia*'s hands were piped to breakfast. 'EIGHT O'CLOCK, SIR!' faced everyone aft to salute the broken-out White Ensign. Then day-men mustered at part-of-ship spaces to be detailed their forenoon duties. Only yesterday *Missouri*'s after-decks and towering upperworks had swarmed with her ship's company and visitors, witnesses to the already 24-hour old Japanese surrender. The great battleship having accomplished its historic mission, would now go down the long trail of States-bound leviathans destined for a knacker's yard; perhaps to be a Bikini Atoll nuclear target; at best to be mothballed pending a yet undetermined future; meantime American and British ships' complements were being pared to peacetime manning, and Claude Mason-Riseborough stood among the first group near *Gambia*'s sea gangway.

An hour ago the 40-knot, 3,000-ton, 3-funnelled minelayer *Ariadne* had secured alongside *King George V*, having arrived to transport BPF men to Sydney for their onward passage home, men well overdue for relief from wartime sea duty. Ships' motor boats were plying back and forth until *Ariadne*'s first load of passengers was inboard and accounted for; but just as she was letting go fore and aft her skipper was signalled to make fast and wait. Head and stern lines were again secured, 'Stop Engines' rang in her engine-room, all passengers were mustered aft, and Admiral Rawlings stepped from his palatial quarters to approach and face them from atop one of *KG V*'s massive bollards: 'I wish to thank you one and all,' the RN Task Force Commander voiced loud enough for men on *Ariadne*'s far side to hear, 'for holding the ships of my Strike Force together. This you have accomplished virtually with bits of string and wire. And for the first time in many years, guns throughout the World have fallen silent. And the killing has stopped.'

He paused. Then as he continued, men standing near saw tears in his eyes, heard a tremor in his voice when he bade everyone farewell. A spontaneous round of cheers rent the air for this paternal naval man who had so ably commanded British fleets in other oceans, and recently this one in the north-west Pacific. Many faces showed both sad and thoughtful when the 'Still' sounded and *Ariadne* moved away; a poignant closure to a chapter in those mens' lives, looked down upon with Oriental equanimity by Fuji, impassive.

EAs Ken (Hoot) Gibson and (Lofty) Jack, Steward Lyndsay (Brigham) Young, Petty Officers Des Grant, Claude Mason-Riseborough, and Leading Seaman Clarrie Johnson had done sea-time on *Achilles* and *Gambia* reaching back to pre-war days; they'd heard the thunder of *Achilles*' guns at the 'Plate', seen her wrecked X-Turret in which some of their mates died at Guadalcanal, fought determinedly against Kamikaze attacks on *Gambia* in the Ryukus; and now they were standing together on *Ariadne* when she picked up speed through Uraga Strait, decks vibrating to the surge of power from her whining turbines as foc'sle spray sent men below; the Kiwis to their allocated hammock spaces in the port mine-passage.

Some Einstein-minded Pom had devised a Heath Robinson latrine made from a discarded toilet-basin frame with all the basins removed. This had been slung outboard right forward on the foc'sle with a sack-cloth wind shelter erected behind the edifice for comfort, but whoever authorised it hadn't considered the effect of wind velocity on gravity, so the first time it was occupied all except those on the foremost long-drop had their protruding backsides fouled by wind-blown excrement. It didn't need a second attempt for the ex-*Gambians* to avoid that experience as *Ariadne* drove south, and this they accomplished by turning out early each Morning Watch to do their ablutions and evacuations in the POs' bathroom and heads.

One forenoon they were piped en masse to report to the CO's cabin, only to find that instead of an expected reprimand, they were greeted by Captain Lloyd RN who had pre-war been *Achilles'* Navigator and, in remembrance of those halcyon peacetime days he spent a pleasant hour sharing reminiscences of New Zealand and its tropical dependencies. The nine-day run south with a refuelling pause at Guam, ended on 11 September at Sydney; but hours prior to entry Captain Lloyd cleared lower deck and apologised for making it at economical speed over the past twenty-four hours: 'Evidently,' he said, 'Admiralty had circulated a signal to all Commanding Officers, ordering ships to proceed at economical speed unless individually instructed otherwise. This my Yeoman tells me was made before we sailed. But I must have mislaid it somewhere,' he grinned in mock contrition.

Ariadne had earned admiration for the power which drove her so fast for most of the journey, and the skipper's grin broadened at an audible Cockney remark from the rear: 'If that were slow Oid like to see tuh old tart runnin' wiv 'er knickers orf.' Captain Lloyd laughed outright with the assembled men, waved farewell to them and disappeared below to generous applause.

Clarrie, Des, Claude, and Ken Gibson were drafted to *Golden Hind*'s 4,000 already waiting for transport home to their bomb-devastated towns and cities, to undamaged homes in South Africa, Canada, even a few to Malta. At parades when names were announced there was discontent about some thought to be jumping the gun; blatant derision when the Camp CO introduced Dad's Army musket drill to counteract growing boredom. Three weeks dragged, then Claude and his mates boarded a 'War Wounded Special Train' loading for Melbourne, an embarrassing series of station stops where gifts of fruit, cakes and chocolates were pressed on them by patriotic Australians thinking they too were wounded men on passage. Then finally on their arrival aboard *Oriana* at Port Phillip, the big liner cast off for New Zealand.

She already creaked at the seams with servicemen from Italy and the Middle East, so when an army lieutenant regretted that berths had not been provided for them: 'Sorry fellahs, see what you can find for yourselves,' they did. They opened occupied door after door, trailed through passage after cabin passage, deck after deck until Des tried the door knob of an unoccupied Bridge Deck cabin: 'Hey Claude,' quietly, 'this one's empty.' After some heartbreaking coaxing the charge Steward said he'd turn a blind eye as long as they vacated it between 0900 and 1600 daily. This was done, beds made and everything left tidy each morning of Grant and Mason-Riseborough's Tasman crossing, in the cabin kept available for an occasional passage by the P & O Line Commodore.

In mid-October 1945 the returning *Gambians* stood among throngs of excited troops pointing to their New Zealand coast, long Moana Kiwa rollers launching themselves in an eternal onslaught against the rocks and cliffs guarding northern Wai Pounamu; the long curve of Farewell Spit; Cook Strait's Stephen's Island with its lighthouse and tuataras; Sinclair Head washed by the Pacific Ocean; and Barretts Reef treacherously close to starboard as men peered through the Prom Deck's salt-blurred windows. Then Eastbourne, and on the other side Marsden Point around which *Oriana* helmed for the slow approach, soldiers hanging half out of every available port waving their hats; decks and lower mast a waving khaki festoon; shouting to waving wives and friends as the liner berthed; gang-ways disgorging laughing men including Claude and his mates with leave passes; travel and pay warrants; petrol, clothing, meat and cigarette coupons to cover their ninety days overseas leave about to begin.

Back in Tokyo Bay in early September 1945 while *Gambia* waited for Lt Cmdr Davis-Goff's and Lieut John Washbourn's occupation parties to be relieved by US Marines, groups were taken ashore to see Yokohama's wrecked dockyards and derelict streets, also to Tokyo where few buildings remained intact amid the rubble and stench of death. Civilians in unkempt military garb looked suspiciously at these victors inspecting the ruin they had brought about. Mile after mile, block after block one saw desolation, apart from General MacArthur's Imperial Hotel Headquarters, the Palace, and the Diet. Pathetic beggars proffered cracked porcelain and family heirlooms for food. It was a relief to return to the sanity of one's messdeck.

And it was a relief on Wednesday, 12 September when the Cable Party mustered on the foc'sle, when hoses blasted Tokyo mud from the surfacing anchor; more so when HMAS *Nizam* cut *Gambia*'s wake en route the Inland Sea. Men with binoculars commented on the similarity to New Zealand's shores, not the cramped housing expected but endless miles of afforested hills rolling down to stretches of lowland bathed in autumnal sunshine; it could have been the varied parts of our South Island east coast except for the strings of American landing craft passed. At night there were more showing on radar plot screens, invisible to all except lookouts who saw them as ghostly images through night-glasses, or the occasional fully laden troopship on its way to occupy Japan, much closer with illuminated upperworks now that blackout regulations no longer applied.

Gambia and *Nizam* awakened to a pine-covered headland as they turned north into the Inland Sea then navigated toward Wakayama, at times easing through safe channels still being cleared by Starred & Striped minesweepers, and finally dropping anchor a mile offshore among an American task group including a Woolworth carrier, several destroyers and landing craft, a gaggle of moored flying boats, two hospital ships, and the flagship cruiser USS *Montpelier*.

'Where's this?' a kitted-up lad was asking Wally Nielsen.

'Wakayama, mate.'

'Waka what?' in brow-furrowed incomprehension.

'Wakayama! W-A-K-A-Y-A-M-A. That's where we'll be going when that landing barge gets alongside.' Wally's patience had come to an end in this geography lesson, so he distanced himself from the slow-learner while edging to the boarding gangway. It had now been eased onto a big US landing craft, upward of a hundred men including two surgeon lieutenants, several officers and Sergeant-Bandmaster Norman Gray's Royal Marine Band, crossed over, and the powerful diesel-motored boot-box surged shoreward.

As soon as its ramp crunched down on beach shingle, landing party groups dispersed about their individual duties. Paymaster Lt 'Mack' McFlinn and Surg Lt Pat Dunn with their writers and sick bay attendants again being issued .38 Webleys by Gunner's Mate Des Grant: 'Only to be used if things become sticky,' then escorted by Gunnery PO Len Jacobs to a hotel commandeered by the US 1st Cavalry Division. Only 100 yards from high tide, its flimsy timbered structure leaned hard up against a sheer rock-face which seemed to be the main support, but already seven successive floors of the eight storeys had been occupied by US Seebees noisily removing all partitions. Oil-fuelled and electric ranges now stood wall to wall on the ground floor, some in operation. On the next floor familiar Japanese 4-feet-square wooden baths were being replaced by showers and, as the New Zealanders arrived heavy laden with typewriters and essential medical equipment they looked around for lifts. 'Lifts, sailor?' from a head-scratching Seebee. 'Awh yeah, yuh mean elevators, those there stairs is thu only ways up this goddam outfit, buddie.'

So they lugged their gear up eight rises and set up shop – three desks near the staircase, barely separated from eight Yanks issuing US Navy shoes and uniform to 'Walking POWs' who'd been deloused and showered, medically examined, fed and questioned about brutality, *then* sent top-floor! 'Oh well?' Personal NZ messages home were typed onto master copies for micro-filming to Navy Office Wellington, while those from US servicemen were channelled by radio to US Navy HQs San Francisco for ASAP delivery to next-of-kin.

Almost hourly trainloads of emaciated servicemen were arriving at the local platform from camps located throughout southern Honshu, being heartened by Norman Gray's Royal Marine band as they shuffled along or were stretcher-borne through delousing tents, then assisted into buses. If American they were driven to a US Contact Center for first aid and initial register, prior to a metal road ride to landing craft nosed in along the waterfront, ramps down, waiting to take them out to large transports bound for Guam. If British, Indian, Netherlanders, Australian or New Zealanders, they went through a similar British system, up landing craft ramps and out to Hope and Charity, the nicknames of two big US Hospital ships *Sanctuary* and *Consolation*, about to depart partly filled with Americans for Okinawa and now completing with allied POWs. Onboard they were given packs of cigarettes, fruit and Moro bars; but not only did they crave for food, they'd been starved of news.

'Did the bastards really sink *Prince of Wales* and *Repulse*, guv?' Then from a nearby GI: 'Say, pally, is that right Roosevelt's kicked it in?' They asked about their country's sport, politics, conditions in English towns and cities, anything unheard by them for years. These wretched skeletons mouthed Japanese atrocities into War Crimes Commission recorders, tried to complete Commission forms, then were taken through hospitalisation routine, until noon on Saturday, 15 September when *Sanctuary* sailed out between lines of cheering warships. *Consolation* however was still embarking, but on asking for clearance next day it was refused due to an approaching typhoon.

All that afternoon *Gambia*'s part-of-ship men had been securing their boats and exposed equipment with extra storm lashings and, with the barometer bottoming dramatically Captain Edwards signalled *Montpelier* for permission to proceed to sea, but this was also declined by the Task Group Rear Admiral so Edwards instructed his 'Weather Deck' officers to prepare for a real twister.

Shortly after dark it rose to hurricane force, a Whirling Dervish flailing spume high over the bridge; thrashing ships with stinging sleet and horizontal rain-sheets in its 90-knot frenzy about the anchorage. Even though *Gambia*'s two forward anchors were dropped and the ship eased astern to lie her cables along the seabed for greater adhesion, she pitched and yawed in those fierce wind shifts, but apart from being uncomfortable below, the messdecks were warm and dry; that is until the foc'sle party was piped to muster, and Ray Goddard grabbed his oilskins before clambering topside with his mates. They edged forward against the shrieking gusts, lifeline attached as each man crawled along the sloping deck, unable to hear commands whilst grasping hand-holds when successive waves cascaded over the foc'sle. Captain Edwards needed assurance that the anchors were holding and an inspection was essential. Huge boiling seas pounded the ship but the task was accomplished; then when they were hand-signalled to retire, a roaring wall of water crashed onboard, injuring an officer and two seamen when it threw them against the foc'sle shearwater.

All permission to venture topside was now refused and within minutes another raging gust veered *Gambia* almost beam-on, bringing mens' gear down from locker tops and breaking messdecks crockery as it leapt from racks. This violent swing had to be corrected by revving the port turbines for 15 knots, and as she came back she ran her taut cable over the slackened one, causing a tangle unable to be dealt with in such dangerous conditions. The anchors *had* been dragging, so *Gambia* was kept steaming ahead sufficiently to counter her movement astern, until near 0200 when the typhoon swung inland and the barometer gradually rose; yet those enormous swells continued to roll in and endanger ships with worse cable problems.

Daylight showed that *Montpelier* was only tens of yards from a reef after colliding with one of her US destroyers. Others less fortunate had been driven ashore, one landing craft having lost four of its crew drowned; small naval and coastal craft were strewn along the shingle foreshore, and an amphibian rode belly-up among several damaged at their moorings. Now with the storm reduced to ineffectual gusts, ships and landing-craft blown haphazard about the anchorage began to winch in and steam back to their moorings, and *Gambia*'s anchor-watch who'd been preparing their gear to rectify their crossed cables, attached a wire to the seaward link of a coupling, held the inboard cable at the Blake Slip then slowly eased the outboard length down to lie along the bottom. Once the wire was brought back under the port cable, it was winched in until the detached seabed end of the starboard cable reappeared, both links were recoupled and presto, everything resumed normality.

Normality? The Inland Sea was anything but normal when Wally Nielsen looked over the side; he could have gone down a Jacob's ladder and walked ashore on jellyfish. Every medusal polyp and nettle-fish in the Inland Sea had been blown into Wakayama Bay, the shore and road were carpeted deep with them, so it must have been a headache for engine-room staff on ships and barges with low draught-cooling water intakes.

And what of the below-deck men that night? Let us go back a few years. *Gambia* was a big cruiser built to withstand a lot of punishment, atmospheric or enemy. Her Main, 2nd, and 3rd W/T Office telegraphists operated in soundproof compartments; so did her gunnery men deep in the ship's bowels at their Transmitting Station computer; but her stokers in their boiler rooms would in later years suffer ear defects from the eternal Devil's Orchestra of screaming forced-draught fans, roaring fuel burners, and air pressurised to stop flames jetting out from furnace apertures. Mechanician Ron Kirkwood's early experiences as a stoker, and later at his starboard after turbine might well speak for many. Months under war conditions requiring prompt obedience to speed changes: throttle manipulation for 'Up X-amount of revs' – 'Down so many revs' – continually – unaware of events topside; just the muffled thump of the ships's guns, the concussion from an enemy's near miss, adrenalin pumping; then soul-destroying West

Country Watchkeeping – Afternoon, Last Dog, Middle, Forenoon. Next day – First Dog, First, Morning. On and on, additional to Dawn Stand-to, then the uncertainty during Kamikaze attacks off the Sakishimas while supporting the Okinawa campaign.

And now this bloody typhoon, hour upon hour keeping the revs down to 80 per minute to maintain Captain Edwards' required 10 knots, apart from the 15 he urgently demanded when that howling gust almost swung *Gambia* side on. With Ron's opposite number ERA Jack Bryant on the port turbine throttle, there was no evidence down there of the elements raging above; both relieved their monotony by verbally solving obtuse mathematical equations in mutual contest. Throughout the night they recorded revolution changes, temperatures and pressures, but at those low revs both 20,000 horse-power after-turbines seemed strangely quiet, no longer that intensifying whine as high-pressure dry steam impinged on whirling blades; just tedium, silent noise sans the trauma of action or the thrill of a chase.

CHAPTER XXV

The Final Reckoning

A LTHOUGH RISKING REITERANCY, here it might be relevant to stress what Hirohito's Defence Council had prepared to counter America's imminent invasion of Japan's home islands. But first let us see what the US Joint Chiefs of Staff had been planning since early in the Pacific War.

On 18 April 1942 only four months after 'Pearl', US Captain Marc A. Mitcher took his carrier *Hornet* to within 800 miles of Honshu. From there Lt Col James H. Doolittle led a sixteen B–25 bomber raid on Tokyo, Yokohama, Kobe, and Nagoya; after which the aircraft flew west to China.

But two years eight months elapsed before another bomber flew over Japan, this one on 1 November 1944 being a Mariana-based B–29 reconnaissance bomber which did a return distance of 3,000-plus miles, equivalent to Auckland-Melbourne-Auckland non-stop, to test the feasibility of proposed strategic bombing as an alternative to troop invasion to enforce a Japanese surrender. Washington's top brass then appointed USAAF General H.H. Arnold to supervise the 20th Bomber Command being established at urgently constructed airfields in India and coastal China. Ineffective B–29 raids of Kyushu's Sasebo and Nagasaki shipyards exposed the difficulties of air-freighting fuel, ammunition and heavy bombs over the 'Hump' from India; and high losses were lowering the morale of US aircrew averaging sixteen raids before the 'big chop' – eighteen of the seventy B–29s over Kyushu on one raid being brought down by more than 200 enemy fighters.

Inspiration came with the March 1945 capture of the Bonin Islands' Iwo Jima, only 700 miles from Tokyo. Now with long-range P–51 Mustangs and radar-fitted P–61 Black Widow night fighters as escorts, the number of high-level raids increased, and in a 7 April daylight raid 100 P–51s shot down considerably more Japanese interceptors than the overall US loss. Then with a European fire-bombing strategy in mind, USAAF General Le May arrived to take over the combined 20th and 21st Bomber Command. He immediately ordered a low-level night attack on Tokyo – less fuel allowing each bomber to carry 6 tons of M–69 6-pound fire bombs in thirty-eight cluster containers. Altitude switches would release them at 5,000 feet to rain jellied petroleum over a wide area and ignite on ground contact. On that 10 March night 348 Superforts flew at 7,000 feet from the Marianas, dropped their individual 6-ton loads pre-dawn then flew back in daylight.

Seventeen square miles of Tokyo were incinerated as a thermal wind

roared in, spreading the conflagration as it replaced the vacuum of consumed oxygen. Le May remembered Hamburg – 1942 – when a similar
fire-storm devastated the German city; but this one on Tokyo outshone it,
killing 100,000 and terribly injuring a further 100,000 all for the loss of
fourteen B–29s. This henceforth became Le May's modus operandi over
ensuing months' fuel build-up on Tinian for the 3,000 mile return trip, load
incendiary jellied cluster containers and give the 'LET'S GO!' order.

Nagoya burned throughout the night of 12 March; Osaka during the
13th; then Kobe and other cities in turn; the last of that ten-day series being
a 20 March return to Nagoya.

By mid-1945 long-range escort P–47 Thunderbolts flew the shorter 700
miles from the Bonin Islands side by side with Mustangs; assisted in July
by Halsey's, Spruance's and Mitcher's TF58 carrier-borne fighters and
fighter-bombers, and by those from the BPF TF57's four big carriers.

The escorted Superforts' traditional and incendiary mass bombing
together with the carriers' pin-point targeting, was gradually bringing many
of the enemy's cities, factories and transport systems to a virtual standstill
in preparation for the 'big push'. Commencing at 0001 on Monday, 1
October 1945, fourteen US Combat Divisions were to be launched ashore
at designated Kyushu beaches and the invasion, code-named OLYMPIC,
would be under way. But.

Made aware of the heavy Navy, Marine and GI losses suffered on
encountering fanatical resistance at Guadalcanal, Tarawa, Iwo Jima, then
Okinawa where top strategists had estimated US losses at 1 to 3 in favour,
now they were facing 3 to 2 against. They knew Japan would use every
trick in the book and a lot not yet published. OLYMPIC would be a long
and bloody series of air, sea, and land battles just to occupy Kyushu and,
if successful it would be followed in December by CORONET, a twenty-
two division attempt on the Emperor's main island, Honshu. Overall would
be involved the entire US Combat Navy aided by Britain's growing Eastern
and Pacific Fleets; all of the US Marine Corps; the massive USAAF 7th,
8th, 20th, 21st Groups, and other US Far Eastern Air Commands, encom-
passing a total of some 4.5 million US servicemen plus whatever the
Western Allies would be contributing. Allied casualties were guesstimated
to be in excess of a million men by the North Pacific autumn of 1946.

On Tuesday, 24 July 1945 President Truman had furrowed his brow
whilst scanning this lengthy summation; he then asked each attendant
strategist relevant questions in turn, bent forward over the documents and
appended tentative approval of their nuclear easy-out alternatives. Truman
then advised United Nations members of his advisers' recommendations,
and at the Potsdam Conference an ultimatum was issued to agents
for transmission to Japan: 'SURRENDER UNCONDITIONALLY OR FACE

ANNIHILATION'. In reply on Saturday, 28 July Japan's Premier Suzuki stated that his cabinet would *mokusatsu* the ultimatum. Truman's translators took this to mean 'ignore', so the question of 'Invasion' or 'Drop the Bomb' still awaited a Presidential answer, this becoming more imperious days later when Intelligence monitored internal Japanese radio broadcasts directing schools to close, followed by an order that the public arm itself with whatever weapons and implements were available.

Already much of Tojo's overall plan for home defence, code-named KESU-GO, was known to US High Command. It divided the main islands into military districts, each with camouflaged airstrips, underground hangars, command centres and shelters interconnected by tunnels to fortified caves storing fuel and ammunition. It was estimated in July 1945 that there were 13,000 enemy aircraft of all types, with an additional 1,100 being assembled and armed monthly, even taking account of USAAF and Allied bomb destruction at that time. Each village was manufacturing components in disused mines, road and rail tunnels, under viaducts, in department store basements and in private homes. The piloted OKHA rocket-propelled bombs so effective at Okinawa were being mass produced; at Kyushu they would have less distance to be air-lifted before being released on their suicidal plunge; and it was now learned that they would concentrate on approaching troopships instead of previously being piloted at escorting warships, so many thousands of troops and their equipment would be lost before hitting the beach.

Apart from air defence against enemy aircraft and piloted bombs there would be the need to protect ships from Japan's two-man KAIRYU mini-subs, these craft carrying 600 kg of explosive in the nose for ramming attacks, there being an estimated 300 presently at strategic bases with another 200 under construction, in addition to 115 KORYU five-man versions operational and 500 building, plus 40 conventional submarines being held in reserve. Also there were the most feared, 60-feet long KAITEN piloted torpedoes, whose 1,600-kg warheads had sunk or crippled the largest of America's naval vessels off Okinawa. Then the last-known attack craft to date were some 4,000 SHINYO fast motor boats laden for'ard with HE for night-ramming against troopships.

Landing craft surviving these offshore hazards would then encounter a network of beach defences – remote-controlled mines to be electronically detonated just beyond the shallows – thousands of male and female pearl divers accustomed to lengthy periods submerged, now named FUKARYU and armed with limpet mines powerful enough to blast large sections from the bottoms of landing craft; and finally the beaches had been sown with countless magnetic and pressure mines to kill or maim troops, wreck invading tracked or wheeled vehicles and mobile guns.

Beyond all this would be line after line of Japan's 28-million 'National Volunteer Combat Force', suitably armed for delaying-operations and 'Banzai!' charges against units making the beach. Then as a last resort in this KESU-GO plan were the millions of guerilla-type populace individually armed with ancient muzzle-loaders, Molotov cocktails, home-made grenades, crossbows and longbows, swords, bamboo spears, slashers and axes, all ready to die fanatically for their Emperor.

One may imagine the carnage awaiting Olympic, the invasion of Kyushu. What would await Coronet, the invasion of Honshu? If there were major Allied setbacks, would that give Japan time to recall her tens of million forces spread throughout Asia? Harry Truman considered profoundly, came to the only sane conclusion and summoned his Chiefs of Staff. As soon as meteorological conditions permitted after 2 August 1945 the bomb should be dropped on Hiroshima.

That nuclear bomb dropped on Hiroshima, then the second one on Nagasaki, killed and maimed tens of thousands but saved the lives of millions, American, Allied, and Japanese. Within a month of the US President's momentous decision the Pacific War was over, Surrender Documents signed or in more remote areas being signed and witnessed.

On 19 August *Gambia*'s Captain's Secretary Lieutenant Tom McFlinn had asked for inclusion in Lt Cmdr Davis-Goff's Yokosuka Naval Base occupation party, but right then vital correspondence demanded precedence. His request was declined but Captain Edwards included him in Air Vice-Marshal Leonard Isitt's New Zealand representative group, taken aboard USS *Missouri* on Sunday, 3 September 1945 to witness the prime Surrender Ceremony. By 13 September he and other *Gambians* were established as a rehabilitation centre on the 8th floor of a Wakayama shorefront hotel and days later all work stopped. Occupants of each floor leaned out from open windows to hear the swirl of bagpipes, distant but growing louder. Landing craft ramps had slammed down on the shingle beach and out marched a fully dressed Highland Band, heart-lifting and magnificent in their tribal tartan, kilts aswirl, bagpipes at full blast as they approached and entered the hotel. But under their colourful kilts, jackets and busbies there were gaunt frames of once sturdy pipers, and on enquiring from one of the officers Mack was told they'd been taken intact at Hong Kong in early 1942, then shipped to Osaka for employment in the coal mines. Reasonably treated as miners they'd received extra but scanty rations, and apart from unprocessed rice and beriberi their faith in eventual release had upheld their Highland morale and their tartans and pipes had recently been returned.

On Thursday, 20 September *Gambia* lay anchored several miles off Yokohama, Japan's greatest seaport with its million-plus inhabitants gradually returning. From this distance one could see little but Schoolie answered his Seaman Boy class queries – what was the history of this enigmatic chain of islands stretching along the eastern coast of Asia, from north of the Sakhalins almost down to Formosa?

It was generally accepted that some time after the Ice Age, Siberian invaders called Ainos overcame the few encountered cave dwellers. In turn these tall hirsute tribes were driven north by newcomers from Korea and Manchuria, later still by armed groups from Southern Asia and Malaya. Several hundred years BC a feudal system evolved with initially independent leaders acknowledging the first Emperor, Jimmu. Under their Shinto belief they revered their ancestors, their Emperor was accepted to be the Son of God, given the name Mikado and gradually he and his successors were enshrined, sacred, unapproachable to all but the highest. These elite were called Shoguns, ruling Japan in much the same manner practised by Britain's early tribal kings, living in castles surrounded by lesser shoguns whose subjects were rallied to oppose a common enemy. Perhaps the last invader was Kublai Khan, Mongol Emperor of China near the end of our thirteenth century AD, who amassed a great armada of Chinese and Koreans to sail east across the Sea of China; but as with the Spanish Armada his fleet foundered in a devastating storm.

Five or six hundred years earlier, Buddhism had encroached from China and Korea to continue alongside the older Shinto religion; then, excited by Marco Polo's tales of a rich land called Cipango, lying close across the sea east of China, Francis Xavier brought Catholicism to Kyushu, and Portuguese traders ventured there to trade through Nagasaki. But to curb the growth of Christianity, a ruthless Japanese soldier, Hideyoshi, who had razed Korea and planned an invasion of China, created a dynasty of shoguns sworn to execute all Catholics and destroy their churches. This done he excluded all foreign ships except the Dutch who alone were sanctioned to trade through Nagasaki.

And that was the status quo until 1853 when US Captain Perry anchored his fleet in Tokyo Bay. By coercive displays of Western hardwear and arms he obtained treaties which opened trade to foreign countries through Yokohama, and since then there'd been an avalanche of commercial, industrial, and military activity within Japan. Her goods competed on shelves throughout the world. Her warlords invaded China and Manchuria. Her Navy destroyed the Russian fleet at Port Arthur. She became an ally in the First World War. But for the moment she lay exhausted, a defeated enemy at the end of the Second World War; and here, eighteen days after the surrender aboard *Missouri*, was New Zealand's most powerful naval contribution to the conflict, HMNZS *Gambia*, now anchored off Yokohama with the victorious US fleet occupying the length and breadth of Tokyo Bay.

As Mechanician in charge of *Gambia*'s boilers, Ron Kirkwood had shut down three for daywatch maintenance, rostered petty officers and stokers for normal boiler-room and ancillary duties to ensure hot water and steam distribution from the fourth, then reported to his Lieutenant (E) 'Snow' Price – a 1920s HMS *Chatham* stoker – that he was going ashore. Under Fujiyama's influence the weather was bleak, overcast and showery for the liberty men in a huge US landing craft on its one-hour journey to Tokyo, fumes from its powerful diesels adding to their discomfort as it smashed through wave after oblique wave. Only its coxswain and crew saw anything but the steel walls of this great naval shoe-box until it crunched against a mess of tyres draped along the landing stage. Men scrambled out to a dockyard of deserted vessels, joined an ant-trail for the city centre but saw only utter desolation in the Superfort fire-bombing aftermath; collapsed multi-storey steel skeletons, acres of crumpled roof rusting among rubble being scavenged by survivors. They were erecting shelters reminiscent of aborigine humpies at Botany Bay's La Perouse native settlements, and showed no interest in Ron Kirkwood and his mates.

A tram rattled by encouraging *Gambians* to leap aboard ignoring the Crusher's warning on leaving the ship: 'No fraternising!' he had shouted at the line of liberty men, 'We don't want you coming off with VD!' There wasn't room on the tram for fraternising as he'd envisaged, just cramped swaying room and the body stench of unwashed Japanese. There was forbidden fruit another tram ride out in the suburbs and, as for fraternising – US Navy and Army patrols were turning a blind eye as their countrymen passed ignoring the edict; Auckland's Queen Street invasion was repeated, a girl on each arm, but this time they were Oriental, negotiating boardwalks over rain-filled subsidence either side of the city's ruined streets.

Most Kiwis knew that New Zealand was getting closer in terms of days, refrained from searching out the fleshpots, and were more interested in seeing the Imperial Palace partly obscured in park-like grounds protected by a sizable moat, and accessible only by one guarded bridge. Mindful of rumoured cruelties committed medieval European-style within its dungeons, Ron's group blasphemed about the inconsistencies of war, turned a back on the Emperor's sanctity and sauntered back with souvenirs in discussion.

One of the few standing emporiums, mindful of Auckland's Smith & Caugheys or Christchurch's Ballantynes, enticed them in to its high-ceilinged clinical atmosphere with its wares tastefully displayed, and its young Japanese female attendants courteous without being obsequious. They looked ravishing and their evocative body perfume tantalised but it was a case of look but don't touch.

Another tram rattled by; they were outside, tempted but determined to arrive home free from social problems. Late afternoon dusk had them top-buttoning their greatcoats as cold sleet drove against their faces. This time an RN destroyer awaited returning BPF stragglers, and within a quarter of the time taken going ashore *Gambia*'s liberty men were back aboard. Warm.

All ships had reverted to peacetime harbour routine with regular runs ashore for men to view or photograph the devastation. Tokyo's weather was similar to Auckland's autumnal warmth and humidity, but occasionally cold enough for some to prefer their No 1 blues in lieu of their naval khaki shorts and shirts. Those going ashore went unarmed, trams and buses were infrequent, but typical matelot ingenuity soon made contact with US 1st Cavalry personnel who picked up hitch-hikers in their jeeps and trucks. By this means many were conveyed into the heart of Tokyo; out into burnt and flattened districts; and to Hirohito's Palace or the Parliament Buildings and Imperial Hotel which had either strategically or fortuitously been left undamaged.

Together with wardroom mates Mack McFlinn visited the palace, photographed unsmiling US sentries at the one bridge over a wide moat populated by gold, white, red, pink and black carp drifting lazily among flowering water-lilies, but were not permitted entry through the high stone wall's ornate gate. They *were* allowed inside the Diet, no longer in session, its Parliament Chamber furnishings dark red with velvet upholstery. 'What diabolic resolutions echoed from those walls?' Mack thought without comment, 'What fateful decisions by Prime Minister General Hideki Tojo, since 1928 when he threw mainland Asia into desperation; again in 1941 when he threw his country into a Pacific war!' Now he had no army, no navy, no air force, and he had no freedom to see quiet Japanese civilians wearing Red Cross armbands, subdued as were the throngs of bewildered survivors.

There was no entry to the Imperial Hotel, which had been appropriated by General Douglas MacArthur as Supreme Allied Commander to accommodate his Headquarters staff, plus his family and those of his Chiefs of Staff. However Mack did get the opportunity to go inside. US currency being the forces only legal tender he went with two Royal Marines and Paymaster Commander Bob Allen to replenish *Gambia*'s cash reserves, this negotiation taking place in the hotel's US 1st Cavalry Division Base Accounts Office. One would have thought they were breaking into Fort Knox, stone-faced checking at each successive door, the transaction enacted by stone-faced military clerks, barely time to appreciate the masterpieces and design incorporated in its early 1930s decor by the renowned American architect Frank Lloyd Knight.

No currency other than yen had been available to the Japanese but they quickly organised a $US black market with American servicemen, and a barter trade in which *Gambia*'s entrepreneurs participated. Gas masks were official impediment so their satchels became one method of rabbiting goods ashore; now instead of containing masks and filters they hung heavy with soap, chocolate, packeted sugar and packs of cigarettes, anything known to be sought by shopkeepers and stall dealers in exchange for silks, porcelains and other Japanese arts.

One day when ashore with Sub Lt Monty Hirtzell, Lt John Washbourn, Middies Younger, Etherington and the enigmatic Surg Lt Reg Hamlin, Mack asked: 'Hey, fellas, anyone see where Reg went?' A succession of 'Noes' then a decision to keep together but look for him on their way back to the landing.

'Say, look at that will you,' by John Washbourn. 'There's Hamlin in that queue of bloody Nips.' And sure enough he was, lined up outside a partly restored cinema billboarding a Japanese war film, unconcerned that he'd be the only Allied serviceman among a theatre full of enemy citizens, laconically evasive when he yelled back to his mates: 'Thought I'd like to see things from the other side.' A comment which thereafter stuck him with the nickname 'Honshu'.

They returned onboard to ponder next morning the bewilderment of a nearby Oz destroyer Skip when he emerged topside – there on a long runner of deep-pile red carpet gracing the quarterdeck stood a magnificent red velvet armchair, until yesterday both part of the Diet furnishings but obviously harpooned by members of his crew last night. US guards must have averted their eyes, though not as many as were necessarily focussed elsewhere when the US cruiser *San Diego*'s power boat furtively towed a complete Jap mini-sub alongside to be craned inboard. *San Diego* had led Halsey's Allied fleet into Tokyo Bay on Monday, 27 August 1945 and maybe she'd got the nod to take home a suitable trophy.

But swinging round the buoy aroused scant excitement, morale was seen to be waning so an effort was made ashore to get a Yokosuka brewery back in operation; by a miracle it had been spared during US bombing and within days it was in limited production, sufficient for a BPF daily ration much appreciated by small vessels, and large.

In early October *Gambia*'s W/T 'LOTE' network operators were copying messages broadcast for *Achilles*, this reinforcing upperdeck buzzes that their relief was on the way. Then on Saturday morning 6 October 1945 there she was, sidling close to fire across a line to establish a Flying Fox, so close now that semaphore wasn't necessary for the exchange of signals, close enough for the usual rash of intership comments and enquiries. *Gambia*'s role as a fighting ship in Admiral Rawlings' TF37 attached to Halsey's TF28, or at times Rawlings' TF57 attached to Spruance's TF58 when the USN command was temporarily relieved, had come to an end and her guardship duties evolved onto New Zealand's veteran cruiser *Achilles*. At mid-fore-noon on Thursday, 10 October *Gambia* weighed anchor and steamed out through Uraga straits, en route Manus for a pit stop before requesting permission to proceed further south. When this was granted, Captain Edwards summoned his Secretary to the bridge and informed him that by sailing immediately after refuelling, and by maintaining more revs than officially sanctioned, the ship would be arriving earlier in Sydney than previously scheduled; 'I hear you plan to marry a Wren member of Lord Louis Mountbatten's staff, you'd better get a signal off to her with my amended ETA and arrange accordingly.' A lengthy message was trans-mitted, addressed to Leading Writer Jay Manning WRNS, BPF HQ, Navy Office Sydney; and shortly after the ship's arrival Paymaster Commander Bob Allen gave the bride away in Saint James Anglican Church, King Street, a ceremony witnessed by an enthusiastic Australian public: the splendour of naval officers in full dress; the emergence of the happy couple through an avenue of dress swords crossed overhead; the parade of shining limou-sines back to a floodlit wedding breakfast and dance on *Gambia's* flag-draped quarterdeck.

Stanley J.F. Hermans, born in Carterton on Friday, 17 March 1916, was educated at Wanganui's Queen's Park Primary, Wanganui Technical Col-lege, then Wellington's Victoria University prior to teaching at Wellington Tech until 7 May 1939 when he joined the NZDRN as a *Philomel* Warrant-Schoolmaster. Within weeks he was a passenger on RMS *Akaroa* for courses at HMS *Defiance* and Greenwich Naval College, followed by appointments to *Ganges* and *Vernon* Schools, and in mid-1940 embarking at Gourock onto the liner *Queen Mary* for passage to *Leander* at Aden to be her Schoolie and Cypher Officer. In this latter duty he became popular with our PO Tels in the Coding Office, a cordial acquaintance which we renew at each Ex-Lean-der annual reunion. Stan was promoted Instructor Lieutenant in October 1946, Instructor Lt Cmdr in January 1951, Instructor Commander appointed Education Adviser to NOIC Auckland in December 1957, and various promotional appointments at Navy Office Wellington until Friday, 17 March 1967, when he assumed Director of Manning and Staff Officer Organisation on CNS Staff HMNZS *Wakefield*, Navy Office Wellington, an appointment held until Wednesday, 17 March 1971 when he was placed on the Retired List as Commander RNZN (Retd).

Back on 15 September 1945 as a Commissioned-Schoolmaster Stan Hermans had joined *Achilles* to replace Ron Wardell, an Hostilities Only officer who returned to his pre-war occupation as a Staff Senior at Well-ington's Seddon Memorial Technical College.

The day after *Achilles'* Yokohama arrival, Captain Butler organised a landing party to occupy the pre-war British Embassy in Tokyo and establish a W/T Station cum Cypher Office, this involving Stan Hermans. They found everything left exactly as it had been when the Ambassador departed on Japan's declaration of war in December 1941: Visitors' Book in the foyer still open at that day's last entry, four years before Lieutenants Lawry Carr, George Shotter, John Washbourn, Schoolmaster Hermans and the Marine Captain now appended their signatures with the 1945 update. Furnishings had remained covered with white sheeting and a Humber limousine still stood on jacks in the garage. *Achilles'* Marine Guard was stationed outside in their peacetime regalia, to become a mini-Buckingham Palace entertainment for American servicemen and a multitude of Japanese civilians who gathered at each changing of the guard. And to cap this British Empire revival, Lieut (E) Shotter 'found' a recharged US battery, had the tyres inflated, magicianised a tankful of gasoline then invited his associates for a hood-down tour-de-Tokyo in aristocratic demeanour; that was until the perished tyres deflated one by one, and even unemotional Nipponese bystanders grinned covertly as the NZ Ensigned highly polished Humber was towed ignominiously behind a US jeep back to the embassy.

Weeks earlier on the Auckland-Wellington Express, Seaman Boy Max Mains had looked askance at the interior destruction wrought by Air Force lads boarding at rail stations on the way south; then he saw similar vandalism by troops back from Italy and Europe and now travelling by train south from Christchurch. At every platform some alighted to be greeted by family and friends; at Maheno seven miles from Oamaru pre-dawn, a family grouped about a mid-level-crossing fire, snow on the road when the driver stopped his train to disembark its awaited soldier. Memories of home, then back aboard *Achilles* en route Japan; Boys' Messdeck doubts about their future; Yokohama cold as *Achilles* lay among other warships outside the breakwater with snow-covered Fuji as a backdrop. Max and his Seaman Boy mates were given a few hours ashore where Yank patrols abounded, where scruffy Japanese proffered silk shawls and ornaments for packs of Woodbines smuggled ashore in their caps or stuffed inside their stockings, and where someone looked through a flimsy fence on hearing Oriental chatter around a communal bath: 'Hey you fellas, cop this lot!' Boys' eyes were glued to apertures in the palings, ogling cavorting girls' naked bodies until a Japanese attendant waved them away. Their first glimpse of undressed females, lumpy and disappointing, nothing like magazine pin-ups at all.

Came Christmas Day onboard, a small bottle of Aussie Pilsener per boy in their Capstan Flat messdeck, but Max had just started drinking his when; 'Right, you lads,' from their instructors, Petty Officers Bert Cope and Maxie Larsen, 'See how you can handle a tot.' They did and some drank more from those who'd refused the gift; 'Woow, this stuff's great.' And so Max found it for half and hour, then he spent the rest of Christmas Day in the heads groaning and retching before collapsing under A-turret overhang, head pulsating as he called for 'Herrrbb' while the world gyrated madly. To this day Max gets a throat spasm when he sniffs navy rum: 'Stomachs never forget!' But there was work to be done on *Achilles'* oil-darkened foc'sle and quarterdeck, years of applied engine-oil to be removed with Chippie Jim Dobbyn's invention – blocks of hand-sized Kagoshima scoria to wear away the layers so that the ship's decks could be returned to their pre-war holystoned lustre, and they did so at the expense of torn and blistered palms.

Another freezing day the boys were mustered to rig the cutter for sailing; in due course it was brought alongside the quarterdeck gangway to await the bright idea-ed two-ringer; in a longer due course he arrived obviously affected by pink gins, stumbling aboard and grimly hanging on to the tiller as they were lashed by fierce gusts of stinging sleet. It didn't take long for him to sober sufficiently to realise his stupidity, grasp an opportunity to go about and head for the squall-obscured cruiser. He ascended the gangway much steadier than he had descended it, now thoroughly soaked as were Max and his messmates who spent cold hours storing gear, rowing the cutter back to its boom billet, then climbing inboard with sailing added to rum on Max's 'Never again' list. On yet another occasion the Boys' Divisional Officer, Lewis King, decided to take the lads up Minami Dake overlooking Kagoshima: 'How about coming along with us, Schoolie?'

'Uhmmm, not a bad idea, Lew. Yes, count me in.' So Lieutenant King's expedition started out with not only the Boys' Division but also many of the ship's company. Most discovered how unfit they were, but with mandarine orchards skirting the base, and picturesque shrines and temples among rock and distorted tree settings, the climb was made worthwhile with a summit view of snow-covered country so beautiful that normal men were waxing lyrical. Six years later when Max Mains flew directly over Kagoshima on his way back home from Korea, he looked down at lava flows from Minami Dake's recently erupted crater, thoughtfully recalled the huge scoria boulders he and his mates had rolled down inside the scrub-lined dormant volcano, as 'Hope we weren't responsible by blocking the vent' passed through his mind.

While in Japanese waters *Achilles* cruised to Sasebo, Nagasaki and Nagoya, giving her complement an opportunity to tour the countryside by train or jeep. On request US depots readily loaned vehicles filled with petrol, accommodation was no problem and a beer-carton of tea, sugar and canned foods more than satisfied innkeepers as payment for a night or two, massages included. Naval officers were allocated recreational leave in the Fuji Ya Hotel up Fujiyama slopes, a hot spring resort appropriated by US

Command to give three-day spells of sheer luxury on its golf links and in its hot pools. At Nagasaki men saw tall smokestacks rising from undamaged factories near hillsides of waving grass, yet beyond those hills lay Urakami Valley, destroyed in aim-error by 'Fat Man' on Thursday, 8 August just fourteen weeks past. It wasn't difficult to imagine its terrorised victims, the immediate death of workers in collapsed and blasted buildings throughout the impact area, the horror among survivors whose skin was flaying to expose raw flesh, the queues of walking wounded with their blackened faces swelling as they were guided towards Nagasaki University Hospital and Nagasaki Medical College, unaware that both had been eradicated.

Came a day when the Dido Class cruiser *Argonaut* arrived as *Achilles'* relief, when she cruised down through the China Sea to anchor off Hong Kong's capital Victoria. A century of British Navy occupation had established local maintenance contracts, Chinese painting parties, laundry and tailoring firms swarming aboard the moment 'Blackie' swung his cable-release mallet. The flagship *Duke of York* had circulated a C-in-C requirement that all ships should prepare a pyrotechnics display marking the forthcoming Chinese New Year. Rockets, flares and thunderflashes were to be mounted about foc'sles according to the Manual, and firing would commence on receipt of *Duke of York*'s Execute Signal. Commissioned Gunner 'Nippy' Watts told P/O Chippie Jim Dobbyn to construct and mount rocket-firing frames, handy to the capstan on which an enormous box of rockets would be placed for ready use; 6" rockets were aligned on the frames and spaced along port and starboard guardrails in proper naval fashion, then as a 'clever lad notion' one of the Gunner's Mates withdrew all wooden safety plugs to speed up *Achilles'* firing rate – which unfortunately it did!

All manner of daytime dragon boat activities entertained spectators afloat, Hong Kong's streets jangled and belled as monstrous dragons writhed and snorted smoke, then as dark descended it was time for the C-in-C to show what the British Fleet could do. 'YEOMAN! MAKE THE EXECUTE!'

Yes, you guessed it! The General Signal! A rocket near Nippy's box of spares jammed in its frame. Jet flames thrashed in all directions spewing sparks into the box; everything ignited and WHHHOOOSSSHHH!!! All hell broke loose as men dived for cover. Thunderflashes boomed and leap-frogged about the foc'sle, unrestrained rockets and flares shot outboard horizontally towards the Admiral's battleship while some screamed down-harbour past cruisers' and destroyers' upperworks, and liberty men in Victoria's Fleet Club reckoned *Achilles'* display far eclipsed all others even if it wasn't what Bruce Fraser had intended. Luckily men of the display party had worn their anti-flash gear so relatively few attended Sick Bay with burns and abrasions; Commissioned Gunner Watts was measured for a uniform to replace his badly scorched one, and Captain Butler demanded answers to the questions he anticipated shortly from the C-in-C.

Soon after and much to everyone's relief *Achilles* wended her way home, waists piled with stores for *Black Prince* at Subic Bay; then off to Morotai Island in the Moluccas, in response to a Netherlands request for the White Ensign to be shown against Indonesian radicals at Menado who'd been revolting about Dutch Authority being re-established in the northern Celebes. But after embarking an official Netherlands liaison group and heading for the Indonesian port, Captain Butler received a cypher from the County Class cruiser HMAS *Sussex* saying Admiral Lord Louis Mountbatten would in no way permit the use of an HM ship for any Dutch enterprise. 'You are to return your passengers to Morotai.'

Now petulant about the Hong Kong fiasco, the Dutch *and* the Lord, *Achilles* raced at 28 knots through oncoming whitecaps, instructed to pull a water-tanker off Biak Reef near north-west New Guinea. But before the cutter had towed a line across, a US tug arrived and *Achilles* departed for Manus, there to refuel before towing a battle-practice target all the way to Sydney from where Captain Butler took passage back to England, his cabin being released to Captain W.E. Banks CBE DSC RN, a First World War submariner who in 1942/43 had commanded the 12th S/M Flotilla and from 1944 to recent months supervised Mediterranean Landing Craft.

Achilles' 17 March 1946 arrival in Auckland was to be her penultimate appearance in Waitemata Harbour as a unit of the RNZN; she departed 29 May to be farewelled at Dunedin, Bluff, Stewart Island's Oban, the West Coast Sounds, Nelson, Picton, New Plymouth, Lyttelton, Timaru, Wellington, Napier, then back alongside Calliope Wharf for a week among wellwishers.

In late March 1936 as an eighteen-year-old Telegraphist, I was among the first to hump my bag and hammock down *Diomede*'s midship gangway and along a cold, wet, granite Sheerness wharf, to be guided up *Achilles'* gangway, forward under her 4" gundeck, through the Sick Bay and Canteen Flat, Seamens' Messdeck, and down a wide serrated-steps hatchway into our Communication Messdeck. Within days a 570 complement of NZDRN New Zealanders, RN Foreign Service men, Royal Marines and Royal Marine bandsmen, plus a Wardroom full of RN officers, had been registered in the Captain's Office. Since then we had left her for Higher Rate courses in Australia and the UK, returned to her books, been drafted to *Leander*, come back to her again, been drafted to *Gambia*, and now while awaiting 'Time Expired' discharge at HMNZS *Philomel* barracks, saw our *Achilles* secured at the new Cruiser Wharf, about to pay off out of our lives. Only the previous week in Wellington her Sunday, 7 July Divine Service had been attended by Lady Freyberg and her husband the 'Baron of Wellington',

Lieutenant General Lord Bernard Cyril 'Tiny' Freyberg VC, GCMG, KCB, KBE, DSO and three bars, six times m.i.d, Knight of St John, New Zealand's 7th Governor General.

Wednesday, 17 July 1946 dawned crisp and clear when back alongside the Base Cruiser Wharf *Achilles* prepared for sea. About mid-forenoon the tug *William C Daldy* stood by as Base seamen slipped the last noose off a bollard connecting her to New Zealand; muddied foam whirlpooled around the thundering propellers when Captain Banks manoeuvred her stern first out into the Waitemata harbour, brought his cruiser to a standstill, then conned her downstream past a waterfront of Devonport farewellers, some running, others sadly waving as she gathered headway. They lost sight of her passing beyond the Ferry Buildings, glimpsed her again off Torpedo Bay as her long paying-off pennant dipped and rose far astern, saw her finally turning to round North Head into Hauraki Gulf, taking with her ten and a half years of New Zealand naval history.

And what of *Gambia*? It was known that soon she would be replaced 'on station' by a Dido Class cruiser, a condition of New Zealand's Loan Arrangement with Admiralty being the return in sound state of each cruiser so loaned; so a day or two homeward bound from Sydney it was decided to conduct an official Power Trial, in which every ounce of power would be extracted from each of the ship's four 20,000 shp turbines. Previously there'd been short full-speed bursts during action, but this would be an orchestrated effort – one hour working up, one hour maintaining maximum power, then the gradual working down to her economic 14 knots. But when advised of the proposed trial, Chief Mechanician Ron Kirkwood conferred with PO Stoker Peter Corbett, the ship's furnace bricklayer, who agreed that the many hours of steaming done without dockyard mainten-ance made this most inadvisable: 'No, Ron, those bloody bricks won't stand up to it!'

This was passed on to higher authority to no avail: 'Oh very well, Chief, but I'm afraid the bally show must go on', which it did with the forewarned result. The rear wall of No 2 furnace collapsed, its boilers were immediately shut down and Captain Banks radioed a re-evaluated ETA based on con-servation of the rest of his so far unaffected power plant.

Tuesday, 30 October 1945's *Auckland Star* headlines read:

WARM WELCOME. RELATIVES GO ABOARD.

An editorial then described *Gambia*'s homecoming, Dockyard Gates opened to admit a flood of next-of-kin and public, the welcome by ships' horns and train whistles, the disembarkation of a hundred navymen and ex-POWs passengered from Sydney, plus C-in-C BPF's Chief of Staff, Commodore Evans-Lombe, here to discuss the future with NZNB, and Lieutenant

Commander S. Polkinghorn RNR who'd been a POW since 1941, when he fought his Yangtse River gunboat HMS *Peterel* to a gallant end against heavily armed Japanese warships. Not until met by VIPs did he know that a DSC awaited his arrival home.

'Dailies' and 'Weeklies' emblazoned *Gambia*'s public and official acclamation for one issue before they featured other items of topical interest, while the ship's Regulating Office was besieged by Hostilities Only ratings, Short Service recruits, RNZNVRs, RNRs, and Time Expired Long Service Men, all seeking their discharge papers, ration coupons and travel warrants to distant hometowns. In droves they handed in returnable kit, donned their personal No 1s then quipped the grinning OOW and Gangway Corporal when finally stepping ashore to resume their civilian life. But those years of war service had injected salt water into their veins, bringing a lump in their throats while crossing the Waitemata and looking back at that 'Grey-funnelled bastard', their home over the past two and a half years. Admiralty Steps for some, for others the Ferry Buildings opening out to Queen Street, Auckland Railway Station's luggage attendant checking their suitcase in to be retrieved at stations along the line to Wellington, or to be on-forwarded to rail destinations throughout the South Island. One after

Gambia arriving Calliope Wharf, Devonport Naval Base Auckland, assisted by *William C. Daldy* (Tug). Vehicle ferry passing astern.

another, messmates left thinning carriages until the last one or two got out at Invercargill. There would henceforth be the need to resume family life, work interspersed with moments of nostalgia.

Manned by an RNZN and Imperial Loan Rating steaming party, *Gambia* departed Auckland on Monday, 12 February 1946 after loading 2m pounds sterling of gold bullion for England's vaults. At Sydney she replaced some of her RNZN by RN officers and rates awaiting passage to the UK; at Melbourne she onloaded another 3m worth of gold bars; then at 20 knots she steamed west via Fremantle, Trincomalee, Aden, Suez Canal and the Med to arrive in Portsmouth on Wednesday, 27 March 1946 – two years six months and four days since commissioning in Liverpool for the RNZN. However it would be another four months before she went off NZNB's books, months in which the Board and Admiralty agreed that *Achilles* and *Gambia* would be replaced by the loan cruisers *Bellona* and probably *Black Prince*, improved Dido Class, 5,700 tons, eight dual-purpose 5.5″ guns in four turrets, six 21″ torpedo tubes, 32 knots and each requiring only half the complement of *Gambia*.

So the 1939–45 War was over, men and officers throughout the Allied navies were returning ashore, wondering perhaps how the Pacific War had evolved?

Becoming Japan's Prime Minister on 3 June 1937, Prince Fumimaro Konoye had formed an aggressive cabinet which invented pretexts for the invasion of China, simultaneously ordering their Admirals to blockade all ports from Shanghai south. British protests and those of other 'Nine Power Signatories' were ignored and the Asian situation deteriorated. On 21 June 1940 Prince Konoye formed a new cabinet, with its War Minister, General Hideki Tojo, demanding that Britain stop supplying arms and material to China via Burma and Hong Kong. He also declared that East Asia and regions of the Pacific were geographically, historically, and economically within the sphere of Japan's 'Unified Territorial Nationality'. Unwilling to enforce her protests, Britain's grip on her Asian interests weakened, American diplomats tried to impress Konoye's henchmen without success, and putting aside more detailed implications the 'effluent hit the punkalouvre'. In hindsight Japan had no possibility of success as history made evident, her 'Sphere of Asian Prosperity' had ballooned then burst, and her perpetrators were sought to exact International Justice – more precisely, vengeance.

An American dragnet was cast across Japan on 11 September 1945, the day *Gambia* left Tokyo Bay for Wakayama. Some of the Emperor's leaders had died in action, others had committed *seppuka* as absolution from their failures, but many were taken into custody, with one, Hideki Tojo, shooting himself in the chest when US Military Police knocked at his door.

Operations on his punctured lungs saved him for eventual trial and sentence, but his superior, Prince Konoye, dodged the inquisition by taking poison on the eve of his arrest. However, by the end of April 1946 twenty-eight leaders and conspirators were arraigned pending War Crimes Commission judgement, their names and status being tabulated below:

Name	Status	Age	Previous appointments etc
ARAKI Sadao	General	71	War Minister 1931 during Manchuria affair. Education Minister, anti-West views.
DOIHARA	General	65	Named 'Lawrence of Asia' in 1930s.
HASHIMOTO Kingoro	Colonel	58	Ordered 12/12/37 bombing of US gunboat *Panay*, Yangtse Rvr, and rape of Nanking.
HATA Shunroku	FM	69	War Minister July 1940, forced ineffectual Cabinet to resign.
HIRANUMA Kiichiro	Baron	81	Premier 1939, anti-West policy.
HIROTA Koki	Politician	70	Prime Min early 30s, insisted on expansion.
HOSHINO	Politician	56	Manchukuo Planning Board.
ITAGAKI	General	69	War Minister 19??.
KAYA	Politician	59	Finance Minister 19??.
KIDO Koichi	Marquis	59	Lord Keeper Privy Seal. Responsible for prolonging Pacific War.
KIMURA Heitaro	General	60	Vice Min War. Led army in Burma. Defeated by General Slim.
KOISO Kuniaki	General	68	P.M. 1944, Defeated at Saipan.
MATSUI	General	70	Commanded 1937/38 army at Nanking.
MATSUOKA Yosuke	Diplomat		1932 League of Nations. New Order advocate Aug 1940. Rome talks with Mussolini Apr 1941, then Berlin talks with Hitler, then Moscow to sign five-year pact with Stalin. July 1941 advised a hard line with America.
MINAMI	Politican	74	War Minister, 'Unofficial Emperor'.
MUTO	General	56	Tojo's Chief of Military Affairs.

Name	Status	Age	Previous appointments etc
NAGANO Osami	Admiral		10 Apr 1941 replaced Prince Hiroyasu Fushimi as Chief of Naval Staff, to strengthen 'Warhawk' Cabinet.
OKA	Vice Adml	58	Tojo's Chief of Navy Affairs.
OKAWA	Agitator		Fanatical propagandist; arrested by US Military Police Sept 1945 but considered psychotic and committed to an asylum.
OSHIMA Hiroshi	Baron	62	1940/41 Ambassador to Germany. Backed Adml Raeder's request for Singapore attack.
SATO Kenryu	General		One-time Chief of Military Affairs.
SHIGEMITSU Mamoru	Politician	61	Early Ambassador to USSR, UK, China. Foreign Minister at USS *Missouri* surrender.
SHIMADA Shigetaro	Admiral	61	Navy Minister July 1944. Foreign Minister July 1944.
SHIRATORI	Politician	61	Ambassador to Italy 1941.
SUZUKI Teichi	General	60	Created Pro-Jap Burmese Independence Army, posing as Rangoon news reporter December 1941.
TOGO Shigenori	Politician	66	For'n Min 1941, ousted by Gen Tojo 1/9/42.
TOJO Hideki	General	64	War Min June 1940. For'n Min 1942. Over Mins of Commerce & Industry 1943. Chief of Genl Staff Feb 1944. Sacked 18 July 1944.
UMEZU Yoshijiro	General		Ranking Official China. Assumed all Tojo's responsibilities 18 July 1944.

Apart from the twenty-eight named as Class 'A' War Criminals there were some twenty field commanders in a 'B' category, then thousands in Class 'C' being tried for common crimes against POWs and internees. More than 3,200 arrested outside Japan were arraigned before British, French, American, Chinese, Dutch, Filipino and Australian military tribunals, 732 being sentenced to death, 2,072 given jail terms and 396 acquitted. As one example General Tomoyuke Yamashita, to whom Lt General A.E. Percival had

War Crimes Tribunal, Tokyo, Monday, 12 November 1948.
Accused rise as judges enter to deliver sentences.

Front row: General Doihara, Field Marshal Hata, Politician Hirota, Politician Minami, General Tojo, Vice-Admiral Oka, General Umezu, General Araki, General Muto, Politician Hoshino *Back row*: Colonel Hashimoto, General Koiso, Admiral Nagano, Politician Baron Oshima, General Matsui, Politician Baron Hiranuma, Politician Togo, Diplomat Matsuoka, Politician Shigemitsu, General Sato, Admiral Shimada, Politician Shiratori, General Itagaki

surrendered Singapore, was accused of sanctioning brutality in such detention centres as Changi Jail, sentenced to death in February 1946 and summarily hanged. And that same month at Manila, Lt General Masaharu Homma, who took the Philippines from General MacArthur, was accused of ignoring Corregidor Island atrocities, sentenced to death and next day faced a firing squad.

At the Nuremberg trials there were four judges; at the Tokyo hearings eleven plus one each from India and the Philippines. Australia's Sir William Webb who'd been investigating Japanese atrocities in Papua New Guinea, was appointed Chief Justice by General MacArthur, with New Zealand's Judge-Advocate-General, Harvey Northcroft, as Webb's Deputy. The British Judge was Lord Patrick and the American, John Higgins. Short-titled IMTFE this International Military Tribunal for the Far East was approved in January 1946 by General MacArthur, the Supreme Commander Allied Powers, SCAP, who became the sole authority for appeals against death or life sentences. There ensued the usual wrangles endemic in multi-national proceedings and gradually, as prosecutors departed Japan on conclusion of their particular duties, substitutes were sworn in.

The courtroom within Japan's War College on Ichigaya heights over-looked central Tokyo's Imperial Palace and as public interest grew, a black market trade developed for official balcony passes to view the East-West pageantry being enacted among glass-proofed cubicles, highly-polished benches, and an array of instant-translation gadgetry highlighted by flood-lights focused on an isolated defendant box. There was utter contrast to the Nuremberg trials where Nazi Germany's Air Marshal Hermann Goring's colourful hauteur had entertained judges, accusers and spectators. Here were tiny Japanese politicians and militarists, wizened by age, standing impassive in baggy prison garb; Tojo an emaciated 5 feet 4 inches matched against Australia's bull-headed hectorial Chief Justice Webb, and Prosecutor Keenan who refused to acknowledge Tojo as a General but continually referred to him as: 'The accused Tojo.'

Initially Japanese public anger at its Government and Service Chiefs saw justice in the trials; but as month succeeded uninteresting month there came an increasing ennui up to April 1948 when the 416 courtroom sessions ended. The Tribunal then recessed to compose judgement, a formal 1,200-page document which took six months to detail the many verdicts. The eleven judges and their staff returned to Tokyo and sat through a week in which the long findings were read and translated page by page, then the sentences were announced to the court on Monday, 12 November 1948: 'Tojo, death by hanging. Kimura, death by hanging. Hirota, death by hanging. Matsui, death by hanging. Muto, death by hanging. Doihara, death by hanging. Itagaki, death by hanging.' Total disgrace by ignoring their ranks or titles.

Matsuoka and Nagano had cheated the gallows by dying before sentence. Okawa had been taken protesting to an asylum for the insane. Fifteen were sentenced to life imprisonment; Shigemitsu got seven years, and two were acquitted on Count 1 – overall conspiracy.

On Thursday, 12 November 1948 General MacArthur reconvened the tribunal to discuss the findings, their recommendations being as shown below:

USA, China, New Zealand, Philippines, USSR, Britain – 'No change.'

France – 'No change, but an appeal for clemency?'

Australia – 'No change, but would oppose reduced sentences.'

Canada – 'Not opposed to reduced sentences.'

India – 'All death sentences should be commuted to life imprisonment.'

Holland – 'Mitigation of five sentences, Hata, Hirota, Shigemitsu, Togo, Umezu.'

On Saturday, 24 November 1948 MacArthur ruled that there be 'No change' to any of the Tribunal's verdicts, his US Eighth Army Commander, Lt General Walker, would carry out the decisions commencing next morning.

Tojo had sat dejected throughout the final hearings, unemotional, stoic when he stood in the dock for sentence, defiantly refusing earphones to hear in Japanese the translation of his fate. One after another those sentenced to death stood facing floodlights, rivetted by a thousand eyes. Several had bowed to the court after hearing its verdict. Itagaki had sneered derision. But outside in an ante-room Tojo was heard to say in his mother-tongue: 'I am so sorry to have involved you. I expected to die but not to be humiliated by hanging. I never thought they would also sentence you to be hanged.'

Unpublicised on Tuesday evening, 22 November 1948 all representatives were summoned to Sugamo Prison. Utmost secrecy had prevailed throughout preceding weeks. At the final condemned mens' call to the gallows, all seven shouted 'BANZAI. FAREWELL AND DETERMINATION TO THE EMPEROR.'

In their drab US Army salvage dress they shuffled single file to the death house mouthing prayers. Between 0007 and 0013, Doihara, Tojo, Muto, and Matsui had the knot adjusted to where it would break the spinal column. Trap doors swung down and the four dangled broken-necked. When declared dead their bodies were removed and the trap was set for Itagaki, Hirota, and Kimura.

The execution chamber was pregnant with silence, its clock ticked past 32 after midnight. The three condemned had been aided up and onto the re-set trapdoor. They had muttered prayers while nooses were adjusted round their necks. Some of the witnesses shut their eyes at the final command, opened them again to see that it was now 0035.

Photographing had been forbidden and the bodies of the executed were cremated immediately, their ashes being scattered secretly to avoid any future attempt to sanctify their graves.

What were the condemned men's thoughts as they stood on those trapdoors only seconds from eternity? Did they recall the horror and bestiality their actions had inflicted on countless mainland Asians? Did they regret the subjugation and beheading of helpless Chinese in public for trivial offences? Or did they see before them the spectre of unfortunates whose bodies had dropped rotting from gibbets erected as examples to townsfolk in Korea, Manchuria, Mongolia, everywhere their Japanese 'Sphere of Prosperity' encroached?

History indicates that warnings intended to deter aggressors such as '*der Fuehrer*' Adolf Hitler, '*Il Duce*' Benito Mussolini, '*The Razor*' Hideki Tojo, fell on ears deafened by egotistic grandiosity, eyes which coveted the world.

So it might be hoped that the leaders of future British, American, Australian, New Zealand and other nations' generations, will heed the adage that 'The pen is mightier than the sword.'

In the case of New Zealand, especially, the Asian pen poised to sign cheque after cheque with which to stealthily occupy the land we strove to make inviolate.

Glossary

AAAA	Merchant ship W/T signal; 'Am being attacked by aircraft'.
QQQQ	Merchant ship W/T signal; 'Am being approached by suspicious vessel'.
RRRR	Merchant ship W/T signal; 'Am being attacked by raider'.
SSSS	Merchant ship W/T signal; 'Am being attacked by submarine'.
SOS	Merchant ship W/T signal; 'Am in danger of sinking'. All followed by ships's name and position.
A/A	Anti-aircraft.
AB	Able Seaman, qualified in general duties.
ABSD	Able Seaman, qualified in submarine detection equipment.
ABST	Able Seaman, qualified in torpedoes.
ACO	Aircraft Control Officer. Launching and retrieving.
Admiralty	Governing Body for British and Dominion Navies.
AFO	Admiralty Fleet Order. Distributed to all naval ships and shore establishments.
AMC	Armed merchant Cruiser. A liner fitted usually with eight 6″ guns and torpedoes.
APD	US Navy destroyer converted to fast troop transport.
A/S	Anti-submarine.
Asdic	Echo-sounder, devised by 'Anti-submarine Detection Investigation Committee'.
AWOL	Absent without leave.
3-badge man	A.B or Stoker who had continued after first 12-year engagement; called 'Stripey', badge was term for good conduct service, V-shaped stripe/s worn above left elbow.

485

Bandit	Aircraft identified as enemy.
Bogie	Suspected enemy aircraft.
Bosun/Buffer	Petty Officer i/c of upper deck and ship's side.
BPF	British Pacific Fleet.
Bunts	Naval signalman; from flag material, bunting.
Cable	(i) As a nautical distance: 200 yards. 10 cables = 1 nautical mile; 2,000 yards. (ii) As equipment; anchor chain.
Can	US Navy term for destroyer.
CAP	Combat air patrol, flown from carrier for close protection of fleet from enemy aircraft.
CCNZ	Commodore Commanding New Zealand Station.
C-in-C	Commander-in-Chief (Admiral rank) of a Fleet; or Naval Station, e.g. Atlantic, Med, Pacific.
CNS	Chief of Naval Staff, Commodore to Admiral rank.
CO	Commanding Officer, Senior officer of ship, flotilla etc.
Corned dog	Messdeck term for navy issue of corned beef.
Coxswain	Petty Officer i/c of ship's routine duties. Takes wheel when entering or leaving harbour.
CPO	Chief Petty Officer, i/c of a Department, e.g. W/T, Gunnery, Torpedo, Engineroom, etc.
Crabfat	Slang term for grey paint; same colour as anti-lice ointment.
Crusher	Slang term for Regulating Petty Officer.
CS7, 15, etc.	Senior Officer of 7th, 15th, etc. Cruiser Squadron.
D7, 15, etc.	Senior Officer of 7th, 15th, etc. Destroyer Flotilla.
DCT	Control Tower with rangefinder to pass range, direction, etc. to Gunnery computer.
Degauss	Low-volt cable around ship, nullifies inherent magnetism & avoids triggering magnetic mines.
Desron	US Navy term for a destroyer flotilla.
D/E	Destroyer Escort. Small destroyer fitted with A/S gear & depth charges for escort duty.
D/F	Direction Finding W/T equipment.
Dhobying	Washing of clothes.

Drop tank	Releasable fuel tank fitted under long-rang fighter aircraft; jettisoned when empty.
DSC	Distinguished Service Cross, awarded to officers. DSM (Medal) awarded to ratings.
& bar	2nd award of above.
DSIR	Department of Scientific & Industrial Research.
E.A.	Electrical Artificer.
ERA	Engineroom Artificer.
ETA	Estimated time of arrival.
FAA	Fleet Air Arm. Aircraft, pilots and crew, borne on catapult-fitted warships or aircraft carriers.
FDO	Flight Direction Officer.
Fleet Train	Back-up carriers, fuel tankers, ammunition and store ships attached to a fleet.
GI	'Government Issue' slang term for US soldier.
GOB	God's Own Boy; US Navy term for enlisted man.
Goffers	Cordial and water soft drinks.
H/A	High-angle capability A/A gun.
H/A L/A	Dual-purpose A/A and surface-action gun.
Hard Tack	Ships' biscuit, dehydrated vegetables, dried beans, peas, etc.
Hawse	Hole in bows through which anchor cable runs.
HDML	Harbour Defence Motor launch, fitted with depth charges and light armament.
H.E.	High explosive.
Heads	Ship's company lavatory.
H/F	High frequency, 6,000 to 30,000 kilocycles.
HMAS	His Majesty's Australian Ship.
RAN	Royal Australian Navy
HMCS	His Majesty's Canadian Ship.
RCN	Royal Canadian Navy.
HMIS	His Majesty's Indian Ship.
RIN	Royal Indian Navy.
RN	Royal Navy. Also NZDRN until Oct 1941.
RNZN	Royal New Zealand Navy from Oct 1941.

HMSAS	His Majesty's South African Ship.
RSAN	Royal South African Navy.
HMS	His Majesty's Ship.
HMNZS	His Majesty's New Zealand Ship.
HIJMS	His Imperial Japanese Majesty's Ship.
HOD	Head of Department.
Jacob's Ladder	Suspended down ship's side to climb inboard from ships' boats.
Jimmy	Ship's executive officer.
Jumping ladder	Suspended from boom to climb inboard from ships' boats.
Ki	Navy issue slab of hard bitter chocolate 18″ × 12″ × 1″ for making watchkeepers' cocoa.
KR & AIs	King's Rules & Admiralty Instructions. RN guide to discipline and punishments.
Leatherneck	Royal Marine.
Lt (A)	Lieutenant/ or other rank/ in Royal Naval Air Force.
MAA	Master at Arms 'Jaunty' (keep clear).
Make & Mend	Traditional day for washing or repairing uniform. usually a Wednesday for early shore leave.
M/F	Medium frequency, 100 to 1,500 kilocycles.
m.i.d.	Mentioned in despatches for exemplary conduct in action; m.i.d. (2) second award of m.i.d.
M/S	Minesweeper, minesweeping.
MTB	Fast naval motor boat fitted with torpedoes.
M.V.	Motor vessel, diesel powered.
NAAFI	Navy Army & Air Force Institutes. Generally applied to Service Canteen.
Nelson's blood	Daily rum issue to all below officer rank. Neat to POs & CPOs; diluted to lesser rates on cruisers & shore establishments, but usually neat to all on small ships.
NNF	Netherlands Naval Force.
NOCA	Naval Officer in Command, Auckland.
NOi/c	Naval Officer in charge, e.g., Lyttelton, or wherever referred to.

NOW	Navy Office Wellington.
NZDRN	New Zealand division Royal Navy until October 1941; then RNZN, Royal New Zealand Navy.
NZEF	New Zealand Expeditionary Force. 1st NZEF (WW1), 2nd NZEF (WW2).
NZNB	New Zealand Naval Board.
OOB	Out of Bounds
OOD	Officer of the Day, OOG Officer of the Guard, OOW Officer of the Watch.
Pom-pom	Multi-barrelled A/A mount firing 2lb shell.
Powder monkey	Supplier of charges from magazines. Traditional name since Nelson days.
Pusser	From Purser; anything relating to naval issue.
Q-ship	Merchant vessel fitted with concealed guns and torpedoes to sink attacking submarines.
R/A	Repel Aircraft stations manned at dawn until CAP is airborne over fleet.
RAAF	Royal Australian Air Force
RCO	Remote Control Office; able to operate apparatus in ships' main and secondary W/T offices.
RFA	Royal Fleet Auxiliary: oil tanker, store ship, ammunition ship, etc.
RMS	Royal Mail Ship; British passenger ship authorised to carry mail.
RN	Royal Navy.
RNR	Royal Naval Reserve, Mercantile officer with RN status.
RNVR	Royal Naval Volunteer Reserve.
RNVR (NZ)	NZ Volunteer Reservist prior to OCT 1941. RNZNVR after Oct 1941.
RNZAF	Royal New Zealand Air Force.
Rockie	Term for naval reservist, possibly from 'Rookie', Oxford Dictionary: army slang for recruit.
RPO	Regulating Petty Officer. 'Crusher'. 'Jaunty's right-hand man'.
Scuppers	(i) Openings in solid railing to let water drain from deck.

	(ii) Offer of rum issue to messmate for a service done or to be done.
SDO	Signal Distributing Office.
Seafire	Spitfire adapted for aircraft carrier service.
Seebees	US Army, Navy, Airforce, construction gangs.
Seppuka	High-ranking Japanese atonement suicide by self-disembowelment.
Sheet	Rope for controlling sail set.
Shrouds	Mast stays.
Sick Bay	Ship's hospital.
Sippers	Offer of a sip of rum issue to messmate for a service done or to be done.
SMO	Senior Medical Officer, ship, or fleet.
SMP	Special Military Police; landed to enforce law, etc.
SMS	Sie Majistat Schiffe; German equivalent of HMS.
Snafu	Senior naval, army, or airforce blunder.
Sparkie	Wireless telegraphist; from days of spark-gap transmitters.
SRE	Sound Reproducing Equipment; for entertainment or orders to messdeck loudspeakers.
TBS	Talk Between Ships; American VHF transceiver distributed to Allied ships in Pacific.
TF57 e.g.	Task Force distinguished by numerals.
TG57.3 e.g.	Task Group; numbered unit of designated Task Force.
TGI	Torpedo Gunnery Instructor; Petty Officer Torpedoman.
TGM	Torpedo Gunners Mate; Chief Torpedoman.
Ticklers	1lb tin of Navy issue unnamed cigarette tobacco. In the lat 1930s, 2/6d per tin. Good for trading ashore.
Tinfishman	Slang name for torpedoman.
Tot	Daily neat rum issue. Eleven days filled an 1,100 ml gin bottle. Very good for trading ashore, or to the USN when it came on the scene, in NZ or up in the Pacific.
USAF	United States Air Force.
VHF	Very High Frequency 30,000 to 300,000 kilocycles.

VJ Day	Japanese unconditional surrender, 15 August 1945.
V/S	Visual signalling by semaphore, by flag hoists, by flashlamp morse.
W/T	Wireless telegraphy by keyed morse, as opposed to R/T, radio telephone by microphone.
WW1	World War One, 1914 to 1918.
WW2	World War Two, 1939 to 1945.